YESTERDAY IN MEXICO

Ex-President Alvaro Obregón *and* President Elías Calles *at Chapultepec Castle*

JOHN W. F. DULLES

YESTERDAY IN MEXICO

A Chronicle
of the Revolution, 1919–1936

UNIVERSITY OF TEXAS PRESS, AUSTIN

Library of Congress Card Catalog No. 60–14309
© 1961 by John W. F. Dulles

Manufactured in the United States of America

Second Printing, 1967

91

Preface

When the Carranza Government was toppled in 1920 by an armed revolt carried out by men whose views were expressed in the Plan of Agua Prieta, a group from the state of Sonora rode to power in Mexico. Its leaders became known as "El Triangulo Sonorense": De la Huerta, Obregón, and Calles. During the course of the ensuing story, which takes us into 1936, each of these three leaders, in a different way and at a different time, is forcibly eliminated.

This period bridging the latter part of the Carranza Administration and the early part of the Cárdenas Administration was one in which those who had contributed to the successful revolutions against Porfirio Díaz and Victoriano Huerta figured prominently.

Victorious young generals, self-made during Mexico's bloody up-heaval, found reasons for disagreeing among themselves. The discontented frequently complained of dictatorial practices not unsimilar to those they had earlier fought to eradicate. In a number of convulsions large ranks of the Revolution's heroes passed out of historical view.

When battles were not fought by armies they were fought in the field of politics, a game at times so rough-and-tumble that a contemporary publication suggested a coat of armor as the sensible attire for a congressman.

Those who had success in the struggle for power were rewarded with the opportunity of directing the development of Mexico. In any evaluation of performance in this field during the sixteen-year period, consideration should be given to conditions as they existed at the start. In 1920 Mexico's new rulers took over the guidance of a nation which was bankrupt after years of bloody civil strife and which was without diplomatic recognition from the "Great Powers." These new rulers found in Mexico many who were clamoring for practical application of the Revolutionary principles which had been included in the Constitution of 1917; they also found in Mexico some who refused to accept the new regime and who were not unwilling to use force to dislodge it. Official reports showed that illiteracy among persons of ten or more years of age was 67 per cent. Communications were primitive by 1936 standards. Using a special train proceeding at full speed from the capital of Sonora, De la Huerta in 1920 could not reach Mexico City in fewer than seven or eight days. It is also important to consider that Mexico in 1920 was practically without paved roads; beasts of burden had to be used to get to most of the interior parts not touched by the railways. The railways themselves assumed a position of supreme importance, commercially and militarily.

I have chosen to limit myself to a rather detailed description of events which transpired between the presidential campaign of 1919 and the early days of the Cárdenas regime, a regime which is touched on in this study only to the extent necessary to describe fully the fall of that member of the Sonora "Triangulo" who remained a political factor the longest. Faced with the problem of whether to ease the reader's burden by eliminating the names of many of the military and political figures who were involved in the victories and defeats, I have decided against the reader and in favor of a rather complete roster.

PREFACE

Almost in their entirety the accounts of these events have heretofore been unavailable in English and are available in Spanish only if one has access to old newspapers, to conversations with those who helped make the history, and to a very special library—which in no small part will turn out to be a collection of conflicting, passionate, and prejudiced publications. In an effort to present the chronicle with as much accuracy as possible, I was fortunate in receiving the assistance of ten individuals, Mexican historians or participants in the events, who studied my manuscript in careful detail before submitting their observations. I am also indebted to over sixty persons who reminisced and answered questions, and often helped also by tendering me memoranda and letters. But these individuals, often representing vastly different viewpoints, have no ultimate responsibility for what was finally put together. Obviously the decisions about what to tell were necessarily mine.

Most of those to whom I am grateful for help are named in the list of Sources of Material, to be found toward the end of this volume. Some whose assistance has been highly valuable are not included in that list. These include Daphne Rodger, my secretary in Rio de Janeiro, Brazil, and Dorothy Ross, of Monterrey, Mexico, whose helpful suggestions were rendered after careful readings of the manuscript. More than to anyone else I am grateful to my former secretary, Elva Jiménez, also of Monterrey.

Should a greater effort have been made in these pages to interpret all of the material? The president of an American university, in discussing the period covered in this volume, once said that he had seen many books by Americans who chose to interpret Mexico for American readers; he wanted a new book, a chronicle with all the facts. A distinguished writer on Mexico remarked, when he wrote about this work: "You have certainly taken much time and trouble to get at the facts. I still think Mexico is too complicated to understand."

Perhaps, by presenting an objective account, this book can contribute to that understanding. Perhaps the reader, given the facts as best I was able to establish them, will be in a better position than before to interpret for himself, to make his own generalizations, to reach his own conclusions about this period of transition. I hope at least that this work will make available a body of raw material which may be useful to those who are anxious to engage in the difficult task of historical evaluation. I do feel that a few of the more general evaluations which have been published in English have dealt a bit lightly with some of the men who were suddenly faced with difficult problems, and I hope that this book may help to effect a fair consideration of those who in less detailed writings have sometimes been unflatteringly dismissed with readable generalities. Anyway, it did seem logical to gather the information at the particular time when I did it, that is, when many of those who helped shape the events were still living and could be consulted, but when enough time had elapsed to allow some of the passions to cool.

The most reasonable excuse for adding these many pages to the already heavy shelves of literature about Mexico is to make available in English accounts of the principal episodes of a rather hectic era. In 1959 I concluded a period of sixteen years of work in the mining business in Mexico, where I was a happy guest and the recipient of kindnesses I shall never forget. My interest in Mexico's past turned into a particular interest in the fairly recent past, in which many of the friends I had the good fortune to know figured prominently. The publication of this volume allows me to share, with others who are interested in the story of Mexico, the information which I gathered.

But it would be foolish to pretend that any very noble purposes inspired the writing of the chapters which follow. And if this Preface does not succeed in justifying from a scholarly point of view what has been set down, it is probably because putting together these accounts of Obregón, Calles, and their contemporaries was done simply as an enjoyable pastime.

J. W. F. D.

Caixa Postal 898
Belo Horizonte, M. G., Brasil

Contents

CONTENTS

Illustrations

xiv

ILLUSTRATIONS

Maps

YESTERDAY IN MEXICO

1·

General Alvaro Obregón and the Constitutionalist Revolution

General Alvaro Obregón would occasionally explain what happened after he lost his right arm while fighting the Villistas in 1915. All was yet in confusion when the soldiers started a search for the missing arm. They were hunting all over the battlefield. "I was helping them myself, because it's not so easy to abandon such a necessary thing as an arm." But the searchers were not having any luck in finding it. They were just about to give up when one of his companions got the idea of trying a final decisive test. According to the General he was well qualified to determine the nature of the test: "He was one of my most intimate friends and knew me thoroughly." Out of his pocket this friend pulled a nice shiny gold piece, an *azteca*. He raised the coin high in the air, where it glittered attractively in the sun's rays. "And then everyone saw a miracle: the arm came forth from who knows where, and came skipping up to where the gold *azteca* was elevated; it reached up and grasped it in its fingers—lovingly—That was the only way to get my lost arm to appear."

The tough and brilliant teller of this story on himself was born in 1880 on a ranch along the Mayo River in Sonora, the sunny state which lies south of Arizona and borders the Gulf of California. The youngest of eighteen children, he picked up a bit of schooling from his older sisters and then went to work, exhibiting soon a mind which was active, inventive, and, above all, practical. After building up a reputation in the district as an expert with farming equipment, and after engaging in chickpea production on some of the flourishing haciendas, he was able in 1906 to acquire from the federal government a small property near Huatabampo, Sonora. This he named "Quinta Chilla" (Penniless), and with his savings he proceeded to farm there.

While Obregón was busy raising chickpeas at "Quinta Chilla" and caring for his two small children, whose mother had died, the Mexican Revolution of 1910 broke out in opposition to the regime of old General Porfirio Díaz, who had been dictator of Mexico for countless years. Obregón, somewhat to his later regret, did not participate in these early events which revealed popular desire for a change and which showed that the troops of the dictatorship were unexpectedly weak. In May, 1911, Díaz was forced to depart for Europe, and about five months later the presidency of the Republic was taken over by Francisco I. Madero, who had led the movement against the eighty-year-old dictator. Madero, however, was not to have an easy time of it.

Obregón's military career had its inception early in 1912, when General Pascual Orozco, who had contributed mightily to the fall of Porfirio Díaz, took up arms against President Madero. The governor of Sonora, José María Maytorena, endeavored to co-operate with the Madero Government as well as protect his state from the Orozquistas. He offered the rank of lieutenant colonel to all *presidentes municipales* (mayors) who would assemble 250 men to defend the state.

Obregón, who had recently become *presidente municipal* of Huatabampo, left his children under the care of his sisters and presented himself at the state capital, Hermosillo, with about 300 farmers who were ready to fight. Thus he became a lieutenant colonel in the "irregular forces" of Sonora. In Obregón's Fourth Battalion was one man who had had military experience, Captain Eugenio Martínez, and this man set to work training Obregón's farmers in the art of warfare.

The group was joined by other contingents, including Major Salvador Alvarado and his 150 men. Soon was created the Sonora Column, in which Lieutenant Colonel Obregón commanded the cavalry. Suspecting that Orozco, whose forces in Chihuahua were retreating before federal troops under Victoriano Huerta, would seek to invade Sonora by the Púlpito Canyon, the Sonora Column marched into the mountains which separate Sonora from Chihuahua. These men were undeterred by the forebodings of disaster uttered by Revolutionary General José Garibaldi, grandson of the Italian hero.

At Ojitos, ten days' march from Agua Prieta, the Sonora Column met and defeated the Orozquistas in an action in which Obregón distinguished himself. When Obregón's victorious commanding general had the opportunity of presenting members of his staff to General Victoriano Huerta, who was on his way to Ciudad Juárez in his special train, he said to Huerta: "*Mi General*, I have the pleasure of introducing to you Lieutenant Colonel Obregón, who captured the enemy's artillery in the battle of Ojitos." Huerta expressed the hope that this young new leader would become a "promise for the nation."

When Obregón, a full colonel, had returned home after further successes against the Orozquistas, he was called almost immediately to Hermosillo because of serious events in the nation's capital: Victoriano Huerta had turned against President Madero and overthrown him. Maytorena seemed uninterested in taking a stand against Huerta, and when Madero was assassinated in Mexico City on February 22, 1913, Maytorena left the Sonora governorship and was succeeded by his local rival, Ignacio L. Pesqueira.

Pesqueira and the state legislature called on Sonora to rebel against Huerta, a step welcomed by men such as Plutarco Elías Calles, the police commissioner of Agua Prieta, Manuel M. Diéguez, the mayor of Cananea, and Alvaro Obregón. Colonels Obregón, Salvador Alvarado, Benjamín Hill, and others of the region, including Maytorena's jovial private secretary, Francisco R. Serrano, were swift to take up the fight against the hard-drinking Victoriano Huerta. At this point the Mexican Revolution entered a particularly bloody stage.

In another northern state, Coahuila, Governor Venustiano Carranza had taken a similar step after Huerta grabbed the presidency. Assuming the title of First Chief of the Constitutionalist Revolution, this majestically bearded politician and landowner left military operations in the northeast to Pablo González, a deliberative general whose tenacity may have helped the cause but who was to become known as "the general who never won a battle." In nearby Chihuahua the impetuous and daring ex-bandit, Pancho Villa, built up h:s own Army of the North, in which cavalry predominated, and set to work to battle wildly against Huertista elements.

In the south of the country Emiliano Zapata had, like Orozco in the north, been in arms against the late President Madero on the grounds that his administration had been insufficiently revolutionary. Now the Zapatistas continued their already well-known custom of seizing lands from the owners of large estates and fighting against any and all central governments on behalf of drastic agrarian reform. Zapata's informal collection of peons became known by Carrancistas as the Liberating Army of the South; it continued to call itself the Liberating Army of the Mexican Nation.

At Monoclova, Coahuila, in April, 1913, representatives of the Coahuila and Sonora governments and some Constitucionalistas from Chihuahua subscribed to Carranza's stand against Huerta, recognizing Carranza's title of First Chief. The Coahuila Legislature promptly gave its backing to the "Monoclova Convention," and in the summer of 1913 the Sonora Legislature did the same.

As leader of the Constitucionalista forces in the west the resourceful Obregón went from victory to victory, demonstrating qualities which were to make him the greatest military commander in Mexico's history. Besides providing strong leadership and intelligent military planning, he exhibited qualities of unaffected comradeship, which inspired much devotion to him among the rank and file. One of his early victories over the Huertista Federals was that in May, 1913, at Santa Rosa, Sonora, and the list of Obregón's subordinates there was studded with the names of those who were destined to go far. After this triumph Colonels Obregón and Alvarado were promoted to brigadier generalships by First Chief Carranza.

On southward went Obregón's enthusiastic west coast Constitutionalists in a campaign which did much for the reputations of such future stars as Lucio Blanco, Rafael Buelna, Juan Carrasco, Angel Flores, and Enrique Estrada. There was some action at sea when the Constitutionalists disabled the gunboat *Morelos* off Mazatlán, Sinaloa, when the Huertista warship *Guerrero* devastated the *Tampico* (whose captain committed suicide as she sank), and when an expedition took from the Federals the control of the island penal colony at the Islas Marías in the Pacific. There was even a little action in the air. For the first time in history, in April, 1914, a plane was used for warfare, when Constitutionalist Captain Gustavo Salinas and his assistant flew the *Sonora* over the sea near Topolobampo, Sinaloa, in order to drop bombs on ships of Victoriano Huerta. Shortly after that these same flyers used the *Sonora* to bomb the Federals at Mazatlán, the west coast port which was held by Huertistas and which Obregón left in a state of siege while he took most of his warriors further south.

In the north and center of the nation roughrider Pancho Villa faced what was by far the greatest Huertista strength. During the campaign against Orozco in the previous year Villa had served under Huerta, but Huerta had wanted to shoot him for insubordination. Huertistas and Orozquistas were now associated, and against them Villa directed the most thunderous and the most important campaign. His securing possession of the border city of Ciudad Juárez, Chihuahua, in November, 1913, came as a surprise to First Chief Carranza, who by that time had been forced out of Coahuila and was in Sonora, issuing decrees and paper money, and who was in a position to cross to the United States in case of disaster. There followed Villa's capture of Chihuahua City early in December and then, in the spring of 1914, his successful eleven-day attack against the finest flower of Huerta's army: the 12,000 Federals in the Torreón district who were commanded by generals trained at the nation's military college. Villa's Army of the North, which showed little mercy to Spaniards, to Orozquistas, or to Huerta supporters, prepared to push on southward toward the nation's capital, paralleling the march down the coast by Obregón's Army of the West.

But not all was harmony in the ranks of Constitucionalismo. More serious than Obregón's brief altercation with Generals Blanco and Buelna was the bickering between Carranza and Villa and the struggle that developed between Plutarco Elías Calles and May-torena, whom Carranza had set up again in the Sonora governorship. Calles had been placed in a strong military position in Sonora and he removed the governor's personal escort until ordered by Carranza to furnish a new one. But as Maytorena and Villa were in close alliance, and as Salvador Alvarado's men, laying siege to the

Generals Obregón, Villa, *and* Pershing. *Behind Obregón's right shoulder* (*far left in photo*) *is* Francisco Serrano. R. Topete.

port of Guaymas, seemed more partial to Maytorena than to Alvarado, Carranza decided that as a means of insuring the presence of some pro-Carranza troops in Sonora, Calles and his forces should remain in that state instead of joining Obregón.

Villa, now the invincible savior of Constitucionalismo, became disrespectful of the First Chief's orders, particularly as it became clear that if he followed these orders he would not make any rapid headway toward Mexico City. Wishing to move southward on the city of Zacatecas, and win for himself another spectacular victory, he disobeyed Carranza's command that he simply dispatch reinforcements for those who were unsuccessfully trying to oust the Federals there. After offering in a rage to resign as head of the

Army of the North, he had the surprise of finding his offer accepted. Intermediaries finally persuaded him to agree to accept again Carranza's leadership in return for his reinstatement.

To the disappointment of many of the Mexican Catholic clergy and those of the wealthy landowners who did not relish the idea of revolution, Victoriano Huerta found himself forced to flee from Mexico City. Eventually he reached the United States. Thanks to the squabble between Villa and Carranza (who withheld coal for Villa's trains), it was the Army of the West which made the victorious entry into the nation's capital in August, 1914. On this occasion General Obregón visited the grave of President Madero. There, as part of the ceremony, he praised a woman, María Arias, for her constant struggle against the Huerta Administration at a time when many men in the capital had hesitated to take a clear stand, presenting her with his pistol and declaring her to be the one most worthy of receiving it. When Carranza paraded into the city,

Alvaro Obregón *and* Venustiano Carranza. *Enrique Díaz.*

Pablo González refused to participate in the event, resenting the idea that he ride at the First Chief's left while Obregón was honored with the place on his right.

From the capital Carranza now sent representatives into the state of Morelos to try to persuade Zapata to accept his leadership. But all conversations with Zapata proved fruitless. The agile horseman

Venustiano Carranza at his office in the Faros Building, Veracruz. 1915. Enrique Díaz.

of the south, who called for recognition of himself as the Revolution's head, was being more pleasantly wooed by Villa's emissaries from the north.

In Sonora, in the meantime, Maytorena made a prisoner of Alvarado and other Carranza supporters. Obregón therefore set out to negotiate personally with Villa on behalf of the First Chief. As Carranza correctly foresaw, Obregón ultimately failed in his mission to Villa, an effort in which Obregón very nearly lost his life at Villa's hands when in September, 1914, he visited him in Chihuahua in a vain attempt to reach a settlement. Maytorena and Calles then took to the battlefield to settle their differences, Calles receiving considerable assistance from Arnulfo R. Gómez and from Maytorena's failure to follow up an early advantage.

Generals Pablo González, Lucio Blanco, Antonio I. Villarreal, and others were working for a solution through the retirement of both Villa and Carranza. When Enrique Estrada, a close friend of Obregón, realized that Obregón considered Blanco and the youthful Rafael Buelna sympathetic to Villa, he separated his forces from Blanco's division in order to give full and clear support to First Chief Carranza.

Obregón, even after Villa had almost succeeded in assassinating him, persuaded Carranza to agree to the meeting of the Aguascalientes Convention of October, 1914. Accordingly representatives of the different factions met under the chairmanship of Villarreal to settle the differences. The Convention, which placed General Eulalio Gutiérrez in the nation's presidency, proved to be more a victory for the Villistas and Zapatistas than a forerunner of peace. In November Carranza withdrew to the port of Veracruz, on the Gulf of Mexico. Lucio Blanco, who had taken a large contingent out of Obregón's Army of the West, assumed the military control of Mexico City on behalf of the Aguascalientes Convention. In a famous photograph Villa was pictured in the presidential chair with Zapata at his side.

Obregón and his associates were soon busy warring on behalf of Carranza against Villistas, Zapatistas, and the setup which resulted from the Aguascalientes Convention. Probably Obregón's most famous victory was that over Villa in the battles at Celaya, Guanajuato, during April, 1915. There, on April 6 and 7, as the Obregón forces repulsed formidable cavalry attacks by Villa, more than 550 of Obregón's men met their death, most of these casualties being suffered by the brigade of General Fortunato Maycotte. Among the 350 defenders who were wounded was General Eugenio Martínez, trainer of Obregón's first fighting farmers. Undismayed by the fact that about 1,800 of his attackers had been killed in this unsuccessful encounter, Pancho Villa again, and on an even grander scale, tested the merits of furious assault as compared with Obregón's more scientific warfare. This time, on April 13, 14, and 15, against Celaya he threw forces which were estimated at about 25,000 but which were not as well organized or as well armed as Obregón's 15,000 defenders. With the exception of the Civil War in the United States, the American continent has seen no encounter as colossal or sanguinary as was this.[1] That the victors could report 4000 Villistas killed and 6000 taken prisoner was due to Obregón's having excellently prepared 9000 men to resist the attack and having hidden Cesáreo Castro's 6000 cavalrymen on the outskirts of Celaya. When Castro closed in at the right moment, Villa (who had sworn he would teach a lesson to his "perfumed" opponent) received the worst surprise of his life. In reporting to Carranza, Obregón explained his great victory: "Fortunately," he telegraphed, "the enemy was directed by Villa."

Later that same spring Obregón was fighting Villista "reactionaries" at Hacienda Santa Ana de Conde, near Trinidad, Guanajuato. (Carranza, Obregón, and all men of the Revolution had the popular habit of classifying their enemies as "reactionaries.") It was there that Obregón lost his right arm as the result of the explosion of a Villista grenade. The loss of blood and the pain were so great that he felt that it was only a matter of a little time before he should die.

The pistol which he had with him was a very small "Savage," his theory being that the size of a pistol carried by a man was in direct proportion to the fear that characterized him. After the loss of his arm he used his remaining hand to fire the pistol into himself in order that his end might be immediate. But it happened that one of his captains had cleaned the pistol on the previous day and had left it without bullets, an act of carelessness which profoundly affected the future of Mexico. Lieutenant Colonel Jesús M. Garza, seeing what was going on, grabbed the pistol from Obregón. Lieutenant Colonel Aarón Sáenz quickly got a doctor to the spot and then passed to General Francisco Murguía the bad news of Obregón's

[1] Juan Barragán Rodríguez, *Historia del ejército y la revolución constitucionalista*, II, 294.

critical injury. Murguía hastened to the side of the commander, with whom of late he had been quarrelling violently.

Still convinced that his end was near, Obregón said to Murguía: "Tell the First Chief that I have fallen fulfilling my duty and I die blessing the Revolution." Then he suggested that Murguía meet with Generals Hill, Diéguez, and Cesáreo Castro to name a successor to himself as Chief of the Army of Operations.

After a surgical operation, Obregón was advised of further defeats of the Villistas, but the first news received by Carranza was discouraging. Since the unsettled conditions had caused an interruption in telegraph communication between Trinidad, Guanajuato, and the port of Veracruz, the news which Carranza received came by way of Villistas in El Paso, Texas, and the Associated Press.[2] Carranza must have been alarmed to hear in this way that Obregón had been killed in combat and his forces wiped out, this latter report being at great variance from information being brought to Obregón by Hill, acting commander during Obregón's illness. Hill told of the Army's success at León, Guanajuato, in a battle as savage as it was important, a battle which followed strategy devised by Murguía, Castro, and Alejo González, and presented by them to Hill and Diéguez. As the Villista general barracks were at León, Villa and Felipe Angeles had been determined to defend the place at all costs. When Murguía was finally able to enter the ravaged city on June 5, 1915, he had the opportunity of renaming streets and avenues which before his arrival had honored the recent occupants.

While Obregón was still recuperating he received advice of the capture of nearby Silao by Generals Joaquín Amaro, Fortunato Maycotte, and Pablo Quiroga. The convalescent received also at this time a visit from his brother José, who was considerably dejected at General Obregón's condition. The General, showing that he was quite himself, remarked to his brother, who had recently shaved off his mustache, that José looked worse without his mustache than did he, the General, without his right arm.

While to the south of Mexico City Pablo González was engaged in a long-drawn-out and plunderous campaign against the Zapatistas, the Villistas, as the result of Obregón's subsequent victories in the Querétaro and Aguascalientes districts, were pushed to the

---

[2] Juan Barragán in *El Universal*, August 19, 1958.

north of the country. San Luis Potosí, Zacatecas, Saltillo, and Torreon were occupied by the Obregón forces in the months of July, August, and September, 1915; this was during the latter part of this successful campaign against Villa, a campaign in which the name of General Manuel M. Diéguez, ex-mayor of Cananea, Sonora, was added to the list of those who were injured in action.

With Carranza thus placed in control of Mexico's destinies in August, 1915, Salvador Alvarado was assigned the task of ruling the far-away Yucatán Peninsula, and Diéguez that of governing the state of Jalisco. Benjamín Hill took over military control of Mexico City, where the food shortage had been so acute that 1915 was to be remembered as the "Year of Hunger." But Villa made one more stab at disturbing the new order. Hoping for assistance from his Maytorenista allies, he crossed Chihuahua's western mountains in order to conquer Sonora, whose defense on behalf of Carranza now lay in the hands of Calles. In earlier struggles with Maytorena, who was now in the United States, Calles had become an expert at fortification and at the construction of trenches, and he was exceptionally well prepared when Villa, in his typical fashion, assaulted the border town of Agua Prieta on November 1, 1915. Three days later the once-great Villa had to withdraw, only to suffer later in the month a complete rout at the hands of Diéguez, who had disembarked at Guaymas. Villa's military prestige had fallen far, but he continued at large, able to lead his remaining followers in a number of bloody attacks, some of them against citizens of the United States, whose government in October, 1915, had recognized the Carranza regime.

The Sonora governorship went to the severe and radical Calles, who gave the state an administration noted not only for stern measures against the use of intoxicating beverages, but also for a more successful campaign of building up the Cruz Gálvez Industrial School for the Orphans of the Revolution. To the robust Obregón went the federal Ministry of War, and when, in 1916, he married for the second time, the Hermosillo wedding was attended by Lic.[3] Luis Cabrera, intellectual adviser of the First Chief. But before Obregón retired from the government early in 1917, his relations with Carranza had notably cooled. The victorious campaigns which had placed Carranza in the presidency had faded into the past, and

[3] Abbreviation for *Licenciado*, professional title of lawyers.

the one-armed hero of Celaya was pained to note Carranza's inclination to overrule him to the advantage of a young favorite who served as Presidential Chief of Staff.[4]

Obregón, once again a Sonora farmer, was conversing one day with his friend, Lic. Arturo H. Orcí, in Nogales. He asked Orcí for the titles of the texts which the latter had used in studies preceding his course in law, expressing particular interest in history, geography, logic, and psychology. By the time Orcí returned from California, two or three months later, Obregón had obtained the textbooks and

From left to right: Alvaro Obregón, Venustiano Carranza, Pablo González, *and* Cesáreo Castro. *1916. Casasola.*

covered all the material therein, and in addition he had read an extra series of volumes, César Cantú's *Historia Universal,* to supplement the history texts, which seemed to him to be too elementary. When he asked Orcí to quiz him the lawyer was able to recall enough to ask a few questions, including a particularly difficult one

[4] Ramón Puente, *Hombres de la Revolución: Calles,* pp. 97–110.

which Orcí had been called upon to answer during the time of his school studies. Finding that the General had fully mastered all of the subjects about which he was able to inquire, Orcí concluded that Obregón covered in two or three months what ordinarily required six years.

That Obregón's memory was unusually retentive was frequently demonstrated to his friends during the course of card tricks and tests. Remarkable is the size of the group of collaborators whose expressions confirm the recent statement of Lic. A. Romandía Ferreira: "I believe that in my life I have dealt with many persons of talent but up to now I have met no one with the intellectual capacity of General Obregón."[5]

In combination with a splendid mind Obregón had an excellent sense of humor, occasionally somewhat ironic, and he was happy to be known for the jokes which he so much enjoyed telling. He was an ardent conversationalist, who at times could not resist making startling or theatrical remarks. In spite of his preference for the unimpressive clothing of the simple citizenry, Obregón was far from being a modest person. With an enthusiasm which was sometimes infectious, he liked to speak of his triumphs, and it is probable that this pride in his achievements was a characteristic in which followers rejoiced. He had much ambition.

On the other hand Obregón knew how to be very tough, and he exercised that quality when he felt that the occasion so demanded. From a rough environment of plots and treasons, in which many lives were lost and from which he himself had narrow escapes, he picked up useful ways of acting and thinking. Companions came to marvel at the General's calmness in the face of the greatest physical dangers.

[5] A. Romandía Ferreira in *El Universal*, July 6, 1956.

2.

The Presidential Campaign
of 1919–1920

During the first part of 1919 President Carranza told the Mexican people that it was too early to be concerned with the 1920 presidential election. The active and imaginative Obregón, who continued in voluntary retirement in Sonora after having served as Minister of War, was disappointed to receive no word of encouragement from Carranza. The result was that on June 1, 1919, Carranza was surprised to receive a telegram from Obregón in which the latter advised that he was proclaiming to the nation his candidacy for the presidency. The proclamation itself came as an

A voting booth in Mexico City. 1917. Casasola.

even greater shock to Carranza, for within its many pages there were references to evils of the Carranza regime.

Said Carranza to Roberto Pesqueira: "The candidate to succeed me in the presidency of the Republic was General Obregón, but now this cannot be, for he has referred to my administration unjustly."[1]

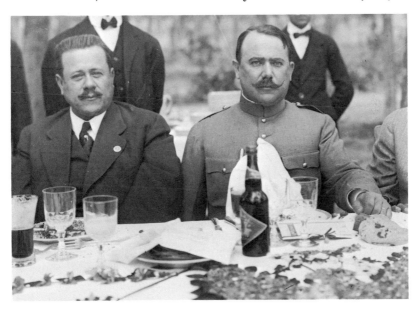

General Alvaro Obregón *just after his retirement from the Cabinet of President Venustiano Carranza. At Obregón's right (on the left side of the picture) is* General Benjamín Hill. *1917. Casasola.*

Whether or not Obregón would have received the nod by remaining more quiet, there thus came into being a serious political contest. Obregón, undoubtedly most serene when in the midst of action, devoted his restless talents to what was for him a new type of campaigning. Carranza looked to Obregón's home state for a candidate worthy of presidential support, and, after learning that Governor Adolfo de la Huerta was uninterested, he sounded out various national leaders on the idea of supporting Ing.[2] Ignacio Bonillas, who was also from Sonora. Few in Mexico were as renowned as Obregón, but certainly Bonillas, the Mexican ambassador to the United States, could not be counted among those few. Pablo Gon-

[1] Miguel Alessio Robles, *A medio camino*, p. 33.
[2] Abbreviation for *Ingeniero*, professional title of engineers.

zález, the warrior from Nuevo León who was Carranza's Chief of Military Operations in the states of Puebla, Tlaxcala, Morelos, Oaxaca, and Veracruz, disappointed the President by refusing to back Bonillas; González announced his own candidacy and engaged in an exchange of open letters with General Obregón.

As a presidential candidate General Obregón might be said to have been the candidate of the Partido Liberal Constitucionalista (P.L.C.). This party was born in 1915 or 1916, very likely as the result of the ideas of General Benjamín Hill, Roque Estrada, Jesús Urueta, and some others.[3] It is clear that during the first part of 1919 Obregón sought affiliation with no political party, and in many ways the wording of his proclamation of June 1 was a blow to the leaders of the Partido Liberal Constitucionalista. But in July, 1919, Obregón did agree to allow the P.L.C. to say that he was its candidate, following some discussions with José Inés Novelo and Rafael Zubaran Capmany in Nogales, Sonora. In September the less important Partido Cooperatista, headed by Jorge Prieto Laurens, came out in favor of Obregón.

Early in November, 1919, Obregón left Sonora in order to tour the nation. Toward the end of the month he reached Mexico City, by which time the voice of his young travelling companion, Luis L. León, had practically wilted as the result of making political speeches along the west coast. Obregón's reception in Mexico City was not particularly warm, although his friends of the P.L.C. did their best to stir up enthusiasm. During the speechmaking which took place on the balcony of the Hotel Saint Francis, the Hero of Celaya had on his right side General Hill and on his left General Plutarco Elías Calles, who was about to resign as Carranza's Minister of Industry and Commerce. Obregón commented after an interview with his former chief: "I cannot hook up my car to the train of Señor Carranza."

As a minister in the Carranza Cabinet General Calles had seemed a rather quiet and somewhat austere figure who was not yet entirely at home with all the rules of etiquette called for in Carranza's top official circles. He had soon become irritated by dishonesty in government and by what he felt to be the Administration's lack of interest in pushing for a really radical and revolutionary program. With the events of 1919 his qualities as a hard-working and astute politician, an associate of labor's cause, became clearly evident. On

[3] Names of others involved in the creation of the P.L.C. may be found in *Los partidos políticos en México* by Vicente Fuente Díaz, II, 15.

behalf of Obregón he got in touch with Luis N. Morones of the Partido Laborista (Labor Party), Felipe Carrillo Puerto of the Partido Socialista de Yucatán, and other important labor leaders, finding little difficulty in persuading them to support Obregón in opposition to the candidate favored by Carranza.[4] Carranza had proved a disappointment to the leaders of Mexico's budding labor movement.

General Benjamín Hill was a forceful and forthright character. and it was his enthusiasm and work, as well as his close association with Obregón, that had much to do with the preservation of the P.L.C. On February 9, 1920, the party gained badly needed prestige when it sponsored the organization of a Centro Director Obregonista to work on behalf of the well-known fighter from Sonora. The president of the Director, Fernando Iglesias Calderón, was highly respected. The membership of the Director included, among others:

Fernando Iglesias Calderón (Pres.)
Plutarco Elías Calles (Vice-Pres.)
Amado Aguirre (Vice-Pres.)
Miguel Alessio Robles
Enrique Colunga
Roque Estrada
Rafael Zubaran Capmany
Cutberto Hidalgo
Francisco R. Serrano
Luis N. Morones
Adalberto Tejeda
Enrique Lieckens

Antonio I. Villarreal
Calixto Maldonado
J. M. Alvarez del Castillo
Claudio N. Tirado
Samuel Yúdico
Manlio Fabio Altamirano
Jesús M. Garza
Luis L. León
Aurelio Manrique, Jr.
Jorge Prieto Laurens
Eduardo Moneda

President of the Comité Obregonista of Guadalajara was Ing. Camilo E. Pani, a distinguished railroad technician who had assisted Obregón during an earlier phase of the Revolution. One of Camilo Pani's brothers, Alberto J. Pani, had in 1915 and 1916 served under Carranza as director of the Constitutionalist Railways and was in 1919 and 1920 serving as Carranza's minister to the French Republic.

When President Venustiano Carranza expressed the reasons which late in 1919 inclined him to favor the candidacy of Ing. Bonillas, they revealed little to indicate that Obregón, with patience, would

[4] Fernando López Portillo in *El Universal*, February 4, 1958.

have received the official blessing. Feeling that peace had been established in the country, the President reasoned that it was not necessary that his successor be an important general. Furthermore, Carranza felt that the keen rivalry among generals would cause trouble if any one of them were favored, and that if Obregón were favored, the men of Pablo González would take up arms. During World War I Mexico had not supported the United States, and, now that the war was over, an important area of Mexico's development would lie in the field of diplomacy. Ing. Bonillas had proved himself an able administrator. He had received a fine technical training in the United States and, as ambassador to the United States, was respected both there and in Mexico. He had not been inactive in working on behalf of the Mexican Revolution. "We should not elect a military man but a civilian, and he must be a man of culture, of ample preparation, able to resolve the great diplomatic problems with which we shall be faced."[5]

The idea of having a well-prepared civilian as Carranza's successor was supported by a large segment of the unorganized civilian public opinion, even if there were those who felt that, in selecting Bonillas, the "First Chief" had in mind his own continuing dominance in the political picture. Bonillas was officially presented as a candidate by the Partido Liberal Democrático late in 1919, and early in 1920 the Partido Civilista was organized to work for his election. Bonillas returned to Mexico from Washington, D.C., in March, 1920. When he crossed the frontier at Laredo he was greeted by a special trainload of supporters headed by General Federico Montes, president of the Comité Civilista. Reaching Saltillo, Coahuila, in this special train on March 19, Bonillas formally announced his acceptance of the candidacy.

Said Obregón: "An excellent person, my *paisano* Bonillas. A man who is serious, honest, and hard-working. The world has lost a magnificent bookkeeper. If I become President of the Republic, I shall offer him the management of a bank."[6] Obregonista campaigner Luis L. León, who does not lack a sense of humor, has retold a story concerning Luis Cabrera, Carranza's Finance Minister. Cabrera, according to the story, remarked at this time: "If González achieves the presidency, I hope I shall not be shot; if Obregón

---

[5] A more complete account of Carranza's views on this matter may be found in *Por la escuela y por la patria* by Andrés Osuna, pp. 237–239.

[6] Vicente Blasco Ibáñez, *El militarismo mejicano*, Art. II.

achieves the presidency, I hope I shall not be exiled; and if Bonillas achieves the presidency, I hope I shall not have to take a position in the government."

By the time that Bonillas made his announcement in Saltillo, the federal government had provoked the hostility of the Sonora state government. The trouble started in 1919 when Carranza declared that the Sonora River was the property of the nation, Sonora's governor replying that it belonged to the state. Not long thereafter, Governor Adolfo de la Huerta became indignant at Carranza's opposition to arrangements he had entered into with his friends, the Yaqui Indians, and he accused the federal government of taking steps to renew an armed campaign against them. Then, when on March 4, 1920, Carranza named Manuel M. Diéguez, head of military operations in Chihuahua, to be head of military operations in Sonora, Governor De la Huerta again protested. As Diéguez prepared to bring Carrancista troops into Sonora, by way of the United States, De la Huerta named General Plutarco Elías Calles to be head of Sonora military operations, and he named General Angel Flores to be head of Sinaloa military operations.

While the controversy between the federal government and Sonora was growing more and more acrimonious, the presidential campaign went forward vigorously. The Bonillas reception in Mexico City was marred by the activities of Obregonistas, who let forth materials of dismaying smell in front of the speakers on the balcony. Vicente Blasco Ibáñez describes the orators, largely generals calling for an end to militarism, fanning the air with one hand and holding their noses with the other. Eventually the disrespectful yells of Obregonistas caused the arrival of the police and the subsequent jailing of the most vociferous offenders.

While Bonillas, with the help of Generals Montes, Aguilar, Barragán, and others, proclaimed the virtues of *civilismo*, political enemies of the candidate referred to him as "Meester Bonillas" and they pointed out that his election would amount to an imposition resulting from the valuable assistance he was receiving from Carranza. They did not doubt that the well-organized Bonillas campaign, with its innumerable posters and leaflets, was financed in large part by government funds. To emphasize that Bonillas was an unknown in Mexico opposition jokesters implied that the candidate was busy learning the Spanish language. They called him "Flor de

Té" (Tea Blossom), which, according to a popular song of the day, was the nickname of a little vagabond shepherd "who knows not whence he came, nor what is his name, nor where he was born."

General Pablo González, now an opposition candidate, was not without money, and posters bearing his likeness found wide distribution. The General got some support from anti-Carrancistas who lacked enthusiasm for Obregón. Like other candidates, he did not picture his candidacy as one of *militarismo*. "In one of the leading theatres of Mexico," wrote Vicente Blasco Ibáñez, "the authors of a review, in which Bonillas appeared dressed as the little shepherd 'Flor de Té' and Obregón spoke of his chickpeas and his firm resolve to occupy the presidency even with blows of a club, presented Don Pablo at the end in a more comic manner. He had on the uniform of campaign; his aspect was threatening; the black lenses and the enormous mustache gave him a fierce air. He advanced slowly shooting a cannon, and on reaching the foot-lights he growled with a cross voice, similar to the roar of a hungry savage, 'I am a pacifist.' "[7]

Obregón's campaign took him to Michoacán, where he got along well with the governor, General Pascual Ortiz Rubio. During part of his trip in the center and north of the nation he was accompanied by General Jesús María Garza and Lic. Rafael Martínez de Escobar; also by those prominent young men of San Luis Potosí, Professor Aurelio Manrique, Jr., and Sr. Jorge Prieto Laurens. General Garza went on ahead to see Lic. Emilio Portes Gil, of Tamaulipas, who organized a reception for Obregón at Tampico. By this time the candidate, a born orator, was becoming ardent. Carrancistas made use of the police, and in Tampico supporters of Obregón were jailed.

During his political tour Obregón took advantage of opportunities to speak with military leaders who were in command of troops and whom he considered to be friendly to him. It was the duty, he pointed out, of good Revolutionaries to prevent the planned imposition, and the generals should be prepared for any eventuality. He sent messages with this import to General Manuel Peláez and to General Arnulfo R. Gómez in the rich petroleum district.[8]

Bonillas likewise undertook an active tour of propaganda, but on occasion found his program somewhat handicapped by misfortunes which occurred to his train. Railroad labor was partial to Obregón.

[7] *Ibid.*, Art. IV.
[8] Fernando López Portillo in *El Universal*, February 4, 1958.

General Obregón had once observed that "the three principal enemies of Mexico are: militarism, the clergy, and capitalism; we can liberate the country from the last two, but who will liberate it from us?" Now he publicly grieved for Carranza's place in history if Carranza could do no more than offer the same tragic result of all previous Mexican revolutions: the failure to allow the country to liberate itself from its liberators.[9]

Early in April, 1920, Obregón was addressing an audience in Monterrey. When some of his remarks were greeted by shouts of "death to Bonillas," Obregón admonished his listeners against such cries. He pleaded with them to show proper respect for corpses. In a more serious tone Obregón told his Monterrey audience that, in response to an official summons from Carranza's Minister of War, he was leaving for Mexico City. This summons ordered Obregón to appear without delay as a witness at the trial wherein the Carranza government was accusing General Roberto F. Cejudo of treason. Under the circumstances there were many who doubted Obregón's wisdom in making such an appearance. Some of the Carranza supporters were surprised that he accepted the summons; perhaps they had hoped that under the threat he would withdraw to United States territory, thus invalidating his candidacy under the Constitution, or else commit the crime of ignoring the summons.

In Mexico City Obregón (and his private secretary, Fernando Torreblanca) stayed at the home of Lic. Miguel Alessio Robles, because General Hill felt that it would be dangerous to stay at the Hotel Saint Francis. Obregón was carefully watched by Carranza's police, and it seemed evident that the purpose of the trial (to which the general public was not admitted) was to show that Obregón had been implicated in a plot against the Carranza Government. The position of the one-armed hero of Celaya appeared to be very dangerous, especially considering what had happened to some of his supporters in Tampico, and the strongly anti-Carranza behavior of his friends in faraway Sonora.

Whenever Obregón moved from the house of Alessio Robles, which he did in order to visit General Hill at his home and also to have a well-publicized conference with General Pablo González, he was accompanied by an escort of government agents on motorcycles.

It was during these days that Obregón had a lengthy lunch at

[9] Carlos Barrera, *Obregón: Estampas de un caudillo*, pp. xi, 24, 101.

Mexico City's Bach Restaurant with Vicente Blasco Ibáñez. The Spanish author, who was picking up material about Mexico, listened for three hours while the modestly attired general spoke with enthusiasm about the Revolution, his experiences as a broker of chickpeas, and his recent campaign speeches. Obregón, as usual, also enjoyed amusing his distinguished guest (and perhaps also himself) with anecdotes:

"You know how they robbed the minister of Spain of his watch?..."

Obregón then described the magnificent banquet which was given at Chapultepec Castle by Carranza in honor of the minister from Spain, the first European nation to recognize the Carranza regime. The white-bearded First Chief had invited the high government officials of the day, among whom was Obregón, then Minister of War. Also among the notables present was Carranza's Chief of Staff, twenty-seven–year–old General Juan Barragán, well known for his good looks and his dazzling uniforms, as well as for the great power that went with his position. At the dinner the Spanish minister found himself seated between Obregón and Carranza's son-in-law, General Cándido Aguilar, who was then Minister of Foreign Relations. Carranza was across the table from the guest of honor.

"Suddenly," continued Obregón to Blasco Ibáñez, "the Spanish minister puts his hand to his waistcoat and turns pale. 'Caramba! They've stolen my watch.' (It was a beautiful old watch of gold and diamonds, a real jewel, a family heirloom.) Complete silence. Everybody looks at me, seated next to him. But it's the side where my arm is missing. So *I* couldn't have stolen the watch. Then they look to see who is on the other side. It's Cándido Aguilar, the son-in-law of Don Venustiano. He's not missing an arm but he has one hand almost paralyzed, by chance the one which is at the side of the Minister. So neither could *he* be the robber.

"By now convinced that he will never recover his watch, the Spanish diplomat spends the rest of the meal muttering to himself: 'They've stolen my watch! They've stolen my watch! This isn't a government, it's a nest of thieves!'

"Upon getting up from the table, Don Venustiano approaches him in his grave and venerable manner. 'Take it and shut up!' he says, and turns the watch over to him.

"The diplomat cannot contain his astonishment. A man who was not at his side but who was facing him! . . . And he exclaims with sincere admiration: 'Ah, Señor Presidente! With reason you are called the First Chief.' "[10]

For those who were more interested in the United States than in Spain, Carranza's belittlers had a tale of John D. Rockefeller's watch which was lost in Mexico. When Carranza returned it to a grateful Mr. Rockefeller, the latter asked how it had been retrieved. Carranza's reply: "I got it from the Minister of Justice, but he doesn't yet know that he has lost it."

As the trial of General Cejudo progressed, the time for Obregón's appearance arrived. Accompanied by Hill, Rafael Zubaran, and Miguel Alessio Robles, and followed by a mass of supporters, Obregón, on the morning of April 11, 1920, entered the military courtroom in the prison of Santiago Tlaltelolco to face the accusation which had been formulated by young General Juan Barragán. On his arrival Obregón was hailed by the Yaqui Indian soldiers who made up the prison guard. The presiding judge was Lic. Pascual Morales y Molina, who had just been made a general in order that he might handle the proceedings on this occasion. During the formalities the prosecution produced a letter which General Cejudo had addressed to Obregón but which had been intercepted by the government. The prevailing sympathy of those present was manifestly pro-Obregón, and Morales y Molina, after conferring with Barragán, quickly suspended the hearing and ordered Obregón to return to the courtroom on the following morning, April 12.[11]

Back at the home of Miguel Alessio Robles, Obregón received copies of decoded telegrams which had recently been exchanged between Carranza and Governor De la Huerta of Sonora. The federal government declared that De la Huerta was no longer the governor and ordered General Ignacio L. Pesqueira to act as military governor of the state.

A telegram from Calles made it known that Sonora was withdrawing recognition of the Carranza regime. Obregón has been reported to have wondered at this moment about the loyalties of Generals Calles and Alvarado,[12] and to have remarked: "This

[10] Vicente Blasco Ibáñez, op. cit., Art. III.
[11] Jorge Prieto Laurens in El Universal, January 15, 1958.
[12] Miguel Alessio Robles, A medio camino, p. 45.

Plutarco wants them to seize me here in Mexico City."[13] Without doubt Calles was extraordinarily active in the decisive actions being taken in Sonora, and in instilling confidence and fight in his friend, Governor De la Huerta.[14]

In Mexico City Obregón told his supporters that if he should be captured and jailed, they were to carry on the struggle. He sent Prieto Laurens to tell General Enrique Estrada, the governor of Zacatecas, that the moment had arrived for the armed struggle to start.[15]

[13] Jorge Prieto Laurens in *El Universal*, January 15, 1958.
[14] Ramón Puente, *Hombres de la Revolución: Calles*, p. 122.
[15] Jorge Prieto Laurens in *El Universal*, January 15, 1958.

3.

The Plan of Agua Prieta

After supper on the evening of April 11 Obregón left the house where he had been residing, making his departure in an automobile with Lic. Alessio Robles, Lic. Rafael Zubaran, and the moonfaced labor leader, Luis N. Morones. Noting that the car was being followed by four or five of the government motorcyclists, Obregón exchanged his prominent straw hat for the hat of Zubaran. Then when they reached one of the parks, Obregón jumped from the moving automobile and hid among the park trees. Soon he got into a Ford which had been placed there in readiness by Margarito Ramírez and Faustino Gutiérrez, who were two railroadmen working with the Mexico City-Iguala train. Obregón went to Margarito Ramírez' house, and when he later left it he was wearing a rail-

Alvaro Obregón (*center*) *and* Margarito Ramírez (*right*), *both with railroad lanterns, at Iguala, Guerrero, after the escape from Mexico City on April 12, 1920. A coat makes Obregón's lost arm unnoticeable. Casasola.*

roadman's hat and carrying a lantern. A large coat made unnoticeable the lost arm. With the help of his friends of the railways he found a hiding place, behind some baskets of chickens, in a railroad car which left the Buenavista Station for Iguala, Guerrero (to the south) at 6:00 A.M. on the morning of April 12.

The police had not noted Obregón's departure from the company of Alessio Robles, Zubaran, and Morones, and when these men went to refresh themselves with cognac at the Café Colón (then on the Paseo de la Reforma) they were interrupted by the police, seeking Obregón.

Before leaving these friends Obregón had asked Morones to cash a check for 500 pesos against the Comisión Monetaria and to purchase for him some medicines and a gadget for cutting hair, using the remainder for the needs of the Morones family. Morones relates that he was able to cash the check in spite of some difficulty which came about when the Comisión Monetaria stated that Obregón had no funds with it.

Early on the morning of the twelfth, when Obregón was supposed to return again to Santiago Tlaltelolco prison, the house of Miguel Alessio Robles was very strongly guarded by the police. Obregón had barely escaped in time, as the intention to jail him would have been carried out, apparently, had he remained a few more hours in Mexico City.[1] Upon learning of the disappearance of the candidate, Carranza sent urgent telegrams to governors and to military commanders, ordering that he be found and arrested.

Such a telegram was received by General Fortunato Maycotte, one of Obregón's former comrades in arms, who discovered Obregón sound asleep under a tree in a very small village near Mexcala, Guerrero, his head resting on a rock covered with his coat.

Upon being awakened, the fugitive said, "It has fallen to you to take me prisoner, I am your prisoner."

"No, *Mi General*," replied Maycotte. "You are not my prisoner; you are my friend and my *jefe*, who on other occasions commanded me in the combats we waged against the Villistas. Thus it is that I am at your orders to serve you and help you in this adventure."

With this defiance of Carranza's orders, Maycotte and his forces were in rebellion against the government. Upon learning of Maycotte's behavior Carranza ordered him thrown out of the Army. The newspapers had just published Maycotte's telegram to Ca-

[1] Vicente Blasco Ibáñez, *El militarismo mejicano*, Art. III.

rranza, reiterating his adherence to the federal government and stating that the President had taken a proper attitude in the case of Sonora and had justice on his side.

The newspapers of Mexico City were full of impressive telegrams of allegiance to the Carranza Government, as well as speculations about the mysterious disappearance of Obregón. While Calles was reportedly busy preparing to defend Sonora, the news about Dié-guez, Carranza's military chief in Chihuahua, was conflicting. Readers could assume that he was either boarding the gunboat *Guerrero* at Manzanillo, Nayarit, in order to invade Sonora at the port of Guaymas, or was moving through Chihuahua. Arizona's Governor Thomas E. Campbell objected to allowing Carranza troops to move through his state. Meanwhile Barragán, the Federal Chief of Staff, forecast an early collapse of Sonora, pointing out that Calles and De la Huerta had few arms, and Bonillas left the capital for Acámbaro, Guanajuato, in a special campaign train.

Obregón had told Morones to join him somewhere between Mexico City and Chilpancingo, Guerrero, and so on April 13 the portly young labor leader left the capital for Iguala, Guerrero. Not finding the candidate there he went on to Mexcala, where he was successful in joining up with Obregón, Lic. Eduardo Neri, and Lic. Mastache. They all continued southward to Chilpancingo, from which point on April 20 various pronouncements and manifestos were issued. In a manifesto to the nation Obregón reached the sad conclusion that, in view of the conduct of the Carranza Government, the political campaign could not be continued and that arms would have to be used to safeguard the virtues which the Government was seeking by arms to destroy; he placed himself at the orders of the governor of the free and sovereign state of Sonora. In a manifesto to the members of the Partido Laborista Mexicano, Morones, Salvador Alvarez, and Ricardo Treviño stated that the Party's Directive Committee would work for Obregón and De la Huerta; all members of the working class were advised to do likewise. And in a speech at Chilpancingo Obregón praised the anti-Carranza attitude taken by Guerreo's governor, Francisco Figueroa, and the chief of Military Operations in Guerrero, Fortunato Maycotte.[2]

[2] Luis N. Morones, letter, February 16, 1957; Miguel Alessio Robles, *A medio camino*, pp. 41–53; Adolfo de la Huerta, *Memorias*, pp. 89–90; *Campaña política del C. Alvaro Obregón, candidato de la presidencia de la República, 1920–1924*, III, 279–355.

Others who fled from Mexico City at about this same time in the spring of 1920 were Benjamín Hill, Cutberto Hidalgo, Rafael Zubaran Capmany, and Miguel Alessio Robles. Luis Morones took a boat from Acapulco to Sonora, but activities that he planned, such as conferences at Cananea, did not meet with De la Huerta's approval.

The Sonora rebellion against Carranza started on April 11, 1920, the same day on which Obregón went into hiding at the home of railroadman Margarito Ramírez. By the fifteenth the rebellion had been backed by the governor of Zacatecas, General Enrique Estrada, and in the south by the governor of Michoacán, General e Ing. Pascual Ortiz Rubio, a staunch supporter of Obregón and one who had had some differences with Carranza.

Movements of armed revolt were customarily accompanied by "Plans," or proclamations which sought to explain and justify what was being done. Those in Sonora who were defying Carranza's efforts to control their state issued their "Plan" on April 23, 1920, at Agua Prieta, Sonora, which touches the United States border. The proclamation of the Plan of Agua Prieta was largely the work of the governor of Sonora, De la Huerta, and of Generals Plutarco Elías Calles and Salvador Alvarado. Credit for its wording goes to that erudite lawyer and speaker, Lic. Gilberto Valenzuela, who was then president of the Sonora state legislature and who had originally drawn it up as the Plan of Hermosillo, only to have it issued, with a few minor changes in wording, at the spot where Calles had defeated Villa and where he had once been police commissioner. Signers included Ing. Luis L. León, Generals Angel Flores, Francisco R. Manzo, Francisco R. Serrano, Roberto Cruz, and Alejandro Mange and Colonels Abelardo L. Rodríguez, J. M. Aguirre, and Fausto Topete. When De la Huerta received it, some days after it was drawn up, with the original signatures, he immediately added his own.

The Plan of Agua Prieta proclaimed that the sovereignty resides essentially in the people. It said further that Carranza had made himself head of a political party and in seeking the triumph of that party he had systematically made mockery of the popular vote and had repeatedly assaulted the sovereignty of the states. Such acts, said the Plan, were absolute treason to the fundamental aspirations of the Constitutionalist Revolution. Since all peaceful means to right the wrongs committed by Carranza had been exhausted, the moment had arrived for the people to defend their sovereignty by means of arms and to remove from the faithless President the powers which had been conferred upon him.

The Plan asserted that, in view of the above, Carranza should no longer be considered to be President of Mexico. Also, the recently announced election results in the states of Guanajuato, San Luis Potosí, Querétaro, Nuevo León, and Tamaulipas should be considered as void. Adolfo de la Huerta was declared to be Supreme Chief of the Liberal Constitutionalist Army. The signers agreed that when Mexico City had been occupied by the Liberal Constitutionalist Army, a Provisional President of Mexico would be selected. He would name provisional governors in those states where the recent results were void, and would call for a new popular election to fill the nation's presidency and the federal congressional chambers. As originally worded the Plan called for the installation of Adolfo de la Huerta as Mexico's Provisional President, but, at the suggestion of General Calles, Ing. Luis L. León arranged to have the wording changed in this respect.

So fast and furious was the allegiance given to the Sonora group by the Revolutionary generals that Luis Cabrera spoke of the movement as "the strike by the Army men." Among those who broke with Carranza late in April were: Arnulfo R. Gómez (with an important command in the petroleum district in the east), Antonio I. Villarreal (Torreón, Coahuila), and Lázaro Cárdenas (Papantla, Veracruz). General Manuel Peláez, who was operating in the east, was already in revolt against Carranza. Chihuahua backers of the movement included Generals Ignacio Enríquez, Francisco Urbalejo, Eugenio Martínez, J. Gonzalo Escobar, Joaquín Amaro, Abundio Gómez, Alfredo Rueda Quijano, and José Amarillas. In the south Generals Fortunato Maycotte and Pascual Oritz Rubio were joined by Alberto Pineda (Oaxaca) and Carlos Vidal (Chiapas). It was no surprise when General Benjamín G. Hill, the commander of forces in Mexico City who had mysteriously disappeared at the same time as Obregón, announced that he had joined the Agua Prieta movement. Then General Carlos Greene, the Tabasco governor, added his name to the list. Greene had, not long before, received valuable political assistance from that loyal Carrancista, Cándido Aguilar.

The break between President Carranza and General Jacinto B. Treviño must have been a cause of sadness to both men. Treviño had been the first to sign the Plan of Guadalupe, under which Carranza started the revolution which toppled Victoriano Huerta. He had early acted as Carranza's chief of staff. As a Carrancista general fighting Villa, Treviño had, in Tampico in 1915, followed the example set in April, 1914, by Obregon's Army of the West in using planes in Mexican civil warfare. The planes had remained for forty minutes in the air, chiefly observing, but also dropping some bombs which Treviño had prepared in the Tampico shops.

General Treviño was a good friend of De la Huerta. Two days prior to the issuance of the Plan of Agua Prieta, Treviño and six others, including General Francisco J. Múgica of Michoacán, called on President Carranza and unsuccessfully tried to persuade him to desist in the steps he was taking with regard to Sonora and General Obregón. Once Carranza had determined on a course it was not easy to get him to change, regardless of circumstances. After Treviño and his companions had thus failed in their efforts to bring about the peace, Treviño transferred his support and his forces to the side of De la Huerta, and these forces were an important factor in the fighting that followed. Although Carranza's former associates, including Obregón and Treviño, clearly endeavored to give their old First Chief an opportunity to assure his own personal safety, Carranza showed no interest in their proposals.

The 22,000 men who were considered to be under the leadership of Pablo González made up the largest military group. Don Pablo remained for a while in Mexico City without making his position clear, merely maintaining his status as opposition candidate to both Obregón and Carranza's man, Bonillas. At the end of April he had a conference with the President, after which it was reported that he had suggested the resignations of two top Cabinet officers (Aguirre Berlanga of Gobernación[3] and Cabrera of Finance), a suggestion which Carranza had rejected.[4] General González then left Mexico City in the evening. Some of his supporters advised that politics had tired him and he was going to rest in the country before resuming his campaign. More astute observers guessed what Don Pablo was up to. And although there were semi-official reports which indicated that his departure was "a good riddance," the truth was that the step taken by Pablo González placed Carranza in a very acute pre-

[3] The Ministry of Gobernación (Government), top-ranking secretaryship in the Cabinet, includes among its functions the handling of the relations of the federal executive branch with the other branches of the federal government and with the state governments. This ministry was interested in the nation's political matters.

[4] *Campaña política del C. Alvaro Obregón*, III, 456.

dicament, and the capital in imminent danger of a devastating attack by the forces of González and Treviño, who promptly occupied the city of Puebla.

During May the bandwagon of rebels became full. Among the few who remained loyal to the old chief were Generals Diéguez (in Jalisco), Cesáreo Castro (in Torreón, Coahuila), Cándido Aguilar (then governor of Veracruz), and Francisco Murguía. General Murguía on April 30 took charge of the Carrancista forces in the critical Mexico City area, having been urgently called there from Tampico. General Pilar R. Sánchez, although he operated under the orders of Pablo González, remained loyal to Carranza, and plans were developed to have him and his men recapture Puebla with help from the numerous forces of General Guadalupe Sánchez, of Veracruz.

Carranza prepared a great departure from Mexico City with the idea of setting up his government in Veracruz, as he had done in 1914 following the Aguascalientes Convention. In spite of difficulties caused by the fact that most railroad employees favored Obregón, a collection of trains, including the presidential *Tren Dorado* (Gold Train), pulled out of the capital city on May 7, 1920. The various trains in the retinue, said to have come to eight miles in length, contained not only Carranza and thousands of government associates but also innumerable friends and friends of friends and their families. Eight or ten thousand persons, half of them women, started out on this exodus, which was not entirely well organized. The trains contained family possessions, government files, fighting equipment, and the Mexican treasury funds amounting to 11 million gold pesos. They contained the dies of the government mint. But they did not contain anywhere near enough water either for the people or the engines. Medical provisions were few.

This departure took place none too soon, coinciding with the entry of Pablo González and Jacinto B. Treviño into Mexico City. Rebel General Jesús M. Guajardo, who had recently arranged the death of Emiliano Zapata, was able to overtake the last part of the group of fleeing trains and, with a locomotive, he managed to derail or otherwise impede about half of the railroad cars. In this process hundreds were killed, and many were injured and taken prisoner. Much fighting equipment was taken.

The trains that escaped Guajardo were soon joined by Carrancista Generals Francisco Murguía, Heliodoro Pérez, and Pilar R.

Venustiano Carranza and his men departing from the presidential train at Aljibes. Mar. 1920. Photo by J. Rafael Sosa. Casasola.

Sánchez and their men. A loyal cavalry squadron of youths from the Government Military School successfully fought off some of the rebels and was able to join the retinue shortly after the exodus began. In the fighting on May 9 the presidential forces were able to repulse attackers who descended on them from Puebla and Tlaxcala.

The catastrophe took place at Aljibes, Puebla. There the presidential trains ran into torn-up track. Besides, the locomotives were out of water and, seemingly, could get none. Rebels from Oaxaca, under General Luis T. Mireles, and from the Valley of Mexico, under General Jacinto B. Treviño, closed in. What contributed mightily to the catastrophe, and was another bitter pill for Don Venustiano, was the action taken by the troops from Veracruz, who under General Guadalupe Sánchez, were also closing in against the faithful. General Sánchez, protégé of General Cándido Aguilar, had recently proclaimed his undying loyalty to Carranza, and it was his control of Veracruz that had persuaded Carranza to move his government to that place. His suddenly joining the others in support of the Plan of Agua Prieta apparently left the Carrancistas with no place to go.

In the fighting which took place at Aljibes on May 13, General Murguía distinguished himself, and, in spite of the fact that many of his own men deserted to the foe, he was able to drive off those who were closing in. But on May 14 a second attack by the rebels caused the rout of the 4000 who had got that far from Mexico City.

Accompanied by his closest advisers and some of his soldiers, Carranza set out on horseback for the north.

On May 9, 1920, following a conversation with Pablo González at Tacubaya, on the outskirts of Mexico City, Alvaro Obregón made a triumphant entry into the capital, whence he had been lucky to escape in disguise less than a month earlier. On his entry he was accompanied by Generals Benjamín Hill, Fortunato Maycotte, Manuel García Vigil, Genovevo de la O (head of the Zapatista fighters), and many others. The Partido Liberal Constitucionalista invited the people to acclaim him as he rode on horseback down the Paseo de la Reforma to the Hotel Saint Francis.

Pablo González, who was now known as the head of the Liberal Revolutionary Army, was not recognizing the Plan of Agua Prieta, under whose banner the Liberal Constitutionalist Army, headed by De la Huerta, had been fighting. On the twelfth of May, in the company of the various generals who supported one or the other of them, Generals Obregón and González discussed this particular point. González, as was his custom, spoke in a manner which indicated that his words and ideas were the result of a very careful mental weighing of the pros and cons. He concluded that the objective of the Plan of Agua Prieta had been achieved with the overthrow of Carranza, and that the proper thing to do now was to submit the Plan to the consideration of the legislative and judicial powers. The practical Obregón thereupon expressed his pleasure at this demonstration of unity, and all agreed that De la Huerta should ask the Congress to name a Provisional President and call for a general election for a Constitutional President. Pablo González was named supreme commander of all the "revolutionary" forces, but as time passed his once-preponderant military advantage in the capital was being reduced by the arrival of forces loyal to Obregón. About a week earlier Obregón, strictly speaking, controlled in that vicinity only the few thousand who were loyal to Maycotte.

After an evaluation of this situation Pablo González issued on May 15 a manifesto to the Mexican people advising that he was withdrawing as a candidate for the constitutional presidency, "sacrificing his political interests for those of the nation." He explained his recent decision not to approve, even with neutrality, Carranza's efforts at imposition, and he added that during the short military campaign he had been meditating on how to establish a solid peace. That opportunity had arrived. If he and Obregón were to oppose each other in the forthcoming political campaign, the resulting division in the Army would be highly dangerous. He concluded by wishing the country well.

As a result of this excellent statement, González received many congratulatory messages, including one from Obregón and one from the Archbishop of Mexico, José Mora y del Río. It was a disappointment to some of the Church leaders that Pablo González, "such a serious man," was the one to express his resolution to step aside.

The governor of Michoacán, General e Ing. Pascual Ortiz Rubio, reached Mexico City on May 20 following a call from Obregón. As chief engineer for the Agua Prieta movement in a number of states, Ortiz Rubio had organized a large army of men[5] and with 2000 of them he entered the capital. Obregón, after remarking

---

[5] José Ugalde, *Quién es Ortiz Rubio*, p. 4.

that these new arrivals had come at a good time, because "Uncle Pablo" González had been seeking to gobble up the command, promised Ortiz Rubio an appointment as Minister of Communications and Public Works.[6]

When General e Ingeniero Amado Aguirre reached Mexico City from Jalisco, he was invited for a meal with Obregón. Aguirre asked Obregón what his plans were for General Diéguez, who, as a result of his recent activities, was now in jail, having been captured in Guadalajara just before that city was taken by the troops of Generals Jesús M. Garza and Enrique Estrada. Aguirre reminded Obregón of Diéguez' important past services to the Revolution. Said Obregón: "To sacrifice these men is to elevate them to the category of martyrs and they do not deserve it, because as revolutionaries they have bungled. This should weigh on their consciences and the best punishment for them is to leave them so that their shame degrade them." As for Diéguez: "Do not forget your old *Jefe*, although had you fallen into his power in recent days, surely we would not be here talking."[7]

Among the men whom Obregón did not forget was Sr. Margarito Ramírez, the railroadman who was working on the Mexico City-Iguala train and who made the arrangements to hide Obregón among the straw baskets when that train went south on April 12. He became Chief of Military Trains, and that post turned out to be the prelude to others: the superintendency of the Guadalajara Division of the National Railways and the governorship of Jalisco.[8]

[6] Pascual Ortiz Rubio, "Medio siglo: Memorias."
[7] Amado Aguirre, *Mis memorias de campaña*, p. 323.
[8] Salvador J. Romero, memorandum, December 20, 1956.

4·

Tlaxcalantongo

Following the disaster at Aljibes Don Venustiano Carranza led his column of about seventy men across the mountain trails of the northern part of the state of Puebla. This bespectacled and white-bearded rider of sixty years was every inch the patriarch, often a very stubborn patriarch. The weather was wet and windy, frequently foggy. The mountain trails were steep and narrow, overgrown with vegetation. And the enemy was all around.

During the long and painful march, Carranza, as always, stayed at the head of the procession. In rejecting enemy offers of safe-conduct, he had made it clear that he would fight to the end and that as long as he had any supporters he would not abandon them. He might now have had with him a greater number had he not recently commanded the group of about seventy-five young cavalry cadets to leave his side rather than to continue exposing themselves to the dangers of useless sacrifice.

What his present column lacked in quantity was made up for in distinguished names. The procession of men on horseback included the great men of the once mighty Carranza regime.

There was General Francisco Murguía, who had fought ably at the side of the First Chief at the recent battles of Rinconada and Aljibes, and who in 1915 had distinguished himself in battle against the Villistas at León, Guanajuato. Murguía was usually to be found in second place, following Carranza, in the single-line formation that the narrowness of the Puebla trails often forced the column to assume.

There was Lic. Luis Cabrera, the Finance Minister and the closest adviser to the President.

There was Ing. Ignacio Bonillas, who Carranza had hoped would be President of Mexico from December, 1920, to December, 1924. Like Don Venustiano, the recent ambassador to the United States was serene and steady in adversity.

There were, in this procession of riders, General Francisco L. Urquizo, who acted as Minister of War, General Juan Barragán, the young presidential Chief of Staff who liked to travel incognito, and General Marciano González, head of the Military Manufacturing Establishments; also Generals Federico Montes, Pilar R. Sánchez, and Heliodoro Pérez. Among the other notables in the group were Lic. Manuel Aguirre Berlanga, who held the top-ranking Cabinet position, that of Minister of Gobernación, Sr. Gil Farías, who was Carranza's private secretary, and Lic. Pascual Morales y Molina, who was handling the government's legal proceeding against the rebels.

The weather in northern Puebla was appropriate for the bitter occasion, and bitter it must have been for the self-confident President who had figured so prominently in the Mexican Revolution, leading the overthrow of the usurper of power, Victoriano Huerta, and then struggling against the activities of both Villa and Zapata. During the campaign against Huerta, Carranza had strongly protested the occupation of Veracruz by the powerful nation to the north, and during World War I he had persevered in a course of foreign policy which was thoroughly disappointing to Washington. Nor had important United States interests found much to cheer about in domestic legislation produced during the Carranza regime, in the course of which had been drawn up and established the Constitution of the Mexican Revolution, that of February 5, 1917, the first Mexican constitution since 1857 and presently the law of the land.

Now as he and his remaining friends went forward through Puebla it was disappointing to find that Lieutenant Colonel Gabriel Barrios, on whom Lic. Luis Cabrera had counted, had followed the action of the majority of the military. Perhaps this was not surprising, because General Francisco R. Serrano, one of the members of the Sonora group, had earlier approached Barrios at Zacatlán, Puebla.

Anyway, General Francisco de P. Mariel, long the military commander of this mountainous region of northern Puebla, remained faithful, and as the presidential contingent passed through his territory he discussed plans and strategy with Carranza and General Murguía. Lieutenant Colonel Aarón L. Valderrábano, he said, was probably loyal and had some men at Villa Juárez, which was on the way to the north. It was very important to determine whether Colonel Lindoro Hernández and his men were still faithful. Hernández, head of a regiment of the brigade of General Mariel, had steadfastly refused to recognize the Plan of Agua Prieta, and from Pachuca, Hidalgo, he had unsuccessfully sought to join the President when the latter was on his way to Veracruz. Unhappy circumstances had recently forced Colonel Hernández to pretend that he recognized the Plan of Agua Prieta. Under Mariel, both Colonel Hernández and Lieutenant Colonel Valderrábano had for years been fighting against the anti-Carrancista groups that infested northern Puebla.

On May 20 at Patla, Puebla, General Mariel introduced Carranza and others to some of the men of General Rodolfo Herrero, men who helped the group in the difficult crossing of a river which had become swollen by the continual rains. With one of these men, Colonel César Lechuga, General Mariel had a consultation in order to select some isolated and protected place where the President and his retinue might spend the night. Lechuga suggested San Antonio Tlaxcalantongo and Mariel approved, ordering Lechuga to arrange that lodgings be prepared in that settlement.

Shortly after the President and his retinue left Patla they were joined by General Rodolfo Herrero himself. Rodolfo Herrero had been one of those who for a long time had been fighting in this region as an anti-Carrancista against Mariel, Hernández, and Valderrábano. Herrero had finally, about two and one-half months ago, agreed to surrender to Mariel, with the understanding that his rank of general would be recognized by the Government and his forces would be included with those of Mariel. The appropriate documents had been ceremoniously signed at a table placed in the principal plaza of Villa Juárez. There had been, between the old enemies, lots of words about future friendship and loyalty, and the district had been pleased at the false prospect of some peace.

Now, two and one-half months after this agreement, Mariel introduced Herrero to Carranza and to Murguía, and as they rode onward there were conversations about the region, possible pasture for the horses, and the merits of Tlaxcalantongo as a stopping place for the night. Mariel left the President and his party in the care of Herrero, who knew this mountainous region as did few others. Mariel himself rushed off to Villa Juárez, through which the presidential party would have to pass on the following day, in order to learn about the loyalties of Colonel Lindoro Hernández and Lieutenant Colonel Valderrábano. No doubt it was also felt that it would be helpful if Mariel could at this moment exchange views personally with Hernández, a particularly bitter enemy of Rodolfo Herrero. Before departing for Villa Juárez, Mariel told the President that, after his investigations, he would send him a message from Villa Juárez to Tlaxcalantongo.

General Herrero escorted his famous new friends to the group of shacks known as San Antonio Tlaxcalantongo. On the way he overwhelmed the President with attentions and assurances of loyalty.

The President and his group found nothing impressive about Tlaxcalantongo, which they reached, with Herrero's help, via a most difficult trail, late in the afternoon in the pouring rain. Tlaxcalantongo consisted of a roofless and ruined old church building and a number of primitive huts of wood, grass, and branches, all on a narrow strip between a deep ravine and the side of a mountain. The place seemed to be vacated, and the presidential party was lodged in the various huts.

Leading the President to one of the shacks, Herrero explained: "For now, Señor, this will be the Palacio Nacional." The President dismounted with an obvious lack of enthusiasm. He was supposed to wait here to receive the message from General Mariel.

The President shared his one-room dirt-floor hut with his private secretary, Pedro Gil Farías, Gobernación Minister Aguirre Berlanga, Telegraph Director Mario Méndez, and two army captains. The others grouped themselves in other such lodgings. General Murguía and Lic. Cabrera shared one hut with Diputado[1] Gerzayn Ugarte and three or four other companions. Generals Barragán, Montes, and Marciano González shared a hut, as did Generals Urquizo, Pilar Sánchez, and Heliodoro Pérez. Ing. Bonillas at first lodged in the dwelling occupied by Lic. Cabrera and others, but later he moved to a hut located almost at the extreme edge of this Indian settlement.

As the only piece of furniture in the presidential shack was a coarse wooden table set in the dirt, the men had to improvise beds. A saddle and horse-blankets were placed against the wall—opposite the door—so that Venustiano Carranza might get some sleep.

While the weary travellers were thus getting settled, a messenger arrived to tell General Herrero that his brother, Lieutenant Colonel Hermilo Herrero, had been wounded in a fight at Patla. The recipient of this news resolved to leave at once. Following Carranza's orders, the presidential party provided some iodine and such bandages as could be found, and with these Herrero departed, leaving behind unrestful guests. The few local people who could be found, and they were very few, seemed unable to provide any pasture for the horses. Members of the President's retinue went to confer with Carranza. Cabrera and Urquizo strongly urged that they all leave Tlaxcalantongo at once, but they found Carranza stoic and lofty, as he was inclined to be in adverse moments. He had a great love for Mexican history as well as a great sense of the historic— and the histrionic. Before leaving the Palacio Nacional in Mexico City on May 7 he had said: "They are going to see how a President of the Republic dies." Now in Tlaxcalantongo he said to his intimates: "We can say what General Miramón said at Querétaro: 'May God be with us during these twenty-four hours.'"

General Herrero, with the message about Hermilo's injury and with the presidential iodine and bandages, rode off to Patla, where he knew that most of his men had been drunkenly shouting "Viva Obregón!" and "Death to Carranza!" Hermilo Herrero had been wanting to attack Carranza's column. Another relative, a nephew

[1] Member of Chamber of Deputies (legislature).

named Ernesto Herrero, had sought to offer the support of Rodolfo Herrero to Obregón and had, like the others, considered Rodolfo to have been foolish to go through with the arrangements of surrender to Mariel just at the moment when their old enemies, the Carrancistas, were to be upset by those who were starting to revolt in Sonora.

At Tlaxcalantongo the Carrancista writer, Adolfo León Osorio, captured a hen, which was forthwith prepared for the supper of the President and the others who shared his hut. Soon Carranza ordered the small remaining candle stub, which had been placed on the middle of the table, to be put out in order to conserve it for use in the early morning. Hours passed while the travellers tried to sleep, sheltered but little from the pouring rains and the cold winds.

Sometime later in the night an assistant of General Murguía ushered into Carranza's shed an Indian messenger and then withdrew. The Indian delivered a written message from General Mariel and then he likewise left, declining an invitation to remain. Carranza, aided by the relit candle stub, read Mariel's message aloud to the group: "Lindoro Hernández is loyal. Very early in the morning a part of his forces will leave to meet the expeditionary column and take it to Villa Juárez." Carranza added: "Now we shall be able to rest." The candle was put out again.

At about 4:00 A.M., on May 21, the presidential retinue in the various huts were rudely awakened by sudden shouting and yelling from without. A number of huts were attacked to the accompaniment of blasphemous cries and shouts of "Death to Carranza!" and "Viva Obregón!" From outside Carranza's hut shots were directed within and downward through the frail boards precisely to the spot where the President had been sleeping on his improvised bed. The President was wounded. He said to Aguirre Berlanga: "One of my legs is broken; I cannot get up," and then he told all those present to save themselves. From outside of the back of the hut there was another discharge of shooting in the direction of the President. While the President's assistant, Captain Ignacio Suárez, was at the side of the fallen leader, striving to move him and uttering words to denote his grief, and while shots were being fired on the other huts occupied by the presidential retinue, Venustiano Carranza died.

The attack on Carranza's hut was made by about twenty or thirty men, led by Facundo Garrido and Ernesto Herrero, while other members of Rodolfo Herrero's force of about one hundred men at-

tacked the other huts. The entire operation was directed by Rodolfo
Herrero, who remained nearby.

Ernesto Herrero, the first of the assailants to enter Carranza's
hut, was followed by the red-headed and insolent Facundo Garrido
and then by more of Herrero's men. Soon Secundino Reyes, old and
loyal helper of the First Chief, came running into the hut, and he
and Captain Suárez, full of emotion, placed a blanket over the bleed-
ing corpse of their fallen leader. Suárez rebuked the assailants, with
the result that both he and Reyes were sent outside. Still more of
Herrero's men entered the place and soon they were busy taking
Carranza's watch, eyeglasses, pistol, horsewhip, and portable type-
writer, as well as some of his clothing such as his hat, jacket, and
leggings.

During the course of the Tlaxcalantongo attack about five Carranza soldiers were killed, and the body of one was hung up. One
who was wounded died on the way to Villa Juárez. Many were
taken prisoner and many others made adventurous escapes.

While General Murguía was putting on his shoes he told two of
his soldiers to flee, but they were less fortunate than he, for they
were shot down a short distance from the hut. Murguía managed
to reach Villa Juárez on the afternoon of May 22.

Lic. Cabrera and Diputado Gerzayn Ugarte, who had shared a
shack with Murguía, fled together, but were separated. Ugarte heard
what he thought was the body of Cabrera, who was handicapped by
the loss of his eyeglasses, falling into the ravine. Ugarte went on,
chased, he says, by three demons crying, "There goes a Carrancista!" At 7:00 A.M. he reached a native's abode hidden in the thick
mountainous growth, and there he was saved from capture when
the native put the pursuers off the track. Days later a guide helped
this collaborator of Carranza find his way to the settlement of Beristáin.

Finance Minister Cabrera might have been killed at the bottom of
the ravine had he not fallen into a tree, in which he remained suspended during the remainder of the assault. After getting out of the
tree he went on foot to Patla, aided by his intimate knowledge of this
region.

Herrero's men showed particular anxiety to locate Bonillas, Cabrera, and Morales y Molina (who had drawn up the legal proceedings against Obregón) but these men were among those they did
not capture. Ing. Bonillas, from the hut to which he had moved and
which was somewhat distant from the others in Tlaxcalantongo,

was guided by a native boy through the ravine. He was able to get all the way to Huachinango. There about 250 natives formed for him an escort, with which he went to Villa Juárez.

Acting War Minister Francisco L. Urquizo, after being awakened from his sleep of bad dreams, just missed being the victim of a bullet which passed his face and went on to break the coffee jar in the hut. He awoke his companions and then took a shot in the darkness at a man who was shouting insults about the President. Rejecting an impulse to seek the side of the President, the General joined his companions who were fleeing to the precipice. Down the cliff they all went in the darkness and pouring rain, prevented from falling by the intense vegetation, and aided in their slow descent by the numerous branches. They were passed by a falling horse and then by a group of ten men who were making the descent much more rapidly. In the woods they were stopped by a strange mustached figure who was carrying two pistols and whose clothing was limited to little more than a bright handkerchief tied around his hair. It turned out to be General Pilar Sánchez, who had undressed before going to sleep at Tlaxcalantongo and who had had time only to grab his shoes and pistols before fleeing.

5.

From Tlaxcalantongo
to Mexico City

General Rodolfo Herrero gave some instructions about moving Carranza's body to Villa Juárez. Then he and his men withdrew with their booty: a large number of horses and about thirty or forty prisoners, including presidential secretary Gil Farías, Gobernación Minister Aguirre Berlanga, General Heliodoro Pérez, and Colonel Paulino Fontes, former director of the government-administered National Railways. This group, with the prisoners in the middle and Herrero at the rear, set out for Mexico City, but after some marching Herrero changed his mind when he received word that General Mariel, with the forces of Valderrábano and Barrios, was after him.

For Herrero and his men the prisoners constituted a problem, particularly as to food, and it was decided to set them free to join those of their companions who had reached Villa Juárez. However, first of all Herrero, who maintained that Carranza ended his own life after being wounded in the leg, forcibly extracted signatures to a "suicide" document, which had been composed by Aguirre Berlanga and written out by Gil Farías. During this episode near Cuanepixca, Puebla, Herrero and his men obtained from the prisoners also a check in dollars and Colonel Fontes' gold watch. One of Carranza's followers received from Herrero the eyeglasses of the late President.

Moments before attacking Carranza and his retinue at Tlaxcalantongo, Rodolfo Herrero had written some letters addressed to Generals Obregón and Mariel advising that he was subscribing to the Plan of Agua Prieta. To Mariel he had included some propositions of a sort that could not have been accepted by a man with any sense of loyalty. Now, following the attack, Mariel received by hand a letter sent by Herrero advising that Carranza had died at Tlaxcalantongo "for the good of the nation."

General Mariel at once sent two men from La Unión to Tlaxcalantongo to arrange to get Carranza's body, with the result that, while Herrero and his men were marching with their prisoners, the remains of Carranza were being conveyed to Villa Juárez accompanied by mourning peasants. On the afternoon of May 22 the body was placed in the sitting room of the home of Juan Córdoba in Villa Juárez. The two cannon, which had some days before been sent from Tulancingo by Lindoro Hernández to strengthen the Carrancistas at Villa Juárez, were used to do the honors for the late President of the Republic.

When the released prisoners reached Villa Juárez they were met by those who had escaped capture, including Bonillas, León Osorio, and Generals Murguía, Urquizo, Juan Barragán, and Marciano González. Barragán and González had been found, drenched and hatless at the foot of a tree, by a young inhabitant who cultivated maize, and subsequently some local people had arranged, without learning who these battered visitors were, to get them to Villa Juárez.

After Colonel Lindoro Hernández had placed himself at the orders of Murguía and had then departed, someone proposed at a meeting that all who were present should accompany Carranza's body to Mexico City. Murguía made some pointed remarks against Alvaro

Obregón and Pablo González, implying that he and certain others could expect in Mexico City an unsatisfactory and perhaps uncomfortable welcome. He suggested that the military leaders might do better to return to their respective states in order to "put things in proper order." But he added that his mission as general-in-chief had ended and he would abide by the opinion of the others.

This picturesque district in northern Puebla is noted as the site of the Light and Power Company of Necaxa, which since 1905 has been providing to Mexico City, over one hundred miles away, power generated by the nearly 3000-foot plunge of the waters of the Necaxa, Tenango, and Xaltepuxtla rivers. On the instructions of Lieutenant Colonel Valderrábano, the doctor employed by the Light and Power Company came from Necaxa to Villa Juárez, where he did his best to embalm the President's body and where he issued an autopsy certificate to the effect that Carranza had died of his wounds.

Then early on the morning of Sunday, May 23, the funeral procession made its way to Necaxa. It was led by twenty or thirty humble workers, some of them bearing the hastily made coffin, covered with flowers. At Necaxa, which was reached early in the afternoon, there were many indications of mourning (black cloths) not only on houses but also on trees. There General Murguía issued his last instructions as general-in-chief of the Columna Expedicionaria de la Legalidad. The column, he said, had left Mexico City with the President on May 7 to fulfill its duty to guard the purity of the nation's institutions. He added that, as the President had succumbed to one of the most infamous treasons, the Column should take to Mexico City the body of the illustrious leader; after the burial of Carranza, the loyal Column would be considered disbanded, and the military members should present themselves to the head of the Mexico City Guard and follow the orders of the Provisional President to be named in accordance with the Constitution.

As a narrow-gauge train took the group from Necaxa to Beristáin, various members of the Columna Expedicionaria de la Legalidad took turns guarding the body of the late President. The first shift to do this guard duty consisted of Generals Murguía and Urquizo, Ing. Bonillas, and Lic. Aguirre Berlanga. Urquizo felt it to be ironic that they guarded now the dead body of the man whom they had deserted in his last living moments. At Beristáin the group met up with some relatives and friends who had come from Mexico City, and they also found there an investigating commission which had been sent forth from the capital to study the recent event at Tlaxcalantongo. All, including the investigating commission, went by standard-gauge train on the slow trip from Beristáin to Mexico City.

At San Cristóbal Ecatepec, just outside of Mexico City, the members of the Carranza Column were ordered out of the train, the civilians being taken to the penitentiary and the military members being placed in the Santiago Tlaltelolco military prison. This step came as a surprise to General Urquizo and others, who had earlier received from Obregonista General Jesús Navoa assurances that Carranza's last companions would not be treated inconsiderately.

Rodolfo Herrero, after sending a telegram to Obregón to report the attack on Tlaxcalantongo, took his followers to Progreso de Zaragoza in the state of Veracruz. There he received a message from César Lechuga advising that General Pablo González was in control in Mexico City and was sending forces to capture him and his chief officers. Herrero therefore changed his course and went with his men in the direction of Papantla, Veracruz, careful to avoid the forces of Barrios, who was one of his various enemies.

Papantla was the headquarters of a military zone whose commander-in-chief was the twenty-five–year-old General Lázaro Cárdenas, who in the past had served under General Calles in Sonora. Lic. Gilberto Valenzuela, author of the Plan of Agua Prieta, tells of receiving from Cárdenas a telegram supporting the Plan and of wiring a reply to "Colonel—now General—Lázaro Cárdenas." Cárdenas had subsequently asked Herrero to join his forces in supporting the Plan.

With Tlaxcalantongo behind him, Herrero now decided to take advantage of the invitation which Cárdenas had rendered earlier, and on May 23, between Comalteco and Coyutla, Herrero and his men were received by Cárdenas and by his chief of staff, Colonel Manuel Avila Camacho. Herrero's men were well impressed with Cárdenas, who revealed himself to be an excellent rider.

Herrero gave Cárdenas his version of the events at Tlaxcalantongo, showing him the document which had been drawn up by Manuel Aguirre Berlanga and Gil Farías. Then the combined forces went to Papantla, where Cárdenas was able to confer by telegraph with General Calles in Mexico City. Cárdenas was ordered to bring Rodolfo Herrero and his principal collaborators to Mexico City for an investigation. The fearful Lieutenant Colonel Hermilo Herrero, whose reported "injury" on the afternoon of May 20 had been nothing but a falsehood and who had been the most ardent instigator of the Tlaxcalantongo attack, refused to make the trip with his brother; but nephew Ernesto Herrero, who had just recently been a civilian and was now called a major, went along. The group, led by Lázaro Cárdenas, included Manuel Avila Camacho and two brothers of Cárdenas.

This trip was made to Tuxpan, Veracruz, and from this port by boat to Tampico; then by train to Monterrey and to Mexico City. The reason for this very roundabout route was to avoid going through the state of Puebla, where they might well have encountered the forces of Lindoro Hernández and Aarón Valderrábano, who were furious with Herrero. The trip from Tampico to Mexico City might have been made by way of San Luis Potosí instead of Monterrey but for the fact that communications, because of the recent strife, had been interrupted.

The travellers spent two days at the port of Tampico, center of oil activity, where Herrero's men were struck by the large amount of gold currency in circulation. Tampico was occupied by two important supporters of the Plan of Agua Prieta: General Arnulfo R. Gómez, young warrior with the Prussian military mustache, who had been a right arm to Calles in struggles against Maytorenistas; and General Manuel Peláez, for years the chief of anti-Carrancista fighters in the "Huastecas" of the states of Veracruz and Hidalgo and a large part of Puebla. Both Peláez and Pancho Villa had in the past conferred upon Rodolfo Herrero the rank of brigadier general in recognition of his activities against the Carranza Government. Peláez had recently received a message from Obregón stating that if Carranza should pass through his zone he should be taken prisoner but should be fully protected and well treated.[1]

After the rest in Tampico Cárdenas and Herrero, with their men, resumed their circuitous journey. Upon reaching Mexico City the two leaders were besieged by newspaper reporters and photographers, who met them and followed them to the Hotel Gillow. Cárdenas, obeying instructions, took Herrero's group to call on General Calles, who heard their story, largely as recounted by Miguel B. Márquez, Herrero's chief of staff. Shortly thereafter, General Cárdenas left Mexico City for Michoacán, his native state, over which the new rulers of Mexico appointed him military commander and acting governor.

[1] Gabriel Antonio Menendez in *Impacto* magazine, July 16, 1958.

As General Murguía had predicted before the Carranza funeral procession left Villa Juárez, he and General Mariel and the other military men who had remained with Carranza did not receive a warm welcome in Mexico City. When Murguía asked for what crime they were placed in jail, the reply, we are told, was, "the crime of loyalty." Rodolfo Herrero, who was left at liberty, testified at the proceedings. But Mariel had with him a letter from Herrero, written after the latter's three-month-old "surrender" to the former. As that letter referred to Obregón, Calles, Hill, and Alvarado in the most disrespectful terms, it was not to be helpful to Herrero.

6.

The Selection
of an Interim President

Now that the Carranza regime had been forcibly removed from power, the federal legislative houses would have to
select an Interim (or "Provisional") President of the Republic to
carry on until a Constitutional President might be elected by the
voters and installed in office. There was talk about this matter
shortly after Carranza's departure from the capital, for, although
he had not resigned, he was no longer President according to the
Plan of Agua Prieta, which called for the selection of a Provisional
President. De la Huerta, head of the Liberal Constitutionalist Army,
was in Sonora, and from there he suggested that the federal Con-

gress select from three names: Sr. Carlos B. Zetina, Senator Fernando Iglesias Calderón, and General Antonio I. Villarreal.[1] Some politicians felt that Villarreal and Zetina were at a disadvantage, as they had been outside the country within the preceding twelve months, and thus Iglesias Calderón was believed to be the most likely choice. Supporters of General Pablo González suggested that General Jacinto B. Treviño and Senator Juan Sánchez Azcona[2] also be considered.

As soon as General González issued the well-considered document whereby he retired from the race for the constitutional presidency, his name became an important factor in the talk about a Provisional President. It was reported that even some "Obregonistas" received this suggestion well. In the midst of the confusion some of the legislators developed a strong boom in favor of Pascual Ortiz Rubio, whose record both before and during his four years as Michoacán's governor was highly regarded. There were some politicians who had thought it would be convenient to send a commission to locate Carranza and secure his resignation. A member of the Supreme Court of Justice affirmed that Carranza was no longer the President of Mexico. All of this was just prior to Tlaxcalantongo.

On May 19 Obregón returned to the capital after a visit to San Luis Potosí. On the following day occurred a preliminary meeting of a quorum of the special session of the Chamber of Deputies, which had been told by De la Huerta, in a message from Sonora, to meet on May 24 to select a Provisional President of Mexico.

According to information provided by General e Ingeniero Pascual Ortiz Rubio, the congressmen were giving consideration to the names of three state governors who had been prompt in defying Carranza's efforts on behalf of Ing. Bonillas. Besides Adolfo de la Huerta of Sonora, they were considering Ortiz Rubio of Michoacán and General Enrique Estrada of Zacatecas.[3] Ortiz Rubio in the past had had some difficulties in his relations with Estrada. Ortiz Rubio writes that he, the Michoacán governor, received a majority of the votes at a secret session of the Chamber, but persuaded his friends to switch their votes to De la Huerta.[4]

By May 20 the contest had boiled down to a struggle between "Obregonistas" who favored De la Huerta (and also thought well

[1] Adolfo de la Huerta, *Memorias*, p. 149.
[2] *Campaña política del C. Alvaro Obregón*, IV, 241, 310.
[3] Interview with Pascual Ortiz Rubio, February 2, 1956.
[4] Pascual Ortiz Rubio, "Medio siglo: Memorias," p. 35.

of Villarreal, Ortiz Rubio, Zubaran Capmany, and Iglesias Calderón) and "Gonzalistas" who supported "Don Pablo" (and also thought well of Treviño, De los Santos, and Sánchez Azcona). Treviño's name was mentioned as a possible compromise. Proposed Cabinet lists were attributed to both González and De la Huerta.

Some Carrancista congressmen who returned from the disaster of the *Tren Dorado* hoped their absence would make it difficult to obtain a quorum on the twenty-fourth. Others who had in the past supported the Carranza Government were felt to have been Gonzalistas at heart, or at least more favorably inclined to González than to the Sonora group. In the Senate's secret session of May 20, sixteen of the thirty-two senators who met agreed to back "Don Adolfo" de la Huerta.

"Congressmen who support the candidacy of Alvaro Obregón" were "kindly invited" to attend a meeting on May 22 in order to determine whom the group would support on May 24.

Senator Iglesias Calderón resigned as head of the Centro Director Obregonista. As a leading legislator he had his hands full reorganizing the Senate, and he was about to undertake a diplomatic mission to the United States. General Plutarco Elías Calles, who had been particularly active in the effort to overthrow Carranza and who was scheduled to take over a Cabinet Post, resigned as vice-president of the Centro Director. General e Ing. Amado Aguirre was named by Obregón to head the Centro, which still had ahead of it the job of winning for Obregón a popular election, a job made much easier on account of recent occurrences. Two new names were added to the Centro's long list of *vocales*: Felipe Carrillo Puerto and Carlos Argüelles.

Obregón was in bed at the Hotel Saint Francis, listening to General Francisco R. Serrano read from a batch of telegrams and advising another general about the replies which should be made. One telegram came from those who had accompanied Carranza into the mountains of Puebla and told of what had occurred at Tlaxcalantongo. Upon learning thus of Carranza's death, Obregón jumped up from his bed, and in no uncertain terms he expressed his indignation.

Generals Pablo González, Jacinto B. Treviño, and Samuel de los Santos, who joined the group, also appeared seriously concerned about this turn in events. After much talk by Obregón and González, it was decided to send to Tlaxcalantongo the investigating commission in order to determine who were responsible. General Amado Aguirre, whose term as federal senator was not to expire until September 1, was originally named to this commission which, besides including two senators, was to include two Supreme Court justices, two federal congressmen (*diputados*), two doctors, and two generals.

But Senator Cutberto Hidalgo joined the group and reminded Obregón that Obregonista senators were badly needed in the capital. The powerful Comisión Permanente[5] of the legislative chambers would, without more help from Obregonista senators, remain in the hands of supporters of Pablo González, and it did not suit Obregón's plans to turn over the nation's Interim Presidency to General González. Therefore General Fortunato Zuazua took the place of Senator Aguirre on the Tlaxcalantongo investigating commission.

More arrivals reached Obregón's hotel rooms, which must have become rather crowded. To the Argentine minister in Mexico Obregón revealed that his idea had been to send Carranza abroad after his capture. When Octavio Amador entered the room, this major, who had been close to Carranza at the end, expressed the thought that Carranza might have killed himself after finding himself wounded in one leg. This report was in contradiction to that which was soon afterwards given out by Lic. Manuel Aguirre Berlanga, and it was in contradiction to reports which were soon published in the newspapers.[6]

Obregón received from Necaxa a telegram signed by one civilian and thirty-two soldiers, including Generals Barragán, Mariel, Montes, and Marciano González. He dictated a reply stating that it was strange that such a group of military men had not fulfilled its duty by risking death to defend Carranza, particularly considering that this group had the greatest responsibility in the unfortunate events which had recently stirred up the nation and had resulted in the unfortunate death of Carranza, abandoned by his friends and companions. Obregón pointed out that on numerous occasions Carranza had been offered full guarantees if he would leave the zone of danger, but that he had declined because he probably felt

---

[5] The Permanent Commission of the federal legislature represents the legislature when it is not in session. This commission is composed of one legislator (federal senator or congressman) from each state. Regular legislative sessions start each September 1 and are not to extend beyond the end of the year.

[6] Amado Aguirre, *Mis memorias de campaña*, p. 325.

that a man of honor should not save himself by leaving his companions in danger. This act, concluded Obregón, "revealed in Sr. Carranza a characteristic of honor and comradeship, not understood by you."

On May 24, 1920, the body of Carranza was buried in Mexico City's Dolores Graveyard. His remains were placed "in a third-class grave, where the poor people are buried" in accordance with the wishes which he expressed to his daughters (Virginia Carranza de Aguilar and Julia Carranza) just before his last departure from Mexico City. A very large number of persons were present for the interment.

On that same afternoon, for the first time in over seventy years, the Mexican federal legislative houses met for the purpose of naming an Interim President of the Republic to serve as the chief executive from June 1 until December 1. By shortly after 5:00 P.M. 187 deputies had been counted to make up a quorum of the Chamber, and by 5:30 forty-seven senators were declared a quorum of the Senate. Cheers greeted a message which had come by wire from De la Huerta.

First it was the senators who deposited their secret votes while the galleries made considerable demonstration: applause for José I. Novelo and Alvarez del Castillo of the P.L.C., hisses for Carrancista Joaquín Aguirre Berlanga. Then under similar conditions the deputies voted. During the counting cheers greeted each De la Huerta vote as it was made known. Finally the presiding officer asked the visitors to stop booing at every mention of the name of Pablo González.

The results were as follows:

Adolfo de la Huerta	224
Pablo González	29
Fernando Iglesias Calderón	1
Antonio I. Villarreal	1

By now it was 7:30 in the evening. After much display of emotion Congress drew up a decree calling on De la Huerta to be at the Congress on June 1. There was some debate as to whether he would arrive from Sonora by that time, but as he had left Hermosillo on the twenty-second in a special train which was making full speed, his arrival on the twenty-ninth or thirtieth was expected.

Somewhat later the Congress declared that the election for Constitutional President should take place on the fifth of September.

With the fall of the Carranza regime General Antonio I. Villarreal and Lic. José Vasconcelos, who had been in exile, returned to Mexico City. Recently these two revolutionaries had, at the invitation of Governor De la Huerta, been spending some time in Sonora. where they found much to admire about the resolution and radicalism of Calles.[7] Now at the Mexico City railroad station they were greeted by Obregón. Another change that Obregón was delighted to see at this time was the end of Carranza's regulation forbidding bullfights.

Ing. Alberto J. Pani, brother of Obregón's friend Camilo Pani, was the Carranza Government's minister to the French Republic. He was considerably surprised at the messages which kept coming to him in Paris, advising him of what was transpiring in his homeland. Then on May 16 a telegram came from General Pablo González, who had taken over Mexico City pending the selection of the Interim President. González asked Pani to support the movement which had overthrown Carranza.

Two days later, in a message from Mexico's acting Minister of Foreign Affairs, Pani was advised of the complete triumph of the Agua Prieta movement and told that within forty-eight hours he should define his attitude. The Mexican Congress would soon name the Provisional President.

Prior to his appointment as Carranza's minister to France Pani had directed the government-managed National Railways and had been Carranza's Minister of Industry and Commerce, having organized that ministry of the Mexican Cabinet. When Pani left for Europe, Calles, recently governor of Sonora, had succeeded Pani in the Cabinet. De la Huerta, close collaborator of Carranza during the Constitutionalist struggle, had at this time taken over the Sonora governorship.

Ing. Pani must have found much to his liking in Paris, for he was a man of considerable culture, with a particular fondness for old oil paintings. He was intelligent and practical, and was now in his mid-thirties. General Villarreal called Pani the man with "the million-dollar smile."

[7] Ramon Puente, *Hombres de la Revolutión: Calles*, p. 123.

He did not change his Carranza colors, and only advised the Mexican Foreign Office that he would "act in accordance with law and popular desire." He felt respect for Carranza, whose government he was now representing in France, and had represented in the past, together with Cabrera and Bonillas, at negotiations in Atlantic City having to do with the presence of General Pershing in Mexico. He maintained, in addition, that diplomatic envoys should not change their colors as easily as others.

Ing. Pani received from Mexico a series of additional messages which put pressure on him. An affectionate greeting from General Obregón advised of the triumph of the Plan of Agua Prieta and invited Pani to return at once to Mexico. Pani, who had known Obregón in Sonora in 1913, merely sent him his thanks for the cable. Soon he received a new message from the Foreign Office recommending that he support the new order of things, but this advice he did not accept. On May 24 we find him studying the following cable from Obregón:

CARRANZA CREATED INTOLERABLE SITUATION, TRYING TO IMPOSE FUTURE PRESIDENT BONILLAS BY BRUTE FORCE. AFTER LONG SERIES OF ATTEMPTS, HE ORDERED THE INVASION OF SONORA SENDING ARMY WITH DIEGUEZ TO DEPOSE CONSTITUTIONAL AUTHORITIES AND PUT DOWN POPULAR WILL WHICH UNANIMOUSLY REPUDIATED IMPOSITION CANDIDATE. THIS EXCITED NATIONAL FEELING AND ALL THE PEOPLE AND ARMY IN TWENTY DAYS OVERTHREW THE CARRANZA REGIME WITHOUT MUCH BLOODSHED. CARRANZA WENT TO THE MOUNTAINS OF PUEBLA. THANKS TO REVOLUTIONARY UNIFICATION, THE REPUBLIC IS IN A NORMAL SITUATION AND THERE IS COMPLETE CONFIDENCE DOMESTICALLY AND ABROAD. COMMUNICATIONS AND TRAINS ARE ALL RIGHT. CONGRESS IS NOW UNITED WITH THE OBJECT OF NAMING AN INTERIM PRESIDENT WHO WILL CALL ELECTIONS. AFFECTIONATELY

Pani advised Obregón that it would be contrary to his sentiments of loyalty to join the Agua Prieta movement just at the moment of its triumph. Then on May 28 a message from the Foreign Ministry advised Ing. Pani of the tragedy at Tlaxcalantongo. This new message reported further that Generals González and Calles were making a thorough investigation and that strong Revolutionary forces sought to capture Rodolfo Herrero in order to try and sentence him.

From Paris Pani condemned the assassination of Venustiano Carranza and announced his resignation as Mexican minister to France, a resignation which was given much publicity in the Mexico City newspapers. Pani did not hurry back to his house on the Paseo de la Reforma in Mexico City. He took his time, He wrote some friendly letters to Lic. José Vasconcelos, who was now in charge of the National University, and to General Antonio I. Villarreal. With his newly collected paintings he arrived home at the end of November, 1920. He was not particularly welcome to many of the Obregonistas.

7.

Adolfo de la Huerta
and Pancho Villa

Late on the afternoon of June 1, 1920, Don Adolfo de la
Huerta, who was just thirty-nine years old, rode in an open carriage
from his lodgings at the Regis Hotel to the Chamber of Deputies.
The presidential sash was across his breast. Before a quorum of congressmen, and in the presence of General Obregón and other military and civilian leaders, Don Adolfo raised his right arm and
promised "to guard and have guarded the Political Constitution of
the United States of Mexico and the Laws emanating therefrom,
and loyally and patriotically to fulfill the position of President of
the Republic which the General Congress has conferred upon me."

While the National Hymn was being played, the new President and his retinue left the Chamber of Deputies to go to the Palacio Nacional.

On the next day President De la Huerta, somewhat tired, appeared on the balcony of the Palacio Nacional in order to review a great parade of about 25,000 soldiers who supported the Plan of Agua Prieta. In the lead were Generals Obregón, Hill, Manuel Peláez, and Jacinto B. Treviño, followed by their men. Next appeared General Pascual Ortiz Rubio at the head of the forces from Michoacán. Then came Generals Guadalupe Sánchez and Rentería Luviano and their forces, and behind them were the Yaqui Indian fighters, not exactly in uniform but accompanied by music. They were followed by the troops of Generals Benigno Serratos and Enrique Estrada, and these in turn were followed by students of the Military College.

While the parade went forward, at the Palacio Nacional the new President was surrounded by a large group which included Generals Plutarco Elías Calles, Pablo González, Genovevo de la O, Salvador Alvarado, and Francisco Serrano, Colonel Benito Ramírez (Chief of Staff), and Lics. Rafael Zubaran Capmany, Gilberto Valenzuela, and José Vasconcelos.

Adolfo de la Huerta made an excellent chief executive during the six-month interim term, and his character well satisfied the popular desires of the time. He was not in any way majestic, austere, or stuffy. He was a frank person who avoided ceremony. He has described the arrival in Mexico of the "envoy extraordinary" from Guatemala to present his credentials. This diplomat wished much formality and a great gathering to which he could read his prepared address. President De la Huerta's insistence on informality for the occasion, he has said, caused the resignation of the Mexican Foreign Minister.[1]

What happened was unique in the annals of diplomatic protocol. The representative from Guatemala had asked the Mexican Foreign Minister for an official appointment with the President of Mexico, and he became somewhat concerned as the latter did not set any date. Imagine his surprise when, entirely unexpectedly, President De la Huerta and his secretary, Lic. Miguel Alessio Robles, arrived at his room in the Hotel Regis. Under these informal conditions the

---

[1] Adolfo de la Huerta, interview, March 22, 1954.

Guatemalan representative made his remarks, commenting on the fact that the Mexican President had come to see him instead of having him come to the Palacio Nacional. De la Huerta replied simply, remarking to the visiting diplomat that he could come to see him whenever he wished to do so. As a result of this incident De la Huerta became the object of much praise in the press of Guatemala.[2]

Feeling that Carranza had been a little bit stingy in the distribution of credit among his associates, De la Huerta sought to be more generous on this score, just as he had done when he was governor of Sonora.[3]

De la Huerta lived quite simply, without fanfare. He had a great fondness for singing, and it is reported that his early ambition in Sonora was to sing for the Metropolitan Opera in New York. He had an excellent voice, coupled with a certain personal dramatic touch which he gave to all occasions. His informality and well-known honesty, and particularly his fondness for general good will, were widely welcomed by a nation that had been through so many years of really terrible fratricidal strife.

Prior to entering public affairs he had been in the banking business in Sonora. De la Huerta, like his grandfather, was held in high esteem by the Yaqui Indians. He took much interest in local politics, and after the triumph of Madero in 1911 he became a member of the Sonora Legislature and played an important role in arrangements leading to the pacification of the Yaquis. During the Constitucionalista Revolution which followed the fall of Madero, De la Huerta as a civilian frequently assisted Carranza and for a while headed the Secretaría de Gobernación. During part of Carranza's term as President De la Huerta not only was Mexican Consul General in New York, but he also went to Washington, D.C., on a mission having to do with Mexico's neutral position in the world conflict. He has told of how in the United States he denied reports that the Carranza Government had used force to confiscate "about 86 million pesos" in gold from the Mexican banks, and how, on returning to Mexico, he was surprised to learn from Lic. Cabrera that what he in good faith had recently denied had been true. De la Huerta told Carranza that this was a terrible thing to have done.[4]

Luis Cabrera had a great talent for writing, and, after the fall of Carranza, he published a daily called *La Vanguardia*, in which he

[2] Miguel Alessio Robles, *A medio camino*, pp. 92–93.
[3] Adolfo de la Huerta, interview, March 22, 1954.
[4] Adolfo de la Huerta, interview, June 6, 1955.

attacked De la Huerta. De la Huerta did not reply or fight back, but assumed a pacific attitude which apparently did not help the circulation of *La Vanguardia*. Although they had differences of opinion, the two men were good personal friends, and De la Huerta soon sent a mutual acquaintance to suggest to Cabrera that he desist from his attacks.[5]

As Interim President De la Huerta was faced with a number of problems related to the transition from strife to peace, and he resolved them all in a spirit of magnanimity. At his first press conference he said that all Mexicans who were living in exile could return to the country whenever they wished.

One problem of his regime was that related to the actors in the Tlaxcalantongo drama. Generals Murguía, Mariel, Marciano González, and others, who had been loyal to Carranza to the end, were questioned and were eventually set at liberty. Among those who obtained their liberty early were General Marciano González, who as a federal *diputado* enjoyed the special protection afforded to members of the legislature, and General Juan Barragán, who made a dramatic escape from the prison of Santiago Tlaltelolco. After Ing. Bonillas was set free he made his way to the United States border, retiring from any further politics. Toward the end of July, 1920, General Rodolfo Herrero was named as head of the military sector of Papantla, Veracruz, the position occupied earlier by Lázaro Cárdenas, and he went there at once from Mexico City, remaining in his new post until worse days befell him shortly after De la Huerta turned over the presidency to his successor on December 1.

Probably the most famous act of De la Huerta during his interim presidency was his handling of General Pancho Villa, who was still very much at large in the north with a loyal force of fighters. Villa's activities had been very disturbing to those who sought to follow peaceful pursuits in the north. But the Obregonista forces now had so much strength that they seemed to be in a position to deal with Villa.

When the Agua Prieta movement began Villa got in touch with his friend, De la Huerta, who asked him to come to Hermosillo with fifty men. Villa also appears to have approached General Calles, pointing out that he (Villa) had long been fighting Carranza and

[5] *Ibid.*

that since the Sonora movement was against Carranza, he would be happy to join up. Calles told Villa to await orders and to cease attacking towns. Villa did not make the trip to Hermosillo.

After a hard-fought battle about the middle of April, 1920, Generals Eugenio Martínez, Joaquín Amaro, José Amarillas, Alfredo Rueda Quijano, Abundio Gómez, and Ignacio C. Enríquez

General Francisco Villa (*center*). *Casasola.*

were able to dominate the city of Chihuahua in the name of the Agua Prieta rebellion. General Enríquez took possession of the governorship of Chihuahua and proceeded, with Calles' authorization, to discuss with Villa terms whereby the latter would lay down arms. Villa and Enríquez came to no agreement, the latter suggesting that Villa go to Sonora with only a few friends and Villa offering to take charge of policing the state of Chihuahua!

Villa was suspicious that Enríquez used the interview to learn about the location and strength of Villa's forces. So he withdrew but left evidence of having remained encamped where Enríquez had met him. Sure enough, Enríquez' forces attacked the abandoned camp at midnight. A week later, on June 2, Villa's forces in revenge attacked the city of Parral, killing many. But Enríquez was not in Parral, and General José Gonzalo Escobar, who defended this mining town, managed to escape.

Ing. Elías L. Torres, a close friend of both De la Huerta and Villa, managed to locate the latter. After a conference with Villa and his intimates he went to Mexico City, where he delivered to the President, with copies for Calles, Obregón, and Hill, a list of conditions under which Villa would agree to become peaceful. Under the proposed terms Villa would be given an estate in Chihuahua and he would head a rural police force of not more than 500 men, to be supported by the state and federal governments. He would make Chihuahua "the most peaceful state of the Republic."

Calles declared that "the Government will accept none of those conditions, nor will it accept anything else but that Villa retire to private life. To enter into pacts with him would be to concede to him a legal position and strength that he does not have." Calles added that the projected armistice was but a maneuver, suggested by politicians close to Villa in order to give him time to reorganize his forces.

Thereupon Villa's representative in Texas declared that if Villa's conditions were not accepted a reign of terror would begin in Mexico. On July 26 Pancho Villa attacked Sabinas, Coahuila, capturing there the garrison of seventy men and three freight trains. He pulled up about fifty kilometers of railroad track to the north of this place, and a similar amount to the south.

Early in the morning following the Sabinas attack Villa sent an urgent message from Sabinas to Mexico City, saying that he wished to confer by telegraph with the President. De la Huerta, General Benjamín Hill and De la Huerta's secretary, Miguel Alessio Robles, rushed to the telegraph office at the Palacio Nacional, the President making the ride from his new official residence, the great castle of Chapultepec.

Villa advised De la Huerta that he wished to surrender to the government, turning over to it all his arms and releasing his men; he said that he wished to have a hacienda where he could work and also a small escort for his protection. De la Huerta at once agreed to enter into negotiations with Villa so as to reach an agreement along these lines, and General Hill backed De la Huerta's decision.

Obregón was then touring the state of Sinaloa as a presidential candidate. For the future peace of Mexico he wanted to see his old enemy wiped out, and he heartily disapproved of the acceptance of

Villa's offer. He wired De la Huerta as follows, sending copies to the state governors and to the heads of military operations in the various districts:

GENERAL VILLA ASSAULTED THE UNITED STATES TOWN OF COLUMBUS, WHERE HE COMMITTED MISBEHAVIORS AND ACTS OF VIOLENCE. IT IS NATURAL THAT THE UNITED STATES FOREIGN OFFICE, ON SEEING HIM PROTECTED BY THE MEXICAN GOVERNMENT, SHOULD ASK FOR EXTRADITION OF THE DU-RANGO WARRIOR. AND WHAT ARE WE GOING TO DO?

In spite of General Obregón's objections, President De la Huerta went ahead with the Villa surrender arrangements. General Eugenio Martínez, head of military operations in Coahuila, was in the Torreón district, and the Interim President instructed him to call on Villa, who wanted a written understanding. As Martínez had been fighting against Villa, De la Huerta found it necessary to assure each of the generals of the other's good faith.

Accompanied by General Gonzalo Escobar and some other government men, General Martínez made the trip to Sabinas, where he met Villa, Ing. Elías Torres, and about sixty Villistas.

There, after long talks, Generales de División[6] Eugenio Martínez and Francisco Villa signed a pact which, in general, followed the terms which had been brought to the meeting by Ing. Torres. The document is dated Sabinas, Coahuila, 11:00 A.M. July 28, 1920. Besides providing that General Villa would retire to private life and be given the "Canutillo" hacienda, where he should reside, the agreement allowed that Villa should have an escort of fifty men to be selected by him but to receive their pay from the Ministry of War. It was further agreed that the War Ministry would pay one year's wages to each of the soldiers that Villa would release. Each of these released soldiers would also receive land at such place as he might desire. Those who wished to continue with a military career could enter the national army. In the force which he was disbanding, Villa had about 700 men of varying ranks.

It was Ing. Elías Torres' idea that the hacienda of "Canutillo," in the state of Durango, would be a suitable place for Villa. It is near the border of the States of Durango and Chihuahua. The suggestion appealed to De la Huerta because its location was far from the Chihuahua and Durango state capitals and also from the main

---

[6] *General de división* is the highest category of generalship. During the Constitucionalista Revolución Carranza elevated Obregón and Pablo González to this rank before so promoting Villa.

railroad lines. Villa's representative (Torres) made that suggestion because Villa, who had been in the region various times, had once remarked that if he ever settled down he would like a hacienda like "Canutillo." In one battle against General Murguía, Villa had defended himself in the hacienda's building and church, both of which had been damaged by General Murguía's cannon. De la Huerta received the impression that "Canutillo" was government property, and when that impression turned out to be incorrect he authorized the government to buy it for 600,000 pesos.

The main building at "Canutillo" must have seemed somewhat deserted when Villa took it over after his agreement with the De la Huerta Government. The previous owner had arranged to sell everything on the place that could be moved. Anyway, for about three years Villa lived the life of a hacienda owner at "Canutillo," where he invested much money in agricultural pursuits and in improvements. He bet with neighbors on cock fights, and he made frequent trips to Parral in search of greater pleasures.

8.

The Interim Regime and Other Restless Generals

Other problems created by adventurous generals included the cases of General Félix Díaz and General Pablo González. The first named was nephew of the former strong man of Mexico against whom the Mexican Revolution had initially been started. General Félix Díaz had played an important part in the lamentable overthrow of President Madero, and he and his followers had been almost continuously in revolt against President Carranza. At the time of the fall of Carranza General Félix Díaz was at the port of Veracruz, and he forthwith sought an interview with the commanding general there, Guadalupe Sánchez, asking to be taken prisoner ("as I do not want to appear as having surrendered") and, as he said, so that his career of uprisings might end. On instructions from Calles, Guadalupe Sánchez prepared to form a military court in order to try and punish Díaz, but President De la Huerta intervened, arranging that the man who became a voluntary prisoner be allowed to leave the country in safety. De la Huerta even offered Díaz 10,000 dollars (20,000 pesos).[1]

The Yucatán socialist leader and federal *diputado*, Felipe Carrillo Puerto, labeled De la Huerta a reactionary for having negotiated with Pancho Villa and Félix Díaz. Carrillo Puerto was seeking the governorship of Yucatán under the banner of his Liga Central de Resistencia Socialista. His motto was: Down with the bourgeois; and his announced plans included collective farms and collective factories. He used propaganda enthusiastically and he had the backing of the radical General Calles. Carrillo Puerto frequently made statements like the following: "If the merchants monopolize the provisions and you lack bread, then go to the stores, tear down the doors and loot all the goods. Let us dynamite the Chamber of Deputies, exterminate at once the Senate, and finish with the Supreme Court. No more peaceful manifestations. No more empty talk. What people need to do is assert themselves. The Bolshevik principles should be put into practice. Let us wave the red flag of replevins."[2]

General Jesús M. Guajardo had in 1919 received his promotion to generalship, together with a monetary award of 50,000 pesos, because he wiped out the life of Emiliano Zapata, whose activities in the south were at that time troubling the Carranza Government. It is not easy to admire Guajardo's method of achieving his prominent rank and well-known place in history. First he had the difficult task of convincing Zapata that he would desert his chief, Pablo González, in favor of Zapata. This Guajardo did by means of attacking a part of González' troops and then having the prisoners shot. After taking note of that piece of evidence, Zapata made the mistake of agreeing to meet Colonel Guajardo, whose men promptly killed the once unconquerable agrarian warrior. Not long after that, as we have seen, González and Guajardo turned against Carranza, with Guajardo derailing the last of the Carranza trains to leave Mexico City on May 7, 1920.

[1] Adolfo de la Huerta, *Memorias*, p. 164.
[2] Rosendo Salazar and José G. Escobedo, *Las pugnas de la gleba*, II, 84.

With De la Huerta in the presidential chair, War Minister Calles ordered General Guajardo to go northward with about 2000 men and join General Joaquín Amaro in fighting against Pancho Villa. This was before Villa's surrender. Instead of joining in the effort against Villa, Guajardo started a rebellion early in July, 1920, against De la Huerta and Obregón in the Torreón, Coahuila, district. A large number of Guajardo's men deserted him and, after he had suffered a defeat at the hands of General Eugenio Martínez, he made his way with his reduced following to Monterrey. There he took up residence in the house of one of his subordinates, but this subordinate revealed his whereabouts to the local authorities, who were after the General not only on account of his Torreón activities but for more recent misconduct in Monterrey.[3] The house was surrounded, and Guajardo was captured. On July 17, by authority of the Nuevo León state government, he was shot.

Guajardo's behavior in Torreón was considered to be part of a more general revolt linked to the name of Pablo González, who, after retiring from the presidential campaign and after making statements about withdrawing to private life, was arousing suspicions in Monterrey. Some minor action at Monclova, Coahuila, and an unsuccessful attack on Nuevo Laredo, Tamaulipas, were considered to be other manifestations of the revolt, and at the same time it was noted that in Tamaulipas the Carrancista General Carlos Osuna was restless.

Things came to a head following a banquet noted for fraternal demonstrations, which was held at Monterrey's Hotel Ancira on July 13 and which was attended by Generals Porfirio González (the governor), Arnulfo R. Gómez, Manuel Pérez Treviño, and Irineo Villarreal and other dignitaries. Amidst the final embraces General Irineo Villarreal received instructions to proceed with his men to Saltillo, but instead of doing this he attacked the city of Monterrey at 3:00 o'clock on the morning of July 14. Whether Irineo Villarreal and his men persuaded Pablo González to join this action against De la Huerta and Obregón in a voluntary way, or whether they involved him by sheer force, became a matter of dispute. But after a great deal of shooting in the early hours of that morning this clear act of rebellion by Irineo Villarreal was quelled by the troops of his recent dinner companions, Manuel Pérez Treviño and Arnulfo R. Gómez. Soon after that the authorities went after Pablo

[3] Faustino Roel, conversation, September 25, 1958.

González, and when they found this prudent man hiding in the cellar of his Monterrey home much was added to suspicions already aroused. He and two other generals were committed to the state penitentiary.

In Mexico City the Ministry of War appointed a tribunal to judge Pablo González, and on the same day that Guajardo was shot it left for Monterrey, where amidst much publicity the trial took place in a theatre jammed with about 3000 spectators. The battery of lawyers which was defending Don Pablo insisted that the trial was improper, as the tribunal was made up of men who were of inferior army rank to the accused; each member of the tribunal was then made, for the duration of the trial, a *general de división*. One of the witnesses was the man who had recently informed on Guajardo, and Pablo González made clear his distaste for this witness. The spectators showed more fondness for the Nuevo León warrior than did the judging body from Mexico City: after considering the evidence against González, including fragments of some proclamation disavowing the De la Huerta Government, the tribunal on July 21 condemned the General to death.

Learning that the death sentence was about to be carried out, Lic. Miguel Alessio Robles went to see General Calles, whom he found in the castle of Chapultepec occupying the bedroom which in former times had been that of the Empress Carlota. Alessio Robles and a friend spent two hours with General Calles arguing that the shooting of General González would be unsuitable politically. Calles then discussed the matter with his close friend De la Huerta, who favored clemency. Subsequently a telegram was sent to General Manuel Pérez Treviño, the chief of military operations in Nuevo León, ordering that González be set free at once. This decision, unlike that relative to Villa, pleased the travelling presidential candidate. Pablo González retired to the north of the border and from there in 1921 he issued from time to time formal declarations against General Obregón.[4]

Zapatista generals, who had not joined Genovevo de la O in supporting the Agua Prieta movement but who had remained behind in the mountains, now ventured to the Palacio Nacional to express their peaceful intentions. They recalled the fairness of De la Huerta in dealing with Zapatistas in Mexico City in 1914.

[4] Miguel Alessio Robles, *A medio camino*, pp. 245–246.

And at length General Alberto Pineda O., who had continued to maintain an attitude of rebellion in the state of Chiapas and had said he would fire upon any further government emissaries, yielded to the magnanimous spirit displayed by the Interim President. A spy of Pineda was caught in the Private Secretaryship of the Presidency, copying the presidential secret codes. Miguel Alessio Robles turned him over to General Hill, a step hardly likely to have aroused in the spy the idea of any agreeable prospects. But De la Huerta intervened in characteristic fashion, giving him 1000 pesos, safe-conduct orders for himself and his friends, and even a key with which to enter the offices of the presidency. The spy returned to Pineda, his ears ringing with De la Huerta's words about the need of "brotherhood for all Mexicans."[5]

The pacification of the northern territory of Lower California, which at the time served as a refuge for some who had felt inclined to be absent from the other sections of Mexico and which included frontier spots not always of the most lofty nature, was another matter. This territory, under the control of Colonel Esteban Cantú, had maintained an attitude of considerable isolation from the Carranza Government, and the latter had made declarations about the faults which it found in the way the Colonel was running things. But after Carranza's death Cantú stated that he was not in accord with the events which transpired at Tlaxcalantongo and that he would remain the only governor in the country faithful to the regime of Carranza. Carrancistas who had recently been defeated elsewhere either sent in their expressions of support, or else made their way into the territory, many of them coming from the state of Coahuila.[6] It being apparent that Cantú had no intention of submitting, the federal government, in an effort to be more persuasive, sent troops.

De la Huerta regarded the expedition of 6000 soldiers to Lower California (via boats from Guaymas or Mazatlán) as one which would not result in any fighting but would simply intimidate Cantú and add its effect to other pressures which the Interim President was busy exerting. He sent Roberto Pesqueira to the United States with the mission of influencing the United States press, and he asked Fernando Iglesias Calderón to get the moral backing of President Wilson. He sought to influence the numerous Villistas, Huer-

[5] Adolfo de la Huerta, *Memorias*, pp. 165–168.
[6] Alfonso Salazar Rovirosa, *Cronología de Baja California*, VIII, 35.

tistas, and Maytorenistas in the territory by enlisting the support of Villa and former associates of Victoriano Huerta and José María Maytorena. He sought assistance from the Mexican consul in Los Angeles. Cantú found he could purchase arms nowhere in the United States.

In the face of various difficulties the military expedition went forward under the leadership of General Abelardo L. Rodríguez. Plans to use the warship *Guerrero* to reach the west coast of Lower California had to be abandoned when it was found that the ship had sunk at Mazatlán, and so the expedition directed itself, by small boats and by hot desert marches (at night), toward the Colorado River. A provisional bridge, for crossing the Colorado, was washed away by a great flow of water.[7] While this delayed the entry into Lower California, it can hardly be doubted that the impending invasion had a formidable effect on Colonel Cantú. Since De la Huerta did not wish to "dishonor" Cantú by turning the government of the territory over to his enemy, he suggested that Luis M. Salazar act as governor. The negotiations were carried out by Ing. Vito Alessio Robles, who represented the federal government. Cantú agreed on August 18, 1920, to turn things over to Salazar. Later that same month the federal troops were able to cross the Colorado and they were in Mexicali on September 1, by which time Colonel Cantú was in Los Angeles, California.[8] General Abelardo L. Rodríguez, who received and discharged the troops of Colonel Cantú, became chief of military operations for the district.

The Mexican Senate met in special session in order to deal with the government of states where, according to the Plan of Agua Prieta, the state constitutional powers had disappeared (i.e., where state governments remained faithful to Carranza). The Senate declared that the constitutional powers of the State of Tabasco had disappeared. De la Huerta, who maintained that the Tabasco state government had efficiently backed the Sonora movement and was therefore legal, used his presidential powers to prevent the Senate from naming a provisional governor of Tabasco.

This action by President De la Huerta prolonged for a short while the term of General Carlos Greene as governor of the State of Tabasco. The campaign of 1919, by which Greene had managed to succeed provisional governor Carlos A. Vidal, had been a rough

[7] Ramón Rodriguez F. in *Excelsior*, February 13, 1958.
[8] Alfonso Salazar Rovirosa, *op. cit.*, VIII, 36.

one, in which General Vidal's father had been killed. In his propaganda General Greene had been aided by Lic. Rafael Martínez de Escobar of the Partido Liberal Constitucionalista. More effective may have been the support which Greene received from General Cándido Aguilar, who seems not to have been overconcerned about the suggestion of his father-in-law (Carranza) that the vote be respected without prejudice.[9]

In spite of the step which President De la Huerta took in 1920 on behalf of General Greene, the latter did not last much longer in charge of Tabasco's affairs. At Villahermosa on October 25 one of Greene's supporters walked into the Tabasco legislative chamber and murdered one of the local law makers who had made some particularly bitter remarks. He killed also another legislator and wounded the presiding officer.

This event gave General Greene's enemies the opportunity they wanted. The federal Senate again declared the disappearance of legal order in Tabasco. Then it named a provisional governor who was to call an election. Greene was captured and placed for a while in Mexico City's military prison of Santiago Tlaltelolco.

The Senate also named provisional governors for the states of Campeche, Guanajuato, Jalisco, México, Puebla, Querétaro, Tamaulipas, and Yucatán. The Chief Executive named governors in the states of Chiapas, Chihuahua, Morelos, Oaxaca, Nuevo León, and, as mentioned above, Michoacán. In the case of fourteen states the local governments were considered to be constitutional, but two of these were torn by rival factions, and so there again the federal government was forced to intervene.

Yucatán had a number of governors during the short time that De la Huerta was President of Mexico, and it also had, in November, a rather turbulent election campaign, in which 160 persons were either killed or wounded. In addition there was much damage to property. When European nations sent in complaints about the socialistic uprising in Yucatán they received a reply from War Minister Calles to the effect that he did not believe that Yucatán was seeking to separate itself from the Republic.

Calles' remark may not have satisfied those abroad who were concerned about the effect of the Mexican Revolution on their investments in Mexico. But it was true enough, particularly as the

[9] Joaquín Ruiz, *La Revolución en Tabasco*, pp. 16–17.

Gobernación Minister was working closely with Felipe Carrillo Puerto and the proletarian Ligas de Resistencia in Yucatán. For that matter, the entire country appeared more united than it had been for some time. Villistas were friendly with the Interim President; Pablo González was no longer a powerful factor; Zapatistas, their leader wiped out, ceased to molest the federal government; even in remote Baja California co-operation could now be expected from those who were in control.

9.

The Election of General Obregón

De la Huerta's Cabinet included a number of the generals who had helped to overthrow the Carranza Government. The following appointments were made:

Undersecretary in Charge of Gobernación
    Lic. Gilberto Valenzuela (until August 3)
    Lic. José Inocente Lugo (after August 3)
Minister of Finance and Public Credit
    General Salvador Alvarado
Minister of Foreign Relations
    Sr. Miguel Covarrubias (until August 4)

Undersecretary in Charge of Foreign Relations
    Dr. Cutberto Hidalgo (after August 4)
Minister of Communications and Public Works
    General Pascual Ortiz Rubio
Minister of War and Navy
    General Plutarco Elías Calles
Minister of Industry and Commerce
    General Jacinto B. Treviño
Minister of Agriculture and Development
    General Antonio I. Villarreal
Governor of the Federal District
    General Celestino Gasca (after July 8)
Mayor of Mexico City
    Lic. Rafael Zubaran Capmany
Military Commander of Mexico City
    General Jesús M. Garza
    General Benjamín G. Hill (after July 11)
Presidential Private Secretary
    Lic. Miguel Alessio Robles

To President De la Huerta, and also to Presidential Secretary Alessio Robles, Obregón indicated his lack of enthusiasm about the appointments of Alvarado as Finance Minister and Calles as Minister of War, feeling that their especially warm relationships with the new President were not adequate qualifications for these assignments.

Obregón maintained that Calles was not a particularly distinguished military figure, and he pointed out that other important generals were displeased at the Calles appointment. To this observation De la Huerta replied: "I did not appoint him because he is a great military figure, but because I have absolute confidence in him."

The appointment of Salvador Alvarado to head the Finance Ministry caused Obregón the greatest distaste, no doubt due at least in part to the personal enmity which had developed between the two generals. At the Hotel Saint Francis, Calles defended the Alvarado appointment, explaining to Obregón that Alvarado was a man of great initiative and that this quality was, at the moment, of greater importance than a question of friendship.[1] De la Huerta also stood

[1] *Impacto,* September 24, 1958.

up for Alvarado, saying that he knew him well and found him very honorable, understanding, and well-intentioned.

Alvarado, who was forty years old when he became Finance Minister, was an ardent socialist, but, as his education had been limited, he hardly qualified as an intellectual socialist. After fighting at the side of Obregón and Hill he had made a name for himself as Carranza's commander of the southeast and as governor of Yucatán, where he attacked the Catholic Church and sought to instill his socialist ideas. He founded the Partido Socialista de Yucatán (Socialist Party of Yucatán), and, with the help of Felipe Carrillo Puerto, he organized the Ligas de Resistencia del Partido Socialista (the Party's Leagues of Resistance) which came to have a large membership. While in Yucatán his most outstanding commercial achievement was the establishment of the Comisión Reguladora del Mercado de Henequén; this organization controlled all the Yucatán henequen sales and was so successful in obtaining high prices during World War I that it was able to make a substantial contribution to the financing of the Carranza regime. Alvarado's attempt to substitute for metallic currency the paper notes issued by the Comisión Reguladora was less successful. Before long he was to die fighting, but not for a cause dear to Obregón.

The socialist regime which Alvarado left behind in the Yucatán Peninsula had serious difficulties during the last part of Carranza's Administration, and was one of the foremost to be affected when De la Huerta issued an executive decree under which the Catholic Church was to receive back the large number of its churches which in earlier days of the Revolution had been seized by governments.

General Alvarado acted as De la Huerta's Finance Minister only for about two months, and then he took off for New York to defend the Reguladora de Henequén, which, having exercised a world monopoly, was the subject of accusations related to the Sherman Anti-trust Act. After his departure the Interim President took direct charge of the Finance Ministry. In that task he received much valuable assistance from twenty-five–year–old Manuel Gómez Morín, one of a celebrated group of Mexican law students who were known as "The Seven Wise Men of Greece" and among whom were Alberto Vázquez del Mercado, Vicente Lombardo Toledano, and Alfonso Caso.

De la Huerta found Mexican banks to be in unsound condition. It had earlier been customary for the Banco Nacional de México, the Banco de Londres y México, and twenty-two state banks, all known as banks of issue, to issue banknotes backed by metal. Later, Victoriano Huerta's principal methods of raising money were to obtain banknotes by legally reducing the guarantee behind the notes and by forcing government loans from the banks, the amount of one such loan to be considered as part of the legal reserve against banknote issuance. While this liberal printing of banknotes reduced their value and also the ultimate ability of the banks to redeem them, Carranza decreed the illegality of these new notes, and he and his forces, and also Villa, put out a series of paper-money issues. At length these copious issues became worthless, including Carranza's "infalsificable" paper issue of 1916, which was to be difficult to counterfeit. Then gold and silver, out of sheer necessity on the part of everyone, including the tax collector, made a return. The Carranza Government was continually at odds with banks, calling them the enemies of the people, and it jailed important bank managers and directors for failing to co-operate. In 1916 it not only ended the rights of banks to emit banknotes but also placed all banks of issue in liquidation because they could not comply with the impossible order that their reserves equal 100 per cent of their notes outstanding.[2]

Shortly before the promulgation of the 1917 Constitution the Carranza Government took from the nation's banks their metallic reserves, in keeping with Luis Cabrera's pronouncement that "money must be taken from where it is." The funds so taken, exceeding 50 million pesos but perhaps less than the 86 million mentioned by the shocked De la Huerta, were to be used to establish metallic currency as the only legal tender in the country, thus giving legal blessing to an accomplished fact. The 1917 Constitution gave the federal government a monopoly in the issuance of metal-backed paper currency, but by 1920, in spite of studies which the Carranza Government had been making, nothing had been arranged in this respect. Nor would the paper money have been popular.

Generally speaking it can be said that during the interim regime of De la Huerta the banks of issue and loan were in bankruptcy, and the only currency that people would accept, after the revolutionary years of indiscriminate paper issue, was metallic currency: gold and silver. Sacks of coins had replaced the wallet. It is true that

[2] A complete account of matters mentioned in this paragraph may be found in Edwin Walter Kemmerer's *Inflation and Revolution: Mexico's Experience of 1912–1917*.

in the early part of 1920 it had been necessary for the Monetary Commission to issue paper notes in one-peso and fifty-centavo amounts, since the price of silver went so high that the silver coins disappeared from circulation; but under the De la Huerta Government these notes were retired because of a drop in the price of silver.

The funds of the Mexican Treasury, estimated at 11 million gold pesos (about $5,500,000), were in Carranza's trains which left Mexico City on May 7, 1920. To a large extent this amount was what remained of 15 million pesos which shortly before had been obtained from banks in exchange for "Cabrera bonds." After the defeat of Carranza at Aljibes on May 14, the victorious forces recovered about 8 million of these gold pesos. Adolfo Ruiz Cortines, who earlier in the Revolution had been associated with Ing. Robles Domínguez and who accompanied General Jacinto B. Treviño in the action at Aljibes, had charge of turning these funds over to the provisional government.

All of this gold was used to pay off the forces of General Pablo González, who had occupied Mexico City with his 22,000 men.[3] Thus a good start was made in the effort to reduce by 50 per cent the nation's total armed forces of 100,000 soldiers and officers, which were costing the nation not a great deal less than a million pesos daily. As another step in this direction, agrarian fighters were provided with lands and with some equipment with which to work them. Besides devoting revenues to the discharge of soldiers and to the payment of government operating expenses, the De la Huerta Administration was able to purchase a few boats for the government and to pay off the 15-million-peso Cabrera bond issue.[4]

De la Huerta's Minister of Communications and Public Works, General Pascual Ortiz Rubio, had the ideal revolutionary record. That is to say, as a youth he opposed the Díaz regime, as a federal congressman he led an anti-Huerta block and was thrown in the penitentiary on Huerta's orders; he had been a member of the Querétaro Congress which drew up the 1917 Constitution, and, while governor of Michoacán (a position which he did not owe to Carranza or Diéquez), he had rejected invitations to support Bonillas.

However, a series of differences developed between De la Huerta

[3] Adolfo de la Huerta (pseud. Alex Hamilton), "Crisis y Cresos," *Nuevos Horizontes*, July 15, 1954.
[4] *Ibid.*

and his Communications Minister. The President removed the provisional governor of Michoacán, whom Ortiz Rubio had left behind, and, as we have seen, named in his stead General Lázaro Cárdenas. Ortiz Rubio maintained that De la Huerta's ultimate plan was to claim the forthcoming Michoacán election void on the basis of Cárdenas' not being properly authorized to be governor, in which case the President could name a provisional governor who in turn would arrange to see that General Francisco Múgica, good friend of De la Huerta, would get the governorship. This objective, said Ortiz Rubio, was precisely the one that Carranza had had. So the Communications Minister made a quick trip to Michoacán, received the governorship from General Cárdenas, and remained in Morelia during the election, which, on account of his presence, was considered legal.[5] Although the election was unsatisfactory to the ambitions of Múgica and to what Ortiz Rubio considered to be De la Huerta's plans, and although the federal Senate failed to recognize Múgica as Michoacán's governor, political conditions were so unsettled in the state that there was a time when Múgica simply took possession of the Governor's Palace and started to dispatch business as governor.

Another difference between De la Huerta and Ortiz Rubio had to do with some payments which De la Huerta wished to have made on account of studies in connection with the selection of the Canutillo hacienda for Villa. This charge was to be made to the National Railways, which were under Ortiz Rubio's jurisdiction, and Ortiz Rubio objected.

Although both Bonillas and Pablo González withdrew as presidential candidates after Tlaxcalantongo, Obregón did find himself with an opponent. The Partido Nacional Republicano met in Mexico City and on July 19 nominated Ing. Alfredo Robles Domínguez, who was also supported by the Partido Católico. While Amado Aguirre of the Centro Director Obregonista asserted that Robles Domínguez was supported by all of the reaction, those who had earlier maligned the reputation of Bonillas now set to work on Obregón's new opponent. The world was advised that Robles Domínguez had recently not only received backing for the provisional presidency from a representative of a foreign country, but

[5] Pascual Ortiz Rubio, "Medio siglo: Memorias," pp. 35–36.

that he had offered the United States military attaché a large sum of money in return for the Mexican presidency![6]

Actually Robles Domínguez could be proud of his Revolutionary record. Before many of his present critics had bestirred themselves on behalf of the Revolution, he was boldly conspiring with Madero and others to topple the Porfirio Díaz regime, helping create the Antire-election Center in 1909, and, later, being caught by the Díaz Administration in the act of purchasing arms for the Revolution. As the result of such activities he was among those considered in the selection of a running mate for Madero in 1911. In August, 1914, he rendered valuable service to Carranza, Obregón, and the Constitucionalista forces: as the Revolutionary Government's representative in Mexico City, he helped arrange for the peaceful occupation of the nation's capital by the victorious Constitucionalista Army.

As a candidate for the constitutional presidency Ing. Robles Domínguez could count on support from those who did not like Obregón, including some of the Catholics, but he could hardly expect to win the election. Obregón made the remark that "the Partido Nacional Republicano was born dead."

In spite of the unlikelihood of defeat at the polls, Obregón made an extensive campaign tour of the republic, starting soon after Congress named September 5 as election day in place of the usual first Sunday in July. He met people in a friendly manner, heard their problems, and consulted about his plans for administration. No doubt the campaign was very worthwhile for Obregón, who was preparing himself for what lay ahead and who had a facility for phrasing things sensibly: "An upheaval such as has shaken our country for ten years inevitably leaves a residue of men who refuse to live by their labor and who foregather to offer incense to those who are on their way to power." And again: "It has been a relatively easy matter for the majority of the peoples of the globe to bring their struggles for liberty to a triumphant issue. But it has been essentially difficult for those same peoples to make a proper use of that liberty when acquired."[7]

Robles Domínguez complained of improper procedures on the part of the commission which was to report the election results, and De la Huerta therefore named three investigators charged with

---

[6] E. J. Dillon, *President Obregón . . . A World Reformer*, p. 204.
[7] Obregón quoted in E. J. Dillon, *op. cit.*, p. 224.

making sure that the reported results would be correct. Obregón in a conversation with De la Huerta made known his annoyance at this step taken by the Interim President,[8] an annoyance not easy to reconcile with his public statements unless he lacked faith in the integrity of De la Huerta's investigators. At a great reception for Obregón at Frontera, Tabasco, a crowd of those who were gathered together broke out and accused Governor Carlos Greene of having placed his own men in municipal positions instead of having relied on the electoral process. Upon hearing these accusations, which were made in the presence of General Greene, Obregón expressed his pain at "the negation of liberty for which we have been struggling for years." Even if the impositions had been carried out on behalf of his own cause, Obregón said, he would favor proper procedures and principles at the sacrifice, if necessary, of his own interests.[9]

At banquets in the vicinity of Mexico City, when it was important to be seen at the candidate's side, Obregón was apt to be flanked by Luis N. Morones of the Partido Laborista Mexicano, Antonio Díaz Soto y Gama and Rodrigo Gómez of the Partido Nacional Agrarista, and by Luis L. León and Emilio Portes Gil. Cosme Hinojosa, Roque Estrada, and Generals Villarreal, Hill, and Miguel Peralta were others who were prominently in his company.

The election of September 5, 1920, was carried out peacefully throughout the country, with important dignitaries photographed depositing ballots in boxes. De la Huerta went to the polls accompanied by Miguel Alessio Robles. Then on October 26, following a cons·derable delay, the Chamber of Deputies declared that Obregón was the victor with 1,131,751 votes against 47,441 received by Robles Domínguez. Miscellaneous candidates, including Lic. Nicolás Zúñiga y Miranda, received 2,356 votes. But not a single person in the state of Tabasco voted for anyone except Obregón. Opposition candidates received goose eggs in General Greene's turbulent state. Tamaulipas also seems to have been devoid of any supporter of either the Partido Nacional Republicano or the Partido Católico: Obregón: 19,029; Robles Domínguez: 0.[10]

One or two days after he was declared President-elect, General Obregón, accompanied by Agriculture Minister Antonio I. Villarreal, appeared in the Chamber of Deputies, where he declared,

[8] Adolfo de la Huerta, *Memorias*, pp. 181–182.
[9] Dillon, *op. cit.*, pp. 225–226.
[10] Amado Aguirre, *Mis memorias de campaña*, pp. 326–327.

"I shall not govern on behalf of a party, but rather on behalf of the entire nation." Foreseeing an agitated future in a strong and independent Congress, he asked the legislators to concern themselves with the future of Mexico rather than the interests of political blocks. He rendered his opinion in connection with the problem of creating small landowners so as to do away with the large estates.

De la Huerta's Minister of Industry and Commerce, General Jacinto B. Treviño, went with President-elect Obregón to represent Mexico at a function in Dallas, Texas, where about 17,000 turned up to greet the distinguished visitors. After some clandestine drinks in someone's cellar, Obregón and Treviño, neither of them short men, were photographed at a ball park on either side of a giant. Fort Worth's residents wanted the Mexican representatives to visit their city also, and this visit was arranged. First they were shown through a large railroad station—from one section to another. Said Treviño in Spanish to Obregón: "I wonder where they are going to take us next." Obregón replied in a jocular mood: "To the Negro section, perhaps!"[11]

[11] Jacinto B. Treviño, luncheon conversation, October 17, 1955.

10·

International Relations during the Interim Regime

The success of the Agua Prieta movement caused Mexico a formal setback on the diplomatic front. Officials of the United States government who had viewed Carranza's policies with alarm and who had become more and more unhappy at the diplomatic recognition given Carranza in 1915, now found that events themselves provided them with a basis for the realization of their wish to withdraw recognition. They had for some time been wanting a number of assurances regarding the effect of Mexico's Revolution on interests which they represented and, with the downfall of Carranza, they found the United States in a position to insist on such assurances as the price of recognition of those who had overthrown the First Chief. England, which had never recognized the Carranza Regime in the first place, showed no disposition to change her attitude about Mexico. France, Belgium, Switzerland, and Cuba were also without formal diplomatic relations with the new Mexican regime.

In June, 1920, Communications Minister Ortiz Rubio dropped in at the office of his good friend, Ing. Félix F. Palavicini. Palavicini was founder and director of the newspaper *El Universal*, which, in contrast to Carranza and Aguirre Berlanga, had supported the enemies of Germany during World War I. When the newspaperman had sought to represent Tabasco in the federal Chamber of Deputies, military men had thrown him into prison and the legislative seat had been awarded to Rafael Martínez de Escobar. Subsequently the editorial policy of *El Universal* had been one of strong opposition to the Partido Liberal Constitucionalista, Obregón, and the participation of generals in politics. Palavicini undoubtedly knew that in 1915, when he was heading Public Instruction in Carranza's Veracruz Cabinet, Obregón had included his name on the list of "pernicious" persons whom he confidentially advised Carranza to "expel" from the Revolution.[1] Appreciating that most of the Obregonistas were unfriendly to him, Palavicini must have been surprised to learn now from Ortiz Rubio that President De la Huerta and General Obregón wanted him to be Mexico's confidential agent to the governments of England, France, Belgium, Italy, and Spain.

Palavicini went with Ortiz Rubio to the Hotel Saint Francis where the matter was discussed with Obregón. "It is not," said Obregón, "a matter of serving me as a politician, but rather of avoiding that Mexico find in the renewal of her diplomatic relations with Europe difficulties which might be of influence regarding the recognition of the new government by the United States."[2]

Predecessors of Palavicini in presenting Revolutionary Mexico's overtures abroad had proclaimed that Mexico sought friendship with Europe to foster a rivalry with the United States. Palavicini set out to destroy this point of view by stating that Mexico sought cordial relations with the whole world, starting with her own neigh-

---

[1] Juan Barragán Rodríguez, *Historia del ejército y de la Revolución Constitucionalista*, II, 207.

[2] Félix F. Palavicini, *Mi vida revolucionaria*, p. 440.

bors, and was not seeking any help from Europe on account of conflicts in which she might become involved with her northern neighbor. He spent about five months on his European mission, receiving, at his own request, no salary.

While Mexican Foreign Minister Covarrubias declared that England had no wish to renew relations with Mexico before the United States did so, Palavicini made calls on Julio Pani, one of the Pani brothers, who was in England as Mexican consul, and on Rowland Sperling, head of the American Section of the British Foreign Office. Sperling expressed thanks for the return to its stockholders of the once-seized Mexican Railway Company, Ltd. (an English concern whose tracks connected Veracruz with Mexico City), but in his note he called particular attention to numerous damages suffered of late in Mexico by British subjects and companies. Sending back Palavicini's credentials, he advised that His Majesty's Government would, before taking a step, await the outcome of the September Mexican presidential election.

Strangely enough, when Palavicini called on Ing. Alberto J. Pani in Paris, his host maintained that diplomatic relations between France and Mexico continued unbroken, wherefore it would be best that the new extraordinary envoy not complicate matters by presenting his credentials. In spite of its polite phraseology the note which Palavicini received from the French government was a strong one showing a desire for more than general assurances. The French listed numerous losses suffered by Frenchmen, including those due to Mexico's total confiscation of metallic reserves, retroactive features of Article 27 of the Mexican Constitution, the suspension by Mexico of foreign debt payments, and damages sustained by the Mexican National Railways (with many French stockholders) under the administration of the Mexican government. With more precise information about how these various matters would be handled, the French government "would be very pleased to recognize the President of the Mexican Republic to be selected by the electors in the forthcoming election."

The Belgians likewise listed numerous claims, but things went more smoothly in Spain and Italy. The Spanish monarch, Alfonso XIII, may have been aware of his guest's aversion to governments run by generals when he suggested the establishment of obligatory military service for everyone in Mexico in order to avoid a military class jealous of its privileges. The Italian Foreign Minister, Count

Sforza, sent General Pepino Garibaldi to Mexico as a special envoy to reciprocate the friendly visit received from Palavicini.[3]

On June 22, 1920, President De la Huerta appointed Lic. Fernando Iglesias Calderón to be Mexico's confidential agent to the United States government. The resignation of Iglesias Calderón, who was succeeded by Roberto Pesqueira, took place in October, when Secretary of State Brainbridge Colby announced conditions for the recognition of the new Mexican regime. These were the conditions: 1) the establishment of a Mixed Claims Commission to establish the claims of foreigners who had been damaged by the Mexican Revolution; 2) the nonenforcement of the apparently retroactive provisions of the 1917 Mexican Constitution (which, among other things, upset the established foreign oil companies by proclaiming that the subsoil mineral values belong to the nation); and 3) the recognition and servicing of Mexico's foreign debt.

Prior to that statement by Secretary Colby, both General Obregón and President De la Huerta had made reassuring remarks. Obregón in September declared that "first of all we shall take care of Mexico's foreign obligations . . . When that is done we shall talk about borrowing money for the rehabilitation of railroads and the building of our ports and other public works which have been allowed to go to pieces." Shortly after Obregón's statement President De la Huerta had made it known that Mexico would pay all she justly owed and that it was not the intention of the Mexican government to give confiscatory effect to Mexican laws.

But De la Huerta insisted that his government should be recognized by the United States without a prior agreement in which Mexico would guarantee various interests of United States citizens or companies in Mexico. When he turned down what he believed to be an offer of recognition in return for a letter guaranteeing United States interests, he did so with expressions of approval from Obregón and Calles.

The government of the Republic of Guatemala was persuaded by the Mexican government to send General Francisco Cárdenas back to Mexico. Francisco Cárdenas had headed the escort which on February 22, 1913, had taken Francisco I. Madero and José María Pino

[3] *Ibid.*, pp. 439–481.

Suárez from the Palacio Nacional to the Penitentiary, and it was during that trip that Madero and Pino Suárez had been assassinated. Following the fall of Victoriano Huerto, Francisco Cárdenas, disguised as a mule driver, fled to Guatemala.

Guatemala agreed to send Francisco Cárdenas back to Mexico in accordance with the Hague Treaty stipulations having to do with those who assault heads of state and then seek asylum in other countries. The idea of returning to Mexico did not appeal to Francisco Cárdenas. Instead, he committed suicide on November 30, 1920.

Following his six months as Interim President, Adolfo de la Huerta turned over to Alvaro Obregón a nation which seemed largely at peace with itself and ready to go ahead with the tremendous task of reconstruction. The ceremony whereby the forty-year-old Obregón became President of Mexico took place at midnight, between November 30 and December 1, 1920, in the Chamber of Deputies. While Obregón raised his left, and only, hand, and made the appropriate solemn promise, all, with the exception of Rafael Martínez de Escobar, the presiding officer of the Congress, stood up.

Some of the many festivities were attended by the governors of Texas and New Mexico, who had made their way to Mexico City to be present at the occasion of Obregón's inauguration. But the presence in Mexico of these friends did not mean that the government of the United States would be easily persuaded to recognize diplomatically the group which had overthrown Carranza. De la Huerta's agents in Europe and the United States had found that the "Great Powers" were insisting on guarantees which where both specific and difficult for Mexico to provide.

11·

General Obregón and the Agrarian Problem

Shortly after Obregón made his triumphant return to Mexico City in May, 1920, following his flight south amidst baskets of chickens, he received a visit from the most famous Mexican orator of the day. Lic. Antonio Díaz Soto y Gama, a man with revolutionary ideals and with a tongue which could be vitriolic, had worked closely with Zapata and had found an enemy in Carranza. He was about Obregón's own age.

What, wondered the visitor, was the point of view of this new *caudillo* from the north? Would he, like Carranza and Madero before him, prove in the eyes of Zapatistas to be deficient in giving

immediate reality to their cry of "Land for the Indians"? Díaz Soto
y Gama had had bitter verbal clashes with Obregón at the Aguascalientes Convention of 1914.

General Obregón, laying his pistol upon the papers that were
piled on his desk, began his conversation with Díaz Soto y Gama
by remarking that he had learned much from his recent flight
south. From the poverty he had seen he had become convinced that
the problem of Mexico was the problem of rehabilitating the Indians, despoiled of their lands.

Díaz Soto y Gama replied that there was, then, no need for a
discussion; they were in agreement.[1]

That the agreement as to how to proceed was at this time a little
less than complete was soon to be revealed. But Antonio Díaz Soto
y Gama kept pushing his ideas, and at the same time this spokesman
for Zapatismo, who was not an easy man to please, came to have
much admiration for Alvaro Obregón.

Sometime after this conference, President-elect Obregón appeared
in the Chamber of Deputies with General Antonio I. Villarreal.
This was just about a month before his inauguration.

The session was under the temporary chairmanship of Professor
Aurelio Manrique, Jr., the orator from San Luis Potosí with the
great black beard.[2] The congressmen were debating a proposed bill
which would break up the large landed estates. Diputado Díaz Soto
y Gama, also from San Luis Potosí, was working on behalf of this
bill which would be welcomed, he knew, by the Zapatistas after ten
years of disappointments.

In his opening remarks General Obregón mentioned that the following bills would be fundamental for the future of the Mexican
nation: a labor law, an agrarian law and the law which would
create the Sole Bank of Currency Issue. Manrique pointed out that
a labor law had been enacted by the deputies and sent to the Senate.
Díaz Soto y Gama said that Article 27 of the Constitution made it
the duty of Congress to enact provisions which would define "large
estates" and allow the parcelling of the excess. The Revolution, he
said, had but one problem: the agrarian problem. "Everyone knows
that Carranza's lack of success was due only to his having been a

[1] Antonio Díaz Soto y Gama, interview, June 10, 1958.
[2] Stenographic text of the session described below may be found in Alvaro
Obregón's *The Agrarian Problem.*

Professor Aurelio Manrique, Jr., *speaking in the federal Chamber of Deputies. Enrique Díaz.*

landowner, as well as on account of his having prevented the solution of the agrarian problem."

The President-elect had much to say about this touchy and important problem, and in considerable detail he discussed its background and economic aspects, pleading with the legislators "to study the cause of an evil in order to fight an evil." After stating that farmers had always been the chief producers of wealth in countries as essentially agricultural as Mexico, he pointed out that in other countries recent times had seen an admirable evolution in which capital and labor, combined with advanced techniques, had increased production and reduced costs. This had resulted in high wages and low prices. "Unfortunately most of the landowners in our country have disregarded the evolution of agriculture, and have stuck to their old-fashioned ways to such an extent that they are always asking for tariff protection." Mexican farm workers, he said, had for generations been in a condition of starvation and had come to realize that the landowners sought a return on their investment not from new methods and implements, but solely from the personal efforts of their laborers. To emphasize this gloomy picture he mentioned the fact that men in the United States paid good wages and travelling expenses to Mexicans to work north of the border and to produce there agricultural products against which Mexican farmers could not compete without import duties.

While Obregón said he agreed with the agrarian principle, he insisted on the need of acting with great caution in order not to endanger the nation's economic welfare. The law-makers, he said, should not begin by destroying the large estates with the idea of creating afterwards numerous small properties. Rather, they should follow a more gradual and less disruptive procedure. If the proposed law was passed, making it illegal for anyone to possess over 50 hectares,[3] property and agricultural credit would be immediately destroyed, much government tax revenue would be lost, and a period of great hunger could easily begin; furthermore, "we would put to flight foreign capital, which at this moment we need more than ever." According to Obregón's statistics, Mexico had 50 million hectares of tillable land and 15 or 16 million inhabitants, of which about 3 million were heads of families. If one million men devoted all their efforts to agriculture they could, with the prevalent primitive methods, cultivate not over 6 million hectares, and so he saw

---

[3] One hectare is equal to about 2.47 acres.

plenty of land available for solving the problem without the need of creating too serious an upheaval. He did favor creating the right of land-ownership for every man who was willing and able to cultivate a piece of land, and the setting of a maximum area to which such a man might be entitled, this land to be taken from large estates "in such a way that with the disappearance of the large estates the output would be replaced, the small property being already created."

Obregón applauded the good intentions of Díaz Soto y Gama, but saw in his proposals "an absolute lack of practical sense." He suggested that it would be wise to act more calmly and consult practical men, "because in many cases practice teaches us things that theory does not." Speaking of himself, Obregón let it be known that he had devoted about three-quarters of his life to farming in regions where colonies had been settled and lands allotted. "About half a million hectares of land have been parcelled throughout the regions of the Yaqui and Mayo Rivers within a period of twenty-five years. I myself was one of the grantees; I received one hectare and a half, which was the tract I could personally cultivate. Therefore I have some experience . . . I am not here to plead for anybody's interest; I come to plead on behalf of the nation."

General Villarreal agreed with Obregón that the ownership of large tracts should not be done away with until small properties had been gradually built. But the ideas which Villarreal expressed on the use of taxation to kill the large estates were hardly such as to prompt their owners to invest sizable sums in more modern farming equipment.

Díaz Soto y Gama then asked Obregón and Villarreal how they reconciled "their pessimistic mind with the optimistic and revolutionary spirit of Constitutional Article 27. Or, in other words, does the triumphant Revolution, scarcely triumphant, step back on its revolutionary principles in the agrarian matter?" In spite of practical details, he said, Russia had attained "the full, absolute, integral realization of the socialistic ideal." "All that Karl Marx pointed out in his great manifesto has come to be without lacking a dot; that is known by everybody who has taken a look into the Russian problem; those who have not done so through fear, or through belief in the mutilated cable messages put out by the newspapers of the Republic, do not understand this, nor want to understand, either, the problem of their own country." Díaz Soto y Gama praised the genius of Lenin. "The agrarian problem in Mexico likewise may be solved with a little good will; it is not true that the problem contains a number of difficulties; it lacks nothing but willingness, a revolutionary spirit, and the determination not to lose heart when stumbling against the first obstacles."

An exchange of views about the merits of parcelling 25,000 hectares among 1,000 inhabitants followed, Díaz Soto y Gama maintaining that such an amount would not be too much and that not all might be tillable. Obregón felt that among 1,000 inhabitants no more than 100 would be able to farm, and he observed that in Mexico to allow a man eight times as much land as he could cultivate constituted a greater evil than the existence of large estates.

Before finishing his analysis of the agrarian problem Obregón made reference to the *ejido*. In the colonial period of Mexico's history the *ejido* was a commonland of a town or village, and so it came to be defined as an area of communal property important for villages or other communities;[4] but as the Mexican Revolution progressed, the *ejido* became more exactly a unit of land turned over to peasants to be worked on a communal basis.[5] Obregón told his listeners that as far as *ejidos* were concerned there need be no discussion: they must be granted to the villages. "No villagers are able even to live, if they have not a place where they can cut wood or get a little water." He described the frightful condition of some villagers in Jalisco who could bathe only when it rained, although in their vicinity the owners of a hacienda operated a mill for which the power was supplied by a flourishing spring which they owned.

Obregón closed his dissertation to the accompaniment of lusty cheers when he criticized a tendency of certain legislators to introduce laws produced in other countries without fully studying the Mexican setting. Díaz Soto y Gama must have felt that he still had some work ahead of him to make of the Obregón Administration a glorious triumph for Zapatismo.

General Amado Aguirre, whose wound during the campaign against the Villistas had not been inconsiderable, possessed at least one feature which distinguished him from the common run of Revolutionary generals: in his appearance the accent was not on youth. His abundant white mustache and his highly elaborate uniform and plumed headgear recalled figures more typical of the last days

---

[4] Charles E. Hughes, letter of January 15, 1924, to Henry Cabot Lodge.
[5] Alberto Jiménez Rueda, memorandum, December, 1956.

of Don Porfirio Díaz. And when his senatorial term came to its close in September, 1920, Aguirre found himself placed at the head of one of the creations of the *científicos* of the Porfirian era: the Caja de Préstamos para Obras de Irrigación y Fomento de Agricultura, S.A. This long-named institution had been brought into being during the Díaz Regime with 10 million pesos of government money. Subsequently Díaz's Finance Minister, José I. Limantour, had borrowed from abroad (through Speyer and Company of New York) 25 million dollars for the Caja, this loan being guaranteed by the Caja's properties and by the Mexican government.

Credits extended by the Caja to stimulate Mexican agricultural production ran into difficulties. Aguirre assumed that the Caja had originally been established to save important banks, which transferred to it their bad risks, and he found that the Revolution made matters worse by causing a great decrease in the production on lands pledged to the Caja. The Caja then came into possession of these lands, but when it sought to cultivate them for its own account the result was a great loss.

When Aguirre took over the Caja's management, he ended cultivation for the Caja's account and rented out the lands. That this experience did not keep the Caja rolling in money can be assumed from Aguirre's conclusion that a farmer would need to have an excellent harvest of corn, beans, and wheat in order to receive as much as 6 per cent annual interest on his investment. General Aguirre felt that no cereal could be a paying proposition when it had to cover the usual interest rates, which approximated 18 per cent annually after considering commissions.

Under Carranza various pieces of legislation had been enacted with a view to solution of the agrarian problem. The agrarian decree of January 6, 1915, provided for the transfer of lands to groups of persons who were in need of them, and it also provided for the "restitution" of lands to the towns and Indian villages which had been "despoiled" of them during many years prior to the Revolution. The famous Article 27 of the 1917 Constitution confirmed ideas expressed in the 1915 decree and proclaimed the right of expropriation in return for compensation. The law of January 10, 1920, authorized an Agrarian Public Debt of 50 million pesos. But under Carranza the agitation of the wild, unsatisfied, and land-hungry Zapatistas had continued, for, in spite of legislation, the annual rate of definite restitutions or gifts to villages came to reach only about sixty, involving each year a total of about 50,000 hectares for the benefit of about 15,000 persons.

During the first year of Obregón's administration General Villarreal was a fairly active Minister of Agriculture who sought to administer a relatively large budget and revise the mechanics of providing lands to the villages. By the Ley de Ejidos of 1921 State Agrarian Commissions and Village Executive Committees were thrown into the picture to work with the National Agrarian Commission, which had already been established under Carranza, but as this new law was both unclear and complicated it represented not much of an improvement. Anyway, under it the redistribution of lands went ahead at almost triple the small rate of preceding years. Expropriations were made of some larger estates, or some sections thereof. The arrangements provided that the parcels restituted or given to the villages were to be worked on a communal basis, and they also provided that for the purpose of compensation the valuation of the lands thus seized would be the latest official tax-assessment valuation plus 10 per cent. Neither the valuations nor the 20-year 5-per-cent Agrarian Debt bonds, which were offered in payment, were attractive to those whose lands were taken.

Late in 1921 President Obregón declared to newspapermen that in principle he defended the Agrarian Law but energetically condemned the procedures followed up to date by some officials in charge of interpreting that law. Generals Villarreal and Obregón were already at odds, and shortly after the publication of this statement of Obregón, Villarreal submitted his resignation as Minister of Agriculture. Under his successor, Ramón P. de Negri, the earlier Ley de Ejidos was replaced by the Agrarian Regulatory Law of 1922, which proved more satisfactory in spelling out the legal procedures for restitution or dotation of lands to villages and in explaining what rights the villages had. Under this law an important consideration for dotations was the number of heads of families of the village.

Then appeared an announcement which made it clear to the public that the government was concerning itself with the holdings of large landowners: plans were under way to expropriate the great estate of Luis Terrazas, whose 2½ million hectares in Chihuahua constituted the largest single landholding in the republic. Thirteen million pesos was the amount mentioned as payable to Terrazas. The matter was the subject of lengthy negotiation, and it was finally agreed that, as the government did not have 13 million pesos available, Terrazas would turn over his landholdings to the Caja de Préstamos para Obras de Irrigación y Fomento de Agricultura, S.A. and in exchange would receive some of the assets of the Caja.

Caution should be exercised before coming to conclusions based on government statistics about the number of hectares redistributed, but the figures do leave no doubt that under Obregón the program which sought to alleviate a tension caused by the existence of large estates did get under way. During his administration about 1,200,-000 hectares went to villages with a total population of about 140,000, indicating an average transfer of between 8 and 9 hectares per inhabitant benefited. Although under Obregón about eight or ten times as much land was redistributed as during Carranza's tenure of office, the practical farmer from Sonora did not push this phase of the Revolution as rapidly as some desired. In addition to the reasons which he presented to the Legislature at the time of his exchange of views with Díaz Soto y Gama, he came to realize that the application of the Revolution's agrarian policies was sometimes accompanied by unwholesome activities wherein gains ended up in the hands of those not supposed to be assisted.

There were loud objections by foreign landholders who were affected, but most of the lands turned over to the villages were expropriated from Mexicans. United States citizens preferred to seek help and protection through diplomatic channels rather than accept what they felt to be unattractive arrangements involving agrarian bonds.

12.

Obregón's Administration Gets under Way during a Depression

The Cabinet with which Alvaro Obregón started his administration contained many of the officials who had collaborated with President De la Huerta. Many of these men of the new regime, which blossomed from the Sonora movement, had a commendable enthusiasm for the construction of values, both material and intangible. But, unfortunately, Cabinet members and legislative leaders were to devote considerable attention to the differences which were now to spring up amongst the Agua Prieta victors. Talents which had brought them to the foreground in the recent conflicts were not always to prove helpful to internal harmony. It would not be long before the Obregón Cabinet bore little resemblance to what it was originally.

At the beginning the following were associated with the new President:

Minister of Gobernación
    General Plutarco Elías Calles
Minister of Finance and Public Credit
    Sr. Adolfo de la Huerta
Minister of Foreign Relations
    Dr. Cutberto Hidalgo
Minister of Communications and Public Works
    General Pascual Ortiz Rubio
Minister of War and Navy
    General Benjamín G. Hill
Minister of Agriculture and Development
    General Antonio I. Villarreal
Minister of Industry, Commerce, and Labor
    Lic. Rafael Zubaran Capmany
Governor of the Federal District
    General Celestino Gasca
Presidential Chief of Staff
    General Manuel Pérez Treviño

Lic. Miguel Alessio Robles, named minister to Spain, made his departure after getting married and after turning over to Sr. Fernando Torreblanca the office of presidential private secretary. De la Huerta's friend Jacinto B. Treviño was given the formidable task of setting up records of the careers of the military personnel.

General Calles, who forgot not his labor friends nor the importance of labor as a political force, had his hands full in the number-one Cabinet post. The Gobernación Ministry handled, among other things, problems related to politics and government, including state governments. During the first nine months of Obregón's administration internal conflicts troubled the states of Tabasco, Puebla, Aguascalientes, Veracruz, Tamaulipas, Nuevo León, México, Jalisco, Hidalgo, and Campeche. In his September, 1921, message to Congress President Obregón stated: "In many local political struggles the contesting parties ask the intervention of the executive power to obtain victory. The federal government asks the states to resolve their political questions in accord with their own laws and has constantly refused to accede to petitions."

Obregon's dour-appearing Communications Minister, General e Ing. Pascual Ortiz Rubio, had no success in his feud with Don Adolfo de la Huerta, who was the most popular man in the Administration and had the important position of Finance Minister. In the Michoacán gubernatorial squabble Ortiz Rubio seemed to be getting little help at combatting De la Huerta-backed General Múgica. But the more serious contest between these two Cabinet officers lay in the province of the National Railways of Mexico, whose management, in government hands as the result of one of Carranza's decrees of 1914, was reporting to the Communications Ministry.

Ortiz Rubio was not satisfied with the way in which the railways were being operated and resolved to replace the railway director, Francisco Pérez, who was a friend of De la Huerta. After discussing

First row: Sr. Fernando López (*railroad expert*), General Calles, General Obregón, Sr. Adolfo de la Huerta, Lic. Gilberto Valenzuela. *Enrique Díaz.*

the matter on two occasions with Obregón and receiving what he thought was the President's approval for the change, Ortiz Rubio asked Communications Undersecretary Faustino Roel to arrange to install a new railway director, Ing. Camilo Pani.

When Camilo Pani and Roel went to the railway offices, Francisco Pérez was out. Roel told the employees there of the change, noting some dissatisfaction on the part of the *Oficial Mayor,* and he sent out the numerous telegrams and papers advising of what had occurred in the railway management. Then he went out to eat, leaving Camilo Pani in charge.

Upon returning after lunch, Roel found the railway office building surrounded by the police, and, as he could not enter, he phoned the police chief, who made it clear that he was following presidential orders. De la Huerta, learning of the change about to be instituted by the Communications Minister, had prevailed on Obregón to transfer the railways to the Finance Ministry.[1]

After this victory for De la Huerta and Railway Director Pérez, Ortiz Rubio's resignation was promptly submitted and accepted, and Ortiz Rubio went to Europe. In Spain the ex-Communications Minister received a cordial message from Obregón assuring him that the Administration wanted him associated with it and providing him with a commission to do a technical study in Egypt. Roel ran the Communications Ministry until General Amado Aguirre left the offices of the Caja de Préstamos para Obras de Irrigación y Fomento de Agricultura, S.A., to take over as the new Minister.

Another who went abroad at this time was the lawyer who in Nogales a few years back had provided Obregón with the list of textbooks for his education and who was now chief legal counsel of the National Railways, Arturo H. Orcí. Advising Obregón that he was leaving for Europe for personal reasons, Orcí found the Ministry to Holland bestowed upon him. As a young Sonora lawyer Orcí had become acquainted with Obregón prior to the Constitucionalista Revolution, and a little later he had come to know two young men who came to Sonora because of Huertista activities in Nuevo León: Aarón Sáenz and Jesús M. Garza. Soon after reaching Sonora Sáenz and Garza joined up with Obregón and both of them became prominent generals during the bitter period of internal

[1] Faustino Roel, conversation, August, 1956.

warfare. Sáenz served as Obregón's Chief of Staff and was minister to Brazil before becoming Undersecretary of Foreign Affairs at the beginning of the Obregón Administration. General Jesús M. Garza, after making a great reputation for valor, and after serving under De la Huerta and Obregón as commander of the Mexico City troops, was campaigning for the Nuevo León governorship early in 1923. He probably would have won had he not committed suicide at Monterrey's Continental Hotel one morning during breakfast, perhaps because of the ulcerous pains which he suffered. His body was buried in Mexico City while President Obregón proclaimed the virtues of this young associate.

Obregón's assumption of the presidential office coincided closely with the post-World War I depression, so that he and various of his collaborators soon found themselves faced with a number of unwelcome problems emanating from the economic collapse that affected much of the world. Among the drains on the federal Treasury in 1921 was the necessity of giving financial help and railroad passage to the many thousands of *braceros* who had immigrated to the United States, attracted by high wages, only to find that the depression there left them unemployed.

The sharp drop in prices of raw materials was ominous. Metal mining was an important Mexican activity as well as a source of tax income and foreign exchange. The year 1920 had been a banner year for metals generally and had seen Mexico export more silver and at a greater value than during any earlier year of the century; the value of copper and lead exports in 1920 was second only to their value in 1918. But 1921 was vastly different, with many mines curtailing production or shutting down on account of the fall in quotations.

	Value of Exports (Pesos)[2]		
	Silver	*Copper*	*Lead*
1920	120,700,000	37,900,000	28,900,000
1921	76,900,000	9,000,000	12,700,000

To alleviate the situation the government was forced to suspend for a time its production taxes on silver, copper, and lead, and to provide help, sometimes including transportation, for many who became unemployed in mining districts. Nor were metals the only raw materials hit, as can be seen from the following tabulation:

[2] Secretaría de la Economía Nacional, *Anuario estadístico, 1938*, p. 254.

		Value of Exports (Pesos)[3]		
	Cattle	Ixtle	Hides	Henequen
1920	1,400,000	3,400,000	4,000,000	43,800,000
1921	400,000	1,800,000	1,400,000	29,400,000

That the picture as a whole was much less gloomy than the above figures would indicate can be attributed to the remarkable performance of Mexico's petroleum industry. In spite of temporary curtailments of operations in both 1921 and 1922, those two years were, respectively, the peak years of Mexican petroleum production and exportation. In September, 1921, exports of Mexican crude oil were over 17,300,000 barrels, a record month, and for the year as a whole the Mexican petroleum output amounted to 26 per cent of the world's production. Thus total Mexican exports did not in 1921 take nearly as sharp a drop as a study of metal statistics alone might imply.

	Total Mexican Exports (Millions of Pesos)	Total Mexican Imports (Millions of Pesos)
1919	404	237
1920	855	397
1921	757	493
1922	644	308
1923	568	315

In order to bolster the sagging revenues of the Treasury there was decreed on June 7, 1921, a special export tax on petroleum and petroleum products. The new oil taxes provoked violent reactions on the part of the oil companies and these reactions affected, on the one hand, the relations between governments and, on the other hand, relations between different political groups which were included in the Mexican government.[4] Important oil companies, controlled in large part by United States and British interests, suspended operations as a protest against the taxes, throwing about four thousand persons out of work. Diputado Emilio Portes Gil of Tamaulipas took charge of the relief which the government gave to this additional group of unemployed.

As the United States warship *Sacramento* appeared threateningly at the port of Tampico, a delegation of foreign oil magnates arrived in Mexico City to discuss the new taxes with the Finance Minister. De la Huerta, animated by a conciliatory spirit, sought to end the opposition of the oil companies and eliminate the other internal and

[3] *Ibid.*   [4] Manuel Gómez Morín, letter, November 24, 1956.

international political consequences by linking the payment of the petroleum export taxes to the redemption of Mexico's defaulted foreign bonds.[5] Oil company representatives and the Finance Minister signed a pact. It was agreed that the new export tax on petroleum would be used by Mexico to make payments on her foreign debt, and arrangements were made whereby increased taxes could be paid by the oil companies in depreciated Mexican foreign bonds taken at their nominal value.

Petroleum operations were renewed, with consequent advantages for the national treasury. In spite of the continuation in most fields of the effects of the 1921 collapse, federal tax collections in 1922 exceeded 280 million pesos, a record high up to that time. The oil companies alone paid 54.7 million pesos in production taxes and 26.4 million in export taxes. Less significant was the federal government's 25 per cent participation in the various local taxes, this participation amounting to 20.7 million pesos.

[5] *Ibid.*

13·

Combatting Francisco Murguía and His Associates

General Benjamín Hill, known as "Obregón's lost right arm," assumed the post of War Minister, which Calles had occupied under President De la Huerta and had relinquished to become Obregón's Gobernación Minister. Early in December, 1920, Hill ordered that Rodolfo Herrero, responsible for Carranza's death, present himself, together with others, including Ernesto Herrero and Facundo Garrido, at a council of war in the capital. These men were placed in military prison to be tried for crimes of "violence against persons in general and homicide." Carranza's secretary, Gil Farías, had died, but Colonel Fontes and Lic. Manuel Aguirre

Berlanga declared that the statement they had drawn up and signed about Carranza's "suicide" had been forced from them. Circumstances, however, were to prevent General Hill's prosecution of the accused men.

Some months earlier, while De la Huerta was still President of Mexico, Calles had made to Generals Hill and Miguel Peralta some disparaging remarks about Lic. José Inés Novelo, who was one of the pillars of the P.L.C. and who in 1919 had helped persuade Obregón to be the P.L.C. candidate. That other pillar of the P.L.C., General Hill, came at once in his usual forthright manner to the defense of his absent friend and associate. As a result of this incident, which became the subject of much discussion, De la Huerta and Obregón decided on an elaborate banquet in order to promote harmony. The banquet, at which the guests of honor were General Calles, General Hill, and Lic. José Inés Novelo, took place in the patio of the old Churubusco Convent, turning out, apparently, as a great success. While members of the P.L.C. consumed fine foods and wines, they listened to well-known orators of the day (among them Manuel García Vigil and Rafael Martínez de Escobar) outdo each other. José Inés Novelo was so moved that he was unable to speak.[1]

But immediately after this banquet General Hill and José Inés Novelo both became very sick. The poet from Yucatán went to the oceanside at Veracruz and recovered, whereas General Hill, after a period of illness during which he received the attentions of Obregón's own physician, died on December 14, 1920. Some were therefore to call the banquet "The Feast of the Borgias."

As Minister of War General Hill was succeeded by General Enrique Estrada. The judge at the trial of Rodolfo Herrero and his group then freed the defendants, but on January 1, 1921, a presidential ruling was issued depriving Rodolfo Herrero of his military rank because in his attack on Carranza he had used dishonorable means and so was unworthy of being in the Army. When Herrero contested the ruling his appeal was denied, and a new order was issued which also fired from the Army all those of rank who had been associated with him at the Tlaxcalantongo tragedy. Herrero remained in Mexico City until 1922 and then retired to his ranch in Puebla for a short while until military restlessness again appeared.

[1] Miguel Alessio Robles, *La cena de las burlas*, pp. 15–26; Miguel Alessio Robles, *A medio camino*, pp. 83–85.

Funeral of General Benjamin Hill. December, 1920. Enrique Díaz.

During Herrero's trial a stir was caused when General Alberto Basave y Piña presented to the Supreme Court a statement dated Suchiate, Chiapas, December 20, 1920, asserting that General Obregón, just prior to Tlaxcalantongo, had sent orders to Herrero (via Basave y Piña) to fight Carranza and his retinue and to have Ca-

At the funeral of General Benjamín Hill, December, 1920: General Antonio I. Villarreal *(second from left)*, President Obregón, Dr. Cutberto Hidalgo, General Enrique Estrada, *and* Lic. Rafael Zubaran Capmany. *Enrique Díaz.*

rranza killed in combat. Among the judicial comments was one to the effect that General Basave y Piña's statement had been worked up by the Carranza supporters who were now active in Guatemala. This was not the last effort to link Carranza's death directly to Obregón, who, writes General Juan Andreu Almazán, "in the fulness of his powers, had no reason to desire, and much less to order, the death of the beaten President Carranza." Efforts were made to implicate others in the death of Carranza. Very recently were displayed pictures of a purported letter of May, 1920, from Cárdenas to Herrero bearing instructions to kill Carranza, but the signature was so obviously not that of Cárdenas in 1920 that the natural reaction has been one of repugnance for the methods used by some to implicate others.

After being freed from the prison of Santiago Tlaltelolco on January 1, 1921, General Francisco Murguía lost little time in working against Obregón. He escaped from a skirmish outside Mexico City, wherein General Heliodoro Pérez was captured, and he made his way to San Antonio, Texas. There he conferred with Lucio Blanco, Marciano Gonzáles, Miguel Alemán, Cándido Aguilar, Alberto Salinas and other military leaders who plotted a movement to overthrow Obregón.[2] General Murguía appears to have been the most precipitous of the group. The month of January had not passed before he was in Coahuila issuing his Plan of Saltillo, which declared that the government of the usurper Obregón was illegitimate and that during the ensuing revolution, which was to re-establish constitutional order, the nation's executive power rested in the hands of Francisco Murguía, head of the Army of Replevin.

Disaster befell the few Carrancistas who engaged in this adventure. Notable was the action of one of Murguía's men who found himself with two companions being threatened if they would not tell the victors the whereabouts of Murguía. This man offered to tell, provided his companions be shot; after his two companions had accordingly been put to death, he made it known that he had requested this in order to be assured that they would say nothing that might lead to the capture of Murguía. He quickly met his own death for refusing to give the wanted information. And so Murguía again reached the Texas border in safety. But not without loss. His own brother had been one of the two unfortunate companions of the man who had taken this drastic step to prevent the government troops from locating the head of the Army of Replevin.[3]

Terminology by now was not what it used to be. General Cándido Aguilar and Carrancista associates of his in Guatemala, who made unsuccessful raids into Mexican territory and who stirred things up in Tabasco, were now called "rebels." Such efforts as were made in Tabasco by Generals Carlos Greene and Fernando Segovia were crushed by the forces of the new government. One of the leaders of the opposition in Veracruz was General Miguel Alemán, who had fought at the side of Obregón during the battles at Celaya. Toward

---

[2] Adolfo Manero Suárez and José Paniagua Arredondo, *Los Tratados de Bucareli*, p. 154.

[3] *Ibid.*, pp. 161–162.

General Francisco Murguía. *Enrique Díaz.*

the latter part of 1921 the unsuccessful presidential candidate, Ing. Alfredo Robles Domínguez, was arrested on the charge of wanting to stir up a revolt in the northern part of the country.

Opposition efforts in 1922 were more pronounced but were just as ineffective. Early in that year Obregón's good friend Francisco R. Serrano took over the War Ministry when Enrique Estrada, no admirer of Calles, was transferred to be commander of military operations in Jalisco. Serrano and his tough young assistant, Roberto Cruz, learned in May of a manifesto issued by Félix Díaz miles away from Mexico—at New Orleans, Louisiana. Díaz declared himself to be "Supreme Chief of the Army of National Reconstruction" and pledged himself to struggle to eradicate the "hodgepodge" Constitution of 1917.[4]

For those with General Murguía across the Texas border, life was not entirely peaceful or necessarily safe. Men close to those in power in Mexico arranged to wipe out the life of General Lucio Blanco, whom they correctly suspected of being involved in the plot of rebellion. This event took place in an unfortunate manner in June, 1922, in the river between Nuevo Laredo, Tamaulipas, and Laredo, Texas, Blanco's body being found in the Rio Grande shackled to that of a friend. Then followed the assassination of the Mexican secret service agent in whose pocket had been found the key to the fetters which bound the wrists of Blanco and his companion. After this event Blanco's mother wrote to President Harding seeking justice as well as protection for her other children, and Calles issued the following comment: "I do not know who will seek to come to Mexico after the tragic end of Blanco's adventure, but surely it will not be General Pablo González, for I consider him too prudent, and sufficiently cautious not to expose himself to a fate similar to that of Blanco."[5]

Soon after that the discontented issued a manifesto to the nation, full of complaints against Obregón and Calles and what the government had done. The leaders of the June, 1922, movement were declared to be: General Juan Carrasco (in the west), General Carlos Greene (Tabasco, Campeche, and Yucatán), General Lindoro Hernández (Hidalgo), General Miguel Alemán (Puebla and Veracruz), General Domingo Arrieta (Durango), General José V. Elizondo (Nuevo León), and a number of others. In the south General

[4] Jorge Fernando Iturribarría, *Oaxaca en la historia*, p. 408.
[5] Adolfo Manero Suárez and José Paniagua Arredondo, *op. cit.*, pp. 163–164.

Lázaro Cárdenas helped to put down this phase of General Greene's uprising.

General Francisco Murguía received numerous pleas to head the movement. He agreed, and in August, 1922, entered Mexico near the port of Brownsville, Texas. Just before he made his crossing óne of the colonels close to Obregón suggested to the latter that Murguía should be captured at once, and he proposed to arrange this by means of an insincere act of sympathy and friendship for Murguía at one of the border points. Obregón declined this suggestion.[6]

In the course of the disturbance in the states of Veracruz and Puebla, Colonel (or rebel "General") Lindoro Hernández' men took Hermilo Herrero and hanged him in a particularly cruel manner and in spite of the pleas of his mother, who was present. Rodolfo Herrero became much alarmed and sought help from General Calles, General Arnulfo Gómez, and General Guadalupe Sánchez. Generals Gómez, Juan Andreu Almazán, and Rodrigo Zuriaga were soon fighting against Lindoro Hernández in a successful campaign wherein Rodolfo Herrero gave assistance to Almazán.

General Murguía found only fifteen men awaiting his orders when he reached Mexican soil. He was able to pick up a few more later and proceeded to Zaragoza, Coahuila, where he issued his Plan of Zaragoza as well as an open letter to Obregón. The authors of the "treason of Tlaxcalantongo" were accused of destroying the moral and just work of Carranza. Activities in the agrarian and labor fields which had been carried on by the Agua Prieta victors were classified as being "falsely radical" and less than helpful outside of attracting votes. The Revolutionary ideal, said Murguía, was a civilian and institutional government rather than governments of absolute militarists. The open letter to Obregón listed assassinations and attempted assassinations in an effort to show that the present government had been "born of crime and sustained by crime." That government was accused not only of following procedures well known to Victoriano Huerta, but of going further and using other "methods which even Victoriano Huerta himself never used."

At the start of the combat at Piedritas, Durango, Murguía had a force of about seventy men, including generals. After the combat was over and his army had been reduced in size, Murguía remarked: "Another victory like this and I am finished." Victory or no victory, he was finished because military men, whose backing he

[6] Faustino Roel, conversations, August, 1956, and June, 1958.

had expected, failed to give active support to his cause. With thousands of soldiers General José Gonzalo Escobar fell upon Murguía and his group at Jagüey del Huarache, near Indé, Durango. Murguía, after the inevitable defeat, was able to escape with his life, and finally, hungry and exhausted, he reached a church at Tepehuanes, Durango. From the church he sought to make some arrangement to surrender to the federal government, and in that connection he sent a message to Lic. Luis Cabrera and other friends in Mexico City. But on October 31, 1922, the Tepehuanes parish priest was surprised by the entry of soldiers into the church while he was in the midst of religious services. Murguía turned himself over to these soldiers, who were part of the forces of General Eugenio Martínez, chief of Military Operations in Chihuahua.

By 2:00 A.M. on November 1 a military tribunal was installed at the Tepehuanes Theatre in order to try General Francisco Murguía, who declared that he had not belonged to the Mexican Army since Carranza had been buried and that he recognized no validity to Obregón's Government as the Constitution allowed no one to be President if he had figured in a military insurrection. The tribunal ruled that Murguía should die and he was taken at once to the Tepehuanes cemetery. "I have been granted," he said, "the honor of directing my own execution, and I have sufficient fortitude to command it, but I shall not do it because I do not wish to commit suicide. For (and hear me well) they are not executing me; they are assassinating me."[7] His last words were "Viva Carranza."

Generals Cándido Aguilar and Miguel Alemán had planned to raise troops in the east to join the movement, but they found no movement to join. One quick to arise in arms was General Juan Carrasco on the west coast, but he was soon defeated and killed by the forces of General Alfonso de la Huerta, brother of the Finance Minister and chief of Military Operations in the state of Nayarit. Carrasco's body was publicly exhibited at Acaponeta, Nayarit, before being buried.

Thus armed efforts in 1921 and 1922 to overthrow the Obregón Government were wiped out without serious trouble.

[7] Adolfo Manero Suárez and José Paniagua Arredondo, *op. cit.*, p. 184.

14·

Combatting Ignorance

The two ministries which, during the Obregón Administration, came to be most favored budget-wise were the Ministry of War and Navy and the new Ministry of Public Education. That the Ministry of War and Navy was the government's most costly department was not surprising. That the Education Ministry came to occupy the second place was a good sign, notwithstanding what truth there might have been in Lic. José Vasconcelos' remark that for propaganda purposes it was customary to approve larger amounts for Agriculture and Education than would be available for spending.

The decision to establish a federal Ministry of Public Education had been made early in the interim regime of De la Huerta. It had meant a revision of the 1917 Constitution and, as the reform had to have the support of the majority of the state legislatures, of which there were then twenty-eight, Lic. José Vasconcelos, head of the National University, spent about three months travelling throughout the country in search of the necessary support. De la Huerta so enthusiastically backed the education plans that, prior to relinquishing the presidency, he left a budget of about 18 million pesos for the University, which by that time, in anticipation of the constitutional reform, had been set up in the manner of a government ministry.

The work performed by Lic. Vasconcelos, who was made Minister of Public Education when this ministry was established in July, 1921, constituted a particularly bright spot in the Obregón Administration. Vasconcelos was an honest, ingenious, and very hard worker, and all of his efforts were directed solely toward the end of doing a great deal for public education. He devoted less time to politics than did some of his associates.

When the education law creating the Ministry was being discussed in Congress early in the Obregón administration, Vasconcelos noted that at least ten congressmen were urging their own particular ideas. Vasconcelos, with the effective support of Obregón and De la Huerta, had already planned the Ministry's organization and its powers, and had in fact already started in a short time some local public schools and obtained an old building which he was to renovate as the Ministry of Education building. Congressmen were quick to approve without change the education law proposed by Vasconcelos after they had seen a school which he had started in a ruined building in a miserable section of town. There, as he pointed out, "the first campaign was not dedicated to the alphabet, but to curing ills and cleaning the clothes of the little ones." Breakfast was given without charge to all the pupils.

Leaders of the powerful Partido Liberal Constitucionalista paid a call on Vasconcelos and invited him to join the Party, indicating that such a step would assure approval of whatever budget he might submit. Declining to accept this opportunity, the Education Minister instead took the matter up with the so-called "independents," who made up the minority in Congress. When Vasconcelos sought out Congressman Vito Alessio Robles, suggesting to him that the new ministry apply for a budget of 20 million pesos, Don Vito advised Vasconcelos to make the application for 30 million, as he felt confi-

Lic. José Vasconcelos. *1920. Casasola.*

dent that he could guarantee congressional approval of the larger amount.[1] Other "independents," or minority party members, such as Díaz Soto y Gama and Roque González Garza, orated in favor of a good budget for the Education Ministry, and it soon became apparent that none of the *diputados* wanted to be on record as favoring a reduction in the work of creating badly needed schooling. It was at about this time that Vasconcelos agreed to act as honorary vice-president of Díaz Soto y Gama's Partido Agrarista.

For the year 1923 Congress, practically without precedent, voted 52 million pesos for Education, which was more money than the Ministry had requested. But on account of troubles and upheavals in 1923, not all of that amount was ever received by the Ministry. (The original 1923 federal budget totalled 348 million pesos. The War Ministry had the highest budget, 113 million. Next came Education's 52 million, followed by 42 million for Communications and Public Works.)

Lic. Vasconcelos knew how to make the funds he administered go a long way. Not only were government-supported schools established all over the Republic, but public libraries were established in the Federal District. There was nothing fancy about them, but they aroused an interest in reading. Presses and machinery obtained from the United States were used to realize Vasconcelos' dream of distributing all over the nation cheap copies of the classics—Homer, Euripides, Plato, Dante, Goethe, and others. From Spanish bookmakers he was able to obtain cheap editions of *Don Quijote* as well as dictionaries of the Spanish language for all the schools. Besides issuing copies of the classics, the Education Ministry edited and gave away two million books on primary reading, as well as hundreds of thousands of geography and history texts.

When Vasconcelos visited the Yucatán Peninsula in 1922, with Jaime Torres Bodet, the poet, and Diego Rivera and Roberto Montenegro, the painters, he was received with acclamation. By this time Felipe Carrillo Puerto, leader of the Partido Socialista del Sureste, had, with the warm approval of Gobernación Minister Calles, attained the governorship of Yucatán. Vasconcelos and his travelling companions found that the public buildings in Yucatán were painted red and the Indians were being called upon to destroy the upper and middle classes.

The socialists of the Peninsula were discussing "rationalistic"

[1] Vito Alessio Robles, interview, January 31, 1957.

education; in this connection Vasconcelos had a word of advice. He tried to warn Governor Carrillo Puerto against the influence in education of "professional atheists," particularly Roberto Haberman ("Long live the Devil—Death to God").[2] Yucatán officials, anxious for federal aid for state education, appeared respectful of the views of the Minister of Education. Their show of respect, however, did not mean that Haberman would not continue a close adviser of Carrillo Puerto. His position was a curious one. Thanks likely to Calles, he was an official in the federal Ministry of Education, and, like other Calles supporters, seemed to Vasconcelos to be using his post to launch political propaganda which would be useful to Calles should the Gobernación Minister make a bid for the presidency. Vasconcelos, who preferred to see his subordinates advancing his own educational ideas, made a public statement disavowing Haberman's pro-Calles agitation among the employees of the Ministry of Education.

The National University, which was under the rectorship of the popular lecturer Antonio Caso, gave Vasconcelos a rough time. Vasconcelos undoubtedly felt that Vicente Lombardo Toledano, who was closely associated with Luis Morones' confederation of labor unions (the C.R.O.M.), was better as a labor agitator than as the director of the University Preparatory School. Early in the conflict that developed there Vasconcelos suspended a number of students who had disobeyed his orders against posting signs on the walls, and one of these students turned out to be a brother of Lombardo Toledano. Considerable complaint against the Minister's so-called arbitrary ways followed, during the course of which Vasconcelos fired three professors, one of whom was the University Rector's brother, Alfonso Caso. The charge: inciting the students against the Minister of Education.

After this a great demonstration occurred at the Preparatoria, students shouting "Death to Vasconcelos." Accompanied only by the Ministry's Chief Clerk, Vasconcelos bravely made an unexpected appearance and pleaded with the students to return to their classes, but at last he had to resort to the usual recourse: the fire department with its water hoses. Subsequently he was pained to note the occurrence of stone-throwing and shooting in the midst of the mêlée. Some students and the leader of the fire-fighting corps

2 José Vasconcelos, *El desastre*, pp. 100–104.

were wounded. Someone blamed labor unionists for the shooting. The students withdrew.

Vicente Lombardo Toledano did not remain in his position as Director of the Preparatoria, and then, after a session in which Vasconcelos refused to reinstate Alfonso Caso, Antonio Caso resigned as Rector of the University. Both Antonio Caso and Lombardo Toledano objected to what they felt to be improper intervention by the Minister of Education in the internal affairs of their domains. Had Antonio stayed on, the situation probably would have been easier for Vasconcelos, but nevertheless the student agitation died down and a student strike was not called.

Obregón said to Vasconcelos in offering his support: "You can make use of all the city troops if necessary to maintain order."

The reply: "All that is necessary is a lieutenant and twenty men to protect the boys who will attend classes at the Preparatoria this afternoon."

When Valente Quintana and police agents showed up at the Minister's offices, Vasconcelos said: "I am not in need of guarantees nor do I want your protection here in the Ministry. Go to the Museum where the students are meeting and protect those who at this moment are threatened by the men of Morones and the C.R.O.M."[3]

Vasconcelos, who in his work was supported by zealous and hardworking helpers, many of them no doubt underpaid, planned, after finishing the work on the Ministry building, for a great public library. He planned a great deal more than either time or conditions allowed him to accomplish. One of his projects was a review called *El Maestro*, which was widely distributed until funds ran short in the Mexican Treasury.

Under the direction of the Minister of Education old ruins and unused patios were turned into useful and charming places where the public could better itself. One of Vasconcelos' more spectacular achievements, completed shortly before he resigned from the Cabinet, was the construction in Mexico City of a stadium for the nation. He had provided small stadiums for each of his new schools but felt that the capital city needed a large one, "an open-air theatre, for dances, gymnastics, and the choruses of various

[3] *Ibid.*, pp. 180–181.

schools."[4] As the work modestly went forward, aided by the Education Minister's ingenious use of the small funds at his disposal, Obregón gradually became enthusiastic. At the inauguration of the stadium, Obregón, Vasconcelos, and other officials joined "over 60,000 persons" in watching the games and exercises; they heard a chorus of 12,000 children, which was followed by dancing by 1000 couples in national dress. Pointing, on this occasion, to an unfinished staircase, Vasconcelos remarked to President Obregón: "Those who follow us will not have the abilities even to finish that staircase."[5]

Vasconcelos was one of those who most decidedly came to lack fondness for Calles, and, in addition, he soon became highly critical of most of his associates, including even Obregón. Toward the end of the Obregón administration his dislike for the regime became so great that he resigned from the Cabinet. When he ran for the governorship of Oaxaca, at a time when political feelings were intense, the federal government did not support his candidacy and his opponent was declared the victor. Vasconcelos next started a publication, which failed. After that, feeling rather bitter and being almost entirely without funds, he took a trip to Europe.

On the lighter side, Hernán Robleto provides us with the account of an incident involving the President and his Minister of Education. On one occasion, Obregón and his party were awaiting a train in a small and deserted railroad station. The weather was hot.

Obregón was in good humor. Eventually he accosted a passing Indian.

"What is the name of this town?" asked the President.

The Indian replied without animation. He said that he did not know the name of the town.

"Where do you come from?" asked Obregón.

"From here, siñor," replied the Indian.

"That's strange. Did you come here recently?"

"No, siñor. I was born here. My parents were born here, siñor."

Obregón shook his head sadly. He had run into much illiteracy, but it was appalling to find a native who was so ignorant that he did not even know the name of the small town in which he had spent all of his life and where he would probably die. He gave the Indian a coin and dismissed him kindly.

[4] *Ibid.*, p. 285.   [5] *Ibid.*, pp. 282–288.

Then, after the Indian had wandered off, Obregón called to one of his companions. In a serious tone he said:

"My secretary must take note that when we get back to Mexico City we must arrange to have sent to this individual *The Dialogues of Plato* and *The Divine Comedy*, which Vasconcelos has published in order to cure the illiteracy of the Indian!"[6]

[6] Hernán Robleto, *Obregón, Toral y la Madre Conchita*, pp. 195–197.

15·

The Death of the Partido Liberal Constitucionalista

It was a tribute to the Partido Liberal Constitucionalista that, when its candidate Obregón assumed the nation's highest office, the presiding officer of Congress was Lic. Rafael Martínez de Escobar, who had recently headed the Party. Having a majority in the Chamber of Deputies and in the Senate, the P.L.C. controlled the all-important Permanent Commission of Congress and thus dominated the decisions of a legislature wherein minorities had no strength. The Congress was at that time quite independent of the executive branch of the government; it was in a position to call for reports from Cabinet members and to institute congressional investigations about their official activities.

The Obregón Cabinet: Antonio I. Villarreal, Adolfo de la Huerta, Plutarco Elías Calles, Alvaro Obregón, Alberto J. Pani, Enrique Estrada, Rafael Zubaran Capmany. *Between Antonio I. Villarreal and De la Huerta can be seen the head of José Vasconcelos. Enrique Díaz.*

Besides being clearly Mexico's most powerful political party, the P.L.C. was noted for having the adherence of the cultured and the intellectual. There was talk of creating a new super-party out of the P.L.C. and some other groups, the new organization to be known as the Partido Liberal Nacional. It was hoped that it might be the bulwark of the Revolutionary institutions.[1]

In President Obregón's Cabinet, however, the strength of the P.L.C. was not so great as in the legislature, although the Party was represented here by three of its important members: Hill of War and Navy, Rafael Zubaran Capmany of Industry, Commerce, and Labor, and Villarreal of Agriculture and Development. The unexpected death of Hill fourteen days after the inauguration of Obregón turned out to be a serious blow to the Party.

And then one morning, when Obregón had been in office less than two months, the President was presented at Chapultepec Castle with a program to be followed by the whole of his Government. This program had been drawn up by the P.L.C., which took its position and responsibilities rather seriously. But Obregón, who would seem to have helped the P.L.C. more than it had helped him, and who had earlier admonished the legislators to work on behalf of the nation rather than political parties, rejected the idea of binding the executive branch to this program which the P.L.C. so boldly and unwisely thrust upon him.

Two who did not adhere to the dominant party were De la Huerta and his friend Calles, and they were among a number of the President's close associates who did not fail to criticize the P.L.C. whenever opportunities arose. Since these two men occupied key Cabinet posts, Calles running the Gobernación Ministry and De la Huerta operating the Finance and Public Credit Ministry, they made a strong combination. In the course of throwing as much weight as he could against the P.L.C., Calles helped Morones build up the Partido Laborista Mexicano into a strong national party, and he supported Felipe Carrillo Puerto and his Partido Socialista del Sureste in the Yucatán Peninsula.

The ill feeling was mutual, and in the Chamber of Deputies in 1921 it was not unusual to hear Calles attacked. After a congressman from Puebla objected to Gobernación's appointment of Claudio N. Tirado as provisional governor of Puebla, Diputado Juan Zuba-

[1] Amado Aguirre, *Mis memorias de campaña*, p. 327.

ran Capmany mentioned what he called Calles' triumphal journey around the Republic, disposing of public funds. Calles, he said, had revealed his savagery in Sonora, when he had ordered an unfortunate wretch shot for taking an alcoholic drink, and he was now sanctioning acts of barbarism in Yucatán.[2]

On the evening of May 13, 1921, when the *diputados* were in the middle of a discussion about the new agrarian law, a mob of about 150 "socialist" workers pushed its way from outside into the legislative precincts, bearing a great red-and-black flag and shouting: "Long live the Russian Revolution! Long live the Red-and-Black Flag! Long live Bolshevism! This is the house of the people and we have the right to be here!" The mob, which in large part was made up of workers of the Military Manufacturing Establishments (headed by Morones) and which included some women and children, went past the seats of the deputies and up the rostrum, there placing the red-and-black banner in the most prominent location.

Taking advantage of this incident, the *diputados* who led the Agrarian Party, Lic. Antonio Díaz Soto y Gama and Professor Aurelio Manrique, Jr., made fiery speeches from the rostrum, praising the name of Emiliano Zapata and attacking the enemies of their party. Men belonging to the mob that had entered praised comrade Celestino Gasca (governor of the Federal District) and Russian socialism, and at the same time they made a few remarks which were far from pleasing to the erudite leaders of the P.L.C.

A few days before, on the first of May, mobs had planted the red-and-black flag on top of the cathedral at the Plaza de la Constitución, but when they invaded the Chamber of Deputies they created what seemed to be more of a problem for themselves. Lic. Juan Zubaran Capmany was the presiding officer of the Chamber of Deputies at the moment, and he and other legislators went to call on Obregón, asking that the authorities take the steps necessary to secure to the legislative power its constitutional guarantees. Otherwise, said Juan Zubaran, the legislature would have to disband.

P.L.C. *diputados* agreed, after a lengthy discussion among themselves, to name General Antonio I. Villarreal, Lic. José Inés Novelo, and Diputado Enrique Bordes Mangel to draw up a memorandum from the Chamber of Deputies to President Obregón. Villarreal declined to participate, because of his position in the Cabinet, but the

---

[2] Alfonso Taracena, *Mi vida en el vértigo de la Revolución*, p. 481.

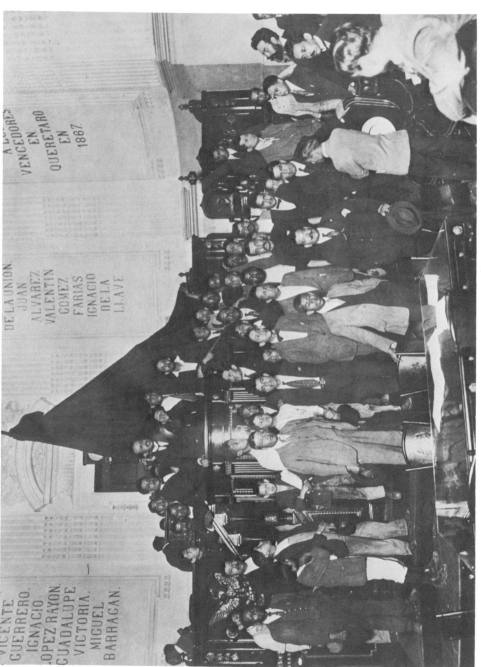

A mob has placed the red-and-black flag on the rostrum in the Chamber of Deputies. Antonio Díaz Soto y Gama delivers a speech. Blackbearded Aurelio Manrique, Jr, who also spoke, can be seen at far right. May 13, 1921. Casasola.

other two men produced a strong document which directly accused Morones of responsibility for the invasion of the legislative chamber on May 13 and which indirectly attacked De la Huerta and Calles. After the Chamber had approved the document, Lic. Rafael Zubaran Capmany, Minister of Industry, Commerce, and Labor, presented it to the President, who subsequently asked the *diputados* of the P.I.C. to call on him at the Palacio Nacional in a body. This call was scheduled for May 18.

On the night of May 17 members of the Labor and Agrarian Parties held a lively meeting in front of the Chamber of Deputies in order to demonstrate their popular appeal and growing strength. The meeting was at last broken up with the help of the forces of General Jesús M. Garza, head of military operations in the Valley of Mexico, in a skirmish in which Professor Manrique was among those who were bathed in water by the firemen.

On May 18 over 100 P.L.C. senators and deputies (including General Manuel García Vigil, Lic. Rafael Martínez de Escobar, Sr. Fernando Iglesias Calderón, Lic. José Inés Novelo, and Sr. Enrique Bordes Mangel) made their call on the President. Bordes Mangel read the memorandum of accusation in a highly dramatic manner, and it might even have seemed that the President himself was being accused.[3] Obregón heard the majority party attack the political methods being used by some high officers in the government and he heard the request that Celestino Gasca be thrown out of the headship of the Federal District and Morones be fired from the management of the Military Manufacturing Establishments. Leaders of the P.L.C. felt that Calles and De la Huerta were fomenting radical movements and using public funds for socialist propaganda.[4]

The President said that justice would be done, and the legislators departed. But from that moment on, Lic. José Inés Novelo, who had been particularly close to Obregón following the death of General Hill, could consider that the President had changed his mind about offering him a position in the Cabinet as Minister of Foreign Affairs.[5]

On May 21, 1921, President Obregón delivered his written reply to the document he had received from the congressmen, and its flavor was far from tasty to the leaders of the P.L.C. He wrote that

[3] Miguel Alessio Robles, *La cena de las burlas*, p. 21.
[4] Alfonso Taracena, *op. cit.*, p. 484.
[5] Miguel Alessio Robles, *op. cit.*, pp. 17, 21.

he considered it dangerous to set up any precedent which would so increase the influence of congressional political blocks that they could encroach upon the prerogatives which the Constitution expressly gave to the other branches of government; he warned against the danger of having the country in the position of being governed at any moment by such a block, "thus upsetting the equilibrium."

As the lack of harmony in the President's Cabinet became more intense, the relations between Obregón and Calles became closer than they had ever been. Rafael Zubaran Capmany publicly proclaimed that while he was not an enemy of the workers, he was an enemy of the exploiters of the workers, such as Diputado Felipe Carrillo Puerto. General Villarreal, who did not keep his fighting qualities under cover, was particularly provoked to note the increasing influence of Calles, and he lost no opportunity to make his acute dislike of Calles embarrassingly evident. Resigning from the Cabinet in order to work against Calles, he sought to represent his state of Nuevo León in the Senate, and the Agriculture post thus made vacant was offered in vain to Enrique Estrada. Shortly after Villarreal's departure, the Attorney General (Procurador General) of the Republic, Lic. Eduardo Neri, found that he was under pressure either to resign from his government post or else get out of the P.L.C. Neri, who blamed the activities of Calles and War Minister Serrano for the break between Obregón and the P.L.C., chose to leave the Attorney Generalship and was succeeded by Lic. Eduardo Delhumeau.

Meanwhile in Congress the P.L.C. was more successful against the men from the northwest. On November 21, 1921, Congress passed a decree whereby the control of the budgets of the various executive departments and ministries was taken away from the federal executive power and placed in the hands of the legislature.[6] And in December, without consulting Obregón, the P.L.C. submitted to Congress a proposal to change the Constitution so as to provide that each Cabinet member would be selected by Congress from a list of three names which the President would submit.[7]

In 1922, after the head of the P.L.C. in Yucatán remarked that Carrillo Puerto had obtained the Yucatán governorship at the cost of many lives, the four minority parties in Congress united to form

[6] Alberto J. Pani, *Memoria de la Secretaría de Hacienda, 1923, 1924, 1925,* I, 46.

[7] Vicente Fuentes Díaz, *Los partidos políticos en México,* II, 17.

the Confederación Nacional Revolucionaria with the objective of wresting the Permanent Commission away from the P.L.C. These four parties were the Partido Cooperatista Nacional, the Partido Laborista Mexicano, the Partido Nacional Agrarista, and the Partido Socialista del Sureste.

While rumors were circulating to the effect that government money was being used to purchase the votes of some of the *diputados*[8] the Gobernación Ministry, under Calles, provided all the help it could to the new combination. By a margin of one or two votes the Confederación Nacional Revolucionaria attained a majority in the Chamber of Deputies. The P.L.C. lost the all-important Permanent Commission and with it the handling of funds and the disposal of many jobs. It forthwith collapsed as a national power, although for a time it continued to play a role in the states of Guerrero, Oaxaca, Tlaxcala, and Zacatecas.

With the election of federal congressmen in 1922, quantities of candidates made a last-minute jump from the ranks of the P.L.C. in order to join up with the Partido Cooperatista Nacional, fearing with reason that otherwise their credentials would be rejected. Thus the Cooperatista came out on top when the Confederación Nacional Revolucionaria fell apart with its only purpose accomplished. The new dominant party had been founded in 1917 and once included prominent Carrancistas, but there had been a split in the ranks in 1920 with Party President Prieto Laurens supporting Obregón, Manuel Aguirre Berlanga supporting Bonillas, and Jacinto B. Treviño supporting Pablo González.[9]

As the P.L.C. leaders fell discontentedly by the wayside, bigwigs in the Cooperatista Party suddenly found their positions enhanced. Mexico would now hear more of Jorge Prieto Laurens, Froylán C. Manjarrez, Juan Manuel Alvarez del Castillo, Martín Luis Guzmán, and Gustavo Arce. Sr. Manjarrez, who had headed the party during its conflict with the P.L.C., became governor of Puebla, his predecessor being thrown out.

In order to prepare for the congressional sessions which were to start on September 1, 1922, the Cooperatista Party held a series of meetings in Mexico City in August, and at one such meeting they approved by global ruling the credentials of 210 future *diputados*, that is, practically all of the members of the Chamber. The new majority block elected as its president Juan Manuel Alvarez del

8 Luis Monroy Durán and Gonzalo Bautista, *El último caudillo*, p. 34.
9 Vicente Fuentes Díaz, *op. cit.*, II, 19.

134

Castillo, and as its vice-president Martín Luis Guzmán. Lic. Ezequiel Padilla, of Guerrero, spoke up to suggest enforcement of the
regulation that those who filled the congressional visitors' galleries
should not participate in the legislative deliberations.

So on September 1 Lic. Alvarez del Castillo sat beside Obregón
while the four-hour annual presidential message was read to the

Gobernación Minister Calles, President Obregón, *and the new Minister
of Industry, Commerce, and Labor*, Lic. Miguel Alessio Robles. *February, 1922. Casasola.*

Thirtieth Congress of the Republic. Subsequently Alvarez del
Castillo resigned to represent Mexico in Germany, and as Party
president he was succeeded by Lic. Emilio Portes Gil, who before
long would struggle with youthful Cooperatista strongman Prieto
Laurens.

In the process of capturing the municipal government of Mexico
City from the P.L.C. mayor, Dr. Miguel Alonso Romero, organized
groups from the Partido Laborista got practice at sabotage when
they cut off the city's water for days. Blame fell on Miguel Alonso
Romero, especially as the Partido Laborista leaders organized a
great demonstration calling for "Water, Water, Water" and demanding the removal of the mayor from office. Mobs, excited by

orators, moved upon the Palacio Municipal, which, like the mayor's home, was being protected by the police. The flash of a photographer's bulb was followed by fatal shootings on the part of the police, and then the mob set fire to the Palacio Municipal, burning up the files and records. Federal troops and the experienced men of the fire department finally dominated this turbulent affair, which contributed to the P.L.C.'s loss of the municipal government.

Rafael Zubaran Capmany of the P.L.C. resigned from the Obregón Cabinet in 1922 and was succeeded as Minister of Industry, Commerce, and Labor by Lic. Miguel Alessio Robles, who had been presidential secretary during the interim administration of De la Huerta. General Antonio I. Villarreal's experience in the 1922 election was not to his liking: his hopes of representing Nuevo León in the Senate went unfulfilled in spite of his popularity in his home state. Villarreal was ready to fight again, and there were other members of the P.L.C. who felt the same way.

16·

Carrillo Puerto and the Ligas de Resistencia de Yucatán

Prior to its collapse in the federal Congress the P.L.C. had failed in its efforts in the state of Yucatán (in the northern part of the Yucatán Peninsula). In the midst of sometimes violent words and actions and in the face of considerable editorial disapproval, victory went to the Ligas de Resistencia de Yucatán, which were associated first with the Partido Socialista de Yucatán and then with the more generally embracing Partido Socialista del Sureste. This victory brought to the governor's chair the colorful Felipe Carrillo Puerto, whose name is among those which today adorn the walls of the federal Congress in gold letters. It was a victory in which the strongest forces in Mexico were seriously interested, and the Revolutionary program which thus received impetus in Yucatán in the early 1920's corresponded closely with the views of those forces.

As the world's greatest producer of henequen fibre Yucatán had richly benefited from the demand which during World War I had sent the price of this product skyrocketing. Progreso, the seaport of the state, was clean and yet bustling with activity, particularly since in those days it was only by boat that goods and persons reached or departed from Yucatán. In a warm climate thirty-six kilometers to the south of Progreso stood the state's capital, Mérida, an attractive city of 50,000, which exhibited a good number of luxurious homes. Progreso and Mérida were connected by the Northern Division of the Ferrocarriles Unidos de Yucatán (United Railways of Yucatán).

As a result of the strong socialistic leadership first of General Salvador Alvarado (during an early phase of the Carranza regime) and later of Felipe Carrillo Puerto, large groups of workers of Yucatán and the surrounding territory became organized for their own material advancement in a manner which would have been unthinkable when the henequen *hacendados* (large landowners) had things mostly their own way under Porfirio Díaz. By the early 1920's Mérida and Progreso were full of socialistic alliances, guilds, and unions. Fifty-eight such Ligas de Resistencia were affiliated with the Partido Socialista, and their enrolled membership of 90,-000 represented a potent force considering that Yucatán's total population, including infants, was in the neighborhood of 300,000.

There were *ligas* of bread merchants, of electricians, of streetcar workers, of students, of milkmen, of newspaper workers, of tailors—in short, of all realms of activity. There were feminine Ligas de Resistencia: the so-called more élite women of the Revolution joined the Liga Rita Cetina Gutiérrez, and the more humble joined the Liga Obrera Feminista. Names of the *Ligas* celebrated national and international heroes as well as local ones: Liga Ricardo Flores Magón, Liga Carlos Marx, Liga Emiliano Zapata, Liga Máximo Gorki, Liga Francisco I. Madero, etc., etc. Some of these groups sought to go beyond protecting and advancing the material interests of their own members: the Liga Edmundo G. Cantón, for instance, carried on a school and a notable baseball team.[1]

---

[1] Juan Rico, *Yucatán, la huelga de junio*, I, 19–27.

Carrillo Puerto, who in his early years had been a train conductor in the Peninsula and who had spent twenty years spreading socialistic propaganda (with occasional t'me-out in jail), took over the Yucatán governorship from his friendly predecessor, Lic. Manuel Berzunza, on February 1, 1922. Speaking to the people in the Maya dialect, he not only promised to guard and to have guarded the political constitutions of the nation and of his state, but he significantly added h's promise "to fulfill and have fulfilled the postulates of the Worker Congresses of Motul and Izamal."

The Worker Congress of Motul, a town to the east of Mérida and Progreso, had been the first general convention of representatives of the Ligas de Resistencia de Yucatán. It took place at the end of 1918 and was attended by 144 delegates. They chose as their president comrade Carrillo Puerto, who had read and reread the Mexican Constitution of 1917. These delegates, most of them in the customary white pants and jackets, filled the Motul Theatre and decided on a course of action for the Mexican Revolution in Yucatán. It was decided that the *ligas* should convert themselves into co-operatives of production so that no one might exploit or be exploited. Although consumer co-operatives had failed in the past (because of the lack, it was felt, of honesty and administrative ability in the managers), Roberto Haberman and others suggested that consumer co-operatives should nevertheless be established. Night schools were to be founded and supported by the *ligas*.

In an effort to get more persons to join the cause, propaganda was to be used and a special assistance for the *ligas* was to be sought from the state legislature; also, the state government was to be asked to favor *liga* members in the granting of jobs. The rights of women were to be pushed; and here again the state government was called upon to help by employing only women who were members of a Liga de Resistencia. After some discussion, membership dues were set at pesos 1.50 monthly for men and half as much for women. Every *liga* was to contribute 20 per cent of its income to sustain the Liga Central de Mérida.

All Ligas de Resistencia were told to celebrate every First of May and also to hold a special observance on May 5, 1918, which was the hundredth anniversary of the birth of Karl Marx.

During the closing session of the Motul Congress speeches declaimed against the use of intoxicating beverages and marihuana. The outstanding woman delegate, Elena Torres (who, like Roberto Haberman, had a good deal to say about new educational ideas), spoke on the subject of religious worship and the state: "I believe this ostentatious worship can be got rid of; and I believe the government could easily stop the call to Mass and other religious ceremonies; let the Catholics attend worship the same way the Protestants do."[2]

Felipe Carrillo Puerto presided also at the Second Worker Congress, that at Izamal, being assisted by Juan Rico of the C.R.O.M. This meeting was not held until August, 1921, one reason for the delay being opposition in 1919 from Carranza officials in Yucatán who were working for Bonillas. At the Izamal Congress the Ligas de Resistencia de Yucatán were federated with those of the state of Campeche and the territory of Quintana Roo to push jointly for proletarian economic advantages in the social struggle. The Liga Central de Resistencia de Mérida became the head of this enlarged federation and also the head of the Partido Socialista del Sureste. The president of the Liga Central was automatically president of the Partido, and he was given broad powers. Speakers at the Izamal Congress called upon the government to socialize such public services as streetcars, light and power, etc. as were still in private hands. They joined tobacco with alcoholic beverages as evils to be avoided. They urged members of the *ligas* to make a fact of Karl Marx's observations that "the emancipation of the proletariat is the work of the proletariat itself."[3]

The first gubernatorial decree signed by Carrillo Puerto provoked much controversy. This law, establishing "rationalistic schools" for the state, was quite in accord with pronouncements made at the Mérida Pedagogical Congress of 1915 and the declarations at Motul and Izamal. Proponents of the new education spoke of the older methods as a "prison system." Comrade Elena Torres called for the suppression of the "disgraceful practices that have been considered good up to now, and which consist of examinations, rewards and punishments, diplomas and titles obtained by these means." "Aptitudes," she said, "will be measured only by the competence which the students demonstrate in practice." Knowledge was to be acquired "in the fields, in the shops, and in the experimental rooms of the school itself." Science was to be derived from daily work, which was to be useful. The schools were to be coeducational and "based on liberty."

[2] *Ibid.*, I, 79–105.   [3] *Ibid.*, I, 105–131.

By Carrillo Puerto's first decree all primary education imparted by the state was to be based on manual work to be carried out by the children in shops, laboratories, and farms. Grading was not to be related to the memorization of precepts but, rather, to the "spontaneous development" of efficiency within the new media. Priests and persons of religious and monastic orders were forbidden to have any place in either official or even private schools.

Many who had in the past been teaching along less "advanced" lines were far from enthusiastic and had for years been working against these ideas of Elena Torres, Roberto Haberman, José de la Luz Mena, Agustín Franco, Edmundo Bolio, and others.

The new governor had a visit with the workers of Muxupip, a small village which was considered as exemplifying the virtues of the Revolution in Yucatán. Here the lands had been expropriated from estate owners who apparently had had small consideration for labor. As in the rest of the Republic, there was in Yucatán very little land redistribution during the first ten years that followed the upheaval of 1910, but considerable progress was made thereafter. Between February 17, 1921, and December 15, 1921, twenty-six towns in Yucatán received 148,400 hectares, and for the year as a whole the state had the Revolutionary merit of being among the five which engaged in the greatest redistribution of land.

The simple and uneducated comrades of Muxupip were advertised as getting along happily on the production from the property they received. They established a school and a fine Liga de Resistencia, "to which all the adults belong, attending the meetings punctually, especially the cultural ones, which take place each Monday."[4] They would hear representatives of the Liga Central speak to them in the Maya tongue. Muxupip, says Juan Rico, got along admirably by expelling gambling, liquor, and the local parish priest, who in the past had "spent most of his time at the table of the landowner, recommending (to the debt-ridden underdogs) resignation, prudence, and goodness."[5]

The Catholic Church fared very poorly in the regimes of Salvador Alvarado and Carrillo Puerto. Alvarado carried out the public destruction of religious art and property. Carrillo Puerto, feeling that his government had the obligation of carrying out the provisions of the 1917 Constitution and of bringing to an end the exploitation of man by man, quickly told the Catholic Archbishop of

[4] *Ibid.*, I, 59–67. [5] *Ibid.*, I, 65.

Mérida that no foreign-born priests could practice in the state. "These 'representatives of Jesus on earth,' " wrote Juan Rico, "lead a life of ease, and harm society by exploiting it."[6]

Let it not be supposed that the only opponents to Carrillo Puerto's regime were the leading newspapers (termed "reactionary") and those who favored the old order of things. In his efforts to alleviate the burdens of the common man and to carry out a constructive administration, Carrillo Puerto could not by any means please every one of the many *ligas* and guilds that covered the peninsula. Not even in Yucatán had there been achieved a paradise completely without jealousies, rivalries, and struggles for the control of the organized groups.

In particular the governor had troubles with the Federación Obrera de Progreso, which, with past backing from the Partido Socialista, now was in complete control of the port through which virtually everything that entered or left the state had to pass. When the henequen price was fantastically high the Progreso dockworkers were in all their glory and were able not only to charge the fanciest prices for every type of work, but also to stipulate who could move what and how far before another specialist had to be called in. After the serious drop in the price of henequen these dockworkers were able to carry on in their former manner on account of the strength of their Federación and Yucatán's dependence upon them. In one of his manifestos Governor Carrillo Puerto pointed out that the conditions then existing required only 500 portworkers whereas the existing system was set up to take care of 2000 members. This situation, he added, fell as a heavy load on all of the other workers of the peninsula.[7] He contemplated establishing a rival port and connecting it by road with Mérida.[8]

The Yucatán state government had come into control of the Ferrocarriles Unidos de Yucatán. While this may have represented a step in the direction of socialism, it developed that the railroad workers would have to make sacrifices if the Railway was to keep on running. By late 1921 the Railway was far in debt to its various creditors and suppliers, and also owed 50,000 pesos in back wages.

The socialist administration of Yucatán and of the Railway could not get the Liga Obrera de Ferrocarrileros (Railroad Workers Alliance) to agree to the needed salary reductions and layoffs. It there-

[6] *Ibid.*, I, 167.   [7] *Ibid.*, II, 104–105.
[8] Ernest Greuning, *Mexico and Its Heritage*, pp. 340–341.

fore signed what it felt to be a satisfactory contract with the new Liga Torres y Acosta, which had been formed a few months prior to the contract negotiations and which almost at once was considered (at least officially) to have more members and better leadership than the older Liga Obrera. The Federación de Progreso backed the Liga Obrera in objections to the contract made by the Liga Torres y Acosta, and the fight was on.

It was at this time that Carrillo Puerto's enemies in the leadership of the Federación de Progreso were planning a super-Federación, the Federación Peninsular, which would include workers at the ports in the state of Campeche (Laguna del Carmen and Campeche), whom they already dominated, as well as railroad and power-plant workers in Mérida.

On May 24, 1922, occurred the murder of two railroad workers who had been instrumental in signing the new railroad labor contract and who were thus considered to be co-operative with Carrillo Puerto's Government. One of the men was first brutally tortured. A worker who was bold enough to attend one of the resulting funerals was murdered on the next day.

Agents representing the Veracruz portworkers, whose previous strikes had been backed by the Federación de Progreso, arrived to investigate the situation. One of these agents had worked with Lic. José Inés Novelo and the P.L.C., and he promptly criticized Carrillo Puerto for being "behind the times" and "for having deceived the workers, because now he does not permit them to do as they like." After the Federación Obrera de Progreso issued a statement declaring that Carrillo Puerto was surrounded by a crowd of reactionaries, comrades arose in public and accused the governor himself of being a reactionary. Some had plans under way to invite Lic. Patricio Sabido, a Supreme Court judge, to take over the Yucatán governorship after the fall of Carrillo Puerto, and thus to "save" the Partido Socialista del Sureste.

At about this time General Francisco R. Serrano of the federal War Ministry arrived on a visit to the peninsula. He conferred with the Governor, who promised him that all the railroad workers, with the exception of those involved in the recent murders and sabotage, would return to work.

Labor leader Juan Rico persuaded the C.R.O.M.'s José F. Gutiérrez and Samuel O. Yúdico to make a hurried trip from Mexico City to Yucatán. The latter was considered particularly well qualified to lend a hand in settling the dispute because he had spent two years in the state and had participated in the Worker Congress of Izamal of 1921. By the time that these distinguished labor leaders reached Progreso, a "general work stoppage" had been declared (on June 5, 1922) at Campeche, Laguna, Mérida, and Progreso, as an act of support for the members of the Liga Obrera de Ferrocarrileros, "whose rights have been villainously outraged by Carrillo Puerto, the satrap who masquerades as a worker." This was in spite of the fact that it had earlier been agreed that of the 1,200 men to be retained by the Railway, 600 would belong to the Liga Obrera, which would conclude a contract similar to that signed by the Liga Acosta y Torres. In Mérida the most important contribution to the strike was made by the power-company workers. The "general" movement was joined some days later by the workers at the port of Veracruz, where the powerful Liga de Trabajadores de la Zona Marítima effected a serious work stoppage, an example followed by other groups in the "heroic city."

In their negotiations, Sres. Gutiérrez and Yúdico of the C.R.O.M. were assisted by the passage of time, which brought forth some discontent with the situation, as well as serious economic difficulties for the comrades in Campeche. It seemed clear that Carrillo Puerto was not yet to fall. The Railway's representatives, ex-Governor Manuel Berzunza, and "rationalistic" Professor José de la Luz Mena, repeated their offer to retain 1,200 men (600 for each Liga), but made it clear that to retain any more would be impossible: the railway lines extended for only 959 kilometers and 900 men would be a more realistic number.

On June 15, 1922, an agreement drawn up at Mérida's Hotel Colonial included a very official recognition of the existence of the Liga Obrera de Ferrocarrileros. Thus the strike of June, 1922, came to an end, although for a while longer the "reds" of Veracruz carried on their stoppage and devoted their time to making verbal attacks on the mayor of that city.

The resumption of work in Yucatán was even followed by a "secret" pact, which was signed on June 27, 1922, and in which the Federación Obrera de Progreso promised "absolutely" not to obstruct the Partido Socialista del Sureste de México "nor the government derived therefrom." For approximately another year and a half Carrillo Puerto was able to carry on conscientiously with his program, the program that he had announced to his followers in the Maya tongue when he took office: the distribution of lands to those who worked them, and the building of roads and of schools;

but, even more important, the building up within the common laborers of an appreciation of their own worth and responsibilities. He pleaded with his comrades not to spend their hard-earned money on intoxicating drinks. He urged them to get to know the Labor Law and the federal and state constitutions. He pointed out that what had been created had been created by labor and therefore rightfully belonged to labor. "If up to now all that belongs to the proletariat has not been realized, it is because you yourselves have contributed to the delay, wasting time in bars and in sleeping."

17·

De la Huerta Makes a Trip to New York

One day during the interim regime of De la Huerta, when José Vasconcelos was in the presidential waiting room, he heard Miguel Alessio Robles, the presidential secretary, dictating a cable to Paris on behalf of Obregón. Alberto J. Pani was being asked to return to Mexico in order to make his services available for the Obregón regime. Recognizing Pani's adroitness, Vasconcelos remarked to Alessio Robles: "If you call Pani here, then it will be he whom we shall have to call upon in order to obtain interviews with Obregón."[1]

[1] Miguel Alessio Robles, *A medio camino*, p. 75.

In view of the hostile attitude of Calles and De la Huerta toward Carranza's Minister to France, a Cabinet position for Pani seemed out of the question at the start of the Obregón administration. Obregón accepted Pani's offer to collaborate unofficially, and he asked him to work out some solution of the problem created by the deplorable condition of Mexican banks. Working hard and somewhat secretly, Pani drew up a plan for rehabilitating the banks by means of payment for their lost money and a system which would make possible the eventual redemption of their paper money. When Obregón asked whether the banks would accept this plan allowing them to renew their operations, Pani was able to advise that they had already agreed to it.

Obregón's Finance Ministry had also been working on a plan for rehabilitating the banks, a plan which was submitted by Finance Minister De la Huerta for discussion at one of the Cabinet meetings. Although approval of the Finance Ministry's plan seemed certain at first, Obregón suddenly suggested to the Cabinet his own new plan, the one he had received from his unofficial collaborator, and it was this plan which was accepted and made official at the end of January, 1921. De la Huerta had lost the first and least important of the series of contests he was to have with Pani.

Minister of Foreign Relations Cutberto Hidalgo felt that Ing. Pani would make an excellent ambassador to the United States, but this assignment could hardly be made as long as the United States refused to recognize the Mexican government.

In the early part of 1921 General Obregón, who was recovering from a recent illness, made a trip to Uruapan, Michoacán, accompanied by his wife, Ing. and Sra. Pani, Miguel Alessio Robles, and the minister from Argentina. Thus the President, who was especially popular in Uruapan, had the pleasure of fulfilling a campaign pledge that he would go there on his first trip for relaxation from the cares of office. A near-tragic incident occurred after General Angel Flores, General Manuel Pérez Treviño, and Ing. Luis L. León joined the President's group in the country. During a swimming party Ing. León was almost drowned, being rescued by General Flores.[2]

Somewhat later on that same trip President Obregón read in a newspaper that the Minister of Foreign Relations had agreed to be

[2] Luis L. León, conversation, June 9, 1958.

a gubernatorial candidate. The President, who apparently shared the opinion of the Argentine minister that Dr. Hidalgo was not the most perfect Foreign Minister, took advantage of this news to make it known that under the circumstances Dr. Hidalgo might resign his Cabinet post. By this time President Obregón was convinced that he had a valuable associate in Pani and he insisted on making him the Minister of Foreign Relations regardless of the opinions of others in the Cabinet. He told Pani that he would mollify the others by explaining the appointment as provisional until conditions would allow Pani to become ambassador to Washington.

As Foreign Minister, Pani pushed for a celebration to commemorate Mexico's one hundred years of independence. Although invitations were accepted by twenty-four nations, and Brazil even declared a holiday in honor of the anniversary, no representatives from the United States, Belgium, Cuba, France, or England appeared at the Mexican festivities. All of a series of functions in the capital displeased De la Huerta with the exception of the performances of an opera company which he arranged for the occasion. The entire idea was disliked by Vasconcelos, who felt that the money spent could better be used for work in the field of education. The Finance Minister did not hesitate to warn the Education Minister to keep his expenses down in order to cover the costs of the celebration sponsored by the new Minister of Foreign Relations.

At Cabinet meetings Pani was usually quiet but coolly smiling. At other times he was busy with the work of his office. He reorganized his Ministry; he also set to work to improve the dilapidated edifice housing the office of Foreign Relations, and he acquired some legation buildings abroad. But his greatest concern was for a matter that seemed more important than reorganizations or centennials: the possibility of renewed diplomatic relations with the United States.

The United States was asking that as a condition of recognition Mexico first conclude with the United States a Treaty of Friendship and Commerce. Mexico objected to this on two grounds. In the first place Mexico felt that she should be properly recognized, on account of the legality of her government and the capacities of her country, without what she felt to be the humiliation of undertaking prior obligations as a condition. In the second place Mexico objected to the proposed Treaty of Friendship and Commerce because, according to Obregón's September 1, 1921, message to Congress, she felt that it created "a privileged situation favoring American residents in Mexico, which would automatically extend to the nationals of other countries."

In the United States Mr. Charles Evans Hughes, with the inauguration of President Warren G. Harding, had become the Secretary of State in the place of Mr. Colby. Nevertheless Mr. Colby's three requirements for recognition continued to be stressed. President Obregón and Ing. Pani insisted that Mexico was already fulfilling these requirements. A National Claims Commission to handle Revolutionary damages already existed, and citizens of certain other nations had already made use of it; furthermore Mexico had invited foreign governments to arrange to establish Mixed Claims Commissions. In reference to the requirement concerning the retroactive features of Constitutional Article 27, Obregón said that the Mexican Supreme Court in its decisions had fully guaranteed that future rulings and applications of the article would be "with full subordination to the mentioned principle of no retroactivity." Mr. Colby's third requirement had to do with the renewal of service on Mexico's foreign debt. This matter was in the hands of De la Huerta. Mexico had formally invited Speyer and Company of New York and the recently formed International Committee of Bankers on Mexico, headed by Thomas W. Lamont, to send representatives to Mexico.

But when Mr. Lamont visited Mexico in October, 1921, and conferred with the Finance Minister little progress was made. Mr. Lamont objected to the arrangements which De la Huerta had worked out with the oil companies, whereby the latter were to buy Mexican government bonds on the market at under 40 per cent of their face value and were to use them at their face value for the payment of taxes on oil. Since De la Huerta insisted that the Mexican government had the right to buy up its defaulted bonds on the market, the negotiations broke down and Mr. Lamont returned to New York.

Then followed considerable correspondence between the International Bankers Committee and the Mexican Finance Ministry, with occasional statements from Mexico to the effect that she desired to resume service on the bonds.

Late in May, 1922, Adolfo de la Huerta made his famous trip to New York in order to continue with the negotiations and to discuss not only the bonds of the Mexican government but also those of the Mexican National Railways and of the Caja de Préstamos para Obras de Irrigación y Fomento de la Agricultura. Obregón emphasized that De la Huerta should bear in mind Mexico's limited economic possibilities, adding that any arrangement made by the Finance Minister should be subject to ratification or correction by the Chief Executive. De la Huerta was also asked to return with a new loan or loans which would permit the construction of badly needed irrigation projects and the establishment of the government central bank for the issuance of currency.

At De la Huerta's first meeting with all the members of the International Bankers Committee on June 2 he was confronted by representatives of the United States, Great Britain, Holland, Belgium, and Switzerland. By June 6 negotiations were going so poorly that De la Huerta fell into a deep depression and planned to return to Mexico. Obregón was backing his negotiator strongly and reiterating his insistence that no arrangement should be made which would not be satisfactory to Mexico. He wired:

THE ONLY STRENGTH THAT WEAK PEOPLE HAVE IS THAT GIVEN THEM BY THEIR OWN DIGNITY AND WE WOULD BE VERY STUPID IF WE RENOUNCED THAT FORCE.

By June 9 the situation had so improved that De la Huerta was able to report to his chief the principal understandings which had been reached. Among these were provisions to exclude from the legitimate debts of the Mexican government one bond issue of the Victoriano Huerta Administration but to include the bonds of the Mexican National Railways which were to escape foreclosure and be returned to the railway company, 51 per cent of whose stock was owned by the Mexican government. When Obregón pointed out that these railways were in debt to the tune of 10 million pesos for construction materials and rolling stock, De la Huerta suggested not mentioning this indebtedness, which would now fall on the owners, and he wired Obregón that it was understood that this indebtedness would be taken care of by the members of the Bankers Committee as important owners.

De la Huerta reported next that the amounts which Mexico would remit for servicing her foreign debt, a minimum of 30 million pesos payable in 1923 and greater amounts for subsequent years, were to be applied only to foreign debts and railway debts but in no part to Mexico's internal public debts.

In reply to his chief's inquiries about the new loans for the Bank of Currency Issue and irrigation works ("both important for the development of our country and to meet our new obligations") De la Huerta wired that after signing the agreement recognizing the old debts it would be "very easy" to get these new amounts. He expected to handle the new credits through the Banco Nacional de México, a private institution, thus avoiding the problem caused by the lack of diplomatic recognition of the Obregón Government. He expected the Bank of Paris, in combination with Morgan or Loeb, to take 49 per cent of the stock of Mexico's proposed new Bank of Currency Issue.

On June 13, when the bankers refused to talk about any new loan prior to diplomatic recognition, De la Huerta was again ready to end the negotiations. He found it hard to describe the "changeability of these men." When the men all kept on talking after De la Huerta suggested the break-up, De la Huerta, as a last resort, proposed that they submit a proposal in writing. De la Huerta quickly received this plan, which he apparently found satisfactory. Once again he became convinced that he could secure new loans—but only after signing the projected agreements. His telegrams to Obregón indicated that he was on the point of signing.

The Mexican President then wired De la Huerta that his government was in very poor financial condition and that the budget was showing a deficit of about 3 million pesos per month. Obregón repeated that he doubted Mexico's ability to comply with the proposed agreement, regardless of its merits, unless the new loans were secured. In view of his concern he asked his Finance Minister to return to Mexico after the project had been drawn up in New York.

De la Huerta persuaded the bankers to agree to say that "the individuals who now make up the International Committee of Bankers manifest their constant interest and their desire to cooperate in a useful form" for the increasing prosperity of Mexico. He now told Obregón that he had assurances of a new loan within a short time; he said that he would have further work in New York after signing with the bankers and felt his immediate return to Mexico would be unnecessary and inadvisable.[3]

On June 16, 1922, De la Huerta signed what is known as the De la Huerta-Lamont Agreement. By this agreement the Mexican government recognized an indebtedness of over one billion pesos (half a billion dollars) on account of bonds and notes issued largely

[3] Alvaro Obregón, *Documentos oficiales relativos al Convenio De la Huerta-Lamont*, pp. 1–16.

prior to the Mexican Revolution, including over a half billion pesos in railroad indebtedness. Mexico also recognized interest arrearages of 400 million pesos and obligated herself to pay this back interest over a forty-year period starting in 1928. She agreed to pay current interest in full after 1928 and until then partly in cash and partly in scrip bearing 3 per cent interest. To assure the cash payments Mexico agreed to turn over to the International Bankers Committee between 1923 and 1927 all of the oil export taxes and also any railway earnings and the proceeds of a 10-per-cent tax on the railways' gross receipts. The minimum cash amounts to be paid between 1923 and 1927 were established: 30 million pesos in 1923 and each year thereafter 5 million pesos more than the prior year. The owners of the railroad bonds agreed not to foreclose on condition that the national railroads, which had been taken over by the Carranza Government, be returned to private management.[4]

De la Huerta sent Martín Luis Guzmán from New York to Mexico with copies of the agreement and he also wired a text of it to Obregón. Upon again being asked to return to Mexico he said he would do so after the following week, which he needed in New York. To dissolve Obregón's reiterated doubts about Mexico's ability to comply with the June 16 Agreement, De la Huerta pointed out that in 1923 the oil export taxes would provide 24 million pesos, and the 10 per cent of the railway's gross receipts would bring the total up to the 30 million. He reminded Obregón that in 1923 the oil people must also pay the Mexican government 20 million pesos for "exploration rights." And he predicted improvements in 1924 both as to oil export taxes and railway receipts for carrying mineral products. He added:

I HAVE STRUGGLED AS YOU CANNOT IMAGINE WITH MEN OF VERY HIGH VISION WHOSE BRAINS ARE TRULY FORMIDABLE; ON PENETRATING THEM WELL ONE GETS A CLEAR IDEA AS TO WHY THEY HAVE ACHIEVED CONTROL OF THE WORLD.[5]

Now De la Huerta pressed for Obregón's rapid ratification of the June 16 Agreement, a ratification that he would pass on to the Committee. But he would allow the Committee to take its time in advising the world. "The idea of the Committee is to communicate little by little the concessions made to the government of Mexico, and after five or six days give the ratification to the press." Obregón

---

[4] See Edgar Turlington, *Mexico and Her Foreign Creditors*, pp. 288–291.
[5] Alvaro Obregón, *op. cit.*, p. 32.

objected to this manner of advising the public, and the New Yorkers dropped the idea. "I only wanted," said De la Huerta, "to give them pleasure in something which means nothing to us and which I understand means much for them on account of the changes on the Stock Exchange."[6]

At this point a shadow fell upon De la Huerta's activities, the shadow of Roberto Haberman, Chief of the Language Department of the Education Ministry, marketer of Mexican henequen, worker for a Red socialistic paradise in Yucatán, and a man who was happy to offer helpful hints to North American writers who chose to render interpretations of Mexico. De la Huerta complained of Mexican and foreign "enemies" who were fighting "tremendously" to avoid a favorable solution, and he was particularly disturbed by the activities of Haberman who, according to reports, represented General Villarreal in striving to have the debt negotiations fail. When De la Huerta told Obregón that Haberman was working with socialistic centers and publications in New York, and was sending messages to induce labor leaders to call strikes in Yucatán and Veracruz should a debt agreement be reached, Obregón replied by advising his Finance Minister that better information awaited him in Mexico.

Eleven days after signing the De la Huerta-Lamont Agreement, De la Huerta advised his chief that he was suspending discussions about new loans because no decision about the ratification of the Agreement had been reported to him from Mexico. He spoke of his embarrassing position and referred to the "work of my enemies."

Obregón asked De la Huerta to maintain his "habitual serenity" and to "place in us the confidence that we always have placed in you." He said that he could not understand De la Huerta's suspending talks about the new loans just because a resolution had not been sent from Mexico City on the same day as Martín Luis Guzmán's arrival there. The Mexican government was concerned about a clause which would obligate it to return the railways, including the rolling stock, in the same condition as that in which the government had taken it over. This would mean the payment of obligations and an expenditure of 8 million pesos for rolling stock. As long as the June 16 Agreement included the provisions about the railways congressional approval would be needed.

[6] *Ibid.*, p. 34.

De la Huerta apologized for his nervousness, which he attributed to the news in the papers about kidnappings and assaults and to the fact that the New York millionaires were "suffocated on account of the asphyxiating heat of this metropolis." The European committee members were, he said, returning to Europe. "We must consider the establishment of the Bank as an accomplished fact." De la Huerta could not, however, return with a signed document confirming this. He pleaded for Obregón's acceptance of the June 16 Agreement, subject, if necessary, to the approval of some railroad clauses by the Congress. Obregón wired doubts about Mexico's ability to comply without the new loans for the bank and irrigation.[7]

Early in July the wires exchanged between De la Huerta and Obregón showed greater strain. Obregón asked De la Huerta not to be surprised at his just doubts concerning verbal promises of new loans. He reminded the Minister of Finance of "the spirit of the small farmer," especially with the experience Mexican officials had had with verbal promises "in certain cases where the interests of high politics are interposed."[8]

De la Huerta complained that Obregón's verdict about the June 16 Agreement had always been conditional. "Never could you give a categoric answer as these gentlemen wanted . . . You put me in a positively embarrassing position . . . I am the first to recognize your extraordinary talent, but it produces its fruits in situations known to you. This setting and these men, how different from our psychology . . ."

And then: "It is intensely painful to me to have to accept the fact of the little or no confidence that I have inspired in you, and the hardness on your part in dealing with one who has been a loyal friend . . . Why not spare me the ridicule to which you have exposed me? What is my fault that merits such punishment from the presidency?" De la Huerta added that the arrangement with the Bank of Paris to establish Mexico's new Bank of Issue was *asegurado* (assured). "I ask you to note this word: *a-se-gu-ra-do*."

Obregón cabled his sympathy at De la Huerta's position in having to struggle with the bankers and at the same time—

. . . TO CONTEND WITH A CHIEF WHOSE LACK OF PREPAREDNESS AND LACK OF INTELLIGENCE DO NOT ALLOW HIM TO GRASP WITH ALL THE NECESSARY CLARITY AND IN AS SHORT A TIME AS WOULD BE DESIRED THE SCOPE OF THE PLAN OF AGREEMENT . . . I HAVE NO MORE FACULTIES THAN THE FEW GIVEN

---

[7] *Ibid.,* pp. 34–45.   [8] *Ibid.,* p. 47.

ME BY NATURE AND THOSE I HAVE USED TO GUIDE ALL THE ACTIONS OF MY LIFE AND THOSE I MUST USE NATURALLY ON THIS OCCASION IN WHICH I AM AWARE OF THE FARREACHING EXTENT OF MY RESPONSIBILITIES. FURTHERMORE, I LACK THAT FRANK KINDLINESS WHICH CHARACTERIZES YOU AND LEADS YOU TO HAVE CONFIDENCE IN THE GOOD FAITH AND SINCERITY OF THE COMMITTEE OF BANKERS, WHOSE GOOD FAITH AND SINCERITY I CONCEDE EACH ONE MIGHT POSSESS INDIVIDUALLY; BUT I HESITATE TO BELIEVE THAT THEY ALLOW THEMSELVES TO BE INSPIRED BY THAT GOOD FAITH AND THAT SINCERITY WHEN IT IS A MATTER OF DEFENDING THEIR INTERESTS IN RELATION TO A GOVERNMENT EMANATING FROM A REVOLUTION WHICH HAS INSCRIBED, AS ONE OF ITS FUNDAMENTAL POSTULATES, THE ABSOLUTE DEFINITION OF THE POLITICAL FEATURES OF OUR NATION AS AN AUTONOMOUS PEOPLE, AND WHICH HAS PREFERRED TO ENCOUNTER ALL KINDS OF DIFFICULTIES AND DANGERS BEFORE YIELDING TO THE PRESSURE WHICH HAS BEEN MADE ON IT TO ACCEPT AN OFFICIAL RECOGNITION AND MATERIAL SUPPORT TOGETHER WITH A DIMINUTION OF ITS SOVEREIGNTY, WHICH PRESSURE HAS NOT BEEN FOREIGN TO OUR CREDITORS . . .[9]

Obregón next noted that the fund for founding the Banco Unico was *a-se-gu-ra-do.* In view of this assurance he agreed that a statement to the press should be released. In this statement the Mexican Chief Executive declared that the Cabinet had found the projected De la Huerta-Lamont Agreement to be fair, generally speaking, and that the difficult and able work of the Finance Minister should be appreciated by all good Mexicans. The statement said further that the executive branch of the government felt that the project needed congressional approval and for that reason executive acceptance was not urgent but could await the return of De la Huerta, who could give full verbal information about the complementary phases of the Agreement.

In stressing the unsatisfactory nature of his relations with Obregón at this time De la Huerta has mentioned assurrances he (De la Huerta) gave to the Bankers Committee that he would keep some matters secret for some days, allowing the bondholders' representatives to play the bond market to advantage in return for their not charging a commission which would have been Mexico's obligation. In his account of this matter Don Adolfo has remarked that a representative of Alvaro Obregón y Compañia of Nogales reached New York with the idea of playing the bond market and became vexed when De la Huerta refused to supply the information which he had agreed with the bankers not yet to divulge.[10]

[9] *Ibid.,* pp. 48–53.   [10] Adolfo de la Huerta, interview, June 6, 1955.

At a Cabinet meeting in Mexico City, Ing. Pani pointed out to General Obregón the financial errors that Don Adolfo had made in his dealings with the International Bankers Committee: (1) the nominal value of the depressed bonds should not have been recognized; (2) the National Railways was an autonomous company (in which the government was a stockholder and originally guaranteed only part of the debt) and its obligations should not have been included with the other debts; and (3) Mexico did not have the capacity to make the payments which the Agreement required. Cables which went from President Obregón to De la Huerta in New York suggested that the agreement about the railroad indebtedness might better have been kept separate from the remainder of the Agreement, and they contained the observation that the payments required under the June 16 Agreement exceeded what Mexico would be able to pay.

During De la Huerta's negotiations in the United States he received from President Harding an invitation to visit Washington. Before making this trip he consulted Obregón, because he wished to take care not to invade affairs managed by Ing. Pani. After some delay Obregón told him to go ahead, and De la Huerta travelled to the United States capital in his special railroad car, the *Hidalgo*. From Washington station, where he received an unexpectedly warm welcome, a motorcycle escort accompanied him to his hotel.

In Washington De la Huerta spent a very pleasant hour at the White House with the President of the United States. The two men got along together in full harmony. The Finance Minister was invited to stay for lunch, but he advised President Harding that he could not do so because he had invited five United States senators to lunch with him in his railroad car. President Harding said that the White House could take care of all of them; but De la Huerta, in his best humor, pointed out that, on account of prohibition, the White House would be unable to accommodate them with respect to "whiskey, cognac, and maybe champagne" which the senators wanted and which had been permitted in the special car.

Harding complimented De la Huerta for having bested the "wolves of Wall Street," for having caused by high taxes the closing down of a Sonora mine in which Harding or some of his friends were interested, and for having, as a Sonora civilian, directed the operations of generals. De la Huerta excused himself from any blame about the mining failure, pointing out that the taxes had been a federal matter which he did not at the time control. He went on to tell his host that the recognition of Mexico should not depend on a prior treaty. Harding, reportedly after expressing sympathy, made an appointment for his guest to discuss this matter with Secretary Hughes.

The discussions which De la Huerta had with Secretary Hughes lasted for about an hour and a half and, according to De la Huerta's account, appear to have covered the most important points of the controversy between Mexico and the United States. When Hughes mentioned the question of the retroactivity of Article 27 of the Mexican Constitution, De la Huerta replied that "every constitution and its articles are retroactive" and he pointed to the effect of United States laws which had abolished slavery. Hughes objected to confiscation, whereupon De la Huerta proposed that while all the Mexican subsoil should henceforth belong to the Mexican nation, regardless of any arrangements made before the 1917 Constitution, on the other hand Mexico would give the oil companies thirty-year concessions. This was not felt to be long enough and so De la Huerta offered fifty years. Secretary Hughes then asked De la Huerta to see the oil people in New York.[11]

A discussion of Constitutional Article 123 brought from De la Huerta a defense of liberal labor legislation and apparently Hughes recognized "the aspirations of the people of Mexico to live within the liberal laws to attain their well-being." In response to Hughes' question as to when Article 27 would be regulated the Finance Minister expressed the belief that this would be one of the first things to be handled by the Mexican Congress after it convened on September 1. De la Huerta quotes Hughes as follows: "I am going to Brazil. I shall return in October; if by that date things develop as you express, nothing will remain but that we send our representative to Mexico and Mexico send hers to Washington, for then we shall be legally friends."[12]

According to a verbal account given by De la Huerta, when he was parting from Secretary Hughes the latter made a remark to the effect that it was too bad that their arrangements leading to the renewal of diplomatic relations would not become effective. "Why?" asked De la Huerta. "Because someone in Mexico is conspiring against you."[13] De la Huerta had no doubt that the reference was to Ing. Pani.

[11] *Ibid.*   [12] Adolfo de la Huerta, *Memorias*, pp. 214–215.
[13] Adolfo de la Huerta, interview, June 6, 1955.

Don Adolfo returned to New York from his Washington visit, which was publicly described as one wherein De la Huerta did not discuss diplomatic recognition of Mexico with either Harding or Hughes. To the oil people in New York he proposed the formation of companies which would exploit Mexican oil, the companies to be owned 51 per cent by Mexican interests and 49 per cent by United States interests, but his hearers declined this offer.

By the time the Finance Minister returned to Mexico, relations between the two countries were rendered somewhat tense by an official statement from the United States government to Foreign Minister Pani pointing out that the De la Huerta-Lamont Agreement had not been ratified and that action had not been taken to protect titles acquired by United States citizens prior to the 1917 Constitution. The statement reported further that oil matters had not been resolved, that it would appear that the court decisions on retroactivity were inadequate, and also that properties of American citizens were being expropriated "without provision for just compensation."

In the face of Pani's criticism of the De la Huerta-Lamont Agreement, Calles loyally backed De la Huerta. Pani admitted that regardless of the defects of the Agreement, it would help relations with the United States and would strengthen the nation's credit. De la Huerta's New York agreement was approved by Congress and was made official by an executive decree dated September 29, 1922.

18·

The Bucareli Conferences

Now it became the turn of the Ministry of Foreign Relations to negotiate an agreement of international scope.

When Pani took over the Foreign Relations Ministry in 1921 the opinion among his colleagues was that if diplomatic recognition of Mexico's government could be secured from the United States it would be easier to repair relations with other nations (England, France, Belgium, Switzerland, and Cuba) which were withholding that recognition. But early in the Obregón Regime, when the President met with De la Huerta and Calles in the Castle of Chapultepec to discuss the insistence of the United States on a Treaty of Friendship and Commerce as a condition of recognition, De la Huerta continued to argue that such an idea was humiliating. The other two felt the same way.

In Washington the Administration of Woodrow Wilson gave way to that of Warren G. Harding in March, 1921. Harding's Secretary of the Interior, Albert Fall, had, as senator, pushed for a break with the Carranza Government. Recently he had written: "So long as I have anything to do with the Mexican question, no government of Mexico will be recognized, with my consent, which does not first enter into a written agreement promising to protect American citizens and their property rights in Mexico."

The proposed Treaty of Friendship and Commerce, which on May 27, 1921, was submitted by the United States chargé d'affaires in Mexico for President Obregón's consideration, contained many provisions which must have caused the Mexican government some concern. Property rights which citizens of either nation had acquired, or might acquire, were not to be violated, even by constitutional precepts. The 1917 Constitution of Mexico was declared not to be retroactive in connection with properties acquired in Mexico by United States citizens, corporations, etc., and such property rights, whether applicable on or below the surface, were not to be disturbed in the future. Mexico was to restore to United States citizens, corporations, etc. any properties, rights, or interests which had been taken away since January 1, 1910, without just compensation. She was, in addition, to pay for any damages suffered on properties being restituted, and was to make fair compensation in those cases where restitution was impossible. United States citizens were to enjoy in Mexico the same rights as Mexican citizens had in the United States regarding religious and educational activities.[1] One Mexican student commented on the suggested treaty by saying: "It was proposed that Mexico's Basic Law should be made inapplicable in its main provisions to North American citizens."[2]

Although Obregón could not have accepted such a prior treaty and although the demands of many in Washington must have seemed rather great to Mexico, there were reasons to feel that a deadlock would not continue indefinitely. Obregón appeared to be more friendly to United States enterprise in Mexico than had been

[1] Secretaría de Relaciones Exteriores, *La cuestión internacional mexicano-americana durante el gobierno del Gral. Don Alvaro Obregón*, 1926 edition, pp. 16–19.
[2] Antonio Gómez Robledo, *The Bucareli Agreements and International Law*, p. 2.

Carranza, and he was interested in having his government recognized by the great powers, "not wanting to end my period heading a government that is not legal before the world." Among the legation buildings acquired by Mexico was one in Washington.

Two days before Obregón presented the 1921 annual presidential message to Congress the Mexican Supreme Court rendered one of its most remarkable and noteworthy decisions. This decision concerned the part of Article 27 of the 1917 Constitution which proclaims that the nation owns the subsoil mineral wealth and cannot part with its ownership but can only grant concessions for exploitation and then only in cases of regular operations. Carranza in 1918 had issued a decree under which denouncements could be made leading to the granting of these concessions; titles to exploit petroleum were accordingly issued to some, who promptly found themselves in conflict with landowners claiming the petroleum rights under the laws of the Porfirio Díaz regime. In ruling on the case of the Texas Company of Mexico the Supreme Court on August 20, 1921, declared that the above-mentioned provisions of the 1917 Constitution were not retroactive for landowning companies or persons who by "positive acts" prior to the issuance of the Constitution had made known their intent to have petroleum extracted.[3]

This decision was to startle some who had felt that the Constitution was clearly retroactive in its intent about this matter of ownership of subsoil mineral wealth, a concept dating from the Ordinances issued in 1783 by Charles III of Spain. Nor was the decision considered entirely satisfactory by those who represented the large oil interests, inasmuch as they felt it unfair in 1921 to make "positive acts" performed prior to May, 1917, a requirement for maintaining rights acquired in accordance with the mining laws of 1882, 1894, and 1909. The Mexican courts during Carranza's administration were not as helpful to established petroleum companies as was the Supreme Court in 1921, but the Petroleum Law which Carranza sent to Congress in November, 1918, had stipulated an exceptional category for oil properties in which capital had been invested prior to May, 1917.

In November, 1921, the United States chargé d'affaires in Mexico, Mr. George T. Summerlin, submitted to the Mexican Foreign Office a suggested convention to create a Mixed Claims Commission to study claims pending between the two governments; this conven-

---

[3] Roscoe B. Gaither, *Expropriation in Mexico*, pp. 35, 184. For a full discussion see *Current Controversies with Mexico* by Guy Stevens.

President Obregón *reading message in the Chamber of Deputies.* Diputado Claudio N. Tirado *and* Diputado Leopoldo Zincunegui Tercero. *Enrique Díaz.*

tion would be signed after the signing of the much discussed Treaty of Friendship and Commerce. Mexico replied by suggesting the establishment of two mixed claims commissions, one to handle claims since 1868 and the other to handle United States claims arising out of damages caused by the Mexican Revolution. Mexico further suggested that with the signing of a treaty concerning these two claims commissions a renewal of diplomatic relations between the two countries should take place simultaneously.

Early in 1922 the United States was insisting on first getting its Treaty of Friendship and Commerce, and Mexico was reiterating its objections. So the United States advised that it would sign a treaty covering the claims conventions provided both parties would agree quickly thereafter to sign the treaty which the United States sought. Mr. Summerlin wrote: "If Mexico is going to continue confiscating property rights, that should be known; if property rights are going to be protected, there should be no objection to an agreement along those lines, and in view of what has happened in Mexico it is manifestly proper that such an agreement should be made."[4]

During the remainder of 1922 and the early part of 1923 the correspondence became long-drawn-out and covered such points as (1) Mexico's foreign debt; (2) negotiations of the oil people to protect their properties; (3) the validity of titles issued before the 1917 Constitution; (4) whether the Supreme Court decisions on the Texas Company and similar cases were sufficiently protective; and (5) expropriations of lands. In connection with the last point Pani maintained that the systematic resistance of the United States was unjustified, especially if one used more of a "human judgment than a legalistic one" and bore in mind that the damages were small compared with the undeferable Mexican needs.

In February, 1923, the American oil companies settled a tax dispute with the Finance Ministry by paying about $6,750,000, which was only about 40 per cent of what had been claimed as due.[5]

The resolution of the many problems related to the possible renewal of diplomatic relations by formal correspondence was slow and tedious. General James A. Ryan, a friend of Presidents Obregón and Harding, suggested that representatives of both Presidents engage in informal talks. This suggestion, which had the backing of President Harding, was accepted by Obregón in a letter of April 9, 1923.

[4] Alberto J. Pani, *Las Conferencias de Bucareli*, p. 36.
[5] James M. Callahan, *American Foreign Policy in Mexican Relations*, p. 592.

In the first draft of Obregón's letter to General Ryan the Mexican President made it clear that the representatives were not to "broach a discussion of the Mexican legislation in force, or touch the point of whether an agreement prior to the renewal of diplomatic relations . . . is relevant or irrelevant." In the letter that Obregón finally signed these stipulations, at the request of General Ryan, were omitted. It is reported that General Ryan nevertheless assured President Obregón "that the Commissioners would adjust their conduct to what was expressed in the deleted part of the letter."[6]

President Harding named Messrs. Charles Beecher Warren and John Barton Payne to be the United States representatives. The Mexican representatives were Lic. Fernando González Roa and Sr. Ramón Ross. Lic. González Roa, named by Ing. Pani, was an erudite, cultured, and hard-working lawyer. He was an expert in international law, and during the conferences he went into many details, some of which seemed to the United States delegates to be irrelevant. Sr. Ross, a merchant and farmer from a small Sonora town, had for years been an intimate friend of General Obregón. He had known Obregón long before the latter first entered the military and political fields, and has been described by Juan de Dios Bojórquez as Obregón's closest friend. Although not well known before the fall of Carranza, Ross was given various public positions by Obregón. According to Pani the United States commissioners acclaimed Ross as "a great listener," and so he must have seemed in comparison with González Roa.

It was agreed to have the talks in the building at No. 85 Avenida Bucareli, in Mexico City.

De la Huerta was in Sonora late in April, 1923, when he read in a New York newspaper that conferences were to take place in Mexico City about matters of dispute between Mexico and the United States. He immediately sent to President Obregón a very confidential telegram, wherein he pointed out that in accordance with understandings reached with Secretary Hughes recognition should follow the regulation of the Petroleum Law, "which is about to be finished in the Chamber of Deputies"; in all other respects De la Huerta considered that the requirements of Hughes had been taken care of. As to the matter of indemnifications to foreigners damaged by the Revolution, De la Huerta wired that the financiers

[6] Alberto J. Pani, *op. cit.*, pp. 90–91.

of the International Bankers Committee would be helpful and this whole matter should be handled together with his proposed conversion and consolidation of the Mexican debt. De la Huerta objected to having United States representatives come to Mexico to discuss Mexican legislation or conditions for recognition.

Obregón wired back that the conferences signified no obligation for the Mexican government and he asked De la Huerta to come to the capital at once. This Don Adolfo did, and again he insisted that Mexico should be recognized prior to any discussions or agreements. Obregón assured the Finance Minister that Messrs. Warren and Payne were in Mexico only to exchange ideas informally, not to make any agreements. De la Huerta suggested that Warren and Payne, since they had already been invited, should be treated "with all kinds of courtesies, as if they were two newspapermen . . . Pani should be in charge of attending them, organizing his little parties for them, and then send them off . . ."[7]

On May 14, 1923, at 10:00 A.M., the delegates started their daily discussions. With them were four stenographers, Juan F. Urquidi, the Mexican interpreter and secretary, a United States secretary, and a United States interpreter. After a few words of welcome by Ramón Ross there was a reply by Mr. Warren, who explained that neither the government nor the people of the United States sought to obtain in Mexico special privileges, or rights which were not to be shared with others. "We do not have the intention or desire to intervene in matters which affect the sovereignty of Mexico." He proposed that the daily minutes in English and Spanish exclude discussion and be limited to cover those portions where the commissioners felt progress had been made. Points of view could be expressed in the minutes or incorporated therein by means of memoranda. The daily minutes were to be signed by the secretaries, with copies given for all the commissioners. González Roa agreed, with the proviso that the Mexicans not exceed their instructions "to exchange impressions about the Mexican-American situation in order to reach a mutual understanding between the two countries, and inform their government for a definite conclusion."[8]

A dramatic crisis was caused by Sr. Ross, who, after having

[7] Adolfo de la Huerta, *Memorias*, p. 220.
[8] Adolfo Manero Suárez and José Paniagua Arredondo, *Los Tratados de Bucareli*, p. 275.

taken a few drinks at the Sonora-Sinaloa Club, was dozing during a debate and who awoke at a time when Mr. Warren was making a reference to the President of Panama. Upon hearing the word "Panama" Ross launched into a bitter attack, condemning the insolence of the United States, criticizing her domination of Panama, and refusing to allow that Mexico be compared with Panama. When Warren disclaimed such an intention and suggested that the confusion perhaps lay in Sr. Ross's imperfect understanding of English, Ross angrily revealed enough English to speak disrespectfully of the lineage of the United States delegates.

After this torrent the session broke up at once and the United States representatives made all preparations for returning home. Their imminent departure was upsetting to General Obregón and to General Ryan, both of whom quite independently communicated with De la Huerta, asking him to do something to save the day. The request from Obregón came as a surprise to De la Huerta, who regarded with displeasure the mission of Warren and Payne in Mexico and who considered the recent incident to be a matter for Pani. Nevertheless Don Adolfo carried out his instructions. He invited the United States representatives to come to his office, and there they agreed not to break off the Conferences of Bucareli. They requested, however, that De la Huerta arrange to have Lic. González Roa carry on the discussions in what they felt would be a more practical manner, with fewer digressions. (De la Huerta quotes Warren as saying in a joking tone: "Why don't you suggest to Lic. González Roa that if he wants to show off his erudition he call a meeting in the bull ring where he can talk all he wants to.") And the diplomats added a request that Sr. Ross leave off visiting the Sonora-Sinaloa Club during the period of the Conferences. Don Adolfo laughed and promised that Sr. Ross would be transformed "into a complete teetotaler."

After that the Bucareli Conferences were resumed, and they continued in a friendly atmosphere.[9] On August 3 all sessions were recessed in respectful observance of the death of President Warren G. Harding.

The Bucareli Conferences came to an end on August 15, 1923, three months after they began, and since that time they have been the subject of considerable debate. Some who have wished to dis-

[9] Miguel Alessio Robles, *Historia política de la Revolución*, pp. 279–289; Adolfo de la Huerta, *op. cit.*, pp. 238–240.

parage the work of Obregón have tried to show that the conferences were injurious to the dignity of Mexico. Lic. Vasconcelos indicates that there was secrecy about what went on, adding that he learned something about the arrangements when he made a courtesy call on Mr. Warren, who told him that as a result of the conferences the lands of United States citizens would not be expropriated unless the proper payments were made in cash, not in bonds. The Education Minister bewailed the fact that a Cabinet member got his knowledge about such arrangements from a casual chat with Mr. Warren.[10]

Lic. Aarón Sáenz, who was serving under Pani as Undersecretary of Foreign Relations, has emphatically denied the existence of any secret treaties or any secrecy about any activity carried on by President Obregón with respect to relations with the United States. "The newspapers of the period gave full information about each and all of the steps that our government was taking in the difficult negotiations."[11] Sáenz also mentions the "frequent consultations which General Obregón had with his Cabinet in order to advise of the state of the talks and the points that were being raised between the Mexican and North American commissioners."[12]

In his message to Congress on September 1, 1923, President Obregón explained that the conferences consisted of an interchange of impressions and reports, during which the Mexican commissioners "after hearing in each case the American point of view, and without originating any discussion tending to modify our laws, explained the parts of these laws related to American interests in Mexico, in connection only with the petroleum and agrarian questions, and also the form in which the present government—in fulfilling its initial political program—has been reconciling the Revolutionary conquests crystallized in our legislation with the principles of international law. Furthermore, the Mexican commissioners ratified the proposition of this government to arrange two conventions—after the normalization of diplomatic relations—for the creation of Mixed Claims Commissions."

Lic. Luis Cabrera viewed the Bucareli Conferences as resulting in three instruments, "two of them of a solemn character, being in the nature of treaties, and one extraofficial pact in the form of minutes."

[10] José Vasconcelos, *El desastre*, p. 289.
[11] Aarón Sáenz, Introduction to Carlos Barrera's, *Obregón*, p. xxiii.
[12] Aarón Sáenz in *Excelsior*, March 2, 1958.

He considered the "extraofficial" minutes to be "the main portion."[13]

That portion which has been called the "extraofficial pact" is in two parts, one of which deals with petroleum and the other with agrarian expropriations. The petroleum section cites the decisions of the Mexican Supreme Court (the Texas Oil Company case, and four similar decisions handed down so as to make the five necessary for decisions of a "general" nature). The document states further that the federal executive power must respect and enforce the decisions of the judicial power and accordingly will continue to support the principles enunciated in the Texas-Oil Company and similar cases. wherein Paragraph IV of Article 27 of the 1917 Constitution is declared to be nonretroactive in all instances where surface owners or oil-right owners had indicated, prior to the Constitution, their intention of working the subsoil oil. In addition, rights to obtain oil were affirmed for all who had received grants under the presidential decrees of January 17, 1920, and January 8, 1921, but who might not have indicated intentions of working oil prior to the adoption of the Constitution. Furthermore, "the present Executive" agreed to continue to make further grants under the above-mentioned decree.[14]

The minutes which are said to make up the "extraofficial pact" on the subject of agrarian reform followed much rhetoric, wherein each side made known its position. The reading of one of Ing. Pani's earlier missives to Mr. Summerlin was reported. This document had pointed out that the Obregón Administration had re-established peace in Mexico not so much by military force and the shedding of blood as by the prompt application of the agrarian laws. "No one doubts that, in the face of such a dilemma, the solution adopted was the most humanitarian and economic—in spite of the inevitable wounding of some national and foreign agricultural interests . . ." Pani had mentioned that the amount of Mexican properties affected was four or five times that of American properties. He had admitted that in view of the required speed of action, the Administration had found it impossible to organize efficiently the personnel administering the program.[15]

The Mexican commissioners stated that the approximate size of an ordinary *ejido*, prior to the existence of the current legislation on

---

[13] Luis Cabrera in *El Universal*, August 2, 1937, quoted in Gómez Robledo, *op. cit.*, pp. 81–82.

[14] Antonio Gómez Robledo, *op. cit.*, pp. 82–86.

[15] Alberto J. Pani, *op. cit.*, pp. 142–144.

the matter, was 1,755 hectares (about 4,000 acres), although in some cases *ejidos* of about 7,000 hectares had been distributed. The Mexican commissioners took note that the American commissioners "reserved the rights" of American citizens regarding expropriation for any consideration except cash.

When it came time to sum matters up in the minutes on agrarian reform, careful wording was used. The minutes presented the first clause in this form:

1. The question of the division of lands is not made the subject of a particular statement here, for the reasons already stated.[16]

In the report of Secretary of State Hughes to the United States Senate this clause, in an expanded form which states the reasons only incidentally referred to in the minutes, becomes the sixth clause. It reads as follows:

The question of the division of large landed estates is not made the subject of a particular statement in view of the fact that the Mexican Congress has not issued any law authorizing the various states of the Republic to create agrarian debts or to issue bonds for this purpose, and in view of the fact that the American commissioners, in behalf of their government, have stated that all the rights of the citizens of the United States regarding such division and the expropriation or sale of lands for bonds or for any consideration other than in cash are reserved, and that the Mexican commissioners, on behalf of the Mexican government, recognize that the American government has reserved the rights of its citizens in this and in other respects.[17]

The second clause appeared in the minutes in this form:

2. The Mexican government does not maintain that the acceptance of federal bonds in payment of expropriation for *ejidos* of a certain area shall be regarded as an acceptance on the part of the government of the United States of the principle that payment in bonds can be made for the expropriation of lands or other property for any purpose.[18]

The third clause largely concerns the bonds. It states that twenty-year 5-per-cent bonds will be issued for the payment of *ejidos*, and that not less than one-twentieth of the bonds outstanding shall be paid each year. The Mexican government expresses its intention of accepting those bonds which are said to be "paid each year" to cover

---

[16] Antonio Gómez Robledo, *op. cit.*, p. 105.
[17] Charles E. Hughes, letter of January 15, 1924, to Henry Cabot Lodge.
[18] Antonio Gómez Robledo, *op. cit.*, p. 105.

all kinds of federal taxes "in the same manner as the coupons." The clause expresses Mexico's hope of negotiating a loan so as to make more cash available for expropriations and bond redemptions.

According to the fourth clause the Mexican commissioners "understand" that in the case of diplomatic recognition and the establishment of a Mixed Claims Commission, the United States will bind its citizens "to accept bonds for *ejidos* of a maximum area of 1,755 hectares on the terms and conditions and with the provisions referred to in Mr. Warren's statement in behalf of the American Commissioners." (The reference to 1,755 hectares is per individual *ejido*.)

The last two clauses declare that United States citizens who have suffered damages due to unjust expropriations for *ejidos* shall have recourse to a General Claims Commission, and that where their property or rights were wrongfully taken during the Revolution these, "where possible," shall be immediately restituted.

According to the interpretation of Professor Antonio Gómez Robledo, by means of the minutes on agrarian reform "The executive branch of the government of Mexico obligated itself . . . to indemnify in cash North Americans affected by agrarian expropriations made for any object other than the granting of *ejidos*, or which, pursuant to that end, might exceed 1,755 hectares."[19] Lic. Vasconcelos may have received some such understanding during the conversation which he mentions having had with Mr. Warren. And when Secretary of State Hughes reported to the United States Senate on the Bucareli Conferences, he advised that the American commissioners had reached a solution whereby the residue of American agrarian properties (the acreage in excess of tracts up to 1,755 hectares) "would be appropriately safeguarded."[20]

Gómez Robledo and the proponents of his thesis have tended to voice their conclusion without presenting convincing evidence. From the six clauses which form the "extraofficial pact" on agrarian reform, it is clear that Mexico agreed not to maintain that the United States accepted the principle of payment by bonds, and, furthermore, Mexico agreed that United States citizens who felt injured could have recourse to a general claims commission. But these agreements alone hardly constitute proof of the categorical statement about Mexico's having obligated herself on the manner of handling the excess acreage.

[19] *Ibid.*, p. 202.
[20] Charles E. Hughes, letter of January 15, 1924, to Henry Cabot Lodge.

What if we disregard Luis Cabrera, who, although no admirer of what transpired at Bucareli, wrote that it was neither necessary nor fair to go beyond the wording of the pact? At the end of the fourth clause there is a reference to "the provisions referred to in Mr. Warren's statement," clearly an invitation to look further into the matter, particularly as the framers of the pact chose not to record in the pact or summation the essence of Mr. Warren's statement. He who limits himself to the six clauses might assume that the reference was to the general rejection of the principle of payment by bonds. During the discussions in July, however, Mr. Warren had declared that a condition for the acceptance of bonds to the extent agreed was a fair and prompt cash payment to United States citizens and companies losing through expropriation tracts larger than the 1,755 hectares specified.[21] This could possibly have been the statement referred to in Clause 4, but it still remains a fact that the Mexican commissioners made no record in the "pact" of agreeing to the terms, conditions, and provisions in Mr. Warren's statement, whatever it was.

The treaty on the Special Claims Convention covered losses sustained by United States citizens, corporations, etc. between November 20, 1910, and May 31, 1920. The claims were to be submitted to a commission of three: one appointed by the United States President, one by the Mexican President, and a presiding commissioner selected by these two or by the Hague Permanent Court of Arbitration. All claims filed were to be decided by the Commission within five years after its first meeting. The Commission's decisions were to be considered as final, and the amounts awarded were to be "paid in gold coin or its equivalent by the Mexican government to the government of the United States at Washington."

The treaty on the General Claims Convention set up a somewhat similar procedure for claims of losses brought by United States citizens against Mexico, and also those brought by Mexicans against the United States, from 1868 on, excepting those claims covered by the Special Convention for United States citizens' losses due to the Revolution.

The so-called "extraofficial" pacts on agrarian reform and petroleum have been recorded by Ing. Pani and others who have written

[21] Adolfo Manero Suárez and José Paniagua Arredondo, *op. cit.*, p. 283.

about the deliberations on Avenida Bucareli. These "minutes" did not go to the Mexican Senate for ratification. Lic. Aarón Sáenz maintains that no document or obligation other than the Claims Conventions was presented to the Mexican Senate, for the simple reason that no other such document or obligation existed.[22]

On August 22, 1923, Secretary of State Hughes wrote to Foreign Minister Pani advising that he had examined the minutes of the meetings which ended on August 15 and that President Coolidge approved the declarations made by the American commissioners; he added that if President Obregón would advise of his approval of the declarations made by the Mexican commissioners the two governments should announce the formal renewal of diplomatic relations as of September 6. On August 24 Pani advised Hughes of Obregón's approval of the declarations made by the Mexicans, and he suggested that the announcement of renewed relations be made on August 31 so that Obregón could mention this in his September 1 report to Congress.[23]

The Mexican government accordingly advised its people that diplomatic relations were to be renewed between the United States and Mexico after an interruption of over three years, and it added that this recognition had not been the result of any compromises or agreements that were counter to the nation's laws or detrimental to its dignity. On August 31 bells were rung in Mexico City in celebration of the event. With the notable exception of Great Britain, other nations which had remained aloof during much of Obregón's administration now promptly followed the United States in recognizing Obregón. The treaty on the General Claims Convention was signed in Washington on September 8, 1923, by Charles Evans Hughes, Charles Beecher Warren, John Barton Payne, and Manuel C. Téllez. The treaty on the Special Claims Convention was signed in Mexico on September 10 by George F. Summerlin and Alberto J. Pani.

All of this occurred before the claims convention treaties were submitted to the Mexican Senate for its approval. There in the Senate an interesting fight ensued.

With the conclusion of the Bucareli Conferences the completed minutes were signed by the United States and the Mexican commissioners "as a record of their proceedings." When General Ryan

[22] Aarón Sáenz, Introduction to Carlos Barrera, op. cit., p. xxiv.
[23] Vito Alessio Robles, Los Tratados de Bucareli, p. 23.

advised De la Huerta that the discussions had resulted in the signing of papers, the Finance Minister in a distressed frame of mind called on Obregón, who authorized him to obtain copies of the minutes from Lic. González Roa, one of the Mexican representatives at the Conferences. This De la Huerta did, and he subsequently found therein a good deal which did not meet with his approval. He considered that the Conferences constituted a treaty which was imposed as a condition of recognition, and which was not only improper but had been made unnecessary on account of his talks with Harding and Hughes. He was not in accord with the nonretroactivity of Constitutional Article 27 and he had objections to the use of mixed claims commissions, which included foreigners, as against the National Claims Commission, established by Madero and made up of Mexicans.

It has been shown by Lic. Aarón Sáenz that Venustiano Carranza had made arrangements for the use of mixed claims commissions, and Alvaro Obregón in his various messages to Congress made reference to the Carranza decrees on the subject, those of May 10, 1913, and December 24, 1917. (Although De la Huerta claimed to have persuaded Carranza to withdraw the 1913 decree, it appears to have been published.) Both Obregón and Sáenz made a point also of the fact that Mexico was interested in settling just claims in an equitable manner. Genaro Fernández MacGregor asserts that the Special Claims Convention resulted from a policy of kindliness toward the foreigner which existed from the start of the Revolution. As for the General Claims Convention, under which both nations were to submit claims, Fernández MacGregor maintains that the will to arbitrate does not impose humiliation or indignity on either of the nations involved.[24]

[24] Genaro Fernández MacGregor in *El Universal*, February 17, 1958.

19.

The Presidential Succession

President Obregón one day discussed the presidential succession with General Calles and Sr. De la Huerta. The conversation took place during an automobile drive through the Chapultepec forest, Obregón being seated between the other two leaders from Sonora, with Calles at his right and De la Huerta at his left.

The President remarked: "You and I, Plutarco, cannot leave politics, because we would die of hunger; on the other hand Adolfo knows how to sing and give classes in voice and music. Under these circumstances who do you feel should follow me in the presidency of the Republic?"

As Calles remained silent and thoughtful Obregón sought the

opinion of De la Huerta, who managed to reply: "Well, after you should come Plutarco."[1]

For a while it seemed that there might be no very serious obstacles to the plans which were under way for the designation of General Calles as the successor of President Obregón, unless it were Calles' poor health, which had made itself manifest not infrequently. True, he was no favorite of Vasconcelos, and no doubt there were Revolutionary generals who for one reason or another, perhaps because of ambition, personality clashes, or past incidents, could be expected to disagree with the idea of placing Calles in the presidential chair. But on the political front the opposition had already been trounced. The disappointed elements of the enfeebled Partido Liberal Constitucionalista now seemed fairly unimportant, and, moreover, they were clearly split in their own views. Some called for General Antonio I. Villarreal, who, like Generals Estrada and Alvarado, refused to back Calles; others suggested General Alvarado or else Villa's old associate, General Raúl Madero. The name of Lic. Roque Estrada, also, was mentioned.

While thus the opposition floundered, it became evident that Calles had built up the enthusiastic support of many political elements which made a point of emphasizing their "radical" position and was backed by the groups which had grown in power during his term as Minister of Gobernación. Short of rebellion, how could anyone push aside a candidate backed by the Partido Cooperatista Nacional, Partido Laborista Mexicano, Partido Nacional Agrarista, and Partido Socialista del Sureste? Luis N. Morones, Antonio Díaz Soto y Gama, and Felipe Carrillo Puerto all used their well-known voices to call for Calles, and so did Cooperatista Party leaders Prieto Laurens and Portes Gil.

Following the collapse of the Partido Liberal Constitucionalista in 1922, the Partido Cooperatista Nacional had energetically pushed itself to the forefront, gaining quick and decisive control over the municipality of Mexico City and the federal legislature. While the Party's ability to rule on the credentials of those who claimed to be elected senators or deputies for the session starting in September, 1922, had been most helpful in creating the Cooperatista majority in the Chamber of Deputies, the *dictámenes globales* (global rulings) which were issued for this purpose did create a certain amount of criticism. In those days the Chamber of Deputies

[1] Jorge Prieto Laurens in *El Universal*, January 15, 1958.

was made up of about 265 members, that is, one representative for each 50,000 inhabitants. Of this number the Cooperatistas claimed the allegiance of about 165 with the remaining 100 being distributed among the other four parties: Laborista, Agrarista, Socialista del Sureste, and Liberal Constitucionalista. Thus the key political figure of the day was twenty-eight–year–old Sr. Jorge Prieto Laurens, the Party strongman, who also held down the positions of federal congressman and *presidente municipal* of Mexico City and who was about to become president of the Chamber of Deputies and candidate for governor of the state of San Luis Potosí. It could not be said that the executive branch controlled the Congress, but it could be said that it would be impossible for anyone to be declared President of Mexico against the wishes of a majority in Congress.

The great "Triangle from Sonora" acted in a united fashion. It was generally accepted that Obregón was supporting Calles, and De la Huerta, who left no doubt whatsoever that his good friend Calles was his choice, described himself as the leader of the Callistas. Early in the game Calles had taken up with Don Adolfo the matter of the presidential succession, indicating that if Don Adolfo was set on returning to the presidency, he himself would not be a candidate. Calles learned directly from De la Huerta that the latter was not interested in running for the position of Constitutional President for the term beginning December, 1924.

Many people thought it was too bad that De la Huerta would not consider the presidency. Some favored him because he was a popular Finance Minister and because his term as Interim President had caused much favorable comment. There were others whose chief concern was their dislike of Calles; they too began to look to De la Huerta. A great deal of pressure was brought to bear on Don Adolfo, who was probably pleased to find himself so popular but who made it clear that he would not run for the presidency and who repeated that his choice was his friend, General Calles.

By July, 1923, the pressure was so great that De la Huerta made the following statement to the press:

Already I have repeated, to a point of satiety and exhaustion, that for no reason will I figure in the list of candidates for the presidency of the Republic in the next elections. All of my friends know that I do not act (as some are seeking to present me publicly) in the manner of a false politician, shamefaced and with hidden intentions; and I believe my background gives me the right to be believed.[2]

[2] Aarón Sáenz in *Excelsior*, March 16, 1958.

It was Felipe Carrillo Puerto's Partido Socialista del Sureste that launched the candidacy of Plutarco Elías Calles for the presidency of the nation. In the federal legislature things went as might have been expected, with a majority of the lawmakers signing the Torregrosa pact supporting Calles.[3]

Lic. Aarón Sáenz, worried by the activities of certain groups who were unenthusiastic toward Calles, paid calls on Finance Minister De la Huerta in order to warn that a split within the ranks would be a serious thing, but might occur if De la Huerta kept on attracting the support of such groups. De la Huerta told Sáenz that he would not accept the candidacy. He had noted, he said, that certain labor groups such as the Confederación General de Trabajadores and the Railway Union and some sections of the Cooperatista Party were not keen on Calles. What he was doing, said De la Huerta, was to gather these groups under his own banner with the idea of obtaining in the end all this additional support for Calles.[4]

[3] Aarón Sáenz in *Excelsior*, March 15, 1958.
[4] Aarón Sáenz in *Excelsior*, March 3, 1958.

20·

The Assassination of Pancho Villa

One who could be expected to be strongly pro-De la Huerta was Pancho Villa. Calles, the fighter against Villistas in Sonora and the victor over Villa at Agua Prieta in 1915, had remained cool to his old foe; De la Huerta, on the other hand, had continued to show the ex-bandit the friendship manifested when he brought about the Villa "surrender" agreement of 1920. Back in 1920, after that agreement, an emissary who brought Villa funds from the federal government brought along also some American reporters who wanted to interview the retired general at "Canutillo." Among the questions asked by reporters was whether he would ever again arise in arms. His reply was that he would do so under either of two conditions: (a) provided the United States should attack, or (b) provided Don Adolfo should need his support. An interesting sidelight was thrown on this interview soon after this reply was voiced: When a reporter asked Villa to perform some cowboy antics, he so enraged Villa that the group had to depart.[1]

Pancho Villa, who was forty-three years old when he retired in 1920, lived in rather grand style at "El Rancho de Canutillo," perhaps better called "La Hacienda de Canutillo." Having acquired a good amount of money, including a substantial sum from the government as a retired general, he spent liberally, particularly for modern equipment and buildings, at his 25,000-acre ranch. With the most modern farm equipment known at that time Villa raised corn, wheat, and potatoes. Among the numerous new buildings was a good schoolhouse for the children of his loyal associates. He also built up the road connecting Canutillo with Parral, Chihuahua.

It was his wont to entertain persons of importance in the business world, in some of whom, at least, he created the impression of being a new and more civilized Pancho Villa. When there was talk of pushing his candidacy for the governorship of Durango, Villa rejected this idea on the ground that he had given his word of honor to De la Huerta not to involve himself in politics during the Obregón administration, but he did cite such talk as a demonstration of the great backing on which he could count.

Villa was inclined to display to visitors two excellent machine guns which, he explained, were gifts presented to him by his old enemy, Obregón himself. These he was in the habit of taking with him when he drove to Parral.[2] His military strength consisted of more than the escort of fifty armed men provided by the Sabinas surrender document of 1920, in view of the fact that his ranching associates were well armed with excellent weapons. Villa spoke of 1,800 men who would follow him should he decide to enter the fray once more.

He still had bitter enemies, with some reason, as a result of the old days, and he became quite accustomed to attempts made on his life. One effort was made to kill him at the Canutillo estate when he was in the act of loading hay, and a number of similar attempts occurred in late 1922 and early 1923 during his frequent visits to Parral. On one such occasion Villa had to call to his side Colonel J.

[1] Daniel P. Fort, conversation, August, 1956.
[2] Rafael F. Muñoz, *Pancho Villa*, p. 185.

Félix Lara, head of the Parral garrison, for protection against his enemies.[3]

Nor was the new Pancho Villa entirely averse to making new enemies. After losing some sums of money to Sr. Melitón Lozoya on cock fights, he learned that this man was the one who had sold all of the furnishings at the Canutillo estate on behalf of the former owner. He thereupon gave Melitón Lozoya one month within which to return the property, which had never been Villa's, "or else—"

The restitution of the furnishings was impossible for Lozoya, who was worried that Villa's threat to assassinate him left him little choice but to kill or be killed. He therefore called together a number of relatives and a few friends, mostly farmers, in order to discuss his predicament. The result was that a group of eight studied the idea of wiping out the life of Villa, and one of the eight, José Barraza, went to Parral to discuss with a relative, Jesús Salas Barraza, plans of possible action. Salas Barraza, who had an old grievance against Villa, was a member of the Durango state legislature and had good relations with important Parral merchants. Not only was Salas Barraza interested, but he furnished the plotters with all they might desire: arms, ammunition, and money. Above all, he let it be known that those who carried out the crime being contemplated would not be punished, but he did not reveal the source of this assurance. Under these auspicious circumstances the conspirators rented, and took positions in, a house in Parral which faced Juárez Street and which Villa customarily passed on his way to amorous adventure.

All was set on the tenth of July, 1923, but, unfortunately, for the plotters, two opportunities were spoiled. On the first such occasion, when Villa went down Juárez Street, there were various children between the would-be killers and their objective, one of them being an adopted son of Lozoya. Later in the afternoon Villa passed the rented house again, but much too rapidly.

Early on the morning of July 20, the men in the house facing Juárez Street received a signal from a confederate who had placed himself outside in order to let them know when Villa was about to pass and what place in the car he would occupy. Villa was in the front seat beside his secretary, Miguel Trillo, and the members of his bodyguard were in the back seat. Windows of the rented house

---

[3] *Ibid.*, pp. 186–187.

were opened and an avalanche of gunfire poured into the car and its occupants, bringing immediate death to Villa and Trillo as the car went into a tree. When General Antonio Medrano, of Villa's escort, passed away some days later in Parral's municipal hospital, only one of Villa's escort survived, a bodyguard who lost an arm in the episode.

After Villa's assassination, Jesús Salas Barraza assumed the responsibility, citing his past grievances. Although it appears that he was the one conspirator who did not sleep in the rented house and so was not there on the early morning of July 20, he wrote a letter of confession, which was delivered to President Obregón.

There were protests against the assassination by some who had been associated with Pancho Villa in his colorful career, as well as by persons who were seeking to interest De la Huerta in the presidency or who disliked Calles. Vasconcelos, who can be classified in the latter group, places the blame for the killing of Villa on Calles and furnishes a report to the effect that following the assassination Salas Barraza went to visit Calles at his "Soledad de la Mota" property in Nuevo León.[4]

At Monterrey, on his way to Laredo, Texas, Salas Barraza was apprehended and sent to the Mexico City penitentiary to serve a twenty-year sentence. He was subsequently moved to the Parral prison. As the Villa strength was great in Parral, Salas Barraza was soon moved again to a safer place, the Chihuahua penitentiary. Later in 1923 President Obregón made arrangements to have Salas Barraza set free.

[4] José Vasconcelos, *El desastre*, p. 240.

21·

The Break between the Partido Cooperatista Nacional and Obregón

Before the Partido Cooperatista had given its official backing to General Calles a storm arose over the gubernatorial election in San Luis Potosí. One of the three candidates, General Samuel M. de los Santos, withdrew from the contest and gave his support to Jorge Prieto Laurens. This left Prieto Laurens considerably stronger than his remaining opponent, Professor Aurelio Manrique, Jr., the Agrarista Party leader and staunch proponent of Calles' presidential aspirations. However, after the turbulent state election, which took place on August 5, 1923, each side claimed victory and two opposing state governments were set up. Prieto Laurens, unlike his rival, set up his administration in the state capital; furthermore, he had the backing of the prior interim governor. The federal Congress could be expected to back him, since he was its presiding officer as well as strongman of the dominating Cooperatista Party; and so Prieto Laurens and almost everyone else must have expected that the *presidente municipal* of Mexico City would have little difficulty in making clear his title to another important political position.

When Prieto Laurens went to visit Calles at "Soledad de la Mota," the discussion concerned not only the governorship of San Luis Potosí but also the position of the Cooperatista Party with respect to the presidential candidacy of Calles. Calles insisted that he could not properly intervene in the San Luis Potosí contest on account of his own position as a presidential candidate.

General Obregón also took the position that he would not intervene in San Luis Potosí because he was not the one to judge whether the election had been won by Manrique or Prieto Laurens.

General Angel Flores, who had been governor of Sinaloa, tried with no more success than others to persuade De la Huerta to become a presidential candidate. Failing in this way to promote a strong anti-Calles movement, Flores decided to enter the fray himself. Accordingly he resigned his active position of *general de división* in the Army in order to accept the presidential nomination offered to him by the Sindicato Nacional de Agricultores. A Liga Política Nacional also proclaimed Flores as its candidate, and Flores-for-President clubs were established in various parts of the country.

But the vice-president of the Partido Cooperatista Nacional, Sr. Martín Luis Guzmán, made it clear that in his opinion the nation was calling for De la Huerta. Sr. Guzmán was the publisher of an afternoon newspaper called *El Mundo*, and he was a close friend of Prieto Laurens. Moreover he had been the private secretary of Ing. Alberto J. Pani, who, in the opinion of some, was not averse to seeing Obregón and De la Huerta fall apart. Martín Luis Guzmán pushed the idea of De la Huerta's candidacy both with Prieto Laurens and with De la Huerta himself.

Shortly before President Obregón was to deliver to Congress his annual message of September 1, 1923, friends of the President sought out the presiding officer of Congress, Diputado Jorge Prieto Laurens, suggesting that he make known to Obregón the text of the reply which he would deliver in the Chamber of Deputies immediately following the presidential message. One of these friends of the President was Lic. Emilio Portes Gil, who at the time, because of a temporary leave granted to Pricto Laurens, was acting as president of the Cooperatista Party. Said Prieto Laurens to Portes Gil: "I am president of Congress, having been elected by a majority of the Chamber, and I have no obligation to make my reply known before the session takes place. If there is a lack of confidence in me, you can immediately call the 'block' to choose another presiding officer."

On September 1, with Congress scheduled to convene at 4:00 P.M., Prieto Laurens took refuge in the Turkish baths at the Hotel Regis until 2:00 P.M. When someone gave him the impression that Obregón was insisting that the congressional leader go first to the Palacio Nacional, if Obregón was to appear at all in the Congress, Prieto Laurens threatened to draw up an official accusation against Obregón should the President not fulfill his constitutional obligation of showing up before the legislative body.[1]

The President appeared before Congress at 5:00 P.M. to deliver the prologue of the annual message, which included mention of the Bucareli Conferences and the renewal of diplomatic relations between Mexico and the United States. In those days it was not unusual for the various Cabinet ministers to read the portions related to their particular fields, and the members of the majority party made a great ovation for De la Huerta.

After the President's message Prieto Laurens came forth with a reply in which he praised the work of De la Huerta and angered Obregón with insinuations to the effect that the Administration was planning to use its power to impose the next President on the nation. Speaking before the Assembly, the young presiding officer told Obregón that the nation's peace depended upon preserving the principle of effective suffrage. "The peoples' representation in the national legislature only points out to you some isolated deeds that might detract from your work," he said, and then listed some bloody local political contests. Turning to the struggle for the nation's presidency, Prieto Laurens referred indirectly to Morones, Salcedo, and

[1] *Un informe presidencial memorable* in *Nosotros* magazine, September 8, 1956, pp. 20–23; also Jorge Carregha in *Excelsior*, January 24, 1958.

Gasca, labor leaders who were respectively heads of Military Manufacturing, Graphic Shops, and the Government of the Federal District, and who were pushing the Calles candidacy. He said in part:

It is clear that there are elements which, abusing the confidence which you have placed in them, take advantage of their official power and soil the prestige of an administration, exhibiting themselves as political-electoral leaders and at the same time heads of very important government departments. No one is better able than you to understand the popular indignation which such a thing arouses, allowing the suspicion that it is a deliberate act suggested by enemies of the Revolution, against yourself and against the political personage whom apparently they flatter and surround.[2]

While applause and ovations from Prieto Laurens' legislative associates interrupted and followed these unusually audacious remarks, Miguel Alessio Robles noted that Obregón's cheeks were red and his eyes were flashing daggers of hate. There was much acclaiming of Obregón and De la Huerta as they left the Chamber. The President departed at once for Veracruz and a trip through various states.[3]

This episode was followed by some desertions from the Cooperatista Party, but other pro-Calles members wished to await the decision which Prieto Laurens announced was to be made at a great Party convention. General Calles, who had been on a leave of absence from the government to receive medical treatment at his "Soledad de la Mota" property in Nuevo León, asked the President on August 30 to accept his resignation from the Cabinet in order that he might fulfill the role of presidential candidate. After Calles on September 5 officially announced his candidacy for the presidency, De la Huerta publicly suggested that it would be well for him to come forth with a clear program as well as a list of the persons who would collaborate in his new government.

Those who wanted to see De la Huerta run for the highest office of the land acted as though he were a presidential candidate instead of the "first of the Callistas." A Comité Pro-Calles had been formed by Portes Gil, Romeo Ortega, J. M. and Carlos Puig Casauranc, and others who were not waiting for the Cooperatista Party to put itself on record one way or the other. Now there was formed a Comité

[2] Jorge Prieto Laurens, *Texto completo del discurso pronunciado . . . el día 1° de septiembre de 1923 . . .*, edition of August 30, 1956.
[3] Miguel Alessio Robles, *Historia política de la Revolución*, p. 262.

Pro-De la Huerta; Roque Estrada was asked to become head of this new *comité* but he declined the honor. There was a moment when the conciliatory De la Huerta, aware of the fast-developing divisions, suggested to Obregón that the apparent deadlock might be solved by the selection of Vasconcelos for the presidency, but Obregón seemed determined to make Calles his successor.[4]

Concerning his own lack of interest in the candidacy De la Huerta gave the press yet another statement, the strongest of them all: "Once and for all, not wanting to concern myself more about this matter, I declare in a solemn and final manner that nothing and no one can make me change my present attitude; I want to demonstrate that among Mexicans we do have men who cannot be led to commit disloyalties to their word pledged before the nation..."[5]

Cooperatista Party supporters of De la Huerta simply kept on campaigning on his behalf, some of them convinced that, in spite of his lack of desire to be a candidate, there might come a time when events would cause him to change his mind. Now and then a remark or two by De la Huerta was interpreted by these supporters in a way which made them feel that it was not useless to continue working for his candidacy.[6]

In reply to a telegram from De la Huerta to Calles on behalf of the Finance Minister's friends in the Cooperatista Party, Calles sent a telegram stating that "I shall not permit any party to take possession of the hegemony in the Congress." This was construed to be a threat to the Cooperatista Party and it very much strengthened its leaders in their determination to work for De la Huerta. When Calles was in the state of Guanajuato, on a visit from Nuevo León, he received a federal *diputado* from Puebla, with an urgent message from De la Huerta. De la Huerta, wishing to make an unequivocal retirement from the presidential race into which he felt he was being swept, asked Calles for a secret conference to discuss matters. Calles' reply was that he would be happy to meet De la Huerta wherever the latter wished, but that the conference should not be secret, since it would deal with matters about which the public had a right to know.

[4] José Vasconcelos, *El desastre*, p. 222.

[5] Adolfo de la Huerta in *El Universal*, September 12, 1923, reproduced by Aarón Sáenz in *Excelsior*, March 16, 1958.

[6] Jorge Carregha in *Excelsior*, January 24, 1958; Martín Luis Guzmán in *Excelsior*, January 27, 1958.

These circumstances on the national level were developing at about the time when Jorge Prieto Laurens took possession of the San Luis Potosí governorship, on September 18, 1923. Simultaneously with Prieto Laurens' action Manrique assumed the duties and prerogatives of the same office, although not at the state capital.

A few days later President Obregón handled the matter of the San Luis Potosí gubernatorial election in such a manner as to rule out both Prieto Laurens and Manrique. He asked the federal Senate to declare that the state's powers had temporarily disappeared, and he set up a provisional government, headed by three men, which was to call a new election.

Recognizing that many Cooperatista Party members in the Senate were not likely to be particularly co-operative with the Chief Executive's wishes, Obregón had already assured himself that in San Luis Potosí there were troops on which he could count. He sent a message to General Luis Gutiérrez, the military commander of the district, instructing him to take charge of the situation and to see to it that Prieto Laurens did not remain in the position of governor.

These steps by Obregón had several results. The leader of the Cooperatista Party declared open battle against Calles and all his supporters in Congress. He immediately called a meeting of the Cooperatista block of the Chamber of Deputies and insisted that each member express his support of De la Huerta in a written memorandum. There were heated and bitter words. Callistas such as J. M. Puig Casauranc, Portes Gil, Luis L. León, and Romeo Ortega insisted on supporting General Calles in spite of violent accusations regarding their loyalty to the Party. Some of them mentioned the Torregrosa Pact.

Said Ortega hotly to Prieto Laurens:

You have no right, Jorge, to call me a traitor! If I am for Calles it's because you, you yourself, inspired my political belief in General Calles, . . . praising him as you did and saying that he alone represents the interests of the Revolution . . . If it was you who asked me to go to Nuevo León to be close to General Calles, then what right do you have now to call me a traitor? On the contrary, I think the traitor is you.

Another result of Obregón's measures was Prieto Laurens' legal action against them. A court whose judge was a Cooperatista Party member granted a stop order against the presidential ruling, point-

ing out that Obregón could not intervene in this state election and
that by doing so he was violating the sovereignty of San Luis Potosí.
But then the federal executive appealed to the Supreme Court,
whose members had just recently been named, for a reversal of the
order of the lower court.

22.

Adolfo de la Huerta Breaks with Obregón

The most dramatic result of the Chief Executive's steps affecting San Luis Potosí was that having to do with De la Huerta.

A few days before Obregón took these steps Don Adolfo had discussed with him the minutes of the Bucareli Conferences. De la Huerta, far from exhibiting his "habitual serenity," referred in the most disrespectful terms to the minutes and to the President's position and attitude in the matter. He was so upset that he spoke about resigning as Finance Minister.

Leading directors of the Cooperatista Party were unaware of this turn in events when they rushed early on the evening of September 21 to see the Finance Minister at his home "Casa del Lago" (on

Chapultepec Lake) in order to advise him that the Gobernación Ministry was about to decide against the Party in the case of contested elections in San Luis Potosí and Nuevo León. They found De la Huerta in his bed, recovering from the strain of recent talks with Obregón and conversing with the governor of Puebla, Froylán C. Manjarrez.

His newly arrived visitors, who included Jorge Prieto Laurens, Martín Luis Guzmán, J. M. Alvarez del Castillo, Gustavo Arce, and others, objected violently to the President's decision regarding San Luis Potosí and Nuevo León, pointing out to De la Huerta that such an act was not becoming to a regime which had made such a fuss at Agua Prieta about the sanctity of the sovereignty of the states. Moreover the Finance Minister's visitors did not fail to point out that Obregón's decision was a blow to the Cooperatista Party and to De la Huerta's position.

After some urging De la Huerta was prevailed upon to go that very night to see Obregón at Chapultepec Castle. There he was delayed briefly when he was advised that the President was sleeping or suffering from a headache, but soon he obtained admission. Going directly to the point, he insisted that the President cancel the orders which had been given by the executive power affecting the state elections. Obregón explained that the question had been carefully studied by the Gobernación Ministry, which was in charge of this matter, and he pointed out that the resolution had already been issued and the appropriate telegrams had already gone out. De la Huerta affirmed that the federal government was illegally intervening.

"That is a matter," said Obregón, "on which I have consulted. My lawyers have advised me that it is all right."

"Very well, you listen to your lawyers. I'll listen to mine."

After Obregón stated that his position was final the agitated De la Huerta made it known that he was leaving Obregón. The President asked him to sit down and stay a little, whereupon De la Huerta pointed out that what he had meant to make clear was his departure from the Obregón Government; he was resigning because he would not tolerate an attack on the sovereignty of the state of San Luis Potosí. The President, feeling that his Finance Minister was momentarily upset, asked him to discuss this whole matter on the following day.[1]

[1] Ignacio C. Enríquez, November, 1923, quoted by Aarón Sáenz in *Excelsior*, March 4, 1958.

Back at his home a few hours later, De la Huerta told his Co-operatista Party friends, who had been anxiously awaiting news of the conference with the President, that he had been unable to convince Obregón, "and, as justice is on your side, I am with you." He said that he was presenting his resignation, and that, as a matter of fact, he had given Obregón oral notice of resigning a few days before because of the Bucareli matter, but that it had then been arranged that he would not leave the Cabinet at once.

Now Don Adolfo's political supporters were satisfied that the Finance Minister was prepared to resign immediately, following his unsatisfactory nocturnal discussion of political matters with Obregón. But, explained De la Huerta, he had, at Obregón's request, agreed that the news of the resignation should not be made public for some time. This agreement for a delayed announcement was not pleasing to the anti-Callistas, since it would prevent the public from appreciating the connection between the resignation and the decisions affecting San Luis Potosí and Nuevo León, and thus would not promote their plans.

On the next afternoon, Saturday, September 22, a huge headline in Martín Luis Guzmán's *El Mundo* proclaimed that "Sr. Adolfo de la Huerta presented his resignation last night." The article under this banner continued: "It has not been possible to confirm the news in official places, but many persons close to Sr. De la Huerta appear to give substance to this sensational rumor, although with reticence."

Following the publication of this rumor, De la Huerta was besieged with newspaper reporters. The result was that on Sunday, September 23, the newspapers published a statement by the Finance Minister to the effect that he had requested of the President a sixty-day leave of absence on account of his health. On that same day Martín Luis Guzmán, the only intimate member of the De la Huerta group who was a friend of Ing. Pani, went to speak with the Foreign Minister, who was felt to be Obregón's choice to succeed De la Huerta. De la Huerta's message stated that he would recommend Pani for the Finance Ministry post provided Pani would not treat his predecessor as an enemy and would allow him to have his papers removed from the Ministry and to receive up to that moment his salary as president of the Monetary Commission.[2] Obregón commissioned Ing. Luis L. León to persuade De la Huerta to join

---

[2] Martín Luis Guzmán in *Excelsior*, January 27, 1958.

the President in Sunday lunch, but after waiting until 3:00 P.M. he had to lunch without Don Adolfo.

On Monday, September 24, De la Huerta dictated his resignation to Froylán Manjarrez, who happened to be at "Casa del Lago," and Manjarrez typed it out after persuading De la Huerta to leave out some harsh phrasing that had been included in the dictation. That evening Martín Luis Guzmán accompanied De la Huerta to the elevator of the Castle of Chapultepec and then at De la Huerta's request went to "Casa del Lago" to await his return from this interview with the President.

On this occasion the President made another unsuccessful effort to convince De la Huerta that the action taken in the case of San Luis Potosí was proper, and he invited him to be his guest at "El Fuerte," his house on Lake Chapala. Although De le Huerta left his written resignation, the two men agreed that neither of them would make it public. De la Huerta left the Castle with the startling impression that Obregón would send him to Washington to revise radically, and in accordance with Don Adolfo's own desires, international understandings which had at long last been reached.

But Obregón's patience with De la Huerta came to an abrupt end on the next day, September 25, when Martín Luis Guzmán's *El Mundo* published the full text of the resignation which had been drawn up and presented on the twenty-fourth. The furious President had his chief of staff, General Pérez Treviño, send a note to Don Adolfo cancelling the invitation to "El Fuerte."

De la Huerta sent an urgent telegram to Lic. Rafael Zubaran Capmany, who had resigned from the Obregón Cabinet with the collapse of the Partido Liberal Constitucionalista in 1922 and who was now a federal senator. Zubaran had early supported the presidential candidacy of De la Huerta as preferable to that of Calles, and he had besought the Finance Minister to enter the contest. As the senator was now out of the country, De la Huerta urged his speedy return to work for the cause. This Zubaran did, and one of his first steps was to make a trip to "El Fuerte," where he had no success in his effort to persuade Obregón to back the ex-Finance Minister. Then Zubaran threw himself into the political contest, raising funds on behalf of De la Huerta and the Partido Cooperatista, and adding his voice to those of the many Delahuertistas in the legislature.

When news of these events reached "Soledad de la Mota" Calles was shocked at the break between his good friends. Speaking with a group of generals and *diputados*, including Emilio Portes Gil, Calles exclaimed that the rupture between De la Huerta and Obregón meant to him "the loss of a brother, for so I considered Adolfo."[3] He issued a statement expressing his approval of Obregón's policies, and he wired De la Huerta advising that he could not at the moment make a trip to Mexico City because he was "surrounded by water," a remark that appeared to refer to the abundant rains which had fallen, but which De la Huerta later chose to interpret as referring to the Obregonistas who surrounded Calles.[4]

Following the retirement of Calles from Obregón's Cabinet, the Gobernación Ministry had been run by its Undersecretary, Lic. Gilberto Valenzuela. This powerful lawyer, who had governed Sonora at the age of twenty-five, had in early days been involved in such sharp differences with Calles that the latter had at one time ordered him out of the state. But Valenzuela and Calles had worked together on the Plan of Agua Prieta, and Valenzuela now backed the presidential aspirations of his recent boss in the Gobernación Ministry.

It gravely concerned Vasconcelos to have the "Ministry of Elections" run by a Calles supporter, whatever his merits, and so alarming did he consider the prospect that he made a trip, together with Education Undersecretary Gastélum, to present his views to Obregón. Near the shores of Lake Chapala, where Obregón was supposed to be getting a needed rest, they saw Valenzuela and Luis L. León come out from the President's improvised office, and they heard León remark that Valenzuela had been appointed Minister of Gobernación. After a further wait while General Serrano was seeing Obregón, Vasconcelos and Gastélum had opportunity to explain to the President how they felt. Vasconcelos was ready to resign. But Obregón charmed his visitors by expressing his appreciation for their frankness and by telling them that he would follow their advice against the Valenzuela appointment, which was the same as that which he had just received from Serrano.

Lic. Enrique Colunga had hardly completed the ceremonies which celebrated his assuming the governorship of Guanajuato, when he had the surprise of receiving a telegram from Obregón congratulating him on his inaugural address and asking him to resign his new post to become Gobernación Minister. Colunga had recently

---

[3] Emilio Portes Gil, "Pani, el villano del drama" in *Hoy* magazine in 1956.
[4] Adolfo de la Huerta, *Memorias,* p. 244.

been Gobernación's *oficial mayor*. Now both Vasconcelos and Agustín Arroyo Ch., a leading Guanajuato politician associated with the Comité Pro-Calles, urged him to accept Obregón's offer. He did accept, with the result that Ignacio García Téllez became governor of Guanajuato. Valenzuela resigned his Gobernación post in view of his announced support of Calles, and subsequently he was made minister to Belgium.

Lic. Colunga must have found his hands full of problems. Alonso Capetillo has written that "surely there is no memory of a parliamentary struggle more cruel, active, passionate, and transcendent than that" of the months of September, October, and November of 1923. "Nothing was lacking: eloquent speeches, terrible accusations, sadistic threats, bribery and inducements, injuries, slander, assassinations, and tumults."[5] The galleries of the Chamber of Deputies were invaded by supporters of the Laborista Party or of the Cooperatista Party. On the floor of the Chamber Emilio Gandarilla accused Calles of being responsible for the death of Villa; Martín Luis Guzmán was accused of having obtained funds from the Finance Ministry for the support of *El Mundo;* and De la Huerta was accused of all sorts of wrong-doings as Finance Minister.

Miguel Alessio Robles resigned as Minister of Industry, Commerce, and Labor when, in October, he clearly felt that Obregón wished to "impose" Calles as the next President. Vasconcelos, who had heartily disliked the *Cromistas* (from C.R.O.M., Morones' confederation of labor leaders) when the Preparatory School students were stirred up against him, told his Education workers that they need not pay the "10" per cent of their salaries which he understood that Morones was seeking to deduct to support the "official" candidacy.[6] (To help support the Partido Laborista deductions were made in 1922 and part of 1923 from the pay of employees of Morones' Military Manufacturing Establishments and from the pay of Mexico City municipal employees.)

Another outspoken enemy of Luis N. Morones was Ing. Vito Alessio Robles, brother of Miguel. Don Vito, as director of the daily *El Demócrata* and as a *diputado* and later as a senator, had attacked the administration of the Military Manufacturing Establishments, pointing to excessive costs. Early in 1923 he had viewed with distaste the government's use of troops against the employees of the streetcar company who were then on strike. The strikers' union,

[5] Alonso Capetillo, *La rebelión sin cabeza*, p. 79.
[6] José Vasconcelos, *El desastre*, p. 220.

observed Ing. Vito Alessio Robles, was affiliated with the Confederación General de Trabajadores, whereas Morones was anxious to have all labor unions become associated with his Confederación Regional Obrera Mexicana (C.R.O.M.).

In view of the sentiments of Vito Alessio Robles, Delahuertistas were disconcerted during the struggle of the fall of 1923 to learn that *El Demócrata* had changed hands and was controlled by friends of Calles.[7] Prieto Laurens stated that Vito Alessio Robles' daily was just about to be purchased by the anti-Calles group for 200,000 pesos when suddenly it was sold to the Comité Pro-Calles for 225,000 pesos.[8] But Ing. Alessio Robles, who was tied to neither side and who delivered frank opinions on the floor of the Senate, was by no means closely associated with Prieto Laurens. He did find it advisable to sell *El Demócrata*, whose presses at that time developed the habit of becoming broken as a result of the activities of political enemies.[9]

Dr. José Manuel Puig Casauranc was pleased and surprised in October, 1923, to find himself appointed by Calles to be Presidente del Centro Director of his political campaign. Dr. Puig, who as a federal *diputado* had been taking part in debates on labor legislation and on a law to nationalize petroleum, had seen Calles but once when he learned of this appointment. Thus he was impressed by the rapidity of Calles' judgment in reaching important decisions.[10]

The Cooperatista Party bloc of Prieto Laurens in the Chamber of Deputies was daily losing adherents and it seemed that unless De la Huerta would consent to be a presidential candidate the Cooperatistas would not have enough strength to control the Permanent Commission. De la Huerta had been offered the candidacy as soon as he resigned from the Cabinet on September 24. If he were going to decide to run for President after all, it would have been pleasanter to do so knowing that his backers already were in command of the federal legislature. But his backers pointed out that without a candidate they were having their difficulties.

On Sunday, October 14, they put on a great public demonstration.

[7] Marte R. Gómez, letter, December 2, 1955.

[8] Jorge Prieto Laurens in Bernardino Mena Brito's *Felipe Angeles, Federal*, pp. 263–273.

[9] Vito Alessio Robles, interview, January 31, 1957.

[10] J. M. Puig Casauranc, *El sentido social*, p. 177.

The Plaza de la Constitución during the pro-De la Huerta manifestation, organized by the Partido Nacional Cooperatista, on Sunday, October 14, 1923. Casasola.

196

Jorge Prieto Laurens (*behind the bell*) *receives handshake of* Adolfo de la Huerta *immediately following the latter's acceptance of presidential candidacy of the Partido Nacional Cooperatista. November 23, 1923. Casasola.*

Masses of people, many of them bearing great banners proclaiming De la Huerta, marched from the Zócalo[11] to the residence of the former Finance Minister. Five days later, on October 19, the same day on which the newspapers carried a statement by Obregón blaming the nation's financial illness on De la Huerta's mismanagement, Don Adolfo made known his decision to be the presidential candidate of the Partido Cooperatista Nacional.

[11] Plaza de la Constitución, Mexico City's great square, on the sides of which are located the cathedral and government offices, including presidential offices.

23.

The Pani-De la Huerta Controversy

On September 26, two days after De la Huerta submitted his resignation, Obregón appointed Alberto J. Pani to be Finance Minister. When Pani heard that De la Huerta had recommended his name to Obregón he concluded that his predecessor must have felt that such a recommendation would only hurt Pani's chances.

The new Finance Minister soon concluded that the nation's financial situation was deplorable. In addition to debts inherited from previous years, he estimated that a deficit of over 42 million pesos had been built up during the first nine months of 1923. Therefore on October 7 he rendered to the President a long report, in which he emphasized the danger of an imminent financial catastrophe, blamed the situation on his predecessor, and suggested the steps that must be taken.

The revenue of the federal government in the year 1922 had been about 284 million pesos, and there was no reason, said Pani, to expect a better income in 1923. For 1923 the Chamber of Deputies had already authorized expenditures of over 356 million, and about 17 million in increases, mostly for the Finance Ministry, were coming up for authorization. The deficit increase approached 3 million pesos with each half month that went by.

Pani also pointed out that the federal payroll had been inflated to the tune of 10 million pesos yearly on account of unwarranted commissions and payments to unnecessary persons, many of whom did nothing more for the government than collect their salaries promptly. Of these 10 million pesos at least 60 per cent was due, said Pani, directly to excessive payrolls in the Finance Ministry.

According to Pani's report De la Huerta was also responsible for having pledged a part of the petroleum production taxes to be collected through January, 1924, for having issued checks against the Mexican Financial Agency in New York, where there were insufficient funds to cover them, and for having pledged oil export taxes which were supposed to be set aside for foreign-debt service.

Pani recommended the suspension of salary payments to useless persons and a general reduction of all salaries paid to government and military personnel. He thought that some government-owned properties might be sold or pledged in order to raise needed cash.

This report to the President by the new Finance Minister was given wide publicity, being released as part of the circular issued to the nation by Obregón at "El Fuerte," Jalisco, on October 16. In some additional comments the President spoke of the complete material and moral bankruptcy which had been caused by De la Huerta through actions taken without the President's authorization or knowledge. He expressed his grave concern at the use of funds which were supposed to service the foreign debt and at De la Huerta's having issued drafts against Mexico's financial agency in New York "knowing ahead of time that the funds were not available and that there was not even a remote probability" of being able to cover the drafts.

The President decided that all employees of the government, including members of the Army, should take a 10 per cent salary reduction.

Those who read these declarations of Obregón and Pani on October 19 had the opportunity on the twentieth of reading De la Huerta's reply to the "disgraceful and unjust" charges. De la Huerta was "not surprised" that his acceptance of the presidential candidacy had brought forth this attack on his honor, and he pointed out that, in addition, cowardly attempts were being made against his life. He pointed out that for three years he had known how to attend to the nation's needs, obtaining for the New York bankers 21 million pesos, which, together with 4 million in the Banco Nacional de Mexico and 5 million expected from October, November, and December oil export taxes, would complete the 30 million due on foreign bonds in 1923. He said that the drafts on New York should have been covered by 2 million pesos loaned by the oil companies, but this loan "was used by my successor to pay salaries, the amount of which he has not known how to raise." Pani, he said, was seeking to excuse himself for his inability to handle the financial problem.

Then De la Huerta hurled another charge against Pani. By the time De la Huerta reached New York in 1922, he said, Pani had already sent there a representative who suggested to the nation's creditors that they not work out the debt arrangements with De la Huerta, for conditions better than those which De la Huerta could offer would be available to them through others. The Cooperatista candidate concluded his reply by promising his readers more sensational revelations, provided his head not be dislodged from his body, as had happened to Pancho Villa's.

Pani answered these remarks by showing that the presidential circular on the nation's disastrous financial condition had not awaited De la Huerta's announced candidacy but had been dated October 16 and brought by Pani from "El Fuerte," Jalisco, with instructions that it be delivered at once to the press. Pani also denied having sent any representative to New York to advise the bankers there not to negotiate with De la Huerta.

Some of the new Minister's suggestions were put into effect promptly. Some 2000 government employees considered as unnecessary personnel were released, thus making a saving of over 800,000 pesos per month. The presidential decree reducing all government and military salaries by 10 per cent was estimated to yield an additional saving of 1.5 million pesos each month.

Not having suffered a violent end to his life, De la Huerta was able on October 30 to issue to the press his main reply to the "deceitful assertions" of Obregón and Pani. He noted that in spite of the four-month petroleum crisis in 1922, the paralysis of some mining and banana operations, and the constant strikes ("produced, often for purely political ends, by some directing elements of the government that have not been able to arrive at the just equilibrium between capital and labor"), he had been able to pay full salaries to all government employees and to the Army. He pointed out that as Interim President he had increased the pay of soldiers, and he criticized the recent "unjust" pay reductions. He referred to the De la Huerta-Lamont Agreement as having cut hundreds of millions from the public debt and as having recovered the Mexican National Railways. He accused Pani of having been bogged down by an economic situation which he did not understand and of having made his attack as political strategy for his superior. De la Huerta pointed to some large financial transactions handled directly by Obregón, such as 2.9 million pesos for the Yavaros Railroad, which was not only a productive investment but was one that "favored . . . the region from which Obregón comes."

How was it that General Obregón did not know what was going on in the Finance Ministry? asked De la Huerta. The President had named and constantly consulted Finance Undersecretary Luis L. León ("presently in charge of propaganda for General Calles"), and had a direct agent in the Nation's Comptroller Generalship which had to approve payments.

De la Huerta classified as "untouchable" the oil export taxes, "delivered directly by the payers to the Banco Nacional de México," adding that only 2.8 million pesos had been borrowed against oil production taxes, which were yielding about 4 million monthly. He pictured Mexico as able to collect in 1923 the 30 million pesos due the New York bankers, although he mentioned rumors that the 10 per cent tax on the Railway receipts might be used for election propaganda.

The ex-Finance Minister blamed the insolvency of the New York financial agency on the Foreign Ministry's "incorrect application" of consular collections, and he revealed that the 3 million pesos owed to local businesses were to have been covered by a 6-million-peso, 6-per-cent, two-year credit which he was about to arrange with the Huasteca Petroleum Company just before he left the Finance Ministry. "How could the financial situation have been less unfavorable than that which was left in Ing. Pani's hands, following the internal rebellions which devastated the country for ten years?"

In answer to this question documents signed by Pani, León, Colunga, and Lamont came to light.

León explained that he had been named Finance Undersecretary by De la Huerta and had collaborated loyally with his chief, for "to act as a spy would be incompatible with my character and background." Becoming aware in May, 1923, of the "squandering of money for supernumeraries," León had suggested reductions but had been told by Don Adolfo that these extra payments were needed for pacification and for creating among discontented persons greater appreciation of the government.

After revealing that as early as April De la Huerta had rejected Obregón's suggestion about salary reductions, León went on to say that at that time he had considered Don Adolfo to be moved by a "passing human weakness, and not by a preconceived plan of presidential propaganda at the cost of public funds and concessions to favorites." The head of Calles' propaganda now declared that he had been deceived by De la Huerta, who, he concluded, by these questionable acts had been preparing for his candidacy for the presidency.

Gobernación Minister Colunga sent to the Supreme Court and to both legislative chambers copies of two telegrams from Thomas W. Lamont. The first of these, addressed on September 20 to De la Huerta, declared that no remittances had been received by the Bankers Committee since June 5, and noted that the payments owing to the Committee through July 1, 1923, amounted to 16 million pesos, this sum being the difference between oil export taxes paid and the amount of those taxes sent to New York. In Mr. Lamont's second telegram, which went to Pani, reference was made to 10 million pesos of oil export taxes held by the bank for distribution to foreign creditors, with the serious comment that of this amount 6 million pesos were tied up as security for a temporary loan which the Mexican government had needed.

In replying to Mr. Lamont, Ing. Pani had passed on a message from the President of Mexico to the effect that there was no argument that could be used to refute the charges and that the former Finance Minister had been publicly rebuked precisely because of such actions as had motivated Mr. Lamont's complaint.

On November 19, just one month after De la Huerta had become a presidential candidate and the newspapers had carried the first strong charges in connection with "material and moral bankruptcy," the former Finance Minister was the central figure in a congressional inquiry. He explained to a group of lawmakers, which included many of his supporters, various aspects of the role which he had played as Minister of Finance. Among the senators present were Vito Alessio Robles, Francisco Field Jurado, Federico González Garza, Fernando Iglesias Calderón, Camilo E. Pani, Tomás A. Robinson, Francisco Trejo, Gerzayn Ugarte, Ildefonso Vázquez, and Rafael Zubaran Capmany.

De la Huerta advised these investigators that as a result of his conversations in Washington with Harding and Hughes he had been able to announce that the State Department had set aside its requirement of a treaty prior to diplomatic recognition.

He had much to say about Lamont's telegram of September 20, which reached him when he was sick in bed on account of an illness which kept him from the Finance Ministry for two weeks prior to his separation from the Government. Remittances to New York had been held up on his instructions when Warren and Payne reached Mexico in June, because he foresaw that a renewal of diplomatic relations would provide a rate of exchange more favorable to Mexico. But, said the Cooperatista candidate, when the Banco Nacional de México heard the President make statements about the seriousness of the situation and declare that funds which had been set aside for the foreign debt had been pledged to cover some of the government's independent indebtedness to the bank, the bank's officials became worried and chose to accept the suggestion.

De la Huerta told the legislators that he had offered to explain the situation to Obregón and Pani. He brought some laughter from congressmen when he remarked that he had even phoned Pani advising of his willingness to help him "because he knew that he was entering a field with which he was not familiar." Pani, who De la Huerta conceded might not have liked those words, never sought help or advice from his predecessor, and Obregón kept himself at "El Fuerte," Jalisco, because of his health.

Two *diputados* were appointed to read letters from Lamont and Jules Chevalier affirming that the ex-Finance Minister had brilliantly defended the interests of Mexico.

Toward the end of this special congressional session the investigators asked some questions regarding Mexico's ability to retain for her own use the excess in case the specified collections should exceed 30 million pesos. De la Huerta concluded by saying that the International Committee was able to concede the excess to Mexico, but that with the recent declarations of the government surely the excess would go to the Committee. With the loss of these millions of pesos, concluded the former Minister of Finance, was purchased the loss of Adolfo de la Huerta's reputation.

Pani, unable to resist replying to all of this, answered on November 30. De la Huerta's telling Hughes that the Supreme Court was judicially in error in disclaiming retroactivity for the Constitution, might, said Pani, have hurt negotiations of the Foreign Office, but, fortunately, the important American officials, whom De la Huerta saw as a private citizen, had the "good sense" not to take into consideration what he said.

Pani published a letter of October 15 from the Banco Nacional de México stating that its temporary advances to the Mexican government had been made, with the authorization of the Finance Ministry, by the use of export taxes which the bank had received from the oil companies. The letter further stated that these advances had been made with the understanding that if the various collections which were to cover them did not do so by the agreed-upon date, then the funds corresponding to the oil export taxes would not be available for remittance to New York until the government made good the deficiency. The bank mentioned also drafts on New York for half a million dollars which had been sold to it by the National Treasury to be applied to the foreign debt, but which had been returned without having been paid in New York.

Had circumstances allowed, De la Huerta and his associates might have prolonged the controversy by issuing a public reply to these points. But by the end of November, 1923, Don Adolfo found himself involved in the most serious matters—matters which had more bearing on the future than on the past record. Thus in its published record of the controversy the Finance Ministry which Pani headed had the advantage of ending up with the last word.[1]

[1] See Secretaría de Hacienda, *La controversia Pani-De la Huerta.* See also Alberto J. Pani, *Memoria de la Secretaría de Hacienda y Crédito Público . . . , 1923, 1924, 1925.*

24.

The Struggle Becomes Intense

Vasconcelos has written that "all the contempt imaginable fell on De la Huerta,"[1] a remark abundantly true in the case of writings by Calles supporters. But even those who most strenuously set their pens to work in this manner could not deny that De la Huerta left the Finance Ministry a poor man in material things. Scrupulously he had paid rent to the government because his "Casa del Largo" home was government property, and now he moved his residence to Insurgentes Street.

In addition to stating that he was most grossly maligned, De la Huerta has mentioned that during this rough period he survived

[1] José Vasconcelos, *El desastre*, p. 228.

several attempts made against his life.[2] Vasconcelos describes an automobile ride which he took with Don Adolfo, in the course of which the Education Minister remarked how much better it would be to die as a campaigning candidate rather than triumph in a military uprising. De la Huerta was mentioning how low he had fallen in the esteem of Obregón, when he suddenly called Lic. Vasconcelos' attention to a pursuing car which he said contained men of the military command who had been paid to assassinate him.[3]

After Diputado Díaz Soto y Gama had consulted with Obregón and heard the President recommend Calles, the Partido Nacional Agrarista called a *gran convención* for the middle of November, 1923, in order to proclaim Calles the candidate of the peasants. Díaz Soto y Gama declared that "we are certain that General Calles will confirm, consolidate, and complete the triumph of the Revolution both in ideas and deeds." The orator attacked "stupid" people who in a Guanajuato town had cried "Long live Christ the King!" and he reminded the gathering of peasant representatives that Christ had many times repeated that "My Kingdom is not of this world." "Christ," he said, "could never be King, because he was always on the side of the people and his mission was precisely to scourge the rich and powerful of the Earth . . . Those same enemies of Christ, his enemies today, are those who proclaim him King, in the manner of [his ancient enemies] . . . Christ was the greatest of the revolutionaries . . . The Revolution is nothing more than the reform of abuses and the correction of injustices . . . We must direct our efforts at one sole point, the correction of the supreme injustice of our history. For this reason the people, with their instinct that does not mislead, elect . . . Plutarco Elías Calles, who has declared and proved with deeds that the interests of the laboring classes are and will be the object of his preferred attention."[4]

Vasconcelos promptly resigned as dues-paying First Honorary Vice-President of the Partido Nacional Agrarista when he learned of this decision of the party to support Calles, a decision made without even consulting the First Honorary Vice-President.

Under the presidency of Jorge Prieto Laurens, the Partido Na-

[2] Adolfo de la Huerta, interview, June 6, 1955.

[3] José Vasconcelos, *op. cit.*, p. 232.

[4] Antonio Díaz Soto y Gama, *Discurso en la gran convención del Partido Nacional Agrarista* (November 12, 1923), pp. 8–13.

cional Cooperatista opened its convention of over 2,000 delegates at the Hidalgo Theatre on November 20. On the twenty-third was finally achieved the objective of Jorge Prieto Laurens, Gustavo Arce, José Villanueva Garza, Francisco Ollivier, Martín Luis Guzmán, Juan Manuel Alvarez del Castillo, and others: with Prieto Laurens at his side, De la Huerta formally accepted the presidential candidacy, promising to carry out "with a highly revolutionary spirit" the program and political platform of the Cooperatista Party.

But this step by De la Huerta did not quite do the trick. The Cooperatista bloc in Congress could muster on November 27 only 122 *diputados*, whereas in order to control the Comisión Permanente 128 were needed. In order to attain as many as 122 it had been necessary to bring in ex-President (and General) Roque González Garza from his sick bed. On the next day when the number had dropped to 114 it began to seem likely that although De la Huerta had much popular support, he could not be placed in the presidential chair by peaceful means.

In writing about the various accomplishments of the federal legislature of this period (the Thirtieth Legislature), Jorge Prieto Laurens acknowledges that a few individuals whose credentials were doubtful had been admitted. He says further that "to be truthful, those persons were the first to desert the Cooperatista majority." He warns against politicians of the type who went from the P.L.C. to the Partido Laborista and then to the Partido Cooperatista "and who, in the end, abandoned us to embrace the cause of the *caudillo*."[5]

General Raúl Madero, who was being mentioned by some as a possible candidate for the presidency, received the suggestion that he back the Administration's plans in return for having his supporters represented in the legislature and maybe even in a governorship or two. But Villa's associate rejected this proposition. He pointed out to Obregón that the situation was dangerous because De la Huerta would react to what he felt to be Administration-inspired attempts on his life. Some kind of a compromise, said Madero, would be a good idea, and as a compromise he suggested to Obregón the name of General Angel Flores, who was engaged in a political campaign against Calles.

[5] See Jorge Prieto Laurens, *Balance moral y político de la XXX Legislatura.*

Other *presidenciables* who discussed the presidential succession with Obregón included Lic. Roque Estrada, federal *diputado* from Zacatecas. These close friends went over the list of opposition presidential timber, which included the names of Angel Flores, Carlos B. Zetina (of Puebla), Raúl Madero, Roque Estrada, Antonio I. Villarreal, and Salvador Alvarado. The President suggested the unsuitability of either Flores or Villarreal in view of the fact that in the past a "Plan" or *manifiesto* issued by Flores, and signed also by Villarreal, had declared that the Mexican Constitution of 1857 should govern instead of that of 1917.

Soon afterwards a discussion occurred among some members of the opposition in an effort to present a more unified front. Among those who sought to determine what to do were General Alvarado, General Villarreal, Lic. Roque Estrada, Lic. Eduardo Neri, and General José M. Carpio of Sonora (*Oficial Mayor* of the National Railways and a leader of the Revolutionary veterans). Roque Estrada had earlier accepted the nomination by the Partido Reconstructor Jalisciense on condition that he might withdraw if by so doing he could help unify the aspirations of the P.L.C. Now he submitted a plan for a deliberation by three representatives each of such leaders as Villarreal, Alvarado, and Raúl Madero, and he himself offered to step aside. But Villarreal was not enthusiastic about Estrada's proposition.

While in this way the contest was unfolding in Mexico, Ing. Pascual Ortiz Rubio, formerly Minister of Communications, was attending to some matters for the Obregón Government in Paris. Suddenly he was instructed to take over the Mexican ministry in Germany from Lic. Juan Manuel Alvarez del Castillo, a prominent Cooperatista and, like most of the Mexican government representatives in Germany, a backer of Adolfo de la Huerta.

With the help of three Mexican officials who were studying in Germany and who had declined invitations to join the others in supporting De la Huerta, Ortiz Rubio took possession of the legation. When he followed Obregón's instructions to fire all who did not present themselves at his orders, he was promptly challenged to a duel by Dr. Guzmán, the Mexican who, because of the absence of Lic. Alvarez del Castillo, felt himself to be in charge. However, during the negotiations which followed the naming of seconds, Dr. Guzmán withdrew his insistence on the duel, and Ortiz Rubio was received by President Friedrich Elbert in spite of all the delay in the arrival of official papers confirming his appointment. Lic. Alvarez del Castillo had joined De la Huerta in Mexico.

For some time there had been rumblings from various of the Mexican Army chieftains who did not view with pleasure the political strides being made by Calles. As early as the spring of 1922 there came to the ears of Obregón a tale of how General Enrique Estrada had approached an emissary of General Joaquín Amaro, introducing him to Salvador Alvarado, José Villanueva Garza, and J. D. Ramírez Garrido, and suggesting that Amaro join up with a discontented group which was said to include Estrada, Alvarado, and Fortunato Maycotte. Amaro not only rejected any suggestion that Estrada may have made, but advised Estrada that he was informing the President about the matter. Obregón, says Luis Monroy Durán, "could not get rid of his friendly affection for many Army chiefs and, full of sentiment, he did not take the reports seriously."[6]

By late 1923 the situation was such that transfers were being considered for generals who were in command of troops and who were felt by Obregón to be seriously contemplating the idea of rebelling. At the same time important sums of government money were used as a means of strengthening the positions and devotions of a number of generals. Some who were close to Obregón cautioned the President against providing Maycotte and Estrada with funds and arms which they had requested for their forces, but Obregón felt it best to send them what they wanted. He doubted that these two, who had collaborated with him so long and so well, would actually rebel, and while he was willing to proceed with full vigor whenever disloyalty seemed clear to him, he did not favor hostility when his mind was not made up that persons were his enemies.[7]

Calles was highly suspicious of the intentions of General Rómulo Figueroa, head of Military Operations in the state of Guerrero, and so in November, 1923, he commissioned the federal *diputado* from that state, Lic. Ezequiel Padilla, to visit with Figueroa in an effort to persuade him to remain loyal to the Obregón government. The somewhat incommodious trip south to Iguala, Guerrero, was made by Padilla, together with General Rubén García and with General Maycotte, whose decision near Mexcala, Guerrero, had saved Obregón in 1920. Regular train service went no further south than

[6] Luis Monroy Durán and Gonzalo Bautista, *El último caudillo*, p. 107.
[7] Faustino Roel, conversation, August, 1956.

Buena Vista de Cuéllar, near which point Maycotte aroused suspicions in the minds of Padilla and García, for he separated himself from them in order to confer privately late at night with Professor Francisco Figueroa, Rómulo's brother.

Padilla's unsuccessful trip was followed on November 30 by the news that Rómulo Figueroa at Iguala had arisen in arms against the government. Some of the best regiments from Puebla were then rushed into Guerrero under the command of General Francisco Urbalejo, who set Figueroa back by occupying Iguala and Chilpancingo.[8]

Obregón could not but be concerned with possible difficulties in Oaxaca. Oaxaca's erudite governor, General Manuel García Vigil, had deeply resented the P.L.C.'s fate in 1922 and he had since then been having a bitter squabble with the federal government; furthermore, García Vigil assumed that men in high places had consented to the attempt which was made against his life early in 1923, particularly as no efforts were made to bring the culprits to justice. Maycotte was the head of Military Operations in Oaxaca and Obregón was counting on him to crush any rebellious designs that García Vigil might have.

The active political supporters of De la Huerta lost no opportunity to work on important Army men who were not sympathetic to Calles. While they were fairly hopeful about General Estrada in the west, they were entirely certain that they could count on General Guadalupe Sánchez, who, as in 1920, was in command of the government troops in Veracruz and the east. Prieto Laurens, Rafael Zubaran Capmany, and Antonio I. Villarreal now had no doubt that there was to be an armed struggle, and they felt that the best time to begin it was before General Sánchez lost his command. Therefore Generals Manuel Chao and José Rentería Luviano were sent from Mexico City on December 3, one to the north and the other to the south, with orders to start rebellions. Sánchez advised De la Huerta that he was ready and anxious to arise in arms and pronounce against the "imposition" of Calles just as soon as Don Adolfo would join him. But in spite of the pleas of Zubaran Capmany and Prieto Laurens, De la Huerta resisted the idea of armed revolt.

During the first black hours of December 4, 1923, Don Adolfo was receiving a report about some plan to do away with his life.

[8] Juan Andreu Almazán in *El Universal*, July 7, 1958.

210

At about the same time General Antonio I. Villarreal was showing Prieto Laurens an order signed by General Arnulfo R. Gómez which called for the arrest of De la Huerta, J. M. Alvarez del Castillo, Prieto Laurens, Rubén Vizcarra, Salvador Franco Urías, and Gustavo Arce.[9] By 2:00 A.M. there was a conference at De la Huerta's Insurgentes Street home, where Villarreal and Prieto Laurens discussed the arrest order, and the latter made it clear that he, for one, was determined to get out of Mexico City. Agents of Guadalupe Sánchez who were present urged the presidential candidate to come at once to Veracruz, where, they assured him, he would be fully protected. Don Adolfo's brother, Alfonso de la Huerta, was head of the candidate's personal escort, and at the conference he added some disquieting news about the maneuvers of Arnulfo Gómez. For a while Don Adolfo spoke of seeking guarantees of the Supreme Court and of holding a meeting of friendly railroad workers, but at length he too resolved to abandon the capital.

A fair demand for compartments on that evening's train to Veracruz developed. In view of the reported order that De la Huerta and his companions be apprehended and in view of the seriousness of the trip, plans to board the Veracruz train were carried out with secrecy and tickets purchased in the names of others than the intended users.

Prieto Laurens arranged to postpone until after midnight a meeting scheduled for that evening at the headquarters of the Cooperatista Party, and he left word so that at this postponed time the remaining party leaders would be advised of the departures. By midnight the train should have safely passed "Boca del Monte."[10]

In a small Ford Don Adolfo was driven around various Mexico City streets in a manner calculated to throw off motorcyclists of Arnulfo Gómez, and then he was taken to Villa Guadalupe and hidden in the house of Antero Roel until the Mexico City-Veracruz train reached that station. With him Don Adolfo brought Rafael Zubaran Capmany, to whom as early as December 1 he had expressed a desire to leave for Veracruz. Aboard the train these new arrivals found Jorge Prieto Laurens, who was in a compartment in another pullman. Jorge provided some cognac (which Don Adolfo felt to be particularly welcome to Zubaran) and sent a telegram to

[9] Jorge Prieto Laurens in *El Universal*, January 12, 1958.
[10] Jorge Carregha in *Excelsior*, January 24, 1958.

Guadalupe Sánchez suggesting that he meet the train on its arrival at Veracruz.

In spite of some trouble at Orizaba, all went as had been hoped, and on the morning of December 5 Adolfo de la Huerta was greeted with cheers as he descended from the train into the heat of the port of Veracruz, together with General Carlos Domínguez, Sr. Prieto Laurens, Lic. Zubaran Capmany, and others. Among those who welcomed the presidential candidate were General Guadalupe Sánchez and his chief of staff, General José Villanueva Garza. Villanueva Garza was a federal *diputado* and a *compadre*[11] of Prieto Laurens, with whom he had been in close touch after recently leaving Mexico City.

The presidential candidate and his retinue established themselves at the Hotel Imperial and there at once they conferred with General Sánchez and his men:

DE LA HUERTA: Confident of your good faith and honor as a soldier, I have come here to take refuge with you and seek those guarantees of life and liberty which the laws provide.

SANCHEZ: Here you shall have them all; if they take you, they'll have to take me first.

DE LA HUERTA: Look here, General, the first thing they are going to do is to order you to turn me over.

SANCHEZ: Well, I won't turn you over.

DE LA HUERTA: You know that's rebellion; better think it over carefully.

SANCHEZ: Well, of course. Everything has been thought out. I knew what I was doing when I sent for you . . . As a Revolutionary I have the obligation to protect you.

DE LA HUERTA: Many thanks, but don't be too confident that it's very safe. You cannot count on your *jefes*.

SANCHEZ: Indeed I can! They are all for me.

DE LA HUERTA: You are very much mistaken. It's because you don't know Obregón. He has them all seduced. Ever since you had your interview with him in Mexico City, telling him you would not lend yourself to an imposition, he started to work on them all. He has sent for some chiefs and I am sure that with the cannonfire of 50,000 pesos he has persuaded them.

Later in the day De la Huerta was called to General Sánchez'

---

[11] When one man becomes godfather to another man's child the two men become *compadres*.

ranch and advised that it had been decided to cut off the train service to Veracruz. During the discussion which ensued, Don Adolfo sought to convince the others that this was not a suitable way to proceed. While he was arguing, someone said "Don't be afraid, Sr. De la Huerta . . ." Don Adolfo reacted to the sting of this remark. "Let's go ahead," he said, although adding ". . . it is a bad step that is being taken because it is premature."[12]

Subsequently telegraphic orders were sent to all those who commanded forces and on whom General Sánchez felt he could count. The orders called for revolt against the Obregón Government and for the support of General Sánchez, the Navy Gulf fleet, and De la Huerta, "who commands the movement to combat the presidential imposition in favor of General Plutarco Elías Calles." Rail, telegraph, and telephone communications between Veracruz and the capital were ordered to be severed.

General Sánchez sent to Obregón a telegram calculated to infuriate the recipient, and then in a proclamation he made known this telegram as well as his communications to other military leaders. Sánchez asserted that he could count on the 22,000 men who were under his orders, and that he had the use of 230 machine guns. "Those of us who fought President Carranza in 1920 would be completely forgetful of what we did then if we would not now fight a government which, without even the virtues of that one, enters into the same evil of impositions, and carries it to the maximum of cynicism."[13]

Colonel Daniel P. Fort, who in the past had served with Obregón in campaigns against Victoriano Huerta, had recently agreed to help organize the De la Huerta presidential movement in the state of Morelos. Now in Mexico City, Fort called at the home of Don Adolfo. This was after De la Huerta, as the Colonel puts it, had been forced out of the nation's capital by the maneuvering of President Obregón, but that departure had been so secret that Fort did not know about it. After the men of Arnulfo Gómez accused Fort of making this visit to Don Adolfo's home, and after the Colonel pointed out that he was a friend of De la Huerta, Fort was placed in the prison of Belén, as were others suspected of favoring the interests of the ex-Minister of Finance. In spite of the efforts of his lawyer and a statement on his behalf made by Lic. Vasconcelos,

[12] Adolfo de la Huerta, *Memorias*, p. 252.
[13] Jorge Prieto Laurens in *El Universal*, January 14, 1958.

Colonel Fort felt very fortunate to escape from Belén with his life. He made his way to Tepic, Nayarit.

General Francisco J. Múgica, whom De la Huerta had backed in Michoacán against Ortiz Rubio, was thirty-nine years old in 1923. He had led an active life. As a fighting captain at Matamoros, Tamaulipas, in August, 1913, he had collaborated enthusiastically with *constitucionalista* General Lucio Blanco's activity in cutting up large estates for the benefit of the poor; he had therefore received a grateful letter from Emiliano Zapata. Prior to the 1917 Constitution he served as Carranza's military comander and governor of the state of Tabasco. His most outstanding achievement was the role he played at the Querétaro Constitutional Assembly of 1916–1917, where he contributed to making the Constitution more revolutionary than Carranza had planned,[14] and where his persuasive guidance and leadership did much to make Articles 27 and 123 what they are. Article 123 as finally drawn up was intended to provide great benefits to the laboring class. For this work Múgica received praise from other members of the Assembly; not only from Obregonistas such as Juan de Dios Bojórquez, but even from Félix F. Palavicini, who at Querétaro represented the Carranza point of view.

General Múgica was one of those who, with General Jacinto B. Treviño, called on Carranza two days before the Plan of Agua Prieta in a vain effort to prevent the armed uprising in which Carranza lost his life. When Provisional President De la Huerta offered Múgica the chief clerkship of the War Department, Múgica declined and set about to become governor of Michoacán, a post he had earlier lost to what he called the "conservatives" backing Ortiz Rubio.

Múgica claimed victory in the 1920 election to succeed Provisional Governor Cárdenas, and he advised both De la Huerta and Obregón that the matter was not one for the federal Senate's decision. When Obregón offered to visit Morelia and participate in the "difficult situation," Múgica replied that he would tolerate no interference. He was soon having such trouble with Obregón's War Minister, Enrique Estrada, and the local head of Military Operations, that a revolt against Múgica developed in February, 1922. Múgica suggested to Obregón that the rebellion be attacked on two

[14] Roberto Blanco Moheno, *Crónica de la Revolución Mexicana*, II, 61.

fronts, the clergy and capitalism, but Obregón replied by telling Múgica that his plan of attack was "erroneous." Complaining of the arbitrary acts of Obregón and Estrada, Múgica resigned the governorship in March, 1922.

After turning down an offer to be Mexico's first representative to Soviet Russia, Múgica sought to reassume the Michoacán governorship in 1923 on the ground that the state legislature had not accepted his resignation but had simply given him a year's leave of absence. He found the revamped legislature unfriendly. On December 4, 1923, he issued a manifesto to the state governors and the press, advising that unfortunately the federal executive power did not back the legitimate governments of Nuevo León, San Luis Potosí, Zacatecas, and Michoacán. He indicated that his predicament sprang from his neutrality in the presidential contest at a time when his opponents supported Calles.

When on the next day Múgica was ordered imprisoned for the crime of usurping the functions of governor, he was placed under the custody of Colonel Miguel Flores Villar, a mutual friend of Múgica and General Lázaro Cárdenas. Cárdenas, who had charge of Military Operations in Michoacán, soon received from Obregón telegraphic orders to have a guard take Múgica to Mexico City. It was decided that Múgica would go to Mexico City guarded by Flores Villar, and with them Cárdenas sent a letter to the President assuring him of Múgica's loyalty.

Although the instructions called for using a train which would stop at Irapuato, where Múgica was to be turned over to General Joaquín Amaro or General Luis Gutiérrez, conditions made this impossible; so they took the train which went more directly from Morelia to Mexico City.

One of the train's many stops was at Acámbaro, and there a telegram arrived for the Colonel, who was sharing a compartment with Múgica. After reading the telegram and turning pale, the Colonel showed it to Múgica. It was signed "Alvaro Obregón" and said:

YOURS OF TODAY. UNDERSTAND THAT GENERAL FRANCISCO J. MUGICA WAS KILLED WHILE ENDEAVORING TO BE FREED BY HIS SUPPORTERS. I REGRET WHAT HAS OCCURRED. PRESENT YOURSELF HERE IN ORDER TO REPORT ON THE CIRCUMSTANCES.

In spite of this ominous message Múgica and Col. Flores Villar decided to go on to Mexico City. At Celaya the Colonel showed the telegram to General Carlos A. Vidal, who followed Cárdenas' example of writing a letter on behalf of Múgica.

In Mexico City Múgica and his guard reported to the Army offices. Arnulfo Gómez, head of the Mexico City garrison, was momentarily absent, and a captain allowed the prisoner to go out to breakfast with his guard. The newspapers were displaying headlines about Múgica being killed when trying to escape, and so when Múgica went to his home he was warmly received by those who had thought him dead. Gómez, furious about Múgica's escape, sent two men to make the capture, but by the time they got into operation Múgica had fled and was in hiding. Colonel Flores Villar lost his rank in the Army.[15]

Obregón could hardly have felt anything but cool to Raúl Madero's suggestion of seeking a compromise in the struggle by placing the administration's blessing on the presidential hopes of Angel Flores. Soon after presenting his suggestion, Raúl Madero left Mexico City by train for the north. When the train reached San Luis Potosí he was told by friends that orders were out to kill him, and so before the train reached Torreón, Coahuila, it was slowed down to allow General Madero to get off. Raúl, brother of Francisco I. Madero, had many relatives and friends at Parras, Coahuila, and any orders against him were ineffective. From there he made his way to the state of Sinaloa via the United States and Nogales, Sonora. He was disguised (with dark glasses and without mustache) when the west-coast train got him to Sinaloa. There he promptly joined up with General Flores.

General Obregón had moved from his "El Fuerte" residence, on the eastern shore of Lake Chapala, and was now seeking good health at Celaya, Guanajuato.

There on the morning of December 7, 1923, he was discussing government matters with Communications Minister Amado Aguirre and Agriculture Minister Ramón P. de Negri, who had come by private railroad car from Mexico City. While Aguirre was in the midst of recommending that Enrique Estrada be removed from his command and perhaps sent on a mission abroad, an urgent telegram arrived. It advised of the revolt by Guadalupe Sánchez and the designation of De la Huerta as head of the rebellion.

[15] Armando de María y Campos, *Múgica*, pp. 189–205; also conversation with Frank Tannenbaum, June 19, 1955.

President Obregón *is received in Mexico City after travelling there from Celaya, Gto., upon learning of the outbreak of the De la Huerta rebellion. December, 1923. Casasola.*

When Aguirre continued to insist on steps against Estrada, Obregón replied:

General Estrada is very much of a gentleman. Besides, do you think he will arise against me when I have promoted him so much, and especially considering that yesterday when he was here to see me he told me that he needed money to carry out his marriage ceremony in the style required by the social standing of his fiancée . . . and that I provided the money with the best of goodwill?

When Obregón's wife joined them and backed Aguirre's idea, Obregón said to her, "You and Don Amado are dreaming."[16]

That same morning Obregón, Aguirre, and De Negri left for Mexico City. Telegraphic orders were dispatched en route. And when the capital was reached at 7:30 in the evening, Obregón went directly to Chapultepec Castle, where he worked late into the night, giving instructions to Generals Serrano, Arnulfo Gómez, Roberto Cruz, Pedro J. Almada (General Inspector of Police), and others. Aguirre wanted a military command, but Obregón told him to remain at his Cabinet post where useful service could be rendered in the interception of rebel communications.

[16] Amado Aguirre, *Mis memorias de campaña*, p. 336.

On the morning of December 8 Obregón was advised of the uprising by General Enrique Estrada.

Among those who were surprised to learn of Estrada's action was his brother, Roque Estrada. Only just recently Roque had pointed out to Salvador Alvarado and Enrique Estrada some reasons why it would be unwise to follow the path of rebellion against Obregón and Calles: (1) as far as Revolutionary principles were concerned, there were no fundamental differences between those proclaimed by De la Huerta and those proclaimed by Calles; (2) a rebellion would be unlikely to succeed because probably most of the Army would support Obregón; and (3) even if a rebellion should succeed, it would probably be followed by a struggle among the differing sectors of the victors. Roque Estrada had offered his support to President Obregón and would have been at the recent conference in Celaya had he not been struck down by an attack of the grippe.

President Obregón pushed for ratification of the Claims Conventions Treaties in the Senate, which now had become much less independent of the wishes of the executive branch of the government. He sent his friend Ramón Ross to deal with the United States government in connection with the assistance that could be expected on account of the recent renewal of diplomatic relations. He resolved to take personal command of the Army forces which remained loyal to his administration. Contrary to Roque Estrada's prediction, at least 60 per cent of the Army was revolting, with the rebels able to count on no fewer than 50,000 men.

25.

The First Stage of the De la Huerta Rebellion

At the Hotel Imperial in Veracruz De la Huerta found that his friends who were critical of his hesitancy to sign the rebel Plan of Veracruz and to make clear his leadership of the revolt were taking many steps in rapid fashion. They pointed out to De la Huerta that numerous persons were counting on him and that the military men who had rebelled needed his presence. The Plan of Xilitla (S.L.P.) was revealed. It was signed by Prieto Laurens, who referred to himself as the "constitutional governor" of San Luis Potosí and who did not recognize the federal powers. After De la

Huerta at length agreed to the Plan of Veracruz he was forthwith called Supreme Chief of the Revolution.

This so-called "Plan," issued on December 7, 1923, in "Heroic Veracruz," was signed by De la Huerta alone and is more formally known as the Revolutionary Declaration of Don Adolfo de la Huerta. The sins attributed to Obregón resemble those attributed to Carranza in the Plan of Agua Prieta. "Never before has there been presented so odious and so intolerable a violation of the sovereignty of the people." According to the declaration, an electoral fraud had been perpetrated in Veracruz in order to consolidate the tyranny of Governor Adalberto Tejeda; the constitutional governor of Michoacán had been seized; the sovereignty of San Luis Potosí had been violated by the Army; the local congress of Zacatecas had been refused recognition in order to set up there a despotic governor who would unscrupulously back the plans for imposition; the constitutional governor of Coahuila had been thrown out in favor of persons supporting Calles.

"In order to kill the independence of the legislative power of the Nation, which has opposed [Obregón's] impositional tendencies with exceptional energy and which has gallantly defended the sovereignty of the people, he [Obregón] has organized plots with the Praetorian Guard (which still soils the honor of the Army), and with the majority of his Cabinet ministers, plots to assassinate deputies . . . " Threats and bribes were also mentioned as contributing to the formation of servile legislative chambers which would "consummate the imposition of a candidacy which was frankly and obviously rejected by the people from the start." The declaration stated that the Supreme Court had been pushed aside.

It declared also that Obregón had not limited himself to violating the sovereignty of the legislative and judicial powers, but moreover had used the immense power which the people had deposited in his hands to place liberties in chains, turning himself into the political leader of Calles' unpopular candidacy with the idea of assuring for himself later on a re-election "which the nation rejects and which our law condemns."

De la Huerta urged that an effort be made to pay for expropriated real estate in cash, and he spoke of credits to increase agricultural production. He called for more intensive education, votes for women, and the abolition of the death penalty except in the case of traitors during wars with other countries. State governors and federal legislators who had worked for the imposition were not to be recognized. Others chosen by popular election were likewise not to be recognized unless within fifteen days they adhered to the De la Huerta movement.

De la Huerta organized a government in rebellion, and, seeking to handle matters in a way which he could consider to be scrupulous, he exerted a restraining influence on associates who felt it to be imperative to grab what they deemed necessary for the campaign. Among the first appointees to high positions were two who had clashed in 1922: Rafael Zubaran Capmany became High Commissioner of Gobernación and Juan Manuel Alvarez del Castillo became High Commissioner of Foreign Relations. Prieto Laurens, who in early reports was mentioned as being in charge of Gobernación, became the rebellion's publicity head. Miguel Palacios Macedo, a young intellectual who was placed in charge of finances, assigned himself a salary of ten pesos daily and endeavored to keep expenses down.

Somewhat later Antonio I. Villarreal was named High Commissioner of Agriculture and Francisco Ollivier was put in charge of Communications and Public Works. When Alvarez del Castillo went on a diplomatic mission to Washington, Zubaran Capmany, then De la Huerta's most intimate and influential advisor, added to his powers those related to foreign relations.

Right after the movement started at Veracruz, rebel generals met with success. Villanueva Garza took the state capital, Jalapa, and Salvador Vega y Bernal took Papantla, Veracruz. After 400 persons had been taken at Jalapa, De la Huerta not only insisted on setting them all at liberty but, when at Veracruz these men agreed to join the cause, he named 100 of them to act as his personal escort.

Once he had accepted the position of Supreme Chief of the Revolution, De la Huerta found himself with a difficult task. A number of jealousies at Veracruz impaired much-needed co-operation, such as assistance for Villarreal at Puebla. On top of that there was a tendency for some members of the Veracruz group to act first and inform the Supreme Chief later, or else perhaps the High Commissioner of Gobernación. In addition to such local difficulties, there was much question as to how loyal to the Veracruz government were the rebels in the south and west. While these revolted at the same time, they carried on independently and did not issue words that could be construed to mean more than that they had a common enemy.

Enrique Estrada proclaimed himself head of the rebellion in the states of Jalisco, Zacatecas, Colima, Nayarit, Michoacán, and Guanajuato, a rebellion caused by the need to overthrow a government "which flagrantly forgets the principles of the Revolution." Salvador Alvarado had for years been quarrelling with Obregón; now Alvarado backed Estrada for military reasons but, like Estrada, he was himself a man of much ambition. Manuel M. Diéguez, who also backed Estrada, did so because this whole episode allowed him to seek to blot out effects of the Agua Prieta movement; as he had opposed that movement he had been in eclipse.

Fortunato Maycotte received from Obregón 200,000 pesos (a good deal better than the standard "cannonfire") with which to crush rebellious developments in Oaxaca. On December 11 he sent a comforting message to Juan Andreu Almazán, ex-Oroquista and ex-Zapatista who was defending Puebla against the De la Huerta movement. But then in Oaxaca Maycotte provided Obregón with a most unhappy surprise: he joined García Vigil and many others in signing an independent plan of rebellion against the Obregón Government.

The Plan Revolucionario de Oaxaca emphasized that the imposition of Calles had been attempted by means of threats, bribery, intimidations, assaults, kidnappings and executions; by means of assassinations like that of General Francisco Villa and the unsuccessful efforts against Manuel García Vigil; by means of the theft of public funds; and by means of the 1922 legislative elections, wherein "was consummated in the most barefaced manner the violation of the principle of effective suffrage . . . for which the nation has struggled with incalculable sacrifices, and those responsible are the President and his then Minister of Gobernación, General Plutarco Elías Calles, who thus prepared the presidential succession."

The Oaxaca Plan was dated December 13, 1923. It recognized "Division Generals Guadalupe Sánchez, Enrique Estrada, and Fortunato Maycotte, respectively, as military chiefs of the regions of the East and Southeast; of the West and Northwest; and of the South and Center of the country." The Oaxaca Plan stated also that "Upon occupying Mexico City and achieving the overthrow of the present government, the three above-mentioned divisionary generals will designate, by a majority of votes, a Provisional President of the Republic, who will immediately call for elections . . ."

Rafael Zubaran Capmany, the High Commissioner of Gober-

222

nación in the De la Huerta rebel government, wrote to the Oaxaca rebels a reply which was signed by Guadalupe Sánchez. It said: "I find myself in the need of declining this unmerited distinction, as I have previously accepted the Plan of Veracruz of December 7 and recognized Adolfo de la Huerta as the Supreme Chief of the Revolution."

The Mexican capital was full of activity. At a Cabinet meeting Serrano of the War Ministry backed the idea of Vasconcelos to the effect that, in view of the presidential campaign, it would be improper to name Calles as head of the government forces. Obregón was voted extraordinary powers. The President decided that he himself would handle the operations against Estrada in the west, and he ordered Eugenio Martínez to bring his division from Chihuahua and direct military operations in Veracruz. (It is interesting to note that De la Huerta hoped that "old" Eugenio Martínez would join up with the rebellion, and went so far as to instruct the rebel forces to receive him and his men "as friends." This instruction of the rebellion's Supreme Chief was ignored.)

General Arnulfo R. Gómez (*with mustache, and wearing dark cape*) *and a group of prisoners during the De la Huerta rebellion. México, D.F., 1924. Enrique Díaz.*

Obregón established himself at Irapuato, Guanajuato, and was seldom seen in the nation's capital. Calles went to Monterrey and San Luis Potosí to recruit forces from among the peasants and to make for added strength in the north, where things remained relatively quiet. The federal government named Aurelio Manrique, Jr., of the Agrarista Party, to be governor of the state of San Luis Potosí and it named General Saturnino Cedillo to be the head of Military Operations in the state.

In Mexico City General Arnulfo Gómez, who had harassed De la Huerta by having him followed by gunmen, now diligently rounded up sympathizers of Don Adolfo. The newspaper *Mañana* came to its end when Luis Morones, dressed in overalls, led his followers in the destruction of the publication's machinery and furniture. A few days later the assassinated body of the newspaper's editor was found in a suburb of Mexico City.[1] A combination of pressures had been used to bring the legislative chambers pretty much into line. But for a while there was such a remarkably determined minority of lawmakers that one could not fully agree with a contemporary anti-Callista when he said that all were declaring themselves in favor of Calles on the theory that if Calles won his enemies would be wiped out whereas if De la Huerta won all would be forgiven.

Besides making life miserable for Delahuertistas in the capital, Arnulfo Gómez sent arms and ammunition to Rodolfo Herrero so that the latter might contribute, as he did, to the recapture of Papantla. Gómez was also successful in having Herrero and others who had figured in the Tlaxcalantongo attack reincorporated in the Army.

Because of its proximity to Mexico City the city of Puebla was of greatest strategic importance, and there the tide went back and forth. Froylán C. Manjarrez, governor of the state since he led the Cooperatistas to victory in the federal legislature, was a close personal friend of De la Huerta and he backed Don Adolfo for the presidency. His efforts in this regard were opposed by Claudio N. Tirado and by the newspaper writer Luis Monroy Durán, who had more admiration for Manjarrez' gubernatorial abilities than he did for De la Huerta's presidential aspirations. Even Gonzalo Bautista, who

[1] Pablo Meneses V., letter in *El Universal*, November 3, 1956.

in 1922 had helped Manjarrez to reach the governor's chair, came out in favor of Calles.

General Juan Andreu Almazán, the head of Military Operations in Puebla, had an uneasy time of it contending with the steps being taken by Governor Manjarrez and by rebel General Antonio I. Villarreal, who was plotting from his hiding place in the home of a general in Puebla City. Already some of Puebla's best battalions had departed for Guerrero to combat Rómulo Figueroa, who had been planning to move on Mexico City at the same time that rebel General Marcial Cavazos was to do so from Pachuca or Texcoco. Almazán was in a difficult position with a number of Puebla's remaining contingents sympathetic to the rebellion and with various army officers not making their position clear.

Manjarrez' first step was to name General Heliodoro Pérez to be Puebla's Police Inspector. This tough general and his companions quickly plotted to bring an end to the lives of Almazán, Rodrigo Zuriaga, and others who were loyal to Obregón. A formal uprising was planned for the morning of December 7, but Almazán beat his enemies to the trigger by being at work earlier on that morning. With the help of 200 loyal soldiers he disarmed mounted police and even arrested Heliodoro Pérez; Almazán might have lost his life, however, had not Colonel Carlos Avilés ignored instructions to shoot his friend during one of the various discussions which took place in these confusing moments.

After Fausto Topete had unsuccessfully pleaded with Manjarrez to mend his ways, Almazán had Zuriaga capture the governor on the afternoon of December 7. Manjarrez resigned as governor within two days and the local legislature promptly accepted the resignation, choosing in his place the twenty-seven–year–old Vicente Lombardo Toledano, who had been recommended to Almazán by General Celestino Gasca. When one of Manjarrez' many pro-Calles friends intervened with Almazán on behalf of the former governor Manjarrez obtained his liberty and was able to join De la Huerta in Veracruz.

Maycotte's telegram of the eleventh, assuring Almazán that the Oaxaca forces would protect southeast Puebla, was followed by similarly misleading messages from Colonel Avilés in Tehuacán, Puebla, and from General Fernando Reyes, Maycotte's right-hand man. The truth was proclaimed on December 14, when Fernando Reyes communicated with Almazán's chief of staff and in lofty language condemned the "impositionists," announcing a movement on Mexico City via Puebla and inviting Almazán to join the "popular" cause, which in fifteen days would "cover itself with glory."

With this development Serrano's War Ministry ordered Almazán to withdraw from Puebla, and, on the evening of the fourteenth, when this order was carried out, Lombardo Toledano and other new officials of the Puebla government went to Mexico City. But Zuriaga did not get far from Puebla, because some of the men who chose this moment to desert Almazán captured Zuriaga, returning him to Puebla and turning him over to Villarreal, who had come out of hiding.[2]

Fernando Reyes and other generals of Maycotte now brought two regiments into Puebla. The state had its third governor in a week in the person of Francisco Espinosa Fleury, who issued a declaration signed by various local politicians, citing the steps taken by the federal government in favor of Calles and against the sovereignties of San Luis Potosí and Puebla. The declaration made it known that Puebla did not recognize the government of Obregón and was supporting the rebellion.

For the rebel cause the importance of controlling Puebla lay in the opportunity it afforded to make a quick attack on the nation's capital. In this endeavor Fernando Reyes, now commander of the rebel garrison, Villarreal, and others might well have received the co-operation of the forces of Villanueva Garza, which, after taking Jalapa, Veracruz, had advanced along the railroad line to Las Vigas and from there well into the state of Puebla, reaching Oriental. But from the port of Veracruz Villaneuva Garza received orders which were not explained and which told him to retreat to Jalapa. Because he obeyed these orders Villaneuva Garza got into a row with his subordinate, General José C. Morán, who was subsequently somewhat appeased by being commissioned to advance on Tampico and the oil fields.[3]

In the meantime the rebel leaders in Puebla, noting that the reinforcements which they were expecting from Veracruz did not materialize, limited themselves to fighting off attacks against them. On December 19 occurred a battle between the rebels and the outnumbered men of Almazán, who was following orders of Obregón

[2] Juan Andreu Almazán in *El Universal*, July 7 and 8, 1958; also conversation with Enrique Casas Alatriste, February 7, 1959.

[3] Jorge Prieto Laurens in *El Universal*, January 14, 1958.

226

and the War Ministry to let his presence be felt by his enemy in Puebla. Almazán almost lost his life.

But on the twentieth Almazán's discouragement vanished when he learned that that veteran Obregonista, General Eugenio Martínez, had arrived from Chihuahua and was in the tiny state of Tlaxcala, north of Puebla's capital. A concentrated and superb array of Obregonista military talent moving against Puebla under Martínez included such troop commanders as Luis Gutiérrez, Francisco Urbalejo, Fausto Topete, José Amarillas, and Federico Berlanga. On the twenty-second, by which time Almazán's men had joined these forces, 9000 men in three armies threw themselves against Puebla's 3500 rebel defenders, most of whom were captured in the act on. While the most telling attack was made by a group of Yaqui Indians under Amarillas, there can be no doubt that Fernando Reyes and his men found the cavalry led by Almazán and the infantry assault led by Roberto Cruz to be devastating, and in addition they had to contend with aerial bombardments made by the government forces. Other government fighters who figured prominently in this battle, which saw about 600 persons killed, were Generals Rodrigo Quevedo M., Pablo Macías, Heriberto Jara, and J. Ríos Zertuche, Colonel Agustín Olachea, and Colonel Adalberto Tejeda, the governor of Veracruz.

After inflicting this setback on the rebels, about 5000 Obregonistas, under such generals as Amarillas, Cruz, Ríos Zertuche, and Pablo Macías, turned westward to reinforce Amaro and Escobar, who were advancing on Guadalajara, Jalisco, in the other important theatre of the war.

Back in the Puebla governor's chair, Vicente Lombardo Toledano refused to recognize the state legislature, since a majority of its members had backed the rebellion. While Lombardo Toledano set himself up with the assistance of peasant groups and the C.R.O.M. labor battalions which General Celestino Gasca directed, Espinosa Fleury set up at Teziutlán a rebel government, which he soon turned over to a new rebel governor named by De la Huerta.

With one or two followers Villarreal reached the port of Veracruz, where he tried to persuade the powers, largely in the hands of Zubaran Capmany, to provide him with a force with which he could operate in the north. It was then that he found himself appointed High Commissioner of Agriculture. After time was lost while he published a manifesto about agricultural matters, Villarreal resigned his new post and was eventually named chief of rebel operations in Nuevo León, Tamaulipas, Coahuila, and San Luis Potosí. Further delay followed until finally in Veracruz about fifty ill-equipped men—almost all of them given officers' rank—were recruited by him. With these he left Veracruz on the steamer *San Leonardo*, landing at Tuxpan, Veracruz, in order to start a new campaign there.

26·

The Last Days
of Carrillo Puerto

Both sides endeavored to get arms and munitions from the United States. Ramón Ross, of the Bucareli Conferences, spent about two weeks in Washington, where, because of the recent United States recognition of the Obregón Government, he had all the advantages. The assurances of moral and material aid with which Ross returned to Mexico were amply fulfilled, except that ships requested by the navy-less Obregón Government were not furnished. President Coolidge cut off United States communications via Veracruz. The Obregón Government quickly arranged to purchase from its northern neighbor about 11 De Haviland airplanes,

33 machine guns, 15,000 Enfield rifles, 5 million rounds of ammunition, and other military supplies.[1]

Seeking aid for De la Huerta, Alvarez del Castillo and other negotiators went to Washington. De la Huerta attributed their failure, and U.S. interference through gunboats stationed at Tampico and Veracruz, to his position with reference to the Bucareli Conferences. Interviewed at Veracruz by United States Consul Wood and Vice-Consul Mayer, De la Huerta condemned "arrangements" worked out between the governments of Mexico and the United States.

Although in the east the rebels occupied sections of the country that offered considerable financial resources, such as oil fields and the important Veracruz customhouse, the scruples of De la Huerta were such that the funds gathered were not as much as they might have been, and the rebel government was far shorter of money than was the central government. But De la Huerta's followers did succeed in providing several hundred thousand dollars to a group of agents who were sent from Veracruz to purchase munitions, particularly in Cuba and New York. Except for 300,000 cartridges secured by Froylán C. Manjarrez, none of these commissioners obtained the sorely needed help for the rebel forces. Eventually De la Huerta had to send his private secretary, Antonio Manero, to Cuba and to the United States to seek to recover funds from the unsuccessful agents.[2]

From the west General Enrique Estrada sent his own commissioner, Dr. Cutberto Hidalgo (Obregón's ex-Minister of Foreign Relations), to purchase war materials in the United States. In Havana on his way to New York, Dr. Hidalgo communicated with the De la Huerta leaders in Veracruz, and in reply he received an urgent wire asking him to stay where he was and await "money, instructions, and fuller powers." The leaders in Veracruz thought it inadvisable to have two separate missions negotiating in the United States for arms for the rebellion, and that arrangements should be made accordingly for work being done in Washington by Alvarez del Castillo to be coordinated with that of Dr. Hidalgo. Estrada did not get his arms or munitions, which is not very surprising in view of Alvarez del Castillo's lack of success, caused by Washington's support of the Obregón Government.

While the C.R.O.M. was sending communications to United

---

[1] Francis McCullagh, *Red Mexico*, p. 368.
[2] Alonso Capetillo, *La rebelión sin cabeza*, pp. 127–132.

States labor leaders to do all possible to prevent the shipment of war materials to the rebels, both the Partido Laborista and the Partido Agrarista, particularly the latter, contributed men for the government's forces. On the financial front, Pani arranged to borrow 10,000,000 pesos from the Huasteca Petroleum Company and 8,000,000 more from businesses in Mexico City. Government salary payments fell behind, and it seemed to be out of the question to make the payments called for in 1924 by De la Huerta's foreign debt agreement.

When Yucatán's Governor Felipe Carrillo Puerto received a telegram from Guadalupe Sánchez, he and Colonel Carlos M. Róbinson, who was head of the Mérida forces, replied by supporting Obregón and Calles. Then Carrillo Puerto and Róbinson, hoping to build up plans for a common defense, sent urgent wires to such Tabasco leaders as Governor Tomás Garrido Canabal and General Vicente González, the commander of Military Operations in Tabasco.

Early on December 12, 1923, Yucatán received a call for help from Campeche, where the troops were rebelling; before noon on the same day assistance went forth in the form of Mérida forces under Colonel Róbinson. Hardly had Carrillo Puerto and some of his brothers and associates seen Róbinson off at the Mérida railway station when the Governor received a telegram reportedly from Róbinson saying that the Campeche rebels had fled and to await his return at the station. What had really happened was that Róbinson had been taken prisoner by his own men, who were now returning in the name of the rebellion.

In Mérida the enemies of Carrillo Puerto's Government, taking advantage of the rebellion to overthrow the Partido Socialista del Sureste, were joined by members of the government itself, such as the State Treasurer, who were admirers of former Governor Salvador Alvarado. Calling on his armed supporters to follow him, Carrillo Puerto left Mérida on the early afternoon of the twelfth in a train which went eastward. This entourage was quickly followed by a trainload of pursuing rebel soldiers sent by Colonel Juan Ricardez Broca, who took over the Governor's office. One hour later, at Motul, Carrillo Puerto was welcomed by three hundred armed workers under the command of his brother Edesio Carrillo, mayor of Motul; at almost the same time another brother, Benjamín Carrillo, joined them with a trainload of his Constitutionalist Police

Force. Although it was reported that Carrillo Puerto was heading eastward to give strength to the organized workers in that part of the state, the Governor had already decided that his Socialistas were insufficiently armed and that a fight from the state's interior would result in useless sacrifice. Bidding his Socialistas disband, he and the Policía Constitucionalista continued fleeing eastward in their trains, while friends in Motul took steps to impede the approach of the train from Mérida with the rebel soldiers.

At Tunkás, further along the railroad route, the Governor asked for the municipal funds. These, amounting to between nine and ten pesos, he received. At this point he had a difficult time ridding h'mself of the Policía Constitucionalista, because the policemen said they would capture the fleeing Governor unless they received their back wages. The police train was dispatched back to Mérida only after these men received the scant funds acquired at successive railroad stations and the government arms which they were carrying. Later other companions were dropped at the Espita station although they strenuously objected at departing from the twelve who stayed with the governor.

At Tizimín, the end of the railroad line, three of the group remained behind, later explaining to the local military commander, Manuel Bates, that they were submitting themselves to the orders of the new state government. With brothers Benjamín, Edesio, and Wilfrido and six other followers, Felipe Carrillo Puerto continued onward with the more tedious part of the journey toward Cuyo, a chicle and lumber port about eighty kilometers northeast of Tizimín. During this part of the flight, which involved the use of beasts of burden, Carrillo Puerto spoke to one who joined up and assisted, pointing out that as his government was one of construction he had now refrained from destroying rail or telephone lines. "I hope," he added, "that you will not place obstacles in the way of our departure from here."[3]

Finally on the afternoon of December 14 they reached the sea at the harbor of Holbox, which is just inside the bounds of the territory of Quintana Roo. The natives appeared unco-operative, and the motorboat which the travellers tried to use turned out to be broken down and insusceptible to repair by the natives. When Manuel Berzunza, Carrillo Puerto's predecessor as governor, left the group to investigate about means of going overland to more southerly

---

[3] "Chato" Duarte, *Fatalismo . . . ? Obra histórica*, p. 31.

parts of Quintana Roo or to Guatemala, he was captured and sent to Manuel Bates at Tizimín. Bates turned him over to Ricardez Broca.

Carrillo Puerto and his remaining eight companions were seized on December 21 off of Holbox when a small boat in which they were navigating went aground. Captain José Corte, whose twenty-eight soldiers made the capture at the beach, got the prisoners to the Tizimín prison, where they were treated courteously by Bates. They were soon taken to the Juárez penitentiary in Mérida by a trainload of rebel soldiers sent by Ricardez Broca to Tizimín for that purpose, and when they reached the penitentiary they found their cell-mates there included two more of Felipe's brothers, Acrelio and Audomaro Carrillo Puerto. While Ricardez Broca, in the face of rumors of tortures and assassinations, made statements that the prisoners would receive all classes of guarantees, soldiers outside of Carrillo Puerto's cell spent their time mocking and insulting the fallen leader.

Felipe Carrillo Puerto explained to a lawyer whom he called to his cell that he was willing to pay 100,000 pesos for his freedom but would have to be set free first in order to obtain the money. The lawyer insisted on a check on a United States bank to cover his professional services, and then, accompanied by Colonel Bernardino Mena Brito, whose Partido Liberal Yucateco had struggled against Carrillo Puerto's Partido Socialista del Sureste, he called on Ricardez Broca. In the Government Palace Ricardez Broca stipulated that the 100,000 pesos be turned over precisely when the liberating papers were signed, adding that this amount was applicable to Felipe Carrillo Puerto alone and that an additional ten thousand pesos would be required for each of his jailed companions. While Carrillo Puerto was negotiating the delivery time of the money, his enemies won the day by offering a larger and countering amount and by making a down payment of 50,000 pesos. Carrillo Puerto's lawyer decided to depart at once for the United States to collect his legal fee before his client might meet his death. As representative of the rebel Veracruz government Gustavo Arce had passed on De la Huerta's suggestion that Carrillo Puerto be shipped to Veracruz, a proposition which the prisoner had declined while he was hoping through the help of legal talent to reach the United States.[4] Now Arce, who could expect De la Huerta to oppose execution of the

---

[4] Edmundo Bolio Ontiveros, *De la cuna al paredón*, p. 83.

Picture issued by the Partido Laborista Mexicano bearing the title: "Felipe Carrillo Puerto, Governor of Yucatán, assassinated on January 3, 1924, on orders of the traitor Adolfo de la Huerta, in connivance with the large landholders of the peninsula."

prisoner, interviewed Ricardez Broca in an effort to forestall any such event. Later he telegraphed De la Huerta that he thought he had done some good in this respect.[5]

Felipe Carrillo Puerto and twelve of his associates, including brothers and a chauffeur, were submitted to a military trial which lasted during much of January 2 and most of the night of January 2–3. For a time Ricardez Broca was present. The accused socialist stated that he was the state governor and president of the Partido Socialista "and as such I energetically protest that this war trial is illegal." Charges which were made and denied had to do with the past shootings of various persons. As an example of what went on, one of the defendants indicated that Wilfrido Carrillo Puerto had ordered some killings and another defendant besought Wilfrido to tell the truth, adding that "you are not to blame because you received your orders from above." Wilfrido then exclaimed: "I never received such orders from my brother Felipe."[6]

The Council of War, under the presidency of Colonel Juan Israel Aguirre, unanimously pronounced death sentences for all the defendants, and in the early hours of the morning they were taken to the general cemetery to be shot. Just before this dismal trip, Carrillo Puerto remarked that none of his companions should be suffering this fate, because he alone was responsible for all that the accusers were seeking to "impute about my government and my party."[7]

When De la Huerta learned about the shootings, which took place at 5:00 A.M. on January 3, he denounced them, but Juan Ricardez Broca was nevertheless promoted to a generalship and made provisional governor of Yucatán. It was not until after these promotions became effective that an agent of Ricardez Broca sought to persuade Don Adolfo that Ricardez Broca had been unable to control the situation, finding himself "almost a prisoner" of local military men whose dislike for Carrillo Puerto was the result of local antagonisms.

These killings in Yucatán caused a great sensation. Calles pointed out that Carrillo Puerto had in all of his life and under all circumstances defended the "humble and working classes" and he called Ricardez Broca a traitor and the "vile instrument of capital." Obregón said: "Don Adolfo de la Huerta will appreciate the magnitude of his crime when he receives the virile protests of the universal proletariat." In Mexico City the men of Arnulfo Gómez and Luis

[5] Luis Monroy Durán and Gonzalo Bautista, *El último caudillo*, p. 477.
[6] *Ibid.*, p. 475.
[7] Edmundo Bolio Ontiveros, *op. cit.*, p. 84.

Morones cited the fate of Carrillo Puerto as they continued their actions against suspected Delahuertistas.

In Yucatán there was good evidence of the handicap which the rebels suffered on account of the poor communications with the United States. After Ricardez Broca became the state's provisional governor, the Ward Line sent no ships there. Yucatán's inability to move henequen not only deprived the rebels of tax revenue but was the cause of increasing restlessness on the part of producers, merchants, and the many others who were affected.

27.

The Assassination
of Field Jurado

The Special Claims Convention, formulated at the Bucareli talks, was approved by the necessary two-thirds of the Mexican
Senate on December 27, 1923, shortly before the end of the regular
legislative session. It became necessary in January to call a special
session of the Senate in an effort to obtain approval of the General
Claims Convention. While Sr. Ross was making known the urgency
of ratification because of his negotiations in Washington, members
of the Senate minority created a stir in Mexico City by insisting that
the General Claims Convention was humiliating to Mexico.

One of those who maintained that Obregón was compromising

the nation's most sacred interests was General Cándido Aguilar. At first, examining the De la Huerta rebellion from outside the country, Carranza's son-in-law concluded that it was a movement by a political group that had been forced to take up arms. But later, when the texts of the Claims Conventions were made known to him, and when he learned of Obregón's negotiations to get arms from Washington, Aguilar decided that Obregón's actions were transforming the rebellion into something more worthy: "a nationalistic movement." From San Antonio he wrote on January 3, 1924, to De la Huerta, expressing his adherence to the movement and offering to collaborate, an offer which was promptly accepted.

Official action by the Senate on the General Claims Convention required a two-thirds quorum of the senators, or thirty-eight in number. Under the direction of Senator Francisco Field Jurado, of Campeche, the opponents of the treaty stayed away so that no quorum could be obtained, in spite of a pro-Calles substitute for the absent Rafael Zubaran Capmany. The majority called other substitute senators to replace those who absented themselves, but Field Jurado managed his men in such a way that no one of them stayed away for the ten consecutive sessions necessary to allow the replacement by a substitute.

In the Chamber of Deputies on January 14 Luis N. Morones orated with his usual vigor, referring to the recent assassination of Felipe Carrillo Puerto and threatening Cooperatista members of the legislature. "For each one of our people who fall like Felipe Carrillo Puerto, there will fall at least five of the gentlemen who are serving as instruments of the reaction." Then on the twentieth, when he was addressing a workers' meeting at the Venecia Movie Theatre, he exclaimed: "the war is without quarter, a tooth for a tooth, a life for a life. The punishment now comes to the senators. Field Jurado and Trejo are collecting funds to be sent to the rebels." In response to this threat, Field Jurado on the following day penned a note to Morones:

Francisco Field Jurado, Campeche senator, has the pleasure of advising you that he has learned of the "enlightening" speech which you pronounced yesterday, Sunday, before your simpletons, and is at your disposition in his home, No. 134 Fourth Colima Street in this capital, where he awaits you and your agents with attentions which are merited.

Also he advises that morning and afternoon he goes to the Senate to protect the interests of the nation which traitors wish to violate, and he will vote against the antipatriotic conventions and he will not leave this capital but will await here the triumph of the liberating army. Your agent, Colonel [José] Preve, has sent me warnings . . .

As he was leaving the Senate on January 23, Field Jurado was followed by two men, who quickly joined three others waiting outside of the Palacio Nacional in a Dodge car (without license plates). When the senator was in front of No. 130 Tabasco Street, the men in the car started shooting at him. He ran, followed by his attackers, but fell dead near No. 86 Córdoba Street with at least eight bullet wounds.

At the same time that this was happening, about 2:00 P.M., in other parts of the city men with automobiles kidnapped Senators Ildefonso Vázquez, Francisco J. Trejo, and Enrique del Castillo. Vázquez was taken to a spot about fifteen kilometers from the city.

While Senators Federico González Garza and Gerzayn Ugarte, also of the opposition, remained in hiding, Ing. Vito Alessio Robles arose in the Senate to point out that, although he himself had never belonged to the Cooperatista group, he severely condemned the recent crimes. "I accuse Morones of being the intellectual author of the assassination of Senator Field Jurado and of the kidnapping of three other senators. Therefore I ask all senators to vote for the arrest of Diputado Luis N. Morones."

Vasconcelos, after being advised that Morones had one of the killers hiding in his own office, wired his resignation to Obregón; he then released this piece of news to the press. From his battle headquarters the President issued a telegram, made public at once, in which he strongly condemned the assassination and kidnappings and ordered that the Mexico City authorities take punitive steps. In a long letter to Morones, which the recipient must have resented, Obregón said in part:

That declaration announcing the unfortunate events which later took place throws a solidarity against the Government over which I preside: to accept it would mean its moral ruin and would surely be more damaging than the treasons of Estrada, Sánchez, and Maycotte.

I have decided in the future to act in a manner which will establish a separation between you and the administration over which I preside, thus ending the charge being made that those assaults were announced and inspired by a high official of the public administration. I ask you only to study conscientiously my situation and tell me if I am not right.

It would appear that the Government used those measures to wipe out its political enemies. This is something that has no place in my conscience and would be a blot on my public life.

In announcing that in defense of the Government acts of that sort would be executed, and then in having them carried out without first finding out how I felt, a lack of consideration was shown, particularly in view of my disapproval of similar acts of much less significance about which you consulted me . . . [1]

At Celaya, Guanajuato, the President received word that Vasconcelos would stay on with the understanding that the recent deeds would not go unpunished. He also received a visit from Dr. Puig Casauranc, who came to make it clear that Calles had had nothing to do with the assassination.

On the floor of the Senate Vito Alessio Robles' motion protesting the fate of Field Jurado was backed by Senator Francisco Labastida Izquierdo; it encountered no apparent opposition, but we are told by its author that many senators supported it grudgingly. After the motion having to do with making an arrest was toned down so that it could be meaningless, the congressional Permanent Commission failed to take any effective action. Don Vito was hardly surprised when the C.R.O.M. renewed its attacks on him, reviving the old charge that he was seeking to take over the control of the Military Manufacturing Establishments.

The kidnapped senators were set at liberty on January 27 but they remained completely silent concerning their recent experiences, and soon minority senators who had not gone into hiding agreed to join the others in informal sessions to study the proposed General Claims Convention. At these meetings the Undersecretary in Charge of Foreign Relations, Aarón Sáenz, assisted by Fernando González Roa, explained in detail all the fine points. No mention was made of the so-called "extraofficial pacts" or "minutes" on agrarian reform and petroleum, and a majority of the senators did not know of their existence. [2]

The fight by Cooperatista senators to alter the Convention was of no avail, as the majority resisted any changes that might call for the renegotiation of matters already approved in the United States Senate. It was finally agreed to leave the text unchanged but to include some covering clause to the effect that "the agreements are not and cannot be contrary to the Constitution." In a secret session Fernando Iglesias Calderón suggested that it would be better to say that "these conventions are good for the nation and in no way

[1] Obregón's letter is reproduced by Alfonso Romandía Ferreira in *El Universal*, August 7, 1956.
[2] Vito Alessio Robles, *Los Tratados de Bucareli*.

oppose the Constitution," a suggestion which was followed by a lively debate. Francisco J. Trejo, recently freed, presented a list of objections to the Conventions, backing up his ideas by submitting a study made by Luis Cabrera. After Sáenz had replied to each of Trejo's objections, Iglesias Calderón had a lot to say to Trejo. He criticized the minority for having earlier prevented the attaining of a quorum, said that Mexico should pay exactly what it owed, and then censured Cabrera. Cabrera, he said, was responsible for many of the claims that Mexico would have to pay, and had fostered a policy ("The Revolution is the Revolution") which had encouraged all sorts of criminal acts. After this the whole matter was put to vote and the General Claims Convention was approved, 28 to 14.

In a court appearance Morones went through the formality of explaining that he had no information which might indicate who had killed Field Jurado and he added that the Directive Committee of the C.R.O.M. could throw no light on the kidnappings. Both he and Colonel José Preve, adventurous gunman of the C.R.O.M., pointed out that in view of the fact that Field Jurado had supported union activities it was illogical to blame the labor organization for the assassination. The senator's death went unpunished.

28·

Military Events;
The Battle of Esperanza

The federal government assigned a difficult task to General Lázaro Cárdenas when it ordered him from Michoacán with his 2000 cavalrymen to combat Enrique Estrada in Jalisco. Learning of the march of Cárdenas and his men, Estrada sent against him General Rafael Buelna with numerically superior forces. Victory went to the larger army in a bloody battle which took place between Santa Ana and Zacoalco, Jalisco, and in which Cárdenas was wounded and federal General Paulino Navarro was killed.

Insisting that "we must make war like civilized people and not like savages," Estrada had instructed Buelna not to follow barbarous customs but rather to treat prisoners like old companions and to attend to the enemy wounded with the same care applied "to our own wounded."[1] From Guadalajara a special train was sent to Zacoalco, eighty kilometers away, to fetch Cárdenas and his men. Prisoners who were not wounded were to be paid thirty pesos each and sent to the town of Ocotlán, Estrada making it clear that he wanted no enemy officer admitted into the ranks of his own followers.

All kinds of considerations were to be shown to Cárdenas, who was met late at night at the Guadalajara railroad station by J. D. Ramírez Garrido, Estrada's chief of staff. After noting that Cárdenas was in bad shape, Ramírez Garrido told him that good doctors and the best room in the military hospital were awaiting him, but that other arrangements could be made if he preferred. Cárdenas, well impressed, named a particular sanitarium he liked and a doctor he knew, and Ramírez Garrido attended to these wishes before returning to the railroad station to take care of the other wounded prisoners. By early January Cárdenas had recovered and was able to be on his way, but long before then he received a visit from Estrada.

As soon as Buelna's victorious column had been reorganized in Guadalajara, Estrada sent it to Morelia, Michoacán, which had been stubbornly defending itself against the forces of Manuel M. Diéguez. Then when Morelia's defending general, who had been wounded, displayed the white flag of surrender, handsome young General Buelna took the lead in entering the city. But all was an ambush. In the furious attack which the government forces unleashed Buelna was killed, and the Estradistas retired again to Morelia's outskirts.

This occurrence brought Estrada himself and his army to Morelia, a movement which weakened the rebel front at Ocotlán, Jalisco. When Estrada subdued Morelia, Buelna's angry men called for the execution of all the government military chiefs who had been taken prisoner. They could not take out their revenge on the defending general, as he had been killed in action, but they did cry for the scalps of the defending general's chief of staff, Colonel Manuel Avila Camacho, and his brother Colonel Maximino Avila Camacho.

[1] J. D. Ramírez Garrido, *Así Fué*, p. 100.

Estrada, however, decided to call the captured officers to his presence and get them to sign a document promising, on their word of honor as soldiers, not again to take up arms against the Estradistas, in return for which they would be set immediately in absolute liberty. Manuel Avila Camacho, the first to be taken to the presence of Estrada, refused to sign the document, notwithstanding the warning that all who would not sign would be shot at once. "General," said the prisoner, "although I know that my words mean that I shall be taken to the wall, I cannot sign, because I gave my word as a soldier to the Government and I have only one word of honor." It was then that Estrada rose from his seat and enthusiastically extended his arms to Mexico's future President. Unconditional release was granted to the Avila Camacho brothers and their companions, and they lost no time in joining the forces of Obregón at Irapuato, Guanajuato.[2]

In the state of Tabasco the revolt against Obregón started at the port of Frontera, where all went well for the rebels. Regiment heads, Generals Alberto Pineda, Gregorio Lozano, Fernando Segovia, Eustorgio Vidal, and Rodolfo H. Vivanco, were quick to declare against the federal government and to join Generals Alberto Segovia and Carlos Greene in an attack on General Vicente González, chief of Military Operations in Tabasco. González and his men, as well as contingents from the Ligas de Resistencia which were headed by Governor Tomás Garrido Canabal and Ausencio C. Cruz, had to withdraw to the state's capital, Villahermosa.[3]

The principal struggle of this period in Tabasco's history then took place. Villahermosa was surrounded by several thousand rebels and remained under siege for over a month. While Vicente González and his chief of staff, Miguel Henríquez Guzmán, directed the defense of the city, Governor Garrido tried to maintain order under progressively disheartening circumstances. After a flurry of unfounded rumors about an impending arrival of a boatload of federals who could come to the aid of the city's defenders, Villahermosa on January 15 had to surrender to the Delahuertistas on account of a lack of provisions and munitions. Tomás Garrido Canabal was able to elude rebel searchers when he hid in Carmela

---

[2] Much in this and in the preceding two paragraphs is based on Salvador J. Romero's memorandum of December 13, 1956.

[3] Baltasar Dromundo, *Tomás Garrido*, p. 24.

Greene's Villahermosa home, and he soon made his way with his two brothers to Ciudad Flores in Guatemala. One of the brothers was then named Mexican Consul in Ciudad Flores by Juan de Dios Bojórquez, the Mexican Minister to Guatemala.

General Pineda and Lic. Zubaran Capmany, who called for "unconditional surrender" of the defeated soldiers, were overruled by the Supreme Chief of the rebellion. General Vicente González declared himself in favor of De la Huerta and then he and 2000 of his men who had been defending Villahermosa were brought by boats from Frontera to Veracruz. The defeated general and his staff were accompanied by Prieto Laurens, Lic. Zubaran, and General Montero Villar when they paid a call on Don Adolfo at the Faros Building. It was a pleasant occasion for the visitors, as Vicente González received 5,000 dollars from the Supreme Chief and members of his staff received promotions in rank. Against the advice of Prieto Laurens and General Segovia, De la Huerta had resolved that those recently beaten in Tabasco should be incorporated into the rebel forces. So González's 2000 men were sent to the Esperanza railroad station to reinforce Guadalupe Sánchez.

In Esperanza, near the Puebla-Veracruz state border, both rebels and federals were building up strength for a possible battle critical to the eastern campaign. Zubaran presided over a brief meeting of rebel leaders at the port of Veracruz, where it was decided to engage in battle at Esperanza, although Don Adolfo seems to have favored Metlac or Fortín, Veracruz, because of better natural defenses and greater proximity to the base of supplies. Another idea which was in the back of De la Huerta's mind was to allow more time for Eugenio Martínez, who was responsible for crushing the rebellion in the east, to incorporate himself and his forces as part of the rebellion.

The battle at Estación Esperanza began at dawn on January 28 when the forces of General Martínez poured their artillery fire into the fortified positions which were being defended by Guadalupe Sánchez, Fortunato Maycotte, Cesáreo Castro, Villanueva Garza, and Alfonso de la Huerta. While important contributions in dislodging the rebels were rendered by Fausto Topete, Rodrigo Quevedo M., and Almazán's cavalry, not the least of the defenders' troubles were caused by the 2000 men who came from Tabasco. Following instructions left with them by General Vicente González and Colonel Miguel Henríquez Guzmán, these men disappointed

Don Adolfo by using their arms not to defend Esperanza but to attack the forces of Guadalupe Sánchez from the rear.[4] Under these disastrous conditions about 400 rebels were killed, 200 wounded, and 1300 taken prisoner. About 1500 rifles and 200,000 cartridges fell to the federals. Among the various trains which were seized was that of Guadalupe Sánchez, which was stopped as it was pulling out of the station in the direction of Veracruz. This prize was captured by Generals Topete, Lucas González, and Quevedo after a terrific struggle in which Sánchez' chief of staff lost his life and from which the rebel leader himself was lucky to make his getaway on a horse. In his report to the President, Eugenio Martínez pointed out that Generals Sánchez, Maycotte, and Cesáreo Castro were fortunate in having good horses and much experience at fleeing.

Vicente González had gone to New Orleans, Louisiana, on a trip which De la Huerta hoped would end up in operations favorable to the rebel cause, and from there he made his way to Irapuato, Guanajuato, where Obregón was directing the western campaign. He was warmly received by the President.

The news of Esperanza brought great relief to the many anxious government employees in the capital, and soon they were learning that the victorious federals were following up the victory by a march toward the port. After Orizaba fell to the government troops, Generals Martínez, Topete, Limón, Lucas González, Quevedo, and others advanced and took Córdoba. The rebels in the east had long since lost their opportunity, which consisted in making an early attack from Puebla on Mexico City, as Villarreal and others had advocated.

After learning of the Esperanza disaster, the Veracruz government at once made plans to evacuate. Since the navy, or rather those who controlled it, had supported the rebellion, a number of good ships were in the harbor. The southeast and the Peninsula, including the states of Yucatán, Campeche, Tabasco, and Chiapas, were dominated by the Rebels, and Don Adolfo was anxious to move to this safer region both his government and the remaining Veracruz troops, consisting of about 2500 men. Villanueva Garza objected to making a flight from the relatively rich customs port, nor did he wish to abandon Guadalupe Sánchez. Other soldiers and sailors agreed on the advisability of a stand, but were overruled by the

---

[4] Jorge Prieto Laurens in *El Universal*, January 15, 1958; also Alonso Capetillo, *La rebelión sin cabeza*, p. 175.

Supreme Chief, who was under the impression that the United States Marines would disembark if the two Mexican factions should get into combat at the port of Veracruz.

The oil boat *San Leonardo* took Prieto Laurens and some others northward to the port of Tuxpan, Veracruz, in the petroleum district. Two armed warships, the *Zaragoza* and the *Agua Prieta*, and various merchant ships (of which the largest were the *Tamaulipas* and the *Tabasco*) were used to take the rebel government and troops to Frontera, Tabasco. They left Veracruz on February 5.

When Martínez and his forces reached Veracruz, not until a week later, cable service to New Orleans was re-established. The government generals must have been surprised, and pleased, to find that the rebels had auctioned off little of the merchandise stored in the port. According to legal custom only such goods remaining after six months of storage could be auctioned, and De la Huerta, in spite of a shortage of funds and of munitions for his troops, had complied with the established regulations. Just before noon on February 12 the army of General de División Eugenio Martínez made its victorious march through the port of Veracruz, and heard the most pronounced spectator acclaim go to the Yaqui Indian warriors. Soon after Martínez made an appearance on the balcony of the Diligencias Hotel commercial houses resumed their normal business.

When Prieto Laurens and Villarreal and the latter's ill-equipped soldiers reached Tuxpan, they found the rebel operations there being carried out by José G. Morán, an unnecessarily rough general, whose drinking was not especially moderate just because he limited himself to Hennessy Extra cognac. Rebel attempts to gain the port of Tampico, the attractive oil center and prize of the north, had early included plans to attack by sea from Tuxpan. Although the Navy, supposedly, controlled these waters, by the time the G-3, a small ship, had gotten into position to make this attack, a message to desist was received from Veracruz, where De la Huerta was concerned about the presence of United States naval vessels at Tampico.

Now, following Villarreal's arrival at Tuxpan, a renewed effort was made to capture Tampico by land. But the campaign was a bad failure, Morán's men being unprepared for the attack inflicted on them by government troops, and Morán himself barely escaping death. As had been his original intention, Villarreal then left for Nuevo León, but there his small force was wiped out; he went into hiding and later turned up north of the border.

General Benito Ramírez G., who had remained in Tuxpan as a link between oil company operators and the rebellion, could not successfully defend Tuxpan with his 200 marines and 100 soldiers. Morán remained in the district, carrying on a losing fight for some time longer, and eventually he surrendered to the federals under terms which, surprisingly enough, were supposed to have allowed him his life and liberty. Nevertheless he ended up in the prison of Santiago Tlaltelolco in Mexico City.

During the course of all these military events Prieto Laurens worked on behalf of the rebel revenue, and with Morán's consent he received a cargo of chicle considered to be a payment of taxes from producers or merchants who were having difficulties in exporting their product. With his chicle he left on the *San Leonardo* for Campeche, where he hoped to sell it, but the rebel supreme command ordered him to return it at Laguna del Carmen to representatives of the original owners, who were claiming it through the American consul on the ground that the federal government, which had taken over Tuxpan, was insisting on the payment of the taxes.[5] This was not the first occasion on which De la Huerta's respect for United States interests and wishes had foiled revenue-seeking plans of Prieto Laurens and Morán. Arrangements made by these men to collect oil taxes were called off by De la Huerta on the grounds that should they be carried out United States forces would disembark and occupy the entire petroleum region.[6]

The defeat at Esperanza and the loss of positions in the state of Veracruz were serious setbacks for the rebel government of De la Huerta; moreover various explanations of the causes of the setbacks gave rise to discords among his followers.

[5] Jorge Prieto Laurens quoted in Bernardino Mena Brito, *Felipe Angeles, federal*, pp. 263–273.
[6] Jorge Prieto Laurens in *El Universal*, January 14, 1958.

29.

The Last Bloody Phases
of the Rebellion

From his headquarters at Irapuato, Guanajuato, Obregón ran the Mexican government and directed operations against the rebels in the west. The great past master at military strategy arranged to have about 400 Mexico City busses used to move more than 3000 soldiers to Irapuato.

The President and general-in-chief, now often rather stern looking, was always active, conferring with an endless succession of visitors, reviewing the troops of numerous generals, and engaging in a series of inspection trips (during one of which he narrowly escaped capture). To Irapuato for consultation came such Cabinet

At Irapuato, Guerrero, in 1924 during the campaign against the Dela-huertistas. Center foreground: Generals Eugenio Martínez *and* Alvaro Obregón. *Behind them* (*on the train*): Generals Plutarco Elías Calles *and* Francisco R. Serrano. *Casasola.*

ministers as Ing. Alberto J. Pani, General Aarón Sáenz, and General Manuel Pérez Treviño (Lic. Miguel Alessio Robles' successor as Minister of Industry, Commerce, and Labor).

At Irapuato the somewhat portly looking President would confer with Generals Francisco Serrano, Plutarco Elías Calles, Joaquín Amaro, J. Gonzalo Escobar, or Luis Gutiérrez. After distinguishing himself in the east, General Juan Andreu Almazán spent some time

President Obregón *in campaign against the 1923–1924 rebellion. Díaz.*

at Irapuato receiving Obregón's instructions before he went off on his campaign in Oaxaca against Generals García Vigil and Maycotte.

A large contingent of rebels, including Generals Salvador Alvarado and Crispiniano Anzaldo, was firmly entrenched at Ocotlán, Jalisco, and much of Obregón's attention was devoted to formulating plans of attack on this stronghold. Ocotlán is on the eastern part of Lake Chapala, one flank being protected by the lake and the other by the Lerma River, whose four bridges were in rebel possession. In order to attack, Obregón improvised bridges made of wooden platforms to which automobile tires were attached. While in this manner the government soldiers sought to cross the Lerma River, advancing directly into heavy fire from the strongly fortified rebels, government planes dropped bombs on Ocotlán's defenders.

The combat started at 6:00 A.M. on February 10, 1924. For hour after hour the government troops, led by Joaquín Amaro, Roberto Cruz, José Amarillas, J. Gonzalo Escobar, Eulogio Ortiz, Luis Gutiérrez, and others, strove to make the river crossing. They received very timely help with the arrival of General Jesús M. Aguirre at the head of over 1000 Yaqui Indian fighters. Hundreds of government soldiers had been killed, and Cruz had been wounded and had lost two of his horses, before the Lerma was finally crossed on the improvised bridges at 4:00 P.M. The fighting continued for two hours longer and then at last Generals Alvarado and Anzaldo withdrew with their remaining men. Among the dead they left behind was rebel General Isaías Castro, associate of Enrique Estrada. After the town's hotels had been turned into hospitals, and after Obregón had sent his cavalry to pursue the fleeing rebel cavalry, the one-armed veteran of countless victories declared: "Never have I found myself in a combat of the magnitude of that in which our troops have just triumphed."

The rebels were now forced out of nearby Guadalajara. Moving largely at night, they tore up railroad lines and burned bridges.

From Michoacán rebel Generals Enrique Estrada and Manuel M. Diéguez reached the region in which the Lerma River flows into the east end of Lake Chapala, near the point where the states of Jalisco, Michoacán, and Guanajuato meet. Although they knew it not, they arrived too late to aid Alvarado at Ocotlán.

Holding a staff meeting at Penjamillo, in the northwest of the state of Michoacán, on February 11, Estrada instructed Diéguez to destroy rail communications at Palo Verde, and he told another general to go to Lake Chapala destroying communication with the town of La Piedad. Both these towns are to the east of Lake Chapala, La Piedad being closer to the lake than Palo Verde, and both are on the railroad line which connects Mexico City with Guadalajara. Other generals, including Estrada and J. D. Ramírez Garrido, were scheduled to take La Piedad from General Enrique Ramírez. Estrada told his hearers that Obregón was between La Barca and Ocotlán (which are also on the railroad line) and that Amaro was attacking Ocotlán. Before the meeting broke up Diéguez sought to help by explaining, and recommending, Pancho Villa's method for successfully destroying communications in Chihuahua:

Cut down the telegraph poles, thus destroying this means of com-

"Las soldaderas" on top of train during the De la Huerta rebellion of 1923–1924. Casasola.

munication, and use these poles as crossbars on the rail line. When the railroad ties are in the air, they are knocked down with other posts. When ten or fifteen ties have been gathered the poles are placed beneath them, and petroleum is dumped thereon and lit. Thus the posts and ties are totally destroyed and the rails, twisted by heat, become useless. This method avoids the difficult task of unscrewing the rail, and doubles the work of repair.[1]

Provided with petroleum, as well as dynamite for bridge destruction, the expeditions set forth on February 12, in spite of a feeling that the federals were familiar with their positions and plans. Ramírez Garrido maintained that the many soldiers' women ("Las Viejas"), who attached themselves to the camp, spread news of plans so well that they served the government better than its own spies or spying airplanes.

While Diéguez went in the direction of Palo Verde, the others struck out for La Piedad. But when it became clear that La Piedad was receiving strong Obregonista reinforcements, Estrada's column crossed the Lerma and went toward the lake. The Villa system of communication destruction was not a success, "no doubt due," says one of those who tried it, "to our lack of practice."

After Estrada's 1500 tired, hungry, and somewhat confused men spent the night near the lake, they set out on the thirteenth to join Diéguez at Palo Verde. There Estrada learned about the Ocotlán outcome of the tenth, but he did not find Diéguez and his force. Diéguez had reached Palo Verde, and destroyed there some communications as planned, but then he had left for Pénjamo, Guanajuato, to the surprise of Estrada. It is interesting to note that Diéguez' occupation of Palo Verde occurred fifteen minutes after Obregón, in the presidential train, passed rapidly through the place on his way from Ocotlán. Had not Diéguez lost forty minutes by straying from his path, he would have been at Palo Verde by the time of the President's arrival, perhaps already at work destroying track.

After government planes had located Estrada's 1500 rebels, entrenched in hills near Palo Verde, J. Gonzalo Escobar and his federals moved on them from La Piedad. At La Piedad, about twenty kilometers west of Palo Verde, Escobar had 6000 soldiers, and it was from this point that government forces had been pursuing those who fled from Ocotlán.

While Estrada tried to get word to Diéguez to come at once, well-

[1] J. D. Ramírez Garrido, *El combate de Palo Verde*, p. 12.

organized government assaults were made on the hill. For a while the morale of the rebels was good, for they had some success in repelling the attack and they wounded Escobar; also, Estrada let his men know that Diéguez was coming. But Diéguez, who was about seven kilometers away, received a panicky report to the effect that Estrada had been killed and his forces routed, and so he prepared to retreat to Zacapu, Michoacán. The success of Estrada's outnumbered men faded fast as ammunition ran out, and many of them fled in spite of orders to the contrary. With the reduced group which remained with him on the hill, Estrada at first refused to depart, exclaiming "I want to be killed here, as I am among cowards." He was eventually pursuaded to abandon his position, none too soon, and without his extra clothing, files, and family pictures.

At a point about ten miles from his recent defeat, Estrada joined up with his 1000 survivors. A government plane was overhead and there seemed nothing left to do but continue retreating. Eventually Estrada made his way to Acapulco, Guerrero, where, not being recognized, he was taken into the federal army as a private. As such he was taken to Mexico City and then he deserted, finally reaching California after barely evading capture at the border. From his exile he wired his brother Roque, admitting that his decision to rebel had been unfortunate and expressing regret for the position in which it had placed Roque.

Manuel M. Diéguez was less fortunate than Estrada. With 600 men who had been defeated in Jalisco he started on a march through the mountains of Michoacán and those of Guerrero, where he hoped to join rebel General Rómulo Figueroa. Learning just before he reached Chilpancingo, the capital of Guerrero, that Figueroa had surrendered, he went on eastward into Oaxaca with the idea of uniting his tired men with the forces of rebel General Alberto Pineda. By the time Diéguez reached Oaxaca City he had 400 men with him. There he found Governor García Vigil preparing to defend the place against an onslaught by Juan Andreu Almazán, who, after recovering Jalapa, Veracruz, for Obregón, had set forth to subdue the rebellion in Oaxaca. Diéguez, by now well impressed with the strength of the federals, persuaded Oaxaca's constructive governor that the evacuation of Oaxaca City would be an intelligent step.

Almazán had already been helped toward his objective in Oaxaca by the pro-Obregón activities of General Onofre Jiménez and his local mountaineers. Now on March 1 his success was made even easier when Diéguez and García Vigil, with 600 men, departed from the capital city of the state and sought to flee eastward into Chiapas, avoiding such federals as Juan Domínguez, who had been operating in the isthmus. But Vicente González was ordered to advance from Tabasco on Diéguez and García Vigil.

Finding himself well surrounded, García Vigil advised his associates that he was going to surrender. Although this step seemed likely to cost his life, the cultured writer who had become a revolutionary general considered this fate preferable to a useless sacrifice of the lives of his followers. Accordingly García Vigil and seventy men, including Diéguez' chief of staff, were soon in the company of Vicente González and Juan Domínguez, who treated the prisoners with considerable respect. But Obregón had his own ideas about dealing with rebel leaders, and late in April both García Vigil and Diéguez' chief of staff were shot. A few days later the federals dealt in a similar way with Oaxaca's Cooperatista Diputado José F. Gómez (Che Gómez), who in the previous year had severely wounded García Vigil, of the Partido Liberal Constitucionalista, while attempting to assassinate him.[2]

Instead of joining in the surrender, Diéguez chose to take his 400 Jalisco riders into Chiapas. But the result was the same: Diéguez and his companions were captured. Diéguez then divided up his 8000 gold pesos among the men who had accompanied him on the long march from Jalisco to Chiapas, and he sent a telegram to Obregón reminding him of the old Revolutionary days when they had fought side by side. The reply he received to his telegram was to the effect that his lack of shame was on a par with his fear of death.[3] In April he and rebel Generals Cristóforo Ocampo and Alfredo R. García were shot by the government forces at San José de las Flores in Chiapas.

Of Oaxaca's formidable rebels, only one now remained at large, Fortunato Maycotte. Even at the cost of getting ahead of our story, we cannot leave Oaxaca without a mention of the struggle to catch this rather young veteran of battles against Victoriano Huerta and Pancho Villa. According to Almazán this was the most fantastic,

[2] Jorge Fernando Iturribarría, *Oaxaca en la historia*, pp. 412–418.
[3] Conversation with Faustino Roel, June, 1958.

best-organized, and most relentless manhunt in the annals of Mexico's history.[4]

Well intrenched in Oaxaca and Puebla, Almazán on April 12 assured Obregón and Serrano that Maycotte would be captured and sent to Mexico City within one month. Maycotte had just caused some concern by taking a town on a railroad line to the east of Puebla City. But, because of the strength of alerted troops in Veracruz, his efforts to penetrate that coastal state were to no avail. So, with 600 men, he struck out for the western parts of Puebla which border on the states of Morelos and Guerrero. There he had to move with agility to escape large bodies of pursuing troops, some of which, unaware of his escape, engaged in fighting each other until one unit discovered that the prisoners being taken were the men of another federal group.[5]

Forced southward into the northwest section of Oaxaca, Maycotte's outnumbered men were attacked and routed by the forces of General Cerrillo, and were reduced in number to 200 by the time they reached Putla, on the fringe of Oaxaca's Mixteca Mountains. There Maycotte broke up his group into small contingents, and he, with about twelve followers, fled on eastward, the only direction open to him. He was believed to be making his way to the Pacific Ocean.

At the small town of San Pedro Mixtepec, Maycotte and his companions were at last captured on the night of May 4. But by the time that other members of the federal troops reached San Pedro Mixtepec, the fugitives had secured their freedom for 300 pesos and had reached the coast. All of the town's municipal authorities were promptly placed under arrest.

Hundreds of patrols were now engaged in the chase. Telegraph messages were widely distributed advising that Maycotte had 23,000 gold pesos in his belt, a sum which would be rewarded to any group or person who could turn him in, dead or alive. Severe penalties were threatened to any who would shelter him. Not only did the War Ministry prohibit all boats from leaving such local ports as Puerto Angel and Salina Cruz, but it dispatched coastguards to aid in the hunt. All roads were watched and every individual in the vicinity was subjected to identification by the authorities.

[4] Juan Andreu Almazán in *El Universal*, July 20, 1958, through August 1, 1958.

[5] Vicente Obregón M. quoted in Almazán's *Memorias* in *El Universal*, July 21, 1958.

General Fortunato Maycotte. *1920. Casasola.*

From San Pedro Mixtepec the pursuers reached the ocean sands of Puerto Escondido ten hours after Maycotte on a mule, with three companions on horse, made their way to the east along the beach. It was thought that Maycotte, who had been pretending to be an engineer, would try for the port of Salina Cruz, where the British consul was related to his wife; but the chances of his reaching this goal seemed slim, as Puerto Angel, which is on the way, was well guarded. Like their intended victims, Almazán's soldiers plodded through the sand, using lanterns at night and being burned by the sun in the day. They could clearly discern footprints of the mule and the three horses where the tide had not blotted them out. But Colonel Cacho Galván and his federals found the coast less attractive than descriptive maps indicated and they could locate no dwellings at all. When their horses could hardly make headway in the sand, the men, trying it on foot, found conditions even worse.

General Benigno Serratos arrived at Salina Cruz with one hundred riders and started to close in from the east. Obregón was reported to be sending more soldiers to Puerto Angel. The searchers included some of the less important rebels who had surrendered and who were considered anxious to redeem their reputations in the eyes of Almazán.

By May 8 Maycotte's three forlorn companions, including his nephew, were taken by those who had been making the slow, sandy march eastward from Puerto Escondido. Maycotte, without his mule, hat, or shirt, fled alone into the mountains on foot. Having negotiated unsuccessfully with a rancher to buy a horse, he was back on the beach on the evening of the tenth, when he spied five men whom he believed to be unarmed civilians.

The bearded fugitive had been without food or water for two days. In addition to the extreme torment of thirst, he was suffering from wounds in the head and shoulder, inflicted by the bites of a large alligator.[6]

Pleading with the civilians for water, they asked him who he was. His agonies increased when he answered "Fortunato Maycotte," for his new acquaintances took to torturing him to get money. But all that the belt could provide was 2500 gold pesos and one gold watch.

At dawn on May 11 Maycotte's new captors turned him over to

[6] Juan Andreu Almazán in *El Universal*, July 28, 1958.

General Luis Alberto Guajardo, who, like General Serratos, had come to the neighborhood to participate in the hunt. Guajardo's nephew, General Miguel M. Acosta, had little difficulty in persuading Obregón that Maycotte should at once be tried for his crimes, at the spot where Guajardo was holding him prisoner. Thus at El Arenal, not far from Salina Cruz, the thirty-six–year–old Maycotte was shot on May 14. When Obregón advised Almazán that those who had participated in the chase should be given promotions, his special praise for Guajardo's contribution was not particularly pleasing to Almazán.

To revive the faltering rebel cause a manifesto to the nation had come out of Frontera, Tabasco, on February 20. Signed by De la Huerta after persuasive arguments in its favor by Cándido Aguilar, Zubaran Capmany, and the Navy commander, it appears to have embodied thoughts which were uppermost in Aguilar's mind: Obregón had turned the civil war into a national war. He had offered the national sovereignty for sale to the most powerful foreign government, at the price of warships, airplanes, rifles, ammunition, and money. In the manifesto the nation's sons were called upon to defend Mexico, notwithstanding official assassinations of deputies and senators, notwithstanding Obregón's use of foreign cannon to spill Mexican blood, notwithstanding Obregón's hiring of United States pilots to pour death on old men, women, and children, as was done "in the city of Morelia."

After about one month at Frontera, Tabasco, Don Adolfo de la Huerta departed by boat for Havana and the United States. He was tired of intrigue and politics and believed he could do some good for his cause through relations he had built up in times past in Washington and New York. At that time—March, 1924—the rebels, with about 6000 men and with the Navy ships, had pretty good control of the states of Yucatán, Campeche, Tabasco, and Chiapas. Near Minatitlán, on the Isthmus of Tehuantepec, rebel General Benito Torruco had recently driven back government forces which sought to penetrate Tabasco. Carlos and Alejandro Greene and their brother, a naturalized United States citizen (he was called "El Gringo") who was on a visit from Washington, expressed the feeling that Don Adolfo might be well advised to see what he could do in the United States.

De la Huerta's departure from Frontera was made secretly in a small motor launch at midnight after he had received about 10,000 pesos. Cándido Aguilar saw him off. Prieto Laurens was at Carmen, Campeche, when the launch stopped there, and the Cooperatista leader was considerably surprised to find the "Jefe Supremo" aboard. After asking Prieto Laurens for the customs money and receiving 14,000 pesos in silver, the traveller said he was on his way to Campeche and Yucatán. Instead, he transferred to the *Tabasco* and went in her to Havana, distributing among the crew the customs money received at Carmen. The *Tabasco* refused to communicate with the *Zaragoza*, which by this time was considered to be unfriendly to the Supreme Chief and desirous of overtaking his means of departure.

The President-elect of Cuba, a close friend of De la Huerta, arranged with a wealthy doctor in Key West, Florida, for Don Adolfo's entry into Key West in disguise, the rebel leader to appear as a man whose passport was available for use in this subterfuge. De la Huerta has enjoyed telling of his arrival there. His Cuban friend advised the doctor to look for a man with a red flower in his buttonhole and to identify himself in the same way. De la Huerta disembarked at Key West and managed to surmount a little difficulty caused by the difference between his signature and the one on the passport. (Extreme seasickness was given as the reason for the difference in handwriting.) There being a bit of time before the train left, the disguised De la Huerta (wearing dark glasses) and the Key West doctor conversed for a while. When the doctor praised the virtues of De la Huerta, not knowing that he was talking with him, Don Adolfo said that De la Huerta was a simple citizen and he played down the other's great admiration for De la Huerta. Later the Key West man advised the Cuban President-elect that the latter had not sent to him a real supporter of De la Huerta. Then, with some geniality, the matter was cleaned up.

Before leaving Frontera on March 11 the Supreme Chief had received a false report about Cándido Aguilar and had got into a hot argument with him. Upon learning that his information had been false, De la Huerta tried to name Aguilar to be Interim Supreme Chief, and he gave him a written appointment placing him in charge of the "Jefatura Suprema" during his absence. Aguilar was reluctant to accept the post unless it were tendered to him by other leading rebel generals who would serve under him, but later such a meeting took place, and then and there Aguilar was named Interim Supreme Chief during De la Huerta's absence.

261

THE LAST BLOODY PHASES OF THE REBELLION

While Zubaran Capmany and Antonio Manero also made their departures from the country, Aguilar was driving back federal forces which tried by land to reach the rebel stronghold. But he was faced with a difficult task. De la Huerta's departure gave the Navy (unable to secure the coal it needed) an excuse to surrender to the federal government, and this allowed the Obregonistas to disembark troops at Sisal, on the Yucatán Peninsula.

Aguilar's problems were complicated when De la Huerta had a meeting in New York with Salvador Alvarado. General Alvarado, after his defeat at Ocotlán, had managed to escape from Mexican soil via Acapulco or Manzanillo, and he was in Vancouver, Canada, when he received the call to come to New York. In New York De la Huerta named Alvarado to be Interim Supreme Chief and he gave him a written appointment which was dated Frontera, Tabasco, March 10, 1924, one day earlier than the Aguilar appointment. (De la Huerta hoped to resolve the resulting complication by asking Aguilar to join him in invading Sonora from the United States.) Alvarado, once the big man of the southeast, managed to leave for Frontera by hiding in the boiler room of the S.S. *Stavangeren* when it left New Orleans. Upon reaching Frontera he immediately carried on in an active fashion as in supreme command.

It can be said to the credit of Alvarado and Aguilar that after a period of misunderstanding, in which their respective followers did not help things, they came to an agreement by which Alvarado took over Tabasco and Chiapas and Aguilar took over Yucatán and Campeche.

The federal government, following the plans of Obregón and War Minister Serrano, was by this time sending more and more well-armed troops against its foes. Eugenio Martínez added to his many laurels by driving the rebels from Yucatán and Campeche, while Vicente González in Tabasco got his revenge at Frontera and Villahermosa for the defeat he had suffered early in the course of the rebellion. Aguilar and Alvarado sought to meet in Chiapas.

For Cándido Aguilar the overland march from Campeche to Chiapas was horrible. Soldiers collapsed and the leader was weakened by exhaustion and fever. For Salvador Alvarado the march was even worse. One of his men, on orders from General Federico Aparicio, tried to take him prisoner; in the scuffle Alvarado was killed.

Aguilar collapsed in a sanatorium in Guatemala after fleeing there with Lic. Rodulfo Brito Foucher, the rebel government's acting director of Gobernación and Foreign Relations. When Aguilar reached San Antonio, Texas, some months later, he was jailed for violating the neutrality laws.

Making his Tabasco revenge fully complete, Vicente González captured the last rebel troops under Fernando Segovia and the two Greene brothers, and he had these three generals shot. The capture of Carlos and Alejandro Greene, who hid in the Chontalpa Mountains instead of fleeing from the country, did not take place until December, 1924, and was carried out by Federico Aparicio of Vicente González' staff. Thus Segovia and the Greene brothers shared the fate of Generals Diéguez, Maycotte, García Vigil, Alvarado, Buelna, Ché Gómez, Benito Torruco, Manuel Chao, and many others.

The number killed in the country on both sides, as a result of the rebellion, was estimated at seven thousand. But the slaughter did not result in fewer generals for the nation. Fifty-four officers were promoted to generalships by President Obregón. Ing. Pani, who drew from Obregón much praise for his contribution in the realm of finances, stated that the rebellion cost the government not less than 70 million pesos, including the loss of tax revenue.

With Vicente González' victories and the shooting of the Greene brothers, thirty-four–year–old Tomás Garrido Canabal was able to resume his constitutional governorship of Tabasco, a four-year term which began on January 1, 1923, when he was declared by Obregón and Calles to be the victor over his cousin, General J. D. Ramírez Garrido. Garrido Canabal, who for much time to come was to be a completely despotic ruler of Tabasco's destinies, came from a family which for years had been the wealthy owner of important haciendas in Tabasco and Chiapas. In Yucatán in 1915 he had become friendly with Salvador Alvarado and acquainted with the philosophy and methods of this socialist; later in Tabasco he served under Governor Carlos Greene and assumed the interim governorship on short occasions when Greene was having troubles with Carranza or others in Mexico City. A staunch supporter of Obregón and Calles, Garrido Canabal became leader of the Liga Central de Resistencia del Partido Socialista Radical, did much organizing of labor and youth, and was to become renowned for his opposition to alcoholic beverages and to the worship of God.

Don Adolfo de la Huerta's efforts to help his cause from the United States were entirely ineffective. Senator Burson of New Mexico advised him that if he were to make calls on officials in Washington he might very well, on account of his illegal entry into the country, be apprehended and deported to Mexico. After being advised to hide, he went furtively from New York to Phoenix, Arizona, but there he had no success in organizing an expedition for the invasion of Sonora. It was a poor time to make such an attempt, as thousands of Mexican federal troops were ready to receive the would-be invaders.

Differences developed between some of the rebel leaders who were now in the United States. In New York Zubaran Capmany, heading a group which sought to reorganize the "Revolution" and direct its politics, endeavored to impart to the "Revolution" an impersonal character. He was acrimoniously attacked in Delahuertista sheets which appeared in the west of the United States. After he and Antonio Manero were accused of selling the files of the "Revolution" to the Obregón Government, Zubaran advised De la Huerta that he was separating himself completely from the movement "which some wish to convert into Delahuertismo." De la Huerta settled down to spend a long period giving vocal training in California, and among his many pupils were a number of outstanding artists.

Not unknown to American readers of Mexican history is Vasconcelos' story of the fate of Lic. Ramón Treviño, captured by the War Ministry after taking part in the De la Huerta rebellion. When the young lawyer pointed out that he was not a military man and so could not be condemned to death, War Minister Serrano resolved the problem by issuing an appointment, which was made known to the newspapers: "Today Licenciado Ramón Treviño is given the rank of general of the Army." Another order was attached: "Shoot General and Licenciado Ramón Treviño."[7]

[7] José Vasconcelos, *El desastre*, pp. 273–274, with modification based on information supplied in 1958 by S. M. Zambrano and Virgilio Garza, Jr.

30·

Obregón Finishes His Term

With the rebellion extinguished a less agitated contest for the presidency ensued: the electoral campaign of 1924. At the end of March Calles announced the termination of his military commission and the renewal of his campaign for votes, and early in April he went to the city of Zacatecas to attend the convention of the Partido Laborista Mexicano. On his campaign tour Calles was in the company of advisers who at times included Carlos Riva Palacio, Luis L. León, J. M. Puig Casauranc, Luis N. Morones, Ezequiel Padilla, Romeo Ortega, and Rafael Martínez de Escobar.

The general from Sinaloa, Angel Flores, who had been quiet during the De la Huerta rebellion, remained as an opponent. Now Flores received such attacks as he might have expected, being called the "standard-bearer of obdurate reaction" and "a deserter of the Revolution." León, who gave particular attention to agrarian matters, sought to show that Flores' record revealed a lack of enthusiasm for the redistribution of land to the *ejidos*. Vasconcelos criticized Flores' candidacy because, he said, it legalized the position of Calles.

The elections took place as scheduled on the first Sunday in July. On September 27 the Chamber of Deputies declared that Calles was to be the next Constitutional President of the Republic, having received 1,340, 634 votes to 250,500 for Flores.

The President-elect did not await this official pronouncement before setting forth in August on a trip to Europe and the United States. In Germany he was welcomed by Ing. Pascual Ortiz Rubio and received by President Elbert. In Paris Prime Minister Herriot conferred attentions on the Mexican general and on his companions, J. M. Puig Casauranc, Arturo M. Elías, and Gilberto Valenzuela. Late in October the Calles party reached the United States. There the functions included a reception in New York, where Calles was greeted by Mayor Hylan, and a stroll in Washington on the White House lawn with President Coolidge.

When the President-elect reached Mexico City in November, Obregón was among the vast throng of friends and supporters who were on hand to meet him.

With the renewal of diplomatic relations between Mexico and the United States on August 31, 1923, George T. Summerlin carried on as the United States representative in charge of affairs in Mexico. This he did until March 31, 1924, when Ambassador Charles Beecher Warren was received by President Obregón and his Cabinet. In October, 1924, Ambassador Warren was succeeded by Ambassador James R. Sheffield.

But during all this period the relations between Mexico and Great Britain were poor. His Britannic Majesty's chargé d'affaires, Mr. H. A. C. Cummins, struggled to protect the interests of British citizens in Revolutionary Mexico. When Obregón, during the De la Huerta rebellion, ordered the requisition of all available horses Mr. Cummins reminded General Sáenz that by the treaty of 1888 British subjects in Mexico (like Mexican subjects in British territory) were exempted from all requisitions of such a nature.

Cummins ran into his greatest difficulty in seeking to help Mrs. Rosalie Evans, American-born widow of a Britisher. During the

Carranza regime she had been asked why it would not be proper to transfer to Indians her hacienda in Puebla, which she and her late husband had happily brought into great productivity. She early let it be known that she was resolved to use every means possible to resist this idea, and she wrote that "Carranza, the old hypocrite, and Cabrera simply sit at home in great luxury and think of laws to rob the people." For a while she considered Cabrera to be her great enemy, but her troubles became more pronounced under the presidency of Obregón, whom she considered "a brute" and to his face accused of deliberately inciting his people to rob her—a woman and a foreigner in his country.

In her determined struggle Mrs. Evans saw much of Ambassador Warren and more of Mr. Cummins. The latter came to feel that land had been promised to agrarians who joined in the efforts to put down the rebellion of 1923–1924, and he noted that far more Mexican properties than those of foreigners were being taken.

Unwilling to yield all that was dear to her in return for the "promise" of "worthless" bonds, Mrs. Evans kept working at producing and selling crops of wheat, and at the same time she engaged in efforts which included a press campaign, occasional exchanges of gunfire, and a number of interviews with people she did not admire. After a session with Pani, who was not favorably impressed at having to listen to Mrs. Evans' defiant words while her dogs glared at him, she described him as "the false one" and "the only one of the new government who attempts society—the diplomats and Baroness X being his friends."

Obregón at length signed orders turning the land over to the villages and General Almazán sent General Benigno Serratos to attend to the formal delivery. In view of these steps Mr. Cummins made an unsuccessful attempt to persuade Mrs. Evans to leave the scene of danger.

The Mexican government advised the British government that it could not tolerate the "insolent attitude of Mr. Cummins, who frustrates all understanding because of his failure to observe a proper attitude in dealing with Mexican authorities," and it cited in particular Mr. Cummins' letter of May 3 to Foreign Minister Sáenz on behalf of Mrs. Evans. In this, one of many letters that Mr. Cummins wrote expressing the deep concern of His Majesty's government about the case, he said: "This whole matter is incredible to His Majesty's government, and the more so to me, in view of the proofs I have had in the past that General Obregón would defend and help a woman, and not set armed and dangerous men against her in a district where already several landlords have been cruelly murdered."

At the request of the Mexican government, the British government had to recall Mr. Cummins, and the United States government agreed to extend appropriate good offices with regard to British interests in Mexico. Ambassador Warren, whom Mrs. Evans described as having "signed a treaty which is a disgrace" and whom she did not consider helpful, spoke of Claims Commissions and hinted of conditions to come that would be more satisfactory to her.

This whole episode, so damaging to the establishment of formal diplomatic relations between Great Britain and the Obregón Administration, ended in tragedy. On August 2, 1924, while riding in a mule-drawn buggy to her hacienda with the payroll, Mrs. Evans was shot at and killed.[1]

Following the resignation of Education Minister José Vasconcelos in July, 1924, President Obregón's Cabinet included the following:

Minister of Gobernación
    Lic. Enrique Colunga
Minister of Finance and Public Credit
    Ing. Alberto J. Pani
Minister of Foreign Relations
    General Aarón Sáenz
Minister of Communications and Public Works
    General Amado Aguirre
Minister of War and Navy
    General Francisco Serrano
Minister of Agriculture
    Sr. Ramón P. de Negri
Minister of Industry, Commerce, and Labor
    General Manuel Pérez Treviño
Minister of Public Education
    Dr. Bernardo J. Gastélum

The President delivered his September 1, 1924, message to Congress under less tense circumstances than had prevailed a year earlier, but that did not mean that the Chamber of Deputies was

[1] See Rosalie Evans and Daisy Caden Pettus, *The Rosalie Evans Letters from Mexico*, pp. 125–185 and 435–457.

not good for scenes of turmoil. At a session in November, after Díaz Soto y Gama had been pointing out that all good Revolutionaries should have economic conditions which they could justify, General José María Sánchez arose and referred to some charges which Diputado Morones had recently made when speaking at the Iris Theatre. When the General objected to Morones' having made accusations behind his back rather than in a straightforward manner, Morones cried: "I am more of a man than you. You are a coward." In the confusion which followed, the presiding officer, Lic. Romeo Ortega, withdrew and his place was taken by Colonel Filiberto Gómez, whose use of the bell was ineffective. While Morones and Sánchez were shouting at each other amidst a general clamor, another *diputado* started shooting and Morones was wounded. (Morones maintains that members of the opposition were seeking an opportunity to assassinate him.[2])

As the Obregón administration drew to its close it issued an *oficio* from the Presidency to Carranza's daughter, Julia. This advised that, as "Venustiano Carranza gave eminent services to the Revolution and to the nation," pensions were to be paid by the Treasury to Julia and her brothers. In reply to this piece of news Carranza's children addressed a letter to the President stating that, although they were not yet of age, they were old enough to appreciate their duty. Rejecting the pension, they suggested that Obregón might better use it for traitors like Hermilo Herrero. Obregón, who in the letter was accused of having ordered Carranza's assassination, was told that not all the gold he could produce, nor all of his blood, would be enough to pay for one drop of Carranza's blood. The letter was signed "Your loyal enemies, Julia, Emilio, Venustiano, and Jesús Carranza."

Plutarco Elías Calles, who in 1920 had declared that the Carranza Administration was "the most corrupt in the annals of the Mexican government," was forty-seven years old when he received the Presidency of the Mexican Republic from Alvaro Obregón. For the inauguration the Congress installed itself on November 30, 1924, in the National Stadium, which Vasconcelos had recently completed, and so the ceremonies were effected before the largest crowd that had ever gathered in Mexico for such an occasion. Among the 30,000 participants and spectators who saw Calles raise his right arm and make the solemn pledge was the United States

[2] Luis N. Morones, interview, January 30, 1957.

labor leader, Samuel Gompers, who had come to Mexico to participate in the festivities.

The members of Congress were very formally attired, most of them wearing top hats. Color was added to the occasion by the presence of Army officers, including a group of such notable *generales de división* as Juan Andreu Almazán, Miguel Acosta, J. Gonzalo Escobar, Joaquín Amaro, Eugenio Martínez, Arnulfo R. Gómez, and Luis Gutiérrez. During the inauguration ceremonies Cabinet appointments were handed out by Romeo Ortega, and later the favored individuals made their way from the stadium to the Palacio Nacional in ornate horse-drawn open carriages. These were the appointments:

Undersecretary in Charge of Gobernación
    Lic. Romeo Ortega
Minister of Finance and Public Credit
    Ing. Alberto J. Pani
Minister of Foreign Relations
    Lic. Aarón Sáenz
Minister of Communications and Public Works
    Colonel Adalberto Tejeda
Undersecretary in Charge of War and Navy
    General Joaquín Amaro
Minister of Agriculture and Development
    Ing. Luis L. León
Minister of Industry, Commerce, and Labor
    Sr. Luis N. Morones
Minister of Public Education
    Dr. J. M. Puig Casauranc

Fernando Torreblanca, who in August, 1922, had married a daughter of Calles, continued in his position of presidential secretary. Ramón Ross, Obregón's old friend who had represented Mexico at the Bucareli Conferences, became governor of the Federal District; General Celestino Gasca succeeded Morones as head of the Military Manufacturing Establishments.

General Calles came to be regarded as having a great deal of executive ability, but it is to be doubted that his technique conformed entirely with the practices of "communication" currently recommended at the Harvard School of Business Administration. To some of his subordinates he displayed at times a tendency to act in an imperative manner, giving orders without giving reasons and requiring that the orders be carried out without discussion. While some who have served under him have pointed out that few cared to argue with him, there can be no doubt that a number of those in the group he favored would disagree with this point.

In the course of demonstrating that Calles was never a Communist, Dr. Puig recalls that during a conversation which he and Lic. Portes Gil had with him in 1923 Calles said that he felt anticapitalist "whenever capitalism obstructs the betterment of the proletariat." Puig commented, "which seems to happen in 80 per cent of the cases," whereupon Calles added dryly, "at least."[3]

[3] J. M. Puig Casauranc, *El sentido social del proceso histórico de México,* p. 178.

31·

Luis N. Morones
and Organized Labor

On the occasion of the transfer of the presidential power Obregón and Calles were riding together in an official car. "Who was that?" asked Obregón when Calles greeted an enthusiastic observer. Calles replied that it was General Francisco J. Múgica, the man whom Obregón had sought to have found and killed.

With this ending of his days of hiding—hiding particularly from Arnulfo Gómez and his men—General Múgica opened up a business office in partnership with Lic. Luis Cabrera. The General was asked to represent the interests of some Mexican oil-property owners who felt themselves to be defrauded of royalties due from a

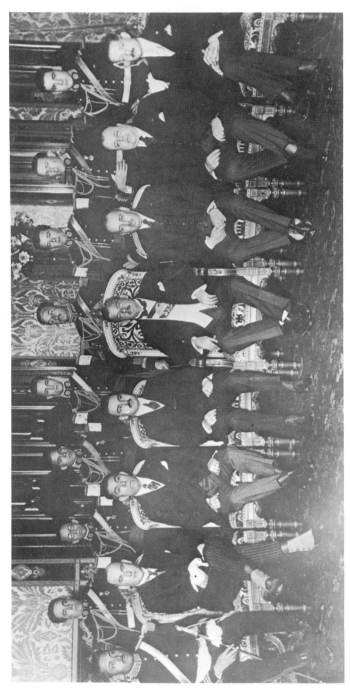

President Calles and his Cabinet. Seated: General Joaquín Amaro (War and Navy), Dr. J. M. Puig Casauranc (Public Education), Ing. Luis L. León (Agriculture and Development), General and Lic. Aarón Sáenz (Foreign Affairs), President Plutarco Elías Calles, Ing. Alberto J. Pani (Finance and Public Credit), Sr. Luis N. Morones (Industry, Commerce, and Labor), Lic. Romeo Ortega (Gobernación). Enrique Díaz.

large company, and when he won the case and collected 50,000 pesos in fees he was able to put behind him the economic difficulties which in hiding he had been experiencing. The petroleum matter took Múgica to the Tuxpan district, where Lázaro Cárdenas was in charge of Military Operations. Múgica subsequently spent two years in this area in the companionship of Cárdenas, and these two friends from Michoacán had considerable opportunity to discuss social problems and to make themselves more familiar with petroleum activities.

The new Cabinet included supporters of Obregón, such as Pani and Sáenz, but it included also one man who was now hardly on warm terms with the ex-President—Luis N. Morones. While some of his unfriendly contemporaries pointed out that Morones was "not a man of culture," it is nevertheless true that of the Cabinet group none was closer to the President. Morones was likely to be present at the poker or baccarat sessions which took place at the Sonora-Sinaloa Club or at the President's home, and Calles frequently attended the great and gaudy parties at Morones' house at Tlalpam. At the age of thirty-five Morones, with the exception of the President, was the most powerful man in Mexico.

The story of Morones' rise is intimately linked with the story of the blossoming of labor organization in Mexico; however, so many had so much to do with that blossoming that it would be highly inaccurate to consider the story of Morones more than a part of the larger story—a story which was full of heroes, many of whom had a difficult time on account of their advanced ideas.

As an electrical worker with the Mexican Light and Power Company and later with the Mexican Telephone Company, Morones devoted much effort to organizing workers and spent much time at the Casa del Obrero Mundial (House of the World Worker), which had been established in Mexico City in 1912. His participation in utility strikes at a time when Carranza was having serious international difficulties brought Morones imprisonment in a military jail. Later he spent some time at Pachuca, Hidalgo.

During the latter part of the Carranza regime Morones became the leader of a movement in which he was associated with such men as Ricardo Treviño, Ezequiel Salcedo, Celestino Gasca. Samuel O. Yúdico, and José López Cortés. There were a few organized strikes, but the strike leaders were handicapped by a lack of sympathy from the Carranza Government. Early in 1918 Morones organized within the Casa del Obrero Mundial a small, informal, but powerful group known as the Grupo Acción. Originally it consisted only of Morones, Ezequiel Salcedo, and one other, but later it came to include such labor organizers as Ricardo Treviño, Salvador Alvarez, and Eduardo Moneda.

On May 1, 1918, labor movement representatives from all the states gathered at Salt'llo, Coahuila, for a National Labor Congress. Mindful of the recent struggles in the United States, the congress expressed its sympathy for the International Workers of the World; it also called on the federal government to parcel the large Mexican landholdings. More important, it created the Confederación Regional Obrera Mexicana (C.R.O.M.) to be a confederation of labor unions, and it elected the following to run the C.R.O.M.'s Central Committee for one year: Luis N. Morones, Ricardo Treviño, and J. Marcos Tristán. The exclusive Grupo Acción, which was for years to consist of about twenty well-disciplined leaders, was strengthened.

In November, 1918, Morones and his associates met at Nuevo Laredo, Tamaulipas, with Samuel Gompers and other leaders of the American Federation of Labor. Labor representatives from other nations of the hemisphere were also present, and there was born the Pan-American Federation of Labor with Gompers as president and Morones as vice-president. The more Communistic labor elements in Mexico were critical of this association. Morones then made a tour of Europe, returning in time to appear in the city of Zacatecas in June, 1919, for the First Annual C.R.O.M. Convention. Among the fifty-odd delegates at Zacatecas a few attacked the C.R.O.M.'s Central Committee, but they were outvoted. They heard it reported that in the year ending June, 1919, C.R.O.M. membership had increased from 40,000 to 70,000.

A Congreso Socialista meeting in September, 1919, was torn by dissension. Present were not only representatives of the Partido Socialista Obrero, which Morones had organized in 1917 but which had not been notably successful, but also well-known leftists such as José Allen, Frank Seaman, Manabrenda Nath Roy (a Hindu), and Linn A. Gale (of the United States). The desire of the assembly to establish a political party of the proletariat was frustrated because of the divergent tendencies among the delegates. Some wanted to see the creation of a Communist Party associated with the International Communist Movement, while others like

Morones and Yúdico had very different ideas. The result was that after the Congreso Socialista broke up two political parties came into existence, the first of these being the Partido Comunista de México, which was established by José Allen and his friends in that same month of September, 1919.

The Grupo Acción sounded out Mexican labor organizations and concluded that 75 per cent of them supported the idea of forming a Partido Laborista Mexicano. Then on December 21, 1919, more than seventy leaders associated with the C.R.O.M. met in Mexico City at the invitation of Eduardo Moneda to bring the party into being. After Morones and Celestino Gasca spoke of the need of worker participation in politics to bring about much needed revolutionary achievements, the group decided that the Partido Socialista Mexicano should consist exclusively of workers, with no professional politicians. An organizing committee was formed.

Under the slogan of "For Justice and Democracy" and in opposition to the presidential candidacy of Ing. Bonillas, the Partido Laborista leaders sought a favorable place for their first convention. The answer came when someone suggested Zacatecas, "where General Enrique Estrada is both the state governor and an Obregonista." Among the forty-four who met at the Calderón Theatre in Zacatecas City early in March, 1920, were not only Morones and his fellow labor leaders but also General J. D. Ramírez Garrido, General Jesús M. Garza, General Francisco R. Serrano, Lic. Emilio Portes Gil, and Felipe Carrillo Puerto. Needless to say considerable opposition to Carranza's efforts to "impose" Ignacio Bonillas as the nation's next President was expressed. Shortly after this first convention of the party Morones participated in Obregón's April, 1920, escape from Mexico City. But in spite of his association with Obregón, Morones in his political speeches made it clear that his backing of Obregón would turn to attack should the candidate ever be unfaithful to the propositions of the Partido Laborista.

By the time the C.R.O.M. held its second annual convention in Aguascalientes at the start of July, 1920, Carranza was dead and De la Huerta was President of Mexico. Great days appeared to be ahead for the labor movement—provided it did not flounder through internal strife. Some at Aguascalientes claimed that Yúdico and Ricardo Treviño were admitted without the proper credentials and that others, whose credentials were in order, were unable to attend. Lic. Antonio Díaz Soto y Gama, as head of a "leftist" group, attacked the centralization of the C.R.O.M. directorship, warning of the dangers of a new caste, the aristocrat of labor. Since the Morones group was the more powerful Díaz Soto y Gama was ridiculed.

Rafael Quintero proposed that the convention send President De la Huerta a message, advising him to ignore the capitalists who objected to Celestino Gasca's appointment as governor of the Federal District. Morones suggested that such a message would be inadvisable because the C.R.O.M. should not participate in political matters but rather should "save the good name and prestige of the organized proletariat." Then exclaimed Quintero: "When Morones, the eternal politician, who has been doing his best to capture congressional seats, talks like this he reminds me of a monk lecturing against his religion." It was voted to send the proposed message to De la Huerta.[1]

When Obregón moved into the Castle of Chapultepec, Morones, Ezequiel Salcedo, and Eduardo Moneda joined Gasca in important government positions. The National Military Manufacturing Establishments, which Morones took over, consisted of eighteen factories producing rifles, ammunition, uniforms, and saddlery and making repairs for larger military pieces obtained from abroad.

Samuel Gompers and others reached Mexico City by train on January 9, 1921, to attend the third convention of the Pan-American Federation of Labor, which also received labor representatives from Mexico, Guatemala, El Salvador, Santo Domingo, Colombia, and Cuba. The meetings, at which the delegates were urged to have their various countries join the League of Nations, received considerable criticism from both Mexicans who were in attendance and Mexicans who were outside of the Pan-American Labor Congress. In *El Demócrata* Vito Alessio Robles pointed to the absence of representation by important South American nations, adding that "in order to obtain the union of the continental proletariat, it is necessary to liberate the Spanish-American people from the American tutelage."

The Mexican delegates got into a dispute among themselves and some of them criticized the parliamentary regulations which governed the right of those present to be heard. Carlos L. Gracidas sought to support Section VI of Article 123 of the Mexican Constitution, which provides that workers shall participate in the earnings of the companies which employ them. Morones argued in favor of a

[1] Rosendo Salazar and José G. Escobedo, *Las pugnas de la gleba*, II, 74–75.

worker security law which Obregón was proposing and which placed on the companies a tax on wages paid as a substitute for worker participation in profits, the tax to provide various "social security" benefits. When Gracidas found himself unable to express his arguments in the convention he released a statement to the newspapers advising that the president of the Labor Congress and a majority of the delegations, including the Mexican, "committed a most reprehensible violation against my free expression. Delegate Morones defined as reactionary that part of the Mexican Constitution which has to do with the participation in earnings, a precept which some seek to change on account of their respect for the capitalists. In order to repel the affront of Morones, I now have recourse to only the Mexican tribune and not the Pan-American."[2]

The rival to the C.R.O.M. was born during the next month, February, 1921. It was called the Confederación General de Trabajadores (General Confederation of Workers—C.G.T.) and grew out of the Convención Radical Roja. This convention declared the true conquests to be those of "anarchical communism" and it called for an end of the "moral and material control exercised over proletarian centers by the directors of the Confederación Regional Obrera Mexicana." The Partido Laborista was criticized for similarity to the British Labor Party, and the C.R.O.M. was censured for associating with the A.F. of L. "Let us show our common opponents how to establish a Confederation free of unworthy tutelages."

Not long after this some of the organizers of the C.G.T. felt the strong hand of the government. With the implantation of the red-and-black flag on the rostrum in the Chamber of Deputies, the Partido Liberal Constitucionalista complained against the Laborista and Agrarista Parties. But after the incident had been studied by the Attorney General's staff eight or nine American and European agitators were thrown out of the country. The C.G.T. pointed out that these foreigners had nothing to do with the flag incident and were all members of the C.G.T.

The C.G.T. held its first convention in September, 1921, and named a number of directors, including the leader of the Mexico City Streetcar Workers. The new organization went on record as believing that "the governments of the world are the instruments of capitalism . . . ; consequently the persecutions and the acts in restraint of liberty which are brought about by Mexico's rulers will be

[2] *Ibid.*, II, 89–90.

considered as arbitrary aggressions on the part of the exploiting and parasitic class." A protest was made against the electrocution of Sacco and Vanzetti. Where labor conflicts might not work out in favor of the workers, the "industry in question" should be managed by a committee of workers. Lands and farm implements should be communized. Neither Obregón's worker security law nor the workers' participation in profits were considered to be good enough. Most of the C.G.T.'s strength came from laborers in the streetcar and textile industries.

On May 1, 1922, in accordance with one of the resolutions of the September convention, the C.G.T. carried out a demonstration by its Rentpayers' Union in Mexico City. The "greedy" landlords were advised: "I am on strike; I pay no rent." After stopping in front of the United States Embassy to condemn the "imperialistic government" of that nation and to demand the freedom of Ricardo Flores Magón and Librado Rivera, the mob turned to demonstrate against the Spanish government and king. Suddenly and unexpectedly it found itself in a fight with the newly-formed Catholic Association of Mexican Youths, led by René Capistrán Garza.

While the C.G.T. was having its troubles the C.R.O.M. was making rapid strides. Reports were issued to show that between 1920 and 1924 the membership in C.R.O.M.-affiliated unions grew from about 100,000 to over one million; but most of the one million were peasants, and only about ten thousand of the grand total paid any union dues.

As Obregón's term drew toward its close the Partido Laborista Mexicano was having disagreements with the President. Obregón denied political posts to some members of the party, some of these posts being the positions of labor attachés at Mexican embassies, appointments Morones very much wanted.[3] Nor is it likely that the Field Jurado assassination, with Obregón's subsequent letter to Morones, brought the letter's writer and recipient closer together.

When Calles took over the Presidency, Morones and Gasca were not the only builders of the C.R.O.M. to receive high posts. Eduardo Moneda, C.R.O.M. general secretary, took over the government Printing Shops, José López Cortés became general secretary of the Mexico City Council, and Ricardo Treviño, Gonzalo González, and Vicente Lombardo Toledano served as powerful members of the Chamber of Deputies.

[3] Vicente Fuentes Díaz, *Los partidos políticos en México*, II, 23.

Although Moscow may have been unfriendly to the C.R.O.M., Morones had enthusiastic admirers among writers in the United States and England. British scholars and labor leaders were especially warm in their praise. Dr. J. H. Retinger states that Morones campaigned against graft, and that he: "never permitted his would-be assassins to be prosecuted . . . He preferred to give the living example of his oft-stated desire that the habit of political vendettas should not be continued in his country." According to Dr. Retinger, Obregón's victory over the De la Huerta rebellion was due mainly to the efforts of Morones and the Partido Laborista. He declares Morones to be more responsible than any other individual for the advance in Mexico's social life and calls him "the greatest moral leader of his country and the object of hero worship of multitudes of his fellow countrymen."[4]

Other Englishmen who chose to enlighten the world as to the Mexican scene were J. W. Brown, secretary of the International Federation of Trades Unions, and George Hicks, chairman of the British Trades Union Congress. After studying the work being done to drive back "the forces of ignorance and superstition," Hicks reached the conclusion that "Luis Morones . . . will surely rank in Mexican history with Benito Juárez."[5]

[4] J. H. Retinger, *Morones of Mexico*, quotation from the Foreword.
[5] George Hicks writing in J. W. Brown's *Modern Mexico and Its Problems*, p. 15.

32.

Government Finances during the Golden Days of President Calles

The Japanese government had a high regard for the military genius of Alvaro Obregón; it therefore conferred a decoration on him, as it did also on Marshalls Joffre and Foch. The Japanese minister to Mexico, a warm admirer of the Hero of Celaya, finding himself scheduled to leave for other lands shortly after Calles took over the Presidency, did not wish to make his departure without paying his respects to Obregón. He therefore set out for Sonora, where Obregón, who had again settled down to the business of farming, had been in the fields for three months (making his home in a tent). Obregón was wearing an enormous beard, a worn-out khaki uniform badly affected by the mesquite bushes, kid-skin sandals, and a broad-brimmed palm hat.

The very correct Japanese diplomat had a difficult time reaching the place, and when he found the ex-President he was taken aback by his appearance.

"Your Excellency," he said, "it was hard for me to recognize you, because you are masquerading."

"No, your Excellency," replied Obregón, "I am not masquerading. This is my normal condition. The Obregón who was masquerading was the one whom you saw before in the Palacio Nacional."[1]

Obregón, who in 1925 received from Agriculture Minister León a prize and public recognition for what he did to produce corn, was not the only one to take advantage of an interval of peace to give attention to agricultural matters. Some of the important generals in the Army, although they had not followed Obregón's example of retiring to private life, became at this time the owners of large land properties.

Men in the government found that they could, if they wished, take some part in the opportunities offered by the new age which they or their companions helped to create. Wits were to state that C.R.O.M. stood for "Como Robó Oro Morones" (How Morones Stole Gold), a slogan to which they were perhaps prompted by the extravagant revelry at Morones' weekend parties and his ostentatious display of automobiles and diamonds. Another who had a fondness for displaying large diamonds was Felipe Pescador, who had built up a reputation as Director of the Railways under Carranza. Ing. Pani's humorous idea of introducing five-and-ten-cent–store glass imitations somewhat backfired when the quality of his "gifts" was not understood.

Finance Minister Pani found in Calles an enthusiastic new chief— especially enthusiastic about irrigation and road construction, and the establishment of the long postponed Bank of Currency Issue. In one of the first statements which Calles, as President, gave to the press, he said: "All the efforts of the new Administration will be directed, ahead of anything else, to balancing the budget. It is imperative that the nation get used to living on its own resources without resorting to help from abroad."

[1] Carlos Barrera, *Obregón*, pp. 78–79.

Thus the first of four financial objectives was the obtaining of federal revenues in excess of expenditures so as to wipe out the cumulative federal deficit which by the end of 1923 amounted to over 58,600,000 pesos. Although in 1924 Army expenses were high, a little headway was made by means of reducing other expenses, instituting new sources of taxation, and the suspension of foreign-debt service payments. By the end of 1924 the cumulative deficit had been reduced to 40,800,000 pesos. The year 1925, a period of peace and excellent business activity, was a glorious one for Pani, and when it came to an end the cumulative deficit of the Mexican government had been entirely wiped out in spite of sizable disbursements called for by the program of the new regime.

The second financial objective was the reorganization of the fiscal methods which over the years had deteriorated into a condition approaching anarchy. The old system of taxation, which gave so much autonomy to the states that there was a lack of co-ordination, was revised to give more control to the central government. Classifications were reformed. But what created the greatest commotion was the firm establishment of income taxes on a permanent basis.

It cannot be said that the Calles Government was the first in Mexico to set up income taxes, because there was in 1921 a one-payment transitory income tax (the "Centenario" Law of 1921) calling for payments of from 1 per cent to 4 per cent on August, 1921, incomes, to be applied to port improvements and the acquisition of ships for the National Merchant Marine. Nor can it be said that the Calles Government first established a permanent income tax, for this was done in February, 1924. The 1924 law, taxing at rates spreading from 1 per cent to 4 per cent, ushered in a period of experimentation and further study. It was followed by the carefully drawn law of March, 1925, a law which provoked energetic protests and which, as originally issued, generally stipulated rates between 2 per cent and 8 per cent for companies engaged in industry and commerce, and between 1 per cent and 4 per cent on salaries.[2] Income taxes, considered by some to be more compatible with the precepts of the Revolution than taxes placed on transactions and on articles for sale, yielded about 13,500,000 pesos in the first six months of 1926, not yet enough to make much progress in the abolishment of numerous stamps called for by the Stamp Tax.

[2] See Secretaría de Hacienda y Crédito Público, *Compilación de leyes del impuesto sobre la renta (1921–1953)*.

The 1925 income tax law was modified from time to time but remained in force until replaced by the law of December 31, 1941.

The Calles Administration's third financial objective was the establishment of a banking system capable of stimulating economic activities. Besides liquidating a few of the twenty-five old banks of issue and helping others of them in their transformation, the government called a National Banking Convention in order to get advice. In January, 1926, was established the National Banking Commission, which included representatives of agriculture, commerce, and industry, to inspect banks and make sure that deposits were protected by good quality loans with at least 33 per cent in metallic reserves. In the short period between January 1, 1926, and August 31, 1926, the deposits in banks rose to over 185,500,000 pesos, an increase of 220 per cent; and the number of these institutions increased from 124 to 185.

A more spectacular phase of the third financial objective was the creation of the great credit institutions to which the government subscribed large sums in return for stock.

In 1925 the Mexican government contributed to the sole bank of issue, which was named the Bank of Mexico, 55,734,500 pesos in return for most of the shares. The International Bankers Committee objected strenuously to the founding of the bank, which it considered to be at the expense of foreign-debt service payments, and through the State Department in August it warned that with such a step the bondholders would "consider faith irrevocably broken and the government finally in default." Nevertheless on August 31, 1925, the inauguration of the Bank of Mexico took place at its provisional home, the main office of the Banco de Londres y México, Pani explaining that the bank was a national need that could not be deferred and that its existence would facilitate the resumption of payments to foreign bondholders.

The inauguration ceremonies included the presentation of the bank's first five-peso banknote to Calles and a certain amount of speechmaking. After the bank's director, Alberto Mascareñas, had finished his address he remarked that were it not a state institution it might appropriately be called the Banco Amaro, as its existence was principally due to economies which had been undertaken in General Joaquín Amaro's War Ministry.

Lic. Manuel Gómez Morín was named chairman of the board of directors, a position which he retained until 1929. He had been

284

Undersecretary of Finance and Mexican fiscal agent in New York during the early days of the Obregón Administration, and in 1924 and 1925 was dean of the National University's Law School. He had been active in drafting the nation's new fiscal methods, including the income tax law, and was among those who had drawn up the statutes of the new bank. The Bank's capital was established at

Gold in the vault, used for the establishment of the Bank of Mexico. President Calles, Finance Minister Pani, and (further to the right) Lorenzo Hernández, Treasurer of the Nation. Early August, 1925. Casasola.

100 million pesos, of which the federal government was to own 51 per cent. After the inauguration, minority shares were purchased by various nongovernment banks.

The Bank of Mexico was authorized to issue notes not to exceed twice the value of its gold and equivalent after deduction of the metallic guarantee of the deposits. These new banknotes were guaranteed by the federal government, were to be acceptable for payments to the federal and local governments, and were to be at any time redeemable in gold by the Bank. As a substitute for coin they were at first accepted only slowly by the public and by August, 1926, only about 3,300,000 pesos were outstanding in banknotes. Other functions of the Bank were to regulate monetary circulation, foreign exchange, and rates of interest; to engage in rediscount operations with other banks; to handle the Treasury's banking operations; and even to engage in operations usual for ordinary banks of deposit.

The Revolutionary program of land redistribution was going forward at a rate more than twice that realized under President Obregón, but the new landholdings which were being created would be unproductive unless agricultural credits were available. To handle this matter the Banco Nacional de Crédito Agrícola was created in 1926, with funds from the federal government, local governments, regional credit societies, and private sources. Although private capital was to have preference as to dividends, most of the funds for creating this bank came from the federal government, which put up 18 million pesos compared with about 2 million subscribed by the public and about 100,000 pesos furnished by some local governments. The Banco Nacional de Crédito Agrícola supplied funds to the local credit societies, which proceeded to make loans to be used for the acquisition of seeds and tools and for the construction of warehouses, dams, and canals.

The fourth and last of the financial objectives of the Calles regime was the "restoration of domestic and foreign credit of the Government by means of satisfying obligations."[3] In Mexico 5-percent ten-year gold bonds of the Caja de Préstamos para Obras de Irrigación y Fomento de la Agricultura, S.A. had been issued to the amount of 11.5 million pesos in connection with the arrangements for the expropriation of the Terrazas estates. Under Calles and Pani some of the Caja's properties were used to redeem part of the bond issue. "Bonds issued for Liquidating the Salaries of Federal Employees," amounting to 20 million pesos, were to a large extent bought in the market by the government at what Pani called "ridiculously low prices." The largest item in the domestic debt was made up of claims by the old banks of issue amounting to 150 million pesos. After a review of these claims, which resulted in the rejection of loans made by the banks to Victoriano Huerta, they were reduced to 76.5 million. A method of amortizing them was then agreed upon: cash and credits to be provided to the banks by the federal government over a number of years.

In the course of seeking a loan in the United States Pani in Sep-

[3] For a detailed account of the steps taken to attain the four objectives, see Alberto J. Pani's *La política hacendaria y la Revolución*.

tember, 1924, signed to get 50 million dollars at 6 per cent annual interest from J. L. Arlitt of Austin, Texas, but as Arlitt did not comply, the agreement was cancelled by Mexico. Nor did Pani have any success in New York in January, 1925, when he tried to borrow 60 million dollars. Both at the time he was there and in succeeding correspondence, Pani maintained that the De la Huerta-Lamont Agreement had been ratified by Mexico because of Don Adolfo's assertions that the Agreement would be quickly followed by a loan much needed for irrigation and for the creation of the bank of issue. He pointed out that the suspension in 1924 of the Agreement of June 16, 1922, had only followed the foreign bankers' refusal to make a fully guaranteed five-year loan of 20 million dollars—a refusal, said Pani, based on a report of the American Association of Petroleum Producers in Mexico "which revealed an absolute ignorance of our legislation and of our political way." Accordingly funds which in 1924 might have gone for foreign-debt service, were used for the discharge of troops and to help pay back salaries of government employees. The new prosperity was used to establish the Bank and to build roads and irrigation works. Then in September, 1925, Pani was ready to return to New York to discuss defaulted bonds, having stated that economies now made unnecessary the loans previously sought.

The trip to New York was rendered sensational because at the Waldorf-Astoria Pani was accused of violating the Mann Act, an occurrence which Pani blamed on a Delahuertista. The Mexican Chamber of Deputies became concerned about the scandal and Pani submitted his resignation, but Calles backed up his Finance Minister, asking if it would please the *diputados* to have "a Cabinet of eunuchs."

On October 23, 1925, the Pani-Lamont Amendment, modifying arrangements made by De la Huerta in 1922, was signed. By this amendment such of the National Railways' indebtedness as had not been guaranteed by the Mexican government prior to the De la Huerta-Lamont Agreement was removed from the Mexican government's responsibility. Thus Mexico's foreign debt, which had exceeded 1.5 billion gold pesos (including about 500,000,000 pesos of interest in arrears), was reduced to about 850 million gold pesos. Overdue interest on account of the Railway debt assumed by the Mexican government in 1922 was, under the new arrangement, to be paid off starting in 1928 by means of about 2.5 million dollars to be taken annually from the Railways' earnings. The Railways were to be returned to private management at the end of 1925 and their net earnings were to be sent each month, starting January 1, 1926, to the Bankers Committee to cover current interest on the Railway debt.

The arrangements of 1922 for non-Railway debt were modified. Mexico had paid 30 million gold pesos in 1923 but the minimum payments for 1924 and 1925 (35 and 40 million gold pesos respectively) were in arrears. This arrearage, plus 3 per cent interest thereon, was to be paid to the Bankers Committee over a period of eight years starting in 1928. As a gold peso was worth half a dollar, this meant 37,500,000 dollars plus 5,025,000 dollars during those eight years. For the current servicing of the Mexican debt there was to be applied not only all the petroleum export taxes, as agreed in 1922, but also 5 million dollars annually from the petroleum production taxes. However, the maximum payments to be made in 1926 and 1927 would be 12,193,000 dollars and 12,512,000 dollars respectively.

The 25-million-dollar face value of bonds issued in 1908 by the Caja de Préstamos para Obras de Irrigación y Fomento de la Agricultura, S.A. had been included among the Mexican government's obligations listed in 1922. Ahead of the government guarantee had been the bondholders' claims on properties of the Caja. Pani arranged to have all the Caja bonds turned in and exchanged for new bonds which were the direct obligation of the Mexican government but were not guaranteed by the properties of the Caja. Mexico agreed to pay $5,000,000 in Treasury Notes, which would become due at the rate of $50,000 monthly and which would be used by the New York Trust Company to purchase on the market the Caja bonds, or the new bonds replacing them, at prices not to exceed 56 per cent of the face value. The bonds so purchased would be cancelled.[4] Pani's maneuver of freeing the Caja's assets of their mortgage under the 1908 bond issue was very satisfactory for the Mexican government, which could as a result do what it liked with some of the best landholdings of the Republic. Agricultural schools were created, low-cost housing projects were started, and scientific societies were benefited.

Congressional debate on the Pani-Lamont Amendment took place during the latter part of December, 1925. In the House of Deputies Díaz Soto y Gama cast a lone vote against the Amendment. In the

[4] Secretaría de Hacienda y Crédito Público, *La deuda exterior de México*, pp. 18–61.

Senate the approval was unanimous, after Pani, with data supplied by Ing. León Salinas, replied to railroad questions brought up by Felipe Pescador.

The National Railways, which had been run by the government for eleven years, were turned over to a management representing the owning company. In an effort to reorganize and improve, technical commissions were set up as stipulated in the Pani-Lamont Amendment.

All in all, the Calles Administration was starting out with a spectacular display of initiative and success in the financial realm. The elimination of an inherited deficit in the federal books, the sound reorganization of tax legislation, the founding of the Bank of Mexico, and the re-establishment of Mexico's credit abroad, all achieved in 1925, did much for the prestige of the President and the nation.

33·

Efforts of the Calles Administration To Develop the Nation

Mexico in the mid-twenties was enjoying growth and material progress, and its government even came to be formally recognized by that of Great Britain. Among the heroes of the day were the bullfighters Rodolfo Gaona, one of the world's greatest until he retired in April, 1925, and Juan Silveti. known as "Fearless John" and "The Tiger of Guanajuato." Although the population of Mexico City had not quite reached one million inhabitants. it did not then embrace the various villages and colonies that have since been incorporated. Leading hotels included the Regis, the Geneve, the Imperial, the Guardiola, and the Princess. The tallest structure in the city remained the cathedral on the Zócalo.

The Palacio Nacional, once the residence of Spanish viceroys, housed the presidential offices and various executive sections, including the Finance and War ministries. Unlike the *diputados*, who had a building of their own dating from the era of Porfirio Díaz, the senators had their session hall and offices in the Palacio Nacional. Under the guidance of Pani this old palace was now enlarged and modernized, one of the principal changes being the addition of a third floor, built in such a way as to belie its lack of antiquity. The Treasury offices also received some badly needed remodeling.

When Calles took over the presidency the nation was practically without roads. Dr. Puig Casauranc pointed out that, with the exception of medium-class highways to Toluca and Puebla, almost nothing existed "except the old roads of the colonial period, which time and negligence had converted into ravines made by torrents."[1] To remedy this situation the Comisión Nacional de Caminos (National Road Commission) was established in 1925 to use the new gasoline tax revenue for road construction. At the start the gasoline tax, 3 centavos per liter, provided less than 400,000 pesos monthly and the executive branch of the government agreed to contribute enough to bring the amount up to one million pesos per month. Thus the Road Commission, under the direction of Ing. León Salinas, soon had about 10,000 men working on three important roads, and between August, 1925, and the end of 1927 it spent almost 23 million pesos.

In 1927 in Jalisco a very significant railway link was completed. The line of the Southern Pacific running southward from Nogales, Sonora, along the west coast was connected with Guadalajara and thus with the extensive National Railways of Mexico. At the same time great strides were being made in long-distance telephone communication. Not long after the inauguration of phone service between Mexico City and San Luis Potosí, President Calles was able to speak by phone with the Tamaulipas governor, Lic. Emilio Portes Gil, and in the months that followed, Mexico City was connected by phone with the United States, Cuba, and Canada.

[1] J. M. Puig Casauranc, *El sentido social del proceso histórico de México,* p. 186.

During the first three years of the Calles administration 2,600,000 hectares of land were redistributed under the agrarian program, an amount double that parcelled during Obregón's four years. While this was going on Agriculture Minister León noted early that production from *ejido* lands was below what had been hoped and that in many cases these lands had simply remained idle. Critics of the agrarian policy called attention to Mexico's low productivity of wheat and maize per hectare in comparison with that of other countries and they editorialized about a decrease in the production from Mexican farms. To remedy the situation the Administration extended credits, revised the organization of the *ejidos*, pressed for increased irrigation, and established agricultural schools.

By March, 1928, the Banco Nacional de Crédito Agrícola had loaned all that it possibly could, although it was, quite naturally, besieged by additional requests for funds. Puig Casauranc not only lamented that more credits could not be made available, but he came to feel that too many of the loans went to medium and large properties. He became critical of "unjustified loans to men of the Revolution, who were becoming holders of great estates."[2]

Addressing the Chamber of Deputies in September, 1925, Luis León stressed that the intended communal or collectivistic administration of *ejido* lands, called for by a National Agrarian Commission circular in October, 1922, was seldom the actual practice. Persons who took leading roles in so-called communal administrations often proved to be factors detrimental to production.[3] On Calles' instructions Ing. Marte R. Gómez and Lic. Emilio Portes Gil (who considered the old agrarian law of Lic. Narciso Bassols to be "frankly anti-Revolutionary" in its tendencies) drafted new legislation which Portes Gil took personally to the Ministry of Agriculture. On December 19, 1925, the Law of *Ejido* Patrimony was enacted. It revised the organization of authorities that were to watch over the *ejido* villages, and provided that, except for certain zones to be commonly used, the *ejido* lands should be divided into lots to be parcelled out to the individual *ejidatarios*. This was a big change.

The Comisión Nacional de Irrigación was created in 1925 to handle irrigation works. After Diputado Díaz Soto y Gama was suc-

---

[2] *Ibid.*, pp. 188–189.
[3] Eyler N. Simpson, *The Ejido, Mexico's Way Out*, pp. 318–322.

cessful in his steps to eliminate from the Comisión any representative of the Finance Ministry, it was fully directed by the Ministry of Agriculture. Calles hoped to provide irrigation for half a million hectares between 1924 and 1928, thus duplicating everything that had been done in this realm in all of Mexico's history up until 1924. In the case of this goal his Administration's achievement came close to 50 per cent.[4] Through December, 1927, the government spent over 15 million pesos on irrigation works, the most important of which were the Calles Dam in Aguascalientes and the Don Martín Dam in Coahuila and Nuevo León.

Recognizing that in addition to such legislative and material steps as were already taken, another factor was needed, the President evolved the idea of establishing central agricultural schools for the sons of *ejidatarios*. Eight such schools, where the students were to spend time both in classrooms and on the farms, were placed in operation in various parts of the country.

The President had ambitious programs where goals turned out to be beyond the possibilities allowed by circumstances. Just as he would like to have seen more than eight agricultural schools, so also did he set his heart on establishing more federal-supported rural schools than came into being. Obregón and Vasconcelos, who inherited from their predecessors no true federal-supported rural schools, were able to leave their successors about 1000 such schools; the number would have been far greater except for the De la Huerta rebellion. Puig Casauranc and his able collaborator, Undersecretary Moisés Sáenz, sought to carry on the work which Vasconcelos started, with a goal of establishing 1000 additional federal rural schools in each year. By the year 1928 about 3,300 such schools were functioning. This number included those which had been set up during the Obregón regime.

With Morones in charge of the nation's Industry, Commerce, and Labor, the Confederación General de Trabajadores had a tough time, while the C.R.O.M. went ahead claiming that more and more laborers were associated with it.

Memberships in unions associated with the C.R.O.M. followed this distribution:[5]

[4] J. M. Puig Casauranc, *op. cit.*, p. 187.
[5] J. W. Brown, *Modern Mexico and Its Problems*, p. 36.

Land workers and peasants	1,215,000
Transport workers	209,000
Textile workers	112,000
Mine workers	75,000
Workers in the building trades	35,000
Metal workers	20,000
Workers in printing, paper and allied trades . .	10,000
Workers employed in public spectacles	124,000
	1,800,000

Groups outside the C.R.O.M. were affiliated thus:

Confederación General de Trabajadores . . .	3,000
Catholic associations	20,000
Railroad Confederation	20,000
Moscow-affiliated section	2,000
	45,000

Eduardo Moneda expressed the hope of showing that two million workers were associated with the C.R.O.M. and a great deal was said about how much the giant confederation of labor unions had done to improve working conditions: working days of eight hours instead of twelve in 1910, Mexico City peon daily wages of 2 pesos instead of 12.5 centavos at the end of the Porfirio Díaz regime. Investors and managers found conditions did not allow them quite as much freedom regarding labor matters as they had been used to in the past. But they could by no means accuse the C.R.O.M. leaders of ties with Russian Bolshevism or of being inspired, as were others in the labor field, by the anarchical ideas of the International Communist movement. It was possible to sit down and deal with those whom Díaz Soto y Gama had termed "the aristocrats of labor." A pronounced decrease in the number of strikes occurred:[6]

Year	Number of Strikes	Strikers involved
1920	173	88,536
1921	310	100,380
1922	197	71,382
1923	146	61,403
1924	136	23,988
1925	51	9,861
1926	23	2,977
1927	16	1,005
1928	7	498

[6] Secretaría de la Economía Nacional, *Anuario estadístico, 1938*, p. 144.

The collapse in petroleum production was to be harmful to both government finances and the economy as a whole:

	Production (barrels)	Export (barrels)[7]	Taxes (pesos)
1916	41 million	———	3 million
1917	55 "	———	7 "
1918	64 "	———	11 "
1919	87 "	———	17 "
1920	157 "	146 million	45 "
1921	193 "	172 "	63 "
1922	182 "	181 "	86 "
1923	150 "	136 "	61 "
1924	140 "	130 "	55 "
1925	116 "	97 "	42 "
1926	90 "	81 "	35 "
1927	64 "	48 "	19 "
1928	50 "	———	11 "

It is difficult to say how much of this falling off was due to the increased necessity of relying on lower-yield wells not so near the coast, and how much was due to the part played by the Mexican government. There is no doubt that the latter factor was of importance, because reinvestments or new investments are vital to production. These hardly came forth in a healthy manner in the face of taxation which the operators felt to be too high when related to the lower-yield wells, and in the face of a controversy which threatened to deprive the operators of their titles.

One evening in September, 1926, Ing. Joaquín Santaella, an important Finance Ministry official, received an urgent call to see Calles in the Castle of Chapultepec. After waiting an hour in the President's reception room, Santaella saw Morones come out of the President's office. Then Santaella was shown in. Calles was highly irritated about an article in *El Universal* which accused Morones' ministry of contributing to the decline in petroleum production and which said that this production decrease was reducing the tax revenue of the states and municipalities. After his talk with Morones, Calles apparently felt that Santaella was responsible for the article. In the face of the President's irate explosion, Santaella found no opportunity to reply or defend himself. He was ordered to resign.

[7] Export figures here are shown only for 1920–1927.

On the next day Santaella advised Pani that he was resigning but he added that he had nothing to do with the article in *El Universal* and was not even familiar with it. After asking Santaella to withdraw his resignation, Pani drew up his own instead and then went to see Calles.

Calles asked: "Has Ing. Santaella resigned? It is the least we could require of him after his disloyal effort to turn the states and municipalities against the federal government."

Pani pointed out that he had asked Santaella to remain at his post, as the accusation was unfounded. "I cannot be a party to carrying out so great an injustice, and if you insist on his resignation you will have to accept mine."

The Finance Minister refused to accept the President's point of view. Instead he traced the authorship of the newspaper article to two lawyers who explained that they had published it in accordance with their duties as the representatives of two state governments. They signed a letter acknowledging their authorship, which Pani took, together with other evidence, to the President. But when Calles asked Pani to withdraw his resignation, the Finance Minister refused to do so, feeling that he could not remain in the same Cabinet as Morones and recognizing that Morones had enormous political strength whereas he himself had none.

Pani carried on as Finance Minister for a few more months, until certain pending legislation had been approved by Congress and the year 1927 was under way. Then he was appointed minister to France and was succeeded in the Cabinet by Luis Montes de Oca, who had been the Comptroller General. In becoming Mexico's minister to a European country Pani was following the example of one of his former colleagues, Gilberto Valenzuela. In 1925 Valenzuela had res'gned as Gobernación Minister when, against his recommendation, Calles had ordered him to proclaim that Carlos Riva Palacio had been elected governor of the state of Mexico.

Montes de Oca took over the Finance Ministry at a time when the golden days of Calles had passed and when the International Bankers Committee must have been wondering how much it could expect to receive in the future as a result of the Pani-Lamont Amendment. The Mexican government's relations with the United States were strained to the breaking point, and its relations with the Catholic clergy had gone beyond the breaking point. Presidential election fever was also once again in the air.

34·

Struggle with the Catholic Clergy

Obregón had sensed in the Catholic clergy a greater sympathy for the "reactionary" Victoriano Huerta than for the Constitutionalist Revolutionaries who struggled to depose this traitor to Madero. After succeeding in that struggle, while Obregón and his men were for a time in Mexico City contending with other opponents in 1915, Obregón issued a decree calling for contributions from those who owned property, in order to "alleviate the present distressing situation of the working classes." The amount demanded of the Mexico City clergy at this time was a half million pesos, and it was pointed out that the clergy had earlier made some such contribution to the cause of Huerta. When the 180 priests who were called in to see Obregón refused to make the payment on the ground that the Mexico City clergy did not have the money, they were placed in jail. Then they were told that if they continued to be financially unco-operative they would have to join Obregón's army, which was on the point of leaving the city. The priests requested physical examinations which, they felt, would show that their state of health made army life impossible. They were examined by an Army doctor, who issued a report advising that 49 out of the 180 were suffering from venereal diseases but that this would not prevent their joining the march.[1]

Generally speaking the Catholic clergy regarded with disfavor much that was done under the banner of the Constitutionalist Revolution led by Carranza, and Lázaro Cárdenas had plenty of company when he expressed the thought that "the priest and the landlord are allies."[2] Catholic leaders could hardly have been expected to be enthusiastic about measures such as those taken by Eleuterio Avila and Salvador Alvarado, Carrancistas sent to govern Yucatán. And when the Constitution of 1917 made its appearance, Catholic archbishops and bishops denounced parts of it which affected religious worship.

Besides repeating the ordinance of the 1857 Constitution prohibiting the establishment of monastic orders, the 1917 Constitution ruled that neither ministers nor religious bodies could establish or direct schools of primary learning, and it made it clear that all acts of public worship were to be performed only within church buildings. Churches were prohibited from possessing or administering any properties or mortgages thereon, and were ordered to turn them over to the government, whether they were held in their own names or in the names of third persons. The federal government, said the Constitution, would also take possession of all bishoprics, curacies, seminaries, asylums, convents, schools, or buildings kept up by religious societies or used for religious purposes. The government would designate which church buildings could continue to be used for religious purposes, and it would see to it that all of the other buildings were used exclusively for public service.

The Constitution enunciated strict rules governing the clergy. They had to be Mexican by birth, were to be considered as persons exercising a profession, and must be subject to laws that might there-

---

[1] Alvaro Obregón, *Ocho mil kilómetros en campaña*, pp. 436–438.
[2] Nathaniel and Sylvia Weyl, *The Reconquest of Mexico*, p. 7.

fore be imposed. A particularly important provision was that authorizing the state legislatures to determine, according to local needs, the maximum number of ministers in each state. Neither in private nor in public could ministers criticize the nation's government, its fundamental laws, or its authorities. Ministers were not to be eligible for public office, nor could they vote; and they were barred from inheriting from ministers of the same sect "or from any other person to whom they are not related by blood within the fourth degree." Religious publications were not allowed to comment on national political matters.

During the Obregón administration there were occasional acts of violence against the Catholic Church, particularly in 1921. A bomb was exploded at the door of the Archbishop of Mexico, Monseñor José Mora y del Río, whose stand against socialism was not highly esteemed by leaders of the Revolutionary government. A week after the Mexico City cathedral had been decorated with a red-and-black flag and its bells rung by those responsible for the incident, the cathedral at Morelia, Michoacán, received a similar treatment. In Morelia a meeting of protest was assaulted by "socialists," with the result that fifty persons were killed. Perhaps the most dramatic note struck in 1921 was the exploding of a bomb just below the altar of the Virgin of Guadalupe at the Guadalupe Church, the great shrine just outside Mexico City. Part of the altar was destroyed. Although candlesticks, porcelain dishes, and a crucifix went flying, the framed picture of the Virgin of Guadalupe was unharmed. Among the many and loud manifestations of protest was the closing up of shops for a five-hour period of mourning.

It was during the next year, 1922, that René Capistrán Garza took part in the founding of the Catholic Association of Mexican Youths, whose members became involved in a fight with the "Reds" on May 1, 1922. During the fight Capistrán Garza was wounded and a reproduction of the Virgin of Guadalupe was destroyed.

Early in 1923 the Obregón Government expelled the Vatican's representative to Mexico, Monseñor Ernesto Filippi. This act followed immediately the role which Apostolic Delegate Filippi played in the ceremonies attending the laying of a cornerstone for the Cristo Rey (Christ the King) monument on the peak of the high hill of Cubilete, near Silao, Guanajuato, approximately at the geographic center of the nation. Over 40,000 pilgrims and other worshippers, including eleven prelates from various parts of the republic, were present at Cubilete to hear the Bishop of San Luis Potosí proclaim Christ the King of Mexico. Monseñor Filippi was expelled from Mexico for violating the constitutional clause disallowing worship outside of church buildings, and Gobernación Minister Calles ordered the governor of Guanajuato to prohibit the carrying forward of any of the work started at Cubilete.

When leaders of the Catholic clergy objected to the expulsion of Monseñor Filippi, Obregón wrote a letter to the bishops expressing his regret that "certain members of the high Catholic clergy have not sensed the transformation which has occurred in the minds of the people toward a modern outlook, in the course of which ineffectively abstract doctrines have day by day lost their influence, while effective social programs have gained strength. To these latter the high Catholic clergy has not only denied its measure of co-operation but has actually opposed their development with systematic obstruction, particularly in those very features which are essentially Christian. It is certainly regrettable that the lack of sincerity in certain members of the Catholic clergy causes a continuation of this ancient struggle, when the two programs could so well co-operate." He called on his readers not to "calumniate nor injure the progress of that essentially Christian and humanitarian program which the government seeks to develop."

Obregón did not look kindly upon some of the manifestations which accompanied the impressive Eucharistic Congress held in Mexico City in October, 1924, and attended by Mexican archbishops and bishops as well as by members of the Knights of Columbus and representatives from various countries of the Americas. Numerous Mexico City homes were adorned in honor of this Congress which, under the presidency of Archbishop Mora y del Río, showed no great respect for some of the articles of the Mexican Constitution. When Obregón asked the Attorney General of the Republic, Lic. Eduardo Delhumeau, to make an investigation and take steps where there were any violations of the Constitution, the organizers of the Congress called off some of the ceremonies which they had planned. Moreover the Congress was unable to hold its closing "literary evening" at the Olimpia Theatre because the C.R.O.M. would not allow the employees of the theatre to co-operate.

Particularly active among the Church leaders who resisted government interferences during the Calles regime was Archbishop Orozco y Jiménez of Guadalajara, who expressed himself strongly and publicly in letters to the Jalisco governor. Another Church leader, active in a similar manner, was the bishop of Huejutla, Hidalgo, José de Jesús Manrique y Zárate. In his pastoral letter of April, 1925, he forbade all priests in his diocese from submitting to government laws about religious matters.

On October 30, 1925, the Tabasco state legislature decreed that no priest could practice unless he be married. This forced the Jesuit who was bishop of Tabasco, Pascual Díaz, to leave the state for Mexico City, where he became secretary of the Episcopate Committee which was set up by Apostolic Delegate Jorge José Caruana. Contemporary observers had not noted any religious problem in Tabasco and they came to feel that Governor Garrido Canabal was taking steps to carry forward a program which he felt would be approved by Calles, a program which was to include the destruction of churches and sacred images in Tabasco.

The Calles Government gave support in 1925 to a schismatic Mexican Catholic Apostolic Church which did not recognize the leadership of Rome and which outlawed as "immoral" celibacy in the clergy. In February, 1925, this new institution took over the Soledad de Santa Cruz church of Mexico City, which had been established during the sixteenth century; the Roman Catholic ministers of La Soledad were forcibly expelled. But when the "Patriarch" of the new Schismatic Church, José Joaquín Pérez, tried on February 23 to perform religious services at La Soledad he was attacked by Roman Catholics of the district, who were furious at the change and at the loss of their temple. After the disorders had been brought to an end with the arrival of the mounted police and the fire department, the federal government asked for reports on the scandal from the Archbishop of Mexico and "Patriarch" Pérez. Presumably after studying these, Calles decreed that La Soledad should be used neither by the Schismatic Church nor by the Roman Catholic Church, but should be turned into a public library. The President next ruled that Mexico City's church of Corpus Christi be turned over to "Patriarch Pérez" as the cathedral of the Cismáticos, and Archbishop Mora y del Río quickly issued an interdict against entering Corpus Christi. This church, which for years has served the Roman Catholics but which of late had been removed from their use, is very centrally located, being on Avenida Juárez across from the Alameda.

When a visitor from Argentina late in 1925 advised Calles to exercise a firmer hand in dealing with the threat by the clergy, the President told his guest that the suggestion disclosed his lack of familiarity with Mexico. "Clericalism now signifies no danger at all." Calles continued that the government would therefore limit itself to its work of administration and of social and economic reconstruction.

But in 1926 the struggle broke out in full force when the Church leaders realized that the President was preparing a lengthy regulating decree to implement the Constitutional provisions about religious matters.[3] At a Cabinet meeting early in 1926 an infuriated Calles called attention to an article in *El Universal* which quoted Archbishop Mora y del Río as stating that the Church would resist attempts to put into effect Articles 3, 5, 27, and 130 of the Constitution. Ignoring Pani's suggestion that the authenticity of the Archbishop's statement first be checked, Calles lost no time in issuing orders for all government employees to comply with all rulings about religious matters. When Pani passed these orders to his Finance Ministry employees with a note to the effect that those who wished to do so could comply, he advised the President of how he was handling the matter and included his offer to resign from the Cabinet. He never heard from his communication to the President.

The Archbishop's first statement as presented in the newspaper was the reproduction of some words he had issued, apparently rather discreetly, about nine years earlier when the 1917 Constitution was formulated. The elderly Archbishop and the government were equally surprised by what they saw on the front page of *El Universal*. The newspaperman who was responsible for digging up an old protest and presenting it as something new, found himself about to lose his job for having displayed a lack of professional ethics. He went to plead with the Archbishop, asking whether "what your Illustrious Person said in 1917 is not true in 1926?" Mora y del Río was not only moved to say that "truth is unchangeable," but he signed a copy of the old protest. So on the following day the situation became more tense when statements again appeared on the newspaper's front page, this time bearing the Archbishop's autograph.[4]

Even if the old protest had not been revived in so unusual a manner on the Day of the Constitution in 1926, the President could have

[3] Arturo M. Elías, *The Mexican People and the Church*, p. 49.
[4] J. M. Puig Casauranc, *El sentido social del proceso histórico de México*, pp. 196–199.

found, sooner or later, declarations by Church leaders showing a clear resistance to the Constitution. A strong pronouncement, signed by a number of archbishops and bishops, had been made public on January 27.

President Calles and Gobernación Minister Adalberto Tejeda asked the Attorney General to study the seditious nature of what had appeared in *El Universal* and to take legal action against Archbishop Mora y del Río. Roman Catholic schools and convents were closed and the buildings taken over. About 200 foreign priests and nuns were thrown out of the country in compliance with the order that they could remain only if they would agree to dedicate themselves to nonreligious activities. The first to be expelled were some Spanish priests, who embarked from Veracruz on February 11. Highly vexing to the Church, although only a taste of what was to come, were early applications of the law which gave each state the right to limit the number of ministers or priests. Yucatán set the limit at sixteen, Durango at twenty-five, and Tamaulipas at twelve.

While Calles complained that the Church was taking advantage of a situation caused by his very considerable difficulties in foreign relations, Catholic leaders were far from silent. In their spoken and written words there was much that was inflaming, but the only bishop clearly to call the religious to fight was José de Jesús Manrique y Zárate, who "indignantly" rejected the laws of the land. In his pastoral letter of March, 1926, he wrote: "We do not fear prisons, nor assassinations, but only the judgments of God. We reprove, condemn, and anathematize each and every one of the crimes and assaults committed by the government in recent days." After he was seized by the authorities in Mexico City about the middle of May he said that he refused to recognize in civilian judges the right to know about purely religious matters. While sympathizers protested, he was taken to Pachuca, Hidalgo.

The hearing could not start before the Pachuca district judge until the bishop had removed his holy garments. Asked by the authorities why he had refused to abide by the ruling to close Catholic schools, he replied: "The special reason of the natural right which allows all men to communicate their ideas about humanity, besides the divine right of the Church to teach the Christian doctrine to all of the world." The press carried a letter from the archbishop of Durango congratulating Manrique y Zárate, also a letter from the Episcopate Committee asking Calles for legal guarantees on his behalf. The publication of a letter of support for the

Church from the Spanish prelates was followed by a letter from Calles stating that any rebellious acts would be energetically punished. Manrique y Zárate was sentenced to prison but continued at liberty, restricted to Mexico City, under bail while his defense appealed his case.

Apostolic Delegate Caruana had not lasted long. He had reached Mexico on March 18, 1926, and within one month had been ordered to leave the country on the charge of having made "false declarations about his birth, profession, and religion." Following Caruana's expulsion, Archbishop Mora y del Río wrote to Calles stating that "for the third time the Mexican government regrettably insults His Holiness [the Pope], the Catholic Church, and our people." There then was organized a League To Defend Religious Liberty (Liga Defensora de la Libertad Religiosa), whose members found gratification in defying actions of the government.

On June 24, 1926, Calles issued his series of penal laws listing provisions about religious matters which are contained in the Mexican Constitution and giving penalties for infractions. Prison terms of from one to five years were to be served by any clergy who criticized the laws, the authorities, or the government. Among the many other offenses for which religious persons might be punished was the "use, outside of church premises, of special garments or badges denoting their profession."

In addition, all priests were required to register with the civil authorities.

These rulings were to go into effect on July 31, 1926.

Already in May the priests in Mexico City had been required to register, and Attorney General Romeo Ortega had imprisoned thirty-seven of them who had been officiating in churches but who had refused to register. The Education Ministry issued a ruling requiring lay teaching in private schools, and it closed schools where religion was taught.

To counter the steps being taken by the government a Liga Nacional Defensora de la Libertad issued a signed circular proposing to the Mexican people a boycott of the Calles government: the limiting of purchases to the necessities of life in order to create an economic crisis, the nonpurchase of periodicals not supporting the Liga, the nonpurchase of lottery tickets, and nonattendance at lay schools, theatres, or dances. The circular, which called on all lovers of liberty to become efficient propagandists against the enemies of liberty, said that the boycott was to go into effect on July 31, 1926, and to remain in force as long as the Calles decree of June 24 was effective.

At the bottom of the Liga's circular was a copy of the letter from the Episcopate Committee approving the projected boycott and signed by José Mora y del Río and Pascual Díaz. Those who signed the circular itself, among them René Capistrán Garza, were placed in the Santiago prison because of the circular's seditious character. Archbishop Mora y del Río and Dr. Díaz were for a time also held by the authorities for their part in the affair.

Following the announcement on June 24 of the regulations and penalties which were to become effective on July 31, the Episcopate Committee met to decide what to do. On April 21 the Committee had issued twenty-four objections to the Constitution. Now it resolved that the priests of the nation should not comply with the ruling that they register, and it further decided on the suspension of all religious services effective July 31.

On July 25 the Committee published a collective pastoral letter, signed by various archbishops and bishops, which made known its decision. Public worship requiring the intervention of priests, it said, had been made impossible and was to be discontinued with the approval of Pope Pius XI. "Have faith in us, beloved children, as we have faith in your unbreakable loyalty, and let us all commit ourselves to God." In a more fighting mood various bishops condemned the penal laws issued on July 24: "Before God, before civilized humanity, before our country, and before history, we protest against this decree. With the help of God and with your help, Catholic priests and people of Mexico, we will labor to have this decree, together with the anti-religious articles of the Constitution, amended, and we will not stop until we see that accomplished."[5]

The last days of July, 1926, were strenuous. So many Roman Catholics wanted to take advantage of the final opportunity to have their children confirmed at the hands of Archbishop Mora y del Río that the crowding became dangerous. The clergy worked overtime to take care of the mad rush for baptisms and religious marriages. At the same time that new leaders of the Liga Defensora de

[5] Wilfrid Parsons, *Mexican Martyrdom*, p. 23.

Long lines of Catholics seeking to be confirmed by Archbishop Mora y del Rio at the Mexico City cathedral shortly before the discontinuance of Catholic services at the end of July, 1926. Casasola.

la Libertad Religiosa were arrested, an organization of Catholic ladies released a testimonial in favor of Mora y del Río.

Calles also received great demonstrations of support. On July 29 over 180 labor union representatives, including Ricardo Treviño, Samuel O. Yúdico, and Eduardo Moneda, called on the President to manifest their allegiance to him and to ask the firing of all government employees who might be supporting the cause of the Catholic clergy. The President made a statement: "You cannot imagine how I am strengthened by the attitude assumed, in this interesting historical moment, by the organized workers of the nation. In the most difficult moments for my government, when international questions which must define whether or not Mexico is a sovereign nation are stirred up, the clergy, with all ill faith, threw a challenge at the government of the Republic and made declarations to the reactionary press of the capital, and ordered the believers to disobey the Constitution."

On Sunday, August 1, Calles greeted a crowd of over 40,000 organized workers jamming the Plaza de la Constitución. This he did from the balcony of the Palacio Municipal, for the Palacio Nacional was at this time undergoing reconstruction and receiving its additional floor.

No bishop registered with the government authorities and, in the face of the threat of excommunication, only two or three priests did so. For the first time in centuries no Roman Catholic religious services were held in Mexico. The Attorney General issued orders for taking over the churches and placing them in the hands of regional committees.

Reams of propaganda were issued by both sides.

Early in August at the Esperanza Iris Theatre a series of public debates about the question was started, with members of the Calles Cabinet arguing against members of the Liga Defensora de la Libertad Religiosa. Education Minister Puig Casauranc took on René Capistrán Garza, Luis L. León opposed Manuel Herrera Lazo, and Morones took the platform to debate with a youthful student, Luis Mier y Terán.

When Bishop Ruiz y Flores, of Morelia, and Pascual Díaz discussed affairs with the President, they were told by him that they had only two ways open to them: "either go to Congress or take up arms."

With the opening of the congressional session on September 1,

A manifestation of support for President Calles during his controversy with leaders of the Catholic clergy. As the Palacio Nacional is undergoing improvement and enlargement, the President greets the labor demonstrators from the balcony of the Palacio Municipal. August 1, 1926. Casasola.

the President said that the executive branch, in the course of enforcing the nation's laws, had closed 129 Catholic schools, 42 churches, 7 convents, and 7 centers of religious propaganda. He added that 185 foreign priests had left the nation as pernicious foreigners.

Five days later the Catholic Episcopate submitted to Congress a petition, on which it claimed to have two million signatures, asking that certain constitutional rulings be repealed and others reformed. But on September 21 the petition was rejected by Congress on the ground that Archbishop Mora y del Río and Bishop Pascual Díaz were not legally capable of presenting a petition in the realm of political matters.

35.

The Cristero Rebellion
and the Case of Padre Pro

Catholic priests were among those who, toward the end of 1926, took part in small armed uprisings in various sections of the country. Under religious slogans, the most prominent of which was "Long live Christ the King," bands of rebels would burn government schools and take small villages. Such activities usually occurred in mountainous, isolated districts and were particularly prevalent in Jalisco, Guanajuato, Colima, and Michoacán. Military men who early took up arms on behalf of the Catholic rebels included General Rodolfo L. Gallegos and General Enrique Gorostieta, Jr., son of one of Victoriano Huerta's Cabinet ministers.

In Mexico City enthusiastic members of the Liga Defensora de la Libertad Religiosa clandestinely sent fighting materials to these Cristero rebels in Jalisco and at the same time sought to outsmart the police, sometimes successfully. Late in 1926 they released over Mexico City six hundred balloons, from which rained down a torrent of colored propaganda leaflets. The police force became lively in tracking down those suspected of responsibility.

The Catholic Episcopate took a stand against violence, a stand which had little restraining effect and which reflected these instructions received from the Vatican: the Mexican archbishops and bishops are to remain aside from the armed struggle, but at the same time are to instill in the faithful "the necessity of taking positions against parties hostile to the Church and of maintaining themselves united."[1] Early in 1927, when the unrest was at its height, the zealous fanatics and others who were in arms against the government numbered roughly 12,000. After a rebel attack on the city of León, Guanajuato, had been repulsed and after the federal troops near Guadalajara killed forty-five Catholics who were accused of sedition, the rebels took to attacking trains. In March General Rodolfo Gallegos led a successful assault on the Mexico City-Laredo train, making off with the government funds and killing the federal escort. More serious was the rebel attack in April on the Mexico City-Guadalajara train. All the cars left the track in an orgy of destruction which cost the lives of about 100 persons, some of them innocent civilians and others soldiers who made up the escort.

In April about half of Mexico's fifteen bishops were advised by Gobernación Minister Tejeda to get out of the country at once on orders from the President. They protested that the Episcopate had not promoted the rebellion, which they considered to be natural self-defense "against unjustifiable tyranny," but nevertheless they soon found themselves in Laredo, Texas. Numerous priests were committed to prison.

Although General Juan Andreu Almazán let Calles know that he would not co-operate in carrying out the "infamous religious persecution," the President found plenty of generals who were not averse to harassing even certain peace-loving Catholics. Among the generals who figured prominently in the campaign against the armed Cristero rebels were Jesús M. Ferreira, Bonifacio Salinas

---

[1] María Elena Sodi de Pallares, *Los Cristeros y José de León Toral*, p. 49.

Leal, and Rodrigo Quevedo M. On May 5 the press carried a bulletin from General Saturnino Cedillo, head of Military Operations in San Luis Potosí, announcing the pursuit of Rodolfo Gallegos by Colonel José María Dávila and his men in the San Miguel Allende district, and the subsequent death of the rebel leader. Enrique Gorostieta, Jr., carried on as head of the rebellion.

Some of the government army men arranged to conduct against their foe a long-drawn-out campaign. One of the federal colonels in Jalisco found he needed to spend but little of the government funds he was receiving, since he could maintain his men and horses by the use of confiscated haciendas. His set-up grew even more lucrative when he began to sell munitions to the rebels between attacks. Some of the government army men remarked that the cartridges used by the Cristeros were manufactured in the National Manufacturing Plant of Arms and Cartridges and were newer than those used by the federal troops.[2] General Ferreira threatened air bombings for an area of 6000 square miles in northern Jalisco unless it was completely evacuated; then, after the area's fifty thousand inhabitants, peasants and hacienda owners alike, had reported, as ordered, to military camps, Ferreira's men moved in on the crops which were just ready to harvest.

By the latter part of 1927 the Cristero rebellion had been somewhat reduced but a fair amount of sporadic plundering and killing by irresponsible persons continued. Many of those who had been active in the campaign of the Liga Defensora de la Libertad Religiosa had served or were serving jail sentences. Some of the members of the Catholic League of Youth, after a jailing in Mexico City, were shipped from Mazatlán, Sinaloa, with other criminals to the Islas Marías penal colony in the Pacific. There for two months they were forced to work at salt collection under the hot sun; then, around the end of the year, they were released in accordance with a pardon issued by Calles.

Government soldiers who were not busy campaigning against the Cristero rebels, or who were not making life difficult for Catholics whom they suspected of favoring the Cristeros, could gild their military reputations by engaging in war on another front. During the summer of 1926 the Yaqui Indians held up a train in which ex-President Obregón was travelling from Nogales, Sonora, to his

[2] Higinio Alvarez García in *El Universal*, October 6, 1956.

Cajeme farm. This incident contributed to the 1926–1927 campaign against the Yaqui tribe, which was once again declared to be in open rebellion. The Chamber of Deputies voted one million pesos to put the Yaquis down "forever," and War Minister Joaquín Amaro left the capital to confer with General Francisco R. Manzo, head of operations in Sonora.

With the aid of military planes, Generals Lucas González, Anselmo Armenta, Antonio Ríos Zertuche, Eduardo García, and J. Félix Lara combatted the hard-fighting Yaquis in remote regions of the Sierra Occidental. The Yaqui fighters finally surrendered to Manzo late in 1927, and not long after that about 600 of them turned up in Mexico City. Through an interpreter their leaders expressed their delight with the railway which had taken them to the focal point of the republic; they did not know where they would go but planned to enter the ranks of the Army.

The most publicized single event of the struggle between the government and the clergy occurred in Mexico City in November, 1927. Jesuit Father Miguel Pro Juárez, a devout and determined young man, had returned to his native Mexico from Europe just at the time when the Catholic Church discontinued religious services. He visited Catholics in jail and threw himself wholeheartedly into undercover activities—providing communions, hearing confessions, and performing religious marriage ceremonies. He was not always successful in eluding the Mexico City police force, which was under the direction of General Roberto Cruz, and he spent some time in jail himself. His younger brothers, Humberto and Roberto, were active in issuing propaganda on behalf of the Liga Defensora, while sister Ana María made a home for the brothers and for their old father.

In Mexico City on November 13 General Alvaro Obregón and two friends, Arturo H. Orcí and Tomás Bay, were taking a Sunday drive around Chapultepec Park prior to attending the bullfights. The three friends in Obregón's Cadillac were being followed by at least two cars. One of these was Orcí's Cadillac, driven by Orcí's chauffeur, and the other was a car which contained Obregón's aides-de-camp, Colonels Juan Jaimes and Ignacio Otero.

From an Essex car which suddenly came alongside Obregón's Cadillac, three bombs were thrown at the ex-President and his companions, who were fortunate not to lose their lives. One bomb went somewhat forward, another somewhat to the rear and the third a little high. Glass was blown to powder, and the Cadillac's occupants, particularly Obregón and Orcí, were covered with blood. After hurling the bombs, the men in the Essex fired some pistol shots on the car containing the intended victims and then sped off.[3]

In the course of the chase which followed, Orcí's chauffeur fired into the Essex, thus aiding the aides-de-camp, who were pursuing it first along Avenida Chapultepec and then along Avenida Insurgentes. Firing on the Essex badly wounded one of its occupants, Nahum Lamberto Ruiz, blinding him, and in a short time both Ruiz and a Juan Tirado were captured. The others in the Essex escaped. Obregón, after being touched up with iodine, proceeded to the bullfights.

The Essex had belonged to Humberto Pro until he had sold it a few days before it was used for the assault. Detective Valente Quintana called on Ruiz, who was in agony at the Juárez Hospital, and by pretending to be a close relative obtained information from Ruiz which he construed as linking to the crime the Pro brothers and Ing. Luis Segura Vilchis, Ruiz's twenty-four–year–old boss at the Light and Power Company. (Contemporary reports state that Ruiz, thinking Quintana to be his brother, told him to tell Segura Vilchis and the Pros to hide.)

Handsome Luis Segura Vilchis, who in religious work had been an associate of Miguel Pro and an effective speaker, was found at his power company desk and taken at once by the police.

Preparatory to fleeing Mexico City the Pro brothers were hidden in the home of Sra. María Valdez, but the activities there were hardly compatible with safety. Padre (Father) Miguel Pro blessed a marriage, celebrated Mass, and heard confessions of penitents who began to arrive. Sra. Valdez' concern about these dangerous proceedings was justified, but Padre Pro had no fear. "For at least a year," his biographer writes, "he had prayed that he might be accepted as a sacrifice for the Faith in his country."[4] Police surrounded the house and took the three brothers, informing Sra. Valdez that she had been "harboring the dynamiters." Although the weather was cold, Padre Pro left for jail without his coat, having given it to the poor.

The Pro brothers and Ing. Segura Vilchis spent six days in cells

[3] Arturo H. Orcí, interview, December 6, 1956.
[4] The story of the life of Miguel Pro Juárez is given in Fanchón Royer's *Padro Pro*.

314

The shooting of Father Miguel Agustín Pro Juárez. November 23, 1927. Enrique Díaz.

at the police station, Humberto occupying a cell with the Pros' charitable Catholic associate, Josefina Montes de Oca, and the other Pro brothers sharing Cell No. 1. Miguel Pro, like his brothers, denied any connection with the plot against Obregón, and he added that he had not engaged in any political activity and was not acquainted with Nahum Lamberto Ruiz. Luis Segura Vilchis assumed the responsibility for the plot and provided testimony which implicated Ruiz, Juan Tirado, and one other who had not been caught. Nothing was said by the Pros or Segura Vilchis which involved the Pros. Nahum Lamberto Ruiz soon died at the Juárez Hospital.

Official reports told of past meetings at the residence of Josefina Montes de Oca, niece of the late Bishop Ignacio Montes de Oca, and mentioned that these meetings had been attended by Ing. Segura Vilchis, Juan Tirado, Humberto Pro Juárez, Nahum Lamberto Ruiz, and José González (the one in the Essex who had escaped).

The tough General Inspector of Police, General Roberto Cruz, was well aware that President Calles wanted the Pros to be shot together with Segura Vilchis and Tirado in order "to set an example." When Cruz pointed out the advisability of giving the sentence "an appearance of legality," Calles simply told him to obey instructions regardless of forms. Cruz thereupon repeated to the press that the Pros were among those involved, adding that the prisoners would be shot on the morning of November 23 in the police station itself, in the heart of the city, before an imposing crowd.

Thus before a gathering of officials, journalists, and photographers, death by shooting came to Miguel Pro, Luis Segura Vilchis, Humberto Pro, and Juan Tirado. Padre Miguel Pro's last words were "Viva Cristo Rey." The youngest brother, Roberto Pro, was about to be fired on when Cruz, who was among those witnessing the proceedings, received a phonecall from Calles: "Let that one off. We'll exile him." The phonecall was attributed to pressure brought on the President by the Argentine Minister to Mexico, Emilio Labougle.

In spite of the numerous constitutional violations in the proceedings against the Pro brothers, photographs of the event were given wide publicity.

36·

The Revolutionary Program
and United States Relations

As the Calles Revolutionary domestic program unfolded, Foreign Minister Aarón Sáenz found his hands full taking
care of the strong objections which came from the United States
Secretary of State, Frank B. Kellogg, and the United States ambassador to Mexico (1924–1927), James R. Sheffield.

Even before the enactment in Mexico of the series of laws which
were to prove most upsetting to the relations between the two nations, Kellogg irked Mexican officials. Speaking to the press on June
12, 1925, in connection with Ambassador Sheffield's visit to Washington, Kellogg mentioned rumors of an imminent rebellion against

Calles and stated that the United States would support the Calles Government only if it lived up to its international obligations. Reference was made to the position assumed by the United States government at the time of the De la Huerta rebellion, when understandings, some of them informal, had been reached by representatives of the two countries. Mexico, said Kellogg, should not only make indemnifications for American losses in Mexico, but should also restore American properties which had been taken illegally. He added a sentence which became well known: "The government of Mexico is now on trial before the world."

President Calles promptly delivered a forceful reply. He felt that as long as the claims commissions had not resolved to abandon their work it was quite improper to charge Mexico with breaking international agreements and with failing to protect American interests. He expressed the feeling that Kellogg had contradicted himself, for he had revealed an interest in the preservation of order in Mexico but at the same time had spoken of news about a rebellious movement; such news "must sow alarm in the world as to the conditions in my country." "The declaration that the United States government will continue backing the Mexican government only if the interests and lives of American citizens are protected and if her international agreements and obligations are fulfilled carries a threat to Mexico's sovereignty. We recognize no right for any foreign nation to intervene in any form . . . If the Mexican government finds itself, as affirmed, subject to the judgment of the world, the same is true of the United States and the other nations; but if it is meant that Mexico stands before the world as accused, my government energetically rejects such an imputation, which only constitutes an injury. To conclude, I declare that my government, conscious of obligations imposed by international law, is resolved to fulfill them, and to provide due protection of the lives and interests of foreigners; that it awaits only that help from other nations which is based on a sincere and loyal co-operation and which accords with international friendship; but that it never will admit that the government of any nation should seek to create in this country a privileged situation for its nationals, nor will it admit any interference against the rights of the sovereignty of Mexico."

Calles' declaration, whatever its impact north of the border, stirred up great enthusiasm in Mexico and brought a pile of congratulatory messages to his desk.

As originally established in one of the treaties of 1923, only one year was allowed for presentation of claims to the General Claims Commission and all claims had to be resolved within three years of the first meeting. The first meeting was held in Washington on August 30, 1924, and soon thereafter both parties dumped upon the Commission such masses of claims that a successful handling of them all seemed most improbable. It was necessary to extend the life of the Commission from time to time. Resignations of presiding officers contributed to losses in time. The following tabulation gives some idea of what transpired, or did not transpire, during the first seven years:[1]

Work of the United States-Mexican General Claims Commission to August 30, 1931

American Claims

Claims filed	2,781 amounting to $513,694,267.17
Claims disallowed or dismissed	50
Awards made	89 amounting to $4,607,926.59

Mexican Claims

Claims filed	836 amounting to $246,158,395.32
Claims disallowed or dismissed	4
Awards made	5 amounting to $39,000.00

The Special Claims Commission, to decide on claims for damages to Americans as a result of the Mexican Revolution, was originally supposed to resolve during five years all claims presented within the first two years. This indicated that the treaty makers felt in 1923 that this Commission would have the heavier load of work. The first meeting took place on August 18, 1924, in Mexico City. Although this Commission had fewer claims than the General Commission, it became involved in more heated discussions. The Mexican representation maintained, with success, that Mexico had not undertaken to cover the damages suffered on account of the acts of illegitimate governments, or, unless negligence or lenity could be proved, those for which bandits or rebels were responsible.[2] This threw out claims caused by acts of the Victoriano Huerta Government and by many acts of the Zapatistas and Villistas. The Special Claims Commission was sorely torn when a majority ruled that Mexico was not liable for the 1916 Villista murder of a group of fifteen American mining engineers.

[1] A full account of the work of United States–Mexican Claims Commissions is given in A. H. Feller's *The Mexican Claims Commissions, 1923–1934,* which is the source of the two tabulations presented in this chapter.

[2] A. H. Feller, *op. cit.,* p.159.

After seven years of wrangling the accomplishments of the Special Claims Commission were as follows:

Work of the United States-Mexican Special Claims Commission to August, 1931

Claims filed	3,176 amounting to $421,300,132.41
Claims disallowed	18
Awards made	none

Mexico's relations with the United States were immeasurably worsened late in 1925 by the enactment of laws regarding those old sores, petroleum and land.

The Petroleum Law of December, 1925, made it necessary for those working petroleum properties to obtain "confirmatory concessions" from the government prior to January 1, 1927. These "confirmatory concessions" would be good for fifty years. Oil companies working claims which they felt they possessed through acquisition prior to 1917 set up a loud cry at the idea of having to exchange their "rights" for such "confirmatory concessions" of limited duration. When operators who were said to control most of the production refused to take the steps which were required of them by the new law, the government denied them drilling permits and advised that they had renounced all their previous rights. The Mexican Petroleum Company of California then went to the Mexican courts and there the case remained during much of 1927.

Although the largest oil company in Mexico, El Aguila, was British, the United States oil interests in Mexico were at the moment the most productive, estimates indicating that United States interests controlled about 58 per cent of Mexico's oil production, British interests about 34 per cent, and Mexican interests about 1 per cent.[3] The director of the Association of Producers of Petroleum in Mexico, Guy Stevens, reported that those producing about 70 per cent of Mexico's oil were not accepting the new Petroleum Law. The Mexican government announced that the "rebellious" companies represented around 50 per cent of the production. The differences in the statistics may have arisen in part from the fact that some producers, including one large British company, first filed applications for "confirmatory concessions" and then decided to withdraw them.[4]

---

[3] J. Fred Rippy in *American Policies Abroad: Mexico*, p. 73.
[4] Guy Stevens in *American Policies Abroad: Mexico*, pp. 209–211.

The argument became hot not only in Mexico but also in the United States. There were writers north of the Rio Grande who were critical of the oil companies and of the stand taken by the State Department, which, they noted, encouraged these companies not to comply with the Mexican Petroleum Law. Mr. Stevens mentioned three major reasons which were responsible for the position of the oil companies: (1) under the Mexican Constitution concessions to exploit mineral fuels cannot be granted to foreign corporations, and so the offered "concessions" would not be valid; (2) in view of their past experience (with particular reference to orders issued under Carranza and the more recent disregard of the Supreme Court decisions of 1921 and 1922) they felt that if they accepted the new arrangement, it could prove to be but one step in a direction that did not appeal to them; and (3) they regarded the issue as fundamentally "a conflict between two economic systems: One is based on respect for private property; the other is the direct antithesis."[5]

The 1925 Petroleum Law was followed by a corresponding *reglamento* which gave great powers over the industry to the Ministry of Industry, Commerce, and Labor, headed by Morones. By this time employment in the industry had fallen to 22,000 after having been 45,000 in 1921.

In December, 1925, and early in 1926 the Mexican government put into effect several laws having to do with land properties. By the law of December 23, foreigners were prohibited from owning land within 50 kilometers of the Mexican coast or within 100 kilometers of the Mexican borders. This was in conformity with the 1917 Constitution, but since the 1857 Constitution had contained no such restriction the delicate question of retroactivity arose. More serious in the eyes of United States authorities were the portions of the Alien Land Law which required that aliens or foreign companies could hold no more than a minority interest in agricultural development companies. In the case of foreign corporations the excess would have to be disposed of within ten years; in the case of alien individuals, within about five years following death. Further efforts were made to prevent foreigners from controlling Mexican companies.

[5] *Ibid.*, pp. 213–215.

To pay for lands which were being expropriated and turned over to *ejidatarios* at a rate theretofore unequalled, the Mexican government began issuing twenty-five-year 5-per-cent bonds of the Agrarian Public Debt. By the end of February, 1928, it had issued such bonds to the extent of 8,650,000 pesos as indemnification for a small portion of the seized properties. The bonds were offered in exchange for the lands valued as for tax assessment plus 10 per cent, but as the tax-assessment valuations were low, and as the bonds sold on the market far below their par value, they were usually not accepted. The former owners of the lands generally preferred to reserve their rights to negotiate further.

Of the 2,600,000 hectares of land redistributed in the first three years of the Calles administration, about 200.000 hectares had belonged to United States citizens who found themselves without any compensation whatsoever.

The foreigner who owned property now learned about the Calvo Clause, which formed a part of Article 27 of the 1917 Constitution and which was included in the Mexican legislation of December, 1925. According to this provision, derived from the concept of the nineteenth-century Argentinian diplomat, Carlos Calvo, foreigners owning property or making contracts were considered to have renounced any rights to call for diplomatic protection. The clause had figured prominently in disputes between the United States and Latin-American nations since 1868, and it made its appearance in the discussions of the claims commissions and in the notes between Foreign Minister Sáenz and Secretary Kellogg.[6] In 1926 Sáenz did agree that "The Mexican Government . . . does not deny that the American Government is at liberty to intervene for its nationals; but that does not stand in the way of carrying out an agreement under which the alien agrees not to be the party asking for the diplomatic protection of his government."

The strongly expressed complaints of Kellogg and Sheffield were based on features of the new petroleum and land laws which, besides revealing retroactive and confiscatory features not in accord with their ideas of international law, were in some parts contrary to their understandings of sections of the minutes of the Bucareli Conferences of 1923. Mexico maintained that these minutes, which

[6] For a complete study see Donald R. Shea, *The Calvo Clause*.

had not attained the status of official treaties, had not been conditions for the renewal of diplomatic relations, and she also pointed out that no minutes could go beyond what the Constitution allowed. Notes from the United States implied the possibility of a withdrawal of diplomatic relations in case American rights were not given the protection which was being relied upon as a result of the discussions of 1923.

While the more technical diplomatic debate was in full swing, a good deal of fuel was otherwise added to already hot fires. During a revolution which was taking place in Nicaragua at this time the United States government backed Adolfo Díaz and was pained when Mexico backed his rival, Juan Sacasa. Mexico did not agree to the United States suggestion of an arms embargo, but instead sent fighting equipment to Sacasa, with the result that the Coolidge Administration accused Mexico of fostering in Central America a Bolshevist hegemony which was a menace to the Panama Canal. United States Marines which were landed in Nicaragua ousted Sacasa, to the annoyance not only of the Mexican government but of Senator William E. Borah and others in the United States.

Much of the United States press became sensitively aware of Mexico, and heated editorials about the situation and the possible break in diplomatic relations appeared. The Hearst newspapers accused four United States senators of having accepted from the Mexican government a bribe of about one million dollars, an accusation which was later shown to have been false. Meanwhile British experts on Mexican labor matters took a dim view of complaints which emanated from United States government sources and which in their opinion threatened the ideals which they attributed to Calles and Morones. "Our whole international movement must say to foreign capitalists and the imperialistic governments: 'Keep your hands off Mexico. Its destiny is in our charge.' "[7]

When Secretary Kellogg submitted to the United States Senate a memorandum entitled "Bolshevik Aims and Policies in Mexico and Latin America" relations were not improved. Loud in calling for intervention were United States Senator Albert B. Fall, Chairman of the Senate Subcommittee of the Foreign Relations Committee, and Mr. E. L. Doheny, of the National Association for the Protection of American Rights in Mexico. While Senator William E.

[7] J. M. Brown, *Modern Mexico and Its Problems*, p. 16.

Borah pleaded for a peaceful settlement, some United States oil interests joined in the clamor for intervention. However, the participation of Fall and Doheny in the Teapot Dome oil scandals, revealed about this time, hardly aroused much enthusiasm for an intervention in Mexico on behalf of United States petroleum interests.

37.

The Arrival of Ambassador Morrow

After having phrased very well the United States position in the controversy—so well, in fact, that a logical impasse had developed—Ambassador Sheffield retired. To be the new ambassador to Mexico President Coolidge late in 1927 appointed his friend and Amherst College classmate, Dwight W. Morrow, who had been a corporation lawyer and a partner in the banking firm of J. P. Morgan.

The new ambassador counteracted in a short time the suspicions which at first prevailed in Mexico at the naming of a Morgan partner, suspicions expressed in the sentence "After Morrow come the Marines." Assuming an attitude which was highly welcome, and which created some surprise, Morrow revealed an enormous and genuine interest in all things Mexican. The enthusiasm of the Ambassador and Mrs. Morrow for Mexico's many delights was that of enchanted and admiring newcomers. During the course of their stay in Mexico they purchased a place in Cuernavaca and spent

General Plutarco Elías Calles *and* Ambassador Dwight W. Morrow. *Enrique Diaz.*

many happy hours arranging their house and gardens there, decorating their home with the Mexican handicrafts which they so much loved to buy in the markets.

From the start Ambassador Morrow's relations with President Calles were on an unusually informal basis. A few days after presenting his credentials on October 29, the Ambassador accepted an invitation to breakfast, unaccompanied by any member of his staff, at the President's country estate ("Santa Bárbara") outside of Mexico City. The breakfast went so well, with Morrow displaying keen interest in the President's plans to irrigate Mexico, that a second such invitation was received within a week.

Calles then arranged to have the Ambassador accompany him

In the stand: Dr. José M. Puig Casauranc, Ambassador Dwight W. Morrow, General Plutarco Elías Calles, Colonel Charles A. Lindbergh. *December, 1927. Enrique Díaz.*

on a six-day train trip which would include visits to one of the land banks, one of the agricultural schools, and the dams which were nearing completion, one in the state of Aguascalientes and the other at Don Martín (near Monterrey, Nuevo León). Some supporters of the recently executed Padre Pro criticized Morrow's participation in this tour of inspection, but the Ambassador profited much from it. Will Rogers also went along and helped make everything a success. As the private railroad cars rolled from one point of interest to another, Morrow observed scenery new to him and conversed at length with the President. Instead of bringing up matters related to the controversy between the two countries, he asked numerous questions about Mexico and sought the President's point of view on

Colonel Charles A. Lindbergh *and* General Alvaro Obregón. *December, 1927. R. Topete.*

ways of bettering the country. Calles spoke at length about the revolutionary program of land reform and its complementary features, and he insisted that government intervention of the type to which his administration was addicted was the way to cure the lamentable conditions which had been inherited from the past.

Following this trip, Colonel Charles A. Lindbergh, at the height of his fame, made a flight in *The Spirit of St. Louis* from Washington, D.C., to Mexico City. This flight was made at the suggestion of Morrow, but the idea of making it a nonstop flight was Lindbergh's. At Mexico City's Balbuena Airfield on December 14 President Calles, seated between Ambassador and Mrs. Morrow, was among those in the grandstand who anxiously awaited the arrival of the "Lone Eagle." After a week of flattering attentions in Mexico City Lindbergh flew to Guatemala.

The irritating oil question had been brought up on November 8, at the time of Morrow's second breakfast with Calles. When Calles asked the Ambassador for a suggestion Morrow replied that the problem was a legal one, and cited the Mexican Supreme Court decision of 1921 in the Texas Oil Company case. With interest the Revolutionary general would listen to the advice of the banker from Wall Street, who seemed to wish to place at Calles' disposal his vast financial experience in order to help Mexico build up her prestige. Vasconcelos, who was now lecturing in the United States, began to criticize Morrow almost as strongly as he criticized Calles.

On November 17, 1927, the Mexican Supreme Court rendered its decision regarding the case of the Mexican Petroleum Company of California, which had, like others, objected to the cancellation of drilling permits following its refusal to exchange its perpetual rights for fifty-year concessions. This decision was favorable to the oil companies, since it declared unconstitutional Article Fourteen and Article Fifteen of the 1925 Petroleum Law and in substance followed the principles laid down six years earlier in the Texas Oil Company case.

Late in December President Calles submitted to the Congress recommendations for new legislation to replace the unconstitutional articles. These recommendations, acted upon at once, provided for new confirmatory concessions which were not to be limited in time and which were to go to those who could demonstrate that they had performed "positive acts" prior to May, 1917, showing the intention of exploiting petroleum. Applications for the new concessions had to be submitted within one year of the new law's effective date, January 10, 1928.

The problem of the objectionable features of the petroleum *reglamento* of the Ministry of Industry, Commerce, and Labor remained. The oil companies submitted a draft of amendments to bring the *reglamento* in line with the new legislation, but this was rejected by Luis Morones. Another draft was then submitted by Morrow and J. Reuben Clark, Jr., who, before the Supreme Court decision, had assisted the Ambassador at informal discussions with Calles about the oil question. Finally, after a period of negotiation, the Mexican government and the oil industry agreed upon a revised *reglamento* which, among other things, prohibited the transfer of the concessions to aliens.

The statement which was issued by the United States Department of State on March 28, 1928, advised that "the steps voluntarily taken by the Mexican government would appear to bring to a practical conclusion discussions which began ten years ago." While it was yet necessary to resolve certain details, such as who had what rights on May 1, 1917, the American statement, which had been drawn up by Morrow, pointed out that these matters could be settled "through the due operation of the Mexican administrative departments and the Mexican courts." Thus at least some of the companies could expect in some cases to obtain perpetual rights, and all of the companies could now turn to high taxation as their principal complaint.

Morrow was also devoting much of his attention to the agrarian program, which, regardless of the Calvo Clause, was the cause of a deluge of complaints received by the Embassy. In certain cases he was influential in having confiscatory decrees reversed, but his principal endeavor was to persuade the President of the advisability of slowing down on the rate of turning properties over to those who, in many cases, were able to make little use of them. He emphasized the financial aspects and even suggested that the amounts promised in agrarian bonds be charged against the federal budget. He sincerely felt that what was needed at the time was not much more land expropriation, but more attention to making that land productive: the credit facilities, agricultural schools, and irrigation projects which Calles loved so dearly.

The Ambassador also quietly explored the possibilities of some kind of settlement of the religious question. Through his mediation, Calles agreed to meet in secret with Father John J. Burke, of the National Catholic Welfare Conference, at the island fort of San Juan de Ulúa, which forms part of the harbor of Veracruz. This was in April, 1928. A proposal for a reconciliation was drafted and Father Burke took it to the Apostolic Delegate in Washington. The various Mexican bishops, who were at the time in exile at San Antonio, Texas, then sent Archbishop Ruiz y Flores to see Calles, and again the bases on which Catholic services might be resumed in Mexico were discussed. The archbishop left for Rome. But unfortunately the publication of an account of an interview which he was said to have had with the press in Paris and which the archbishop later said was unfounded did nothing to help matters.

In accordance with the Pani-Lamont Amendment, Mexico in 1926 paid the interest due that year on her direct foreign debt, and in addition paid over 5 million pesos on account of the bonds of the National Railways of Mexico. The year 1927 was a poorer year because of the collapse in the revenue from petroleum taxes; in order to make the payments on her foreign debt, the Mexican government had to borrow 6 million pesos, partly from the Bank of Mexico and partly from the International Bankers Committee itself. In 1927 no payments were made to the holders of the railroad bonds.

The agreements called for about 70 million pesos in 1928 to cover payments due on the direct foreign debt alone, an amount which Calles and Finance Minister Montes de Oca saw could not be furnished. In the 1928 federal budget, which totalled 290 million pesos, they included an item of 32,500,000 pesos for servicing the foreign debt, and they sent negotiators to New York.[1]

The International Bankers Committee next sent Joseph E. Sterrett and Joseph S. Davis to make an on-the-spot study of the Mexican financial situation. After three months these gentlemen rendered a report advising that a variety of circumstances, which could be considered of a temporary nature, caused Mexico to have at the moment an abnormally low capacity to make the required payments. The Bankers Committee studied the report and then in October, 1928, accepted the invitation of the Mexican government to send representatives to Mexico for discussions. During the talks which followed, Morrow used his influence to stimulate the idea of handling the different bond issues—both domestic and foreign—in a comprehensive way.

Montes de Oca presented his proposals to Congress at the end of 1928. He suggested that payments on domestic government bonds, with the exception of the agrarian bond issue and the debt owed to the banks due to the seizures of metallic reserves, be suspended until an overall arrangement could be made. In the case of the

[1] Edgar Turlington, *Mexico and Her Foreign Creditors*, pp. 313–314.

foreign debt the Finance Minister proposed a consolidation of the various issues into a single issue redeemable in forty-five years or more and calling for an annual interest not to exceed 5 per cent. The holders of the railroad bonds would do their negotiating directly with the National Railways.

Further negotiations by the interested parties ran into delay occasioned by problems of a political and military nature.

38·

The Presidential Campaign of Generals, 1927–1928

General Arnulfo R. Gómez, who in 1923 and 1924 had worked to make Mexico City dangerous for De la Huerta and his supporters, spent the early part of the Calles administration on an official trip of military studies in the United States and Europe. After handing in a lengthy report on his trip he was placed in charge of Veracruz Military Operations.

One morning when Gómez was breakfasting at "Santa Bárbara" with his close friend Calles, the President advised him that Morones appeared to be the most suitable one to occupy the presidency because of his "ample preparation and his familiarity with national problems, and because of his complete identification with the working masses."[1] The large labor leader was a powerful figure whose influence dominated governorships and Cabinet ministries. Although his presidential ambitions were backed by many who owed their posts to him, such as the ambassador to the United States, Morones suffered from a serious handicap in the opposition of Obregón and the many Obregonistas who were in the federal legislature. It seemed likely that if this obstacle should thwart the Morones candidacy the President would support Arnulfo Gómez.

Early in the Calles administration Obregón looked upon his protégé and former War Minister, General Francisco R. Serrano, as possible timber for the presidency. Well known was Serrano's addiction to night life, and few had not heard of how, not long after the triumph of the Agua Prieta movement, Obregón had let the National Treasury take care of a large gambling loss sustained in one night of play by Serrano. After Obregón left the presidency he sent Serrano on a European trip as a means of maturing him. But when Serrano returned from Europe Obregón failed to see in him the necessary presidential qualifications. Serrano on the other hand returned rather enthusiastic about the possibilities, and for a while basked in the approving attitudes of a number of Obregonistas in the Army.

Obregón concluded that the best interests of Mexico would be served by his own re-election, and in that conclusion he had some backing. "We renounced in a conscious manner," says Portes Gil, "the democratic ideal of No Re-election." Although neither Calles nor Morones was enthusiastic about amending the Constitution to permit re-election to the presidency, the Obregonista majority in Congress set to work to make such re-election possible provided the terms of office were not consecutive. When an Obregonista senator, General Higinio Alvarez García of Colima, sought to make this even sweeter by proposing an amendment which would lengthen the term from four to six years, he received some words of caution. Calles sent Luis L. León to object. And Obregón told the senator that while he would have to be a candidate again because neither Serrano nor Gómez was suitable, the proposal to lengthen the term would merely give ammunition to "our enemies." Late in 1926, over the objections of Morones elements, the Constitution was amended to permit nonconsecutive presidential re-elections, and

[1] Fernando López Portillo in *El Universal*, November 1, 1956.

somewhat later Senator Higinio Alvarez García obtained approval of his amendment to increase the length of the term to six years.[2]

Morones was not averse to seeing the pressure kept on Serrano, nor was he disappointed when a few generals signed a secret anti-re-election manifesto. For a while Calles expressed the thought that Obregón was not seriously considering desertion of the Revolutionary ideal of No Re-election. Gómez received some additional encouragement when Calles indicated to him that Serrano was not worthy of the presidency. But as Obregón's intention became clearer, Calles came to realize that if he did not support Obregón there would be a repetition of the Agua Prieta movement and it would be backed by a majority of the Army. In the face of this probability he resolved that the best thing to do would be to cease pushing for his friends Luis Morones and Arnulfo Gómez.[3]

By the first months of 1927 there was considerable opposition from those who said they disliked the idea of presidential re-election. At a banquet commemorating the tenth anniversary of the 1917 Constitution, Lic. Calixto Maldonado said that the recent changes were illegal. Arnulfo Gómez and Francisco Serrano, although now lacking the official support they had hoped to have, found themselves approached by the opposition as possible nominees for the dangerous task of contesting the ambition of Obregón.

Vito Alessio Robles was serving as minister to Sweden when he learned with dismay that Congress had modified the Constitution to make Obregón's re-election possible. In the Senate he had not only irked Morones but had voted against the granting of some concessions which it seemed to him would benefit the Obregón family, and the result of all this had been the offer by Calles of a diplomatic post in Japan or Sweden. Now he returned to Mexico, rejected Aarón Sáenz' offer of a position on the Obregón campaign committee, and instead threw himself into the work of organizing the Gran Convención del Partido Antirreeleccionista. The Antirreeleccionista Party name had been made famous by Francisco I. Madero in the 1910–1911 overthrow of the Porfirio Díaz dictatorship, and there was at this time some popular enthusiasm for the reappearance of the party.

[2] Higinio Alvarez García in *El Universal*, October 5 and 6, 1949 reproduced in part on pp. 47–51 of Alberto J. Pani's *La historia, agredida;* also Higinio Alvarez García in *El Universal*, October 6, 1956.

[3] Fernando López Portillo in *El Universal*, November 1, 1956.

At their convention of June, 1927, the Antirreeleccionistas criticized the operation of the Bank of Mexico and put forth projects to establish Bancos Populares and more agricultural and *ejido* credits. On June 23 the assemblage acclaimed as their standard-bearer General Arnulfo Gómez, who seemed to be concerning himself more with public feeling than was Serrano. Thinking that the support of Vasconcelos would be useful, Alessio Robles sent a telegram to Chicago, but the former Education Minister replied by calling Gómez another "ruffian." When a commission advised the General of his selection, the new nominee showed some caution and stated that as he was military commander of Veracruz he could not at the moment involve h'mself in political matters. He did note that differences of opinion existed and recommended that everyone become united. He added that he felt sure that the President would respect the mandate of public opinion.

Just as soon as the Antirreeleccionistas had concluded their convention, the Comité Pro-Serrano gathered at the Arbeu Theatre. Calling itself the Partido Nacional Revolucionario, this gathering shouted down the name of Obregón and went through the formality of considering the merits of Serrano, Gómez, Vasconcelos, and Gilberto Valenzuela. After Serrano had been nominated, he relinquished the headship of the Federal District in favor of Lic. Primo Villa Michel and dedicated himself to achieving the presidency, a task in which he hoped to be aided by his many friends in the Army.

Then on June 26 Obregón did what was expected of him, announcing his resolve to return to political activities at the call of the nation. In a lengthy proclamation he praised the work of Calles and classified the Antirreeleccionistas as conservatives. He observed that as there were two opposition candidates, evidently they were not sincere about the principle of No Re-election because neither was willing to put his own personal ambition aside in its favor. Had they sincerely opposed the 1926 constitutional changes they should, he said, have taken legal steps against the changes when they were being made, and if their efforts had been unsuccessful they could then have resigned the official positions which they were fulfilling thanks to the support they enjoyed from the Administration.

When asked by Dr. Bernardo J. Gastélum if it were not paradoxical to have to violate the principle of No Re-election in order to assure the principle of Effective Suffrage, Obregón replied that in Mexico one could accomplish nothing when one was out of power. "Once we are in the presidency we shall issue an election law and also a law about political parties, and in this we shall seek the collaboration of the best minds of Mexico, regardless of factions. Quite the opposite of what is being done now, we shall subsidize the opposition, for it is evident that it is a voice that should be heard. It would be desirable to have but two political parties."[4]

Presidential candidates Arnulfo R. Gómez *and* Francisco R. Serrano *at Chapultepec Restaurant. 1927. Casasola.*

Immediately following Obregón's pronouncement of June 26, Gómez suggested that the Hero of Celaya withdraw his candidacy, in which case both he and Serrano would, he felt sure, also withdraw from the race. It was a safe offer.

During July the three candidates, all of them from the northwest, started their campaigning in earnest. Obregón's campaign was under the direction of his former associate in battle, Aarón Sáenz, who had become governor of Nuevo León after resigning as Minister of Foreign Relations in April, 1927. Serrano and Gómez attacked their old leader but were careful not to attack each other. Rather, they embraced each other at a banquet in their honor on July 1.

[4] Carlos Barrera, *Obregón*, p. 156.

Gómez threw caution to the winds. In Puebla he stated that for Obregón and his political supporters he had in mind two places: one at the penal colony of the Islas Marías, and the other two meters underground. Such punishments, he said, would prove fitting examples for those who sought to kill a sacred principle. Serrano expressed his conviction that Obregón had lost his political wisdom and was no longer devoting his talents to the benefit of the poor classes. While some conjectured on the possibility of Obregón and Calles alternating in the presidency for an indefinite period of time, others felt that Obregón was seeking to follow in the footsteps of Porfirio Díaz. Serrano asked Calles how he could contemplate

Ex-President Alvaro Obregón *and* President Plutarco Elías Calles *at the Castle of Chapultepec. Beside Calles is* General Amaro. *April, 1926. Enrique Díaz.*

permitting a presidential re-election, and in reply the President pointed out that his predecessor had a very strong following. Army supporters of Serrano found themselves placed in less important positions.

When Luis Cabrera was asked whether he would be a presidential candidate, he answered by saying that he had not yet signed his last will and testament. Vasconcelos was more rash. He said he would return to Mexico if a group of citizens would put forth his candidacy; but no such group developed.

Gómez, the more active of the two opposition candidates, covered important sections of the country on a speaking tour in the company of Rafael Martínez de Escobar, Francisco J. Santamaría, and Enrique Bordes Mangel. He wore out his health and in his exhaustion seemed at times a different, a more mature and approachable, Arnulfo Gómez than the general who had put fear into De la Huerta. He emphasized the mutilation of the Constitution by "Alvaro Santana" and drew attention to the tactics of "imposition" being used by the group in power. These tactics, he said, not only made the Antirreeleccionista campaign difficult but probably would not allow the true public desire to be respected. "If mockery is made of the vote, the only recourse will be the one which Obregón himself used in 1920: the force of arms."

Obregón made the familiar trip down the west coast in order to reach Mexico City, and there from a balcony of the Centro Director Obregonista offices on Avenida Juárez he and his associates, Aarón Sáenz, Alfonso Romandía Ferreira, and Antonio Díaz Soto y Gama, addressed the multitudes. He visited Michoacán and then went north. After reviewing the struggle in favor of popular rights and against reactionary tendencies, he defined as "reactionary" a good deal of the nation's press, "subsidized by the residues of the conservative elements." Like the gold hoards of the big Wall Street trusts, the attitudes of Gómez and Serrano were "reactionary." These men, said the official candidate, had withdrawn from the Administration's vigorous social program.

Until the end of August, Serrano limited himself to making occasional statements against Obregón in Mexico City. More forceful was General Carlos A. Vidal, head of the Comité Pro-Serrano and once governor of Tabasco and Chiapas. The *reeleccionistas*, he said, consisted of the Congress, twelve or fifteen state governors, three or four Cabinet ministries, the government exchequer and a number of other government offices. "With these elements it is impossible to triumph democratically, but it is possible to carry out a bloody ridicule of the vote." He called the conversion of the Chamber of Deputies into a political party a threat to free expression, and he accused Governors Portes Gil, Garrido Canabal, Manuel Pérez Treviño, and Carlos Riva Palacio of co-operating in the work of "fraud and corruption."

Lic. Antonio Díaz Soto y Gama *making a speech during Obregón's presidential campaign in 1927. Enrique Díaz.*

340

On August 28 at La Bombilla Restaurant in San Angel, on the outskirts of Mexico City, Gómez and Serrano attended a great banquet in honor of Vidal. Speakers included not only the presidential candidates but also General Juan Barragán, Carranza's chief of staff. Gómez accused Aarón Sáenz of having tried to have him arrested in Chihuahua on the charge of "recruiting men," and he affirmed that it was not true that he had been stirring up a rebellion.

The Partido Laborista finally got around to the difficult task of choosing a candidate during the first days of September, although labor groups in Zacatecas and Querétaro had earlier and independently declared themselves for Obregón. At the national convention the delegates considered the names of Morones, Celestino Gasca, Serrano, and Obregón, but regretfully found that the first two could not qualify because they were still holding government posts. The problem that confronted Morones and his companions was finally resolved with the convention's decision to go along for the time being with the Obregón candidacy but to empower the general directive committee to change this decision if the candidate should depart from the "correct" norms.

During the last days of September some meetings were held by representatives of the two opposition candidates in an endeavor to bring an end to the split. Félix F. Palavicini presided over sessions which were attended by three Antirreeleccionistas, including Vito Alessio Robles and Calixto Maldonado, and three Serranistas, including Carlos A. Vidal. Maldonado presented a project whereby one candidate would withdraw in order to become president of the new fusion party. But when he pointed out that Gómez had been the first to campaign throughout the country, Vidal asserted that, while it would be imprudent to mention any names, Serrano was the candidate who had the greater support in the Army. This point, suggested Maldonado, might better be discussed in the presence of both candidates, but Palavicini opposed the idea.

It proved easier to agree that the election would not be honest and that arms should be used to make public opinion effective than to decide on which candidate should withdraw. There was some discussion as to whether Gómez or Serrano could bring off the more successful military movement, the Antirreeleccionistas insisting that public opinion backed Gómez and that a military effort would fail unless it had public support. It was finally resolved that the commissioners would meet again after speaking with their respective candidates to learn from them "which of them had the more certain probabilities of military support."

At the meeting which was held two or three days later, Vidal said that Serrano had the greater military support and Alessio Robles said that Gómez had the greater military support. When Alessio Robles suggested a new convention to put up a third candidate, preferably a civilian, the suggestion was vetoed by the Serranistas, who made it clear that their candidate had given some commitments to supporters and would not abandon them. The Comisión Mixta Unificadora thereupon agreed on one more thing, which was that it would be impossible to get together. Before the group broke up Colonel Carlos T. Robinson said that Serrano was the candidate of a national convention, and Lic. Federico Sodi said that while Serrano had earlier not concerned himself with the "populace" he did nevertheless have much popularity. Alessio Robles, calling himself a socialist, objected to the term which Sodi had used in referring to the "populace."

The Antirreeleccionistas departed with the idea that Serrano was more concerned with a quick military blow than with public opinion, and they guessed that if he realized a military triumph he would install Vidal as Provisional President until an election could be held for the purpose of making Serrano the Constitutional President.

CALIFORNIA
Mexicali

ARIZONA
Tucson

NEW MEXICO

Nogales

Cd. Juárez

SONORA

Hermosillo

CHIHUAHUA

Chihuahua

TERRITORIO
DE
BAJA
CALIFORNIA
NORTE

BAJA CALIFORNIA

GOLFO DE CALIFORNIA

COA

TERRITORIO DE
BAJA CALIFORNIA SUR

SINALOA

Tepehuanes

Torreón

Culiacán

DURANGO

Durango

PACIFIC

La Paz

ZACAT

Zacatecas

Mazatlán

NAY

AGUASCALI

Aguascaliente

Las Tres Marías

I. María Madre
I. María Magdalena
I. María Cleofas

Tepic

Guadalajaj

JAL S

MEXICO

Scale

0   100   200   300

Miles

0   300

Kilometers

Colima

COLIMA

MIC.

O

C

E

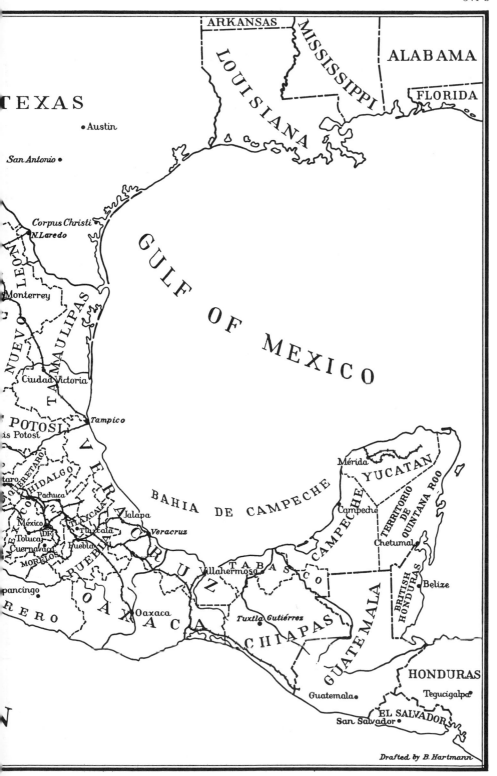

ARKANSAS

MISSISSIPPI

ALABAMA

LOUISIANA

FLORIDA

TEXAS

•Austin

San Antonio •

GULF

OF

MEXICO

Corpus Christi•
•N. Laredo

•Monterrey

NUEVO LEON

TAMAULIPAS

Ciudad Victoria

POTOSI

is Potosí

Tampico

BAHIA DE CAMPECHE

Mérida

YUCATAN

CAMPECHE

VERACRUZ

QUERETARO

HIDALGO

Pachuca

México

TLAXCALA

Jalapa

Tlaxcala

Veracruz

Toluca

DF

Campeche

TERRITORIO DE QUINTANA ROO

Chetumal

Cuernavaca

Puebla

MORELOS

PUEBLA

Villahermosa

TABASCO

BRITISH HONDURAS

Belize

pancingo

OAXACA

Oaxaca

Tuxtla Gutiérrez

RERO

CHIAPAS

GUATEMALA

HONDURAS

Guatemala •

Tegucigalpa•

EL SALVADOR

San Salvador •

N

Drafted by B. Hartmann

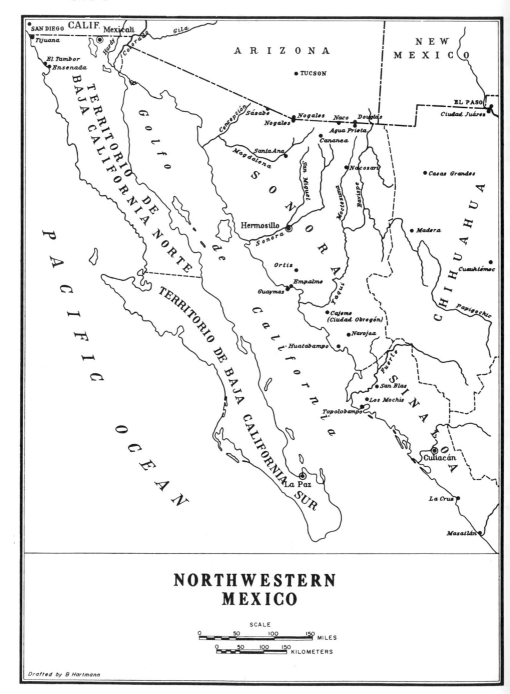

**NORTHWESTERN
MEXICO**

SCALE

0   50   100   150 MILES

0   50   100   150 KILOMETERS

Drafted by B Hartmann

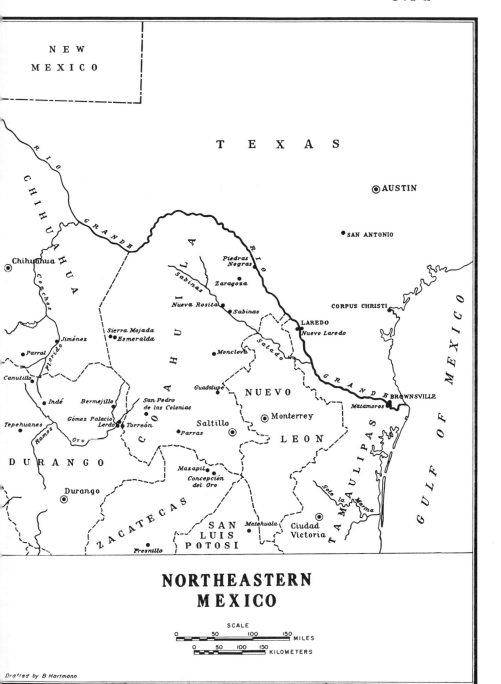

TEXAS

⊙ AUSTIN

• SAN ANTONIO

CHIHUAHUA

RIO

GRANDE

Corchos

⊙ Chihuahua

Piedras
Negras

Sabinas

Zaragoza

Nueva Rosita •

• Sabinas

RIO

CORPUS CHRISTI

LAREDO
Nuevo Laredo

Sierra Mojada

•• Esmeralda

• Jiménez

Florido

• Parral

Monclova

C O A H U I L A

Salado

GRANDE

• BROWNSVILLE

Matamoros

GULF OF MEXICO

Canutillo

Guadalupe

NUEVO

• Indé

Bermejillo

San Pedro
de las Colonias

⊙ Monterrey

Tepehuanes

Gómez Palacio
Lerdo •• Torreón

Saltillo ⊙

LEON

Ramos

Oro

• Parras

TAMAULIPAS

D U R A N G O

Mazapil •

Concepción
del Oro

⊙ Durango

Soto
la
Marina

Z A C A T E C A S

S A N
L U I S
P O T O S I

Matehuala •

Ciudad
Victoria

• Fresnillo

NORTHEASTERN
MEXICO

SCALE

0   50   100   150
                                    MILES

0   50   100   150
                          KILOMETERS

Drafted by B. Hartmann

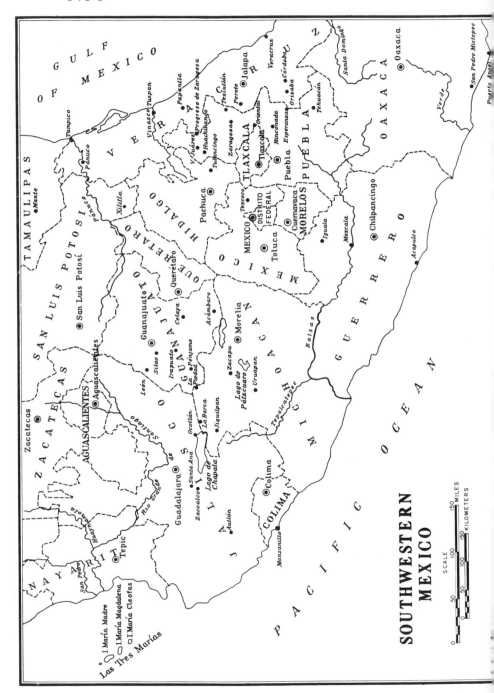

SOUTHWESTERN MEXICO

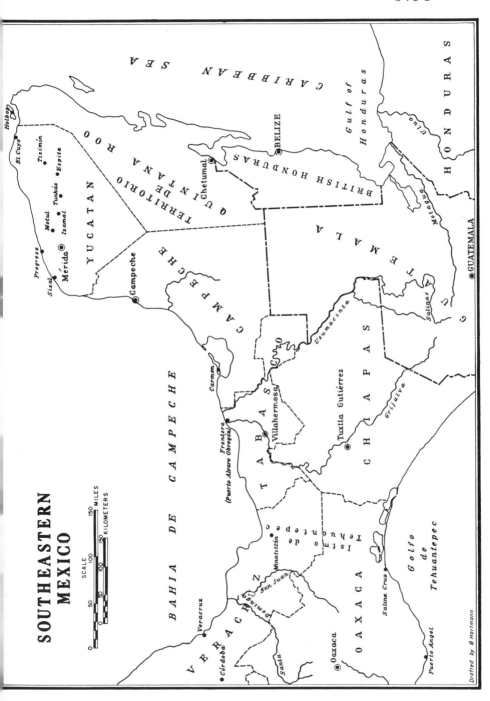

SOUTHEASTERN MEXICO

Drafted by B Hartmann

342

39.

Bloody Climax of the 1927–1928 Presidential Campaign

As early as Saturday, October 1, 1927, Arnulfo Gómez, whose health was rapidly deteriorating, phoned Palavicini to advise that there would be a military uprising on the following day. When Vito Alessio Robles found him preparing to make his departure from Mexico City, the candidate explained that he did not intend to start a rebellion but that, as events outside his control, including the Serrano revolt, were about to take place, he wished to join General Horacio Lucero at Perote, Veracruz, in order to insure his own safety.

Gómez' staunch Antirreeleccionista Party supporters, Lics.

Rafael Martínez de Escobar and Francisco J. Santamaría, were disappointed to learn from the departing candidate that he did not want them to accompany him on his trip to Perote. He explained that the two of them should spend the following day, Sunday, promenading in the streets of Mexico City, being sure to be seen in Chapultepec Park, in order to dispel suspicion. When the two lawyers objected, Gómez remarked: "Your lives are very precious to me and I don't want to see you lose them in this business. I, yes; that's just what is going to happen to me. I know this whole affair has fallen apart but there's no going back now. Serrano has dragged us all into this mess, and I have to leave to see if I can save myself, or else face whatever develops. You two hide here."

On the day before Gómez departed, Serrano, with a number of friends, had left Mexico City for Cuernavaca, Morelos, so as to follow from there the story which was now to unfold. General Juan Domínguez, head of Military Operations in Morelos, was a close friend and *compadre* of Serrano.

Martínez de Escobar, restless and not at all anxious to remain in the capital, observed that people would get a poor opinion of civilians and would say that the soldiers did everything. He asked Santamaría to accompany him and Generals Daniel and Miguel Angel Peralta on a trip into the state of Guerrero, where, he said, Vigueras and Victoriano Bárcenas were already up in arms against the Calles government. Any further convincing needed by Santamaría was provided late that night by General Miguel Angel Peralta, who suggested that they all join General Carlos Ariza in Cuernavaca and then proceed to Guerrero. He spoke with enthusiasm and confidence about the Army revolt, scheduled to take place at 8:00 P.M. on the next day at Balbuena, close to Mexico City. "Serrano has been in Cuernavaca since yesterday, waiting to see what happens here. And it should all go quickly, as everything is very well prepared. General Villarreal has also agreed to join the movement."

Santamaría yielded. But before the night was over he and Martínez de Escobar paid a call on Antonio I. Villarreal, who was in hiding in Mexico City. Villarreal had none of General Peralta's optimism: "I don't have much faith in what is going to happen here; and even if Serrano is in Cuernavaca, I think I had better go to Texcoco [in the state of México] tomorrow and join Rueda Quijano, in whom I have full confidence." But the old Revolutionary commended his visitors for not sticking with Gómez, with whom his relations had been far from cordial. Some of Villarreal's good wine was used by the plotters to toast the coming events, Santamaría becoming convinced that he should play his cards openly and that it would be cowardly to remain in Mexico City.

After but little sleep, Daniel and Miguel Peralta drove with Martínez de Escobar and Santamaría to Cuernavaca. There was much hopeful talk in the automobile on that morning of October 2. The consensus was that General Eugenio Martínez (the man who in 1912 had trained the "Fourth Battalion" of Lieutenant Colonel Obregón) would succeed in quickly crushing just three men who were the main props of the government: Calles, Obregón, and Amaro. The travellers also took comfort in the close association between Serrano and Juan Domínguez, and they agreed that Carlos Vidal, who was working so actively with Serrano, would make an excellent Provisional President.

Upon reaching Cuernavaca they took lodgings in the Moctezuma Hotel, and had a visit with General Carlos Ariza. Someone offered the post of Education Minister to Santamaría. Those prone to conjecture had Serrano planning a government somewhat as follows:

Provisional President	General Carlos A. Vidal
Gobernación Minister	Lic. Rafael Martínez de Escobar
War Minister	General Eugenio Martínez
Communications Minister	General Miguel A. Peralta
Education Minister	Lic. Francisco J. Santamaría
Agriculture Minister	General Antonio I. Villarreal

Noting that neither the Peraltas nor Ariza were taking them on south to Guerrero as originally planned, and beginning to feel that, contrary to Gómez' instructions, they were becoming involved in an unfamiliar and possibly dangerous situation, Martínez de Escobar and Santamaría determined to return to Mexico City if the expedition to Guerrero did not get under way by 3:00 o'clock on that afternoon of the second. But just before 3:00 they received a message saying that Vidal wanted to see them, and as they waited and waited for Vidal it finally grew so late that they had to give up the idea of returning that evening to Mexico City, where the military uprising was scheduled for 8:00 P.M.

Vidal and Serrano were staying at the Bellavista Hotel, not far from the Moctezuma. Vidal's delay in seeing the lawyers was explained as caused by his being tied up in an important conference with Serrano and Juan Domínguez, the latter having come to Cuernavaca for that purpose. What actually transpired, however, was that since Domínguez preferred to stay away from Cuernavaca Serrano therefore had to send the owner of the Bellavista as a messenger to Domínguez to seek assurances of his support. But the military commander of Morelos had bad news for his *compadre*. Pointing out that he could not be a traitor to any government which he served, he told Serrano to expect no assistance from him. The best he could do was to advise Serrano to get out of the state at once.

By the time Domínguez had made his position clear, late on the afternoon of October 2, General Antonio I. Villarreal, who was not supposed to be on Mexican soil, arrived on the Cuernavaca scene. There he and General Benito Ramírez joined up with Colonel Daniel P. Fort. Fort had breakfasted with Calles at "Santa Bárbara" that morning and, against the advice of Calles, had then gone to Cuernavaca to join Serrano for the celebration of the candidate's Saint's Day.

At Cuernavaca a strong warning reached Fort. The situation seemed even more discouraging to Villarreal's companions when they visited Serrano, whom they found playing checkers at the Bellavista. After Serrano let them know of the position which Domínguez had taken, Fort offered to take Serrano into the mountains or to Mexico City, but the offer was not accepted. When Villarreal remarked to Vidal that "things seemed to be going all right, as I notice numerous troops concentrated here, all certainly ready to advance on Mexico City," Vidal replied: "That's the way it should be, but it's just the reverse."

The hour of 8:00 P.M. approached, at which time Army maneuvers were scheduled to take place at Mexico City's Balbuena Field in the presence of Calles, Obregón, and Amaro. One of the most significant aspects of this armed display was that at the last minute it was placed under the direction not of Eugenio Martínez, but of General Héctor Ignacio Almada, Martínez' chief of staff. At the moment when the maneuvers started, General Martínez, relieved of his command, was departing from the capital to undertake a "study mission" in Europe.

Neither Obregón nor Calles had been unaware of what was in the air. Obregón, who had interrupted his campaign tour to come to the capital, participated in decisions which had to do with replacing dubious military contingents with those known to be faithful. But Obregón's greatest contribution was his conversation with

Eugenio Martínez, which resulted in the latter's hasty departure.

Calles and Obregón did not show up for the evening's event at Balbuena, and when Amaro put in a late appearance he was formidably escorted. After he departed, four of the city's military groups marched off from the capital, having noised about their intentions against the government. As these soldiers took the road for Texcoco, thus starting a rebellion under Almada, there were some "vivas" for Serrano and Gómez. Leaders of the four rebel groups were Generals Oscar Aguilar, Antonio Medina, and Alfredo Rueda Quijano and Colonel Carlos Altamira. The head of the presidential military staff announced that no more than 500 had participated in this desertion, but the actual number slightly exceeded one thousand. In the general excitement rumors ran that the story would have been different had Calles and Obregón attended the night maneuvers, and there was talk as to the possibility of yet taking Calles prisoner at Chapultepec Castle after a blockade of the city.

If Gómez and Serrano had as yet committed no step that could be proved rebellious, at least there was a rebellion under way in their names. It was not a very formidable one, particularly as Almada's men lacked arms, ammunition, and money.

If another storm signal was necessary for Villarreal and his companions late that night in Cuernavaca, it came in the form of a report from the Cuernavaca telegraph office that a message had been received from the President to the Morelos governor, Ambrosio Puente, a message ordering the governor to make prisoners of Serrano and all of his companions.

Before Villarreal and his group left Cuernavaca in Fort's car they stopped at the Moctezuma to leave a message for their friends there to get out of town at once. Santamaría, Martínez de Escobar, and Miguel Angel Peralta picked up this message when they returned from the Bellavista. In the meantime Fort had an exciting drive to Mexico City with Villarreal and Benito Ramírez. At one time when they encountered government troops on their way to Cuernavaca, Fort shrewdly left his small grey car to say something to an officer about the advisability of being on the lookout for Serrano, who would be coming along in a red Lincoln. Fort had credentials of a high order and the officer allowed the car and its nervous passengers to go on to Mexico City, although admitting that he had instructions to let no car pass.

After Serrano had left the Bellavista to spend the night hiding in the home of a Cuernavaca friend, Carlos Vidal dropped in at the Moctezuma to reassure his friends there, or perhaps to try to reassure himself. When Miguel Angel Peralta asked him whether the time had come to embrace him as "señor Presidente Provisional de la República," Vidal commented that "as a result of the events in Mexico City, Domínguez will back the movement." Vidal's friends were less optimistic about the outcome at Balbuena and, after Vidal left, they too departed from their hotel, feeling that a safer place to seek a little sleep would be the home of an acquaintance of Miguel Angel Peralta.

Very early on the morning of October 3 the federal senator from Chiapas, General Higinio Alvarez García, heard that General Vicente González, famed for fighting Delahuertistas in Tabasco and now head of the Army's Artillery Department, might be in danger for having sent cartridges to General Luis T. Vidal in Chiapas. Alvarez García went quickly to the home of Obregón, suggesting that his friend Vicente González not be assassinated; that if he had committed any faults they be judged by military tribunals.

Obregón told the senator not to worry: "I am going to Chapultepec Castle right away and Vicente won't be killed."[1]

From his home on Jalisco Avenue Obregón sped to the Castle to be at the side of the President. Among the others who did likewise in the early hours of October 3 were War Minister Amaro, Presidential Secretary Torreblanca, and the head of the presidential military staff, General José Alvarez. Firm measures were to be taken to prevent a repetition of the 1923–1924 disaster.

That morning Cuernavaca was full of soldiers carrying out the orders which Calles had sent to Governor Puente. Santamaría and his friends made a brief return to their hotel, leaving it just before the federal troops took it over, and then they fled through the streets completely disorganized. Cried Martínez de Escobar, who had learned from his cousin about the orders of arrest: "Let those who can, save themselves." The two lawyers followed the Peralta brothers, and in this way they reached a house in which they found Serrano. There in a room with eight beds ranged in two rows Serrano and his companions had been sleeping in their street clothes. The atmosphere was one of deep depression. Said Serrano: "If you are

[1] Higinio Alvarez García in *El Universal*, October 8, 1956.

captured with me here you can say that you came because my friends invited you to attend the dinner being given for me tomorrow at my ranch."[2]

Santamaría expressed doubt that any such reason would be believed, "bearing in mind that they consider you politically as the only one responsible for what may have happened last night in Mexico. I think that we should leave Cuernavaca as best we can, or else put up resistance here."

Addressing all those present and raising his arms, Serrano said: "No one is to resist if they capture us here."

It was twenty minutes after noon; and Santamaría was guessing that not five minutes would pass before they would be captured. Hardly had he expressed his thought when loud knocks on the front door announced the arrival of the federal guard. After an exchange of words with the head of the guard, Serrano made a calm announcement to his companions: "Gentlemen, be kind enough to accompany me." Generals taken with Serrano were Carlos A. Vidal, Miguel Angel Peralta, and Daniel Peralta. Others captured at the same time were Rafael Martínez de Escobar, Francisco J. Santamaría, Captain Ernesto V. Méndez, Antonio Jáuregui, Ing. José Villa Arce, Augusto Peña, and Enrique Monteverde; taken also was Alonso Capetillo, who had participated in the De la Huerta rebellion and had later written on that subject a book which showed Calles in a favorable light.

The head of the capturing guard happened to be Martínez de Escobar's cousin, Major Angel Fernández Escobar, who had previously urged Martínez de Escobar to escape and was consequently most unhappily surprised to find the politician here. As the line of prisoners and soldiers left the house and marched down the sidewalk amidst a mob of observers, Martínez de Escobar carried on a heated discussion with his cousin. Santamaría was the last in the line and directly behind him. At a moment when the debate of the cousins had attracted the attention of the soldier guarding Santamaría, Santamaría stepped into the crowd of observers and thus escaped.

However, three more prisoners were taken elsewhere and added to those who were taken with Serrano. They were Lic. Otilio González, Major Octavio R. Almada, and Carlos B. Ariza, the retired general whom Martínez de Escobar, Santamaría, and the Peraltas

[2] Francisco J. Santamaría, *La tragedia de Cuernavaca en 1927 y mi escapatoria célebre*, pp. 114 ff.

had planned to accompany on a rebellious expedition into the southern state of Guerrero.

Governor Puente, feeling that he had nothing to do with these military matters, left his captives in the hands of General Enrique Díaz González, who was in charge of the garrison at Cuernavaca.

The group at Chapultepec Castle called for General José Gonzalo Escobar and General Claudio Fox, the head of Military Operations in the state of Guerrero. Escobar was ordered to combat the group which had revolted under Almada, and he promptly marched forth with 2000 men.

At dawn government troops fell on the Sixteenth Battalion at Torreón, Coahuila, suspected of being unsympathetic to the ambitions of General Obregón. Lieutenant Colonel Augusto Manzanillo and all the officers of the Sixteenth Battalion were shot. Other examples of federal firmness at Torreón included the shooting of General Agapito Lastra and the arrest of Dr. Rafael Cepeda.

When the news of the capture of Serrano and his companions and of their confinement by General Enrique Díaz reached the group at Chapultepec Castle this group had been joined there by Montes de Oca, Puig Casauranc, and Roberto Cruz. Alvarez García and a fellow senator went to the Castle and found thirty or forty persons in the patio of tall pine trees. Going on into the building they came upon a large oval table, where Calles was seated with Obregón at his left and Amaro at his right.

The chief of staff brought the President an order calling for the shooting of Serrano and his companions, an order which had been agreed upon by the President and the ex-President. In the course of some further discussion Calles stood up and struck the table with both hands, remarking that "they would certainly have shot us if they'd caught us in that trap they set for us at Balbuena."[3]

At that moment General Claudio Fox was seen passing in front of the door giving on to the patio. Fox was summoned; when he reached the table the President was still standing, his hands shaking. Fox, receiving the orders affecting Serrano and his associates, simply said, "Your orders will be carried out, Señor Presidente." Then he spoke with Amaro, who provided him means of transportation to the barracks of the First Artillery Regiment. At the barracks Fox was to receive the necessary funds and was to be joined

---

[3] Higinio Alvarez García in *El Universal*, October 8, 1956.

by Colonel Nazario Medina and an escort of fifty soldiers, all of whom were to proceed under Fox to take Serrano and the other prisoners from General Díaz. A few additional officers were assigned to Fox by Amaro. Fox has stated that on the copy of the telegram which he received, ordering Díaz to turn the prisoners over to him, Calles had written: "Execute the prisoners and bring their bodies here."[4]

In addition to the Lincoln which Fox received from Amaro he had some rented Fords, in such poor condition that the journey to join up with General Díaz was a slow one. Not until about 4:00 P.M. did the soldiers reach the group which was proceeding toward Mexico City from Cuernavaca. Near Huitzilac Fox and his men found the prisoners in three small automobiles and in two postal cars, escorted by a marching group of about one hundred soldiers. The prisoners were taken from their conveyances, and Fox found that all of them, except for a one-armed man, had their arms tied behind their backs with electric wiring cord. Serrano was "smiling and fatalistic," as were the Peralta brothers, but General Vidal appeared to be unnerved. Lic. Martínez de Escobar's request for permission to make a speech to the soldiers was denied. When Serrano asked Fox what had happened to the military uprising in Mexico City, he was told that it had been of no importance. He also asked Fox what his orders were, and Fox replied that he had been ordered to take the prisoners to Mexico City.

Then, following the orders which he had received at Chapultepec Castle, Fox directed the executions. Crispín Marroquín, the colonel in charge of Amaro's horses, was instructed to handle the execution of Serrano; Colonel Carlos C. Valdés that of Vidal. In this way to each prisoner there was assigned an officer and three soldiers. After giving these detailed orders and instructing Colonel Medina that the bodies should not be despoiled, Fox left the scene for a spot over a kilometer away, where he awaited the sound of the execution shots. He heard over one hundred discharges. After an interval he heard a few more. Later he learned that after the executions only thirteen dead prisoners, out of fourteen to be executed, could be found. When the executioners discovered that José Villa Arce had not been killed with the first volleys, they shot him before he could escape.[5]

All this transpired in the woods called "Tres Marías," near

[4] Vito Alessio Robles, *Desfile sangriento*, p. 238.
[5] *Ibid.*, p. 243.

Huitzilac, when the sun was setting on October 3, 1927. Appropriate photographs were taken and displayed by the government. The fourteen bodies were conveyed to the Military Hospital in Mexico City and then turned over to relatives, who later marked the place of their deaths in the shadowed glade with crosses still to be seen from the old road.

On September 21 twenty-three members of the Federal House of Deputies had issued a proclamation attacking the changes of Constitutional Articles 82 and 83—the changes which had made presidential re-election possible. On October 3, in a short session of that legislative body, these twenty-three were thrown out of their congressional positions. Senators and deputies could be tried for crimes only by appropriate congressional committees, and so the loss of a congressional seat meant also the loss of immunity from the usual court procedures.

Dr. Puig Casauranc felt that the lives of Ing. Félix F. Palavicini and Ing. Vito Alessio Robles, one a newspaperman and the other a former newspaperman, might be in danger on account of their earlier involvements with Serrano and Gómez. When he spoke to Calles on their behalf, he found the President interested in seeing that their lives be spared. In the case of Vito Alessio Robles, Calles remarked that "If there is one person who can do what he wants against my government, without my being able to shoot him, it is Vito Alessio Robles, because one of his daughters, Carmen, has been, and I believe still is, an intimate, inseparable friend of my daughter. They love each other like sisters."

Both Vito Alessio Robles and Félix F. Palavicini were jailed. When Alessio Robles was arrested on October 3 he was told that the order for his apprehension had been given at 3:00 a.m. that morning by General Obregón, the presidential candidate. Since unoccupied jail cells were hard to find, Alessio Robles, for a while, shared a cell with General Luis Hermosillo, until the General was taken out to be shot. Alessio Robles was released on October 10.

On Monday, October 3, Ing. Palavicini found in the newspapers some mention, without details, of a military movement in the capital. On the fourth he saw on the first pages the photographs of the bodies of General Serrano and his companions. Like Ing. Alessio Robles, he was surprised to find out that the prominent Antirreeleccionista, Lic. Rafael Martínez de Escobar, had been among those taken with General Serrano. It was not until October 6 that Ing.

Palavicini was arrested and taken by the authorities to Mexico City's prison of Santiago Tlaltelolco. When he first reached the prison the cells were all filled, but before long he was able to occupy the one vacated by General José C. Morán, when he was taken out to be shot. Morán, who was considered responsible during the De la Huerta rebellion for the death of Dr. and Colonel Manuel Izaguirre, father of Amaro's intelligent and attractive wife, had been in jail ever since his surrender in the Tuxpan, Veracruz, district in 1924. Palavicini, after only a few days in prison, was placed on a train for Laredo, Texas, and he later went in exile to Havana and Paris.

Soon after the events of October 3, Calles received a telegram from General Eugenio Martínez, who was on his way to fulfill his military miss:on abroad. Martínez advised that he did not back General Héctor Ignacio Almada's action, and he offered to return and help the government. Calles told Martínez to keep on with his trip, since the rebellion had practically been extinguished and since it had been linked with the name of General Martínez and carried out by men who had served under him.

It was true that the rebellion was faltering. Word of the prompt and firm disciplinary action at Torreón was followed by somewhat similar news which came in from other parts of the country. The Chiapas governor, Luis T. Vidal, and his political associates came out in open rebellion against the federal government; but when Governor Vidal tried to get local guards to rebel he was killed. Unsuccessful efforts to get troops to revolt were made in Pachuca, Hidalgo, by the Serrano supporter and retired general, Arturo Lasso de la Vega. At his side was Enrique Bordes Mangel of the Antirreeleccionista Party. The retired general was captured and shot. Bordes was arrested. In Zacatecas when ex-Generals Alfredo Rodríguez and Norberto C. Olvera made efforts similar to those of Arturo Lasso de la Vega they encountered the same fate. In Sonora General Alfonso de la Huerta (brother of Don Adolfo) and General Pedro Medina were killed on October 6 in what was reported to be a skirmish against the government troops.

After the Balbuena maneuvers of Sunday evening, October 2, General Héctor Ignacio Almada and his rebels started for the state of Veracruz in order to join Arnulfo Gómez at Perote. But the pursuit by Escobar and his 2000 men was quite successful. During the first few days, at San Juan Teotihuacán, a number of Colonel Carlos Altamira's men surrendered to the government forces of General Gilberto R. Limón. At Estación Iturbe men of General Alfredo Rueda Quijano likewise quit the rebellion. The formalities were applied to Rueda Quijano, who had the misfortune of being turned over to the federal forces by some of his own soldiers. He was given an Army trial and on October 5 was executed while making an address to those present.

After these events Almada was left with about 700 men, and with these he kept on going toward Perote, hotly pursued by Escobar, Gilberto Limón, Fausto Topete, Agustín Mora, Félix Ireta, and the commander of Veracruz Military Operations, Jesús M. Aguirre. At Ayahualulco, Veracruz, on October 9 Escobar and his associates had little difficulty in routing rebel troops under Gómez, Almada, and Oscar Aguilar, and these three defeated leaders fled in different directions.

By November 4 the very infirm Arnulfo Gómez was hiding in a mountain cave with his nephew, Lieutenant Colonel Francisco Gómez Vizcarra, and Salvador Castaños. The man who was providing these fugitives with food denoted to General Escobar where they could be found, and, thanks to this advice, Escobar and his men made the capture on November 4. The prisoners were taken to Teocelo, near Jalapa, and from there by train to Coatepec. Execution on November 5 followed a brief trial on the spot.

The burial of General Gómez took place in Mexico City on November 6. At that occasion Vito Alessio Robles made a funeral oration, pointing out that although the body of General Gómez was being buried, his flag, "the glorious flag waved by the apostle Madero . . ." was not being buried. The death of Gómez "does not imply the death of antire-electionism . . ."

After the defeat of the rebels at Ayahualulco, General Oscar Aguilar fled northward, but he was captured in Monterrey, Nuevo León, and there he was shot. General Héctor Ignacio Almada, under whom the rebellion had started at Balbuena, managed to escape from the country.

In connection with the fate of Generals Serrano and Gómez we have the following observations of Ing. Marte R. Gómez: "Both General Serrano and General Gómez realized that the coming struggle meant life or death, but they were willing to risk their own lives in the hope of collecting the lives of their enemies. There was no doubt or secret about the matter. In a dramatic interview with Obregón, Serrano advised that he was going to accept the candidacy and offered to make it a campaign of gentlemen. Obregón explained that this would be impossible, since they were separating in order to fight, and the fight would, of necessity, be the kind demanded by the fatal circumstances then prevailing in Mexico. The banner of the uprising was antire-election, but, in spite of the popularity that this banner has in Mexico, the nation did not follow the rebels, for the wise policy of General Obregón was considered a guarantee for the country, whereas Serrano, whose personal conduct was hardly edifying, and Gómez, with a lightness that gave little guarantee of responsibility, could not be serious opponents of a leader who was at the peak of his maturity."[6]

Lic. Luis Cabrera observed that "Generals Calles and Obregón knew Generals Gómez and Serrano well, and although legally what was done was an atrocity, politically there was no other way to avoid a second Agua Prieta; Obregón and Calles had acquired a healthy experience in this realm from 1920, and it had been reinforced in 1923."[7]

[6] Marte R. Gómez, letter, December 2, 1955.
[7] Luis Cabrera (pseud. Blas Urrea), *Veinte años después*, pp. 135–136.

40·

The Re-election
of General Obregón

Alvaro Obregón spent the early part of 1928 in Sonora.
Then in the spring, after having explained that he had had nothing
to do with the killings of the Pro brothers, he set out to travel
around the country on his campaign tour. He was accompanied
everywhere by the leaders of the Partido Agrarista, Diputado Aurelio Manrique, Jr., who had lost his San Luis Potosí governorship
during the first part of the Calles regime, and Diputado Díaz Soto
y Gama. Lic. Aarón Sáenz devoted his energies to running the
affairs of the Centro Director Obregonista with assistance from

Antonio Valadés Ramírez, Rodrigo Gómez, Ricardo Topete, Arturo H. Orcí, and José Luis Solórzano.

Following an unsuccessful attempt against his life at Orizaba, Veracruz, the candidate went on to Yucatán. While he was campaigning at Mérida near the end of April he became far more concerned than he had been over the Orizaba physical assault. Reading in the newspapers about the verbal attacks by the Minister of Industry, Commerce, and Labor, he became incensed and rushed back to Mexico City.

At Orizaba's Hidalgo Theatre on the evening of April 30 Luis Morones had, as a starter for the Labor Day festivities, delivered a fighting speech which was encouraging to the enemies of Obregón. In it Morones had high praise for Calles, calling him a man with whom organized labor had been pleased and proud to collaborate because he fulfilled his agreements and duties. Morones went on to rebuke the position of others who, he said, were insisting on the imposition of their authority on a self-sacrificing people, and who were making use of slander and persecution. In the face of the attitude of such persons, cried Morones, it is proper "to repeat in front of the scaffold the words that served as a symbol for Napoleon: 'the old guard dies but never surrenders.' Let our enemies take away from us the congressional seats, municipal posts, and two or three governorships that have been controlled by the Labor Party . . . Let them take our positions, . . . but we shall never permit them to attack the right of the worker to organize and to protect his interests."

The conflict which developed between Obregón and Morones, who was expected to lose some of his vast power in case of Obregón's re-election, gave some pungency to the campaign of the single candidate. In a speech delivered at Jalapa, Veracruz, on May 8, Obregón reviewed the situation, pointing out that although local affiliates of the Labor Party in Coahuila, Hidalgo, and Zacatecas had early and on their own initiative backed his campaign, the Labor Party itself did not decide to adhere to his candidacy until late in August, 1927, about two months after he had thrown his hat into the ring. Furthermore, Obregón observed, while the Party's national convention had thus at length backed him, the Party's leaders had expressly reserved for themselves the right to annul this decision of the convention should they find it convenient to do so at a later date. "Our campaign," said Obregón, "gained force each day, and the enemy, its two deluded candidates already beaten, has not dared to present a new one, leaving us in the field without an enemy." But then, he continued, came the recent attack by one of the highest representatives of the group of directors of the Labor Party, who spoke of moral defects in the forthcoming Obregón Administration and who expressed an unwillingness to collaborate with it. Obregón added that he would never attempt to persuade the leaders of the Labor Party to abandon their resolution that they would not collaborate with the next administration.

At the Palacio Nacional the candidate explained to the President that he was surprised at such sharp attacks as were being made against him by a leading member of Calles' official family, and he referred to all the friends that he himself had sacrificed in order to put Calles in the highest office. A number of Obregonistas suggested that Calles should have publicly rebuked Morones. But friends of Calles pointed out that if the President had fired Morones for his speech, he would have "authorized the whole world to say that the government sought to impose Obregón's candidacy."[1]

Obregón left Mexico City in order to await, at his Sonora home, the result of the elections of July 1, 1928.

But before reaching Sonora, via the Cañón del Púlpito in the mountains between Chihuahua and Sonora, he campaigned in May throughout Chihuahua. On his trip to Jiménez, Parral, Villa Cuauhtémoc, and Chihuahua he was accompanied, among others, by Ing. Luis L. León. On their way to Casas Grandes they stopped at Madera, where Obregón promised the workers a fair code of labor laws and a social security system.

Before going to the Casino that night, Obregón and León went for a drive. As they passed among pines and moon-lit mountains in the cool night, Obregón, an able conversationalist, spoke to León about his future plans for Mexico, and, incidentally, for himself.

Obregón pointed out that groups which were taking part in the presidential election were, with the exception of the Army, poorly organized. Improvised parties of scattered groups, which come forth only at the time of each presidential election, cannot be the "cement for a constructive and lasting work of the Revolution. Besides, this system does not offer a suitable climate for the development of new national leaders."

Would Obregón and Calles take turns in the presidential chair?

[1] Alejandro Cerisola speaking in the Chamber of Deputies on October 8, 1928.

Obregón asked himself. No, he answered. "When I conclude my new term of six years, I shall be worn out, if not because of my age, because of the weight of the work. And one must bear in mind that Calles is older than I. That cannot be the solution. That would be no guarantee either for the country or for the Revolution."

Obregón said with emphasis that it was necessary to create a political or social organization with a definite program and permanent action, to "guarantee the survival of the Revolutionary principles by means of democratic paths." He visualized a school for the training of responsible future leaders so that Mexico might be spared the continuance of the present situation, wherein the resolution of each national crisis was dependent on one man or else on violence, and might be guaranteed a peaceful democratic political life.

"We must," he said, "take advantage of the six years of my government in order to create this organization, this political party that should be an expression of our desires and sentiments. And we must also take advantage of those six years to bring forth new men in our ranks, capable of taking over the direction and the responsibility of our movement."[2]

Not long after this conversation Obregón and León parted at the Púlpito Pass, León exclaiming "Viva Obregón!" and the candidate replying "Viva Chihuahua!"

The election returns for President ran as might have been supposed in view of the violent deaths of the opposition candidates.

However, with the attitude of Morones and his friends, the unrest of the militant Catholics, the resentment of the followers of those who had perished in the October and November phases of the campaign, and the breaking down of the Revolutionary principle of No Re-election, a certain amount of uneasiness hung in the air. On May 23, 1928, some bombs had been exploded in the Chamber of Deputies, creating more sensation than damage. One week later a bomb had gone off at the Centro Director Obregonista. Carlos Castro Balda was arrested as responsible for the bombing at the Chamber of Deputies.

At the request of Calles, Obregón had earlier made a statement

[2] Luis L. León, "Las conjeturas del Ing. Pani," reproduced on pp. 69–75 of Alberto J. Pani's *La historia, agredida.*

supporting the policies of the Calles Government with respect to the religious question.[3] Obregón was at this time devoting a good deal of attention to means which would bring the Cristero conflict to a swift termination. He had given Alvarez García, senator from the strife-torn state of Colima, the impression of sharing his view that the Calles-sponsored Law of Religion for Colima was so drastic as to create upheavals with the attendant destruction of wealth and the creation of "new saints" for the inspiration of fanatics.[4] In a letter written on June 1, 1928, to Colonel Jesús Otero, Obregón pointed out that "the pacification of Jalisco should not be entrusted to brute force alone." Calling for the use of some persuasive efforts, he suggested that the lower classes be made to see that the movement fostered by the clergy "goes entirely against the cause of the workers." Obregón told Otero that when he was recently in Mexico City he had found Calles in agreement with his idea of sending peasants, taken as prisoners, to Yucatán or elsewhere where they could find work and yet be unable to reunite with the rebels. Obregón considered the shooting of such prisoners to be unnecessarily cruel and improper, in view of the fact that they were hardly the responsible ones; and he also felt that whereas such shootings would strengthen the determination of the remaining rebels, a more humane treatment would have the opposite effect. As a final suggestion, Obregón called for the enforcement of more discipline among the lower officials in the federal army in order to bring an end to abuses which helped prolong the struggle.[5]

By the time that Obregón was President-elect of Mexico for the second time, Aarón Sáenz was exploring for him the possibilities of an arrangement to end the Cristero conflict.[6] The bases for a settlement which were being worked up by Obregón were such as would, in his opinion, confine the activities of the Catholic Church to the spiritual field.[7] In the meantime the Archbishop of Guadalajara and the Bishops of Tacámbaro and of San Luis Potosí wrote a message to the Holy Father in which they not only expressed their complete lack of faith in Obregón, but also repeated their insistence on the need for Constitutional reforms.[8]

[3] Arturo H. Orcí, interview, December 6, 1956.
[4] Higinio Alvarez García in El Universal, October 6, 1956.
[5] Hernán Robleto, Obregón, Toral y la Madre Conchita, pp. 299–300.
[6] Arturo H. Orcí, interview, December 6, 1956.
[7] Aarón Sáenz, interview, February 2, 1956.
[8] Aarón Sáenz in prologue of Carlos Barrera's Obregón, pp. xxx–xl.

In Paris Alberto J. Pani was told by a member of the United States diplomatic staff that Obregón would never reach the presidency, and he forthwith wired the President-elect advising him to spend outside of Mexico the period remaining until the inauguration. Pani was not the only one to recommend caution. But to follow such advice would hardly have been typical of Obregón, who made up his mind to go at once from Sonora to Mexico City and who remarked that "If I do not go to Mexico City my cause is lost."

Dr. Bernardo Gastélum, who in 1924 had finished out Vasconcelos' term as Obregón's Education Minister, was at this time in charge of the Department of Health. In the *Salubridad* special railroad car he went with Sáenz, Orcí, and other Obregonistas from Mexico City to Culiacán, Sinaloa, to meet the President-elect and accompany him on his trip to Mexico City—that is, if he should not be dissuaded from making the trip.

The group in the *Salubridad* special decided that Obregón should be advised of dangers in Mexico City. It was agreed that Orcí, whose relations with the President-elect were unofficial but close, would discuss the situation with Obregón and suggest that he delay his entry into the capital until such time as he would take over the power.

After these friends met Obregón at Culiacán they went with him in the special railroad cars down the west coast. But from the outset Orcí did not find great opportunities to develop with Obregón a conversation involving his important piece of advice. For one thing, a good deal of time was devoted to local leaders and to the multitudes of people who acclaimed the President-elect. For another thing, the great parties which were staged were particularly gay and went far into the nights. At Mazatlán the travellers went from the Hotel Belmar to a lavish residence where the music and dancing went on so long that Orcí could find no appropriate occasion to discuss with Obregón the dangers which he felt awaited him in Mexico City.

On they went to the warmth of Tepic, Nayarit, and there the late fiestas continued. While Obregón was having his hair cut at what was then the leading hotel in Tepic Orcí slipped him from the barbershop via the kitchen to avoid the crowds. The two men drove up a nearby hill.

Was there danger from the Cristeros of Nayarit? Obregón told

Orcí that the dangers were in Mexico City, thus revealing his awareness of a situation against which his close friends had delegated Orcí to warn him. Although Obregón demonstrated his realization of possible peril to his life, he insisted that he should not retire from danger, and he argued that if someone wanted to take his life, no possible measures could save it.

So the festive arrival occurred in Mexico City on July 15, while Roberto Cruz busied himself with precautions. This was the day, too, of a large reception banquet.

Obregón and Orcí drove to the Palacio Nacional for a call on Calles, a call which Obregón made alone and which lasted for an hour. Calles made a good impression on the President-elect, who expressed to Orcí his feeling that the danger of the situation had been exaggerated.[9]

[9] Arturo H. Orcí, interviews, December 6, 1956, and December 31, 1956.

41·

The Assassination
of General Obregón

S rita. María Concepción Acevedo y de la Llata, known as Madre Conchita, was born in Querétaro in 1891. In 1923, following the instructions of Archbishop Mora y del Río, she came to Mexico City in order to establish and take charge of a convent at Tlalpam. She was a strict disciplinarian. The convent was broken up by the police in 1927, and after that Madre Conchita and her nuns carried on their work more informally.

She was in the habit of visiting prisoners, taking them small presents, and turning their thoughts toward religion. When the Pro brothers were imprisoned, she unsuccessfully sought some arrangement to make a payment to General Cruz in order to obtain the freedom of Padre Miguel Pro. She also planned to provide a communion service for Padre Pro in his cell, as he had requested, but the priest was executed before this plan could be carried out.

In the early part of 1928 Madre Conchita was using her home at 133 Chopo Street in Mexico City for religious purposes. One of the rooms was a chapel wherein Catholic services were performed. In the course of imparting spiritual guidance to the many who came to her house Madre Conchita inspired great confidence, and her influence over at least a few of the younger people was very strong. Indeed, a number of her devoted followers regarded her as a saint. Among those who frequented her house were Srita. Leonor Rubio and Srita. Margarita Rubio and their relative, Carlos Díaz de Sollano.

The young devotees of Madre Conchita possessed great fervor. Many of them were determined to fight for the Church. They desired to be martyrs, to risk and create dangers.

In April, 1928, a few of these ardent Catholics had some discussions in the Chopo Street house in connection with a plan to assassinate General Obregón or General Calles. Eulogio González, Carlos Castro Balda, and Srita. María Elena Manzano received from Carlos Díaz de Sollano some money and a hypodermic containing poison. They took the poison to Celaya, where they expected to find Obregón and Calles. The girl was to hide the poison in her bouquet and, if she could arrange to dance with the General, she was to suddenly inject it into his body. But the plan did not succeed and the disappointed young people returned from Celaya.

Carlos Castro Balda lived close to the Chopo Street house of Madre Conchita, and, with his co-adventurer María Elena Manzano, attended daily Mass at the Chopo Street house. Although it was reported that these two were engaged to be married, the report did not have as much foundation as María Elena Manzano might have wished. This girl, who was an orphan, was devoted to Madre Conchita. Her fondness for the dashing Castro Balda was so great that she was keenly disappointed to realize that he was in love with Madre Conchita and not with her.

Castro Balda fabricated bombs, and so did Ing. Eduardo Zozaya. Although Zozaya made bombs solely for the Cristero rebels, Castro Balda's bombs found wider use. One of them was exploded in the Chamber of Deputies on May 23, 1928. Another youth connected with this explosion was Manuel Trejo Morales, who then went into hiding at the home of Sra. María Peña Vda. de Altamira. Although Manuel Trejo knew Madre Conchita, he was not a frequent attender of worship services, and fellow bomb-maker Eduardo Zozaya was completely dissociated from Madre Conchita.

By May, 1928, the Chopo Street house became the subject of so much suspicion that Madre Conchita had to move to another location, this one at 68 Zaragoza Street. Persons outside of the intimate group had been welcome to attend the services at Chopo Street, but at the Zaragoza Street house outsiders were not admitted.

It was in March, 1928, that Srita. Margarita Rubio introduced to Madre Conchita the twenty-six–year–old José de León Toral, who was currently teaching drawing. Born in Matehuala, San Luis Potosí, this religious young man had been educated in Monterrey and Mexico City, where he had shown an interest in football and had jo:ned a number of Catholic organizations. As far back as 1920 he had been a friend of Humberto Pro, and with the passage of years this friendship, which developed in the field of sports as well as in work, became very close. At the invitation of Humberto Pro, José de León Toral had collaborated with the Liga Defensora de la Libertad Religiosa, and when Humberto Pro met his death Toral succeeded him as head of the Liga in one of the sections of Mexico City.

The killing of the Pro brothers and of Luis Segura Vilches considerably perturbed Toral, who had known Segura Vilches, although not intimately. At first Toral did not think that good Catholics should endeavor to kill. He knew, however, that Segura Vilches had been devout, and he gave much thought to the reasons which might have prompted him to attempt murder. Thus Toral thought of the few who were carrying on the fight on behalf of the Church, and he thought of the religious persecutions and sufferings which he saw as increasing from day to day. One month after the death of Padre Pro he decided to become active instead of passive, and he determined to give his life for Christ. He devoted an increasing amount of his time to religious practices.

During these days Toral received much spiritual guidance from Madre Conchita, to whom he was increasingly attracted and by whom he was much influenced. Once, when he called at her new home early in July, the conversation concerned a bolt of lightning said to have been responsible for the very recent death of the Mexican aviator, Emilio Carranza, when he was starting his return flight from Long Island. Would that God would send such a bolt against the persecutors of the Church, said Toral to Conchita. She said that God knew the answer. She pictured the times and conditions as being a test put to them by God. It appeared to Toral that she would not be upset should death come to Obregón, Calles, and Patriarch Pérez of the Schismatic Mexican Church.

Toral at once set his mind to the manner in which he might kill Obregón. He felt that he had a divine mission; that all other methods having been exhausted, the death of Obregón was necessary in order to solve the religious problem of Mexico. He regarded as martyrs the Cristero rebels. He studied the Bible and read carefully from the book of Judith, resolving to become the instrument of God. He reached this decision within a week of the time when Obregón was scheduled to make his triumphant entry into Mexico City as President-elect.

From Manuel Trejo, to whom he had been introduced by Madre Conchita, Toral borrowed a pistol on July 11 or 12, and at Villa Guadalupe, outside of the city, he practiced the use of it, discovering that he was a poor marksman, unlikely to hit his target except at close range. At about this time Manuel Trejo, who had in June abandoned his hiding at the home of Sra. Vda. de Altamira, went into hiding again at the same place.

Having returned the pistol to Manuel Trejo, Toral borrowed it again. On Sunday, July 15, he left his home early, telling his wife that he was going on an excursion. After attending Mass he sought out Obregón, who on that day was arriving in Mexico City after his trip down the west coast. Among the receptions and festivities which were in store for the victorious candidate was the parade which would take Obregón to the Centro Director Obregonista and the banquet in his honor to be attended by 10,000 persons at the Parque Asturias.

León Toral took Trejo's pistol to the Tacuba railroad station but there missed the opportunity he was looking for. So he next went to the Colonia railroad station in Mexico City, but there the movements were so rapid and the crowds so great that Toral could not achieve his objective. Watching the great parade down the Paseo de la Reforma he could not get close enough to his intended victim. Outside of the Centro Director Obregonista Toral heard a number of speeches, including one by Aurelio Manrique, Jr. Before going home Toral stopped at the home of Sra. Vda. de Altamira to ask Manuel Trejo to let him have the pistol a bit longer.

Back at home Toral told his wife that he was going to a hacienda near Pachuca to spend the week of vacation which he now had from his school teaching. She at first objected, having seen little of him of late, but it was obvious that he needed a rest. He said farewell to his wife and children, and went off with a little clothing. This was on Monday, July 16.

Instead of going to Pachuca, Toral went to a drugstore. There he met Padre José Jiménez, whom he had come to know at the home of Sra. Vda. de Altamira. He asked the Padre for a place to spend that night, and the Padre told him to meet him again in the drugstore that same evening.

Toral spent July 16 unsuccessfully seeking his opportunity at the Palacio Nacional, at the Centro Director Obregonista, and outside Obregón's home at 185 Jalisco Avenue. He purchased a drawing block. He planned to buy a postcard picture of Obregón, use it to make a drawing, and use the drawing as a pretext for entering the Jalisco Avenue house. Returning to the drugstore and failing to find Padre Jiménez, he then went to call on Madre Conchita. By this time Toral was in a depressed condition, feeling that the day had been wasted, but he did not reveal his plans to Madre Conchita. He found her words strengthening to his spirit.

Back at the pharmacy he met Padre Jiménez, who had made arrangements for Toral to spend the night at a room in the Justo Sierra Street home of Sra. Dolores Azcona.

On the morning of Tuesday, July 17, Toral helped Madre Conchita with a religious service and then, assisted by information given in a newspaper, he again sought out the man whom he considered responsible for the plight of the faithful. He was outside of Obregón's home at 1:00 P.M. when the federal *diputado* from Sonora, Ricardo Topete, called there to accompany the President-elect to a banquet being given in his honor by the Guanajuato federal legislators at the La Bombilla restaurant at San Angel. Obregón and the Hidalgo governor, Colonel Matías Rodríguez, joined Topete and two others in the car.

Feeling that Obregón's attendance at the banquet would be unwise, some of his followers, to avoid possible dangers, had worked up a pretext. An urgent appointment with Calles, they explained, made Obregón's appearance impossible. But then members of the Guanajuato group made a great plea. Could not the President-elect at least put in a short appearance? Obregón's secretary, Enrique Torreblanca, telephoned his brother Fernando Torreblanca, the presidential secretary, and arranged for Obregón to attend the affair at La Bombilla and delayed his appointment with Calles.

On leaving his home Obregón was in good humor. He turned to one of his companions and said jokingly, "Aren't you afraid to go with us? Someone might set off a bomb." The laughing reply to the General was that the bombs would be little ones since they were going to La Bombilla (Small Bomb).

Immediately behind Obregón's car went the one containing the bodyguard, which included Colonels Ignacio Otero and Juan Jaimes. These two cars were followed to San Angel by Toral in a taxicab. At the tables in the restaurant's large eating pavilion, in the garden, gathered the dignitaries, including men who could expect to be influential with the advent of the new presidential administration. Seated close to Obregón were Diputado Federico Medrano, president of the Confederation of Socialistic Revolutionary Parties of Guanajuato, Aarón Sáenz, Arturo H. Orcí, Ricardo Topete, Antonio Valadés Ramírez, Supreme Court President Jesús Guzmán Baca, and José Luis Solórzano. Other guests included Antonio Díaz Soto y Gama, Aurelio Manrique, Jr., Ezequiel Padilla, David Montes de Oca, Tomás A. Róbinson, José Aguilar y Maya, and Dr. Alejandro Sánchez. Medrano was on the right of the guest of honor, Sáenz on his left.

A few seats to the left of Obregón was Ricardo Topete. Seeing Toral at the entrance to the patio, he became suspicious and asked someone what the person in the brown suit was doing. He was told that he was a caricaturist, and so he relaxed.

Toral did, in fact, have his pad and pencil. Upon entering the restaurant he had asked for a Sr. Cedillo, and on being told that he was perhaps at the main table, had said he would await the end of the meal. Then he had proceeded to make a few sketches, although making caricatures was not his line. He drew the orchestra leader and General Obregón. Then he drew Sáenz, and another picture of Obregón. He started a drawing of Manrique's whiskers.

Toral decided that the time had come to act, for Topete seemed to be regarding him with greater suspicion. He later said that he then communicated with his guardian angel saying: "You cannot complain; I have raised you very high; soon we shall see each other."

While the guests were eating, the orchestra of Esparza Oteo was playing such popular tunes as "El Limoncito."

General Obregón, a few minutes before his assassination at the banquet at "La Bombilla" restaurant. At table: Octavio Mendoza González, Arturo H. Orcí, Federico Medrano, Alvaro Obregón, Aarón Sáenz, Enrique Romero Courtade, Ricardo Topete. July 17, 1928. Casasola.

Toral came up to Topete and showed him what he believed to be some of the better drawings. Topete was not very well impressed but he made some remark to the effect that they were not bad and heard the artist offer later to make one of Topete. Toral then set about to show his pictures to Obregón. He had a little difficulty in making his way to the President-elect because of the floral decorations on wooden stands immediately behind the more prominent seats.

Once Toral was behind Obregón and Sáenz, the one-armed Hero of Celaya turned his head to take a look. He smiled at the artist. He was the picture of friendliness. Toral shifted his pad to his left hand while General Obregón glanced across the table at Lic. Padilla. Then with his right hand Toral shot into Obregón's face with the borrowed pistol. There were three quick shots followed by two more, and, as the orchestra was playing at that moment, some of the guests thought the noise of the discharges formed part of the music.

Lic. Padilla saw Obregón's eyes grow enormous. The General fell forward onto the table, and, as awareness of what had just happened came over the guests, the pavilion became the scene of wild tumult. Many, including Sáenz and Topete, grabbed Toral, disarming him. Pistols were pulled out.

Manrique shouted to Colonel Jaimes: "Don't kill him!" and his shout was seconded by Topete. It was necessary to find out who sent Toral. Orders were given to guard the exits.

Obregón's body was on the floor, being attended by his physician, Alejandro Sánchez, and by others. But he was quite dead. After Calles had been advised by phone, the body of the President-elect was taken by car to the house on Jalisco Avenue.

Toral put up no resistance and received many rough blows, so many that his face became a welter of blood and wounds. Some identification was sought but none could be found on him. He was taken in a car to the headquarters of the General Police Inspection in the custody of Colonel Jaimes, Colonel Róbinson, and one of the Guanajuato *diputados*.

42.

An Investigation
and Some Accusations

Those who went in the car with Obregón's body from La Bombilla to Avenida Jalisco No. 185 were Sáenz, Orcí, Manrique, Ricardo Topete, and Medrano. This car was followed by an array of others bearing the saddened and irate men who had attended the memorable banquet. The news had already reached the neighborhood of Obregón's home, where, by the time the cars arrived from San Angel, a crowd had gathered in front. Soon there was a brief visit to Jalisco Avenue by Calles, who arrived with Fernando Torreblanca and who was received by the mob in front of the house with cries of "We want justice." The President remained only a few minutes and then with some others went off to the General Police Inspection.

A soldier who had an appointment to meet Obregón at his home at 3:00 P.M. was shocked to find there a multitude of politicians and the body of the late President-elect.

Calles was by now, within an hour of the assassination, at the Police Inspection with Amaro, Orcí, Ricardo Topete, Abundio Gómez, and General Police Inspector Cruz. A conflict on the handling of matters had already begun when a disagreement arose between Cruz's men and Colonels Jaimes and Róbinson as to who should guard the prisoner. Toral was not giving much information and when asked his name he merely replied Juan, which seemed to be confirmed by the initials "J.L.T." found on a piece of his clothing. He said he had carried out the deed for reasons of his own.

Calles asked Toral why he had killed Obregón and not Calles, to which Toral remarked that when undermining a building one attacks the foundations. "We feel that you are the house and General Obregón the foundation." Calles expressed annoyance, struck the table and ordered the prisoner taken away.[1] Topete had grabbed the pistol used by Toral, and now he turned it over to Calles with words hardly calculated to mend the President's ill humor: "Here is the pistol, with which you are familiar." When shortly afterward Calles was telling the press that Toral was one of the clergy, Topete interrupted to say that Calles, not Toral, had so stated.

Calles and some of those who were with him then returned to the Obregón home, which had become more crowded than ever and included such well-known persons as Luis Montes de Oca, Manuel Pérez Treviño, Francisco R. Manzo, Alberto Mascareñas, Juan José Ríos, Eduardo Hay, and Colonel Alexander Macnab of the American Embassy. By now, between 3:30 and 4:00 in the afternoon, the extra editions of the newspapers were making a sensation on the streets of Mexico. Mauricio Magdaleno writes that for the first time in Mexico tons of newspapers were sold. He reviews some of the dramatic news events that future years were to bring: the conflict between Calles and Cárdenas, the nationalization of Mexico's petroleum industry, and the outbreak of the Second World War, and then expresses the belief that none of these events produced "a greater commotion or a more intense state of alarm" than did the news of Obregón's assassination.[2]

[1] Luis N. Morones in *El Universal*, August 12, 1956.
[2] Mauricio Magdaleno, *Las palabras perdidas*, p. 15.

Portes Gil, Orcí, Francisco R. Manzo, Antonio Ríos Zertuche, and Aarón Sáenz, all close friends of Obregón, decided that Roberto Cruz was a Callista who lacked their confidence and should therefore be replaced as Chief Police Inspector. They called on Calles at the Palacio Nacional on that same afternoon of the assassination and found him in a foul mood. When Orcí explained what was wanted, Calles at once snapped: "You, then, are the Chief Police Inspector." Orcí pointed out the need of having a military man, and, as had been planned by the visitors, he suggested General Ríos Zertuche. This made it Ríos Zertuche's turn to hear Calles say: "You are Chief Police Inspector." But the visitors explained that they needed Cruz's resignation and a properly formalized appointment, and so Calles phoned Cruz saying that this visiting group had asked for his resignation.[3]

General Antonio Ríos Zertuche was the head of Sinaloa Military Operations. Associated with him in the direction of the murder investigation were Sáenz, Orcí, and Chief Safety Commissioner Valente Quintana.

That evening Obregón's body was moved to the Palacio Nacional. Before this was done there was a good deal of conjecture on the part of those who filled the Jalisco Avenue house. One could have overheard the aviator, Captain Pablo Sidar, speaking with Srita. Cholita González, private secretary of Calles. The aviator said, "Now they are going to kill Morones." Srita. González replied: "Don't worry, they won't find him; all precautions have been taken."[4] Morones, who had spent the morning in conference with members of the Grupo Acción, departed from Mexico City early on the afternoon of Obregón's assassination, using a Ford station wagon.[5]

While Obregón's body lay in state in the Salón de Embajadores of the Palacio Nacional, a long line of persons made its way past the fallen *caudillo*. Soldiers kept the line moving. Then on July 18 there was a great funeral procession, the coffin being followed by President Calles and others. The coffin, amidst oratory (such as that provided by Aurelio Manrique, Jr.), crowds of persons, and floral wreaths, was placed on a train to be taken for burial in Sonora, in

[3] Arturo H. Orcí, interview, December 6, 1956.
[4] Higinio Alvarez García in *El Universal*, October 4 and 5, 1956.
[5] Pablo Meneses V. in *El Universal*, November 3, 1956.

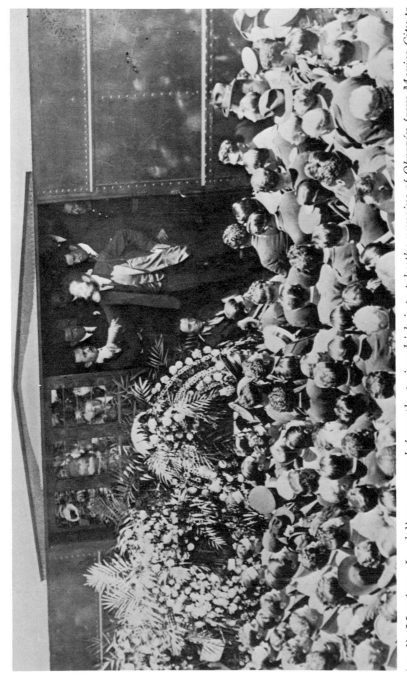

Aurelio Manrique, Jr., delivers a speech from the train which is to take the remains of Obregón from Mexico City to Sonora. July, 1928. Casasola.

accordance with the wishes which General Obregón had often made known.

During the night of the seventeenth José de León Toral was subjected to severe tortures. With his body suspended, hung up by toes and fingers, great suffering was inflicted upon him, but he refused to be informative or even to give his name.

Valente Quintana told Orcí when he was in the Police Inspection Office that they had discovered some clue, and he persuaded Orcí that the clue was important. It was a Chinese laundry mark, which, according to Orcí's account, resulted in the location of the Toral home. When the investigators called on Sra. Toral they found her pregnant and completely ignorant of her husband's whereabouts or of his having killed Obregón. The investigators, acting in a friendly manner, were able to learn from Toral's wife and parents a great deal about the assassin besides his name.

León Toral's father, Aurelio de León, who had recently won an automobile in a raffle sponsored by *El Universal*, was told by Valente Quintana that his son had been the one who killed Obregón. At first the old man had a difficult time believing this tragic news, but before long he was telling Quintana about José's youth and early illnesses. Aurelio and his wife and daughter-in-law were arrested by the police.

Thus on the day following the event at La Bombilla the investigators were able to confront Toral with all that they had learned about him. They not only threatened tortures for his wife and parents, but even simulated such tortures with Toral able to hear what went on.

Toral gave a little information and then asked Quintana for thirty minutes in which to deliberate, a request which was granted. After this interval Toral advised that he could say no more until he had spoken with a certain person, and he asked to be allowed to visit that person at seven in the evening. It was agreed that in this interview Toral would be accompanied only by Quintana. Toral has stated that Meneses and Quintana, by the use of calm reason, convinced him that he should tell all.

The group of persons who went with Toral on the visit saw the lights go on in the Zaragoza Street house. When the windows revealed some nuns moving about, the police agents commented that they were entering "a religious place."

Madre Conchita came to the door and beheld Toral in a badly

wounded condition. "José!" Seeing him as he was she thought to herself: José has returned to earth after death. She apparently had not known that he had assassinated Obregón.

Toral entered the house and was followed not only by Quintana but by a group of police agents, who were fearful of a trap.

Toral spoke to Madre Conchita: "I've come here to see if they believe you. I'm here to see if you want to die with me."

Madre Conchita replied quite calmly: "Yes, with much pleasure." She appeared to be cool and quite satisfied to be a "martyr."

Toral, Orcí, Madre Conchita, and others went into a room described by the lawyer as being "full of saints." With the introduction of Orcí to Madre Conchita, the latter exclaimed that Orcí was himself a saint, adding that she had heard about how in the past he had intervened on behalf of some Catholics who were being treated in a rough and unjustified manner by authorities of Cruz's Police Inspection. Madre Conchita spoke in what Orcí has called "a religious way," mentioning forgiveness.

In the conversation between Toral and Madre Conchita, Toral said that he himself was willing to go through tortures but could not stand the idea of the torturing of his family. Toral referred to his remark of a while back in connection with the death of the aviator Emilio Carranza, when he had said: "Would that God would send a crash of lightning" to wipe out Obregón, or Obregón, Calles, and Patriarch Pérez. Toral now said to Madre Conchita that he had interpreted her reaction as meaning that she wanted Obregón to be assassinated. Madre Conchita was arrested by the police, and so were about twenty nuns.

In the subsequent police investigations Toral spoke freely. He has said that it was untrue that he was identified by a mark on his clothing; rather, he has said, everything was learned from his own lips. According to Quintana, Madre Conchita told them it was unnecessary to look any further: José and I are the principals and we have been caught.

Toral's family was set free two days after arrest and soon after that many of Madre Conchita's nuns were released.

The newspapers were pleased to learn that the suspects would be tried by a jury to establish the responsibilities in connection with the crime, and also the punishments. The trial was to be held at the small courthouse of San Angel, close to the spot of the crime. Some whose testimony was wanted had not been located. Padre José Jiménez had disappeared, and so had Manuel Trejo Morales, who loaned the pistol to Toral. The police offered a reward of 5000 pesos for the capture of Carlos Castro Balda, and this young man voluntarily presented himself to a government official who was a close friend of his and who accordingly received the reward.

Representatives of the Catholic Church made declarations expressing their disapproval of the assassination. In a statement on behalf of the Catholic Subcomité Episcopal, the Bishop of San Luis Potosí made it clear that the Mexican clergy, who were widely dispersed as the result of government policy, were not implicated. He referred to the great sorrows of the times and to the easily influenced character of Toral. As for Madre Conchita, "we point out, in defense of the rest of the religious Mexicans, who have suffered so much but who are so far removed from this sort of action, that it is public knowledge that her brain is not normal and that, unfortunately, in her family there have been some mental abnormalities."[6]

Before the end of July Toral concluded that he had misjudged Obregón and should not have killed him. He said that he would not have committed the murder had he known more about Obregón as a politician and as a family man, and had he known then that Obregón was taking steps to settle the religious question.

Before the trial got under way Toral's mother sent a telegram to Obregón's widow, who had returned to Navojoa, Sonora, asking that Toral be pardoned. The widow of Obregón responded with a telegram to the jury suggesting forgiveness. Díaz Soto y Gama and Manrique showed little interest in the trial, one of these Obregonistas observing that "we shall not repair the great loss that has been suffered by rolling another body into the bottomless grave of our national tragedies. The exemplary nobleness of the widow of the late great patrician has given us now the definitive word." Vito Alessio Robles condemned the tortures which had been applied to Toral and publicly accused Tomás A. Róbinson as one of those responsible for them.

In view of the high pitch of political feelings and the fury of those enemies of Calles and Morones who had been close to Obregón, a welter of accusations arose. Such accusations have continued to emanate from anti-Callistas from time to time up to the present. A target of unfavorable comment has been Morones, who, says Puig Casauranc, was unjustly charged with being involved in the

[6] Bishop De la Mora quoted in Hernán Robleto's *Obregón, Toral y la Madre Conchita*, p. 359.

assassination of the President-elect. Other charges have been directed at Calles, with enemies alleging that he provoked and sustained the Cristero rebellion "to justify Obregón's assassination and in order to blame the clergy." (At this point the usual practice is to take advantage of the opportunity to implicate Calles also in connection with the deaths of Benjamín Hill, Lucio Blanco, Pancho Villa, and Angel Flores, the first- and last-named by poisoning.)

Many words have been written to sustain the thesis that Morones sought to stir up such unrest as to create an atmosphere conducive to the crime. In his exposition of this point of view Lic. A. Romandía Ferreira says that Morones was responsible for the assault on the Soledad church, the bombing at the Basílica de Guadalupe, and the activities of Patriarch Pérez of the Schismatic Church. Romandía Ferreira writes: "I do not deny that José de León Toral was a weak-minded fanatic who was admirably taken advantage of; and I do not deny that some of those called Catholics who at bottom are no Catholics took advantage of the atmosphere created by Morones to serve as instruments of the conspiracy, but the pistol with which Obregón was assassinated had been brought from Spain by one of the high leaders of the Laborista Party."[7] Romandía Ferreira does not accuse Calles, who, he points out, provided the protection of Roberto Cruz and the police department when Obregón went from the Mexico City railroad station to the Centro Director Obregonista.

Ricardo Topete has stated that Manuel Trejo, who loaned the pistol to Toral, was a worker in the Military Manufacturing Establishments.[8] The former "Jefe de Seguridad," Pablo Meneses V., has tried to show that the activities of Madre Conchita were financed by Morones and his group. He tells about the Recamier sisters, Adela, Amanda, and Margarita. The last-named, he says, was Morones' "third or fourth" wife, and he adds that Adela and Amanda were well known at the parties which were held at Morones' residence at Tlalpam. According to Meneses, these three sisters were daughters of a sister of Madre Conchita, and Adela introduced Morones to Madre Conchita. This Obregonista detective even quotes Elena Manzano as having seen labor leader Samuel Yúdico at Madre Conchita's Chopo Street and Zaragoza Street houses prior to Yúdico's death in April, 1928, a death which he feels

[7] Alfonso Romandía Ferreira in *El Universal*, July 4, 1956.

[8] Ricardo Topete quoted in Juan Andreu Almazán's *Memorias* in *El Universal*, November 8, 1958.

was not "very natural." He says that another labor leader, José López Cortés, was a friend of the owners of the Zaragoza Street house and not only vouched for the rental payments thereon but owned the adjoining house.[9]

In maintaining that charges of his foes have been unfounded, Morones points out that he never exchanged a word with Madre Conchita until some time after the events being described. He insists that had there been any truth to the various accusations that have been leveled at him, there was adequate opportunity to make much of these matters in 1928 when the investigation of Obregón's assassination was in the hands of Obregonistas.[10]

"My own group of companions was firmly dedicated to the principle of No Re-election, but when we learned that General Obregón would accept his new candidacy, and realized that failure to back it would break up the unity of the Revolutionary forces, we decided to co-operate for his re-election."[11] So writes Morones, who also tells of conferences between the Partido Laborista leaders and the President-elect a few weeks before the latter's death. Morones explains that in a four-hour conference which he had with Obregón, the President-elect offered to sign a pact which would be satisfactory to the labor group, as had been done in 1919, but that Morones felt the signing to be unnecessary, "for we had full confidence in General Obregón. . . . We also reached the conclusion that our supporters would have to collaborate with the new regime, at the request of General Obregón himself. Unfortunately a few days later he was assassinated."[12]

[9] Pablo Meneses V. in *El Universal*, November 3 and 5, 1956.
[10] Luis N. Morones, interview, January 30, 1957.
[11] Luis N. Morones, letter, February 16, 1957.
[12] Luis N. Morones in *El Universal*, August 12, 1956.

43.

A Memorable
Presidential Address

The naming on July 17 of Obregón's friend, Antonio
Ríos Zertuche, to replace Roberto Cruz as Chief Police Inspector
was one of a series of steps taken to deal with a political situation
which was very dangerous for the Republic. At this time President
Calles displayed much political wisdom. Advice, often conflicting,
he received from a great many sources.

Some idea of the condition in which Calles found himself can be
gathered from Emilio Portes Gil, who points out that in the days
following the crime Calles was deserted and his authority practically extinct. The legislative houses, particularly the Chamber of

Deputies, were strongly Obregonista. Obregonistas were not only saddened, but great ranks of them were furious, in "frank rebellion against President Calles."[1] Some felt that the hand of Calles was behind the assassination of Obregón, and accusations were made to that effect.

At the ceremony at the Mexico City railroad station, when Obregón's remains were being sent to Sonora, Manrique, in front of Calles, indicated that the Calles Government was hiding the true intellectual authors of the crime. At the burial in Sonora, Manrique and Topete unleashed accusations against both Calles and Morones.

Among the many politicians in Mexico City at this time was the Tamaulipas governor, Lic. Portes Gil, adversary of Morones and staunch supporter of Obregón, and from him the President received helpful suggestions about the immediate situation. Calles became sympathetic to the views of Portes Gil and other Obregonistas who did not accuse him of implication in the death of Obregón, such as Aarón Sáenz, Marte R. Gómez, and Luis L. León. León, who had been one of Obregón's close friends dating back from the days when León had demonstrated his skill as a bullfighter, had since May, 1927, been out of the Cabinet, fulfilling a mission in Chihuahua.

Declarations were made to the nation on July 18 and during the succeeding days. The President expressed the view that Mexico had lost "the most complete statesman of recent times." He promised full punishment to the material and intellectual authors of the crime, and he promised that the Revolutionary work would go forward. War Minister Joaquín Amaro called upon members of the armed forces to observe strictly the fulfillment of their duty.

Helpful to the Administration was the attitude taken by the leader of the Centro Director Obregonista, Lic. Aarón Sáenz, who called upon his group to "observe prudence and serenity." Sáenz of course energetically denounced the crime. Referring to "Calles' integrity and pureness of principles" he expressed the hope that the intellectual authors of the crime would be discovered.

Some peasant and labor groups that had supported Obregón let it be known, on July 20, that they felt Luis Morones and his Partido Laborista had had much responsibility for the assassination. They remarked that Morones and a number of his men, besides opposing

[1] Emilio Portes Gil, *Quince años de política mexicana*, pp. 13–20.

Obregón, had indicated that the re-election candidate would never take office.

Shortly after that certain resignations from public office by leaders of the Partido Laborista were submitted to Calles, although they were not at once made known or acted upon. Morones turned in his resignation as Minister of Industry, Commerce, and Labor. Celestino Gasca, head of the Military Manufacturing Establishments, and Eduardo Moneda, director of the National Printing Shops, followed the example of Morones. So did José López Cortés, of the Mexico City Municipal Council. At the same time these men rejected any blame or responsibility for the fate that had befallen Obregón.

Calles, in bed with the grippe at his residence in Anzures Colony, in Mexico City, received on July 27 a visit from Portes Gil, Luis León, and Marte Gómez. This delegation recommended Cabinet changes to the President, with Luis Morones particularly in mind. Calles vigorously supported his friends who held public office and pointed out that, although certain resignations had been submitted to him, this would be a poor time to make them effective. On the contrary he should defend his friends against "unjust charges."

The President, however, soon became convinced that it would be prudent at this tense moment to consider the opinion which was represented by Portes Gil and his associates, and so he accepted the resignations which had been tendered. Ing. Luis León rejoined the Cabinet, again as Minister of Agriculture. And in August Lic. Emilio Portes Gil was appointed to the Number One Cabinet position, that of Minister of Gobernación.

The first act of Gobernación Minister Portes Gil had to do with the religious question. While Portes Gil was a strict upholder of the Constitution and of the program of the Revolution, he recognized, as did many, that a considerable number who were connected with the government were proceeding quite incorrectly against Catholic believers. They were making the situation worse by means of abuses. They concocted ridiculous reasons for fines, or for simply forcing payments; they stole religious relics of value; they sacked homes. The new Minister of Gobernación told his employees and the state governors to see to it that abuses were ended and that procedures were followed correctly.

Not long after assuming his new post Portes Gil received a visit from Lázaro Cárdenas, who was still in charge of Military Operations in the Huasteca Veracruzana. Cárdenas requested that his close companion, General Francisco J. Múgica, who had been out of the picture since the start of the De la Huerta rebellion, be appointed Director of the Islas Marías penal colony. The appointment was made as a favor to Cárdenas, although President Calles expressed himself as being far from enthusiastic about Múgica.

Following Morones' retirement in late July, the Ministry of Industry, Commerce, and Labor was run by its Oficial Mayor until August 22, when Dr. José M. Puig Casauranc took over Morones' old position. Professor Moisés Sáenz, brother of Aarón, ran the Education Ministry, which Puig Casauranc had recently headed.

A meeting of the Centro Director Obregonista on August 3 resulted on August 6 in a statement by Aarón Sáenz to the effect that the Centro, its mission completed, had unanimously resolved to disband. The statement, which contained expressions of confidence in the Congress and in the President, contained also a plea for serenity and for unity on the part of the Revolutionaries of the nation. On that same day the Obregonista blocks in the federal legislative chambers issued a public declaration, signed by Ricardo Topete and many others, in which they took note of the termination of the Centro Director Obregonista. The Obregonista legislators asserted that they were assuming the responsibilities as executors of Obregón's political and social program. Before a picture of the Hero of Celaya, Topete and other important congressional leaders solemnly swore to be faithful to the memory of Obregón and to do away with any of their number who should ever prove a traitor to this promise.[2]

Uppermost in the political debate and thinking was what was going to happen to the presidency. Díaz Soto y Gama and Manrique did not go along with those Obregonistas who expressed confidence in Calles, and immediately after the assassination they approached Portes Gil as a possible candidate for the provisional presidency. They also told Portes Gil that Calles was slow in providing justice to Obregonismo. Portes Gil had a record satisfactory to the agrarian Revolutionaries, but he did make it clear to the Partido Agrarista leaders that he had no intention of breaking with Calles because of unfounded accusations against him.

Generals and politicians poured into Mexico City from all parts of the country. Some favored an extension of time for Calles in the presidency, while others told him in no uncertain terms to get out

[2] Ricardo Topete quoted in Juan Andreu Almazán's *Memorias* in *El Universal*, November 8, 1958.

at the end of his term, or else be forced out. August was a month full of maneuvers preparatory to the September 1 annual presidential message opening the congressional session.

Early arrivals at the end of July were the powers from Sinaloa and Sonora. The respective governors, Manuel Páez and Alejo Bay, went to see Calles. They were accompanied by Francisco R. Manzo, who headed Sonora Military Operations, and Fausto Topete, Ricardo's brother and the governor-elect of Sonora. So emphatically did they insist that Calles ignore those recommending prolongation of his tenure of office, that their message was virtually an ultimatum. This was the viewpoint of those who continued to agitate and to attack Calles. Said Manrique: "Díaz Soto and I, with some others as wildly excited as we, went shouting our passion through the streets of Mexico City."

On the other hand, while the generals and the governors continued to arrive, a number of political groups, feeling that the gravity of the situation required some continuity of administration, recommended that Calles remain in office for at least two more years. The Partido Tejedista Veracruzano (supporting Ing. Adalberto Tejeda for the Veracruz governorship) recommended that Constitutional Article 83, which had been amended to make the chief executive's term six instead of four years, be made retroactive to cover the present incumbent. This suggestion was made on August 5. Among the many who quickly raised their voices in favor of this idea were the governors of Puebla, Yucatán, Nayarit, and Tabasco, the municipalities of Veracruz, Hidalgo, and San Luis Potosí, the Partido Socialista Veracruzano, the Club Unionista Alvaro Obregón of Orizaba, the Comité Pro-Paz of Tuxpan, and the Partido Socialista de Oriente (of Tecamachalco, Puebla). On August 11 supporters of the President announced that more than one hundred political groups approved the extension of Calles' term. Among those who wanted to see Calles continue in office were Luis Montes de Oca and J. M. Puig Casauranc. Also Ambassador Dwight Morrow.

When the Coahuila governor, General Manuel Pérez Treviño, reached Mexico City on August 27, he pointed out that the matter was up to Congress, thus echoing thoughts expressed a few days earlier by Aarón Sáenz. Once again Sáenz appealed for calmness.

Leading generals took to assembling at the Hotel Regis, which daily took on more and more the appearance of a political convention.

Thus the stage was set for the presidential message opening the congressional sessions. In the words of Miguel Alessio Robles: "The session of the Mexican Parliament, which took place on September 1, 1928, was, without any doubt, the most memorable of all in the agitated political history of Mexico." More memorable, he adds, than the occasion five years earlier when Jorge Prieto Laurens defied Obregón and the "imposition" of Calles.[3]

Plentiful military display not only gave a measure of protection to the chief participants but also provided color to the occasion. Soldiers lined the streets all the way from the Palacio Nacional to the Chamber of Deputies.

At this important moment not only senators and deputies gathered in the Chamber to hear the message, but also, as customary, members of the judicial bodies, the diplomats representing foreign nations, the resplendently uniformed generals who commanded troops, and galleries full of politicians and friends. The message was carried all over the Republic by radio. The tone of President Calles' voice befitted the solemn occasion.[4]

The President explained to his listeners that he was submitting in writing the customary reports on the year's activities in the various departments of the administration. Then, using words which had been formulated by Dr. Puig Casauranc to express Calles' conclusions, the President discussed the political situation of the country and the steps which should be taken. While lamenting the loss of the President-elect, he nevertheless saw in the difficult situation an opportunity for Mexico to shake off its tradition of depending on political strongmen. He called upon his listeners to create true democratic institutions. In particular he asked the Army to examine the situation and to act for the country's immediate and future peace. Before speaking further about the "nation of institutions and laws" which he was proposing, Calles made a dramatic and "irrevocable" declaration, one which was influenced by the need to reject governments of *caudillos* (political strongmen). In spite of all the pressure exerted on him to carry on in the presidential chair, Calles pledged his honor "before the National Congress, before the nation, and before the order of civilized peoples" not to serve as President beyond the expiration of his term of

[3] Miguel Alessio Robles, *Historia política de la Revolución*, p. 331.
[4] *Ibid.*, p. 332.

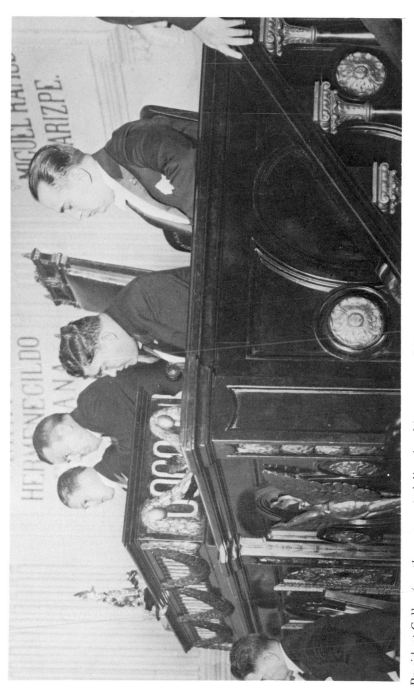

President Calles (on the rostrum) delivering his message of September 1, 1928, to Congress. Also on the rostrum (at top left) is the president of Congress, Diputado Ricardo Topete. R. Topete.

office on November 30, and under no circumstance to return to the presidency.

In accordance with the Constitution Calles called upon the Congress to name a Provisional President, assuring his hearers that the choice of the Congress in this matter would have the material and moral backing of the Army. He asked Congress also to set an election date so that the Provisional President could be succeeded by a properly elected Constitutional President. On this subject Calles gave a good deal of advice. The election date should be such as to allow opportunity for all who aspired to enter the contest. Furthermore, the election should be fair and honest, and so effective should be the vote that the federal legislative chambers should be representative of all the varying political shades and all the legitimate interests of the country. "More dangerous than the acceptance of all kinds of minorities is the continuation of some political methods followed up to now, political intolerance carried to extreme and the absolute domination by one group."

The President's concluding words were addressed to the Mexican Army: "Never have I felt, as I do today because of my irrevocable decision which will last to my death, more logically authorized to establish myself before the Nation, as I do establish myself, as the guarantor of the noble and disinterested conduct of the Army."

While Calles read this message, Manrique interrupted on several pertinent occasions to cheer for Obregón and on one occasion he even made a remark against the President. Ambassador Dwight Morrow was so impressed by the great speech that he warmly clapped, which action was, according to the British ambassador, contrary to proper deportment under the circumstances.

In his reply to the message the presiding officer of Congress, Ricardo Topete, praised the memory of Alvaro Obregón. Then Calles departed from the Chamber as he had entered it, surrounded by protection against any who might make an attempt against his life.

For his thoughts and for his decision, the President received an abundance of congratulations. Some advance had been made in solving the problem of the presidential succession, but the matter was far from settled.

Puig Casauranc was a personal friend of Manrique, having attended medical school with him and having been associated with him in congressional activities in 1923. Fearing that some attempt might be made on the life of Manrique, Puig Casauranc pointed out to Calles that care should be taken. In case of an assault by some foolish person, the Calles Administration would be considered as an accomplice to the crime. Calles, however, assured Puig that: "Manrique is being protected by me and until he revolts nothing will happen to him. And I can tell you this, that he will be the only sincere man and the only man who will revolt in good faith; that I can assure you!"

44·

The Selection of a
Provisional President

As a possible successor to President Calles, the Army men at their sessions at the Regis had been mentioning General Manuel Pérez Treviño, General José Gonzalo Escobar, General Juan Andreu Almazán, Lic. Emilio Portes Gil, and Senator Eduardo Neri.

Recognizing the danger of a prolongation of these debates, which could lead to profound divisions or which could be disastrous if Army leaders should agree on a name unacceptable to Congress and incompatible with concepts put forth on September 1, President

Calles called an unusual meeting of Army generals at the Palacio Nacional on September 5. Among those present were Amaro, Saturnino Cedillo, Abundio Gómez, Limón, J. Jiménez Méndez, J. L. Amezcua, Agustín Mora; also the following active heads of Military Operations: Urbalejo, J. M. Aguirre, Almazán, Francisco Manzo, Escobar, Cruz, Lázaro Cárdenas, and P. Gabay. In addition fourteen other generals, brigadiers, were present.

Calles spoke to them clearly: "My words may sound a little hard but I do not mean to hurt anyone. The Army must keep perfect unity. There are two fundamental questions: the provisional presidency and the candidate for the constitutional presidency. We do not want disunity in the Army. I think in this period the Army should stay out of the situation; that none of its members should present himself as a candidate, for that will only bring division in the Army . . . If anyone thinks I am in error, my words signify no agreement binding on those who hear them."

Calles said that in the selection of a Provisional President the Congress should provide the legal solution and the Army should respect and sustain the designation. He said, "Up to now I have, frankly, no candidate and have recommended none." Then he added: "I have noticed that groups are being formed in the Army, two or three currents of different opinion, the start of division. I will drop this point if it is thought that what I am saying might cause division . . . I want to hear your opinion."

In reply to a question by Almazán, Calles made it clear that in his opinion no active Army man should figure in either the provisional presidency or in the campaign for the constitutional presidency. General Amezcua said, "It would be good if we could convince Calles to stay in power." General Madrigal suggested that Calles mention one, two, or three names of those who might well fill the highest office.

After some discussion General Juan José Ríos said: "I do not think we are sticking to the point. I am in accord with the views of the President in his Saturday address. I am entirely in accord with the views expressed here that no military chief should aspire to occupy the presidency. Those also agreeing will kindly arise."

With that, all of the generals arose. Then General Escobar said: "I think, frankly, we should all have absolute confidence in the President. He knows that I do not have the intention of committing a servile act, but I do consider that he has a political vision much superior to ours, for he is a specialist in political questions. I feel that the President is completely right." Escobar then gave assurances that the much-feared rebellion would not take place. "I wish to make it clear that barrack uprisings have passed into history. The Army has been definitely purged of such shameless men. The words 'Army uprising' should be absolutely thrown out. If the President, in his address to Congress, made himself guarantor of the Army, he did so because he considers that the present army is not an army of uprisings."

General Cedillo referred to the day's issue of *El Universal,* wherein it was reported that "during a meeting in the Regis a candidate for the presidency was selected." He asked that this matter be cleared up. General Escobar retorted that he and Generals Ferreira and Manzo had had meetings with the President's blessing.

General Almazán rejected the idea of asking the President for names, because, he said, the matter should be resolved by the congressmen as they saw fit. As for the divisionary generals, he said: "I deem any divisionary more able to occupy the presidency than any civilian." Escobar, who was quick to agree with this appraisal of the merits of *generales de división,* remarked that the President should not now be asked for names of candidates, but, rather, the matter should be left fully in his hands; his responsibility "is historically enormous."

Madrigal and Cruz felt that the generals should send some suggestions to Congress, the former pointing out that it would not be at all patriotic to leave to such as Manrique and Díaz Soto y Gama "the resolution of such an important matter." But after hearing Escobar, the generals reached the conclusion that the situation should be left up to Calles. "He will see how to orient those in charge of designating the new Chief Executive." Said Roberto Cruz: "I, too, think the President should be the one to guide Congress, for we are only Revolutionary soldiers, and we should back his action."

Calles, following the suggestion of the generals, agreed to "come to an understanding with Congress and to give it the guidance most suitable for the designation of the Provisional President. I am going to accept this responsibility, as by doing so I can wipe out the differences of opinion. . . . I foresaw this patriotic stand of the Army; it could not have been more patriotic or more disinterested; its action demonstrates that we are now on the path of peace and prosperity for the Nation. . . . I congratulate the Army."

In the new Thirty-third Legislature, which, together with Obregón, had been selected in the July elections, Obregonistas who did not favor working closely with Calles had a nominal advantage in that Ricardo Topete headed the Obregonista bloc and was president of the Chamber of Deputies. This advantage became more and more tenuous because of the attitude of Aarón Sáenz, Portes Gil, and other leaders, and also because of the way in which Calles was handling the situation. Opponents of Topete claimed that the young Obregonista was running things in a dictatorial manner, and they expressed the fear that he might even go so far as to call at some unexpected hour a meeting of legislators and somehow arrange to name the Provisional President of Mexico without taking into consideration the views of all.

On the day on which Calles called his meeting with the generals, September 5, occurred also a meeting of politicians who were resolved to work against the Topete faction. To Ing. Marte R. Gómez was assigned the responsibility of bringing an end to Ricardo Topete's congressional power. Present at this meeting were four state governors, five senators, and seven deputies, including Manuel Riva Palacio, Gonzalo N. Santos, Melchor Ortega, and Marte Gómez. The governors who participated were Aarón Sáenz (Nuevo León), Saturnino Cedillo (San Luis Potosí), Carlos Riva Palacio (México), and Agustín Arroyo Ch. (Guanajuato).

Although Calles' friends recognized the possible necessity of creating a new legislative bloc in opposition to the anti-Calles Obregonistas, developments showed such a step unnecessary. On September 7, 154 deputies belonging to the Bloque Revolucionario Obregonista elected Diputado Miguel E. Yáñez as their leader in place of Topete. The Bloque issued a manifesto which proclaimed that henceforth, in order to make its leadership more democratic, it would select each month a new director. It declared that its "components live in a century of socialism." It made known its "great desire to discuss the petitions of the Catholics as soon as they are ready to condemn the anti-Christian and even criminal methods they are using today to make their power felt." It maintained as its program "the ideas contained in the report of the President." A corresponding group in the Senate agreed to "act with Calles, who made clear in his message to Congress his noble qualities."

The next step was to remove Topete from the presidency of Congress. In the warm sessions of the legislature, Topete, who felt that he had been double-crossed by some of his former comrades, stated that he was not in agreement with the resolution calling for his resignation. But he did not long delay his departure for Sonora to join his brother the governor, General Fausto Topete.

By now the President had made it clear that someone not in active military service ought to succeed him on December 1. The strongest pressures were those on behalf of Gobernación Minister Portes Gil and Coahuila's Governor Manuel Pérez Treviño. A number of worker organizations which were not controlled by Morones sent in messages favoring Portes Gil and so did the Veracruz party of Adalberto Tejeda, which a month before had proposed two more years for Calles. On the other hand some of the President's intimate friends, such as Carlos and Manuel Riva Palacio, Puig Casauranc, and Montes de Oca, were not especially enthusiastic about seeing the Gobernación Minister placed in the presidential chair.

Besides showing pictures of John Gilbert and Greta Garbo, the September 6, 1928, issue of *La Prensa* commented on the political situation. The Tamaulipas federal *diputados*, headed by Marte Gómez and joined by three or four from Jalisco, backed Portes Gil for the presidency. The *diputados* from the state of México, plus two or three from Veracruz, backed the governor of the state of México, Carlos Riva Palacio. The *diputados* from San Luis Potosí backed General Cedillo. The largest congressional group, said *La Prensa*, backed the Coahuila governor, Manuel Pérez Treviño, for the presidency. *La Prensa* assured its readers that Manuel Pérez Treviño would be selected.

On September 19 President Calles received a delegation representing the federal deputies and senators. The President advised that he had no candidate to recommend. In the long discussion that followed it was decided that all would agree on Portes Gil, the civilian of unmistakable Obregonista antecedents who in 1923 had broken with the Cooperatista Party when Prieto Laurens worked for De la Huerta. He had made a name for himself as an ardent pusher of the agrarian program of land redistribution. That he was not a friend of Morones did not mean that he did not have a record satisfactory for the working classes; Tamaulipas was one of the first states to get a labor law such as that called for by Article 123 of the federal Constitution.

After this conference with President Calles only formality remained. Three days later the Gran Comisión of the Chamber of Deputies declared that Obregón had been legally elected Constitutional President, but that since he had died a Provisional President should be chosen by the deputies and senators on September 25, pending new general elections for a Constitutional President.

On September 25 Lic. Portes Gil, without a dissenting vote, was named Provisional President to take office on the following December 1. He received 277 votes. Antonio Díaz Soto y Gama and Aurelio Manrique, Jr., did not vote.

At the same session Congress selected a date, November 20, 1929, on which the nation should elect a new Constitutional President to fill out Obregón's term by serving from February 5, 1930, to December 1, 1934. The November, 1929, date would allow enough time for candidates to fulfill the Constitutional requisite (Article 82) that prior to elections they reside in the country for one year without being during that time in active military service, or in a governorship, or in a Cabinet post as minister or undersecretary.

Lic. Portes Gil was officially notified of his selection by a congressional commission headed by Ing. Marte R. Gómez. At a banquet in his honor at Chapultepec Castle on September 29 speeches were made by General J. Gonzalo Escobar, General Manuel Pérez Treviño, Ing. Luis L. León, Dr. Alejandro Cerisola, and Senator Bartolomé García Correa. Escobar told the gathering that the Army was the true defender of the institutions of the Republic, and in Lic. Portes Gil it saw these institutions. General Pérez Treviño, who warmly congratulated Lic. Portes Gil, received loud cries of "Yes!" when he asked whether Lic. Portes Gil represented public opinion. He added that he was referring to Revolutionary and Obregonista opinion; "it is of no concern at all to us whether other opinion, which we call the reaction, is satisfied or not."

Lic. Portes Gil replied to his well-wishers by inviting all Mexicans of good will to co-operate in the program of the Revolution. He assured his hearers that he had never desired the post that he would take over on December 1. "But I am cheered because all the Revolutionary factions are with me." He promised that the political and social program of Alvaro Obregón would guide his steps "because this program is the same as that developed . . . by that great Revolutionary and austere statesman, Plutarco Elías Calles."

Shortly after his selection Portes Gil objected to the agrarian provisions of the budget being drawn up by Montes de Oca for 1929, in which 10 million pesos were set aside for pay for lands to be expropriated. Portes Gil objected on two counts: (1) it was unnecessary to debit the budget with the amount of agrarian bonds to be issued because it was unnecessary to pay in cash; and (2) 10 million pesos was ridiculously small, being closer to the amount involved in one month of expropriations rather than one year. Although Calles favored Montes de Oca's plan and advised that it would be well to slow down with land expropriations, Portes Gil got his way. He indicated that, if he did not, he would decline the provisional presidency.

Of "the great political debate" which took place in the Chamber of Deputies on October 8, 9, and 10, 1928, Professor Aurelio Manrique, Jr., said, "This is the first debate in the very short history of this legislature that has provoked the attention and interest not only of Mexico City but of all the nation." Numerically the debate was lopsided. Manrique and Díaz Soto y Gama explained to their fellow *diputados* why they did not vote for Portes Gil although they had been his original supporters.

Said Manrique: "We could not support Portes Gil, the candidate of Calles. Portes Gil owes his election to two factors: to his definite and undeniable Obregonista antecedents, and to his selection by Calles, a selection perhaps veiled, perhaps able, perhaps clever, but real and positive, that no one can honestly deny; no one here can say that Portes Gil was elected in spite of Calles. For us it is enough to think that Calles, whom we have attacked following the death of Obregón, influenced even slightly the selection of Portes Gil. Our propriety is such that that thought alone forced Díaz Soto y Gama and me to stay out of the *salón* at the hour of voting."

Díaz Soto y Gama justified his independence by referring to the recent speech of Calles in the halls of this same Congress: "If Calles and Obregón wanted the national, the impersonal, why do our companions seek to personalize? . . . Do not convert yourselves into a government of faction or into a sectarian party. . . . Let us," he said "put ourselves in a rational and human terrain, in the terrain of free discussion. To be a Revolutionary it is not necessary to be furiously pro-Calles. I, for example, am not a fervent admirer of Calles, frankly." (Applause from the galleries.)

The expression *jefe máximo* came up. Díaz Soto y Gama argued against a *caudillo* hidden behind a national party; "a man who without having the responsibility of power, has all the power—a man behind the throne." He quoted what Calles had just said against indispensable men. "And nevertheless" he went on, making reference to the earthquake that had just shaken the Chamber, "here Marte Gómez and Gonzalo Bautista, and all the others come to scare us with something worse than the earthquake: that if we lose sight of the personality of General Calles and do not accept him as the infallible director of the Revolution—as *jefe máximo*—we are lost, and he who does not admit it is to be hated, excommunicated."

If the legislative power is to name the Provisional President, "why," asked Díaz Soto y Gama "these trips and return trips to the Palacio Nacional?" Diputado Cerisola pointed out that Calles had limited himself to saying: "I have no candidate; I shall accept the selection made by Congress."

When Manrique said that Obregón reaped hates he did not sow, he opened up a topic that was good for hours of oratory by the lawmakers. Marte Gómez, Melchor Ortega, and others referred to the "insidious work of Manrique, who seeks to provoke a split between Callismo and Obregonismo."

Manrique and Díaz Soto y Gama received some support from the galleries, but on the floor they were called "frauds of agrarianism and Obregonism." Professor Leopoldo Camarena, speaking as a member of the Partido Agrarista, said that "we think differently from Manrique and Soto y Gama" and he let it be known that the Agrarian Party had high regard for Calles.

45.

The Murder Trial

A manifesto to the nation, dated Los Altos, Jalisco, October 28, 1928 (Fiesta de Cristo Rey), and signed by Division General Enrique Gorostieta, Jr., appeared. This document, circulated rather clandestinely in the nation's capital, referred to the civil strife which for over two years had been going forward against the "tyranny" of Plutarco Elías Calles. It noted that the "Liberators," because of all the material resources on which the oppressors could count, had not yet obtained final victory; the "Liberators" had, however, generously given their blood to write brilliant pages in the book of struggle against Bolshevik barbarianism. Reference was made to the efforts of Francisco Serrano and Arnulfo Gómez.

The manifesto noted that those who fought under the slogans of

"Viva Cristo Rey" and "Viva la Virgen de Guadalupe" had, up to then, lacked a Supreme Chief, or *Caudillo*, as well as the customary "Plan" and program. It then suggested remedies for these deficiencies: the Liga Nacional Defensora de la Libertad Religiosa had decided to name General Gorostieta as the Military Chief of the Liberating Movement, with all necessary authority in the realms of finance and war. General Gorostieta was accepting with the understanding that, as a soldier, he would place himself at the orders of the Civilian Chief when the latter had been named.

The "Liberators" declared that they did not recognize federal or state powers which had been usurped. The manifesto decreed the re-establishment of the 1857 Constitution without the inclusion therein of the Reform Laws; it claimed that these laws had been modified by "the national plebiscite" of September, 1926 (which backed the policy of the Mexican clergy) as well as by the Memorial de los católicos presented to Congress on September 3, 1928. The Constitution, said General Gorostieta's manifesto, could be reformed by national plebiscites or referenda in which women would have the right to vote.

The manifesto commented on the expropriation of lands for *ejidos*, saying that the Liberating Government would adopt adequate procedures for indemnifications, which should be just and effective. The Civilian Chief of the Liberating Movement would be named by the Directive Committee of the Liga Nacional Defensora de la Libertad Religiosa, after consulting with the National Guard. The Plan proclaimed by this manifesto was not to be altered unless changes were jointly approved by said Directive Committee and the Military Chief. When Mexico City was taken and order re-established in the nation Mexico would be reconstructed in accordance with the 1857 Constitution.

General Gorostieta called upon his companions in defeats, in sufferings, and in victories at Troneras, San Julián, Jalpa, Manzanillo, and Asís to raise the war cry: "Viva Cristo Rey! Viva la Virgen de Guadalupe! Death to the bad government!"[1]

On November 2, 1928, several days after General Gorostieta issued his manifesto, the sensational trial of José de León Toral and Srita. Concepción Acevedo de la Llata (Madre Conchita) began at the courthouse of San Angel.

[1] Enrique Gorostieta, Jr., quoted in Manuel González Ramírez (ed.), *Planes políticos y otros documentos*, pp. 280–294.

During the period before the start of the trial Madre Conchita, in the municipal jail of Mixcoac, received among a number of callers her mother and one of her sisters. Some of her recent companions were free and some were in the penitentiary. One of Madre Conchita's visitors, Father Ignacio Flores R., caused her to feel that while she would probably be pronounced not guilty in the San Angel civil trial, she could expect the religious authorities to try her and punish her by sending her to a strict European convent. Her lawyer, Lic. Fernando Ortega, was receiving letters from priests asking that he not defend her.

Madre Conchita felt that generally speaking she lacked the support of the members of the Association of Catholic Women (Damas Católicas). In this connection she was to point out that in the visits she had made a year before to the cell of Roberto Pro he had appreciated her visits more than those made by the Damas. At the Police Inspection she had been a frequent visitor of Roberto Pro and of Father Paredes before each was expelled from the country. Some of the Damas Católicas, who almost invariably encountered official difficulties, had remarked to her that she seemed to have a much easier time in making such visits than was the case with them. In reply Madre Conchita had remarked: "I believe that God is good to me and He helps me." The Damas felt suspicious; at that time it had even been rumored that Madre Conchita must be a girl friend of General Cruz![2]

Needless to say, Madre Conchita, now herself in a cell, was hurt by the public reference which Bishop De la Mora of San Luis Potosí made to mental abnormalities in herself and in her family.

On November 1 the names of the jurors were drawn by lot. They were mostly workmen and peasants from around San Angel. In spite of the desire of many thousands to watch the proceedings, the decision to hold the trial in the small San Angel courthouse limited to only about two hundred the number that could be accommodated.

On the morning of November 2 Toral and Madre Conchita were taken from their cells and, surrounded by soldiers, were conveyed in large police trucks to the courthouse. As they reached the neighborhood of the courthouse, where photographers and movie cameras were working away, double rows of policemen held back crowds of the curious, some of whom had waited for hours to catch a glimpse

[2] María Concepción Acevedo y de la Llata, *Obregón: Memorias inéditas de la Madre Conchita*, pp. 94–98.

of the prisoners. Two women who threw some flowers at Madre Conchita were taken and held for a while by the police. On the whole the crowd appeared to be more curious than friendly.

Toral smiled to the public, and then he gave his arm to Madre Conchita to escort her up the steps of the building. She, too, smiled upon the onlookers. When Margarita Pacheco, one of her companions who had recently been set free, urged her not to be dismayed, Madre Conchita raised her arms in a sort of general greeting to all.

During the first days of the trial, when much information obtained during the police investigations was made public, Toral described in great detail his actions, and even his thoughts. He admitted that if Madre Conchita had asked him not to commit the crime he would not have undertaken it.

In the eyes of Madre Conchita the atmosphere "began to darken" with the session of Monday, November 5, the day she took the stand. The audience developed the habit of applauding remarks of the prosecution and hissing statements by the defense, as Lic. Juan Correa Nieto, Attorney General of the Federal District, brought out details having to do with the manufacture of bombs, the journey with poison to Celaya, and the influence of Madre Conchita over various young people who frequented her house and were involved in such activities.

It was on that day that Lic. Correa Nieto revealed that Madre Conchita had had made a branding iron, presumably used to brand herself and her nuns with a cross and the letters "JHC." In seeking to show that Madre Conchita exerted great influence on Castro Balda (who was involved in the Celaya poisoning effort and in exploding bombs) the prosecuting attorney revealed that Castro Balda bore on his chest the mark of the branding iron. Madre Conchita pointed out that the prosecutor had earlier assured her that this "intimate" matter would not be brought out during the trial. When asked if her "nuns" were branded she rather heatedly replied that "these matters are the secrets of my nuns."

Ricardo Topete testified. So did Arturo H. Orcí and Valente Quintana. Madre Conchita was not impressed with the truthfulness of their testimony. One youth after another was subjected to cross-examination: María Elena Manzano, Eulogio González, Jorge Gallardo Pavón, Carlos Castro Balda, Leonor Rubio, Margarita Rubio, and Eduardo Zozaya. These witnesses, who for the most part

Senorita De la Llata (Madre Conchita) *and* José de León Toral *with Toral's lawyer*, Demetrio Sodi (*standing*). *At the murder trial, November, 1928. Casasola.*

had already signed statements, revealed great devotion to Madre Conchita and denied that she was involved in the effort to poison Obregón and Calles at Celaya. Eulogio González told the court that in the Police Inspection he had been compelled to make false declarations. It was during his testimony that Toral's defense lawyer was shouted down with insulting words, and then cries of "Catherine de Medici!" and "Lucrecia Borgia!" were made with reference to Madre Conchita.

A call of "Viva Obregón!" was followed by cries of death to Toral and to the "prostitute Concha." When the Federal District's Attorney General implied that Madre Conchita was deliberately telling untruths, some in the courtroom threatened to take in their own hands the matter of providing justice on behalf of Obregón, "vilely assassinated by a prostitute and a crack-brain." About fifty congressmen were present. One of them shouted at the jury, "If you will not do justice, then we shall punish them!"

Toral's chief of defense, Lic. Demetrio Sodi, agreed after hearing the plea of Toral's wife to defend the assassin at no charge. Sodi was not a young man, having served under Porfirio Díaz for twenty-three years, some of the time as president of the Supreme Court and a part of the time as Minister of Justice. Sodi maintained that religious persecutions caused the crime committed by Toral, and he also argued that the crime was entirely of a political nature and thus, under the laws, punishable by imprisonment but not by a death sentence.

The trial was the object of great public attention. In spite of all the noises in the courtroom and all that was being revealed, Calles was not sure that things were going too well. He noted some sympathy for Toral, a genuine religious fanatic and very well behaved. In an unusual step he called on the Attorney General of the Nation, Ezequiel Padilla, to step down from his high position and speak in court on behalf of the case of the State. After the President had expressed the thought that although Toral was on trial it was beginning to look as if the government was on trial, Padilla agreed; then in three days this great orator studied as fully as he could the numerous records on the matter.

Most of the members of Congress went to the San Angel courthouse to hear Padilla's speech closing the government's case. Padilla, who found himself arguing against his old teacher, a man he much admired, did not go into details of the case which had been carefully examined by others. To the accompaniment of great ap-

plause from an overwhelmingly partisan audience, he opened up
his discussion by pointing out that the crime committed by Toral
and Srita. de la Llata "not only is a crime against the Republic,
against society, and against the law, but is also a crime against their
own religion."

After demonstrating this point by referring to religious writings,
Padilla turned to the broad question of the Catholic religion in the
Mexican state, and he distinguished between the fervent Catholics
and the clergy. With Mexico's independence, he said, the Mexican
clergy became something different from the silent, humble, and
poor group that had been obedient to the King of Spain. It became
rich and even insolent. There came the laws of 1856, the laws of
Juárez directed at the moneyed clergy, and the 1857 Constitution.
However, with the conciliation of the Porfirian Dictatorship, the
clergy constantly violated the laws of the 1857 Constitution and
obtained new acquisitions. "When our Revolution came," said Padilla, "it was natural that the Laws of the Reform, which had not
been obeyed, be restored in the Constitution of 1917. . . . The
Catholic clergy then began to declare itself in rebellion."

Padilla pointed out that the vigilance of the laws "has been secured for the benefit of the humble people," adding that "a government that does not know how to implement its laws does not deserve
to govern." He declared that the assassins of Obregón were in error
if they thought that the fall of that great mountain would mean the
loss of the Revolution. Obregón, he asserted, had through the Revolution guarded "the great and noble spirit of the socialism of
Christ . . . Obregón was the first who said that his greatest leader
was Christ himself." Other mountains would arise, like Calles and
Portes Gil.

The clergy, said Padilla, protests the limitation of the number of
priests in Mexico. But he pointed out that in Spain the clergy "is
an official institution" with a limited number of priests. As for the
disallowing of foreign priests in Mexico, Padilla declared that the
same rules applied in Spain, and that in France such rules applied
not only to the clergy but to the members of the various professions.

Developing his point that it was false to maintain that the nation
opposed the government, Padilla asserted that Mexico was largely
a nation of Catholics, but of "Catholics who have found it their
Christian duty to resist the worldly tendencies of the clergy, and
defend the doctrines of Christ . . . The people have understood this
problem and so to them the death of General Obregón is a terrible

thing. . . . That figure of Obregón was not that of a politician, nor that of a military leader; it was that of a man who carried in his bosom precisely Christ's socialistic virtue; who had as his mission on earth to reject what is called aristocracy in the clergy, or what is called aristocracy in capital, and descend to what is called democracy in religion, to what is called democracy in the division of wealth." Obregón favored the oppressed masses.[3]

After a tremendous ovation had demonstrated support for Padilla's observations, Demetrio Sodi sought in reply to speak on behalf of his client. The defense lawyer wanted to make it clear that a very real religious persecution existed in Mexico and that this had caused the crime. But the shouts and insults that interrupted his words became in almost no time so pronounced that he was unable to make himself heard, and he was forced to leave his thoughts unspoken. He had to say: "I have finished, Señor Presidente, because I cannot continue." Shouts of "Death to Sodi!" were his reward.

Padilla took his old teacher by the arm and the two men went out together. The government had an escort for the protection of Sodi on his way home, an escort which his daughter points out might better have been used to preserve order in the room of justice.

José de León Toral was found guilty and condemned to death. His codefendant was also found guilty, but her death penalty was revised, since she was a woman, to read twenty years in jail with no reduction in time.

While his defenders unsuccessfully sought to have the verdict changed, Toral spent time in his small cell writing notes and making numerous sketches for his friends, his wife, and his children. Another child was born, and was named Humberto Toral, in memory of Humberto Pro. There was some excitement in the penitentiary when a nephew of Obregón tried to assassinate Toral and, when his effort failed, committed suicide.

In one of his letters to a friend, Toral wrote: "I have learned very beautiful things about the life of Señor Obregón, his friendliness, helpfulness to those in need, his forgiveness of his enemies; his projects and intentions for the nation, etc., and I can truthfully say that if before July I had had these talks with his friends, I never would have taken his life."[4]

---

[3] Ezequiel Padilla's speech and everything recorded in the course of the trial may be found in the stenographic text, *El jurado de Toral y la Madre Conchita.*

[4] María Elena Sodi de Pallares, *Los Cristeros y José de León Toral*, p. 127.

404

46·

President Portes Gil
and the C.R.O.M.

Following his selection as Provisional President Lic. Portes Gil, in a press statement, gave assurances that the federal officials in his forthcoming administration would not intervene in the election which was to take place in November, 1929, for Constitutional President. The election, he said, would be "a true expression of liberty." When Calles and Portes Gil went on a tour to inspect the progress of the Calles and Don Martín dams they discussed this coming election, which was by now a matter of much public interest. Lic. Aarón Sáenz, the candidate of many Callista-Obregonistas, was urged to act with discretion.

Portes Gil talked over with Calles the need for new blood in the federal government. He ordered Ing. Pascual Ortiz Rubio and Lic. Ramón P. de Negri back to Mexico to take over, respectively, the ministries of Gobernación and of Industry, Commerce, and Labor in the new Cabinet. As Mexican minister to Germany, Ortiz Rubio in 1924 had received in Berlin a visit from General Calles, during the three months which the then President-elect was spending in Europe studying socialism and economics. After serving in Germany, Ortiz Rubio had been named Mexican minister to Brazil. In Brazil he found he had no small task in seeking to better relations which had become very delicate because of Brazilian sympathy for the Mexican Catholic clergy. On November 20, 1928, he received a telegram telling him to come to Mexico at once.

Shortly before this message was sent to Ortiz Rubio, President Calles held a remarkable meeting at the Mexico City home of Agriculture Minister León. All the prominent Revolutionaries were asked to remain in their Cabinet or Army posts, or governorships, until November 21, 1928, thus making them ineligible to partake in the presidential election of November 20, 1929. The reason which Calles gave for this drastic step was the same one he had given to Army leaders in September. He wanted to "avoid divisions in the Revolutionary groups."[1] Since Aarón Sáenz, who had been absent from his Nuevo León governorship for some time, was not affected by this step, his presidential chances were immeasurably strengthened by the elimination of so many from the field. All agreed to comply fully. The failure of anyone to agree, or to keep the agreement, would have been clear indication of his intention. Once the deadline had passed, those who had maintained their high positions, including those in the command of troops, would have had recourse only to rebellion.

There was distinct possibility of a rebellion by those who dissented from current developments and who saw only one way to make their opinions count. Some of the warm words expressed by some of the generals when Calles had his September meeting with them were considered, with reason, to be insincere. The events of 1920, 1923, and 1927 were not forgotten. War Minister Joaquín Amaro, the self-educated general of much discipline, who had reorganized the Army, was carefully planning ahead for an adverse eventuality and was concentrating forces in the central plateau. Montes de Oca was building up reserves for possible war expenses.

[1] J. M. Puig Casauranc, *Galatea rebelde a varios pigmaliones*, p. 309.

A crowd had assembled at the National Stadium on November 30, 1928. Not only did they witness the act whereby the thirty-seven–year–old lawyer took over the presidency from General Calles, but immediately thereafter they heard the new executive set a precedent by outlining the program that his administration would follow. Portes Gil emphasized that the most important problem of his government would not be that of the coming election. He said that his administration hoped to consolidate the Revolutionary gains made by acts under Obregón and Calles and it hoped to advance "to the extent possible." He spoke of complying with foreign

Lic. Emilio Portes Gil *makes the pledge of the office of President of Mexico, November 30, 1928*. Plutarco Elías Calles, Manuel Riva Palacio (*behind Calles' left shoulder*), Antonio Juárez (*left of Riva Palacio*), Marte R. Gómez (*behind microphone*), Congressional President Arturo Campillo Seyde (*seated*), Emilio Portes Gil (*arm extended*), Melchor Ortega, Eduardo Hay (*a bit to the rear and left of Ortega*), *and* Fernando Moctezuma. *Enrique Díaz.*

and domestic obligations, and he lauded the good understandings developed by Calles and Dwight Morrow. As for the men of his new regime, he proclaimed that "men who know how to be loyal to men should be replaced by men who know how to be loyal to institutions." He referred to the "just criticism levelled at those who were using influence and public posts as instruments for obtaining wealth."

Included in the Cabinet of Portes Gil, who was scheduled to serve for fourteen months, were a number of men who had been in the Cabinet of the outgoing chief executive: the War Minister, General Amaro; the Finance Minister, Luis Montes de Oca; the Undersecretary in Charge of Foreign Relations, Genaro Estrada; and the Comptroller General, Julio Freyssinier Morín. Dr. Puig Casauranc became head of the Department of the Federal District, Portes Gil later pointing out that Calles "was vitally interested in this [appointment] and felt a paternal fondness for" Puig.

It is not likely that Montes de Oca would have remained on as Finance Minister had Obregón started his second term as Mexico's President, for differences had arisen between Pani's successor and the Cajeme chickpea broker. Nor was Portes Gil entirely enthusiastic about Montes de Oca, whose ideas about land redistribution were distant from his own, and with whom he was to have disagreements during the course of the provisional presidency. But the new President recognized the Finance Minister's honesty and appreciated the fact that he was highly conversant with the financial program that had for some time been going forward under the previous administration.

Sr. Ramón P. de Negri took over from Puig Casauranc the Ministry of Industry, Commerce, and Labor, and Ing. Javier Sánchez Mejorada became Minister of Communications and Public Works. Others who were brought by Portes Gil to the headships of ministries were Ing. Marte R. Gómez in Agriculture, Lic. Ezequiel Padilla in Public Education, and Lic. Felipe Canales who, as Undersecretary, headed the Gobernación post. Pascual Ortiz Rubio, scheduled to be the Gobernación Minister, had been delayed by his inability to obtain a boat from Brazil promptly after receiving his instructions to return to Mexico.

As promised in his inaugural address, Portes Gil endeavored to hold back the tide of corruption in public men. He named a commission (Montes de Oca, Sánchez Mejorada, and Freyssinier Morín) to study a dredging contract which involved Arturo Elías and which had already been approved by the Calles Administration. In connection with that case Portes Gil agreed with the feeling that "much money went to officials of the government and of the congressional chambers." Marte Gómez cancelled contracts which the previous administration had made with Santiago Smithers who was close to Calles. Portes Gil points out that, while neither Carranza nor Obregón nor De la Huerta can be accused of business dealings nor of being immoral heads of state, "all three acquiesced in overlooking the crowd of men beside them who dedicated themselves unrestrainedly to every kind of money-making. This state of corruption continued to increase during the administration of General Calles and in the following periods. In the interim administration, which it befell me to fulfill, I did my best to hold back this increasing wave of immorality of officials and with pride I can declare that at least my immediate collaborators, my intimate friends, and my relatives abstained . . . Unfortunately it was not possible to prevent others, accustomed to the game of big interests, from managing to profit from official favor."[2]

A step forward was the inauguration of a system of federal judges with status secure from the whim of the executive. This system had been recommended to President-elect Obregón by a number of lawyers, including Ezequiel Padilla and Portes Gil. Gilberto Valenzuela pointed out its advantages, provided a good and careful selection of judges was made. The arguments had convinced Obregón, who was responsible for the incorporation of this change into the law of the land, effective on January 1, 1929. Following a careful study of the honesty, ability, and dependability of the many who were suggested for positions on the Supreme Court and the top courts of the territories and Federal District, Portes Gil in December, 1928, sent his nominations to the Congress, where they were ratified.

Since delivering his September 1, 1928, message to Congress, General Calles had been studying the creation of a Revolutionary political party, in which he might play a part following his departure from the presidency of the nation. With the formation of such a party he hoped to contribute further to Mexico's transition to a regime of institutions. He asked Puig Casauranc to study the histories of French, English, and United States political parties, with particular emphasis on the two leading parties in the United States.

The time was particularly propitious for the development of the new party that Calles had in mind—an idea, it will be recalled, which had also been brought up by Obregón in a conversation which

[2] Emilio Portes Gil, *Quince años de política mexicana*, p. 99.

he had had with Luis León just before his re-election. The Centro Director Obregonista had been dissolved; the nation was looking forward to a new future based on the ideas expressed on September 1; and arrangements had to be made for a party to nominate a

Organizers of the Partido Nacional Revolucionario. Front row: Bartolomé García Correa, Aarón Sáenz, Plutarco Elías Calles, Luis L. León, Manuel Pérez Treviño. *Second row, third from left:* Manlio Fabio Altamirano. *December, 1928. Enrique Díaz.*

constitutional presidential candidate who would carry the banner of the Revolution.

The country was full of political parties, the large majority of them being local groups. Previous efforts to consolidate various important parties under one organization had not been successful. For a while in 1922 three leading non-sectional parties (Cooperatista, Agrarista, and Laborista) had consolidated as the Confederación Nacional Revolucionaria but this union had been primarily a congressional device to overthrow the Partido Liberal Constitucionalista, and after its success this opportunistic confederation had soon fallen apart, to the temporary advantage of the Cooperatista leaders.

On December 1, with Portes Gil starting his new labors, the nation learned about the organization of the Partido Nacional Revolucionario from a manifesto signed by General Calles, Lic. Aarón Sáenz, Ing. Luis L. León, General Manuel Pérez Treviño, Professor Basilio Vadillo, Professor Bartolomé García, Senator Manlio Fabio Altamirano, and Lic. David Orozco (in the order indicated). It mentioned the need for the "organization and foundation of political parties of definite principles and of permanent life." Dr. Puig Casauranc, who had been helping Calles to develop his ideas, declined to be the new party's secretary general, because he did not agree with what he felt to be Calles' interest in having the party nominate Aarón Sáenz for the constitutional presidency.

"Rudimentary logic," said the manifesto, "permits us to consider that the multiple tendencies and opinions which presently divide the nation should be organized into two strong currents: the innovators, reformers, or revolutionaries; and the conservative and reactionary tendency . . . To bring together all the first-mentioned, that is to say, of the revolutionary tendency, following the suggestions contained in the [September 1] message to Congress, and using the rights which as citizens we receive from our laws, the undersigned have united to constitute the Organizing Committee of the Partido Nacional Revolucionario."

The organizing committee invited "all the parties, groups, and political organizations of the Republic of revolutionary belief and tendency to unite and form the Partido Nacional Revolucionario" and it proposed "to call soon a convention of representatives of all the existing organizations who desire to form part of the P.N.R., where will be discussed" the statutes and constitution, the principles, the presidential candidate, and the national board of the party. It added that the manifesto's signers "cannot and should not work for any candidate."

A few days before leaving the presidency Calles had called a meeting at the home of Industry Minister Puig Casauranc in an effort to achieve a peace between the C.R.O.M. leaders and the President-elect. Portes Gil attended, and so did the C.R.O.M. leaders (such as Eduardo Moneda and Ricardo Treviño) with the exception of Morones. After a due interval of complaints by each side—particularly regarding the conflicts in Tamaulipas—peace and cooperation were agreed upon between the C.R.O.M. labor leaders and the new administration. Former foes embraced each other in amity.

This achievement and the inauguration of Portes Gil were followed, on December 4, 1928, by a gathering of the C.R.O.M. at the Hidalgo Theatre for its ninth annual convention. On December 6 Calles greeted and praised the labor organization which had always been so faithful to him. He also recommended calmness, a recommendation hardly followed by another orator, Luis N. Morones, who attacked President Portes Gil and took advantage of Calles' friendly speech in order to strengthen his own position. Others who, like Portes Gil, were attacked at the labor convention for appearing to be enemies of the C.R.O.M. were the well-known governors of Coahuila and Guanajuato, Manuel Pérez Treviño and Agustín Arroyo Ch.

The C.R.O.M. delegates passed a resolution calling upon President Portes Gil forcibly to bring to an end a performance ("El Desmoronamiento de Morones") at the Lírico Theatre, a production which Morones highly resented. The show at the Lírico pictured Morones as a gangster at his Tlalpam estate, reveling there in great orgies with companions among whom were some high in the preceding administration. Portes Gil would not comply with the C.R.O.M. resolution; and, since the C.R.O.M. had said that it would itself take the necessary steps if the President would not, Portes Gil arranged for police protection at the Lírico Theatre and also at another theatre whose performance was classified by the C.R.O.M. as anti-labor. The new President spoke about freedom of speech.

Because of this attitude on the part of Portes Gil, subsequent resolutions made by the C.R.O.M. included one calling for the resignation of any C.R.O.M. member in a public position. Portes Gil's Secretary of Industry, Commerce, and Labor accepted the resignations and stated that he would proceed to fill the posts thus made vacant. Another resolution of the C.R.O.M. was to withdraw its delegates from the Convención Patronal y Obrera, which was working on the formulation of a federal labor law.

As a result of this struggle between the President and Morones, the position of Calles became not only difficult but also a matter of considerable conjecture. In the Chamber of Deputies Aurelio Manrique, Jr., stated that Calles was with the C.R.O.M. against the federal administration, and President Portes Gil asked Luis L. León (of the Organizing Committee of the Partido Nacional Revolucionario) to have Calles clear up the matter of where he stood.

General Calles, says Puig Casauranc, "fell into a state of depression, one of the most profound we have ever known."

War Minister Amaro stated that whatever might be the conduct or attitude of General Calles regarding the C.R.O.M. attacks on the President, he (Amaro) would fulfill his duty and support the Chief Executive. In the Congress commissions were delegated to advise Portes Gil that the senators and deputies supported him. Upon being officially notified, the President declared: "I am convinced that General Calles will not support the policy of any who attack the Administration without reason."

Then on December 8, just one week after Calles had announced the formation of the P.N.R. Organizing Committee, two statements appeared in the press defining his position. One of the statements was worded by Puig Casauranc, expert in phrasing the General's statements concerning his highly purposed self-sacrifices. In it Calles announced his retirement from politics and from the P.N.R. The signer analyzed the existing situation and decided that he was probably not the right person to be creating the P.N.R. He said further, in conclusion: "I should retire absolutely and definitely from political life and return, as I do return today, to the condition of the most obscure citizen who now does not want to be, and never will be, a political factor in Mexico." He added that only in the unfortunate case of a threat to the country's institutions would he place himself at the orders of the legitimate government, to serve it as it might indicate, and that once the crisis was over he would return again to the unpretentious position he was now assigning to himself.

Calles' second statement of December 8, an explanation of his appearance at the C.R.O.M. convention, was less dramatic. After speaking of his affection for the C.R.O.M., "because I consider that it is one of the crystallizations of the Revolutionary ideals," he added:

my presence at the convention was erroneously taken advantage of . . . because instead of social themes, political themes were developed, opinions in which I have no participation. Yesterday a commission named by that convention came to notify me of the decisions which had been reached, and I answered, with my usual frankness, that I regretted profoundly the situation created, which was not in accord with my recommendation of serenity, moderation, and prudence.

Before this commission from the labor convention Calles had defined as groundless its fears about the attitude of the Portes Gil Government. He said that "the present government is revolutionary and must be revolutionary, as I believe the future governments in this country must be."

After Portes Gil had thus triumphed over Morones, General Manuel Pérez Treviño was named to succeed Calles as head of the Partido Nacional Revolucionario's organizing committee. Luis León was the secretary general; Professor Basilio Vadillo, the Committee's secretary of the interior; Dip. David Orozco, the secretary of organization; and Senator Manlio Fabio Altamirano, the secretary of propaganda.

The Convención Patronal y Obrera, from which the C.R.O.M. decided to withdraw its delegates, was a series of meetings at the Palacio Nacional attended by representatives of labor and capital. These meetings had been organized by Portes Gil, who kept pushing for a federal labor law in accordance with Constitutional Article 123. State labor laws already existed in Sonora, Veracruz, Yucatán, and Tamaulipas, and it was the President's desire that the meetings at the Palacio Nacional would produce a proposed federal law. Regardless of the attitude of the C.R.O.M., the sessions continued.

47·

Background for the
Querétaro Convention

During this first month of Portes Gil's administration
it appeared that General y Lic. Aarón Sáenz, who had been the
leader of the Centro Obregonista and who since July 17 had coun-
selled his followers to co-operate with the Calles régime, was the
obvious one to be the presidential candidate of the P.N.R. Following
a banquet given in his honor by supporters in Nuevo León, Sáenz
made a statement for *El Universal* saying that, in connection with
the work being done on his behalf, it would be best to postpone
action until after an expression of public opinion from all parts of
the nation and until after completion of the organizational work of

the P.N.R. On December 5, 1928, the "railroad" bloc of the federal congress gave a banquet in his honor.

A few, of course, besides Puig Casauranc, felt differently about the candidacy of Lic. Sáenz. According to Portes Gil, Colonel Adalberto Tejeda (governor of Veracruz), General Saturnino Cedillo (governor of San Luis Potosí), General Manuel Pérez Treviño (governor of Coahuila), and *Diputados* Luis L. León, Melchor Ortega, and Gonzalo N. Santos "did not favor Sáenz, the first three because they themselves aspired to the post, and the others because they felt Sáenz was not a guarantee of the advanced principles of the Revolution." Some who were bold enough to generalize with respect to classifications which were easier to use than to define, expressed the thought that Sáenz was a Revolutionary moderate rather than a Revolutionary radical. For the moment, however, some of those who may have been seeking a more extreme "radical" either kept quiet or felt they had nowhere to turn. It is reported that Melchor Ortega and Gonzalo N. Santos attended the banquet of December 5 honoring Sáenz.[1]

December saw the return to Mexico of two who had represented Mexico abroad. On account of the November pact whereby much of the nation's presidential timber had made itself unavailable for the high office, these two were immediately regarded as possible presidential candidates, particularly as service abroad in representation of Mexico during a part of the twelve-month period preceding the election was not considered a reason for disqualification.

The first of the two to arrive in Mexico was Lic. Gilberto Valenzuela, who came from England, where he had been the Mexican minister. When this Sonora lawyer left the Gobernación post in 1925 he was not in sympathy with the policies of President Calles. He had remarked at that time that a Cabinet minister's resignation was likely to occur when the President had no confidence in his minister, or else when the minister had no confidence in the President, and that the latter situation was the case.

After landing at Veracruz on December 6, Lic. Valenzuela repeated observations which he had earlier made in London: "Since I left Mexico I have remained away from the politics of the

[1] Archivo Casasola, *Historia gráfica de la Revolución*, p. 1851.

country to such an extent that I do not know the background and characteristics of the present situation and of the leaders . . . I do not seek or desire to be Chief Executive and much less do I desire to be an element of division and discord in the Mexican family . . ." He spoke of the need for honorable collaboration "in this historic moment."

Lic. Valenzuela was nevertheless subject to some pressure to be a presidential candidate, particularly by his discontented admirers in Sonora, and Diputado Ricardo Topete was able to convince him that he should "enter the fray." Manrique and Díaz Soto y Gama joined with Diputado Ricardo Topete in acclaiming Valenzuela. Some of his old friends who associated themselves with the P.N.R. also favored him at the start, but after a talk with Calles, Valenzuela accused the latter "of planning an imposition."

In spite of pleas by Manlio Fabio Altamirano of the P.N.R., Valenzuela declined to put his presidential hopes in the hands of the forthcoming convention at Querétaro. Also declining Portes Gil's offer of the presidency of the Supreme Court, he remained loyal to Topete, Manrique, and Díaz Soto y Gama, and became an eloquent candidate in opposition to the P.N.R. It was reported that he took with him, in his movement to the camp of the dissenters, at least fifty federal *diputados* and some senators.

On February 21, 1929, Valenzuela left Mexico City on a campaign tour which brought him to Sonora via Durango, Torreón, and Chihuahua. With terrific vigor the author of the Plan of Agua Prieta spoke out against Calles, and in Sonora he used his rich vocabulary to attack "the intrigue, the baseness, and the crimes that have prevailed in the government program." He asked for a better era, "without agrarianism á la Calles, which has killed agriculture . . . , without a political economy which consists only in . . . reducing wages of miserable employees, allowing the amassing of fortunes to be converted into estates such as 'Soledad de la Mota,' 'Santa Bárbara,' 'La Hormiga,' and palatial residences for immodest courtiers like those of Anzures and the Hipódromo subdivisions." He called for an end to the importation of quantities of contraband by relatives and protégés, adding that some sons-in-law who now found themselves millionaires were "actual tramps" a short while back. The new era, he proclaimed, would be one which would approve an army of patriotic and conscientious soldiers rather than unscrupulous slaughtermen and assassins who were made rich in the fulfillment of their odious commissions.

Valenzuela promised to reveal "how the coward, the assassin, the Borgia of the present epoch, Plutarco Elías Calles, plotted and brought about" the murder of Obregón with the twofold purpose of justifying his hateful, unpopular campaign of religious persecution and of removing the man who was going to reduce him to nothing.

Ing. y General Pascual Ortiz Rubio touched New York and Havana on his way from Brazil to Mexico. At New York he received a suggestion that he make no statement. Both at New York and later at Havana he received information which made it clear that he might be a strong presidential possibility.

He reached Mexico City on December 26, at a time when opposition politicians and generals were becoming particularly restless and bold in their ideas. During a chat with Portes Gil at the Palacio Nacional it was arranged that Ortiz Rubio would confer with Calles at Cuernavaca, Morelos, before deciding whether to accept the Gobernación post. From Portes Gil he received the escort which he requested for the trip to Cuernavaca.

The conversation between Ortiz Rubio and Calles has been variously described. There seems no doubt that Ortiz Rubio left Cuernavaca enthusiastic about his chances at the P.N.R. Querétaro convention. Some of the party felt that a candidate who had remained for so long a time "isolated from the political atmosphere" might hold some advantages. The restless generals were forecasting the "imposition" of Aarón Sáenz. Apparently Ortiz Rubio heard from Calles a great deal about "institutional government" wherein the P.N.R. would be a powerful factor. He learned that the P.N.R. at Querétaro would select its candidate "freely and democratically." He learned enough to decide not to accept Portes Gil's offer of the Gobernación post, and of this decision he advised the President before December was ended.

As soon as Ortiz Rubio declined the Cabinet post talk began as to whether or not he was to be a really important contender for the P.N.R. nomination. Many felt that the grooming of Ortiz Rubio as a contestant was being done to create at Querétaro an atmosphere of democracy which would have been lacking had Aarón Sáenz been the only candidate. But this point of view could easily have been disputed by those who noted that early serious backers of Ortiz Rubio were Governor Lázaro Cárdenas of Michoacán, and Governor Carlos Riva Palacio of México, the latter being a particularly intimate friend of Calles.[2] Cárdenas, in now supporting Ortiz Rubio, was disregarding differences which he had had with the engineer during earlier phases of Michoacán politics.[3]

While the official party debated the relative merits of Sáenz and Ortiz Rubio, and while Valenzuela campaigned with strong anti-Calles phraseology, two others were making independent efforts to reach the presidency. They were Lic. José Vasconcelos, Obregón's Minister of Public Education, and General Antonio I. Villarreal, who for a while had been Obregón's Minister of Agriculture and later had associated himself with De la Huerta in rebellion.

Not long after refusing to support the Antirreeleccionista candidacy of Arnulfo R. Gómez in 1927, José Vasconcelos had moved from his lecture post at the University of Chicago to give a course at Stanford University. He was in California when Obregón was assassinated. Asked to comment on Obregón's death, he said: "The principal guilty one is one who will preside at his funeral." He kept up his attacks on Calles, Obregón, and Dwight Morrow, particularly the first-mentioned.

In California he conversed with General Enrique Estrada and he addressed meetings of many exiled Mexicans. Los Angeles, he has pointed out, "was the most populous Mexican city after Mexico City, with 200,000 Mexicans." He lent an attentive ear to those who suggested that he return to his homeland as a presidential candidate; and he went from city to city in the southwest of the United States arousing audiences of his countrymen against Calles and the P.N.R.

At Laredo, Texas, he had an important conversation with another dissenter who had a clearly anti-Calles past and who also seemed eager to be the opposition candidate, General Antonio I. Villarreal. Lic. Vasconcelos proposed that they work independently for the nomination by the Partido Antirreeleccionista, and that whoever won that nomination would be supported by the other. They would both start their prenomination campaigns "on the day when the year within which the candidates must be on national soil starts"; General Villarreal would enter Mexico at Nuevo Laredo, Tamaulipas, close to his home state of Nuevo León; Lic. Vasconcelos would enter Mexico at Nogales, Sonora, and work south via the west coast. Vasconcelos wanted to stir up the people of

[2] Mauricio Magdaleno, *Las palabras perdidas*, pp. 79, 50.
[3] Luis Montes de Oca, handwritten observations.

Mexico, rather than seek to win the politicians. With characteristic self-assurance he told his supporters: "I shall be present at the meeting to which destiny calls me."

Vasconcelos started his campaign with an address at a Nogales theatre on November 10, 1928. He called for the people to act on behalf of effective suffrage and no re-election. Religious fanaticism, he said, "should be fought by books, not by machine guns." After referring to Mexican defeats in international relations, he added: "the truth is that most of our Revolutionary illusions have been extinguished; . . . a nation divided cannot face up to the rival interests abroad . . . The only danger is that the public may not feel the call . . ."

Even before Vasconcelos' entry at Nogales, there were many students in Mexico City who enthusiastically felt the call to campaign for a vital new national leadership. Under Lic. Octavio Medellín Ostos and Abraham Arellano such pro-Vasconcelos organizations as the Frente Nacional Renovador and the Comité Orientador Pro-Vasconcelos soon sprang up in Mexico City. Arellano, a former Villista, had worked with Vasconcelos in the Education Ministry. Octavio Medellín Ostos was leader of the Comité Orientador. Most of their ardent associates were very young. Some of the many who participated in the early planning were: Enrique González Aparicio, Angel Carvajal, Salvador Azuela, Alejandro Gómez Arias, Adolfo López Mateos, Antonio Armendáriz and Vicente and Mauricio Magdaleno. Germán de Campo, only twenty-five years old, developed into a moving speaker.

Among the many women who devoted themselves to Vasconcelismo perhaps the best known was Antonieta Rivas Mercado, who appears to have been relatively well off financially and who at this time switched from being a devotee of intellectualism and advanced writings to becoming a devotee of Vasconcelos and of his cause. She often invited the members of the Frente Nacional Renovador to her house.

Abraham Arellano helped persuade the Centro Revolucionario de Principios (a small group of dyed-in-the-wool Maderistas) to back Vasconcelos. Some of the young Vasconcelistas joined up with the Partido Nacional Antirreeleccionista, in which figured such older and more experienced men as Vito Alessio Robles, Francisco Vázquez Gómez, Victorio Góngora, Calixto Maldonado, and José G. Aguilar. They hoped to win the party away from

General Villarreal, to whom it seemed to be heading. Others were not attracted to the party whose recent candidate had been the late General Arnulfo R. Gómez.[4]

Vasconcelos followed his Nogales effort by a really strenuous campaign of travelling and speaking. He covered the states of Sonora, Sinaloa, Nayarit, and Jalisco, stimulating the creation of pro-Vasconcelos political clubs. These were to form a new party, the Partido Democrático Sonorense, which, at least for the time being, was kept independent of the Partido Antirreeleccionista. The former Minister of Education did not think highly of the candidacy of Valenzuela because of what he considered to be Valenzuela's earlier association with Calles. Vasconcelos criticized the candidacy of Aarón Sáenz, saying that "Sáenz has no credentials other than the recommendation of Ambassador Morrow."[5]

From Mazatlán, Sinaloa, Vasconcelos wrote to his young admirers in Mexico City, replying to their question about the relationship with the Partido Nacional Antirreeleccionista. He did not preclude the possibility of an arrangement, but insisted that it be on the basis of a judgment by a fair convention and not on the basis of some political maneuver.[6]

Vasconcelos and his coworkers ran into assaults and fighting in Guadalajara, where clubs and boiling oil were used against them. While official versions blamed the Vasconcelistas for the rioting, the candidate denounced Margarito Ramírez, the railroad worker who had arranged Obregón's escape from Mexico City in April, 1920, and who was now governor of the state of Jalisco. Ramírez' paid hands, said Vasconcelos, were responsible for the hostile acts, and he sent off a wire of protest to President Portes Gil. The President did his best to make it possible for Vasconcelos to hold as many meetings as he desired and he censured the acts in Guadalajara. He constantly strove to give Vasconcelos all the protection guaranteed by the laws, but it was not an easy matter.

At Guadalajara Vasconcelos received a visit from Vito Alessio Robles, who wanted the former Education Minister to submit his independent candidacy to a decision which would be forthcoming when the Partido Antirreeleccionista held its convention in the capital. According to Vasconcelos, Alessio Robles confided: "Don't worry about Villarreal, we have him under control; the whole

[4] Mauricio Magdaleno, op. cit., pp. 24–26.
[5] José Vasconcelos, El proconsulado, p. 45.
[6] Mauricio Magdaleno, op. cit., p. 39.

General Antonio I. Villarreal, *candidate for the Mexican presidency. January, 1929. Casasola.*

party is for you . . ." Vasconcelos agreed to the ideas of Alessio Robles provided that the Mexico City convention be one of various parties among which the Antirreeleccionistas would have a leading but not a dominant position. This satisfied Alessio Robles, who thereupon issued newspaper statements praising Vasconcelos and criticizing the Jalisco governor. Representatives of General Enrique Gorostieta and the Cristeros were also at this time received by Vasconcelos, who suggested that armed uprisings be held back until after the election. "When I take the field I want to be a President-elect and not just a candidate heading a movement."[7]

Vasconcelista campaigners quickly acquired experience. Under the slogan of "With Madero Yesterday! With Vasconcelos Today!" they covered the country, putting up posters, organizing political clubs, and preparing towns for the arrival of their candidate. Although obstacles were furnished by inhospitable local politicians, and although sometimes it was hard to gather a crowd to hear the former Education Minister, the young workers were generally enthusiastic about what they regarded to be the true feeling of the people. They crusaded for what they called a much-needed change . . . for a sort of revolution within the Revolution. They pointed to the evils of a dictatorship. In their movement they saw great similarities to the popular Madero movement of 1910.

As the time approached for the P.N.R. to pick its candidate, General Antonio I. Villarreal was campaigning in Nuevo León for the Antirreeleccionista nomination, and the Communist Party was busy with an independent effort in Mexico City. The painter Diego Rivera was among those present at a gathering to honor General Pedro Rodríguez Triana, the presidential candidate selected by a group of Communist representatives of laborers and peasants.

General Villarreal was acclaimed by his supporters at Monterrey's Hotel Continental on January 27, 1929. He was greeted by officials of the Partido Social Republicano, Lics. Felipe B. Martínez and Alfredo de León, Jr., and of the Centro Antirreeleccionista de Nuevo León, Professors Antonio Moreno and Fortunato Lozano. When he refused to make a speech from the Hotel Continental's balcony that in previous campaigns had been used by Madero, Carranza, Obregón, Calles, and Arnulfo Gómez, that balcony was

---

[7] José Vasconcelos, op. cit., pp. 111–119.

used by Professor Fortunato Lozano. Then General Villarreal appeared on another balcony. He said that the failure of the Revolution was not due to a lack of ideals, but rather was due to the fact that many of those at the top saw in the postulates of the Revolution a rich vein to be selfishly exploited.

At this time an open rupture took place between General Roberto Cruz and Lic. Portes Gil, who had been among those who insisted, following Obregón's assassination, that Cruz be replaced (as Chief of Police) by Ríos Zertuche. As President, Portes Gil appointed Colonel José María Tapia to be Presidential Chief of Staff, a post to which some felt Cruz had aspirations. Cruz, who at this time was head of Military Operations in Michoacán, put in an appearance at the C.R.O.M.'s Mexico City convention, where he proclaimed that he was a friend of the workers because they represented a world movement. He added that his sword was at the disposition of the worker organization represented at the meeting.

President Portes Gil was not happy about some of Cruz's statements at the C.R.O.M. convention, but Cruz refused to retract anything that he had said there. Nor was the President happy with what he considered to be the insolent manner of the young *general de división*. Feeling that Cruz was criticizing the Government for planning to impose the next President, he called Cruz to his office, where something was said about the possibility of Cruz's going on one of those well-known missions abroad. By the time the unsatisfactory interview had ended Cruz was no longer connected with the government and was in a position to devote, if he wished, all of his time to supporting the candidacy of Gilberto Valenzuela.

The General then followed Portes Gil to Calles' home. About twenty minutes later, when the President had left the house at the Anzures Colony, Cruz went in to pay a call on Calles, who made it obvious that his friendship for Cruz had ended. When Calles told his visitor that he had apparently been very disrespectful to the President, Cruz agreed and added that because of the unbearable situation in which he found himself he had submitted his resignation.[8] He left for his ranch in the north of Sinaloa, and the President instructed Cárdenas to assume the headship of Michoacán Military Operations.

[8] Roberto Cruz in *El Universal*, August 19, 1949.

The positions of some of the suspected generals were less clear than that of General Cruz. They were so eagerly expressing their loyalty to President Portes Gil that they could hardly be separated from their posts. On January 28, 1928, Jesús M. Aguirre, head of Military Operations in Veracruz, came to the capital to convey to the President the respect of the Yaqui Indian battalions. Early in February, Escobar, considered by some as disappointed at not being named War Minister, was careful, during a trip with the President to Ciudad Victoria, Tamaulipas, to express his loyalty to him. On February 7 Aguirre assured Portes Gil that he could count on him in case Escobar, Manzo, and Topete should try anything. On February 13 General Marcelo Caraveo, the governor of Chihuahua, assured the President that he was loyal and would be of assistance in case the Chihuahua military head, Jesús M. Ferreira, should revolt.

That General Fausto Topete, the Sonora governor, was highly discontented was generally recognized, and nothing that was done by him or his brother was calculated to allay the concern of the Administration. Nor were either of the Topetes, inactive. Ricardo Topete writes that "it went better for us when Fausto, my brother, persuaded General Enrique Gorostieta to come over on our side; the Catholics were very suspicious, but as Fausto is very Catholic, it appears that they believed him, so that Gorostieta went to Mexico City to speak with General José Gonzalo Escobar, who named him Chief of the Army Corps of the Center . . ."[9] Plans were being hatched to start a *coup d'état* in the capital as early as December with the seizure of Generals Calles and Amaro, but the opportunities were not good enough and General Escobar decided to delay.

General Abelardo Rodríguez, governor and military commander of the northern section of Baja California, received from Fausto Topete an invitation to join forces with the discontented. Rodríguez rejected the proposal and wrote to Escobar: "I have been invited to take part in these conspiracies mentioning your name. But I doubt that it can be true, for I know you as a sound and intelligent person, who foresees the sad consequences which a new revolution would have for the country." In a similar vein General Rodríguez

[9] Ricardo Topete, quoted in Froylán C. Manjarrez' *La jornada institucional*, II, Appendix, lix.

wrote to other generals whose names were linked to a possible uprising.[10] Portes Gil told Governor Caraveo about the attitude General Rodríguez was taking, and he suggested that Caraveo handle Chihuahua Military Operations in such a way as to be able to help Rodríguez and others close in on Sonora.

On his way from Ciudad Victoria to Tampico, President Portes Gil received a telegram from Toral's lawyers asking that clemency be shown in the case of Toral. This was followed by a letter signed by some claiming to be representatives of the League of Defense of Religious Liberty which threatened the lives of Portes Gil, his mother, his wife, and his daughter, in case Toral was not pardoned.

Portes Gil denied the pardon and on the morning of February 10 the presidential train was dynamited in the state of Guanajuato. Among those aboard were the President, his wife and daughter, General Amaro, and Valente Quintana (head of the Safety Commission). Dynamite had been placed under a bridge across which the train had to pass. One person was killed, two Pullman cars were destroyed and the locomotive exploded.

Valente Quintana, directing a successful investigation, learned that a prominent woman of Mexico City was among those involved. Most of those who were responsible for this grim affair were sent by the President to the Islas Marías penal colony but were set at liberty shortly before the end of the provisional presidential term. One guilty individual who could not be apprehended later lost his life in the Guanajuato Cristero fighting.

On José de León Toral's last night on earth, the guard, who should have been watching over the prisoner, fell asleep. From a supervisor there came the call: "Who goes?", which the guard was supposed to answer, thus revealing his presence and alertness. Toral answered the call, as the guard would have done had he been awake, and the supervisor continued with his routine in the belief that the guard was fulfilling his functions.[11] On the next day the prisoner was taken from his cell at the Federal District Penitentiary and was executed by a firing squad. Before he died Toral started to cry "Viva—" but death cut off the last words. So many thousands of persons were present at his burial that the police and firemen had a hard time preserving a semblance of order.

[10] Francisco Javier Gaxiola, Jr., *El Presidente Rodríguez*, pp. 84–85.
[11] Ezequiel Padilla, conversation.

Somewhat later Ricardo Topete declared that the killing of Toral had been faked by the Government and that no one had positively identified the person who had been executed and buried as Toral. Topete stated further that Toral was in the United States "peacefully enjoying the reward of his crime."[12]

[12] Ricardo Topete, quoted in Juan Andreu Almazán's *Memorias* in *El Universal*, November 8, 1958.

48·

The Querétaro Convention of the Partido Nacional Revolucionario

About nine hundred representatives of the Partido Nacional Revolucionario poured into the city of Querétaro, where they met on March 1, 1929, in accordance with the call which had been issued by the organizing committee on January 6. At the same theatre at which the Constitutional Convention had held its sessions in 1917 these delegates subscribed to a political program so far to the left that Vasconcelistas were somewhat concerned, finding it to be similar to the "advanced" program that they themselves had prepared.[1]

A majority of the Querétaro delegates were considered to be pledged to nominate General y Lic. Aarón Sáenz as the presidential candidate of the P.N.R. On January 27 he had already been nominated for the nation's presidency at the convention of the Partido Nacional Agrarista. So assured were his supporters that they brought to Querétaro great banners proclaiming him to be the P.N.R. candidate, banners which they were ready to unfurl after the formality of the secret voting.

But behind the scenes last-minute maneuvering away from Sáenz was taking place. That such a movement could favor only Ortiz Rubio was clear.

For one thing, outside of Sáenz, Ortiz Rubio was the only heralded P.N.R. presidential possibility who could qualify under the constitutional requirement that a candidate hold no governorship or important federal or Army position for one year prior to election. In the second place, Ortiz Rubio's long absence from the turbulent political scene caused him to have few enemies and few known ties, making him an ideal "element of conciliation between conflicting groups."[2] And in the third place, the record of Ortiz Rubio denoted devotion to the ideas which were considered to be the noblest of the Revolution. He had been an early supporter of Madero and later jailed by Victoriano Huerta. He was considered a valorous Revolutionary organizer. His action in the Agua Prieta movement was so early that it was perfect. His conflict with De la Huerta was considered by some as the conflict of a radical revolutionary against a moderate. Ortiz Rubio in Germany had rendered service to Obregón and to Calles, and he never wavered from absolute loyalty to these two. He had endured poverty. He was known to be honest and serious, but he was not too well known.

Why the maneuvering away from Aarón Sáenz?

Some of the more radical speakers felt that Sáenz was a definite moderate. Puig Casauranc, who had told Calles that he did not see Sáenz as the one to fulfill the hope and desire for the "acceleration of the social rhythm of the Revolution," insisted that it would "be

[1] Mauricio Magdaleno, *Las palabras perdidas*, p. 51.
[2] Francisco Díaz Babio, *Un drama nacional*, p. 115.

very difficult to cause the large masses of the nation, those in the workshops and in the fields, to believe that Lic. Sáenz in 1928 was the standard or guide in the realm of social revolution."[3] Portes Gil felt that Sáenz lacked the "indispensable knack of speaking about national problems with the fortitude and energy of a revolutionary radical ... When he did speak he addressed a large group of businessmen of Monterrey ... with phrases of great respect for the capitalistic interests."[4] In a similar vein Abraham Arellano stated that Sáenz did not help his cause by "proclaiming himself an associate of the Monterrey capitalists."[5]

Calles, according to Vito Alessio Robles, was reported to have felt that Sáenz's Protestantism hurt his popularity.[6] Melchor Ortega believed that Sáenz could have co-operated to a greater extent with important party leaders, such as Gonzalo N. Santos and himself, when at an earlier stage they were preparing to launch his candidacy.[7]

While the above factors were perhaps being given some consideration, the plans of various discontented generals to revolt were coming close to realization, and the effect of these ominous clouds was decisive. There was need to give as little excuse as possible for rebellion, either to those generals who disliked Sáenz or to possible followers of these generals if they did revolt. Puig Casauranc had told Calles that "under familiar conditions the candidacy of Lic. Sáenz would appear as a typical example of imposition or of a desire for 'continuism'; that if we committed that political error the rebellion which was coming might triumph very easily ..."[8]

President Portes Gil and Dr. Puig Casauranc had discussed the problem on January 1, 1929, and had said good things about Ortiz Rubio's record. According to Puig's account of this discussion Portes Gil had said that he thought a candidate other than Sáenz would "give fewer pretexts for the rebellion." Above all, Portes Gil did not want an uprising to be developed by "some chiefs of agrarian tendencies who have no confidence in Aarón." The President, well-known for his Revolutionary agrarian ideas and for his political astuteness, is said to have resolved to use all of his strength to op-

[3] J. M. Puig Casauranc, *Galatea rebelde a varios pigmaliones*, p. 284.
[4] Emilio Portes Gil, *Quince años de política mexicana*, pp. 143–144.
[5] Mauricio Magdaleno, *op. cit.*, p. 80.
[6] Vito Alessio Robles, *Mis andanzas con nuestro Ulises*, p. 187.
[7] Melchor Ortega, conversation, September 13, 1956.
[8] J. M. Puig Casauranc, *op. cit.*, p. 285.

pose Sáenz's candidacy, and there can be little doubt but that, in situations like this, the Chief Executive is likely to play a role which is not insignificant.[9]

Lic. Sáenz has confirmed that the threatened rebellion was quite a blow to his candidacy.[10]

Not only was Sáenz unpopular with those restless Obregonista generals who had not cared for the idea of co-operating with Calles, but, most important of all, he was not wanted as a candidate by four supremely powerful generals, whose assistance to the government was to be hoped for in case of trouble.[11] Clearly the situation was delicate, and at this particular moment the views of these important generals, whatever their motives, as well as the views of politicians who might cry out against "planned impositions" and "moderates," required careful consideration. Reasons can be found for rejecting any candidate, even as hard-working and able an administrator as Sáenz, particularly if he has been on the national scene for some time. Nor do expressed reasons always represent the fundamental motives for opposition. Under the circumstances the key to the choice of a nominee at Querétaro lay as much in the hands of generals whose support would be needed during the expected rebellion, as it lay in the hands of politicians, many of whom were sensitive to the military situation.

With the registration of the credentials at the start of the convention it became clear that Sáenz did not have his expected majority support from the delegates. One of the first groups to shift from Sáenz to Ortiz Rubio was the Coahuila group, led by that important politician, Pérez Treviño. Another state which backed Ortiz Rubio early was his home state of Michoacán, among whose delegates was Melchor Ortega. Ortega, although a native of Guanajuato, was a resident of and federal *diputado* from Michoacán. Ortega's opinion was not shared by the Guanajuato governor, Agustín Arroyo Ch., who had been one of the organizers of the Bombilla banquet of July 17, 1928. Arroyo Ch. recognized in Sáenz a sound man of the Revolution and an upholder of the principles of General Obregón,

[9] *Ibid.*, p. 212; Agustín Arroyo Ch., conversation, August 16, 1956; Melchor Ortega, conversation, September 13, 1956.

[10] Aarón Sáenz, conversation, February 2, 1956.

[11] Antonio Díaz Soto y Gama, conversations, October 3, 1955, and June 10, 1958. The four generals mentioned by Díaz Soto y Gama were Almazán, Amaro, Cárdenas, and Cedillo.

and he and the Guanajuato delegates faithful to him supported Governor Sáenz.

To the surprise of Sáenz and Arroyo Ch. the Ortiz Rubio trend became overwhelming, and not long after the official opening of the Querétaro convention Sáenz withdrew his name as a candidate, de-

Lic. Aarón Sáenz (*fourth from right, front row, hat in left hand*) *just before his departure from the P.N.R.'s Querétaro Convention, March, 1929.*

claring that he and the delegates who continued to support him would make their departure. Ing. Alessio Robles attributes to Lic. Sáenz the following remark at this exciting time: "No one is ignorant of the fact that Ortiz Rubio does not know the situation of the country, lacks a place in public opinion, and is not well versed in the problems of the people."[12]

Accordingly, after a few farewell words to his remaining backers, spoken in front of the convention hall, or theatre, Aarón Sáenz left Querétaro in a special train on March 2, and his supporters returned to their respective states. Ortiz Rubio delegates at once criticized the absence of the Guanajuato delegates; Melchor Ortega and

[12] Vito Alessio Robles, *op. cit.*, p. 185.

his Michoacán associates declared that if the victory had gone to Sáenz the Ortizrubistas would have accepted the decision with less annoyance. Other Ortiz Rubio backers stated that "the attitude of Lic. Sáenz is inexplicable. In our judgment it implies that Lic. Sáenz is attempting to hinder the unification of the Mexican Revolutionary element." The head of the Yucatán delegation, Senator Bartolomé García Correa, pointed out that the delegates of the Partido Socialista del Sureste had been committed to support Sáenz, but that since Sáenz had withdrawn, they were free to support whomever they wished.

On March 3 the president of the Party, General Pérez Treviño, addressed the convention, announcing that he had just received official advice of a military uprising. In his speech Pérez Treviño said that the uprising was "without a cause, without a flag, for what possible inscription could a banner bear to turn the people against the government of the Republic?" The General expressed his confidence in the enormous majority of the Army, which, he said, would fulfill its duty in upholding the institutions of the Republic, represented by President Portes Gil. He said: "We are living in an historic moment of enormous importance. At the head of the National Army is a civilian . . . who . . . , like the best of soldiers, has engraved upon his conscience love for the Revolution."

On March 4, 1929, when President Hoover was taking office in the United States, the presiding officer of the Querétaro convention, Diputado Filiberto Gómez, declared that the Partido Nacional Revolucionario was now official. After the legal constitutional act was read to the assembly, the discussion of candidates for the Mexican presidency was opened. A Zacatecas delegate proclaimed that everyone knew that only Ortiz Rubio could save the country. The delegates dispensed with the secret voting which was called for, and Ortiz Rubio was nominated by acclamation. Colonel Filiberto Gómez named a committee (Manuel Pérez Treviño, Manuel Riva Palacio, Gonzalo Santos, and Praxedis Balboa) to invite Ortiz Rubio to appear and give the required pledge.

Ing. Ortiz Rubio appeared fifteen minutes later. He was asked: "Citizen Ing. Ortiz Rubio, in case a majority of the unified citizens of the Republic ratify by their vote the selection of this assembly, do you swear on your honor as a Mexican citizen, to obey and to have obeyed the Constitution and the laws emanating therefrom and to bring to realization the program of this convention, taking care to watch over the well-being and progress of the Republic?" The candidate made the promise.

Then Ortiz Rubio gave a short talk to the gathering, his main point being to invite the return of all the delegates who formerly had supported another candidate and to assure them that they would find him a friend who respected their convictions. After a

Foreground: General Manuel Pérez Treviño; Sr. Melchor Ortega (*slightly behind*); General e Ing. Pascual Ortiz Rubio; Ing. Luis L. León. *1929. Enrique Díaz.*

speech by Ing. Luis L. León relative to the military uprising, the P.N.R. appointed an executive committee to serve until the next convention. Besides General Pérez Treviño, its president, it included León, Colonel Filiberto Gómez, and Diputados Gonzalo N. Santos and Melchor Ortega.

General Pérez Treviño returned to Coahuila on March 7, having been absent, with permission, from the governorship since November, 1928. Somewhat later Lic. Aarón Sáenz took over again the governorship of Nuevo León, his various activities on the national scene since the start of Obregón's campaign for re-election having taken him away from his Monterrey post for some time.

People with a close view of the picture have stated that Calles "decided to elect Ortiz Rubio,"[13] or that Calles, being sympathetic to the more radical point of view which prevailed, "backed Ing. Ortiz Rubio."[14] Puig Casauranc speaks of Ortiz Rubio's nomination

At the front: General Plutarco Elías Calles *and* General *e* Ing. Pascual Ortiz Rubio. Ing. Luis L. León *is behind General Calles' right shoulder.* Sr. Gonzalo N. Santos *is between General Calles and Ortiz Rubio. Between Sr. Gonzalo N. Santos and Ortiz Rubio (behind Santos) appears* Sr. Manlio Fabio Altamirano. *Enrique Díaz.*

"with the acquiescence (voluntary or forced) of Calles." Portes Gil, however, advises that it is not true that Calles participated in the change against Sáenz, and he adds that "Calles sincerely wanted Lic. Sáenz to win." (Calles was a close personal friend of Sáenz, and his son, Plutarco, Jr., was married to the sister of Sáenz.) Furthermore, Portes Gil denies Puig Casauranc's assertions that he (Portes Gil) had anything to do with the candidacy of Ing. Ortiz Rubio. It must be admitted, however, that in opposing Sáenz the President rather effectively served to assist the engineer from Michoacán.

[13] Francisco Díaz Babio, *op. cit.*, p. 115.
[14] León Salinas, interview, January 16, 1956.

Following the financial system of the Partido Socialista Fronterizo of Tamaulipas, President Portes Gil decreed that the Partido Nacional Revolucionario should be financed by deductions from the salaries and wages received by federal government employees: seven days pay per year. Some protests arose. Both in his own name and in the name of the Mexican legation in France, Ing. Alberto J. Pani sent a telegram objecting to these salary deductions, on the ground that they were not constitutional. He received no reply to his telegram.[15]

The blossoming of the Partido Nacional Revolucionario appeared destined not only to remove from the Ministry of Gobernación much of its authority in the field of federal and local politics, but also to affect the office of the presidency itself. It seems that Ortiz Rubio, when he interviewed General Calles at Cuernavaca after reaching Mexico in December, 1928, agreed to Calles' proposition to him about "the exercise of an institutional government in which I [Ortiz Rubio] would divide the power with the P.N.R." if nominated and elected. After that interview Ortiz Rubio observed: "I was given to understand the inconvenience of building up new personalities . . . I must go along strictly united with the P.N.R. and I must therefore sacrifice my friends . . . with the objective of avoiding ties which would be inappropriate for a well-functioning democracy."[16]

[15] Alberto J. Pani, *La historia, agredida*, p. 92.
[16] Francisco Díaz Babio, *op. cit.*, p. 120.

49.

The Outbreak of the Escobar Rebellion

As we have seen, while the P.N.R. convention at Querétaro was in the midst of its deliberations, the long-expected rebellion broke out. It broke out on March 3, 1929, in a somewhat confused way.

General Calles had much faith in General Jesús M. Aguirre, head of the government's Military Operations in Veracruz. General Aguirre was instructed by the War Department to send from Veracruz to Mexico City one battalion and one regiment to strengthen the position in the capital. From Veracruz early on March 3 he wired the presidency advising that these two units were on their way to Mexico City. Another telegram from Aguirre soon followed:

DURING THE NIGHT THE GOVERNOR, HAVING BEEN IN THIS PORT, LEFT FOR
UNKNOWN PARTS, TAKING MOUNTED POLICE, ALSO MARINES OF THE WAR-
SHIPS, AND THEY PROCEEDED TO EMBARK. FOUND ALL THIS VERY SUSPICIOUS.
AT THE SAME TIME THE YAQUIS AT PEROTE BECAME FRANKLY HOSTILE,
WHEREFORE I FOUND MYSELF OBLIGED TO DETAIN THE MARCH OF THE FORCES
WHICH WERE TO GO TO THE CAPITAL.——AGUIRRE

Although it was soon noted in Mexico City that the trains from
Veracruz were not arriving as they should and that the military in
Veracruz had taken over various telegraph offices, President Portes
Gil could not believe General Aguirre's news that the Veracruz
governor, Ing. Adalberto Tejeda, was disloyal. His suspicions were
confirmed when he received from General José María Dorantes a
message advising that General Aguirre was the one in revolt. Like
the Delahuertistas in 1923, Aguirre's men quickly seized the governor's palace at Jalapa and gained the adherence of the leaders of
the war fleet at the Veracruz harbor.

According to statements which Ricardo Topete made later, Generals Aguirre and Claudio Fox (the latter in Oaxaca) had planned
to move quickly on Mexico City on the night of March 9, capturing
there Portes Gil, Calles, and Amaro and placing General Escobar in
the provisional presidency; this move was to have coincided with
attacks on various cities and on loyal generals by certain others who
were implicated. The War Department's call on General Aguirre
to have two of his contingents leave his command for Mexico City
precipitated the revolt to such an extent that it got under way before the Querétaro convention had nominated a presidential candidate.

In this connection it is interesting to note that in Governor Fausto
Topete's undated and unsigned memorandum inviting General
Abelardo Rodríguez to rebel, the writer not only referred to the
"multiple defects" of Lic. Sáenz, but stated that "If General Calles
had chosen another person more capable and more appropriate to
occupy the presidency of the Republic, you know that I and all our
friends would have joined the ranks of his party." (In this memorandum, General Topete made known that he felt he could count
on Generals Escobar, Ferreira, Caraveo, Amaya, Aguirre, and
Cruz.)[1]

[1] Manuel González Ramírez (ed.), *Planes políticos y otros documentos*,
pp. 301–303.

Even though the Querétaro convention had not named its presidential candidate, the rebel's Plan of Hermosillo (Sonora) cried out against "imposition." This Plan, drawn up by Lic. Gilberto Valenzuela and issued on March 3, was the call to the people to revolt. It was largely a recital of the "crimes" of General Calles. It said in part:

. . . Bastard passions, unbridled ambitions, criminal and cynical impostures, criminal lusts and acts of comedy and farce performed systematically, have made of the government and the institutions a school of mercantilism and of corruption and of mean actions . . . The majestic precinct of the public powers has converted itself into a vulgar market where everything is for sale, from morals and the written law to the honor and dignity of the citizens . . . The soul of this corruption, of this source of vice which overflows, of this insatiable thirst for power and riches, the great master of mystification and of farce, the supreme administrator of this wicked market of moral values, the diabolical inspirer of inhuman and savage persecutions, the inventor of . . . delinquency and crimes: Plutarco Elías Calles, the Judas of the Mexican Revolution . . .

Calles was described as wishing to continue at all costs on the throne of the Caesars, where he could enforce the whim of his will. He was pictured, therefore, as using bayonets and crime to impose in the presidency "one of the members of his troupe of comedians." Mention was made of some of the methods of "imposition": the stopping of pensions, the crimes and "outrages" practiced against conscientious citizens; and the bribes and grants provided to all who "slavishly incline their heads before the gesture of Caesar."

The Plan of Hermosillo did not recognize the provisional presidency of Lic. Portes Gil, nor any officials who might, directly or indirectly, oppose the movement which the Plan proclaimed. It declared General José Gonzalo Escobar (who, at Torreón, headed the federal Military Operations in Coahuila) to be the Supreme Chief of the liberating movement and of the Ejército Renovador de la Revolución. General Calles was declared to have been a vile traitor to a group which included Generals Obregón, Flores, Villa, and Serrano. The Plan was signed by a great many, including Francisco R. Manzo, Roberto Cruz, Ricardo Topete, and Aurelio Manrique, Jr.; also Sonora's new governor, Fausto Topete, and his predecessor, Alejo Bay, brother-in-law of Obregón.

The attitude of the discontented in faraway Sonora was less unexpected than that of General Jesús M. Aguirre. General Francisco

R. Manzo, in charge of the government's Military Operations in Sonora, wired that he was pursuing the "rebel" General Antonio Armenta Rosas; it was no surprise to learn that General Armenta Rosas was the loyal one and General Manzo the rebel. Armenta Rosas had to flee with his men over the mountainous terrain of Sonora into the state of Chihuahua, where, after that painful march, he fell into the hands of Chihuahua's governor, General Marcelo Caraveo.

The part played by General Caraveo turned out to be disappointing both to his close friend, General Juan Andreu Almazán, and to President Portes Gil. Almazán had conducted a lengthy correspondence with Caraveo, in the course of which the Chihuahua governor expressed the feeling that the Querétaro convention would not be fair and democratic. Almazán, who had been forecasting the neutrality of Calles with respect to the convention and who predicted that Ortiz Rubio would win out, had urged Caraveo not to join up with the discontented of Sonora. Lic. Portes Gil had suggested to Caraveo that he take over the Chihuahua military operations from General Jesús M. Ferreira, of whom the President was suspicious. But it was Caraveo who led the Chihuahua troops in rebellion. General Ferreira, who had made a name for himself by his conduct of the campaign against the Cristeros in Jalisco, was taken in Mexico City and placed in jail, where he made an unsuccessful attempt at suicide.

When General Roberto Cruz rebelled in the state of Sinaloa he found himself fighting together with a veteran of somewhat different background, General Ramón F. Iturbe, who had been governor of the state early in the Revolution but who had never recognized the Plan of Agua Prieta. Soldiers of northern Sinaloa who were loyal to the Portes Gil regime received instructions from the War Department to strengthen the port of Mazatlán, which was soon being defended by General Jaime Carrillo against attacks under the direction of Manzo, Cruz, and Iturbe.

The young Vasconcelista, Mauricio Magdaleno, had been encountering difficulties in the course of organizing receptions for Vasconcelos in some Guanajuato towns and expected that a "reign of terror" would make Acámbaro as difficult to crack as Celaya. But at Acámbaro he boldly interviewed General Jesús Palomera López, a man with a very tough reputation, who had served in Mexico City under Roberto Cruz as chief of the Mounted Police. Palomera

López astonished Magdaleno with his friendliness and assured the young man that the Vasconcelistas would be guaranteed by him against any unpleasant incidents. He sent his regards to Vasconcelos, who expressed less surprise than Magdaleno: "The Obregonista generals will not be long in rebelling and they consider us as their allies."[2] When the Escobar rebellion broke out General Palomera López was seized in Mexico City, and at 5:00 A.M. on March 7, 1929, he was executed on the charges of being disloyal to the government and of planning to lead his regiment in Ciudad Hidalgo, Michoacán, into rebellion with him.

By March 3 Vasconcelos had reached Michoacán, where his supporters found that Governor Lázaro Cárdenas, although an early advocate of Ortiz Rubio, offered ample freedom to their efforts. With the commencement of the armed rebellion Lic. Medellín Ostos let it be known at once that the Vasconcelistas did not support it, and Vasconcelos himself, who was at Uruapan, made it clear that he had no intention of following the example of the other opposition candidates, Gilberto Valenzuela and Antonio I. Villarreal, who had become involved in the revolt. To one of his audiences Vasconcelos said: "This rebellion in the north is a very bad thing for the country, since it is simply a dispute between the Callista military group and the Obregonista military group. If there is to be any revolt at all it should come from the people if they find after the elections that their votes have been disregarded." He asked his supporters to continue with the election work and stay out of the military struggle. He recommended support of the Portes Gil Government which, "with all of its defects, represented a bridge to the legal government which would be created by the elections." "Furthermore, I recognized that ever since we started developing the electoral campaign a tacit agreement had existed between ourselves and the government." The government spread far and wide Vasconcelos' advice to his supporters to stay out of the armed struggle.[3]

The Communist National Worker and Peasant Bloc, which was backing General Pedro Rodríguez Triana for the nation's presidency, likewise came out in opposition to the rebellion, pronouncing it to be the beginning of a "frankly reactionary movement." The Cristeros, on the other hand, continued to harry the government in their rather informal way, and now found themselves

[2] Mauricio Magdaleno, *Las palabras perdidas*, pp. 68–77.
[3] José Vasconcelos, *El proconsulado*, pp. 128–130.

fighting a common enemy together with others who had formerly battled against them.

General Raúl Madero had been out of the country since the Serrano and Gómez uprisings. Although he had been on good terms with Carlos A. Vidal, he did not favor Serrano's plans for rebellion. When those who were planning a Serrano rebellion began to include Raúl Madero's name among those supporting the 1927 uprising, Madero left for Texas. He was there in the first part of 1929 when his close friend, Antonio I. Villarreal, called him to Monterrey. Madero advised Obregón's Agriculture Minister of the political disadvantages of joining the Escobar rebellion, but Villarreal joined the rebels anyway. Madero, finding himself in Torreón when the Escobar uprising broke out, participated in some actions with Escobar.

After the government's head of Military Operations in Durango, General Francisco Urbalejo, received the President's telegram concerning the situation, he replied as follows:

RECEIVED YOUR MESSAGE OF TODAY ABOUT THE DISOBEDIENCE OF THE JEFE OPERACIONES MILITARES VERACRUZ, ALLOWING MYSELF TO MANIFEST THAT, AS A SOLDIER, I AWAIT YOUR ORDERS.

But General Urbalejo had already become one of the rebels!

Early on the morning of March 3, 1929, President Portes Gil conferred with General Calles, who placed himself at the orders of the President. General Joaquín Amaro had recently suffered a painful injury when struck in the face by a ball during a polo game, and the accident, which cost him an eye, had made it necessary for him to seek medical attention at Rochester, Minnesota. In consideration of the state of Amaro's health, President Portes Gil named Calles to be Minister of War and Navy and put him in charge of the military campaign against the rebels.

The President issued to the nation a declaration in which he explained who had rebelled and where, and why they had no reason to rebel. He had high praise for the loyal ones and stated that "the Government is certain to count on enough men to put down the rebellion in a short time." He expressed confidence in the support of laborers and peasants.

Lic. Portes Gil has stated that altogether the rebels included almost 30,000 well-equipped men. (Numerically this was a good many less than the 50,000 who are said to have arisen in the De la Huerta rebellion.) General Calles later wrote as follows about the Escobar rebellion: "When the rebellion broke out twenty-two battalions, one regional fixed company, and twenty-one cavalry regiments, or 28 per cent of the total effects of the Army, were apparently removed from the authority of the government." To these contingents, amounting to about 17,000 men, there should be added the Cristero rebels and also the fleet. The federal government, besides controlling about 72 per cent of the troops, could count on all of the air force and, as during the De la Huerta rebellion, much assistance from agrarian and labor groups.[4] In San Luis Potosí General Saturnino Cedillo organized on behalf of the government a division of 5000 agrarians.

A statement given out by President Portes Gil late in March, 1929, indicated in round numbers the forces of the generals who were in command of troops when they revolted:

General Francisco R. Manzo (Sonora) 5,000
General Jesús M. Aguirre (Veracruz) 3,500
General J. Gonzalo Escobar (Coahuila) 3,500
General Francisco Urbalejo (Durango) 2,000
General Marcelo Caraveo (Chihuahua) 3,000

From Torreón on March 3 General Escobar wired to Portes Gil, placing himself at the President's orders, and then at once he took his men by train to make an attack on Monterrey. His activities were carried on in such a way that some people in the district got the mistaken impression that Escobar was fighting on behalf of the government and that General Juan Andreu Almazán was in rebellion. The loyal Almazán was at the moment away from Monterrey, having just reached Mexico City in order to start a campaign against the rebels in Veracruz. Much of the Monterrey guard was absent and there had not been time to bring it together before Escobar struck. At the Monterrey penitentiary building on March 4 General Rodrigo Zuriaga tried to put up a defense with only about 100 men but he lost his life in the effort and Monterrey was taken by Escobar in the name of the uprising.

Almazán now had to change his plans. He was ordered to advance on Monterrey from Tampico, and Eulogio Ortiz, head of

[4] Froylán C. Manjarrez, *La jornada institucional*, II, 30–31.

Tamaulipas Military Operations, was ordered to lead the vanguard of this movement. Cedillo was ordered to bring his agrarian fighters from San Luis Potosí to Saltillo.

Escobar stayed in Monterrey long enough to take money from the banks there (as he also did from Torreón banks) and to ravage the home of Almazán. Then he retired in the direction of Saltillo, tearing up intervening railroad track, prior to General Ortiz' arrival in Monterrey from Tampico on March 6 with 840 men. Almazán and Benigno Serratos also occupied Monterrey on behalf of the Portes Gil Government.

As soon as the rebellion broke out, J. Gonzalo Escobar and Fausto Topete made pronouncements to the effect that their movement had control of nine states: Sonora, Sinaloa, Durango, Coahuila, Nayarit, Zacatecas, Jalisco, Veracruz, and Oaxaca; on March 4 they could have added Chihuahua. Escobar, as Supreme Chief of the Ejército Renovador issued a number of decrees. One of these reimplanted the principle of No Re election, and another pleased the clergy and the Cristeros, by revoking the laws which regulated religious worship. He also named, as diplomatic agents to represent the cause in Washington, Mariano Montero Villar, Gerzayn Ugarte, Francisco Santamaría, and J. M. Alvarez del Castillo; and he established a number of consulates at cities in the United States. However great the experience of Lic. Alvarez del Castillo, obtained during the De la Huerta rebellion, in pleading for an official attitude north of the border which would be acceptable to Mexicans in rebellion, he and his fellow negotiators were no more successful than he had been five years earlier. Co-operation between Calles, Montes de Oca, and others on the one hand, and Ambassador Dwight Morrow on the other, had resulted in benefits for the Calles Administration, and a continuation of this co-operation proved helpful to the Portes Gil Administration. There were a number of instances of United States assistance in the efforts made against the Escobaristas, and not the least of these was the Mexican government's privilege of purchasing war materials in the United States. Mexico paid out over 1½ million dollars for such planes, arms, and munitions.

50·

The Campaign East and North; The Battle of Jiménez

Following the orders of Calles, General Miguel M. Acosta advanced on Veracruz with a great force which amounted to about 8000 men, including troops from Puebla and Oaxaca.

The position of rebel General Jesús M. Aguirre in Veracruz was bad from the start because very important groups, in Esperanza, Córdoba, and particularly Orizaba, on whose support he had counted, failed to stick with the rebellion. A few in Córdoba did arise on March 3 in favor of General Aguirre but they were overwhelmed on the fifth by soldiers who decided to remain loyal to the government. Calles tried to worsen Aguirre's position by moving troops, under General Alejandro Mange and José Juan Méndez, to cut off any retreat he might seek to Chiapas or the Tehuantepec Isthmus.

Not only did neighboring contingents fail to behave as hoped for by the rebels, but also numerous units of Aguirre's Veracruz force (such as the one headed by Colonel José W. Cervantes) preferred to be loyal to the government. Under these circumstances and in the face of Acosta's strong and fast-moving advance on Veracruz, Aguirre and his companions fled from the port. This was on March 6, just three days after the rebellion got under way. The federals promptly took over the city and were joined there by Governor Tejeda, who brought with him about one thousand armed agrarians. The naval fleet, which had been out at sea, returned to Veracruz to reincorporate itself with the federal government, and some of those who were responsible for its early defection were sent to the prison of Santiago Tlaltelolco in Mexico City. Calles then ordered Acosta to return to Mexico City.

Again we hear of Rodolfo Herrero's old enemy, Lindoro Hernández, the man who not only remained loyal to President Carranza at the Tlaxcalantongo finish, but who, in 1922, joined General Murguía in an armed uprising against President Obregón. By now (1929) Lindoro Hernández was a general in the government army. His forces, together with the agrarians, knew the Veracruz mountains well, and they sought out Aguirre, who was with his companions, Generals Miguel Alemán and Brígido Escobedo.

General Miguel Alemán, a Revolutionary of the Madero and Constitucionalista periods, had been associated with General Lindoro Hernández in the 1922 revolt in which Generals Murguía and Juan Carrasco had been killed. During the Veracruz governorship of Ing. Adalberto Tejeda he had re-entered the Army of the Republic and had been elected a *diputado* in the local Veracruz congress. He had objected to the changes in Constitutional Articles 82 and 83 which permitted presidential re-elections and had therefore supported Generals Gómez and Serrano. Now he supported General Aguirre.

Learning the whereabouts of Aguirre, Alemán, and Escobedo, the troops under Miguel Acosta and Alejandro Mange set fire to the woods. On March 19 Alemán and Escobedo were killed, and on the following day Lindoro Hernández' men captured Jesús M. Aguirre. Aguirre, after being tried by a council of war which consisted of an impressive array of generals (such as José Juan Méndez and Samuel M. de los Santos), was sentenced to death and executed early on the twenty-first. In his final remarks he somehow sought to justify his own action and at the same time recommend loyalty to the government.

After studying matters for long hours and with great care and energy in Mexico City, War Minister Calles departed on March 9 for the north, accompanied by a staff which included his close friend Colonel Carlos Riva Palacio. The Veracruz rebellion had been extinguished by a large force in a record time, and so now the government controlled the Gulf of Mexico as well as the southwest. Monterrey had been regained, but much remained to be done in the north (Chihuahua, Coahuila, and Durango). It was on this problem that Calles was now determined to concentrate, knowing that the rebel movements from the far northwest (Sonora and Sinaloa) could be expected to be slow.

At first Calles established himself and his Consejo Superior de Guerra at Aguascalientes, where Lázaro Cárdenas had organized an important force. The Consejo Superior de Guerra included Generals Cárdenas, Cedillo, Genovevo de la O, Anselmo Macías, Manuel F. Enríquez, and Guillermo Palma and Colonel Juan Antonio Domínguez.

The first decisions of the High Council of War had to do with steps to bottle up Escobar's men at Saltillo. From Aguascalientes General Pablo E. Macías and Nazario Medina were sent to join Almazán, who was in charge of chasing Escobar and who was ably aided by Eulogio Ortiz and Benigno Serratos. Cedillo was moving against Saltillo from the south, but before he arrived there the rebels retreated westward toward Torreón.

In the Saltillo district the rebels were joined by General Eulalio Gutiérrez, a former President of Mexico. According to Lic. Vasconcelos, his friend Eulalio Gutiérrez "attracted by his brother, allowed himself to be involved . . ."[1] A prominent participant has related that Eulalio Gutiérrez, who received some of the erroneous reports which were floating around, had wanted to support Generals Almazán and Cedillo in case they should revolt, and when he became aware of the action in his district he joined the rebels, thinking they represented Almazán and Cedillo in an uprising.

There was a little action when some of Cedillo's men did some

---

[1] José Vasconcelos, *El proconsulado*, p. 130.

bridge-burning so as to prevent the rebels from getting from Saltillo to Torreón in trains: about eighty men were killed at San Juan de la Vaquería, about seventy of them being rebels. Trains had to be abandoned by Escobar's forces.

To Colonel Juan Antonio Domínguez, head of the Twenty-eighth Cavalry Regiment, was assigned the task of attacking the city of Durango, which was controlled by rebel General Francisco Urbalejo, a Yaqui Indian from Sonora and close friend of the late General Obregón. In four hours Domínguez won a victory over Urbalejo, and the defeated general took the train for Torreón. The rebellious Durango governor, General Juan Gualberto Amaya, tore up tracks on the line to Aguascalientes in order to delay the approach of Cárdenas' division, but the federals took Durango quickly with the aid of agrarian fighters, and established Lic. Alberto Terrones Benítez as interim governor. The division of General Cárdenas kept on going toward Torreón. So did the Minister of War and his staff.

The new interim governor of Durango, Alberto Terrones Benítez, had been a federal senator from his state and had on principle opposed the idea of re-election for General Obregón. Terrones Benítez knew his state well and was well liked, particularly by natives in the mining and timber districts (such as the Mezquital Indians), whose interests he studiously tried to protect. He received word from President Portes Gil to endeavor to resolve the religious question, for the armed conflict by religious "fanatics" was as important in Durango as the difficulties caused by the Escobaristas, or even more important. The interim governor called for the return of the exiled Durango archbishop, José María González Valencia, and the two men quickly and intelligently brought an end to the local religious conflict.

After Terrones Benítez took over the Durango governorship he was left with few soldiers, since most departed in pursuit of the Escobar forces to the north. He found that some of the remaining *campesinos* were spending their time marking horses and equipment with the hammer and sickle, instead of fighting the Cristeros. The new governor took a stand against Communism, and eventually President Portes Gil sent Ing. Marte Gómez to investigate this matter.

As Escobar and his men retreated northward in order to join the rebels of Governor Caraveo in Chihuahua, all the federal forces

448

were able to establish their headquarters at Torreón. Benigno Serratos entered Torreón on March 18 and his men were soon joined
by Cárdenas' division, which had entered Durango on March 15.

War Minister Calles now put Almazán in charge of the Northern
Division, whose task was to battle Escobar and Caraveo in Chihuahua. He sent Cárdenas, commander of the Northwest Division,
off on a long trip, via Zacatecas and Jalisco, to fight the rebels on
the west coast, where there was some activity at Naco, Sonora, and
where the loyal General Jaime Carrillo was defending the port of
Mazatlán. Calles kept Cedillo in Torreón in order to help Almazán
if necessary; otherwise to follow the route of Cárdenas, combatting
Cristeros in the Republic's center and rebels on the west coast. The
Cristeros, in keeping with their attitude of hostility to federal troops,
burned a railroad bridge between Irapuato and Guadalajara.

North of Torreón there was by this time a conglomeration of rebels
under such generals as Escobar, Caraveo, Urbalejo, Villarreal,
Cesáreo Castro, Miguel Valle, and Raúl Madero. Escobar had requested reinforcements from Sonora, and some of Manzo's men had
started to Chihuahua (via the Cañón del Púlpito) under Fausto
Topete, but developments on the west coast caused a cancellation of
these plans. There General Agustín Olachea and Colonel Vicente
Torres Avilés, although they had signed the rebel Plan of Hermosillo, gave Manzo and Topete a jolt by taking Naco, Sonora, in the
name of the Portes Gil Government. The only men to join Caraveo
from Sonora were those under Armenta Rosas, who fled from the
rebels there and took twenty days to reach western Chihuahua. The
Chihuahua governor got these exhausted men because Armenta
Rosas had supposed that Caraveo was fighting against the rebellion.

At Ciudad Juárez, Chihuahua (across from El Paso, Texas), two
or three hundred men who remained faithful to Portes Gil and not
all of whom were members of the Army, engaged in an uneven
fight against a far larger number of rebel soldiers. Arrangements
were quickly made by General George V. H. Moseley (Fort Bliss
Commander), General Matías Ramos (*oficial mayor* of the War
Ministry), and Roberto Pesqueira for this outnumbered group to
enter United States territory and return into Mexico three days
later near Piedras Negras, Coahuila.

At Jiménez, Chihuahua, about 150 miles northwest of Torreón, the
rebels had gathered together about 8000 men. The railroad line

between Torreón and Jiménez had been very effectively destroyed by Escobar, and so the pursuing federals encountered a severe problem in getting about 9000 men and 5000 horses across the Mapimí desert. General Calles, in one of his many interesting dispatches to President Portes Gil, discussed the water problem and the possibility of the manufacture in Torreón of movable water tanks. After a slow and particularly dry march, Almazán's Northern Division reached the Escalón station. Although the rail to the south continued out of commission, Escalón had a rail communication in the direction of Sierra Mojada, Coahuila, and the federals could in this way receive provisions.

Calles had advanced from Torreón to Bermejillo, Durango, and was giving much attention to the reconstruction of the railroad line which Escobar had destroyed. He also showed a keen interest in the activities of his air force, which was rendering valuable service by indicating watering places to the troops crossing the desert and by reporting fully on the location and estimated size of enemy forces. In addition, the aviators dropped bombs on rebels who were found in Escalón before Almazán's men got there, and on the large rebel gathering at Jiménez.

The federals, although weary and thirsty, performed at Jiménez a surrounding movement in which Generals Anacleto López and Rodrigo Quevedo Moreno took an active part, and the result was a decisive battle at last. In the course of describing the fighting, Almazán has written: "The action started in Corralitos at 9:00 A.M. on the 30th of March and ended at Reforma Station at 2:00 P.M. on April 3." The cornered antigovernment men let loose a furious attack against those hard fighters, Rodrigo Quevedo and Eulogio Ortiz, but they were finally repulsed after the forces of Gilberto R. Limón entered the fray to assist the men of Ortiz. Quevedo and his men did much to force the rebels out of Jiménez and Benigno Serratos' tired soldiers battled with success against fleeing rebels, who were no doubt also near the point of exhaustion.

At this point steps were taken by Almazán and his staff to make the victory complete by seeing to it that the defeated foe did not once again escape. After federal planes had noted Escobaristas repairing rail to the north, Almazán sent Anacleto López and Rodrigo Quevedo with their cavalries along one side of the rail line, and Ortiz and Serratos along the other side. Almazán led forces along the rail. The federals pounced on the pursued and their trains at the point where the line was undergoing repair, and for this reason the battle of Jiménez cost the rebels about 6000 men. Almazán has estimated that over 1000 of his enemy were killed, over 3000 surrendered and about 2000 disbanded, whereas federal losses were 161 dead, 312 wounded and 79 missing. The destruction of the rail line to the north, which caused the rebels such catastrophe, had earlier been carried out by Benigno Serratos and Jesús García Gutiérrez.

While Almazán was arranging to have the federal and rebel wounded conveyed to Escalón for movement by rail to hospitals in Monterrey, and while General J. Félix Lara set to work strengthening the government's position in Chihuahua and repairing communications, Escobar was fleeing with his cavalry. To the north he picked up about 2000 men, whom he led on the mountainous march into Sonora, the last remaining stronghold of rebellion.

51·

The Campaign in the West

Cedillo's division of agrarian fighters, now in excellent shape and no longer needed around Torreón, was named the Expeditionary Division of the Center. It was sent on April 3 against Cristeros in Jalisco and surrounding states. The Cristeros were particularly active in the Los Altos sector of Jalisco, and there Cedillo's men took strong measures.

Almazán's Northern Division subdued rebel bands in Chihuahua. Ciudad Juárez was retaken. The Chihuahua state legislature was deemed not to have participated with Governor Caraveo in the revolt, and it proceeded to name Luis L. León as interim governor in his place. Then Almazán and his division prepared to cross the mountains into Sonora.

On April 5 Calles moved his general barracks from Bermejillo, heading for the west coast. On the eleventh at Culiacán, Sinaloa (which he reached via Irapuato), he joined up with Cárdenas, who had been successfully moving through Nayarit and Sinaloa, repairing railroad lines and rebuilding bridges. Marching also to Sinaloa was General Espiridión Rodríguez, whose troops, together with those of General Manuel Avila Camacho, found some rebels to defeat at a battle at El Limón, Sinaloa.

In Sinaloa, prior to the arrival of Cárdenas, the federals at the port of Mazatlán had been successful in their defense against the attacks of Manzo, Cruz, and Iturbe, attacks which had continued for a while despite Manzo's departure for the north after some disagreements with Cruz and Iturbe. Assistance in the defense of Mazatlán had been furnished when the loyal warship *Progreso* had taken shots at the attackers, and now, as Cárdenas pushed the Sinaloa rebels further northward, the *Progreso* and the *Bravo* went on ahead in order to shell from the sea at the trains of retreating Escobaristas.

Much further north, General and Governor Fausto Topete of Sonora tried to retake Naco, Sonora, whose fall to loyal forces, as a result of the position taken by Agustín Olachea, had caused Topete not to join Escobar in Chihuahua. The Governor hurled against Naco's defenses a car with dynamite, but it was stopped a kilometer short of the defenders' trenches by a car which the federals had derailed for that purpose. In a formal attack on Naco on April 8 Topete's men used seven armored tractors protected by cavalry and infantry. Formidable attacks were repulsed during a twenty-four-hour struggle which started early in the morning and in which both sides made some use of planes for bombing. The unsuccessful rebels withdrew, and troops organized by General Lucas González, who had been in charge of Naco's defense, then pursued them. Besides sending help to Naco's defenders, General Abelardo L. Rodríguez, of Baja California, organized volunteers, who took from the rebels the frontier town of Sásabe, Sonora, on April 19.

The state of Sinaloa fell completely into the hands of the troops of Cárdenas, whose march to the north brought them into Sonora late in April. In one of his descriptive reports to the President Calles spoke of the successful shooting of enemy trains by the *Progreso* and the *Bravo*. He added that he ordered the commanders of these gunboats to hold off for twelve hours before bombarding the rail-

453

road mechanical shops at Empalme so that Empalme's inhabitants could get out of their homes to safety, and that, as the workers then abandoned the shops, the step had the desired result of bringing to an end the repair of the rolling stock of the "traitors."

Rebel Generals Francisco R. Manzo and Benito Bernal fled northward to the United States, and at Nogales, Arizona, on April 14, 1929, they issued a manifesto to their "companions" in which they said that they had concluded that they had been misled by "a group of ambitious military leaders and perverse politicians" and on that account had forgotten their "duties." They announced that since they had reached this conclusion, and because they opposed the useless shedding of blood, they were abandoning the rebellion.

In his letters to Portes Gil, Calles was particularly lavish in his praise for Cárdenas. Other generals who contributed to the government's cause during this part of the campaign were Juventino Espinosa, Jaime Carrillo, and Rodrigo Talamante. From Sonora the War Minister wrote of wholesale desertions from the enemy camp and of the great desire in the state for the re-establishment of order and peace. "Of the 700 men that Topete raised in this region, mostly Mayo Indians, not a single one is still with him; they have all gone back home, very angry at the traitors who brutally forced them to leave their farms." Over 3000 rebels, said Calles, had been occupied for over a week building trenches and other defenses at Masiaca, Sonora, but most of these, he said, fled suddenly "full of panic" with the arrival of the government forces. In describing the flight of Fausto Topete, Francisco Bórquez, and Miguel Guerrero Verduzco and their men from Masiaca, Calles did not fail to mention that the "infidels" followed the practice of Escobar in destroying the railroad line. As for the cavalries commanded by Cruz, Manuel M. Aguirre, and Crisóforo Vázquez, they were, the President learned, almost completely demolished, their leaders fleeing with about one hundred men. "Roberto Cruz, who is hated among the rebels themselves, could not even command his assistant, who remained in this place and turned over the *charro* costume which Cruz had left with him, this then being shown in public exhibitions." To complete the picture, the rebel merchantships *Bolivar* and *Washington* surrendered to the *Progreso* and *Bravo*, which were now in Guaymas bay, blocking the port.

Leaving General Matías Ramos in charge of Military Operations in the state of Chihuahua (by the War Department's decision),

Almazán, accompanied by Quevedo and others, progressed rapidly toward Sonora, establishing a base at the Las Vargas ranch near the Sonora-Chihuahua border. From Las Vargas planes bombed those rebels who occupied strong positions in the mountains and canyons and who were said to be determined to prevent the westward passage of the federals. Almazán had learned, he says, "that the enemy might be 2500 to 3000 men commanded by Caraveo, Román Yocupicio, Bernabé González, Jacinto B. Treviño, and others." Almazán's army got through the Púlpito Pass, going along the sides of the canyon instead of through the center. At Los Azogues, Jesús García Gutiérrez and his regiment, at the vanguard of the Serratos Brigade, engaged in strong fighting before the rebels fled and the march could be continued.

With the arrivals in Sonora of Cárdenas' Division of the Northwest and Almazán's Division of the North the last of the rebellion there was extinguished. Messages of surrender were received from Francisco Bórquez, who had 600 men at Ortiz, Sonora, and from Miguel Guerrero Verduzco, who had 400 at Potan, Sonora, these rebel fighters commenting that they had been abandoned by their leaders. Indeed, the Mexican consul, Enrique Lieckens, was busy reporting arrivals of prominent rebels at Nogales, Arizona. Manzo, who had crossed to United States soil on April 12, was followed on the twenty-second by Urbalejo and on the twenty-sixth by Fausto and Ricardo Topete, Ramón Iturbe and the family of Francisco Bórquez. Gilberto Valenzuela, who reached the United States at the same time as Manzo, advised that he was representing Escobar in a confidential diplomatic mission to Washington. Enrique Estrada, who had been in the United States and not heard from since the rebellion of 1923–1924, now let it be known that he had been in Sonora during the revolt and had offered his services to General Manzo without getting much response.

In the state of Chihuahua the men of loyal General Matías Ramos fought those of ex-Governor Caraveo, who was soon forced to include himself among the new Mexican refugees in the United States. At the time of his flight he received another letter from his *compadre* and voluminous correspondent, General Almazán. As long as he could General Caraveo had maintained the situation in the state of Chihuahua in fairly good order.

Professor Aurelio Manrique, Jr., critical of what he felt to be the way some rebel generals had abandoned the cause, made his way to

California. Among his new occupations was to be the taking of "bit" or "extra" parts in the United States movie industry, in which endeavor, perhaps, he was assisted by his magnificent black beard. Diputado Ricardo Topete was also to take parts in movies that were produced in California.

General Calles and his staff treated rather generously the troops which surrendered, distributing pardons and payments and railroad passes so that the men could return to productive work. Calles was flown to Hermosillo (capital of Sonora) by the air-force squadron commander, Lieutenant Colonel Pablo L. Sidar. He went next to Nogales, and from Nogales by plane with Abelardo Rodríguez

General Plutarco Elías Calles *in campaign against the Escobar rebellion. Behind Calles' right shoulder is* Sr. Manuel Riva Palacio, *who is between General Calles and* General Macías Valenzuela. *The tall aviator to the right in the photograph is* Pablo Sidar. *Enrique Díaz.*

to Agua Prieta to confer with Almazán about the handling of the government's forces. To succeed Fausto Topete, the federal legislature named Francisco S. Elías to be the interim governor of Sonora.

456

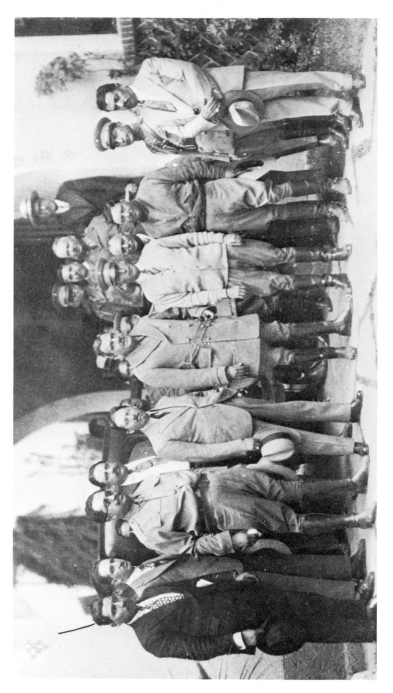

At the home of General Calles at Anzures Colony, following defeat of the Escobar rebels. Third from left (in uniform and with glasses) is Manuel Riva Palacio. Then (moving to the right): Carlos Riva Palacio (behind Manuel's left shoulder), Lamberto Hernández, Calles, General Eulogio Ortiz (wearing sweater), and Melchor Ortega. May, 1929. Casasola.

Lic. Portes Gil has stated that the cost of the government's military campaign was about 13,800,000 pesos, which was paid for by economies in the federal budget. He adds that the destruction of railways and trains, the sacking of banks, and other such rebel activities cost the country another 25 million pesos. But in his opinion the most censurable thing was the nation's loss of close to 2000 persons who were killed. These, he says, included only two or three rebel generals, whereas the rest, "enriched at the cost of the nation and truly responsible for this new shame in our history, took themselves to safety, either hastily crossing the frontier or giving themselves up to the loyal forces with a request for mercy, since they already knew that the provisional government, in spite of the law, would not soil its hands with blood."[1] Lic. Luis Cabrera has described the Escobar rebellion as follows: "This rebellion, known as the Railroad and Banking Rebellion, was simpler than that of 1923, for all that it amounted to was the rebels taking money from the banks and withdrawing to the United States by the Central line and by the Southern Pacific line, destroying the railway communications as they went."[2]

Back in Mexico City, the highly successful General Calles issued another important statement, again worded by Dr. Puig Casauranc, and published on May 22, 1929. In it he announced his resignation from the War Department and his return to private life. He took advantage of this opportunity to refer to "the political failure of the Revolution." Whereas he expressed satisfaction with the progress made since 1910 in the "economic-social" field, in administration, and in construction, he pronounced the Revolution to be a failure with respect to democracy and the vote. Analyzing this shortcoming, he found it to be not only something outside the scope of the Army, but practically impossible for the President to remedy either, inasmuch as fraudulent election returns were submitted in such apparently legal form that any intervention by the President would be considered as an act of imposition. He concluded that "true political parties" were the ones to remedy the situation and therefore called upon the P.N.R. "to repair the errors which the Revolution has committed in the political realm." The National Party, he said, should take advantage of the period of material peace, achieved at so much sacrifice, to create a period of "true peace in

[1] Emilio Portes Gil, *Quince años de política mexicana*, pp. 280–281.
[2] Luis Cabrera (pseud. Blas Urrea), *Veinte años después*, p. 138.

the consciences" wherein all legitimate opposition victories would be accepted in politics. Only then, when a fair handling of the vote would permit the revolutionary conscience of the nation to be satisfied in the political realm "as it is now satisfied in the field of social reform, shall we be able to say that we have triumphed fully . . ."

52.

The Resumption of
Catholic Services

Mention has been made of the negotiations between Father John J. Burke and President Calles in the spring of 1928 regarding the possibility of some arrangement which might bring to an end the conflict between the Mexican Catholic clergy and the Mexican government. Father Burke, in those talks which preceded the assassination of Obregón, expressed the belief that the Mexican Catholic bishops wished to renew public worship and would do so "if they be assured of a tolerance within the law which would permit the Church the liberty of living and exercising its spiritual offices." He had pointed to the Church's fear of certain regulations, such as the registration of priests and the fixing of their number by the states, "if made effective in the spirit of antagonism that threatens the identity of the Church."

Calles had said in his reply to Father Burke: "I take this opportunity to express with full clarity, as I have done on other occasions, that it is not the idea of the Constitution or the laws, or my own to destroy the identity of any Church, or to become involved in any way with its spiritual functions."

That there was no further progress at that time was due, says Portes Gil, to "the lack of judgment of the dignitaries of the Catholic clergy, and the intemperance of some of the bishops residing in the nation and abroad." It will be recalled that a press statement attributed to Archbishop Leopoldo Ruiz y Flores, when he was on his way to Rome, had an unfortunate effect.

In the spring of 1929 ideas were again exchanged, this time between President Portes Gil and Archbishop Ruiz y Flores. Statements indicated that the government and the clergy not only wanted a better situation but also felt that much could be achieved.

In an interview with a newspaper correspondent, President Portes Gil opened the door. He praised the secretary of the Oaxaca Catholic bishopric who gave orders to his religious followers to respect the nation's constituted authorities. Portes Gil said that it was unfortunate that this example had not been more widespread and that representatives of the Catholic clergy had not reproved acts of violence which, in the absence of such reproval, had become more frequent. He admitted that high Church authorities had generally remained above the acts of violence. The exception, he said, was Archbishop Orozco y Jiménez, of Guadalajara, "who does direct these irresponsible groups and even covers regions in Jalisco to stir them on to continue their seditious attitude." The President agreed that "one cannot, in any way, ascribe to the Catholic Church the responsibility for those acts, nor should it be made responsible, since the individuals who commit them operate outside of all principle of Christian morals, order, and rectitude." Nor in his opinion was the Catholic Church involved in the Escobar rebellion.

The President advised that: "On the part of the government there is no objection that the Catholic Church renew its worship when it desires, with the assurance that no authority will be hostile to it, whenever the representatives of the Church are ready to subject themselves to the existing laws regarding worship." He said that

"The Mexican government, as it has often repeated, does not in any manner persecute religion."

Archbishop Leopoldo Ruiz y Flores was at this time in the United States, having returned there recently following a discussion with Pope Pius XI. On May 2, 1929, he gave to the press a statement referring to the remarks which Portes Gil had just made. The Archbishop explained that Mexican legislation had made necessary the suspension of public worship and he asked for a "reconsideration" of the existing laws "with a spirit of sincere patriotism and good will." He expressed the thought that the conflict could be "corrected by men of good will." He said that the Catholic Church was not asking for privileges, adding: "The Catholic citizens of my country, whose faith and patriotism are beyond doubt, will sincerely accept any arrangement that can be made between the Church and the government."

Then on May 8 the President spoke again to the press, this time commenting on the Archbishop's words and stating that "If the Archbishop wishes to discuss with me the method of obtaining co-operation as to a moral force for bettering the Mexican people, I would have no objection to dealing with him."

Archbishop Ruiz y Flores referred Portes Gil's statements to Rome, and later in May he was appointed Apostolic Delegate to Mexico for the purpose of handling the matter. To go with him to Mexico and assist him he called on Bishop Pascual Díaz, the Jesuit who had left Tabasco in 1925 when that state decreed that only married priests could practice; Pascual Díaz was at the time in Louisiana.

Before these two prelates came to Mexico in June they had an opportunity to discuss the matter with Ambassador Morrow, who was in the United States for the marriage of his daughter Anne to Colonel Charles A. Lindbergh. To the Ambassador they explained that of course the Catholic Church sought a change in the Mexican laws, but that if this could not be taken care of at once, perhaps a temporary arrangement could be effected on the basis of a clear recognition of the Church's status and rights, including its rights to own buildings and give religious education.[1]

The Ambassador reached Mexico City on June 10. Soon afterward Ruiz y Flores and Díaz arrived there without any publicity,

---

[1] Joseph H. L. Schlarman, *Mexico: A Land of Volcanoes*, p. 522.

having been met just outside of Mexico City by Father Edmund Walsh (who had been communicating in code between Mexico City and Rome). Morrow arranged secret accommodations for Ruiz y Flores and Díaz, and on June 12 these prelates called on President Portes Gil and presented such thoughts as they had earlier given to Morrow.

Some days later Morrow discussed with the Catholic representatives a statement by the Mexican President to the effect that the Church could renew religious service in accordance with the law. Apparently neither Morrow nor Father Walsh felt that much more could be obtained. When the matter was referred to Rome, the Pope cabled back insisting on the return of religious buildings, the respect for Church property, and an amnesty for the Cristeros.[2] Then on June 21 Ruiz y Flores and Díaz paid another call on the President. The result was that on June 22, 1929, President Emilio Portes Gil and Archbishop Ruiz y Flores made announcements which were generally received with much joy. The President made it known that the Church authorities felt public worship could be renewed provided that "the Church can enjoy liberty under the law to live and exercise its spiritual offices." He declared that neither the Constitution nor the laws nor the government wished to "destroy the integrity of the Catholic Church, nor any other church, nor to intervene in any way in its spiritual functions." He had a responsibility to see that the laws were upheld and to hear complaints based on "improper application of the laws." He went on to clear up some articles which had been "poorly understood": (1) the government was not to register ministers who had not been named "by the superior hierarchy of the respective religious creed"; (2) religious education could be given in churches but not in government or private schools; (3) all can request "the reform, repeal, or issuance of any law."

The Archbishop expressed pleasure at the evidence of good will, and announced that, as a result of the President's declarations, "the Mexican clergy will renew religious services in accordance with the laws that are in effect."

It is to be noted that the Mexican government had not in any way receded from its original position about the Constitution and the laws, including those regulations which caused such strong protests from the prelates in 1926. Since Father Burke had started

[2] *Ibid.*, p. 523.

his exchange of views in 1928, with help from Ambassador Morrow, the Church had received a few more statements denoting that the government did not want to destroy the Church or intervene in its spiritual functions; in this respect the words of Calles to Burke in April, 1928, were practically identical with those of Portes Gil in June, 1929. In 1928 Father Burke had indicated that much depended on a certain tolerance that could well be admitted "within the law." In the summer of 1929 it seems to have been felt that the necessary good will existed on both sides. No doubt the Catholic bishops hoped that limiting measures and regulations would not be carried to what they felt to be stifling extremes, and that uncalled-for actions on both sides, which went beyond the laws, would cease.

Calles kept in close touch with the progress of the "settlement."[3] Portes Gil denies that his friend Ambassador Morrow "intervened" in connection with the Mexican President's efforts in this matter, and points out that in those days he had but two interviews with the Ambassador. The first concerned some other affair, but Morrow did then congratulate Portes Gil on his talks with the Church representatives. In the second interview Morrow was able further to congratulate the President: on the conclusion of the "bloody conflict."[4] Harold Nicolson writes of the Ambassador: "Again and again did he urge on President Calles and upon his successor, President Portes Gil, the necessity of resuming negotiations." Morrow's biographer calls the arrangement "The Morrow Armistice" and quotes Dwight Morrow as telling Mrs. Morrow: "I have opened the churches in Mexico."[5]

The congratulations given by Ambassador Morrow to President Portes Gil were in order. According to Portes Gil 14,000 men surrendered to the government. The War Ministry estimated that between 800 and 1000 had lost their lives in the Cristero struggle. Catholic churches which had not been officially turned into non-religious buildings were made available to the clergy for the renewal of worship services. Bells rang out on Sunday June 30, 1929.

[3] Aarón Sáenz, interview, February 2, 1956.
[4] Emilio Portes Gil, *Quince años de política mexicana*, p. 318.
[5] Harold Nicolson, *Dwight Morrow*, pp. 345–347.

53·

Autonomy for the National University

At precisely the time when he was stating the government's position on religious matters President Portes Gil was handling another problem in which there was also much popular interest. In some respects it appears to have been a more difficult problem.

The rector of the National University, Lic. Antonio Castro Leal, ruled that the professional school students would have to take written examinations, although in the past only oral examinations had been required of them. The Law School students in protest called a strike on May 6, 1929, and promptly the Law School was closed by the President of the Republic. Soon there was a general student strike accompanied by disorders. The rector took disciplinary steps and students resorted to violence.

The rector appealed to the higher authorities, particularly to Education Minister Ezequiel Padilla. Former Education Minister Puig Casauranc was now Head of the Federal District, and he gave orders to the members of the fire department to turn their hoses on the students, an act so handled that the public believed this step ordered by Padilla. The strike became worse, and on May 23 several students were wounded in the battles which students had with police and firemen. Lic. Narciso Bassols resigned the directorship of the University of Law.

In the face of all this violence President Portes Gil on May 24 ordered the withdrawal of the police and firemen and announced that order at the University was now up to the honor of the students, who would not be molested. He asked the students to deliberate and present to him, personally, the fundamental reasons for the strike.

The students named a commission, which presented a petition to the President. The petition included requests for the resignations of the top education authorities: Lic. Ezequiel Padilla (the Minister), Professor Moisés Sáenz (the Undersecretary) and Lic. Antonio Castro Leal (the University rector). It requested the dismissal of Valente Quintana (the District police chief) and Pablo Meneses (head of the Safety Commission). Resignations were requested of those associated with the Education Ministry and the University who had taken "reprisals" against the striking students. The students asked that the University Board be established in such a way that the student representatives would never be outvoted by representatives of teachers and directors. This new board, they suggested, should name three candidates for rector (to replace Lic. Castro Leal), and the President of the Republic should select one of the three.

On May 28, 1929, President Portes Gil pointed out that he could not agree to the requests which the students had made. "Some of your petitions are the fruit of the heat coming from violence." He did express regret for excesses of repression against the students.

He saw the unrest as stemming from an old desire of the University to be autonomous, instead of a section of the federal government. As far back as the time of Lic. Justo Sierra, Porfirio Díaz's renowned expert on education, there had been clamor in favor of separating the National University from the executive branch of the government.

Lic. Portes Gil chose this moment to announce the establishment of the University's autonomy. This was such an important step that it resolved the problem. "The University will freely determine its programs of study, methods of teaching, and the application of funds and resources." In the case of naming the University rector and directors of the various school faculties the President of the Republic was in each case to submit three names, one of which would be selected by the University Board. "The University Board, made up of the rector, the directors of the faculties or schools, the delegates of the teachers, students, and graduate ex-students . . . will be the supreme authority of government of the University." It was also resolved that the President of the Republic had the right to veto Board resolutions in a few realms, and that the funds to be administered by the autonomous University would be supplied by the federal government.

On June 4, 1929, Congress authorized the President to draw up the law creating the University's autonomy, and in the succeeding days the students, who were in control of the University, forced Professor Alfonso Caso and others to listen to strong speeches demanding the resignations of Caso, Castro Leal, Ezequiel Padilla, and Moisés Sáenz. Lic. Castro Leal did resign as rector on June 13 and then the striking students turned over the University to the authorities. The new presidential decree was issued on July 9, and on the tenth Lic. Ignacio García Téllez (who had governed Guanajuato) was provisionally placed in charge of the University's affairs. On July 11 the student strike finally came to an end after sixty-eight days' duration.

When the University Board (which was established on July 31) rejected all three candidates for the rectorship which the President had submitted, Portes Gil refused to change his list. Lic. Salvador Urbina was then selected by the Board, but he declined the honor. Finally, on September 4, the Board chose Ignacio García Téllez, who accepted.

Dr. Puig Casauranc, as President Calles' Education Minister, had pushed for the autonomy of the University, and during the May, 1929, student strike he made to President Portes Gil an un-

467

solicited recommendation that this step be taken. Regardless of incidents which created no great cordiality on the part of Portes Gil or Ezequiel Padilla for the activities of Dr. Puig Casauranc in connection with the unfolding of this affair, the fact is that the arrangement for the autonomy of the National University at this time was another dramatic and popular achievement for President Portes Gil. Large groups of students favored the campaign of Lic. Vasconcelos. The more political-minded of the young Vasconcelistas regretted seeing any end of the student strike, as its continuation would have provided Lic. Vasconcelos and his followers with more ammunition for their speeches.

Ezequiel Padilla, who had such hearty backing from the President that Diego Rivera murals were placed on interior walls of the Palacio Nacional in spite of opposition by Montes de Oca, presided over the Education Ministry at the time when it instituted the so-called "circuit schools." Although a large number of federal schools had been started during the presidential administration of Calles, there was still a lack of available teaching for the many wanting and requiring the fundamentals of education, reading and writing. The "circuit school" plan called for advanced students to make the rounds (on weekends or at other times when they were free) to little schools of rural communities, each to teach reading and writing in a number of such schools and to receive some remuneration for this service. Several thousand school groups were thus aided.

	1928	1929
Total federal schools	4,076	6,925
Federal rural schools	3,303	6,106
Student enrollment in federal rural schools	278,137	384,328

By 1930 there were 2,242,000 children between the ages of six and ten, and of these 942,000 attended school. Illiteracy in persons ten or more years of age declined from 70 per cent in 1910, to 67 per cent in 1921, and to 59 per cent in 1930.[1]

There was by now an immensely high regard for President Portes Gil. "The situation of the President," says Puig Casauranc, "was a

[1] Secretaría de la Economía Nacional, *Anuario estadístico, 1938*, pp. 42–49. The table given above is from the same source, pp. 92 and 99.

honeymoon with the politicians, the Congress, the governors, and the Army."[2] General Calles, just before departing for Europe in order to see what well-known doctors abroad could do for his poor health, made a declaration in which he said: "I believe that the future of Mexico is guaranteed."

[2] J. M. Puig Casauranc, *Galatea rebelde a varios pigmaliones*, p. 336.

54·

The Vasconcelista Campaign of 1929

By the end of May, 1929, Ing. Pascual Ortiz Rubio had embarked on a campaign tour which was to take him and his secretary, Colonel Eduardo Hernández Cházaro, together with such P.N.R. bigwigs as Manuel Pérez Treviño and Luis L. León, all over the nation. Early on the tour, when he was visiting points which had served as the setting for the 1920 tragedy at Tlaxcalantongo, Ortiz Rubio emphasized construction "as the magic word of our epoch." As he went on he had words for the farm-workers ("I shall work that the peasants might have water") and for laborers (whom he advised to group themselves around honest leaders), and he called upon the people to interest themselves in public questions and to vote. Stressing the need of co-operation by all in order to attain progress in modern times, he advocated "schools and more schools"; then "roads, roads, and more roads."

Vasconcelistas kept on with their political activities, which during the Escobar military uprising had been highlighted by the addition to their ranks of many Mexico City Valenzuelistas and by a relative freedom from interference by official elements. In order to help raise funds, Lic. Vasconcelos appeared at two great meetings in Mexico City where attendance required pay. He said: "to those who call us idealists I ask what have the practical ones done? We, in the opportunity we had, knew how to found schools, not palaces for officials." Then he followed these words with an announcement which brought great concern to the Antirreeleccionistas; he announced the creation of a new political party: the Partido Nacional del Trabajo. To add to the confusion quite a rivalry had by now blossomed between the two groups which were pushing his candidacy, the Comité Orientador Pro-Vasconcelos, which was headed by Medellín Ostos, and the Frente Nacional Renovador, in which Antonieta Rivas Mercado was active.

After two months of preparation the Antireeleccionista convention opened on July 2, 1929, at the Frontón Hispanomexicano in Mexico City, and by that time Vasconcelos did agree to seek to be that party's candidate, although he did not fail to mention that the Antirreeleccionista leaders had not supported him in 1927. Under the presidency of Ing. Vito Alessio Robles, aided by secretaries Calixto Maldonado and José G. Aguilar, the convention was made up of about 835 delegates from all over the country. In a passionate speech at the opening session Alessio Robles reviewed the unfortunate events of 1927 and maintained that the enthusiasm kindled by General Calles' September 1, 1928, message to the nation had been wiped out by the sad facts: opposition representatives had been thrown out of Congress; Calles, abandoning Don Aarón Sáenz, prepared the farce of Querétaro in order to impose the most ambiguous, the least plausible, and the most unable citizen as presidential candidate. Besides framing in Río de Janeiro, Brazil, a memorial by inhabitants there in memory of Obregón, what, asked Alessio Robles, has Ortiz Rubio accomplished? The orator proclaimed that Ortiz Rubio had been chosen because, having no abilities, he was perfectly equipped to obey hidden orders.

Vasconcelos saw the convention, which by now had moved to the Hidalgo Theatre, as a coalition of parties, and he kept pushing for his idea of a new party name: Partido Nacional del Trabajo. However, Alessio Robles succeeded in preserving the old name that had

In the center is Lic. José Vasconcelos *at the time of becoming presidential candidate of the Partido Nacional Antirreeleccionista. To the right (Vasconcelos' left) is* Ing. Vito Alessio Robles *(with arm extended). At extreme right (and partly cut off from picture) is* Lic. Calixto Maldonado. *July, 1929. Enrique Díaz.*

brought triumph to Francisco I. Madero, although Vasconcelos pointed out that the problem was not one of re-election.

By his participation in the recently quelled Escobar rebellion, General Antonio I. Villarreal had disqualified himself from the presidential race, but nevertheless two names were presented to the Antirreeleccionista gathering: those of Lic. José Vasconcelos and Dr. Francisco Vázquez Gómez. Vasconcelos was nominated by frenzied acclamation, while his supporters, to the tune of "La Cucaracha," burst out in song:

> Los diputados, los diputados
> ya no pueden mangonear
> pues Vasconcelos, pues Vasconcelos
> ya los vino a fastidiar.

More internal friction developed when Vasconcelos suggested that Manuel Bonilla be named substitute candidate to take over in case the first candidate should lose his life in the campaign. Ing. Alessio Robles suggested that the convention choose the running mate from Bonilla and Lic. Calixto Maldonado, who had been associated with Don Vito in the days of General Gómez' candidacy. A rupture among the Antirreeleccionistas was averted only by the decision not to name any "vice-candidate." At the same time the Frente Nacional Renovador and the Comité Orientador Pro-Vasconcelos found a point about which they could agree with each other: the program of Vasconcelos must be socialistic.

After being nominated by the Antirreeleccionistas, Lic. Vasconcelos resumed his campaigning throughout the nation, with some financial assistance from Manuel Gómez Morín, Federico González Garza, Luis Cabrera, and others. Apparently considering Ambassador Dwight Morrow to be his most formidable opponent, he accused the P.N.R. of following "the Morrow plan: fool the people with a change of person which will make the prolongation of a system more bearable." He blamed Morrow for the "disloyal arrangements of the religious question" and had a lot to say against them. They were, he maintained, purposely consummated some months before the electoral test with the aim of demoralizing the opposition through the surrender of the Cristeros, and he listed the Cristero leader, General Gorostieta, as a victim "of the famous arrangements." Gorostieta, according to Vasconcelos, was largely abandoned, and, after agreeing to a parley under terms which guaranteed the life of himself and his men, was shot to death in ambush.

In July, 1929, Vito Alessio Robles accepted the Antirreeleccionista candidacy for the governorship of the state of Coahuila. Vasconcelos, who learned about this in the newspapers, believed that he should have been consulted, but he agreed to the accomplished fact. Don Vito explained that the Coahuila elections were to take place two weeks before the presidential elections, and since they would both officially be declared the losers, Don Vito could use the two weeks to prepare Coahuila so that it would be the first state to rebel.

For the governorship of Coahuila, Ing. Alessio Robles faced Nazario S. Ortiz Garza, who had been *presidente municipal* of Torreón and later president of the Coahuila state congress. The chief object of Alessio Robles' attack was General Manuel Pérez Treviño, who as president of the P.N.R. was again temporarily absent from the governor's chair. Pérez Treviño was accused by the Antirreeleccionista of having enriched himself at the public's expense and of seeking the continuance of a disastrous regime for Coahuila in his protégé Don Nazario S. Ortiz Garza. Alessio Robles also blasted the Riva Palacio brothers and criticized Garrido Canabal's Tabasco dictatorship. On the less negative side he offered a program of financial honesty in government, and of respect for votes, institutions, and laws; he sponsored a new dignity for the free municipality ("now tied down and ridiculed by official political directors"), and he came out in favor of voting by women.

The opposition candidates gave attention to the question of whether certain men had served at any time in the past under Victoriano Huerta, and Ing. Alessio Robles addressed to "Sr. Ingeniero Topógrafo Don Pascual Ortiz Rubio" a number of open letters in which he presented evidence to the effect that the P.N.R. candidate had during part of 1913 done some work for the Victoriano Huerta Government. Vasconcelos, besides calling some important government officials "ex-Huertistas," mentions that Vito Alessio Robles, the accuser of Ortiz Rubio, was himself for a while a professional in the army of Victoriano Huerta. But there was, according to Ing. Alessio Robles, quite a difference in this respect between himself and Ing. Ortiz Rubio. Ing. Alessio Robles, an army engineer, resigned in 1913 from his position of lieutenant colonel in Huerta's army, explaining to Huerta that he did not agree with him. He was subsequently jailed, and in the Mexico City Penitentiary met Ortiz Rubio, who as a federal *diputado* had incurred Huerta's disfavor. When Alessio Robles got out of jail he carried on against Huerta and was for a time an associate of Pancho Villa. Ing. Alessio Robles has stated that Ortiz Rubio, after his release from prison, was for a time a member of Huerta's forces.[1]

Vasconcelos and his supporters, including such campaigners as Alejandro Gómez Arias, Adolfo López Mateos, Germán de Campo, Angel Carvajal, and Mauricio Magdaleno, put an enormous amount

[1] Vito Alessio Robles, interview, January 31, 1957.

of energy into their crusade to arouse the people. Abraham Arellano sought out his cotton and mining friends of Coahuila and Chihuahua. Monterrey gave the Vasconcelistas no trouble, although at
first the people there seemed rather indifferent. Vasconcelos leaders
visited Santa Engracia, Tamaulipas, where young Vasconcelistas
expressed the thought that land should be worked collectively, and
Saltillo, Coahuila, where they called on Julia Carranza, daughter
of Venustiano Carranza. In spite of the fact that Vasconcelos had
once been loudly critical of Don Venustiano, the campaigners were
able to enlist the support of Julia, who said something to the effect
that the ideal of Vasconcelos was the same one for which her father
had given his life.[2]

With the approach of election day the Vasconcelistas ran into
troubles. In San Luis Potosí, bulwark of General Cedillo, some of
them were thrown out of the state, and at León, Guanajuato, some
of them were jailed. Notwithstanding President Portes Gil's efforts
to attend to the various complaints which he received from the
Antirreeleccionista candidate, acts of repression increased in September, when there were some victims in the mountains of Puebla,
Oaxaca, Hidalgo, and México. Vasconcelos at length gave up formulating denouncements and complaints, having reached the conclusion that "war to the death was declared." He feared precipitating
a pretext for calling off the elections or for "disqualifying" the opposition candidate. He had absolutely no admiration for General
Amaro (now back in the War Ministry) and felt that Amaro was
"scheming a military blow under the pretext of disturbances which
would make it impossible to hold elections."

Greatly mourned by their many coworkers and friends were
Aurelio Celis, of Tampico, and the young speechmaker Germán de
Campo, both assassinated during the course of the political campaign. Germán de Campo met his death on the evening of September
20 in front of the Jardín de San Fernando in Mexico City. Not without some disturbances he had been speaking to some workers from
a high place on the Teatro Nacional (now the Palace of Fine Arts),
and he and his friends were on their way back to the office of the
Comité Orientador when they heard some "vivas" for Ortiz Rubio.
From cars which drew up alongside they were shot at by some
Thompson repeaters, and in this way Germán de Campo and two
others were killed. A federal *diputado* was considered to have pro-

[2] Mauricio Magdaleno, *Las palabras perdidas*, p. 120.

voked this clash. Antonieta Rivas Mercado provided cognac for some of the survivors. President Portes Gil promised to investigate.[3]

Lines of people passed before the three bodies at the offices of the Partido Nacional Antirreeleccionista. Then a funeral procession through the main parts of Mexico City was followed by speeches by Medellín Ostos and others at the graveyard. When Vasconcelos reached Mexico City to be welcomed by about 90,000 on October 6, he paused at the place where Germán de Campo had been murdered. In reply to a query as to the attitude which the United States might take with respect to the Mexican electoral struggle he said: "The United States is against anyone that cannot be handled."[4]

In the street fighting which took place in Mexico City in the days just before the election, Valente Quintana, head of the Federal District police, received a blow on the head. On one occasion crowds of Vasconcelistas burned down the door of a P.N.R. office and took over the office.

On the eve of the November 17 election Vasconcelos was at Mazatlán, Sinaloa, where, he says, "groups of *pistoleros* in the municipal trucks went back and forth in front of our balcony . . . shooting into the air, giving 'vivas' for Ortiz Rubio and Calles."[5] President Portes Gil had sent instructions to the military commanders of Sinaloa and Sonora to preserve order, following the receipts of Vasconcelos' complaints from Nayarit that force had been used against him and his supporters by official elements.[6]

Abraham Arellano was in Coahuila ready to join a revolt. Vicente and Mauricio Magdaleno went from Mexico City to Tampico, and as their train passed through San Luis Potosí freight cars full of armed agrarians were attached thereto. By November 17 Tampico was full of men with rifles and machine guns. During the voting in Mexico City nineteen people were reported killed and nine wounded.

On election day Vasconcelos went by train north to Guaymas, Sonora, where he awaited the election results and drew up his Plan of Guaymas. This Plan was to be circulated in case the announced election results were unfavorable, an eventuality which seemed probable in spite of Mauricio Magdaleno's feeling that public opin-

[3] *Ibid.*, pp. 173–174.
[4] José Vasconcelos, *El proconsulado*, p. 296.
[5] *Ibid.*, p. 295.
[6] Emilio Portes Gil, *Quince años de política mexicana*, pp. 182–183.

ion was overwhelmingly in favor of the Antirreeleccionista candidate. Vasconcelistas point out that a fair voting was effectively prevented. The candidate himself got the understanding that one telegram with favorable election news was intercepted by the government and falsified, and the promptness with which the press reported an Ortiz Rubio victory made him more than skeptical. He has called attention to the fact that this news was published in New York before the voting booths were officially closed.

On November 28 Congress issued a decree declaring that Ortiz Rubio was President-elect, following the official announcement of the voting results by its Gran Comisión:

Ortiz Rubio	1,948,848
Vasconcelos	110,979
Rodríguez Triana	23,279

Alessio Robles' choice for the vice-presidential spot, Calixto Maldonado, declared: "Democracy has been assassinated; there were no elections; the assaults prevented them." On the other hand Antirreeleccionista Party President Góngora asserted that Vasconcelos was President-elect, having won the majority of votes. In Los Angeles, Generals Francisco R. Manzo and Fausto Topete inquired about this inconsistency.

Disguised as a woman, Alessio Robles had departed from Saltillo after his defeat in Coahuila, going quietly to San Antonio, Texas.[7] Insofar as journeying to the United States was concerned, Vasconcelos resolved to follow the example of Alessio Robles. He recalled the fate of Angel Flores, who, not long after losing the 1924 presidential election to Calles, had passed away—poisoned, according to many. Although Manuel Gómez Morín advised Vasconcelos against rebellion, and although no rebellion seemed to be starting, Vasconcelos appeared determined to carry out his "plan of war" based on the declarations of the Plan of Guaymas (dated December 1, 1929) which was being circulated privately. This Plan stated that Vasconcelos was Mexico's President-elect and expressed lack of recognition of the federal, state, and municipal powers that had "made mockery" of the public votes. It concluded by stating that "The President-elect is now leaving the country, but he will return to take direct charge of the mandate as soon as there is a group of free armed men who are in condition to make the mandate respected. Circulate this and comply."

[7] Alfonso Taracena, *Los Vasconcelistas sacrificados en Topilejo*, p. 13.

Vasconcelos' decision to go to the United States received some co-operation from the government armed forces. He found himself with an escort.

Before leaving he received, he explains, a most interesting caller who said he wished to speak to him on behalf of Morrow. This caller, says Vasconcelos, offered him the rectorship of the Autonomous University and also offered for his supporters one or two posts in Ortiz Rubio's Cabinet. In return, Vasconcelos tells us, he was asked to sign a telegram advising that although the elections were not properly carried out, he was, for patriotic and peaceful reasons, recognizing Ortiz Rubio's victory and recommending that his supporters back Ortiz Rubio. Vasconcelos tells of how he stoutly turned down the offer and predicted that an armed rebellion was at hand. His caller accompanied him northward to Nogales, together with a special car containing the escort of forty government soldiers.

In Nogales, Arizona, Vasconcelos was joined by Vito Alessio Robles, who was accompanied by Gerzayn Ugarte. Alessio Robles hoped for an uprising in Coahuila. Vasconcelos hoped for something in Sinaloa or Sonora. The only real hope at the moment for an armed uprising rested with General Carlos Bouquet, who was in Sonora and was an ardent Vasconcelista.

The Plan of Guaymas was published in San Antonio, Texas, and in some unimportant newspapers of Mexico, although Ing. Alessio Robles was not enthusiastic about the wording. After this had been arranged, Vasconcelos took a train for New York, explaining to Alessio Robles that he was being urged by Sra. Antonieta Rivas Mercado and Lic. Manuel Gómez Morín to go to Washington, D.C. He told Alessio Robles to await his orders in San Antonio.

In New York Vasconcelos listened to Sra. Riva Mercado's pleas that he have discussions in Washington with important members of the United States Congress and the Administration,[8] but he took great care not to follow what he considered to be a dishonorable path such as had in the past been taken by others hoping to attain the Mexican presidency.[9] Through an intermediary he received word which was said to come from President Hoover to the effect that the United States government would remain neutral if a rebellion broke out prior to Ortiz Rubio's proposed visit to Washington, whereas it would back Ortiz Rubio should there be no rebellion in Mexico prior to that visit.[10]

[8] Manuel Gómez Morín, letter, February 4, 1957.
[9] José Vasconcelos, *op. cit.*, p. 319.   [10] *Ibid.*, pp. 322–323.

In Washington Sra. Riva Mercado was able to bring the Vasconcelistas' problem to the attention of some women's groups but she did not succeed in having any official interviews with members of the United States administration. In New York Lic. Gómez Morín tried to persuade Vasconcelos to continue with the efforts which he had made in Mexico, using a permanent opposition party, but this idea did not appeal to Vasconcelos, who felt himself committed to push now for a revolutionary uprising such as had taken Madero to the presidency.

The hopes that Vasconcelos placed in General Carlos Bouquet were short-lived. Vasconcelos had returned to Arizona and was in Tucson when he learned that in the neighborhood of Nogales, Sonora, Bouquet and his companions had been captured while trying to cross to the United States, an event which was followed by the killing of Bouquet and the freeing of the companions. In denouncing this "new crime" Vasconcelos pointed out that the order to shoot Bouquet came from War Minister Amaro. Vito Alessio Robles has written that the "imprudent declarations" of the Plan of Guaymas resulted in the death sentence of General Bouquet,[11] and he has added that Vasconcelos did not help things when he arranged to send "by express" four machine guns from north of the border to Bouquet in Sonora.[12]

The days passed but no rebellion developed.

Ing. Ortiz Rubio left Mexico City for New York on December 3. When he entered the United States at Brownsville, Texas, he was greeted by Arthur Bliss Lane and presented with a letter from President Hoover inviting him to visit Washington. On his tour in the United States he was accompanied by General Pérez Treviño and Dr. Puig Casauranc, as well as his secretary, Colonel Eduardo Hernández Cházaro.

Before making the Washington visit, Ortiz Rubio proceeded to New York, where he was the city's "guest of honor" on December 12 and where he had important conversations with General Calles, who docked there on the fourteenth after a stormy passage from France. These conversations, which took place in a room at the Hotel Pennsylvania, concerned the Cabinet of the forthcoming administration and they have been described as not entirely pleasing to the President-elect. Hernández Cházaro, who alone witnessed

[11] Vito Alessio Robles, *Mis andanzas con nuestro Ulises*, p. 327.
[12] Vito Alessio Robles, interview, January 31, 1957.

the most important discussion between the two men, mentioned that they agreed to go down the list of positions, taking turns at making suggestions. At least Ortiz Rubio was able to place Almazán in the Communications post in spite of Calles' desire to see either Adalberto Tejeda or Saturnino Cedillo there. Ortiz Rubio accepted the suggestion that Gonzalo N. Santos head the congressional Permanent Commission. Santos was closely associated with Pérez Treviño; Santos and Melchor Ortega, during December's maneuvers in Congress, had been struggling against a group which was expected to support Ortiz Rubio and which was led by Arturo Campillo Seyde and Ignacio de la Mora.[13]

Calles was back in Mexico on December 18. Ortiz Rubio went on to Johns Hopkins Hospital at Baltimore and there his future Cabinet was discussed again, this time with Pérez Treviño and Puig Casauranc; for the most part this discussion consisted in going over what had been decided in talks with Calles in New York.

From Baltimore the President-elect went to Washington, D.C. Here he was given a fine reception at the White House, a dinner by Dwight Morrow, and an honorary degree of Doctor of Laws from George Washington University. He went on to Buffalo, Niagara, and Detroit (where he was the guest of Henry Ford). During January, 1930, he was travelling through Kansas, New Mexico, and Arizona. Before crossing to Mexican soil at Nogales, in order to be honored by numerous receptions in his own country, Ortiz Rubio heard rumors about a plot to finish his life.

When General Calles returned to Mexico after his trip to Europe and his chat with Ortiz Rubio in New York, he found President Portes Gil and Agriculture Minister Marte R. Gómez carrying out land expropriations at a record rate. Whereas in 1928 about 640,000 hectares were redistributed, in 1929 over one million hectares with an official valuation of 80 million pesos were redistributed to the benefit of over 100,000 persons. These figures hardly represented a slowing up of the program, which Calles, Montes de Oca, and Dwight Morrow felt at this stage might be wise.

Men close to Calles, such as Carlos Riva Palacio, the governor of the state of México, complained bitterly to the General about the agrarian policy of the Administration. Portes Gil has pointed out that a number of the friends of the ex-President were adversely af-

[13] Juan Andreu Almazán in *El Universal*, February 11 and 12, 1959.

fected by the land redistributions, but that Generals Amaro and Pedro J. Almada (head of Military Operations in Puebla) cooperated fully with the program and with some parcelling of their own estates.[14]

One of the last acts of the Administration of Portes Gil was to break off diplomatic relations with Russia. Russia's representative to Mexico, Alexandra Kollontai, had in 1928 been replaced by the more aggressive Dr. Alejandro de Makar, who used the Soviet Legation as a center of intrigue and propaganda to stir up Communist violence and attacks on Mexico and her government. That relations were not cordial could perhaps be sensed from the Russian reaction to the appeal made by Mexico, as a signer of the Kellogg-Briand Pact outlawing war, that China and Russia resolve their differences in a peaceful way.[15] That relations were becoming intolerable was clear from the insults to Mexico in the Russian press, accusations by the Communist Party of Moscow, which labeled Mexico "an instrument of American imperialism and of the bourgeois," and from the experiences of Mexico's minister to Russia, Professor Jesús Silva Herzog, who reported spying on the mission's personnel. In reply to official complaints, the Russian government blamed the Communist Party of Moscow and said that nothing could be done about the vigorous attacks on Mexico.

Then Lic. Portes Gil came into possession of a confidential Russian document which the Mexican Foreign Ministry had been able to obtain and which provided some explanation of the aggressive attacks by Russia against Mexico. The document contained instructions of the Russian Interior Department to its agents to create not merely public agitation, but a revolution, all for the purpose of indirectly hurting the United States and giving a blow to petroleum production. The document revealed detailed plans about spying, and also mentioned the need to attack the lives of Ortiz Rubio, Portes Gil, and others.

After Mexico terminated diplomatic relations, Russia intensified her disagreeable attitude and gave instructions to her agents to stone the Mexican embassies and consulates throughout the world.[16]

[14] Emilio Portes Gil, *op. cit.*, pp. 366–367.
[15] Luis G. Franco, *Relaciones exteriores en una actuación histórica*, pp. 24–25.
[16] Emilio Portes Gil, *op. cit.*, pp. 373–389.

55.

A Bad Inauguration Day for President Ortiz Rubio

General e Ing. Pascual Ortiz Rubio took over the presidency from Lic. Emilio Portes Gil in the midst of a setting in which political intrigue was rampant. Supporters of Portes Gil were, generally speaking, not getting along well with those who were now classified as Ortizrubistas. Some of the Portesgilistas expressed fears about certain tendencies on the part of supporters of the new President. A number of those who were due to leave office wished to continue their influence.

These differences were manifest in political maneuvering and in struggles in the federal Congress, where the so-called "Whites" supported Ortiz Rubio, and the "Reds" supported those who to date had been in power.

When General Calles returned from his trip to Europe and New York he found himself in a strong position politically, since the two opposing groups of intriguers sought to base much of their strength on his support. He was besieged by politicians who either wanted to use his name as an aid in the attainment of favors, or brought to him complaints and suspicions in connection with others. The relations between Portes Gil and Calles, both experts in politics, were at this time good. Ortiz Rubio, far from experienced in these political stratagems and far from having a strong bloc of personal political addicts, accepted the idea of influence by Calles—or the P.N.R.—in the political aspect of his Administration. But by the time of his inauguration it was apparent that he did not take a great liking to submitting to ideas and influences classified as Portesgilista.

On February 4, 1930, one day prior to the inauguration, the press received the names of new Cabinet ministers and other officials:

Gobernación
    Lic. Emilio Portes Gil
Finance and Public Credit
    Sr. Luis Montes de Oca
Foreign Relations
    Sr. Genaro Estrada
War and Navy
    General Joaquín Amaro
Communications and Public Works
    General Juan Andreu Almazán
Agriculture and Development
    General Manuel Pérez Treviño
Industry, Commerce, and Labor
    Ing. Luis L. León
Public Education
    Lic. y General Aarón Sáenz
Federal District
    Dr. J. M. Puig Casauranc
Attorney General of the Nation
    Lic. José Aguilar y Maya
Statistics
    Ing. Juan de Dios Bojórquez

President's Secretary
Colonel Eduardo Hernández Cházaro

The public found this list to be full of familiar names. Generally speaking these well-known figures who occupied the important ministries and who promised to support the new President were strong Callistas who had collaborated with Calles over the past years and who had attained stature through that collaboration. Aarón Sáenz agreed to serve in this new Cabinet because of Ortiz Rubio's persistent urging, but he declined the Foreign Relations post, which he had handled for so long, and instead took over the Education Ministry. Later writers have observed that probably Ortiz Rubio would not have named Portes Gil to be Gobernación Minister if he had felt himself entirely free as to the selection of his collaborators. He found it advisable to rely on Calles for guidance in political matters; and he resolved to proceed in the presidency along new lines, a course of action that at the moment was interpreted by some as a sharing of powers which had earlier been concentrated in the hands of the President.

On Sunday February 5 the capital was adorned for the ceremonies. Many soldiers were in evidence. Uniforms were especially concentrated on Avenida Madero, Paseo de la Reforma, and Avenida Orizaba, through which the presidential car passed on its way to the National Stadium. The car left the Palacio Nacional at 11:00 A.M. bearing President Portes Gil, President-elect Ortiz Rubio, and Diputados Gonzalo N. Santos and Pedro C. Rodríguez.

Rumors had been circulating as to a possible attempt to assassinate Ortiz Rubio. The President-elect had arranged to have his own supporters organize a protective force, in which he had more confidence, and members of that force occasionally had clashes with the regular police, although the latter had been placed at the disposal of the President-elect by President Portes Gil. Intimates of Ortiz Rubio were full of alarm.

By noon the National Stadium was jammed with over 35,000 persons who were to have the privilege of witnessing the transfer of the executive power and of hearing Pascual Ortiz Rubio make the official pledge of office and outline the program he hoped to follow. *Generales de división* attending the inauguration included those who had distinguished themselves in the recent rebellion, such as Miguel Acosta, Alejandro Mange, Eulogio Ortiz (who had been placed in charge of operations in the Valley of Mexico) and Matías Ramos (who was about to serve as War Undersecretary). Among the governors present were Alberto Terrones Benítez (of Durango), Agustín Arroyo Ch. (of Guanajuato), Lázaro Cádenas (of Michoacán), Saturnino Cedillo (of San Luis Potosí) and Francisco Elías (of Sonora). Also present was Nazario S. Ortiz Garza, who had in the recent Coahuila gubernatorial race been declared the victor over Ing. Vito Alessio Robles after a campaign which was hardly indicative of the warm friendship and mutual admiration that was to develop between those two contestants with the passage of years and the calming of political passions.

The arrival of the outgoing and incoming Presidents at the stadium was announced at 12:15 P.M. Bands played the national hymn and Portes Gil and Ortiz Rubio took their places on the central platform, one on each side of the president of the Federal Congress, Diputado Melchor Ortega. Behind Ortiz Rubio was his secretary, Colonel Hernández Cházaro. In accordance with protocol, all stood, with the exception of the president of the Congress, while the new President promised to uphold the Constitution and the laws emanating therefrom. The new President of the Republic also read a speech, in which he pledged his efforts on behalf of the social program of the Revolution.

At 12:50 President Ortiz Rubio left the stadium in the company of Portes Gil, Hernández Cházaro, and the presidents of congressional commissions, Senator José J. Reynoso and Diputado Manuel Riva Palacio. At 1:20 P.M. they reached the Palacio Nacional, where some champagne was tasted in celebration of the moment and where the new Cabinet ministers were sworn in, they also having come directly to the Palacio from the stadium. After this ceremony the new Cabinet members departed, Portes Gil going with his wife and mother for a ride in the park of the Bosque de Chapultepec.

President Ortiz Rubio, his wife, his niece, and Colonel Hernández Cházaro entered a closed Cadillac in the Palacio's Patio de Honor and were driven off. Just as the car came outside the Patio it was fired upon.

Six shots were fired. One of them first struck the President's wife above the right ear, at a moment when she was turned toward her husband, and then it struck the President in the right jawbone. The shattering of glass wounded the President's niece.

The youth who had fired the shots was at once apprehended in the midst of the tumult. Hernández Cházaro took the President immediately to the Red Cross Hospital, at San Jerónimo Street, and there, holding a bloody handkerchief against his wound, President Ortiz Rubio was able to climb the steps and enter the building. Near the Fountain of the Frogs in the Bosque de Chapultepec General Juan José Ríos gave the news to Portes Gil, who rushed immediately to the Red Cross Hospital, as did Joaquín Amaro, J. M. Puig Casauranc, and other Cabinet members.

At the President's bedside, just as Dr. Julián Villarreal was about to start giving the anaesthetic prior to operating, occurred the sort of incident which in tense moments was apt to be blown up so as to create difficulties. Portes Gil ordered Valente Quintana to investigate the crime and Puig Casauranc observed that Quintana was no longer General Inspector of Police. On the previous evening Ortiz Rubio had told Puig Casauranc to be sure to put General José Mijares Palencia in the place of Valente Quintana, but this was unknown to Portes Gil or to Quintana. Portes Gil, besides remarking that he had issued his instructions because no one had seemed to be concerned about the matter, said also that he had not known about the changes. Then a technical point came up. Puig Casauranc on February 4 had issued the orders replacing Quintana as of February 5. But Puig Casauranc had not yet formally gone through the ceremony of becoming President Ortiz Rubio's Head of the Federal District. The wounded President was therefore asked, perhaps by General Amaro, to take the pledge of office of Dr. Puig Casauranc, and this he did just before his operation. Puig Casauranc writes: "Then, the last formal requisite having been complied with, in the presence of Lic. Portes Gil we ordered Sr. Quintana 'not to make any official investigations of any sort, since he was no longer a police official.' "[1]

Wildest rumors flew about concerning the possible intellectual authors of the crime, and, even among some close collaborators of the President, the names of Lic. Portes Gil, Ing. Marte R. Gómez, General Calles, and General Cedillo were mentioned.

On the day of the assault against Ortiz Rubio, Portes Gil issued a circular for the state governors. Urging the nation to be calm, he

[1] J. M. Puig Casauranc, *Galatea rebelde a varios pigmaliones*, p. 366.

pointed out that fortunately the wounds had not been fatal and he gave assurance that people who committed such crimes as this would be energetically punished. Lic. Portes Gil has been accused by Ing. Francisco Díaz Babio and by Dr. Puig Casauranc of calling a Cabinet meeting on the day of the assassination attempt, but he brands as false the charges of these writers.

The youth who had attempted to kill the President turned out to be Daniel Flores, twenty-three years of age. Although he was at once questioned by many, including General Amaro, Dr. Puig Casauranc, and the new Police Inspector, General Mijares Palencia, he was not at all loquacious, refusing to give even the name of his father. Investigating officers found on him a billfold and an image of the Virgin of Guadalupe.

According to some announcements, Daniel Flores had been a zealous Vasconcelista and was not one of the Cristeros. Among many others who were taken by the police was Señorita Guillermina Ruiz, Secretary of the Women's Committee of the Partido Nacional Antirreeleccionista. Mauricio Magdaleno and his friends of the Vasconcelista campaign went through the lists of their Mexico City associates but they could not find anyone named Daniel Flores.

The crime became the cause of an intense secret investigation in which many persons were arrested and molested but were found to have had no connection with it whatsoever. By means of a photograph in Flores' Colonial Hotel room in Mexico City showing a house at Charcas, San Luis Potosí, the sleuths were able to locate his family. Newspapers announced that the police were investigating connections in San Luis Potosí and in Los Angeles, California, and subsequent elaborations in the press indicated that the Los Angeles connection was considered to be a supporter of Vasconcelismo.

Very cruel tortures were applied to Daniel Flores. In addition, the would-be assassin underwent the agony of seeing a faked shooting of his father. But all the efforts to show that any person or group had been behind the action of Flores were fruitless. After mentioning physical tortures and describing mental tortures that were applied to Flores in order to cause him to give names of those "intellectually" responsible for the crime, Portes Gil writes: "If I did not then resign as Minister of Gobernación, it was so that I would not be thought to be trying to escape the judgment of responsibility, to which I had already practically been submitted." Portes Gil provides his readers with a letter showing that officials were seeking to link the crime to himself, Calles, Cedillo, Marte R. Gómez, and Gonzalo N. Santos.[2]

At a meeting of the Partido Laborista Mexicano on June 8, 1930, Luis N. Morones hurled one of his verbal blasts at Portes Gil, mentioning also the names of Cedillo, Marte R. Gómez, and Gonzalo Santos. The labor leader accused Portes Gil of sending, when he was Provisional President, Gobernación employees to Los Angeles, California, in connection with a plot to kill Ortiz Rubio.

On the next day Portes Gil made public a letter which he wrote asking President Ortiz Rubio to investigate the accusation of Morones. He sent copies of his letter to Foreign Minister Genaro Estrada and Carlos Riva Palacio, who had by then succeeded Portes Gil as Ortiz Rubio's Gobernación Minister. The President replied that he could not "give credit to the accusation which Sr. Morones has publicly made," and those who had received copies of Portes Gil's letter agreed that they had no data supporting the accusation of Morones. In a press declaration Portes Gil called Morones a "vile slanderer."

A number of persons who had favored Vasconcelos and strongly criticized the "Callista despotism" were arrested in Mexico City even before Ortiz Rubio's woeful inauguration-day experience. But after that event Vasconcelistas had a much rougher time of it, as military authorities stepped up their activities under the orders of General Eulogio Ortiz, the fierce military commander of the Valley of Mexico. Antirreeleccionistas mysteriously disappeared, and, their whereabouts and condition unknown to their families, they underwent unpleasant pressures by investigators who sought to get them to confess that conspiracies had been hatched at the office of Lic. Medellín Ostos. Detectives found it expedient to pretend that they were Vasconcelistas planning a rebellion, and to note the reaction of their intended victims. Under these circumstances the old Revolutionary general, León Ibarra, was grabbed at Texcoco.

Ibarra and scores of others were ordered to be interned at the Hacienda de Narvarte, barracks of the Fifty-first Cavalry Regiment

[2] Emilio Portes Gil, *Quince años de política mexicana*, pp. 402, 410–430.

(commanded by General Maximino Avila Camacho). There in incommodious and gloomy cells they bore with questioning and tortures. A little later a great many of them were carted in trucks at night to a hill near the town of Topilejo, between Mexico City and Cuernavaca. After helping dig their own graves (an impossibility for the infirm and tortured Ibarra), the prisoners were hanged and then buried. Such, we are told, was the industry of Eulogio Ortiz and his collaborators that this was the fate of about sixty Vasconcelistas.

Unlike the shooting of Francisco Serrano and his companions, an event quickly publicized by its authors, the Topilejo slaughter was a matter of deep secrecy so that relatives and friends of the victims knew no more than that they had simply vanished. But the principal fact, that of their ultimate fate, accidentally came to light on Sunday, March 9, when a hungry dog unearthed pieces of bodies at the Topilejo hill. The subsequent search resulted in press releases which mentioned over one hundred bodies. Relatives of missing Vasconcelistas went to the Juárez Hospital, where the remains of the Topilejo victims were taken after the discovery. Although the corpses were in a condition of extreme disintegration, post-mortems disclosed that the victims had been strangled about a month earlier. By means of remains of clothing a number of bodies, including those of General León Ibarra, an engineering student named Ricardo González Villa, and a laborer, were identified.

After Ibarra's body had been identified by his daughter, his brother filed an accusation against Eulogio Ortiz. Lic. José C. Aguilar had a long and unsatisfacory interview with Attorney General Aguilar y Maya; and Antirreeleccionista Party President Victorio E. Góngora sent Ortiz Rubio a telegram asking for an investigation and pointing out that the victims had been seized quite unconstitutionally. The Senate received a strong protest which stressed that relatives of those who had been hanged were finding the "doors of justice" solidly closed against them. The Senate did not act nor did the press publish this protest.

Eulogio Ortiz issued a statement in which he said that investigations had followed the attempt to assassinate Ortiz Rubio. He explained further that the preposterous and contradictory accounts of events were a manifestation of the "reaction's" desire to discredit the governmental institutions emanating from the Revolution. These malevolent rumors, he said, were absolutely false; and he asserted that the splendid principles which united the members of the Revolutionary family would never succumb to the contamination desired by the "reaction."[3]

An armored car with bullet-proof glass one inch thick was now constructed for the use of President Ortiz Rubio.[4]

[3] Something about the Topilejo killings may be found in Mauricio Magdaleno's *Las palabras perdidas,* but the most complete account is that given in Alfonso Taracena's book on the subject, *Los Vasconcelistas sacrificados en Topilejo.*

[4] Archivo Casasola, *Historia gráfica de la Revolución,* p. 1935.

56·

Rough Times
for the Convalescent

In the weeks during which President Ortiz Rubio was secluded in the Castle of Chapultepec, recovering from the physical effects of the assault by Flores and under doctors' orders not to use his voice, appointments were made to the secondary positions in the Administration. The friends of Don Pascual complained that they were given no consideration by the Callistas in the case of these appointments and they noted that, in contrast to the quiet at the President's residence, there were "continual political comings and goings" at Calles' house in the nearby Anzures Colony. "Calles," insists Puig Casauranc, "was the one who in those weeks instilled

491

First Cabinet meeting ("*Acuerdo Colectivo*") of President Ortiz Rubio. *Clockwise around table:* J. M. Puig Casauranc, Juan de Dios Bojórquez, José Aguilar y Maya, Luis Montes de Oca, Juan Andreu Almazán, Aarón Sáenz, Manuel Pérez Treviño, Julio Freyssinier Morín, Emilio Portes Gil, President Pascual Ortiz Rubio (*bandaged*), Joaquín Amaro, Luis L. León, Agustín Mora (*Jefe del Estado Mayor*). *March 20, 1930. Enrique Díaz.*

confidence, implanted discipline, calmed the friends of the President, and at the same time placated certain friends of Portes Gil who were (like Morones in 1928) unjustly, absurdly pointed to now as being the instigators of the crime."[1]

One morning about two weeks after the assassination attempt, this verse painted in clear red letters appeared on one of the walls of Chapultepec Castle:

> AQUI VIVE EL PRESIDENTE;
> Y EL QUE MANDA VIVE ENFRENTE.
> (Here lives the President;
> He who rules lives across the way—
> reference to Anzures.)

A few months after the inauguration, Ing. Pani was back in Mexico for a vacation from his ministry abroad. No admirer of Ortiz Rubio, he maintains that the President might well have taken advantage of the crime to consolidate his position. "If on the following day or a few days later he had walked—bandaged in case his wound would make that necessary—entirely alone in the streets which took him to his office, he would have been followed by a multitude acclaiming him." His seclusion "behind bricks and mortar," according to Pani, "was considered as a manifestation of fear, . . . enough . . . to lose all the authority of his office. More than that, the people got fed up with his considerable ability to isolate himself."[2]

On February 26, three weeks after the attempt on his life, President Ortiz Rubio let it be known in a radio message that his health had improved sufficiently to allow him to work. He reaffirmed his determination to follow the constructive program announced in his inauguration address. His first public act was to attend, on March 3, a ceremony wherein a flag was presented to athletes departing to participate in the Central American Olympic Games in Cuba.

Ortiz Rubio was still bandaged (across the head and around the neck) when he appeared at his first Cabinet meeting at the Chapultepec Castle on March 20. He called his Cabinet meetings *acuerdos colectivos* (collective agreements). Calles, although he had no official position, was present then (as he was at a similar meeting on

---

[1] J. M. Puig Casauranc, *Galatea rebelde a varios pigmaliones*, p. 364.
[2] Alberto J. Pani, *Apuntes autobiográficos* (one-volume edition), p. 393.

April 25). A social security law was discussed; also a federal labor law, on which much work had been done during Portes Gil's Administration.

The Revolutionary agrarian program called forth heated debate. At the *acuerdo colectivo* of March 20 Calles spoke. Following his recent return from Europe he had made some statements criticizing the agrarian program in Mexico. Now, surrounded by President Ortiz Rubio and his Cabinet, he expounded his new point of view, forcefully criticizing, "in a serene and measured tone," all that had been done to date. The division of lands, he explained, was hurting the nation's economy.

Portes Gil replied to Calles and advised the President that the government was pledged to support the Revolutionary program of land division. Pointing out that 15,000 or 20,000 towns had received no land, he suggested that the President proceed with the program more rapidly than ever, adding that what failures there might be were due to those in charge of executing the program, but not to the program itself.

Luis León and Pérez Treviño backed Portes Gil. Finance Minister Montes de Oca and others agreed with Calles. President Ortiz Rubio, says Portes Gil, "limited himself to making notes on what happened in the meeting and nothing was definitely resolved."[3]

Whether or not anything was definitely resolved about the agrarian matter at that or at subsequent *acuerdos colectivos*, the program of land redistribution was soon slowed down. Such redistributions, which had exceeded one million hectares in 1929, approximated 740.000 in 1930, 610,000 in 1931, and 348,000 in 1932. Early in 1931 the federal government gave Zacatecas thirty days and Coahuila sixty days within which to present remaining requests for land redistribution; after the time limits the local agrarian commissions were to be dissolved. So it was for various states.

It is rather interesting to note, however, that it was during the Ortiz Rubio administration that some agrarian leaders in Congress were able to push through, at the end of 1931, a decree which realized the aims of Lic. Lauro Caloca and which ended any further possibility of the *hacendados* continuing to use *amparos* (injunctions) to tie up expropriation rulings in the courts. The original law of January 6, 1915, had allowed those losing property to make use of *amparos*. During Portes Gil's Administration the Supreme

[3] Emilio Portes Gil, *Quince años de política mexicana*, p. 407.

Court judges whom he named had resolved against the Supreme Court's granting *amparos* in *ejido* cases; but *amparos* continued to be granted by the lower courts until the Congress acted in December, 1931.

The presidential bandages were removed on April 1, 1930.

While the President was inspecting the construction of the Gran Boulevard across Lake Texcoco, Díaz Babio had occasion to discuss with his fellow engineer, President Ortiz Rubio, the crime of inauguration day. The President appears to have been happiest when concerned with new public works, and unhappiest when concerned with politics.

Here is the conversation as recorded by Ing. Díaz Babio:

THE PRESIDENT: I called that poor Flores—talked with him. General Carlos Real, the director of the Prison of Santiago, brought him to me at Chapultepec. They had treated the poor boy very badly, so I have given orders that he be given every consideration compatible with his situation.

DIAZ BABIO: Didn't you feel like killing him when you saw him?

THE PRESIDENT: No, I didn't. He's the least guilty of all.

DIAZ BABIO: Then who *is* guilty?

THE PRESIDENT: Congress. I brought up serious charges about improper conduct there, and this was the result [pointing to his wound]. That is, you know what they say about Calles, Morones, and the C.R.O.M. with respect to the assassination of Gen. Obregón?

DIAZ BABIO: Why, yes—that they set up a favorable atmosphere for the committing of the crime.

THE PRESIDENT: Well, this was exactly the same thing.

DIAZ BABIO: You can count on me, General; let me help you.

THE PRESIDENT: No. I would rather nothing be said. The wound is mine. It isn't wise to talk now; it would just complicate the political situation all the more. We must have peace if we are going to develop our activities for the good of the Mexican people. Look here, if it weren't for the complications my resignation would make, I would have resigned already. If I had known all this, I never would have gotten into this. There is a remedy for all this but I don't want bloodshed; it doesn't help the country. Perhaps next year—

DIAZ BABIO: You know, General, that I am your friend and I promise you that I shall never say anything that would harm you or break your confidence. Tell me who attacked you—

THE PRESIDENT: It was when I was in Baltimore, recovering in Johns

Hopkins Hospital. The Congress was completely made up of Callistas, managed by Melchor Ortega, Gonzalo N. Santos, and Manuel Riva Palacio. These men were wasting the internal budget of the Congress and I couldn't tolerate it. As our plans for reform included the moralization of politics, I tried to end that group, in agreement with Diputado Federico Medrano, an honest and honorable man. So a movement was started to knock out the profiteering leaders. Good progress was being made, with a congressional split developing: the "Whites," headed by Medrano, and the "Reds" headed by the trio I just mentioned. This was the situation when Pérez Treviño, president of the P.N.R., joined me in Baltimore. All of a sudden he invented some pretext to leave me and came back to Mexico. Melchor Ortega, having investigated the situation, had got in touch with Pérez Treviño in Baltimore to tell him that the "Whites" had won and that he was almost certain to be expelled, together with Santos and Riva Palacio. Pérez Treviño intrigued with Calles and various other influential politicians, who came close to winning, but the triumph of the "Whites" was too definite. I have good reason to believe that these were the events that brought on the attack of which I was the victim.[4]

After recording this interview, Díaz Babio notes that President Ortiz Rubio did not have Flores killed. However, Daniel Flores was not long for this world, for he died in his cell on April 22, 1932, after being sentenced on March 1, 1931, to spend 19 years, 9 months and 18 days in prison.

Less than one week after the President received his wound, Professor Basilio Vadillo was named head of the P.N.R., a position left vacant when General Pérez Treviño became Minister of Agriculture. Sr. Matías Rodríguez succeeded Ing. Luis León as the Party's secretary.

It has been explained that Ortiz Rubio had a hand in these appointments of the P.N.R.'s new leaders. For those who were concerned about the President's political strength and prestige, it was hard to overemphasize the importance of having the P.N.R. headed by Professor Vadillo, who came to be regarded as a "man of the President." Elections to the federal Congress were to take place on the first Sunday of July, 1930, and the President's political future would very considerably depend upon the outcome. In spite of beautiful statements about how all were either working together or

[4] Francisco Díaz Babio, *Un drama nacional*, pp. 167–169.

496

should work together, the truth of the matter is that the struggle between the "Whites" and the "Reds" could hardly have been more acrimonious.

It was advisable that the relations between the president of the P.N.R., now a political factor of tremendous weight, and the Minister of Gobernación be such that the two men work as a team. But this was in no way the case. Vadillo co-operated with Ortiz Rubio. He also worked closely in Congress with Colonel Ignacio de la Mora, who was one of the "Whites" battling Santos, Riva Palacio, and Ortega and whose efforts in behalf of bettering things took the form of charges implicating Calles in the receipt of 80,000 pesos.

Unlike Professor Vadillo, Gobernación Minister Portes Gil did not get along at all with the President.

Early in March, 1930, Vadillo stated that in the July congressional elections "candidates of conviction and true representatives of the people" must be chosen. At the offices of the P.N.R.'s executive committee it was announced that "President Ortiz Rubio does not recommend candidates, staying clear of electoral matters; the people have absolute liberty to place their confidence in those who deserve it." Then early in the next month the P.N.R.'s executive committee accused the congressional Permanent Commission of seeking to eliminate it.

At this point Calles, perhaps forgetting some of his earlier words about not being a political factor, stepped into the picture in order to bring to an end the unhappy situation created by the P.N.R.'s differences with the Gobernación Ministry and the Permanent Commission. Much to the annoyance of the "Whites" he arranged, late in April, to have Portes Gil replace Vadillo as president of the Party. He also arranged to have his friend Colonel Carlos Riva Palacio become President Ortiz Rubio's Gobernación Minister. Professor Vadillo was given the honor of representing Mexico in Uruguay.

Ortiz Rubio, whose "Whites" had thus been badly whipped, accompanied the Cabinet and a large bloc of congressmen as they heard the words of the P.N.R.'s new president at the Teatro Ideal. There Portes Gil proclaimed that the July 6 elections would be the last ones in which the re-election of representatives and senators would be allowed.

These July congressional elections were an overwhelming triumph for the P.N.R. Not a single opposition candidate got a seat, with the result that not a few felt that all the hopes expressed by

Calles in 1928 and 1929 as to the vote were unfulfilled in this congressional election, the first since those statements.

Not long after the congressional election, Dr. Puig Casauranc resigned as head of the Federal District. He left for Europe. ("One of my purposes in leaving the country one week after the election was to avoid any seeming intervention by leaders of Calles' campaign at the time of discussing the congressional credentials.") The President's friend and secretary, Colonel Hernández Cházaro, who for the many who were maneuvering against Ortiz Rubio was the center of dislike, lasted as Federal District head only a few hours; then he, too, sailed for Europe. When Hernández Cházaro returned from abroad it was to "withdraw to some state capital," following Calles' advice. He joined Colonel Ignacio de la Mora, once the active congressional "White" and by then governor of Jalisco. There, in Guadalajara, Hernández Cházaro spoke out against Calles, whom he accused of not allowing Ortiz Rubio to govern in peace. After that he left for Texas, where he took the position of Mexican consul in San Antonio. De la Mora before long was deposed from the governorship. President Ortiz Rubio had lost, in "thin man" Hernández Cházaro, a man who worked in his behalf without much hesitation. To make matters worse, the President found himself with a new private secretary who was "an element put there by Calles."[5]

Shortly after the inauguration of Ortiz Rubio, Russia's recent representative to Mexico, Dr. Alejandro de Makar, made his turbulent departure. From Mexico City he reached the Hotel Imperial in Veracruz on February 9. There he was advised that his baggage had been stolen. His interpretation was different. Officials, he complained, not only took his baggage keys but took also Dr. Makar himself, holding him for three and one-half hours while they went through most of his books and documents. He complained that his baggage, which had not been stolen, was opened against his protest. As far as his mission was concerned, he declared to the press: "I received instructions to go."

One of the most publicized achievements of the Ortiz Rubio Administration in the field of foreign affairs was provoked by revolutions in Argentina, Bolivia, and Peru which set the President and his Foreign Minister, Genaro Estrada, to considering the question of the recognition of governments following such uprisings.

[5] J. M. Puig Casauranc, *op. cit.*, p. 399.

498

Recalling all that had preceded the recognition of the Obregón Government by the United States and other world powers, they issued in September, 1930, the "Estrada Doctrine." In it Mexico declared that "No country should ask for that which, because of the sovereignty of her own people, she already possesses through inherent right." Others in Latin America hailed Mexico's insistence that powerful nations should not interrupt diplomatic relations with their weaker sisters merely because of some revolutionary changes in administration. The great powers, they said, should not impede such changes nor use the threat of nonrecognition as a means of unjustified intervention in internal matters. By some of its admirers the "Estrada Doctrine" was also called the "Mexican Doctrine," or even the "Ortiz Rubio Doctrine," and was ranked along with the Monroe Doctrine and Woodrow Wilson's Fourteen Points.[6]

When Ortiz Rubio offered a diplomatic post to General Francisco J. Múgica the offer met with a cool reception. As head of the penal colony at the Islas Marías in the Pacific, Múgica had been having ample correspondence with his friend Lázaro Cárdenas, part of it about projects for their state of Michoacán. He received also a letter from Ortiz Rubio, his old rival in Michoacán struggles. The President, wishing to let bygones be bygones, expressed a "special desire" to name Múgica minister plenipotentiary and envoy extraordinary of Mexico to the Republic of Salvador; but the desire went unrealized when Múgica declined the offer, requesting that he be permitted to continue with his work in the penal colony.

Newspaper headlines in the late 1920's frequently featured the exploits of aviators who sought to follow in the footsteps of Charles A. Lindbergh and who were daring pioneers in the new skill of linking distant points. During the first part of 1928 Roberto Fierro was enthusiastically acclaimed by President Calles and others after he made a fourteen-hour nonstop flight from Mexicali, Lower California, to Mexico City, not only because he gave prestige to Mexican aviators but also because his plane had been constructed on Mexican soil.[7] About two months later crowds of people in Mexico City attended the burial of Captain Emilio Carranza, whose remains were brought back after he had flown from Mexico to Washington, D.C., and then suffered a fatal accident.

[6] See discussion of this doctrine in Luis G. Franco's *Relaciones exteriores en una actuación histórica*.

[7] Enriqueta de Parodi, *Abelardo L. Rodríguez*, pp. 322–323.

During the first part of 1929 the Mexican "aces" were useful and busy making trouble for the Escobar rebels. Captain Manuel Robles M. lost his life in the action at La Cruz, Sinaloa, but Lieutenant Colonels Pablo Sidar and Roberto Fierro were living heroes by the time the rebellion was suffocated, and they were ready to risk their lives in peaceful but dramatic endeavors. Pablo Sidar, who had been quite often in the company of Calles, spent the month of September, 1929, on a triumphal flight through the nations of Central and South America. Miguel Colorado, using a plane belonging to Calles, tried to make a nonstop flight from Mexicali to Mérida, Yucatán, and although the plane crashed at Los Mochis, Sinaloa, the aviator escaped unharmed.

Early in the regime of Ortiz Rubio, Pablo Sidar was commissioned to make a nonstop flight, together with Captain Pablo Rovirosa, from Mexico to Buenos Aires. These aviators, who were to take a message of friendship to the Argentine people and army, left Mexico City's Balbuena Airport in the plane *Morelos* on May 2, 1930. They landed at an airfield which had been prepared on Cerro Loco, Oaxaca, on the Isthmus of Tehuantepec, and there they made the arrangements necessary for the nonstop trip to Buenos Aires. They set out again on the early morning of May 11, but unfortunately the plane fell into the sea during a storm off of Costa Rica and both aviators were killed. After recovery of the bodies military honors were provided by the government of Costa Rica. Later the bodies lay in state for a while at Mexico's Palacio Nacional before being buried at the Dolores graveyard.

Undeterred by this disaster, Roberto Fierro in the next month flew from Los Angeles to New York on a flight which lost much of its glamour when motor trouble made a number of stops necessary. However, Fierro's flight from New York to Mexico City was made without stops and upon his return to the capital he was warmly received by Mexican officials.

57·

The Great Depression Sets In

Under the direction of Luis Montes de Oca, a man of intelligence, culture, and honesty, the Finance Ministry was performing a good job. In 1929 the federal books showed, in spite of the Escobar rebellion, a surplus of 24 million pesos. As far as cash on hand was concerned, the Treasury and some dependencies reported 18 million pesos at the end of 1929, then 20.5 million on the day that Ortiz Rubio took office, and on July 31, 1930, about 29.5 million. Economies necessitated by the rebellion had a beneficial effect and much attention was given to tax collections. Tobacco taxes were increased. Income taxes, which amounted in those days to about 7 per cent of net income, were simplified.

But the financial results mentioned above were attained by means of Mexico's failure to make payments due on foreign bonds and on most domestic bond issues. With certain exceptions, payments on federal domestic bond issues had been suspended in 1928. The arrangements for servicing foreign bonds, made in 1925, had not produced any remittances since 1928, and the holders of bonds of the Mexican National Railways had received no payments since 1926. Montes de Oca, as has been noted, had in 1928 proposed the consolidation of the various federal direct foreign debt issues into one issue bearing no more than 5 per cent annual interest redeemable in no fewer than forty-five years. On January 25, 1929, the Portes Gil Administration had authorized the Finance Minister to deal with foreign creditors about the foreign debt but before anything could be done the Escobar rebellion had broken out.

By the early part of 1930 economic conditions in Mexico did not, generally speaking, seem to be bad. True, there were some clouds on the horizon. Exports such as oil, metals, and cotton were reflecting weaknesses in the world markets and were being afforded some special assistance in the fiscal legislation which went into effect on January 1, 1930. (Reductions were made in the taxes affecting petroleum and cotton production; low-grade mines, new mines, and mines which had not been worked for at least ten years were given the opportunity to receive some production tax reduction.) But the government's income continued to exceed its disbursements and the situation at least appeared healthy enough in the middle of 1930 for Montes de Oca to follow the footsteps of Adolfo de la Huerta and Alberto Pani in making a trip to New York to negotiate pending matters with the International Bankers Committee.

On foreign debts Mexico's position in 1930, as the result of the 1922 and 1925 agreements and of the passage of time, was as follows:

Debt owed	$274,700,000.00 U.S.Cy.	(railway debt not included)
Back interest	211,100,000.00 " " "	(accumulated and due)
	$485,800,000.00 " " "	
Railway debt	$239,600,000.00 U.S.Cy.	(separated from above, in 1925)
Back interest	147,500,000.00 " " "	(accumulated and due)
	$387,100,000.00 " " "	

The Finance Minister considered the foreign debt to be just one phase of an integrated plan covering all aspects of the public debt, a plan which would be unfolded step by step. In addition to foreign obligations, the Mexican government had as of 1929 debts of about

600,000,000 pesos owed to its own citizens, of which amount about 400,000,000 pesos consisted of the agrarian debt and the interest.[1]

Ambassador Dwight Morrow, who had been away from Mexico when President Ortiz Rubio took office, returned on June 3, 1930, from his successful New Jersey senatorial campaign and at once interested himself in the negotiations about the Mexican debt. Giving particular attention to the Mexican internal debt and to obligations which were being discussed by the Mixed Claims Commissions, he came out in opposition to the plans being developed by Montes de Oca in his conversations with Lamont. Morrow felt that these plans discriminated against the holders of other Mexican obligations who were not represented by the strong International Bankers Committee.[2] It cannot be said that Morrow held with President Ortiz Rubio the same cordial and confidential relationship which he had had with Presidents Calles and Portes Gil. Nor had his usefulness in Mexico been increased when on April 23 Colonel Macnab, in the course of Morrow's recent political campaign, made a speech in which he described the Ambassador as having directed the departments of the Mexican government, taught finance to the Mexican Finance Minister, and "put Mexico on her feet and given her a strong government."[3]

On July 25, 1930, the Finance Minister signed the Montes de Oca-Lamont Agreement. The fifteen different issues making up the nonrailway debt were consolidated into a new issue bearing 5 per cent annual interest and amounting to $267,493,250.00 U.S. currency. The large item for back interest was cancelled. It was arranged that interest and principal on the new issue would be paid off in a series of annual installments of 15 million dollars each, starting in 1936. Prior to 1936 the payments were not quite so great, e.g., 12.5 million dollars were called for in 1931. (At the time it was felt that these annual payments would amount to about 10 per cent of the Mexican annual federal budget.) The guarantee was to be all the foreign trade taxes. The agent of the International Bankers Committee was eliminated. Starting in 1936 the payments were to be handled by the Bank of Mexico, acting as agent of the Mexican government.[4]

The direct debt agreement was accompanied by a memorandum

[1] Edgar Turlington, *Mexico and Her Foreign Creditors*, p. 334.
[2] Harold Nicolson, *Dwight Morrow*, p. 385.　　　　[3] *Ibid.*, p. 382.
[4] Secretaría de Hacienda y Crédito Público, "Convenio Montes de Oca-Lamont," typescript in the official files.

concerning the railways. The financial obligations of the railways were to be reduced to $225,000,000.00 U.S. currency in bonds of a new issue. The executive branch of the Mexican government planned to reorganize the railways by forming a new company in which the government would have 65 per cent of the shares of stock, instead of its former holdings of slightly over 50 per cent. Efficiency was to be studied by a Comisión Reorganizadora, which, rather than reduce personnel, would arrange to invest, over six years, up to 24 million dollars in badly needed new works. This new 24-million-dollar debt was to be a preferential mortgage debt.

During the days which preceded the signing of the agreement in New York on July 25, not only did Montes de Oca receive from Morrow a clear expression of opposition to what was being negotiated, but he also found himself receiving from Mexico reports which were not heartening; financial reports from Undersecretary Rafael Mancera O. and reports showing a drop in railroad carloadings. Toward the end of his stay in New York, Montes de Oca expressed to Lamont some apprehension regarding Mexico's ability to comply with the new agreement, which he said had yet to be presented to the Mexican Congress for its approval. It was arranged that from the Mexican government's cash surplus of 30 million pesos (that is, about fifteen million dollars) five million dollars would be placed in the Banco Nacional de México to be available to the International Bankers Committee in case this congressional ratification should be forthcoming.

In Mexico on August 15, 1930, a presidential *acuerdo colectivo* approved the Montes de Oca-Lamont Agreement, but thereafter things took a decided turn for the worse with the federal budget and cash position. As revenues began to decline in August, 1930, it became clear that the 1931 federal expenditures, budgeted in July, 1930, at about 300 million pesos, would not be covered by revenues.

The year 1931 was quite a year.

Following an *acuerdo colectivo* in January, drastic steps were taken to reduce budgeted expenditures in all the ministries. As the year went on it appeared that revenues would fall short of the 300-million-peso budget by about 80 million pesos. It became necessary to reduce government personnel to a minimum, and in addition to reduce military and bureaucratic salaries of all who were getting over three pesos daily. Wage reductions were 10 per cent, 12.5 per cent, or 15 per cent, depending on what wage was received. These steps became effective on August 1, 1931.

Since such savings were estimated to amount to 60 million pesos annually it became necessary to make some increases in taxes, which to date and in order to stimulate business had been relatively low. New emergency taxes were placed on tobacco, matches, beer, pulque, sparkling water, and woolen goods; also on the production of electric power and on the use of federal waters. Taxes were placed on incomes received by Mexicans abroad, and studies were made regarding taxes on inheritances and gifts. One of the emergency taxes, the 1 per cent tax on the gross incomes of industry, commerce, and agriculture, resulted in the assembly of a convention of protest, but was upheld by the Executive. During the difficult days of balancing the 1931 budget Montes de Oca put in long hours, many of them with such hard-working assistants as Joaquín Nortega, acting head of the Technical Fiscal Department, and Gustavo R. Velasco, Director of the Budget.

The Mexican silver peso, which had for so long held at nearly fifty cents U.S. Currency began to decline. During the latter part of June, 1931, while President Hoover was speaking of a one-year moratorium on all inter-government debts, the U.S. dollar was quoted as worth 2.04 gold pesos and 2.55 silver pesos. The quotation for silver had dropped to 28⅞ cents U.S. Currency per ounce. Copper was quoted at 8¾ cents U.S. currency per pound; lead, at 4.4 cents U.S. currency; and zinc, at 3.95 cents U.S. currency.

Books and articles which came out against the ratification of the Montes de Oca-Lamont Agreement included the attacks by Lic. Toribio Esquivel Obregón, a noted lawyer and historian who had been Finance Minister in the Cabinet of Victoriano Huerta. Ing. Francisco Vázquez del Mercado pointed out, in *La Deuda Exterior de México*, that the International Bankers Committee did not represent the bondholders. In *Las Objeciones al Convenio Montes de Oca-Lamont* Salvador Mendoza showed that whereas in July, 1930, the cost of 12.5 million dollars was 27 million silver pesos, the cost in December, 1930, was 34 million silver pesos. In the Veracruz state legislature there were objections to the Agreement and there were suggestions for postponing payments on the foreign debts.

On January 31, 1931, the Finance Ministry received an irrevocable *acuerdo* to advise officially the International Bankers Committee that due to the drop in the value of the peso the government had not submitted the Agreement for congressional ratification and could not do so while it stood in its original form. At the same time the Finance Minister was authorized to sign a Supplementary Agreement with the committee whereby the payments due in 1931 and 1932 would be made in silver money, using the exchange rate which had been in effect on July 25, 1930.

In his September 1, 1931, report to the Congress, President Ortiz Rubio touched on other government debts. In connection with the National Banking Debt he cited the August 30, 1930, decree liquidating the old banks of issue if said banks were not in complete solvency. In connection with the agrarian debt, he remarked that normal service payments had been made except in 1931. He added that now projected was a new law to take care of pending and future indemnifications by issuing bonds in excess of the 50-million-peso amount provided by the law of January 10, 1920. (This step, incidentally, would seem to have been long overdue.) Payments awarded by the Mixed Claims Commissions needed attention. The Congress, said the President, had spent practically all of its extended special session of 1931 in debates about the new federal labor law, in spite of the fact that in asking for the special session the President had requested that matters related to the foreign and domestic debt also be studied. He hoped, he said, that these financial matters would be studied in the regular session which he was opening.

The Comisión Reguladora de Cambios, created at the end of 1930 to work with the banks in an attempt to stabilize the peso's relation to the dollar, had a difficult and unsuccessful time. Mexico had an unfavorable balance of trade, and capital was fleeing the country. Gold, which had become scarce and of high value in relation to silver, was smuggled out of the country and became more of an international merchandise than a monetary factor.

In view of these circumstances an important new monetary law was issued on June 25, 1931. It was called the "Plan Calles" and was the work of Luis Montes de Oca, aided by such experts as Manuel Gómez Morín and Luciano Wiechers. In it gold was demonetarized, and its free commerce was authorized, domestically and abroad. Free and unlimited power of legal tender was given to the silver *peso fuerte* with the old parity of 0.75 grams of gold.

In order to sustain the value of the silver peso and not to increase the circulating stock, the government had for some time adopted the policy of not coining new silver pesos. (As early as March, 1930, the Executive had issued a decree prohibiting the reimportation of silver coins exported earlier when the silver price had been higher.) The Plan Calles included a prohibition against coining new one-peso silver pieces.

At the same time considerable attention was given to the Bank of Mexico and to its issuance of bank notes in accordance with the needs of commerce. The Bank was deprived of its functions of an ordinary bank competing with private banks. It was to give attention to its duties as a central bank of rediscount. Occupying itself with monetary problems, it was "to issue notes against gold, at the legal parity, whenever this was made possible by the state of our balance of accounts or from the rediscounting of commercial paper; but, always, against an additional metallic reserve of 50 per cent."[5]

A Junta Central Bancaria was created to watch over the common reserves which backed public deposits. This "Junta," presided over by the Finance Minister, included representatives of private banks and of the Bank of Mexico.

General Calles became president of the Bank of Mexico.

The Plan Calles eliminated the disturbing factor caused by the new relation between silver and gold. It contributed to a monetary contraction which it attributed to "the period of liquidation which we are going through, which would be grave if permanent, and so the law has left open the possibility of creating new moneys."[6] It did not claim to be a cure-all of economic problems which were dependent on production, etc.

The Plan Calles was acclaimed by Congress, where there were shouts of: "Long live silver!" and "Death to gold!" Later in the year the governors of twenty states gathered in Mexico City in order to honor General Calles at a banquet given for the purpose of expressing the governors' appreciation to him for having formulated the Plan Calles.

On July 27, 1931, the newspaper *Universal* announced the obligation of banks and others to receive the legal amount of silver in payment of obligations contracted in gold. Dollars continued to be quoted as worth 2.04 gold pesos and 2.55 silver pesos.

Following the example of the United States, Mexico reformed its customs tariffs on a basis which was frankly protectionist.

[5] Secretaría de Hacienda y Crédito Público, *La Hacienda Pública a través de los informes presidenciales*, p. 549.
[6] *Ibid.* See President's message to Congress, September 1, 1931.

58·

Pani Returns
to the Finance Ministry

D uring his vacation in Mexico Ing. Alberto J. Pani was honored by an impressive banquet attended by the President. Then he returned to his Paris post, going by way of New York, where he boarded the *Bremen*. Before setting sail he received from Mr. Lamont a confidential copy of the Montes de Oca-Lamont Agreement. After studying it on the ship he sent a long memorandum from Paris to President Ortiz Rubio, criticizing this new foreign-debt arrangement. He objected to the fact that the debt being assumed by Mexico considerably exceeded the prevailing market quotations for the defaulted bonds, and he also objected to the payment base in dollars. To leave no doubt about this whole matter Pani followed up his memorandum with a series of letters to the President.

With the fall of the Spanish monarchy Mexico raised its diplomatic post in Spain from a ministry to an embassy. Pani received a telegram from Calles asking him if he would like to be the first Mexican ambassador to Madrid. After replying that he would, Pani received official advice of the appointment from President Ortiz Rubio.

It was therefore in Spain that Pani learned about the new Mexican monetary law known as the Plan Calles. Feeling that his missives to Ortiz Rubio about foreign debts had proved fruitless, he wrote to Calles at length, pointing out that the monetary steps which had been taken were having the opposite of the desired effects, since they were deflationary and created "a notorious insufficiency of circulating medium."

As we shall see, changes in Cabinet positions during the administration of Ortiz Rubio occurred very frequently. Although the President was remarkably steadfast in his efforts to co-operate with Calles, the relations between these two men appear to have been largely formal. Calles shuffled ministers around like a deck of cards, and in the course of one such change, that of October, 1931, Calles himself became Minister of War.

As he should have done, Luis Montes de Oca gave his loyalty clearly to President Ortiz Rubio. This became more and more evident, and a few have tried to show that his relations with Calles became less warm than formerly they had been. Montes de Oca was not lacking in loyalty to Calles, but by supporting the President he did not endear himself to various politicians who surrounded Calles. When Montes de Oca's name came up in connection with political matters, friends of Manuel Pérez Treviño and Carlos Riva Palacio intimated that the Finance Minister was opposing the work of Calles, and they made the Finance Minister a center of political agitation, creating, says Ortiz Rubio, "another problem for the government."[1] All of this was at a time when intriguers were running to Calles, bringing him stories which would make the President appear foolish, and when incidents were carefully analyzed and blown up so as to give rise to "crises" in the Cabinet. We find Puig Casauranc analyzing the part played by Montes de Oca in two such incidents.

[1] Pascual Ortiz Rubio quoted in Juan Andreu Almazán's *Memorias* in *El Universal*, February 12, 1959.

As President of the P.N.R. Portes Gil in 1930 had made his remarks against the advisability of re-election of members of the legislative chambers. Late in 1931 Calles' oldest son Rodolfo (Sonora's governor) undertook the generally popular task of getting the Constitution amended to do away with re-elections, including presidential re-elections. In this effort Montes de Oca associated himself somewhat with Rodolfo, who had brought a group of fellow-governors with him to Mexico City. Montes de Oca and Rodolfo Calles were among those who at this time called on Almazán to try to persuade him to help them obtain the support of a few governors who were friends of his. But Puig Casauranc chose this occasion to tell the "Jefe Máximo" that his sons ought not be prominent in national politics. At the same time, and probably with more effectiveness, many federal congressmen made it clear that they deplored the step which was being taken. Whatever had been the original feeling of the "Jefe Máximo" about Rodolfo's crusade, he now suddenly brought down his "iron fist" against it in a manner which looked like a rebuff to Montes de Oca and Almazán.[2]

For the twelfth of December, 1931, the Catholic Church planned a service of commemoration at the Basilica of the Virgin of Guadalupe, this being the fourth centennial of the appearance of the image in the Cerro de Tepeyac. Some made a small fuss because the Finance Ministry arranged that a splendid organ to be played at the brilliant ceremony might be imported free of duty. (Sr. Montes de Oca has pointed out, in connection with this duty-free importation, that this was the forty-eighth incident of this nature, and, furthermore, that the objects used by the Church are the properties of the government.[3]) Railroad fares were reduced in order to allow the faithful to come to the ceremony. Among the many who attended this service at Guadalupe were members of the diplomatic corps and even some members of the Cabinet of President Ortiz Rubio. At the solemn ceremonies the officiating clergyman was the Archbishop of Mexico, Monseñor Pascual Díaz, who some months before had criticized the extinction of religious customs and had recommended the intensification of Catholic education. On the occasion of Ortiz Rubio's next Cabinet meeting, Calles rebuked those Cabinet ministers who had appeared at the Guadalupe service.

In a talk with Puig Casauranc Calles referred to the necessity of

---

[2] J. M. Puig Casauranc, *Galatea rebelde a varios pigmaliones*, pp. 395–397; also Juan Andreu Almazán in *El Universal*, January 28, 1959.

[3] Luis Montes de Oca, conversation.

"seeing that justice was done to men who had been away a long time, especially when, in the concrete cases of their separations, they were in the right." Calles made it clear that he was referring to Pani. He mentioned "the case of Morones, in which Pani was right . . . we must have him return to Hacienda." Soon after this the President, hoping for less political agitation, agreed to dump his Finance Minister and loyal supporter.

The next Cabinet revision after that of October 21, 1931, was announced on January 20, 1932. Those who were then replaced were Genaro Estrada (Foreign Relations), Aarón Sáenz (Industry, Commerce, and Labor), Freyssinier Morín (Comptroller) and Montes de Oca (Finance).

Pani received a telegram from Calles asking him whether he would again head the Finance Ministry. He accepted and a few days later received a telegram from President Ortiz Rubio advising that he had been named to succeed Montes de Oca. Some of the more pronounced leftists, who had objected to Montes de Oca on account of his moderate views, were not entirely appeased by reading in the newspapers that Pani was a "most extreme leftist radical."

Lic. Eduardo Suárez, who was later to become Finance Minister, feels that the shift from Sr. Montes de Oca to Ing. Pani was occasioned by the failure of the Plan Calles to give the desired results. Steps taken to give strength to the peso created such a scarcity of pesos that General Calles, says Suárez, was interested to see what the great critic of the Plan Calles, Ing. Pani, might be able to do.[4] Lic. Manuel Gómez Morín, who worked closely with both Montes de Oca and Pani and who might have been Finance Minister had Vasconcelos reached the presidency, also received the impression that the switch in Finance Ministers was based on difficulties caused by the extreme scarcity of money.[5] The silver peso in January, 1932, when the New York silver quotation was thirty cents U.S. currency per ounce, had the same relation to the dollar that it had when the Plan Calles was first issued, but such was the situation that federal government employees were sometimes behind in receiving their salaries, teachers in San Luis Potosí claimed to be 100 days behind in receiving their pay, and great demonstrations were made by the large ranks of unemployed. The C.R.O.M. petitioned the President to take steps against the closing down of places to

---

[4] Eduardo Suárez, interview, June 23, 1955.
[5] Manuel Gómez Morín, interview, September, 1956.

Labor leader Luis N. Morones *in jail, following his speech at a labor gathering at Los Mochis, Sinaloa, in the latter part of 1932. Casasola.*

work, and Sr. Morones criticized the Secretary of Industry, Commerce, and Labor, Lic. Aarón Sáenz.

The effect of the great depression on the National Railways of Mexico, whose 45,500 employees in 1930 were receiving about 63 million pesos in salaries, can be appreciated from the following tabulation:[6]

Year	Gross Revenues in Pesos
1928	112,264,723
1929	112,921,197
1930	107,520,558
1931	88,356,558
1932	73,460,461

To difficulties caused by the start of highway competition had been added the destruction of railroad property during the Cristero and Escobar rebellions; and following the last-mentioned, which had seen preferential use of the system given to the military, the government evaluated the damages at a figure considered by the railway management to be 2.5 million pesos too low. During 1930 a lack of rain decreased the movement of agricultural products, and as the depression unfolded there was a sharp drop in the movement of mineral products, which in 1929 had represented 26 per cent of the freight carried.

During 1928, 1929, and 1930 the Mexican railroad problem had been studied by various experts from the United States. A semiofficial Mexican commission to recommend reorganization and improvements was established in 1929. It was headed by General Calles and included Finance Minister Montes de Oca and Communications Minister Javier Sánchez Mejorada. During 1930 this commission came out with some recommendations which Ing. Javier Sánchez Mejorada, by then president of the railroad company's board of directors, proceeded to put into effect. A number of subsidiary railway lines or divisions were merged, and quite a few workers were laid off. As a result of this the Confederation of Transportation and Communications, representing the railroad employees, made various complaints about the unfairness of having the workers alone contribute to saving the National Lines, and it pointed to what it considered an unsatisfactory fuel contract with

[6] Vicente Fuentes Díaz, *El problema ferrocarrilero de México*, p. 105.

the Huasteca Petroleum Company. It asked for a new study by a "mixed commission" with delegates of the company, the laborers, and the government. Finally the labor representatives went directly to President Ortiz Rubio asking that the railroad reorganization be carried out without laying off any workers. The President, it is reported, "interpreted the words of the laborers as a threat" and on January 3, 1931, denied the formation of the "mixed commission," adding that the reorganization would be carried out as planned by the Calles commission.[7]

By 1932 the National Railways of Mexico had only about 35,000 employees, a reduction of over 10,000 since 1930.

After the representatives of laborers and business owners, who at Portes Gil's suggestion met in 1928 and 1929 to draft the labor law which Constitutional Article 123 called for, came up with some suggestions, Portes Gil was able to present his cherished project to Congress when it convened in September, 1929. He has stated that if no federal law was passed during his presidency, it was because of political maneuvers on the part of those who were to succeed the provisional government, and the projected law caused uneasiness "because of its advances in favor of workers."[8]

During the presidency of Ortiz Rubio not only was Avenida Nuevo México renamed Avenida Artículo 123, but representatives of labor and business drew up a new project for a federal labor law. It was based on the so-called Portes Gil Project, and those formulating it utilized the experience gained by various states in the application of their own labor laws, often quite at variance.[9]

As we have seen, President Ortiz Rubio in his September, 1931, message remarked that the 1931 special congressional session had been devoted almost entirely to debating the new federal labor law, to the exclusion of various urgent financial matters. Anyway, the special session, which started on May 22, accomplished something. The new labor law was approved by the Chamber of Deputies on July 20, 1931. On August 13 it was approved by the Senate, which, after many years in Empress Carlota's chapel in the Palacio Nacional, had just provisionally transferred its activities to the Green Room of the *diputados* prior to occupying its own new building.

[7] *Ibid.*, p. 119.
[8] Emilio Portes Gil, *Quince años de política mexicana*, p. 130.
[9] Alfonso López Aparicio, *El movimiento obrero en México*, p. 195.

And on August 28, 1931, the nation at last received, in the *Diario Oficial,* its Federal Labor Law which put into legislative form the provisions of Article 123 of the 1917 Constitution.

This famous article includes a call for a minimum wage, an eight-hour day, a six-day week, and double pay for overtime, and it also stipulates that employers shall be liable for accidents and occupational diseases and shall at their own expense provide comfortable and sanitary dwellings and compulsory schooling. It proclaims the legality of strikes, except when a majority of the strikers resort to violence or except in case of war when the strikers are in services dependent on the government. It speaks significantly about the handling of disputes between labor and capital. Such disputes, it says, shall be submitted for settlement to a board of conciliation and arbitration "to consist of an equal number of representatives of the workmen and of the employers and of one representative of the government." It says further that if the workmen should not accept the board's decision the labor contract shall be considered terminated, and that if the employer should refuse to submit the dispute to arbitration or should refuse to accept the board's decision, not only shall the labor contract therewith terminate but also the employer shall be bound to indemnify his workmen by the payment to each of three months' wages plus such additional liability which the dispute may have caused.

Such other liability was, in Articles 601 and 602 of the 1931 Federal Labor Law, established to be twenty days of salary for each employee for each year which he had worked for the employer in the past. Article 576 of this law gave, in the case of labor disputes, very broad powers to the boards of conciliation and arbitration so that they could in the case of each dispute order the institution of all sorts of conditions of work, among them wage scales, hours of work, and the increase or decrease of personnel. Among the Federal Labor Law's approximately 700 articles were important provisions leading to compulsory trade unionism. Unions were empowered to require that in the future employers hire only union members and fire such workers as might withdraw from the union.

Ing. Pani did not get to Mexico until the middle of February, 1932. He writes that he found conditions deplorable. "The illness of the public treasury at the start of 1932, I repeat, was incomparably more serious and difficult to cure than that of 1923. . . . acute monetary deflation; international instability of our exchange and total disappearance of credit; progressive paralysis of industry and commerce; lowering of salaries and increase in the number of unemployed; and as a consequence of all this, a precipitous decline in the federal income and an increasing deficit in Hacienda."[10]

The new Finance Minister calculated that the 1931 federal deficit was 28 million pesos. The difference between expenditures and receipts was actually 4 million, but Pani added about 24 million to take into account some overdue notes and advances and also some payments due on the agrarian and banking debts. The estimated deficit for 1932 was to be covered by using the fund which had been deposited with the Banco Nacional de México as a result of the Montes de Oca-Lamont Agreement, since no agreement concerning foreign debts had been approved by Congress. This sum of 5 million dollars had been returned to Montes de Oca by the International Bankers Committee when it was clear that general economic conditions then made absolutely impossible any agreement involving payments on the foreign debt.

On March 9, 1932, was issued a new law of monetary reform to replace the Plan Calles of the previous July 25. Quite unlike the Plan of 1931, Pani's new law provided for silver coinage by the Casa de Moneda at full capacity. In fact, control of coinage was taken from the Bank of Mexico and placed in the hands of the Finance Ministry. From the annual presidential message of 1933 we read: ". . . with the Secretaría de Hacienda authorized by the Law of March 9, 1932, to order an extraordinary coinage to the amount which would strictly correct the scarcity by means of exchange occasioned by the Law of July 25, 1931, confidence reappeared . . ."

The profit which was derived from producing silver coins containing less silver than the marked value was to be added to the legal reserves of the Bank of Mexico, allowing for the issuance of more paper currency. This paper money was freely convertible into the legal money, silver. The public could accept it if it wished, but government offices were obliged to accept it for all kinds of payments.

In announcing the new measures to the press on March 9, 1932, Pani expressed hope for an improvement in the silver price with respect to gold, a rather important matter for Mexico, whose currency was now on a silver basis and whose silver product was the

[10] Alberto J. Pani, *Mi contribución al nuevo régimen, 1910–1933*, p. 332.

world's largest. He referred to international efforts to persuade world opinion in favor of the rehabilitation of the white metal. Such a rehabilitation, he said, would greatly contribute to stabilization and should be pushed by the Mexican government by every means possible.

Pani also issued the following statistics showing the total of peso sight deposits in all of the banks of the Republic: [11]

June 30, 1931	143 million pesos
July 30, 1931 (5 days after Plan Calles)	115 million pesos
March 9, 1932 (presently)	95 million pesos.

The constitution of the Bank of Mexico was amended by a law of April 12, 1932. This amending act reduced the Bank's capital from 100 million to 50 million pesos and at the same time confirmed provisions established in the previous year to the effect that the Bank was no longer to carry on business directly with the public. Some large loans which it had made in the past, such as one to Cia. Azucarera del Mante, S.A., had become the subject of criticism.

The Monetary Reform Law of March 9 and the Law of April 12, which changed the central bank's constitution, were followed by a series of other new laws, those of May 19, June 28, and August 26, which also affected banking and credit. In the course of formulating all of this legislation Pani adhered to his custom of relying heavily on the collaboration of numerous experts. Before the Monetary Reform Law of March 9, 1932, was issued, with the approval of Calles, Pani gave careful study to Gómez Morín's memorandum, unfavorable to the coinage of silver at full capacity directly under the authority of the Finance Ministry; in this particular case the Finance Minister decided not to be guided by the recommendation of an assistant who contributed mightily to the financial reforms of these days.

As was to be expected, the monetary reform of March 9, 1932, depreciated the peso in terms of the dollar, and by September, 1932, the exchange rate had settled so that the dollar would purchase about 3.50 pesos. The Monetary Reserve Decree of March 22, 1933, returned to the Bank of Mexico the control over the coinage of silver. Circulating paper money, which had amounted to only one million pesos at the end of 1931, amounted to 26 million by September, 1932, and 78 million by September, 1933.

[11] Secretaría de Hacienda y Crédito Público, *La crisis económica en México y la nueva legislación sobre la moneda y crédito*, pp. 15–21.

Speaking on July 15, 1935, Lic. Eduardo Suárez explained: "Mexico, in seeking to solve its crisis, turned first, in July, 1931, to deflationary steps, but later, in March, 1932, it corrected this, reversing the policy, and this, put into action with decision, is the principal cause of the good condition of the nation."[12]

[12] Eduardo Suárez quoted in Alberto J. Pani's *Mi contribución al nuevo régimen, 1910–1933*, p. 344.

59.

Some Cabinets
of President Ortiz Rubio

When in March, 1930, Luis N. Morones returned from a European trip, he took advantage of the welcoming receptions to make life as difficult as he could for Portes Gil. At an evening meeting given in his honor by the Partido Laborista Mexicano Celestino Gasca and Vicente Lombardo Toledano were among the speakers. It was clear that the Partido Laborista Mexicano planned to return to the political struggle and was backing President Ortiz Rubio but was opposing Portes Gil's P.N.R.

Two days later the Federation of Labor Unions of the Federal

District, affiliated with the C.R.O.M., gave a demonstration of welcome to Morones at the Iris Theatre in the capital. Then the political meeting of the Partido Laborista occurred on June 8, 1930, at its offices, where Morones and Vicente Lombardo Toledano attacked the P.N.R., and where Morones accused Portes Gil of having tried to arrange the murder of Ortiz Rubio.

Morones maintained that Portes Gil sought to promote Communism in Mexico and the United States; during Portes Gil's visit to Cuba he accused the head of the P.N.R. of seeking to use Communism to overthrow President Machado's Administration.

Back from Cuba in August, 1930, Portes Gil blasted away at Morones. Speaking before the P.N.R., its president referred to the "unprecedented triumph" of the recent congressional elections. He spoke of the social work to be done. He asked the "false leaders" of labor what had become of various funds collected by the C.R.O.M. "from the suffering laborers and peasants." "These leaders," he added, "before the national conscience, have a great responsibility in the assassination of Obregón."

Portes Gil was soon off for Europe, serving some diplomatic missions. His reason for resigning the Party presidency on October 15, 1930, had to do with his "unbearable" situation in the Ortiz Rubio Government. Action, he says, was made impossible not only by the "furious attacks of Ing. Ortiz Rubio's intimates" but also by "the steps taken by friends of General Calles [Riva Palacio, Morones, Puig Casauranc, Montes de Oca, and some others] whom General Calles himself frequently disclaimed."[1] At about the same time, that is, in October, 1930, Luis L. León resigned as Minister of Industry, Commerce, and Labor, being succeeded by Aarón Sáenz. Puig Casauranc, who in June had left the headship of the Federal District, was recalled to take over the Education post vacated by Sáenz.

In Italy we find Portes Gil, who had succeeded Pani as minister to France, discussing Mexican politics with his close friend Ezequiel Padilla, who had been minister to Italy since the start of the Ortiz Rubio administration. Portes Gil was conjecturing about who might be the Party's next presidential candidate: "General Calles now is thinking of Pérez Treviño or Carlos Riva Palacio . . ."

Lic. Portes Gil resolved to return to Mexico early in 1932 to run

[1] Emilio Portes Gil, *Quince años de política mexicana*, p. 444.

again for the governorship of Tamaulipas. But while he was still in Paris he received a visit from Colonel Carlos Riva Palacio. This large man with the impressive mustache brought a message from Calles to the effect that the antire-electionist feeling in Tamaulipas was so deep that Portes Gil would fail, news which Calles was providing frankly as a friend. Portes Gil, who took this to mean that Calles did not favor his candidacy, has observed that Calles was already laying the groundwork to provide one of his sons, young Alfredo Elías Calles, with the Tamaulipas governorship in some future year.[2]

Portes Gil resolved, however, to face the official machinery rather than let down friends and supporters who were counting on him. After returning to Mexico from France he paid a call on Calles at Cuernavaca:

PORTES GIL: Yesterday I went to see President Ortiz Rubio to say hello and to give him my reasons for resigning the diplomatic post to which he had appointed me, and at the same time to notify him that I have accepted the candidacy for the governorship of Tamaulipas. The President told me frankly that he knows nothing about these matters and that I should discuss this with you.

CALLES (annoyed): I'm surprised that Ing. Ortiz Rubio told you to speak to me about this. I have no official position in the Government.

PORTES GIL: General, I would like very much for us to speak as completely frankly as we always have. I know, as the whole country knows, that you are the one who decides all government business. I want you to listen to me for a few moments so that I can tell you what I think and feel. That's why I came to see you.

CALLES (dryly): Go ahead.

PORTES GIL: . . . If in other states impositions have not had repercussions, in Tamaulipas one will. With the accomplishment of such an imposition you will suffer more than anyone else, and in Tamaulipas you will definitely lose your prestige. I do not believe that any force exists capable of making you turn aside from your duties as a sincere and patriotic revolutionary. Nevertheless, those of us who have been your sincere friends note sadly that you are allowing yourself to be influenced by a group of persons who do not add to your renown and who are using you in such a way that, if continued, in a few more years they will destroy you.

CALLES (more friendly): It is not true that I have the slightest interest in the Tamaulipas elections. You must have confidence that the Party

2 *Ibid.*, pp. 452–459.

will work with the most absolute impartiality and will recognize the victory of the one who attains it. I have spoken with Pérez Treviño about this so that, as president of the Partido Nacional Revolucionario, he will observe these instructions.[3]

Portes Gil did not feel that Calles was speaking sincerely. He did fail of election in spite of the efforts he made. "The Partido Nacional Revolucionario," he writes, "declared my opponent victorious: Dr. Rafael Villarreal, the man chosen by General Calles to confront me on that occasion."[4]

The Michoacán governor, General Lázaro Cárdenas, in October, 1930, was notified by telephone that he had been chosen to succeed Lic. Portes Gil as President of the P.N.R. This seems to have been a happy selection. Cárdenas was highly respected in the Army and elsewhere as a man more dedicated to work than to words, and he was known to be enthusiastic about the principles of the Revolution. He was a youthful newcomer to the intricacies of top-level politics. From the Islas Marías penal colony Múgica wrote to Cárdenas, remarking that surely his "diplomacy and wise principles of loyalty would establish anew the connection between our strong and vigorous *caudillo*, General Calles," and the President.

Cárdenas handled his post well, displaying much-needed loyalty to the President and trying to eliminate some of the intrigues against him. When in December, 1930, a number of senators attacked in strong language the executive of the nation, with particular emphasis on what they called the "right-ism" of Finance Minister Montes de Oca, Cárdenas took the drastic step of expelling these senators from the official party.

By this time General Calles was generally referred to as the "Jefe Máximo de la Revolución." This title, which was not particularly helpful to the prestige of the presidency, has been attributed to Luis L. León because he was managing *El Nacional*, the daily paper put out by the P.N.R., when it began using this designation frequently in referring to Calles. Activities seemed to confirm the title. The press reported important commissions first calling on the "Jefe Máximo" and perhaps then calling on the President. If, as Puig Casauranc affirms,[5] the Cabinet in May, 1931, adopted a resolution prohibiting members of the Administration from consulting

---

[3] *Ibid.*, pp. 453–455.   [4] *Ibid.*, p. 455.
[5] J. M. Puig Casauranc, *Galatea rebelde a varios pigmaliones*, Chapter 39.

Calles unless so ordered by the President, it can be added that there was a lack of compliance with any such agreement.

Late in August, 1931, just before the President was to open the regular session of Congress with his annual message (his second), an affair in honor of the Ortizrubista governor of Jalisco, Colonel Ignacio de la Mora, ended up in a shooting. One *diputado* from Jalisco was killed and two were gravely wounded. That scuffle, or the motive behind it, was considered sufficient reason for important political changes. General Cárdenas was transferred from the Party presidency to the apparently then less critical post of Gobernación Minister, a post from which Colonel Carlos Riva Palacio had resigned a few months before. General Pérez Treviño returned to his place as Party president, and General Saturnino Cedillo, strong man in San Luis Potosí, replaced General Pérez Treviño as Minister of Agriculture. An attempt was then made to improve political matters by issuing an agreement to the effect that "all political actions" should be "the joint resolution of the Party and the Secretaría de Gobernación."[6]

Shortly after the above-mentioned changes in the Party presidency and in the Cabinet, Puig Casauranc resigned as Education Minister. Calles, whose health was now such that from time to time he suffered severe pains, asked Puig Casauranc to formulate a plan for the reorganization of the executive branch of the government. President Ortiz Rubio had appointed Puig Casauranc ambassador to the United States; but another Cabinet crisis occurred before this active politician left for Washington. This was the crisis of October, 1931, and it was by all odds the most sensational of all these Cabinet "crises."

Leading politicians and Cabinet ministers were worrying about what other important politicians and Cabinet ministers might be doing to achieve the highest office in the land. For some time Communications Minister Almazán, while hard at work on public construction, had felt that Pérez Treviño and Carlos Riva Palacio, besides failing to co-operate with Ortiz Rubio, were "conspiring" for the presidency. As far back as March, 1931, Almazán had suggested that the entire Cabinet resign and be replaced by men who would work harmoniously, and of whom none would be available for the presidency.

[6] *Ibid.*, Chapter 40.

What Ortiz Rubio learned from Calles early in October, 1931, was that one of the four active *generales de división* in the Cabinet had the idea of bringing about certain important maneuvers to usurp the presidential functions, or at least "provoke some political phenomenon of unexpected scope."[7] The President replied that he wished to "continue outside of all political incidents," leaving with the Jefe Máximo all authority and responsibility for handling the awesome matter.

Ortiz Rubio, like his secretary, Hernández Cházaro, had long believed that War Minister Amaro could be expected to use the great strength of his position fully on behalf of Calles.[8] But some of the politicians who were closer to Calles than to Ortiz Rubio were concerned lest Amaro take a dramatic step to strengthen the President's position and weaken that of Calles. Calles had even mentioned to Montes de Oca a rumor about Amaro's having planned to assassinate the Jefe Máximo.[9] Those who were notably loyal to Ortiz Rubio, such as Montes de Oca, Genaro Estrada, and Aarón Sáenz, felt that the four active generals in the Cabinet (Almazán, Amaro, Cárdenas, and Cedillo) formed with them a sort of group—a group on which the President could count had he wished to do so in the course of his endless difficulties with legislative and Party leaders.

Almazán suggested to some members of this group that if Calles was concerned about a maneuver by the War Minister, the simplest solution would be to have Almazán return to Military Operations in Monterrey, thus allowing Amaro to move to Communications. But Cárdenas objected to Almazán's being the only one to be sacrificed to the work of "the intriguers." It was decided that the four generals all resign on the pretext that they were in the difficult and undesirable situation of receiving support as presidential candidates, whether or not they wanted such support. So when Calles told Ortiz Rubio that the prevention of the "political phenomenon of unexpected scope" would best be accomplished by calling for the resignation of all four generals so as not to hurt the feelings of the one he had in mind, he came out with a suggestion that the generals themselves were independently considering.

Almazán noted that Calles was openly handling this "crisis." When Calles angrily told Almazán to be sure to join a meeting of

<hr>

[7] See the account of the crisis given by Francisco Díaz Babio in *Un drama nacional.*

[8] Juan Andreu Almazán in *El Universal*, February 11, 1959.

[9] Juan Andreu Almazán in *El Universal*, January 7, 1959.

524

other Cabinet ministers at the home of another member on October 12, as any Cabinet member who did not attend would have to "abide by the consequences," the Jefe Máximo also remarked that the P.N.R.'s Pérez Treviño and certain Cabinet members had been complaining that Ortiz Rubio would not let them work in peace. Almazán retorted that on the contrary a number were working too freely and were trying to get Ortiz Rubio's position. It is interesting to note that among those who did not attend the meeting were two whose positions made them central figures in the "crisis," Amaro and Cárdenas. Unlike Almazán, Amaro did not get a stern warning to be present. On the contrary his absence "on account of illness" had been suggested to him by Calles.[10] Puig, although not a Cabinet minister, was invited "in the name of General Calles" to be present "as a founder member of the P.N.R.," and he attended with the approval of the President. In Puig's opinion the crisis had been caused by the Party being under Pérez Treviño, "inspired by Calles," whereas Cárdenas, in Gobernación, was "inspired by the Chief Executive."

Nothing was settled at this meeting and it is not clear who presided, as neither the President nor Calles was there. But at another meeting called the next day at Amaro's home both Amaro and Cárdenas were present. Having noted that Calles, in spite of his past promise not to be a political factor, seemed determined to maintain a strong position, Almazán had revised his earlier ideas about what should be done. He now read a memorandum stating that if his companions were considering the advisability of Ortiz Rubio's resigning they should bear in mind that the President was not entirely responsible for the crisis, and that it would be unsuitable for him to be succeeded by someone in the present Cabinet, which was supposed to be supporting him. As Almazán saw it, the fundamental difficulty lay in differences between the executive and legislative branches. He considered that it would be lamentable if the legislature prevailed, and he warned that care had to be exercised to prevent a bloody civil war.

The solution which Almazán now propounded to the gathering was that Ortiz Rubio resign, as on past occasions he had suggested he would like to do, and that the Congress should insist that Calles take over the presidency.

Some of the President's official collaborators commented on the

[10] Juan Andreu Almazán in *El Universal*, January 7, 1959.

Ortiz Rubio Administration, and Cedillo took advantage of the discussion to brand as false the charges that the Government was "anti-agrarian." The efforts made by Ortiz Rubio to develop policies in the realms of labor and agrarianism were reviewed, and the President's exploration of the possibility of greater social action on the part of the Bank of Mexico and his suggestion that the Bank's funds be used for such objectives as "ejidal" financing were brought out. (It was also brought out that the Bank's manager, Alberto Mascareñas, had showed himself to be less than enthusiastic about all of this.)

Almazán and Amaro made statements as to their loyalty to the President, and Cárdenas remained silent on this point, perhaps feeling that his record spoke louder than words. The Cabinet ministers concluded the meeting by resolving to resign in a body and to meet for the last time with the President and with Calles, in case the former so desired.

They had this last meeting late on the next day at the Anzures residence of Calles, who had a few hours before suffered a particularly painful attack of his illness. There Dr. Puig Casauranc presented a long memorandum about the situation, one which he had reviewed that morning with Calles. The possibility of a presidential change before the end of the constitutional term (December, 1934) was brought out in one of Puig's many recommendations: "Of the present military chief Cabinet ministers, retain Generals Cedillo and Cárdenas because of their agrarian representation, unless it is felt advisable to do otherwise on account of considering them as presidential possibilities for 1932 in case the presidential succession should then be open." Ambassador Puig had some suggestions regarding the role that should be played by Calles: "the right of planning the general lines of governmental action with reference to the large objectives of the Revolution, and when he is expressly consulted by the President of the Republic"; also: "when the concrete, more frequent actions are involved in any section of government, General Calles should engage in them only as a definite member of the Administration, in the section which corresponds: War, Hacienda, etc."

The outgoing Cabinet was advised that Calles would become Minister of War in the new Cabinet. Genaro Estrada and Puig Casauranc were told to draw up, for the President's signature, an announcement to the public. The meeting ended.

In the announcement the President spoke of the perfect collaboration he had found in his associates. Referring to Calles he said that the Executive was in need of the decided co-operation of the Jefe de la Revolución, to reach "not only a solution of the immediate crisis, but also a basic realization of the permanent direction . . . and to have a definite cohesion and political harmony, so much required by the present conditions of inequilibrium, not only national but world-wide." The announcement made known that Calles would serve as War Minister and advised that other appointments would be revealed later.

Puig and Estrada also formulated a public message, which Calles signed and which spoke of the "disinterested and patriotic attitude of Citizens Generales de División Amaro, Andreu Almazán, Cedillo, and Cárdenas." Calles advised: "I shall contribute all my decided force and give my complete backing to the realization of a work of co-ordination and energetic construction, along the lines of my Revolutionary convictions and my message to Congress of September 1, 1928."

The Cabinet had resigned on October 14, 1931. On October 21 the following Cabinet took over:

Gobernación
    Sr. Manuel C. Téllez
Finance and Public Credit
    Sr. Luis Montes de Oca
Foreign Relations
    Sr. Genaro Estrada
Communications and Public Works
    Ing. Gustavo P. Serrano
War and Navy
    General Plutarco Elías Calles
Agriculture
    Sr. Francisco S. Elías
Industry, Commerce, and Labor
    Lic. Aarón Sáenz
Public Education
    Lic. Narciso Bassols
Comptroller of the Federation
    Sr. Julio Freyssinier Morín
Head of Federal District
    Ing. Lorenzo Hernández
Attorney General
    Lic. José Aguilar y Maya

After scolding those who had attended the Guadalupe ceremony, Calles suggested further changes in the Cabinet. President Ortiz Rubio was not much inclined to object, but rather continued his policy of seeking to keep the peace even at the expense of his own immediate prestige. These changes took place on January 20, 1932, and they resulted in the departures of Montes de Oca, Genaro Estrada, and Aarón Sáenz, three who in the course of past incidents had shown particular loyalty to the President. Ortiz Rubio hoped that these changes, like the exit of the four generals who were said to be ambitious, would allow administrative work to go forward "without agitations."[11] The new changes brought the following men to the following positions:

Gobernación
    General Juan José Ríos
Finance and Public Credit
    Ing. Alberto J. Pani
Foreign Relations
    Sr. Manuel C. Téllez
Communications and Public Works
    General Miguel M. Acosta
Industry, Commerce, and Labor
    General Abelardo L. Rodríguez

The new Minister of Industry, Commerce, and Labor, General Abelardo L. Rodríguez, had just served as Undersecretary to War Minister Calles and made a fine impression on his chief. The new Gobernación Minister, General Juan José Ríos, had been Director of the Military Manufacturing Establishments and then had succeeded General Agustín Mora as Presidential Chief of Staff. In March, 1932, General Rafael Aguirre Manjarrez, a close friend of Amaro and for over seven years Quartermaster General of the Army, was appointed Comptroller General of the Nation, succeeding Sr. Freyssinier Morín.

[11] Pascual Ortiz Rubio quoted in Juan Andreu Almazán's *Memorias* in *El Universal*, February 11 and 12, 1959.

60·

Acute Religious and
Political Problems

During 1931 the newspapers were full of reports about two state governors who barely escaped attacks on their lives. Shortly after an Indian took four shots at Colonel Adalberto Tejeda of Veracruz, supporters of the governor began burning churches and taking whatever violent actions against the Catholic Church as occurred to them. However, this assassination attempt which wounded Tejeda on July 25 by no means started the series of actions against the clergy of Veracruz; occurring at a time when strong anti-Catholic measures were being taken in that state, it served as a reason for their intensification.

The shots which "thieves and bandits" took on October 10 at the automobile in which rode Dr. Leonides Andreu Almazán, governor of Puebla and brother of General Almazán, opened up a storm of scandal when Diputado Manuel Riva Palacio was formally accused of being intellectually responsible for the attack. When the congressional grand jury found no reason to proceed against Manuel Riva Palacio, some of Puebla's representatives objected to the decision and submitted a memorandum to President Ortiz Rubio. Various federal *diputados* then made accusations against Governor Leonides Andreu Almazán and the way Puebla was being administered. A group of Puebla politicians, claiming to speak for over fifty Puebla revolutionary organizations, pointed out that the Governor was not a revolutionary and was unfit to rule because he adorned his home with religious images, permitted all kinds of Catholic activities, and even made a public declaration of his religious faith.[1] The Almazán brothers, like their father before them, did not hesitate to protest against governmental decrees which seemed to them to interfere in an unwarranted manner with the activities of the Church.

Throughout part of 1930, as well as in 1931, the Mexican Catholic clergy were busy preparing for the celebration of the four-hundredth anniversary of the appearance of the Virgin of Guadalupe. Funds were raised to make the December 12, 1931, ceremonial as fitting as possible. Catholic leaders were also telling their followers not to comment unfavorably on the arrangement made with Portes Gil, and they were asking the priests to register in accordance with the government regulations. The Archbishop of Mexico did recommend the intensification of religious education so as to combat what he felt to be a trend toward the extinction of religious customs.

If things in early 1931 were quieter in this realm on the whole than they had once been, the noisy exception was certainly the state of Veracruz, whose Governor Tejeda had strongly rebuked Portes Gil for having made any arrangement at all with the clergy about the "religious problem." In March, 1931, a bomb was exploded in the cathedral at the state's capital, and, as this happened during the celebration of Mass, many people were injured. Then in June, 1931, Colonel Tejeda decreed a limitation on the number of priests in the state: one for every 5000 inhabitants. This ruling was

[1] Daniel Blumenkron and Luis Campomanes (eds.), *Puebla bajo el terror Almazanista*, pp. 37 and 68.

followed by a battle on the occasion of the burial of the Curate of Huatusco, Veracruz, who had died of injuries inflicted upon him; during the funeral about twenty, including the commander of the local police, were killed.

Women from Veracruz went to Mexico City to beseech the Minister of Gobernación to do away with Tejeda's ruling limiting the number of priests. But the bloc of the official party in the federal congress came out with a pronouncement backing Tejeda in his efforts to regulate worship. With the reassurance of his backing, Governor Tejeda issued a decree which showed the religious Catholic pleaders where they stood and which was about as unacceptable as possible to the Catholic clergy: there should be only thirteen Catholic priests for the entire state. As the state had a population of 1,380,000, this was less than one priest for every 100,000 persons.

On the day when the shots were fired at Colonel Tejeda, some Veracruz policemen entered a church and fired at two priests who were busy teaching the catechism, with the result that one of the priests was killed and the other wounded. In the days that followed, the dynamiting and burning of churches in Veracruz became frequent. Churches were burned at Medellín, Villa Cuauhtémoc, Otatitlán, Villa de Xico, and San Juan de la Punta, all in Veracruz. In a bloody encounter at Tlapacoyan, Veracruz, twelve persons were killed. The destruction of religious objects was a common practice.

Following the ceremonies commemorating the four-hundredth anniversary of the appearance of the Virgin of Guadalupe, ceremonies which were attended by thousands of pilgrims, the federal congressional chambers condemned the Catholic clergy for their attitude on that occasion. While the nation's lawmakers took steps to teach the clergy a lesson, Guadalajara's Archbishop Orozco y Jiménez was thrown out of the country for "subversive activities."

Earlier, according to Puig Casauranc, 400 churches had been openly "tolerated" in the Federal District, where the official limitation called for no more than 125 priests. But now the federal Congress limited the Federal District to 25 priests (one for every 50,000 inhabitants) and set out to enforce the ruling sternly. Catholic services were suspended in the District on New Year's day, 1932, until on February 18, 1932, the first 11 of the 25 were authorized by the government to officiate. In the following days the number was brought up to the limit of 25.

Various state legislatures were quick to follow examples which had been set in Veracruz and Mexico City, passing laws which were severe in limiting the number of priests who could practice, and taking steps to secure strict adherence to these new laws. Chihuahua set its limit at one priest for every 45,000 persons and later reduced even further the number of priests. Querétaro set the limit at one priest for every 8000 persons, later making it one priest for every 60,000 persons. The state of México limited to 34 the number of priests who could practice in that state, these to be distributed so that each district would have two priests, except for Toluca, where four could officiate. The state of Hidalgo decreed that only two priests could function in the city of Pachuca. Hidalgo later set the state limit at one per 50,000 inhabitants. In Sonora, where Rodolfo Elías Calles was governor, the limit was one priest for every 20,000 inhabitants. Durango and Michoacán set the state limits at 25 and 33 respectively.[2] Chiapas ruled that there could be one priest for every 60,000 inhabitants.[3] (María Elena Sodi de Pallares, daughter of Toral's defense lawyer, pointed out that the 1925 statistics for the United States showed one Catholic priest for every 601 Catholics.[4])

During 1932 the church at Pánuco was added to the list of those burned in the state of Veracruz. Other manifestations of violence throughout the nation included the death of one person and the injury of several during a demonstration in front of the cathedral at Morelia, Michoacán. Tragically, two nuns, who had been sleeping, were burned to death when fire was set to a church in Guadalajara.

Officials sought to do away with the names of places that had a religious connotation. Villa de Guadalupe Hidalgo, D.F., was renamed Colonia Gustavo A. Madero. San Angel, D.F., was renamed Villa Alvaro Obregón. The governor of Chihuahua decreed that all towns that had been named after saints should be given new names based on revolutionary ideas.

But now, as the situation unfolded in a manner not to the liking of many of the clergy, Monseñor Leopoldo Ruiz y Flores, the Apostolic Delegate in Mexico, came out clearly and repeatedly against any acts of violence by those who might seek to use arms to defend what they felt to be the rights of the Catholic Church. Statements

[2] María Elena Sodi de Pallares, *Los Cristeros y José de León Toral*, pp. 151–156.

[3] Félix Navarrete. *Sí hay persecución religiosa en México*, p. 44.

[4] María Elena Sodi de Pallares, *op. cit.*, p. 56.

which he made in June, 1931, February, 1932, and July, 1932, were to this effect.

The schismatic Mexican Catholic Apostolic Church came to an end in 1931. It simply disappeared, and before Schismatic Patriarch José Joaquín Pérez died in October he expressed regret at the steps which he had taken. The church of Corpus Christi, which had been received by the schismatic organization in 1925, was in July, 1932, taken away from an organization which had ceased to exist. Today this church building serves as a museum, the Museo Nacional de Artes e Industrias Populares at Avenida Juárez #44.

General Pedro J. Almada, head of Military Operations in the Valley of Mexico, heard rumors that General Calles had resigned as War Minister. Early the next morning he went to call on President Ortiz Rubio, whom he found still hoping to persuade Calles to stay on for at least six more months. "For this reason I have sent for General Amaro," said the President. After Amaro and Eulogio Ortiz had joined Ortiz Rubio and Almada it was decided to send a commission to see Calles and persuade him to remain at the head of the War Ministry. Among those who went to Cuernavaca to discuss the matter with the Jefe Máximo were Miguel M. Acosta, Joaquín Amaro, Pedro J. Almada, Abelardo L. Rodríguez, and Eulogio Ortiz. Their expressions supported the wishes of the President.

Calles had been out of the picture for a month during the spring of 1932 when, as his second wife's health was failing fast, he took her to Boston, accompanied by Colonel Carlos Riva Palacio and the Mexican ambassador to the United States, Dr. Puig Casauranc. Upon his return to Mexico he did not find things in the War Ministry going as well as they had gone before General Rodríguez was transferred to Industry, Commerce, and Labor, and, as neither his own nor his wife's health would permit him to spend much time running the Ministry, he determined to resign. Now he explained to the delegation which had come to Cuernavaca that he did not want to continue with the responsibility of signing papers which he did not even read, and he added that his personal affairs were requiring all of his attention.[5]

After it was clear that Calles would not change his mind, Amaro spoke to the group, suggesting three possibilities for the War Minis-

[5] Pedro J. Almada, *Con mi cobija al hombro*, pp. 292–294.

try: "In first place, Abelardo L. Rodríguez; second, Pedro J. Almada; and third, Andrés Figueroa." "Very well," said Calles, "on to the President."

Pedro J. Almada describes the trip then made from Cuernavaca "to inform the President." He was in the car with Abelardo L. Rodríguez, to whom he remarked: "You'll be Minister of War. But what crazy chance made Figueroa and me opponents? They couldn't have chosen worse opponents. I think this was something that was planned so as to have you grouped with some of us who would not outshine you." Almada goes on to say that "Abelardo laughed, but my prophecy came true."[6]

Calles told Puig not only to advise the President of his decision to resign from the War Ministry, but also, on seeing the President, not to leave him, "even if it took hours to convince him," until the President agreed to make Abelardo Rodríguez the next War Minister.[7] In five minutes Ortiz Rubio agreed to this appointment. When Rodríguez learned from the President about his new appointment, as he did at once, he accepted. And when he suggested that his Undersecretary in the Ministry of Industry, Commerce, and Labor, Lic. Primo Villa Michel, continue in his post, Ortiz Rubio promoted Villa Michel to fill the post being vacated by Abelardo Rodríguez.

With the completion of the first three years of the six-year presidential term to which General Obregón had been elected, a change in the presidency of the Republic would not require that a Substitute President be followed in office by another Constitutional President popularly chosen in a special election, all of this simply to fill the period ending on December 1, 1934. In case Ing. Ortiz Rubio should not complete his term, it would now be possible, under the Constitution, for Congress simply to name an Interim President to complete the period started by Lic. Portes Gil. Late in 1930 legislators had fixed this matter up by amending Constitutional Article 84.

This possibility was in the minds of many, not excluding Ortiz Rubio. But it was Calles who forced the issue on August 22, 1932, after an ugly upheaval in the General Hospital when some of the doctors there who were closer to Calles than to the President resigned in protest against the appointment of a new Hospital di-

[6] *Ibid.*, p. 295.

[7] J. M. Puig Casauranc, *Galatea rebelde a varios pigmaliones*, p. 450.

rector. Since the General Hospital operated as a section of Benefi-
ciencia Pública, headed by the President's brother, Francisco Ortiz
Rubio, much scandal was made out of the incident.

After this unfortunate affair, President Ortiz Rubio sought to
name, as head of the Federal District, General José María Tapia,
considered to be unquestionably a Callista. This should have been
pleasing to Calles. But when Puig Casauranc took this suggestion to
the residence in Anzures Colony on August 22, Calles made it
known that from that date on no friend of his (Calles) should occupy any high position in the Administration of Ortiz Rubio. This
new decision would leave to the President, said Calles, the complete
responsibility for his political and administrative acts.

General Tapia and Lic. F. J. Gaxiola, Jr., went to the Castle of
Chapultepec to notify the President of Calles' decision. Ing. Ortiz
Rubio, considerably upset, then discussed matters with Calles at the
Casino Sonora-Sinaloa. Gaxiola states that there "it was made
known to Ing. Ortiz Rubio that neither General Calles nor his
group could assume the responsibility of the situation nor lend personal co-operation to the Government."[8] Ortiz Rubio had gone to
the Casino to ask Calles about some troop movements ordered by
War Minister Rodríguez without consulting the President, and this
at a time when agitators were whispering to congressmen that the
President might be planning to pull off a *coup d'état*.[9]

A few days later President Ortiz Rubio asked Dr. Puig Casauranc
to take over the headship of the Federal District which General
Tapia had just refused. Dr. Puig likewise declined the offer, and
made it clear to the President that it "would be useless to offer that
post or any other place of importance in his government to anyone
allied to General Calles or to any prominent member of the P.N.R.
who presently had a voice in its direction."[10]

At this time there was considerable excitement as the congressional groups, generally unfriendly to Ortiz Rubio, prepared to assemble for the Thirty-fifth Legislature, whose sessions were to begin
on September 1, 1932, with the reading of the annual presidential
message. Rumors were flying about that the President, with the
help of some loyal generals, would prevent the installation of
Congress.

[8] F. J. Gaxiola, Jr., *El Presidente Rodríguez*, p. 37.
[9] Pascual Ortiz Rubio quoted in Juan Andreu Almazán's *Memorias* in *El Universal*, February 11, 1959.
[10] J. M. Puig Casauranc, *op. cit.*, p. 454.

61·

The Resignation
of President Ortiz Rubio

Among those who were having differences with Ortiz Rubio was the Finance Minister, Ing. Alberto J. Pani.

Considerably earlier in the Ortiz Rubio administration the President had unsuccessfully offered to Pani the headship of the Federal District. Pani had turned the position down because of a legality requiring residence in the district prior to the appointment. When Ortiz Rubio suggested that this legal requirement could be surmounted, Pani replied that perhaps the Paris legation could be considered part of the national territory but hardly could it be considered part of the Federal District.

As Finance Minister, Pani one day received a report that the President had told the members of the Supreme Court that their lack of a Supreme Court building was due to the "vanity" or "emptiness" of the Finance Minister. After checking this story, Pani called on Calles to tell him of his determination to resign. Calles persuaded Pani to postpone such a decision.

A few weeks later the Finance Minister received, he says, a visit from an American who claimed to be a close friend of President Ortiz Rubio. This American said that his company, the Amasco Corporation, had been commissioned by the President to construct all of the highways of Mexico. He showed the Finance Minister a pile of stock shares which he said he had set aside for him. When Pani said that he had not the money for the purchase of these shares, the American, Pani recalls, replied that the shares were to be a gift to him, similar gifts having been made to other high government officials. Pani became irate and said that as Finance Minister he would never approve any contract with the Amasco Corporation for road building in Mexico.[1]

Pani at once asked Communications Minister Miguel M. Acosta to help him fight the proposed contract. General Acosta agreed that if he received the contracts he would forward them to the Finance Minister, who could turn them down. And that is just what happened. On July 14, 1932, Pani received an executive *acuerdo* signed by President Ortiz Rubio which called for a contract with the Amasco Corporation involving 18,620,000 pesos. Pani points out that his refusal to sign such a document, already issued by the President, was unique.

Again Pani saw Calles about resigning from the Ortiz Rubio Cabinet. This time the Jefe Máximo indicated that in a short while a suitable occasion would arise. In the meantime Pani co-operated with the President in connection with the forthcoming message to Congress, that of September 1, 1932.

Dr. Puig Casauranc made daily notes of many of his conversations during the critical days of August, 1932.

After Puig advised the President that it would be useless for him to offer any important post to anyone allied with Calles or to any prominent member of the P.N.R., Ortiz Rubio revealed that under

[1] Alberto J. Pani, *Apuntes autobiográficos*, II, 165; also Alberto J. Pani interview, *El Universal*, August 6, 1949, p. 1.

such conditions he could not and should not govern. Admitting his inability he asked: "Where am I going to find Revolutionaries for my government if I eliminate all the men of Calles?" His feeling that he should not govern stemmed, he said, from the fact that he "had arrived at the presidency by the aid and will of the General and not through my own popularity or personal strength, even in the Party." Then Ortiz Rubio asked Puig to perform a last service for him: draw up the resignation of the President of the Republic and take it to Calles with the recommendation that it go into effect immediately after the presidential message of September 1, if Calles should not change his attitude about not permitting his friends or personal allies to form part of the Government. The President continued: "I only ask that in the formulation of this resignation, a very difficult task, since the Constitution requires that serious reasons will have to be found for it, neither should General Calles be hurt nor should it be inferred that my attitude is a result of any ideological discrepancies in the revolutionary philosophy."

Calles had gone from Anzures Colony to Cuernavaca. So Puig at once went to Cuernavaca, where Calles thanked him for having rejected the headship of the Federal District. The General added that precisely because such offers by the President were to be expected, he (Calles) had made clear two days before at Anzures what he expected of his friends. Calles agreed that the resignation of the President was inevitable if the President did not wish to form a government outside of the influence of Calles. Puig was asked by Calles to read the first draft of the resignation.

Puig discussed with frankness the historical position of Calles, and secured from the General a promise to the effect that, even if his men were not to collaborate in high government positions, neither he nor his intimates would "oppose" the government.

This piece of news was then taken (on August 25) to Ortiz Rubio by the recent ambassador to the United States. The President asked: "But where on earth would I find men identified with the Revolution who would not have those personal ties with General Calles?" Puig suggested "In the Supreme Court of Justice, which is composed of men named by Lic. Portes Gil without the intervention of Calles."

The President liked the idea, and so on August 26 Lic. Manuel Padilla, of the Mexican Supreme Court, became head of the Federal District. The President made an effort to persuade Dr. Puig Casauranc to be Gobernación Minister in the Cabinet he sought to form, "if only for a few months" and "making just this one exception to General Calles' orders." Puig Casauranc had to refuse. However, he left saying that he would forget about the matter of drafting a resignation unless he received new instructions.

But on August 27 President Ortiz Rubio advised Puig that he had definitely decided to resign. The resignation should be drawn up and also arrangements should be made so that Ortiz Rubio and his family might leave the country just as a new President took the oath of office. As Ortiz Rubio saw it, the nation was faced with a choice between the bloodshed that would have to take place to establish the President in his proper position, or else his own withdrawal to give Mexico a chance to solve its problem peacefully.

Puig's draft of a resignation statement to be presented to Congress was approved by the President and by Calles. It referred to the "frequent crises in the past" and declared it to be the signer's duty to resign "so that the ends we all seek may be achieved with greater unity in the future." It said further:

I believe in this way to seal with a definite flourish of declared loyalty my modest term as President; I believe thus also to contribute to the consolidation of the Calles Doctrine, to that saving doctrine of 1928, ratified today as yesterday by deeds of its creator, which establishes that personal sacrifices mean nothing before the need of making Mexico a land of institutions and laws . . . Without pretending that the second very real reason of my resignation—my failing health which does not allow me, as I would wish, to dedicate either the energy or necessary time to the serious attention of my job; without pretending, I repeat, that the cause of health deserves to be called a serious matter because the presidency implies the sacrifice of life itself, I want to present my resignation because of the grave political reason previously pointed out . . . The guide to the Revolution is found and is made concrete in the presidential message of September 1, 1928, by the present head of the Mexican Revolution. PASCUAL ORTIZ RUBIO.

Calles asked Puig Casauranc to let General Joaquín Amaro in on what was transpiring. Amaro was now head of Military Education and of the Military University, and Calles wanted his "understanding and acceptance of the happenings." Said Amaro to Puig: "What you tell me agrees exactly with what the President did us the honor of telling us this morning. So I'm with you and you can advise *mi General* Calles that, as the President wishes, I will do everything in my power to see that the change in First Executive is made without the slightest difficulty or trouble."

War Minister Abelardo Rodríguez took measures to assure the installation of Congress on September 1, 1932, even should there take place, as rumored, efforts by the President and his supporters to prevent the legislative houses from meeting. Possible bloodshed was foreseen.

General Pedro J. Almada formed three columns: the first under Emilio N. Acosta, the second under Ignacio Otero, and the third under his own orders at the Palacio Nacional. Almada adds that the forces from the general barracks were to be placed by the President in the stadium or wherever he felt it to be best. In the previous year Ortiz Rubio had made the suggestion that the annual message be delivered in the National Stadium, a suggestion which Cárdenas had backed but which did not become effective because federal legislators had opposed it.

General Almada further reports: "At the sacred place of the Chamber the arrival of deputies and senators was slow and without any agitation or manifestation; but with the arrival of General Abelardo L. Rodríguez a tremendous acclamation that attained the heights of emotion was heard." Then, after this highly significant demonstration, appeared the P.N.R.'s president, General Manuel Pérez Treviño. He was greeted with much applause, but his face reddened when he heard from the galleries a loud shout: "Viva el Presidente—del Partido Nacional Revolucionario!" (Long live the President—of the P.N.R.). When Ortiz Rubio arrived he received, says Almada, "a demonstration of the support his high office merited, principally, however, because it had been so ordered by General Calles, through the President of the P.N.R."

Without any untoward happenings, President Ortiz Rubio read his September 1, 1932, message to Congress. A large part of it was devoted to the activities of the Finance Ministry.

On the next day the city was full of rumors to the effect that "the President would not surrender." General Almada called on the President and said: "Do not resign, Mr. President. The Army must be with you, otherwise it would be even lower than the one that assassinated Madero. I assure you that there is not one single *jefe* who will lend himself to these machinations and personal quarrels. We are for the Constitutional President of the Republic."

The President replied: "No, Almada, I admire your loyalty, and by the same quality, I also wish to be loyal to General Calles. He created this situation; he is the one to resolve it. I do not wish to be responsible for disturbances in the Nation."[2]

On September 2 President Ortiz Rubio called to the Castle of Chapultepec the high officials of his administration. He made known the text of his resignation and asked for opinions. Ing. Pani, who after the September 1 address had been advised by Calles of the President's decision, reports on the Chapultepec Castle meeting. He says that following the President's announcement there was a rather obvious silence on the part of all except Attorney General Aguilar y Maya, who asked the President not to carry out his plan of resignation and who reiterated his loyalty to him. Gaxiola describes the resignation as being opposed only for constitutional reasons by Aguilar y Maya and Nicéforo Guerrero, whose arguments were refuted by those of Narciso Bassols.

The resignation was signed by President Ortiz Rubio on Friday September 2 and presented to the Congress on the next day.

By this time there was much activity regarding the selection of a successor.

Pani has described another Cabinet meeting which also took place on September 2, this one at the home of Calles at Cuernavaca. Calles informed the ministers that, in order to determine who should succeed Ortiz Rubio, the names of three candidates would be presented to Congress by General Manuel Pérez Treviño. Calles then made known the following three names: Ing. Alberto J. Pani, General Joaquín Amaro, and General Abelardo L. Rodríguez. Pani remarks on Calles' order of listing the names that, "considering the characteristics of the age," the fact that his name was in the first place "was more than an insinuation by General Calles that I had the absolute preference."[3]

On the morning of September 3 a group of congressmen came to call on Pani and to assure him of their support. Pani asked them not to vote for him. "For whom, then?" they asked. Pani advised them to add their votes to the majority, and the congressmen left, somewhat perplexed.

Pani next sped to Cuernavaca, where he advised Calles that he was not enthusiastic about being the favored one. "Why not?" asked the General. "Because," replied Pani, "I would not be pleased

[2] Pedro J. Almada, *Con mi cobija al hombro*, pp. 296–298.
[3] Alberto J. Pani in *El Universal*, August 6, 1949.

to be favored for that post simply because of an order of yours to a flock of Congressional lambs." The General then asked the financier about what he thought should be done. Pani suggested the name of Abelardo Rodríguez, whom he believed to be "interested in the position." He relates that Rodríguez, accompanied by General Miguel Acosta, had by then come to call on Calles and that these two were in the waiting room when he left.[4]

Late on the morning of Saturday, September 3, while Ing. Ortiz Rubio was bidding farewell to collaborators and friends, a short meeting of the majority group of the Chamber of Deputies took place. It became known that as far back as August 24 Ortiz Rubio had expressed his intention of resigning. General Pérez Treviño said to the majority block of congressmen: "The deputies and senators have in their hands the resolution of this present conflict." There was great applause. He added: "I think the President's resignation should be accepted."

Four Party-member names were presented by Pérez Treviño to the majority bloc of *diputados* as possible successors to President Ortiz Rubio. To the three names mentioned by Calles on the preceding day was added the name of General Juan José Ríos, who was backed by the representatives from the state of Veracruz.[5] Before mentioning the four names, Pérez Treviño stated that the Party did not favor any one name, and that those present were free to vote for whomever they wished. Such a great ovation greeted the name of General Rodríguez that it appeared clear that he would be the choice. The meeting ended with the announcement that the majority bloc of the *diputados* would meet that afternoon with the corresponding bloc from the Senate in order for the official party to make a decision.

The afternoon meeting of the P.N.R. blocs of both houses of Congress was a little delayed and did not get under way until 5:30 P.M. Attending were 132 *diputados* and 18 senators. After the reading of Ortiz Rubio's resignation statement, General Pérez Treviño suggested that the resignation be accepted "for the public tranquillity of the country." Lic. Aarón Sáenz praised the patriotic attitude of Ing. Ortiz Rubio and asked for applause for him. Dip. Luis L. León expressed his satisfaction at being present at one of the moments of "Mexico's institutional life," opened four years earlier

[4] Alberto J. Pani, conversation, June 1, 1955.
[5] Steps taken by the P.N.R. to select Pascual Ortiz Rubio's successor are described in *La jornada institucional del día cuatro de septiembre de 1932*.

by General Calles. He accepted the words of Sáenz in praise of Ortiz Rubio's patriotism, but added that they "should also appreciate the attitude of General Manuel Pérez Treviño, who is perfectly prepared to occupy the Presidency of the Republic but who, however, is fulfilling his duty." This expression was followed by a great ovation honoring Pérez Treviño. Then all four of the candidates to take over the provisional presidency of the republic were praised as "true Revolutionaries."

At a joint meeting of the two houses of Congress, General Abelardo L. Rodríguez was officially elected Substitute President of Mexico, and to advise him was named a commission, which included Diputados Luis L. León, Ezequiel Padilla, and Gonzalo N. Santos and Senators Carlos Riva Palacio, Aarón Sáenz, and Federico Medrano.

The congressmen met again on the next morning, Sunday. Ing. Ortiz Rubio's resignation having been officially accepted and General Rodríguez having been officially named to succeed him, more commissions were formed. One was to advise the judicial power of the recent change. Another, to which Pani has called particular attention, was to advise Calles of the selection of a Substitute President. (Pani says it was a commission to advise Calles that "his orders had been faithfully carried out."[6]) A commission to advise Ortiz Rubio of the acceptance of his resignation was also named.

Pascual Ortiz Rubio, with his family, was escorted from the country on the *Tren Olivo* by General Eulogio Ortiz. The train departed from Mexico City's Buenavista Station just before noon on Sunday, September 4, and headed for New York.

While the congressmen awaited the arrival of Abelardo Rodríguez, Lic. Ezequiel Padilla, recently returned from Italy, stepped forward to address them. He praised Ortiz Rubio for his patriotism in resigning when "he felt that he lacked popular backing"; he also pointed out that Congress had fulfilled its duty in accepting the resignation and in selecting as a successor a man who did not find himself in such a condition. "We are not," he added, "a democracy of individuals, but rather a democracy of masses, of multitudes— but organized, disciplined, compact multitudes, and the men who represent the nation should get this backing whenever they want firm results. Rudyard Kipling and Karl Marx have upheld the necessity for the organized masses to point out the road of the people . . ."

[6] Alberto J. Pani, *op. cit.*, II, 171.

The applause which followed Lic. Ezequiel Padilla's oration was interrupted by bugle calls announcing the arrival of General Rodríguez. He came into the Chamber of applauding deputies with General Pérez Treviño, General Amaro, and Ing. Pani, the inclusion in the group of the two last-named making it clear that other candidates presented by the P.N.R. were backing the selection of General Rodríguez. While General Rodríguez made the pledge called for by his new high office, all stood up except the president of Congress, Lic. Flavio Pérez Gasga.

After the pledge, General Pérez Treviño was the first to embrace the new President, who then left for the Palacio Nacional. This historic congressional session ended at 12:10 P.M., just as the *Tren Olivo* was starting on its way to the United States border.

The Mexican peso strengthened. The dollar was worth 3.50 pesos just before Ing. Ortiz Rubio left office. With the change in the presidency, this figure dropped at once to 3.41 and then to 3.36 and to 3.34. In the next month it went to 3.16.

62.

Pani's Departure from President Rodríguez' Cabinet

After the brief ceremony in the Chamber of Deputies President Rodríguez and various other generals, among them Amaro, Almada, and Azcárate, called on General Calles at Cuernavaca. Subsequently the public learned the names of the new President's administrative associates:

Gobernación (Undersecretary in Charge)
  Lic. Eduardo Vasconcelos
Foreign Relations
  Sr. Manuel C. Téllez

President Abelardo L. Rodríguez *and members of his Cabinet. Seated:* Attorney General General Portes Gil, War Minister Cárdenas, Gobernación Minister Eduardo Vasconcelos, President Rodríguez, Finance Minister Pani, Foreign Minister Puig Casauranc, Communications Minister Miguel Acosta. *Standing:* Chief of Staff Juan F. Azcárate, Presidential Secretary Francisco Javier Gaxiola, Jr., Head of Military Manufacturing Establishments Gilberto R. Limón, Health Chief Gaston Melo, Education Minister Bassols, Agriculture Minister Elías, Federal District Department Head Aarón Sáenz, Statistic Head Bojórquez, Industry and Commerce Minister Villa Michel, Attorney General for the Federal District José Trinidad Sánchez Benítez. *1933.*

Finance and Public Credit
    Ing. Alberto J. Pani
War and Navy (Undersecretary in Charge)
    General Pablo Quiroga
Agriculture
    Sr. Francisco S. Elías
Communications and Public Works
    General Miguel M. Acosta
Industry and Commerce
    Lic. Primo Villa Michel
Public Education
    Lic. Narciso Bassols
Attorney General of the Republic
    Lic. Emilio Portes Gil
Head of Comptroller's Department
    General Rafael Aguirre Manjarrez
Head of Statistics Department
    Ing. Juan de Dios Bojórquez
Head of Military Manufacturing Establishments
    General Gilberto R. Limón
Head of Federal District
    General Juan G. Cabral
Presidential Secretary
    Lic. Francisco Javier Gaxiola, Jr.
Presidential Chief of Staff
    General Juan F. Azcárate
Attorney General of the Federal District
    Lic. José Trinidad Sánchez Benítez

Promptly created was an important new department called the Labor Department, of which, instead of Statistics, Ing. Juan de Dios Bojórquez was placed in charge. Industry and Commerce was re-named the "Secretaría de la Economía Nacional" and the Statistics Department was made a dependency of this new Ministry. Several other changes in the Cabinet's personnel occurred before the end of 1932. Lic. Aarón Sáenz replaced General Cabral as Head of the Federal District, and Dr. Puig Casauranc, in accordance with his own request, became Foreign Minister when Sr. Téllez resigned. General Cárdenas became Minister of War and Navy, and his as-sociate, General Manuel Avila Camacho, became the War Undersecretary instead of General Quiroga (who was promoted to be a *general de división*).

In direct contrast to the system of *acuerdos colectivos*, which had been established by Ortiz Rubio, President Rodríguez made it clear at once that he did not consider his Cabinet to be a group of persons collectively responsible for the Administration. The Chief Executive, said Rodríguez, was the bearer of the executive power. In a circular of November, 1932, he pointed out to his ministers, attorneys general, and department heads that "the political Constitution of February 5, 1917, frankly establishes the presidential regime of the government," and he went on to show that the President is constitutionally authorized "to name and freely remove his ministers," etc., and is "implicitly responsible for each and all of the acts which the different dependencies of the executive power develop." General Rodríguez told his subordinates that all important matters should first be submitted to his consideration, so that "it shall be the President who directs and orients the policy of the government in the different realms of public administration which constitutionally are incumbent on him." He concluded his circular with these words: "Please acknowledge receipt."

Finance Minister Pani, who was directing certain physical improvements in Mexico City, hoped to create an institution which would consist of a number of buildings and which would house artistic collections, as in other cultured capitals of the world. At the moment the heart of this scheme was the finishing of the Palace of Fine Arts (Palacio de Bellas Artes). This beautiful and imposing structure of white marble had been started as the Gran Teatro Nacional in 1904 under the guidance of Porfirio Díaz's Finance Minister, José Ives Limantour, aided by his architect, Adamo Boari. Prior to the suspension of this work in 1913, as a result of the Revolution, one of Pani's early engineering jobs had been connected with the construction of this building. Work was resumed in July, 1932.

Using their own blood instead of ink, the Comptroller General and the Finance Minister had signed a pact wherein they agreed not to attack each other.[1] But this did not prevent a dispute between Pani and Aguirre Manjarrez about the Italian marble blocks which were located in the Mexico City district and which Pani planned to

---

[1] Rafael Aguirre Manjarrez, conversation, June 11, 1956.

have moved by convicts to Bellas Artes in order to complete the construction. The Comptroller Generalship, which was independent of the Finance Ministry and which had received a clear definition of its powers in 1926, now refused to approve Pani's purchase requisitions, pointing out that the government had already bought the marble blocks from Italy in the time of Porfirio Díaz. When the Finance Minister maintained nevertheless that it would be necessary to make some additional payments to certain people in Mexico City in order to obtain the blocks, Abelardo Rodríguez took steps which ended controversies of this nature. In December, 1932, he stated that the Comptroller Generalship had been slow in providing reports, had at times made it difficult for other departments to fulfill their public services, and had not succeeded in ending graft. Pointing out also the increased duplication of work since the 1928 Law of the Federal Administrative Department of the Budget, he now abolished the Comptroller Generalship and sent Aguirre Manjarrez on a mission to the United States. In this move to simplify things, the functions of the Comptrollership were absorbed by Hacienda.[2]

Other aspects of Pani's campaign for adding beauty and culture to Mexico City were his project for a large popular theatre for low-cost performances and his project for doing something about the structural remains at the Plaza de la República. During the era of Porfirio Díaz work had been started on an elaborate Palacio del Poder Legislativo at the Plaza de la República, but from time to time during the Revolution this metallic structure had been partially dismantled. Ever since his days as Foreign Minister, Pani had tried to have the remains utilized, and he had even commissioned the original architect, Emile Bénard, to draw up some expensive plans for converting it into a Panteón Nacional (National Mausoleum). Pani says that he dropped the idea of creating a national pantheon "because, unfortunately, the men who rule Mexico frequently put transitory, political, or personal expedience ahead of the permanent interests of the nation, so there would be no guarantee of any historical or sacred dedication as to admissions to such a monument."[3]

Early in 1933 he learned that the remaining dome of the Palacio del Poder Legislativo was about to be sold as scrap iron. He had

---

[2] Secretaría de Hacienda y Crédito Público, Comisión de Revisión Contable, *Informe sobre la revisión de la contabilidad del gobierno federal*, pp. 47–49.

[3] Alberto J. Pani, *La historia, agredida*, pp. 159–160.

Making the Monument to the Revolution out of the remains of what was once going to be the Palace of Legislative Power. 1933. Casasola.

architect Carlos Obregón Santacilia prepare a drawing to show how this remainder could be made into a monument to the Revolution. President Rodríguez and ex-President Calles were both agreeable to this suggestion of Pani. Thus, instead of the cupola's being sold as scrap iron, the Gran Comisión del Patronato del Monumento a la Revolución was created to preserve it in a new form. Pani, however, was not entirely satisfied with the architecture of the monument as it was later finished.[4]

In the spring of 1933, which saw the arrival of Ambassador Josephus Daniels to represent Franklin D. Roosevelt's Administration, and also the return of Jorge Prieto Laurens from his long exile, Finance Minister Pani left for the United States to discuss in Washington matters which would come up at the London Economic Conference. He went by way of Lower California, where he exchanged impressions with Calles. In Los Angeles, when asked about his availability for the nation's presidency in 1934, he replied: "I am busy with important things."

At the World Monetary and Economic Conference, held in London from June 12 to July 27, 1933, Ing. Pani presided over the Mexican delegation (which included Lic. González Roa, Lic. Eduardo Suárez, and Ing. Marte R. Gómez) and was on the directive board of the Conference. When speaking before this international gathering of financial experts, Pani pointed to the similarity between the agenda and the Mexican program of national economic rehabilitation which he considered had been started in 1924 and renewed in 1933. Pani offered the Mexican economic advances as support for the agenda's suggested procedures. He said also that the only thing now holding Mexico back was the lack of prosperity outside of Mexico. He added that Mexico was willing to accept whatever sacrifices might be necessary "to save civilization and to mitigate the present sufferings of humanity."

By August 1, 1933, Pani was back in Mexico, reporting on the Mexican mission to London. He had with him some paintings which he had purchased on behalf of the Mexican government not only in London, but also in Madrid, where he had spent a week following the conclusion of the London Conference. These were for the galleries of the Palacio de Bellas Artes, whose completion was fast approaching.

[4] *Ibid.*, pp. 161–162.

During August, 1933, the discord between Finance Minister Pani and Education Minister Narciso Bassols became "intolerable." Presidential Secretary Gaxiola wrote that "their mutual antipathy and their contact on the Commission of the Six-Year Plan were upsetting to the nerves..."[5]

The Six-Year Plan was to be a program of the government for the 1934–1940 period and was to be presented at the second national convention of the P.N.R., at the time when it met to choose a new presidential candidate. The plan was originally the idea of Calles, who, on May 20, 1933, called for the formulation of a detailed program of action based on reason, statistics, and the lessons of experience. In the course of his declarations, Calles, always willing to be critical of the Revolution in realms where he thought it had failed, pointed out that defeat of the Revolution's greatest constructive proposals was due to a complete lack of co-ordination and to the failure of high-placed persons to work for the undertaking with love, capacity to understand it, and a disinterested spirit. After declaring that "to make social experiments at the cost of hunger for the masses is a crime," he added that very small properties seldom lend themselves to modern agricultural techniques. He recommended that large landowners be forced to divide their lands and sell them in sections, not small sections of three or four hectares but areas sufficient to stimulate men of ambition.

By a presidential order of July 18, 1933, the government ministers and department heads were made technical collaborators in the formation of the Six-Year Party Program. President Rodríguez stated that in the formulation of the program consideration should be given to the economic and financial capacity of the federal government, and he specifically asked for the direct intervention of the Finance Minister. He added that the program should consider the four foremost problems of the nation, which he felt to be (1) public education, (2) the agrarian program, (3) labor, and (4) communications in the nation's interior. When on July 24 he inaugurated the work of the Comisión de Colaboración Técnica, Rodríguez suggested the possibility of creating national mineral reserves "to prevent the limitless exploitation of these materials by private parties with prejudice to the economic system of the nation."

[5] Francisco Javier Gaxiola, Jr., *El Presidente Rodríguez*, p. 97.

In Pani's absence the Undersecretary of Finance, Ing. Octavio Dubois, presided at the earlier sessions. By the time of the meeting on August 7 Pani was back from Europe and able to preside, but the differences that then arose between him and Bassols obstructed progress by the Commission. Gaxiola attributed the mutual dislike to "essential differences of character." The specific bone of contention at the moment was the rapidly terminating construction of the Palacio de Bellas Artes under the direction of Pani and aided by the architect, Federico Mariscal. Bassols maintained that the construction of the Palacio should have been under the direction of the Ministry of Communications and Public Works, and its administration and organization belonged to the Education Ministry.

This matter came up at one of the rare Cabinet meetings, where, as Pani describes it, the President referred to a legal study which supported the thesis that the construction should be handled by Communications and Public Works. Pani not only maintained that there was no legal reason why the President could not leave this work in the Finance Minister's hands, but added that, in view of his own relations with the Education Minister, a presidential decision favorable to Bassols would hurt his "personal dignity" and oblige him to resign. Gaxiola tells us that the President quite properly ordered that the Palacio de Bellas Artes be turned over to the Education Ministry once the work of construction was terminated.

By this time Bassols, whose work in education had the strong backing of the President, concluded that it was impossible for him and Pani to exist in the same Cabinet. He decided to resign and asked to be sent to Brazil, but the President informed him that any of his associates who left his government would never go to foreign diplomatic posts. Finally Gaxiola persuaded Bassols to withdraw his idea of resigning and go instead on an official trip to purchase, in the United States, machinery for industrial schools, returning in time for the opening of Congress on September 1, 1933. The President appointed Gaxiola to substitute for Bassols on the Six-Year Plan Commission.

Prior to the delivery of the presidential message to Congress on September 1, the presidential retinue, including Cabinet members, met in the President's office. Bassols arrived later than the others. Pani relates that Bassols, with whom he says he was having difficulties "for trivial reasons," started to greet those present—the President, General Acosta, Lic. Sáenz; then he passed by Ing. Pani without a greeting and without extending his hand. Pani thereupon came forth with a verse which he says so "annihilated" the Education Minister that he ended his round of greetings to retire to a corner.[6]

In those days (and this occasion was the last time) the presidential message was started and concluded by the President, but often various ministers spoke about their own fields. Pani writes of how his own section, on finances, was received with much more applause than any other, including those portions read by the President himself.

In an informal visit to Calles, Pani discussed with him how to improve the lot of the proletariat. Pani told the General that "the cause of the failure" was a false handling of the problem: the simple raising of salaries, without the prevention of the inevitable repercussions in the increase of living costs. "What it is important to increase is not the nominal value or monetary expression of salaries, but their acquisitive power."

As governor of the northern part of Baja California, Abelardo Rodríguez had succeeded in having municipal commissions there set a four-peso daily minimum wage. One of his first steps as President of Mexico was to create a commission to study Mexican wages in general, in order to better the lot of the working men by means of "real" increases in salaries, better production, and better educational opportunities. Among the many who served on the commission were Marte R. Gómez (president), Rafael Sánchez Lira (vice-president), Guillermo Flores Muñoz (secretary), Francisco Trejo, Adolfo Ruiz Cortines, Federico Bach, and Carlos Prieto. The work of the commission ran into obstacles.

The President then carried on a personal campaign, suggesting minimum wages to the various governors. On September 7, 1933, he issued an *acuerdo* expressing his satisfaction that considerable and enthusiastic approval had backed the idea of establishing 1.50 pesos and 1.00 peso as minimum wages in different states, because, as he had often made it clear, he considered that the fundamental contemporary problem was the bettering of life for the working classes. He formed a special commission to co-ordinate all efforts to establish minimum salaries. Head of this new commission was the Minister of Economía Nacional, Lic. Primo Villa Michel; other members were Senator Carlos Riva Palacio, head of the P.N.R.,

[6] Alberto J. Pani, *Apuntes autobiográficos* (one-volume edition), p. 485.

Agriculture Minister Francisco S. Elías, Labor Minister Juan de Dios Bojórquez, and Diputado Guillermo Flores Muñoz. On September 12, 1933, Congress amended the Labor Law so as to include minimum wages. For the municipalities in most of the states minimums notably higher than the 1.00 peso or the 1.50 pesos mentioned by the President were established.

After Pani had discussed with Calles the means of increasing the workers' purchasing power, as distinct from nominal salaries, Calles showed himself interested. The General explained that he was about to leave for a few days at Tehuacán to receive medical treatment and at the same time have some discussions with President Rodríguez. He added that he would then bring up Pani's observations and that Pani would no doubt be called to join them so that he might amplify his exposition about wages and help dictate resolutions to define a rational policy.

But Pani was not called to Tehuacán. The discussions there between President Rodríguez and General Calles took place while cyclones and overflowing rivers brought unprecedented catastrophe to the port of Tampico and parts of the state of San Luis Potosí.

When President Rodríguez got back to Mexico City on September 27 he asked Lic. Gaxiola: "How good are you at requesting resignations?" He instructed him to obtain at once the resignation of the Finance Minister, explaining that it was not right for Pani to continue occupying a post of confidence close to the President when his son, "with the tacit approval of his personal secretary," was criticizing the President's social manners and affirming that the Finance Minister did not recognize the authority of the President nor resolve with him the business of his office.

On that same day General Rodríguez also sent a strong directive to his colleagues. In that directive, which Puig Casauranc says[7] was provoked by the conduct of Agriculture Minister Elías and had already been shown to Calles, the President observed that it had come to his attention that ministers of state and department heads frequently consulted Calles about matters related to the administration of the government's executive branch. While recording his own high opinion of Calles' advice, of which he said he made frequent use, the President explained that what had been happening was not proper. Since the President was responsible for all the acts

[7] J. M. Puig Casauranc, *Galatea rebelde a varios pigmaliones*, p. 468.

of the executive branch, the members of his government, said Rodríguez, should in the future abstain from submitting to Calles, unless called upon to do so by Calles, matters which the Chief Executive and his ministers were supposed to handle. Rodríguez also pointed out that he had no reason to retain as his direct appointees any who felt that the President was incapable of directing the progress of the public administration. Should any colleague want to know the opinion of Calles about administrative questions, he could learn of it through the President.

After this memorandum was issued, Gaxiola called on Pani and asked him for his resignation. The Finance Minister was surprised not only at the unexpectedness of the blow, but more at the unfairness of the reasons for it. He felt that he had never gone to Calles on government matters except when ordered to do so ("as in the case of my suggestion to call upon Lic. Sáenz to fill the vacancy of the Headship of the Department of the Federal District"). And he considered that the comment about his son's speaking discourteously of the President at the Cuernavaca banquet was quite unjustified. (According to Pani, his son should have been able to be free to say whatever he wanted to, and besides, writes Pani, his son had not even been in Cuernavaca at the time of the banquet; moreover, the young man liked General Rodríguez.) [8]

Anyway, Ing. Pani submitted his resignation on September 28, 1933. In his covering letter to the President he expressed the supposition that there must be additional reasons. If, he said, it concerned the problems created by his disagreements with the Education Minister, "you have a perfect right to select, from among two of your associates, the one who seems most useful to you, and it is certainly your right to keep your reasons for your preference to yourself."

Pani's resignation was accepted at once. The press proclaimed the news that Calles had agreed to be the Finance Minister, and that with this step the crisis had passed. News dispatches went on to say that in the absence of Calles, who remained at Tehuacán, the Finance Undersecretary, Marte R. Gómez, was taking charge of the Ministry.

Pani then sent some documents to Calles. The news which he received in reply was that Calles had not known about the impending change in the Finance Ministry when the President left Tehua-

[8] Alberto J. Pani, *La historia, agredida*, pp. 181–182.

cán and that the step had been a surprise to him; that he had placed himself at the President's orders and had agreed to accept the position of Finance Minister provided it be of a transitory nature, that is, until the President named a permanent Minister.

Pani next became quite annoyed when his "ex-colleague," Foreign Minister Puig Casauranc, took steps against his two brothers, Arturo and Julio Pani, who had been in the Foreign Service for fourteen years and who were now with the consular service in Paris and Hamburg. Julio Pani also represented Mexico at the League of Nations. Dr. Puig wired to Dr. Francisco Castillo Nájera, the Mexican minister in Paris:

THE PRESIDENT HAS ASKED FOR ING. PANI'S RESIGNATION. CONSIDERATION OF THE UNSUITABLENESS OF HAVING HIGH POSTS ABROAD OCCUPIED BY PERSONS WHO HUMANLY MUST RESENT DAMAGING ATTITUDES TO CLOSE RELATIVES, FORCES THE PRESIDENT AND ME TO END THE CONSULAR COMMISSIONS IN PARIS AND HAMBURG . . .

On the other hand, Pani much appreciated the commissions which the Finance Undersecretary, Marte R. Gómez, gave at this difficult time to Arturo and Julio Pani. He also was no doubt happy to receive from Ing. Gómez an appointment to continue with the direction of the construction of the Palacio de Bellas Artes.

On New Year's Day, 1934, Ing. Marte R. Gómez succeeded Calles as Finance Minister. Sections of the financial part of the subsequent presidential message to Congress, that of September 1, 1934, displeased Pani, who therefore wrote an eighty-page memorandum containing his corrections. For reasons of courtesy, however, he delayed releasing it and for the moment limited himself to corresponding with Ing. Gómez about the matter.

Ing. León Salinas, who in many posts contributed significantly to the development of Mexico during Revolutionary governments, has this to say about the role of Ing. Pani: "Ing. Alberto J. Pani was the man of the most outstanding intelligence and constructive spirit among the many who figured in the Revolution of 1911 to date (1956); although Lic. Luis Cabrera had a more brilliant intelligence and more political ability, the results of his efforts have been less beneficial to Mexico than those of Pani. I was a close friend of both and knew them exceedingly well."[9]

[9] León Salinas, letter, January 30, 1956.

63.

Narciso Bassols and the Catholic Clergy

Ambassador Josephus Daniels came to Mexico with the idea, which was widespread, that Calles was the "Iron Man" of Mexico. "He makes and unmakes Presidents and Congress does his bidding," he was told. Members of his staff said to him: "Mr. Morrow got nowhere until he had won Calles."[1] The Ambassador's concept was in no way diminished by the publication of books such as *El verdadero Calles*, which contains the contemporary eulogies of hundreds of leading Mexicans about the "Chief of the Mexican

[1] Josephus Daniels, *Shirt-Sleeve Diplomat*, p. 45.

Revolution, and day by day 'The Strong Man of the Continent,' "
and which, incidentally, lists seven "political enemies": Vito Alessio Robles, Antonio Díaz Soto y Gama, Jorge Prieto Laurens, Calixto Maldonado R., Octavio Medellín Ostos, Antonio I. Villarreal, and
Aurelio Manrique, Jr.[2]

In March, 1934, Foreign Minister Puig Casauranc created a problem when he asked Gaxiola to advise President Rodríguez of a lunch
to be given in honor of Josephus Daniels at the home of Calles in
Cuernavaca. For this occasion, on which the Ambassador was to
speak, Puig was going to extend invitations to foreign representatives.

After consulting with the President, Gaxiola told Puig that Rodríguez did not authorize him to issue the invitations because Calles
"was simply a private citizen." By that time Dr. Puig had already
invited some foreign ambassadors and ministers; furthermore it
was learned that at the proposed lunch Ambassador Daniels would
present to General Calles a letter from President Roosevelt congratulating him on the "peace and growing prosperity of Mexico."

General Rodríguez then ordered Dr. Puig to withdraw the invitations which he had given out. In the presence of Marte Gómez
and Gaxiola, the President phoned Calles to let him know that if
the party took place and if Roosevelt's letter were publicly and officially delivered to Calles, he, Rodríguez, would fire Puig and any
of his associates who attended the function; he would also publicly
condemn the attitude of Calles and Puig, for he could in no way
permit his authority to be broken. The President maintained that
if any such luncheon were to be given it should be given by him
and that if a message should come from President Roosevelt it
should come to the President of Mexico.

Calles agreed that the lunch would not take place. Explaining
that Calles had suddenly fallen ill and was to leave for treatment
and rest in California, Puig called in the invitations, already received by the English minister and the ambassadors from Argentina and Spain, among others. Calles received Roosevelt's letter

[2] Much less pretentious than *El verdadero Calles* was the anti-Callista *El Turco*,
a magazine of few pages which at least got as far as issuing Vol. I, No. 1.
"El Turco" (The Turk) was a name applied to Calles by some who maintained
that Calles was of Turkish descent and that this explained his attitude toward
the Church. In *El Turco* cartoons showed a grim Calles handling "El Nopalito"
with little consideration. "El Nopalito" (little prickly cactus) was a name used
by some when they referred to Pascual Ortiz Rubio.

privately and in reply he wrote, in part: "I appreciate very sincerely your congratulations, and of course I do not need to tell you that inasmuch as I have not formed part of the government as a collaborator of President Rodríguez in any concrete post, my contribution has been developed only along lines of general co-operation, inspired by my past responsibilities, my convictions and political commitments, my respect and affection for President Rodríguez, and my sincere esteem for the exemplary government work which he is developing . . ."

Some months later Ambassador Daniels, after an interview with General Calles, was quoted in *El Nacional* as calling him "the strong man of Mexico." General Rodríguez wrote to the Ambassador, explaining that administrative matters were not in the hands of General Calles and that "we are now living under a well-organized political regime in which all democratic institutions function normally."[3] The Ambassador wrote back to tell President Rodríguez that he had been misquoted.

After describing these two incidents Mr. Daniels adds that Dr. Puig and General Calles "knew that the man in Chapultepec Castle was the President of Mexico."

With Pani out of the Cabinet, Narciso Bassols carried on as Education Minister. This he did in an aggressive manner which was not entirely popular, but he had the President's full support. Daniels tells us that Methodist Bishop Pascoe felt that Bassols, who "comes . . . from a very strong Catholic family, . . . extends no favors or considerations to Protestant churches and schools."[4] But certainly the program of Bassols, who was considered to be well to the left, brought little comfort to those who spoke for Catholicism. His reorganization of Mexican education brought from Catholic circles an avalanche of very hostile criticism.

Schools which had theretofore been under the control of the states were placed under federal control. Official documents pointed out that many of the schools which had been established in accordance with labor legislation "were not developing uniform activities that could bring about a social transformation directed to benefit the masses of workers; they were not adjusting their functioning to definite purposes, nor were they concerning themselves about

---

[3] Josephus Daniels, *op, cit.*, p. 51.   [4] *Ibid.*, p. 152.

preparing the students to achieve a better form of family and collective life. Moreover, this class of schools has been converted, actually, into centers of antirevolutionary and clerical [Church]
propaganda . . ."[5]

Having extended the federal control so that in addition to the
federal rural schools it now covered all the state schools, and having
made it clear that all secondary schools as well as primary schools
should not be under any Church influence, Bassols arranged to have
a constitutional amendment proclaim that in all schools the point
of view would be that of socialism. He increased teachers' salaries
but got into a row with the so-called leaders of teacher groups when
he sought to reduce their influence.

Bassols had his troubles with student agitation at the autonomous
University, and even with opinion in his own Ministry. Particularly he had his troubles with the press—to such an extent that the
President asked Gaxiola to persuade the leaders of the principal
dailies to limit their criticisms to charges that had foundation. The
establishment of "sexual education" in the schools, which were to
be scientific and practical, caused the greatest storm. After attacks
by the press and the clergy on this "sexual education," parents' as-
sociations started a sort of strike by their children, whom they
would not allow to attend the schools.

The agitation became so great that on May 9, 1934, President
Rodríguez made a shift in his Cabinet. Lic. Bassols was given the
top-ranking Cabinet post, that of Minister of Gobernación. The
Gobernación Minister, Lic. Eduardo Vasconcelos, became the Minister of Education.

On his way back to Mexico City from a trip to the west of the
United States, Gobernación Minister Bassols stopped at El Tambor,
Sinaloa, to speak with Calles and with Cárdenas, who was also considered to be anticlerical and is reported to have once remarked
that "Every moment spent on one's knees is a moment stolen from
humanity."[6] Then at a Cabinet meeting in Mexico City, Bassols
told President Rodríguez that it was urgent to enter into a period
of great activity against the clergy. Otherwise, Bassols told the
President, his "reputation as a revolutionary would be broken to
smithereens."[7] But Rodríguez refused to go along with this idea and

[5] Departamento del Trabajo, *La obra social del Presidente Rodríguez,* p. 575.
[6] Nathaniel and Sylvia Weyl, *The Reconquest of Mexico*, p. 153.
[7] Francisco Javier Gaxiola, Jr., *El Presidente Rodríguez*, p. 108.

pointed out that the religious problem was being handled with all the "decorum and dignity of a revolutionary government." The President also remarked that the strong steps advocated by Bassols would provoke difficulties for the incoming President, and that with such a program "I would be the one to leave the Palacio Nacional in smithereens."

Lic. Bassols then resigned as Gobernación Minister, being succeeded by General Juan Cabral.

Manuel Trejo Morales, who had loaned the pistol to Toral and who had been captured after four years of hiding, was sentenced in August, 1933, to serve six years in prison because of his past collaboration with Carlos Castro Balda and because of his involvement in the May 23, 1928, bombing of the Chamber of Deputies. Some months before this sentence was handed down, Padre Jiménez, who had been very close to Toral prior to the assassination, was arrested.

Early in 1933 a weekly published at La Piedad, Michoacán, came forth with the news that Srita. María Concepción Acevedo de la Llata ("Madre Conchita") had married General Francisco J. Múgica, former governor of Michoacán and director of the Islas Marías penal colony. This news item came to the attention of Luis L. León, who was directing the publication of the P.N.R.'s *El Nacional*. León got in touch with Múgica, who issued a statement of denial and who branded the false report as a step taken by reactionaries in order to attack his convictions and his social ethics.

In July, 1934, Madre Conchita and Carlos Castro Balda were shipped with other convicts to the Islas Marías penal colony. There Múgica persuaded Madre Conchita to speak fully, in articles which were published in Tampico's *El Mundo*, about the assassination of Obregón. The federal *diputado* from Michoacán, Ernesto Soto Reyes, wrote to Múgica to advise that Calles was very pleased with these revelations, which were so valuable for the good name of the Revolution and which destroyed the "coarse slander" of the clergy to the effect that the assassination of Obregón was political and inspired by Calles himself.[8] Later in that same year Madre Conchita, who was devoting much of her time at the penal colony to sewing, cooking, painting, and writing, became the wife of her fellow-prisoner, Carlos Castro Balda.

[8] Armando de María y Campos, *Múgica*, p. 238.

Difficulties for the Catholic Church had become immense during the Ortiz Rubio Administration, largely on account of restrictive legislation which was hardly in accord with the hopes of the church leaders who agreed in 1929 to the resumption of services. Difficulties and incidents carried over into the Rodríguez Administration. In the almost priest-less state of Veracruz, where Governor Tejeda's revolutionary manifestations had taken the form of expropriating textile plants for the workers as well as fighting the Catholic Church, a circular was now issued requiring the renaming of all Veracruz towns and ranches which bore the names of saints or which in any way commemorated the Catholic Church in their names. Officials of the Veracruz government soon had the additional pleasure of attending what was called a "socialistic baptism" of thirteen children, without benefit of clergy.

In the nation's capital Díaz Soto y Gama, who was never afraid to speak his mind, created excitement in the Chamber of Deputies when he made an oration attacking Lombardo Toledano and urging religious teaching in the schools so that children might learn Christian morals. There was more excitement when the lawmakers read a recent encyclical letter issued by Pope Pius XI ("Acerba Animi") which objected to the Mexican legislation affecting the Catholic clergy. The Pope was bitterly attacked in the Mexican Chamber of Deputies. President Rodríguez made a statement revealing his surprise at the Pope's remarks, which, he said, were full of falsehoods and would incite the clergy to disobey the Mexican rulings. In referring to the clergy, the President said that they "cannot resign themselves to losing domination of souls and the possession of worldly properties, by virtue of which the proletarian classes were held in complete lethargy and were impiously exploited." Apostolic Delegate Leopoldo Ruiz y Flores, who had forbidden criticism of the arrangement made with Portes Gil and who had strongly forbidden the use of arms on behalf of the Church, now affirmed that the Pope's message had been misunderstood by the Mexican government. But the congressmen demanded that Monseñor Ruiz y Flores be expelled from the country. He was therefore put on a plane, and his only farewell remark to the press was to the effect that he had never flown before.

Priests were also having a hard time in Jalisco, where their number was limited to one for every 25,000 inhabitants and where the state government had turned over twenty-seven church buildings to nonreligious functions. The police in Guadalajara closed all of the city's churches and not until twelve days later, after Catholics made an appeal to the President, were some church services resumed there.

In 1933 the state of Chiapas reduced to four the number of priests who could officiate in that state. Good Catholics were probably not the only ones to be somewhat startled when they read in the press the latest decree of Lic. Tomás Garrido Canabal, the governor of Tabasco: mausoleums, inscriptions on tombs, crosses, and names on gravestones shall be abolished; on each grave there will be placed only an order number which will be assigned to each dead person; present tombs will be demolished.[9] Of the numerous thefts made from churches during this period, the most noteworthy was that from the Basilica of Guadalupe: the Virgin lost her beautiful and valuable crown.

Apostolic Delegate Ruiz y Flores was at last provoked into coming out with a strong statement. Explaining that all his hopes had been in vain, he pointed out that he would be failing in his duty were he to keep silent any longer. He said that the experience of five years demonstrated a lack of sincerity on the part of the government with regard to "agreements" reached in 1929. To prove his point he maintained that the Veracruz state laws had inspired similar restrictive actions in other states, especially with the urging of the federal Congress, which had "unconstitutionally" reduced the number of churches in the Federal District and the territories. To all this, he said, had been added the project of placing in schools the "so-called sexual education, which had better be called the corruption of the children." Bearing in mind these violations of the most sacred rights, rights which he claimed were superior to any Constitution, Ruiz y Flores stated that no Catholic could be a socialist or belong to the P.N.R., which ". . . itself openly socialistic and, what is more, atheistic . . . , with unheard of tyranny obligates the teachers and employees to adhere to its theories and approve its policy." The Apostolic Delegate called on all Catholics to organize without awaiting orders of their ecclesiastic superiors. "Each Catholic should be converted into a school of Christian doctrine—into a real apostle—and we shall see that the persecution is converted into blessings from Heaven."

[9] Antigua Librería Murguía, S.A., *Colección de las efemérides publicadas en el calendario del más antiguo Galván*, p. 747.

The Bishop of Huejutla, Monseñor Jesús Manrique y Zárate, came out with his "Third Message to the Civilized World." He said that he was taking up the glove thrown down by General Calles. "If the Bolshevik revolution attacks us in the field of letters, we shall create periodicals to face periodicals—school to face school. If in violence, there also must we defend ourselves and our children, in spite of our meagre resources of force. The fathers of families should convert themselves into lions, and homes into fortresses. We have reached such a stage in our appeasement of our enemies, that one more step along that road would see us actually contributing to the degeneration of Mexican children and youths. And you, oh civilized world, will you again remain impassive before . . . the struggle between truth and error, civilization and barbarity, between unarmed justice and armed crime, between the true Mexican people and their bloody oppressors . . . ?"

President Rodríguez received, through General Cárdenas and Colonel Carlos Riva Palacio, a message from General Calles suggesting that Monseñor Ruiz y Flores and the Archbishop of Mexico, Pascual Díaz, be thrown out of the country at once. The President replied that he could not act in such an arbitrary fashion. He turned the matter over to Attorney General Portes Gil for his study. Portes Gil made a careful legal investigation, in which he mentioned "acts contrary to the public order and the integrity of the social and political institutions of the nation." He recommended the arrest of Ruiz y Flores and Manrique y Zárate, but, since these men were already outside of the country, he recommended that they be seized should they endeavor to enter Mexico.

The President, who was about to leave for Baja California, authorized Portes Gil to discuss his report with Calles, who was at Cuernavaca and who was greatly interested in the matter. After hearing the report's conclusions, Calles remarked to Portes Gil: "I don't think that's good enough. The government should act with full force, expelling the bishops, as I did in 1926 when the government closed the churches." Portes Gil reminded Calles that ". . . it is not true that you expelled any bishop nor that the churches were ordered closed in 1926. They did so because they wanted to, you yourself at that time explaining that the curates had declared a strike and closed the churches but that the government put them in the possession of regional groups so that they could stay open for worship." Then Portes Gil read all of his study (it took him until 3:00 o'clock in the morning), and Calles was so enthusiastic that he said "it should be translated into various languages and spread all over the world."[10]

Later, at Mexicali, President Rodríguez likewise listened for four hours as Portes Gil read his report. He authorized the legal steps to be taken against the two prelates. The Attorney General's report was issued in Spanish, English, and French and 600,000 copies were printed.

Although Lic. Bassols may have regretted that the federal executive did not engage in greater activity against the clergy, he could perhaps console himself a bit in the thought that high dignitaries of the Catholic Church considered conditions appalling in much of the country. Hopes of Church leaders, born of the announcements made on June 22, 1929, by President Portes Gil and Archbishop Ruiz y Flores, had most certainly not been fulfilled.

[10] Emilio Portes Gil, *Quince años de política mexicana*, p. 492.

64.

The Official Party Selects a Presidential Candidate

Early in 1932 the state legislatures met in a national assembly for the purpose of unifying the election rules affecting the various units of the republic. At that meeting the principle of No Re-election was considered. The president of the P.N.R. declared that "the general conventions of the Party are the only assemblies that can establish this mandate." Accordingly the Party's Executive Committee called a Party convention, which, after some preliminary work in April, 1932, met six months later in Aguascalientes. There the delegates—all politicians—adopted by acclamation the principle of No Re-election. Subsequently a majority of the state legislatures ratified the idea. On March 2, 1933, the Permanent Commission of the federal Congress met in a special session and amended again the 1917 Constitution, this time to prevent the re-election of Mexican Presidents and governors. As it was arranged that congressmen and senators could be re-elected after an intervening term, some federal legislators developed the practice of representing their constituencies rather consistently first in one chamber and then in another.[1]

Partly because of the differences between Pani and Bassols, and partly because of presidential campaign activities, the commissioners appointed by President Rodríguez to work on the Six-Year Plan met only four times. On October 2, 1933, President Rodríguez took the group to Tehuacán in order to finish the program there with Calles, who, as Finance Minister, had replaced Pani as the president of the commission. Since Gobernación Minister Eduardo Vasconcelos was then in Tampico inspecting cyclone damage, the President appointed in his place Gaxiola, who has made it clear that the commission finished its project as a result of the efforts, principally, of Bassols and Villa Michel.[2]

The Plan that was sent to the second national convention of the P.N.R. at Querétaro in December, 1933, was somewhat modified at that convention by some left-wing elements. While the convention was debating the Plan and preparing to nominate a presidential candidate who would be guided by it, the president of the convention, Lic. Sebastián Allende, received a message from President Rodríguez:

I judge it necessary in the projected Six-Year Plan which the convention discusses, that regarding the activities of the Labor Department a paragraph be added as follows: "The State itself will see to it that the labor unions carry out as efficiently as possible the function under their control, without said unions going beyond their proper limits and converting themselves into instruments of oppression within the classes they represent."

The Plan called for 12,000 new rural schools. It called for more federal control over schools, and said that education was to be secular and socialistic. In the field of labor the Plan called for collective bargaining and insisted that "a clause obligating the employer not

---

[1] Francisco Javier Gaxiola, Jr., *El Presidente Rodríguez*, p. 145.
[2] *Ibid.*, p. 160.

to accept nonunion workers shall be made compulsory in all collective labor contracts." Co-operatives were to be stimulated, and middlemen were to be eliminated as much as possible. The machinery for land redistribution was to be simplified (with more power going to the federal government) so that this division could proceed more rapidly. "The only limit to the distribution of land and waters shall be the complete satisfaction of the agricultural needs of the centers of rural population." Stimulation was to be given to Mexican-owned mining, petroleum, and power production. The Plan pointed out that "the state is an active agent, moving and controlling the vital processes of the country, and not a mere custodian of the national integrity and keeper of the public peace and order." It added that "the system of property should be conditioned to make it available to the greatest number of people." More roads and railways were to be built; among the highways called for was one in the west to connect Sonora with Guatemala.[3]

After the Ortiz Rubio Cabinet crisis of October, 1931, wherein all the Cabinet had resigned in order that four *generales de división* (Almazán, Amaro, Cárdenas, and Cedillo) would lose their posts, General Cárdenas had returned to the governorship of Michoacán. When his term as governor came to an end, on September 16, 1932, he was succeeded by General Benigno Serratos, who was not of the Cárdenas-Múgica school of thought. Serratos was a devout Catholic and was reputed to have been much less to the left in labor matters than was Cárdenas. Relations between the former governor and the new governor were far from perfect, with Cárdenas firm in the belief that his progressive program was being slowed down. Serratos wrote to President Rodríguez about the "systematic opposition which has arisen since the start of my administration and which has been helped by local political elements of muddy background and by a group of pseudo-leaders who have used every unpleasant method to reduce the prestige of the present regime in the eyes of the national revolutionary opinion."[4] Serratos was no doubt referring to the Confederación Revolucionaria Michoacana del Trabajo, which Cárdenas had helped build up into a powerful organization.

Cárdenas was made military commander of Puebla. Although he was not in the original Cabinet of Abelardo Rodríguez, the latter thought enough of him to appoint him to the important post of War

[3] Nathaniel and Sylvia Weyl, *The Reconquest of Mexico*, pp. 118–120.
[4] Francisco Javier Gaxiola, Jr., *op. cit.*, p. 175.

Minister at the end of December, 1932. Then President Rodríguez invited Cárdenas to accompany him in February, 1933, on a visit he was making to the states of Jalisco and Michoacán. The President hoped that he might effect a reconciliation between Generals Cárdenas and Serratos. This proved impossible.

When Rodríguez and Cárdenas were in Guadalajara, political groups surrounded Cárdenas, offering him the candidacy for the presidency. In an offhand manner President Rodríguez mentioned this matter to his companion. Cárdenas replied that he was not considering these overtures of the politicians because he had no personal ambitions, desired to continue collaborating in the government, and did not want his fellow soldiers and the nation itself to think that the War Ministry was a "nursery of Presidents." Then Cárdenas modestly added that he did not think he had the capacity or knowledge necessary for the presidency. Gaxiola reports that President Rodríguez, on his return to Mexico City, "made up his mind about the personality of General Cárdenas and felt it to be almost a certainty that he would be presented as a candidate."[5]

In April, 1933, Calles left Mexico City to spend the summer at President Rodríguez' "El Sauzal" property at Ensenada, Lower California. Before leaving he recommended that all political leaders absolutely refrain from laying any groundwork in connection with the presidential succession. Portes Gil has made it clear that "El Sauzal" forthwith became "a Mecca" of politicians who wanted guidance to begin work for the future, but that "the hundreds of politicians who made trips to 'El Sauzal,' by every means of travel, returned unconsoled and always with the recommendation that it was 'unpatriotic to proceed in an effort so prematurely.' "[6] Late in April the President declared that his government would keep outside of politics and remain strictly neutral in order that the public might be able to express its opinion freely with regard to the election of a new President.

Colonel Adalberto Tejeda, who had served as President Calles' Gobernación Minister and who had twice been governor of Veracruz, was a particularly active politician who was making much progress in turning the means of production over to workers. Both he and Tabasco's Tomás Garrido Canabal were considered to be well regarded by Cárdenas. Whereas Garrido Canabal was the acknowledged top man among Tabasco's organized "Red Shirts," it

[5] *Ibid.*, p. 176.
[6] Emilio Portes Gil, *Quince años de política mexicana*, p. 462.

was Veracruz that contributed the first federal *diputado* to wear a red shirt in the Chamber of Deputies when Lic. Eugenio Méndez Aguirre took his seat so attired in April, 1933.

In spite of its leftist advances, however, Veracruz was in such a state of confusion that the new governor, Lic. Gonzalo Vázquez Vela, could not govern. The state's Liga de Comunidades Agrarias recognized only the authority of Colonel Tejeda. President Rodríguez had to take the step of sending General Miguel M. Acosta, famed for his Veracruz campaign against Aguirre in 1929, to carry out the difficult task of disarming the state's so-called "rural defenses." The local groups were well armed, and President Rodríguez felt that the arms should be under the control of the federal government.

Again, the President had to intervene in Veracruz when two different peasant groups, each claiming to be the Liga de Comunidades Agrarias, set up for the state two distinct governing bodies. The President wrote to Governor Vázquez Vela to say that he felt that the Liga de Comunidades Agrarias should separate itself from all official action of the state government and should not be considered as an organization for the fulfillment of political ends, but rather as an institution created for the benefit of the peasants and for their exclusive use.

Ing. Alberto J. Pani found himself nominated for the presidency by the Partido Civilista Renovador, whose directors he did not know. He turned the nomination down and pointed out to President Rodríguez that his nomination by such a party had been a plan of Lic. Napoleón Molina Enríquez, an agent of Colonel Tejeda, who sought to help Tejeda's candidacy by setting up a party and candidate of less radical tendencies. Although Pani claimed that his own position was as far to the left as the Revolution permitted, he felt that other "leaders and demagogues" went even further to the left, and "as they could not understand my lack of personal political aspirations, they classed me as a reactionary and attacked me, doing me the honor of considering me the most serious enemy of the new Communist tendency."[7]

Late in April, 1933, and early in May, the candidacy of General Cárdenas was pushed by Lic. Portes Gil, who continued to have the feeling that General Calles might pick either the man who was con-

[7] Alberto J. Pani, *La historia, agredida,* p. 169.

sidered to be his most intimate friend, Colonel Carlos Riva Palacio, or else the president of the official party, General Manuel Pérez Treviño.

From President Rodríguez, Portes Gil got approval of his plan to launch the candidacy of the Michoacán general. Then after consulting with Cárdenas, Portes Gil read to the President a manifesto dated May 1, 1933, which was worded by Marte R. Gómez and which was promptly published in the newspapers. It was signed by the Leagues of Agrarian Communities of Tamaulipas, San Luis Potosí, Michoacán, Chihuahua, Tlaxcala, and others. These leagues declared that the agrarian elements had decided to unite in order to be a factor in the coming presidential contest, and were joining with the Liga Nacional Campesina Ursulo Galván to declare in favor of General Cárdenas. It also suggested that the industrial labor elements likewise unite. The Liga Nacional Campesina Ursulo Galván (which in 1929 had combatted General Jesús Aguirre's Veracruz uprising) was asked to get in touch with the city workers.

Before this pro-Cárdenas manifesto was published Portes Gil had sent Enrique Flores Magón to Palomas, San Luis Potosí, to get the opinion of Saturnino Cedillo. This important army leader, who was considered to be pro-Catholic and less radical than Cárdenas, expressed his enthusiasm for the manifesto.

Some of the state governors were resolved to back the candidacy of Cárdenas. At the beginning of May President Rodríguez received a coded letter from General Agustín Olachea, who had done much to set back Manzo and the Topetes in Sonora in 1929 and who was now the governor of Northern Baja California. Dated as far back as April 19, it said:

A few days ago when Rodolfo [Elías Calles, governor of Sonora] was here to visit General Calles he indicated to me that the three candidates of the Party would be Manuel Pérez Treviño, Carlos Riva Palacio, and General Cárdenas; that he thought it would be wise for us to bring together a number of the governors so that the state representatives might launch the candidacy of General Cárdenas at the end of May. I told Rodolfo that I wanted to know nothing of politics, only what you or General Calles may want me to know, and he said to me that was impossible, but that he knew who, because of his civic and patriotic virtues, was the most feasible of the three. I exceedingly beg of you to give me your opinion on the matter . . .

On May 3 President Rodríguez sent a ciphered reply in which he repeated that the government supported no candidate for the presidency, it being Rodríguez' desire that the citizens freely elect the leader best satisfying their needs.

Among those with Calles at "El Sauzal" was Pérez Treviño, who now made a statement declaring that, having exchanged impressions with Calles, he felt that the time had come to initiate "the presidential efforts." The important federal *diputado* from Oaxaca, General Rafael Melgar, advised that another pro-Cárdenas manifesto would soon be launched. The newspapers reported that "politics is in full effervescence" and "the presidential campaign cannot be delayed any longer."

In the meantime Cárdenas was busy reorganizing the Ministry of War and Navy. Francisco J. Múgica, who had been in California for three months trying to buy a warship for the use of the Islas Marías, was in May, 1933, appointed Quartermaster General of the Army.

In writing about the political activities of those moments Múgica points out that Calles, who was in Lower California, had by no external act indicated his good will toward the candidacy of Cárdenas; that Cárdenas did not feel that there was much likelihood of success, "for at that time it was indispensable to be able to count on the good will of the Gran Elector"; and that although Cárdenas had sufficient prestige to arouse the nation in his favor, he lacked the necessary accompaniments, money and political connections, with which to swing an election.

But then, Múgica continues, a son of Calles acted in favor of the candidacy of Cárdenas, a candidacy which quickly "found wide response from the people."[8] Although Múgica appears to be speaking about the pro-Cárdenas sentiment of Diputado Plutarco Elías Calles, Jr. (who was in Monterrey at the time of these events), greater importance must be given to the part played by another son, Rodolfo Elías Calles. Gaxiola writes that "the letter of General Olachea leaves no doubt that the launching of the candidacy of General Cárdenas was done by a group of governors at the initiative of the Sonora governor, Rodolfo Elías Calles, and as the invitation to Olachea himself was made after an interview of the Sonora governor with his father, General Calles, it was logical to suppose that the work of development, if not done in accord with his will and under his direction, was at least carried forward with his tacit approval."[9]

[8] Armando de María y Campos, *Múgica*, pp. 249–250.
[9] Francisco Javier Gaxiola, Jr., *op. cit.*, p. 179.

Some politicians assumed that Rodolfo Elías Calles had spoken for his father and were impressed on that account. Nor was President Rodríguez' favorable opinion of Cárdenas an unimportant factor. Of the four outstanding generals who had dramatically departed in a group from the Ortiz Rubio Cabinet (Amaro, Cedillo, Almazán, and Cárdenas), Cárdenas alone was holding a post in the Rodríguez Cabinet, a fact which made it unlikely that his name would be ignored. Other politicians, not moved to act on the basis of guessing the opinions of Calles or Rodríguez, but simply because of their own high esteem of his record, were pleased to be able to jump on the Cárdenas bandwagon.[10] In the minds of many Lázaro Cárdenas, who was a more astute politician than some of them realized, had something fresher to offer than did older political leaders who for so many years had been prominent in running the official machinery. In Michoacán, and as a soldier, and in his short span on the national political scene, Cárdenas had revealed serious enthusiasm for the Revolution; he had revealed personal attributes of energy and honesty which seemed likely to attract a popular following.

Those who supposed that Calles' sons were expressing opinions at their father's suggestion were wrong. The ex-President was content at a rather early date to indicate three candidates, Pérez Treviño, Carlos Riva Palacio, and Cárdenas, and leave it at that, expressing the wish that the most favored one win even if it should be necessary to await the formal nominating convention to find the answer. Calles' sons and everyone else were perfectly free to carry on as they wished, and this they did. The result was a hearty popular acclaim for Cárdenas, an acclaim which was perhaps surprising to some, and one in which Aarón Sáenz raised his voice at an early stage.[11]

President Rodríguez, who had resolved to administer the nation's business and leave the "political nuisance" in Calles' hands, asked Calles whether it would be advisable for Cárdenas to resign his War Ministry post and dedicate himself to the campaign. Calles agreed that this action would be good.

[10] Agustín Arroyo Ch., interview, August 16, 1956.
[11] Plutarco Elías Calles, Jr., interview, January 19, 1959; Francisco Javier Gaxiola, Jr., interview, January 14, 1959; Alberto J. Pani, op. cit., pp. 169–170; Ezequiel Padilla, conversation, January 16, 1959. See Nathaniel and Sylvia Weyl, op. cit., p. 108; also Emilio Portes Gil, op. cit., p. 468.

Cárdenas' resignation, effective May 15, was announced by the press on May 8. Newspapers guessed that his successor would be Miguel M. Acosta, who had been disarming peasants in Veracruz, but they found themselves mistaken when the appointment went to Pablo Quiroga, who had been in charge of the War Ministry before Cárdenas had taken it over.

On May 12, 1933, General Manuel Pérez Treviño resigned as president of the P.N.R. in order to carry on his campaign for the presidency of the nation. The Guanajuato governor (1932–1935), Melchor Ortega, became the new head of the Party in a move that was satisfactory for Pérez Treviño. During the presidential term of Ortiz Rubio differences had arisen between politicians who then dominated Guanajuato, on the one hand, and Cárdenas and Ortiz Rubio, on the other. The political group which was in power in Guanajuato and was associated with Ortega now supported Manuel Pérez Treviño for the presidency of the republic.[12]

As Cárdenas prepared himself for two days of rest in Cuernavaca, it was announced that Calles would be present at the next national convention of the P.N.R. in Querétaro, and there were reports that he would soon return to Mexico City from Baja California, where he was surrounded by politicians. In the meantime various political groups came to the public's attention as they pushed for various candidates.

Leftist groups of agrarians and railroad workers came out in favor of the candidacy of Ramón P. de Negri, who had served as head of the National Railways and as Minister of Agriculture and of Industry, Commerce, and Labor. But De Negri announced that he had been unable to convince himself of the effectiveness of the vote, and added that "the existence of political democracy is impossible while economic democracy does not also exist." A Comité Pro-Luis Cabrera was organized to support Carranza's Finance Minister, who in January, 1931, had declared that "there is not a single public official who has been really elected by the people."[13] A new party, calling itself the Gran Partido Revolucionario Institucional, came out with a manifesto in favor of Cárdenas.

While Generals Cárdenas and Pérez Treviño were carrying on political activities late in May, politicians arrived in Mexico City from Baja California. These were Melchor Ortega (Party president), Eduardo Vasconcelos (Gobernación Minister), Bartolomé

[12] Melchor Ortega, interview, September 13, 1956.
[13] Hubert Herring and Herbert Weinstock (eds.), *Renascent Mexico*, p. 153.

García Correa (Yucatán governor and a leader of the Socialist Party of the Southeast), Filiberto Gómez (governor of the state of México) and various federal senators and deputies. Melchor Ortega and Eduardo Vasconcelos went at once to confer with Senator Carlos Riva Palacio.

A serious problem at this time was the control of the Permanent Commission of the Congress. The new Cardenista bloc of Congress called on President Rodríguez to advise that they had a majority in the Congress and in the Permanent Commission. But the supporters of Pérez Treviño also claimed control of the Commission. Gaxiola reports that "ten days after the resignations of Generals Cárdenas and Pérez Treviño, the political discomposure had reached such an extreme, the attacks were so violent, and sectarianism was so passioned, that the Permanent Commission . . . was on the verge of dissolving because each of the two contending groups sought to rule."[14] President Rodríguez told the deputy secretary of the Commission that the Commission's disintegration would "constitute a grave political threat."

A pro-Cárdenas propagandist was assassinated in Tlaxcala. In Mexico City Arturo Flores López and Bartolo Flores called a meeting of about forty politicians who had been members of the Thirty-second Congressional Legislature (1926–1928) and who were now gathering in a reunion in order to discuss their position in the presidential campaign. A number of these former congressmen mentioned the possibility of this group's coming to an agreement in favor of Cárdenas.

The P.N.R. announced that the forthcoming national party convention at Querétaro would take place on December 3, 1933. At the same time it announced a national P.N.R. plebiscite for August 6. At this plebiscite, which would take place in all the districts of the Republic and in the presence of the municipal Party members, the delegates to the national convention would be selected. There would be one delegate for every 10,000 inhabitants (or fractions thereof greater than 5000). "In this form each of the 170 electoral districts of the Republic will send ten delegates, all of them with perfectly defined affiliation." All of a district's delegates would vote for the pre-candidate who was the strongest in the district. "It will be unnecessary to count the votes one by one, but rather 10 by 10—170 tens."

[14] Francisco Javier Gaxiola, Jr., *El Presidente Rodríguez*, p. 181.

576

On the last day of May, 1933, General Cárdenas officially agreed to run for the presidency in the campaign which was to be concluded with the national election of July 1, 1934.

While the battle was still apparently hot, while Melchor Ortega was having his troubles running the Executive Committee of the P.N.R., and while the congressional Permanent Commission was in

General Calles, Ing. L. L. León, General Abelardo L. Rodríguez, General Manuel Pérez Treviño. *Enrique Diaz.*

a state of suspension, General Manuel Pérez Treviño withdrew as a presidential candidate. Gaxiola, who states that Pérez Treviño did this because of the high point reached by passions and the persistency of attacks, adds that his sacrifice assured for the P.N.R a unified and consolidated position. Pérez Treviño took this step on June 7, and on the eighth it was announced that he was to return to the leadership of the Party and that Ortega would return to the Guanajuato governorship. Ortega proclaimed his mission terminated on account of Pérez Treviño's decision to withdraw as a candidate in the contest, and from "El Sauzal" Calles wrote to Pérez Treviño congratulating him for his patriotic conduct.

At a meeting of members of the P.N.R.'s Executive Committee Ortega presented his resignation as Party head. But although 17 members were needed to make up a quorum, only 14 showed up, including Pérez Treviño, Ortega, Flores Muñoz, Manuel Riva Palacio, and Luis L. León. Of the total membership of the committee, five were absent from Mexico City and of the remainder about one-half were on one side and one-half on the other with regard to the struggle between Pérez Treviño and Cárdenas. Since nonattending members who were in Mexico City were largely considered to be Cardenistas, Cárdenas was asked whether he had authorized the absence of the large bloc. He replied that he had not.

When the P.N.R. Executive Committee could gather a quorum, Pérez Treviño was for the third time chosen to be its president, to which step Gaxiola attributes the end of the danger of the disintegration of the congressional Permanent Commission. But political passions and disagreements within the Party did not altogether die down, and in August, following the P.N.R. plebiscites, Pérez Treviño had to abandon his post. As possible successors General Múgica, Lic. Sáenz, and Senator Carlos Riva Palacio emerged, and it was the last-named who was selected to act as conciliator.

65.

Efforts by the Opposition in 1933 and 1934

The opposition parties were having no fewer troubles in deciding among candidates.

Following reports that Veracruz' Colonel Adalberto Tejeda and Michoacán's General Lázaro Cárdenas had not reached an agreement to join forces, the Partido Laborista Mexicano held its convention at the Capitolio movie theatre. This was in June, 1933. Candidates whose names were considered were: Luis N. Morones, Celestino Gasca, Adalberto Tejeda, and Lázaro Cárdenas. A great many delegates were from the state of Veracruz, and, at least at the outset, much enthusiasm existed for the "red-shirt, radical labor leader," Colonel Tejeda. Then Sabino Calderón, of the Córdoba delegation, made a sensational speech in which he accused Tejeda and Vicente Lombardo Toledano of having sought to use the administrations of the C.R.O.M. and of the Partido Laborista Mexicano for personal ends, that is, as means for attaining the nation's presidency. Calderón added that Tejeda's work in Veracruz had been anarchical. After this there was a great acclaim for Cárdenas.

Early in July, 1933, the Partido Nacional Antirreeleccionista held a preliminary session at which Lic. Luis Cabrera and General Antonio I. Villarreal received much support. Ing. Vito Alessio Robles spoke against Lic. José Vasconcelos, saying that the 1929 Antirreeleccionista candidate had taken advantage of his candidacy merely to make money and live well. By acclamation the Antirreeleccionistas agreed not to recognize Vasconcelos, who was living in Spain following his failure to organize a Mexican rebellion from Guatemala and who had been writing under the name of "José Vasconcelos, President of Mexico."

Late in July Calles and Cárdenas reached Mexico City after a trip down the west coast in the *Tren Amarillo* (yellow train). But soon after this Calles' health was again reported to be poor, and he had to postpone a meeting with Cardenista senators and *diputados*. Although General Villarreal had a meeting with Colonel Tejeda, no political pact was agreed upon, and on August 4 Villarreal recommended the candidacy of Lic. Cabrera.

Early in October Governor Rodolfo Elías Calles went to join his father, who, it will be recalled, was at this time receiving medical treatment and conferring with President Rodríguez at Tehuacán. At the Anzures residence large groups of senators and *diputados* had called on Rodolfo. Having been one who formally initiated the candidacy of Cárdenas, he was looked upon as one of the principal political leaders of the moment, and he was reportedly slated to head the Agriculture Ministry or the P.N.R.

Also in October enthusiasts of Colonel Adalberto Tejeda held their own convention without awaiting the P.N.R. convention, and so they were thrown out of the official Party. Colonel Tejeda was nominated for the presidency by the Partido Socialista de las Izquierdas (Socialist Party of the Leftists). "We, the leftists," said Tejeda, "have made ourselves heard, and we know how to make ourselves heard both by our supporters and by our enemies."

One political party, which called itself the Partido Pro Patria, had the idea of somehow nominating President Rodríguez for the presidential term of 1934 to 1940. Both Cárdenas and Senator Carlos Riva Palacio congratulated Rodríguez for advising this group that he would not accept its strange offer even if the no re-election clause were not in the Constitution.

Luis Cabrera considered that in the latter part of 1933 the opposition consisted of a number of minor groups and two major groups. Minor groups included Tejeda's Party of the Socialists of the Left; also the Partido Social Democrático supporting Lic. Gilberto Valenzuela, a small group which backed Lic. Enrique Colunga, and some agrarians who wanted Lic. Román Badillo. The major opposition

Foreground: General Lázaro Cárdenas, General Abelardo Rodríguez; Lic. Narciso Bassols (*at far right*). *Enrique Díaz.*

groups consisted of the Partido Nacional Antirreeleccionista, which favored Cabrera, and the Confederación Revolucionaria de Partidos Independientes, which supported Antonio I. Villarreal and which included among its leaders Aurelio Manrique, Jr., and Díaz Soto y Gama.

The Antirreeleccionista Party and the Confederación Revolucionaria de Partidos Independientes on November 19, 1933, had a lively meeting at the Politeama Theatre before it was broken up by gases which made it impossible for the anti-P.N.R. crowd to remain in the hall. Díaz Soto y Gama differentiated between those whom he considered to have failed to live up to purity, and those who were the great idealists of the Revolution which they were commemorating. In the first category he included Plutarco Elías Calles ("the greatest magnate and Mexico's greatest capitalist"), Aarón Sáenz ("the regent"), Carlos Riva Palacio, Luis León, and Narciso Bassols. "The struggle today," he said, is against these men and against the "quack" Vicente Lombardo Toledano, whom he considered "an instrument of Calles."

In the second (the praiseworthy) category, Díaz Soto y Gama included Aquiles Serdán, Belisario Domínguez, Ricardo Flores Magón, Madero, Juan Sarabia, Zapata, and Praxedis Guerrero and all of the martyrs. Someone in the audience shouted "Francisco Villa" and the orator added his name. Another from the audience then cried "Carrillo Puerto" and Soto y Gama added: "Carrillo Puerto, also." The crowd was very vocal throughout the speech. "Is there liberty in Mexico?" "No." "Who has the sugar monopoly?" "Calles." "The milk monopoly?" "Calles." "Who seeks the salt monopoly?" "Calles." "Who uses the railroad for his personal business?" "Calles." "We have a Wall Street here; it is Callismo." "Death to Callismo."

In November, 1923, just ten years before, Lic. Díaz Soto y Gama had praised Calles at a Partido Agrarista meeting and had at the same time spoken to the peasant representatives about the virtues of Christ and the foolishness of those who proclaimed Christ to be King. Now Díaz Soto y Gama spoke again about the greatness of Christ. "I tell you sincerely and with all the frankness of my conviction: between Christ and Lenin, I choose Christ." One of the listeners shouted, "I choose Lenin."

Professor Aurelio Manrique, Jr., introduced General Antonio I. Villarreal, who mentioned the assassinations of Lucio Blanco, Arnulfo R. Gómez, Francisco R. Serrano, Martínez de Escobar, and the poet Otilio González. Someone shouted "Villa" and someone else added "Obregón." When Villarreal asked what had been accomplished during ten years of Callismo, a listener replied, "Robbery." The Nuevo León general told his listeners that the 30 million pesos spent on the Don Martín Dam had been largely wasted to irrigate land that was no good. The only result, he said, was the creation of an artificial lake, good for recreation and for impressing tourists, but practically useless for the district.

Villarreal made sarcastic remarks about the El Mante sugar *cooperativa* established by "that humble farmer," Plutarco Elías Calles, and the "poor" Aarón Sáenz. He pointed out that the nation had spent another 30 million pesos in creating that *cooperativa*, whose members included the sons and sons-in-law of Calles and relatives of Sáenz.

Just before the meeting was broken up, General Villarreal was pleasing his audience with a description of the dynasty of "His Majesty" Calles, "the supreme maker of Presidents." He mentioned "Prince" Rodolfo Elías Calles, "ruler of the principality of Sonora," Plutarco Elías Calles, Jr., who headed "the principality of Nuevo León," and the third son, Alfredo, "destined to take over the principality of Tamaulipas, where he exercises so much influence that the present governor, from week to week, goes to seek his advice and orders." He called Fernando Torreblanca the "prince consort" in charge of Foreign Relations. He discussed the "grand dukes," Francisco Elías, Minister of Agriculture, and Arturo M. Elías, head of the postal and telegraph services. Villarreal was advising his listeners that Arturo M. Elías had been a Mexican consul in the Porfirio Díaz regime when the explosion of gas bombs broke up the meeting. Without success Villarreal sought to calm the crowd and carry on. Nor was Aurelio Manrique, Jr., able to prevent the crowd from scattering from the gases which had been let loose.

The speakers and the crowd had praised Cabrera,[1] Villarreal, Manrique, Díaz Soto y Gama, Valenzuela, Tejeda, Vito Alessio Robles, and José Vasconcelos. The audience (or a part of it) had cried "Death to Morones," apparently not sharing the views propounded in 1926 and 1927 by Dr. Retinger and Mr. Hicks to the effect that Morones had been his country's greatest moral leader, whose name would surely rank in history with that of Benito Juárez.

---

[1] Luis Cabrera had got into trouble with the Ortiz Rubio Administration in a dispute involving the creation of an underground passage at the busy section of Mexico City where the wide street of San Juan de Letran intersects the Avenue of 16 de Septiembre. By means of this underground passageway people could cross either San Juan de Letran or 16 de Septiembre without concern about automobile traffic. Some detractors of Ortiz Rubio proclaimed the construction of this underground passage to be the greatest achievement of Ortiz Rubio's administration.

It remained to be seen whether the two leading opposition groups, who had sponsored the November 19 meeting, could get together for a general convention. The convention, originally set for January 1, 1934, was first postponed until February 5, and it was between these two dates that Lic. Cabrera drew up his statement, published on January 25, announcing his decision to decline the nomination which the Antirreeleccionistas wanted to give him. His reasons were many. Under the circumstances it was most unlikely that an opposition candidate would attain the presidency. Although General Villarreal had recommended Cabrera, the Confederación Revolucionaria de Partidos Independientes was apparently determined to go ahead with the candidacy of Villarreal, an action which would result in two opposition candidates. And as for Villarreal, Cabrera could not forget that this General represented a wing of Obregonismo, enemy of the Carrancismo represented by Cabrera.

In his letter of January 31 to Díaz Soto y Gama, Cabrera denied that he was guilty, as charged by Díaz Soto y Gama, of egoism or cowardice. "I do not wish to take part, least of all as the central figure, in the democratic farce which is being prepared for July." He pointed out that the current situation was not the result of the political Revolution of 1910, nor of the social Revolution of 1913, but was the result of the Agua Prieta movement, and he added that he could not accept the leadership of a group that in substance was no more than a branch of Obregonismo.[2]

The convention of the united stronger opposition groups suffered another postponement, this time until March 1. Finally two separate conventions were called for April 1, and so it was not until the spring of 1934, after Cárdenas had been formally nominated by the P.N.R. and after he was well into his very strenuous campaign, that the stronger opposition groups got down to the business of selecting from among candidates.

The Partido Nacional Antirreeleccionista was joined by some other non-P.N.R. groups to form the Consejo Nacional de la Oposición, whose directors, in March, 1934, asked for and received the government's permission to hold a convention. This they did in the Salón Palacio on San Miguel Street. Besides including representatives of the Partido Nacional Antirreeleccionista, this new Consejo

[2] Luis Cabrera (pseud., Blas Urrea), *Veinte años despues*, p. 170.

was formed of representatives of the Partido Acción Nacional (organized by Lic. Octavio Elizalde, and not connected with today's party of the same name), the Confederación Nacionalista Democrática, and the Social Anticomunista. General Villarreal and his supporters refused to attend this convention, which favored Lic. Gilberto Valenzuela, who had been out of the country since the collapse of the Escobar rebellion. Following the suggestion of Ing. Alessio Robles, the delegates at the Consejo did not vote candidate by candidate, but left all voting to follow the discussion of all candidates. The assembly refused to discuss the absent Gen. Villarreal. Much was said for and against Lic. Cabrera.

Lic. Gilberto Valenzuela was nominated and the well-known agrarian leader, Lic. Román Badillo, was named "vice-candidate." Then the Confederación Nacionalista Democrática asked President Rodríguez' permission for Valenzuela to return to the country, and advice of these events was sent to the nominee in El Paso, Texas. Valenzuela accepted the nomination, expressing his gratitude for the honor, and said that he planned to enter the country as soon as possible.

A few days later the Villarreal supporters, led by Professor Aurelio Manrique, Jr., proceeded to hold their own convention. This was the convention of the Confederación Revolucionaria de Partidos Independientes. Antirreeleccionista delegates from Tamaulipas, who had walked out of the convention that had nominated Valenzuela, hesitated to appear also as delegates to the subsequent convention which nominated Villarreal for the presidency. General Villarreal proceeded at once to campaign throughout the nation, accompanied by Antonio Díaz Soto y Gama and by Aurelio Manrique, Jr.

Meanwhile there was a great controversy about Gilberto Valenzuela's return. Lic. José G. Aguilar, president of the Consejo Nacional de la Oposición, tried to show that since the penalty for rebellion was a prison term of one to six years (and a fine of 100,000 pesos), the average was three and one-half years, and as five years had passed since the Escobar rebellion, there was no reason for Lic. Valenzuela not to return now. Gobernación Minister Eduardo Vasconcelos stated that the government never had prevented Lic. Valenzuela from returning, but that certain antecedents made it seem that he would not return since charges against him for his responsibility in connection with the Escobar rebellion were still pending. One anti-Calles writer, J. Manuel Corro Viña, states that

Calles, acting through President Rodríguez, prohibited Valenzuela's entry into Mexico because Valenzuela was so thoroughly aware of the looting that had been carried on by Callismo and its leader.[3]

Early in April, 1934, Gilberto Valenzuela sent from El Paso, Texas, to Mexico City his resignation as an opposition candidate, after having assured himself that the authorities would not permit his return to the country to conduct an active campaign. Román Badillo, the "vice-candidate" of the Consejo Nacional de la Oposición therefore claimed the mantle of Valenzuela and announced that he would start campaigning as candidate for the presidency. But the elements that made up the Consejo Nacional de la Oposición began to fall apart. Not only did the ties which held the four groups together collapse, but internal divisions within each group also developed. When some stated that Valenzuela was going to enter the country after all, Badillo said that he would return to his position of "vice-candidate" should the Sonora lawyer actually show up. Then when Valenzuela made it clear that his resignation was irrevocable, the Valenzuelistas announced that they would refrain from voting at the election.

While in May and June, 1934, Generals Cárdenas and Villarreal and Colonel Tejeda were busy campaigning, the third vice-president of the Partido Nacional Antirreeleccionista said that he and the president of the Partido Acción Nacional were going to phone Lic. Valenzuela to learn of his reasons for resigning. When Antirreeleccionista Party officials then announced that the party was not going to vote, but would limit itself to "watching over" the elections, other Antirreeleccionistas protested against this announcement by the Party's directors. Some Antirreeleccionista campaigning in favor of Lic. Badillo occurred, but at the end of June (just prior to the election) the press indicated that not many were backing Badillo and that the Confederación Nacionalista Democrática, the Partido Acción Nacional, and the Partido Nacional Antirreeleccionista were without a candiate.

Late in June, 1934, Colonel Tejeda, of the Partido Socialista de las Izquierdas, explained that he had begun to part company with the government when Lic. Portes Gil engaged in discussions with churchmen to end the religious difficulties. The Veracruz leader attacked the P.N.R., but he did not attack General Cárdenas, and it is reported that Cárdenas asked his followers not to make attacks

[3] J. Manuel Corro Viña, *Cárdenas frente a Calles*, p. 87.

against Tejeda. Although Tejeda was praising Communism, the Communists had their own candidate in the well-known Communist leader, Hernán Laborde, who as far back as April, 1933, had been nominated in the Salón Palacio by the Communist National Convention of Laborers and Peasants.

Cárdenas, in an amazing campaign, had covered about 18,000 miles, and much of the journey had been slow going because the official party's candidate had visited the people in the smallest villages. He is an indefatigable worker with an extraordinary memory. He listened with real sympathy to the problems of the Indians, the peasants, the laborers, and the poor people, and when he spoke to them they were impressed by his sincerity. "To the Mexican people I do not offer the empty phrases of 'freedom of conscience,' 'freedom of teaching,' and 'economic freedom.' For I know that the first represents the dictatorship of the clergy; the second represents the dictatorship of the reaction which seeks to oppose the labor of the revolutionary regime on behalf of popular culture; while the third represents the capitalist dictatorship. . . . One of my greatest desires is that the working class should have the doors of power frankly opened to it. . . . If I am elected President . . . , all closed factories which cannot be reopened by their owners will be rented and turned over to the workers organized in co-operatives, so that under government direction they may produce for their own benefit. . . . The Revolution wills that the agrarian principles be accomplished faithfully throughout the country."[4]

H. F. Hurley tells of Cárdenas' visit during the campaign to the San Luis Potosí smelter of the American Smelting and Refining Company. While he and Cárdenas were observing the 275-foot stack at the plant Hurley told the candidate of how ten years earlier Aurelio Manrique, Jr., then governor of the state, had expressed a desire to climb the stack, and of how Manrique and Hurley had returned to the ground before reaching the top. With some satisfaction Hurley noted that Cárdenas' interest in the stack was limited to the story about Manrique but did not extend to following his example by making the climb. The presidential candidate was, however, full of interest in what was being done at the smelter on behalf of the workers.

[4] Nathaniel and Sylvia Weyl, *The Reconquest of Mexico*, pp. 129–130, 137.

Lázaro Cárdenas campaigns for the presidency in remote districts and hears about the problems of the poor. 1934.

On the eve of the election, radios brought to the nation the voice of Cárdenas, speaking from Durango. The thirty-nine–year–old candidate discussed the government program which he would follow, if elected, and which had been drawn up in the Six-Year Plan.

To the agrarians he promised an intensification of land distribution and of *ejidal* restitution. He supported more credit facilities, more irrigation, more roads; also the organization of co-operatives so as to do away with speculation by intermediaries.

To the workers he said that collective labor bargaining would be strengthened until it became exclusive. Co-operatives, he told the workers, would bring them the progressive conquest of the productive machinery, a conquest which he defined as the ideal of the socialistic doctrine of the Revolution. While this was going forward, said Cárdenas, a national economy, directed and regulated by the state, must be formed.

We must free ourselves of the capitalism that exploits, that makes Mexico a nation of a colonial economy, that leaves behind waste, impoverished subsoil, hunger, and ill-being, such as precede public unrest. The candidate added that the national sentiment of such an economic policy did not close the door to national and foreign business organizers, provided that these adjusted themselves to the laws of the Revolution and respected the government.

The state, said Cárdenas, must direct private as well as public education; and it must fight against the ideological chaos which results from attacks on the state by the defenders of the past and the enemies of the Revolutionary call to social solidarity. The Plan calls for the socialistic school.

Turning to religion, the candidate proclaimed that the government must continue with its pledge on behalf of the spiritual and material emancipation of the Mexican population. At this point the speaker returned to the subject of education and pointed to the necessity of stimulating utilitarian and collectivistic teaching. Such teaching, he said, prepares the students for co-operative production, which develops the love of work as a social duty.

Cárdenas did not finish this election-eve radio address without making it clear that he would continue the policy of creating additional irrigation, roads, railways, and airways. He would also seek a resurgence and nationalization of the merchant marine.[5]

[5] Lázaro Cárdenas quoted in *El Universal,* July 1, 1934.

On election day General Cárdenas cast his own vote in favor of Tabasco's "Red Shirt," Lic. Tomás Garrido Canabal. In the course of the following days, various announcements of the election results were made, one such announcement showing these figures:

Antonio I. Villarreal	24,690 votes
Adalberto Tejeda	15,765 votes
Hernán Laborde	1,888 votes
Lázaro Cárdenas	2,268,507 votes

In some preliminary returns, made public on July 3, Laborde was given as many as 6,406 votes. On the other hand a later tabulation shows: Laborde 539, Tejeda 16,037, Villarreal 24,395, and Cárdenas 2,225,000.

Some election-day disorders were reported in Tampico and in Monterrey between Cardenistas and Villarrealistas struggling for possession of voting booths, and Villarrealistas phoned from various places to say that no opposition ballots had been available at booths and that "independents" had been violently ejected. While Cárdenas and Calles, at Ciudad Obregón, Sonora, were receiving many congratulatory visitors, reports varied as to whether Villarreal was in Monterrey or the United States. Lic. Díaz Soto y Gama and Professor Aurelio Manrique, Jr., were in San Antonio, Texas, ostensibly resting, and it was later learned that these two politicians planned to go to Los Angeles, California, to give some lectures. The government said that, as far as it was concerned, there was no reason for General Villarreal to leave the country.

The propaganda secretary of the Confederación Nacionalista Democrática announced what he called the "true results": 2,873,-118 votes for Lic. Gilberto Valenzuela. Valenzuela, he said, is the President-elect.

Officials announced that the election had been the most peaceful one in recent times, and that of 150 congressional credentials, only six duplications had occurred through the presentation of credentials by non-P.N.R. persons. This was the least such duplication since the start of the Constitucionalista Revolution in 1913.

On July 23 General Calles arrived in Mexico City together with the P.N.R.'s chief, Senator Carlos Riva Palacio, and the governors of Jalisco and Sinaloa, Sebastián Allende and Manuel Páez. But General Cárdenas continued his journeying throughout the Republic. He left on a "study" trip to visit Colima and parts of Michoacán.

66·

Negotiations with the United States under President Rodríguez

At the London Economic and Monetary Conference of July, 1933, Mexico entered into a silver agreement signed by China, Spain, and India, as silver consumers, and by Australia, Canada, the United States, Mexico, and Peru, as producers. This agreement to "rehabilitate and stabilize the price of silver" was designed to stimulate the world's use of silver for coinage, and may have been helpful to Mexico, whose annual production of 100 million ounces made it the world's greatest silver producer. Otherwise the London Conference, where various nations assumed protectionist policies, did not appear very helpful to Mexico—or to anyone.

Although 1933 showed some financial and commercial improvements over the low points reached just before General Rodríguez assumed the presidency, it turned out to be another deficit year for the Mexican treasury, with receipts totalling about 233 million pesos and expenditures roughly 240 million. The next year was very much better, as is evident from the jump in the value of Mexican exports in 1934 to 645 million pesos over a figure of 365 million in 1933. It also turned out to be a year of surplus for federal finances, with receipts of 296 million pesos against expenditures of 265 million. Some of the effects of the business improvement and of the new Mexican monetary policy are revealed in the following statistics:[1]

Year	Average Monthly Rediscounts by Bank of Mexico (thousands of pesos)	Number of Credit Institutions	Number of Auxiliary Credit Institutions	Money in Circulation % in Coins	% in Banknotes
1931	3,964	65	....	99.44	0.56
1932	22,988	53	10	86.17	13.83
1933	25,021	68	21	79.82	20.18
1934	34,205	77	29	68.74	31.26

The National Railways of Mexico also were able to report improvements. Gross revenues which had amounted to 73,460.461 pesos in 1932, were reported as 81,815,366 pesos in 1933 and 104,-211,822 pesos in 1934. (The 1934 figure was still below that for 1930, nor were the pesos, affected by regulations of 1931 and 1932, equivalent to the earlier ones.) The amount of freight carried increased from 5,003,554 metric tons in 1932 to 7,475,362 tons in 1934.[2]

Petroleum production, which had dropped from 193 million barrels in 1921 to 50 million barrels in 1928, had continued to fall off, although at a slower rate, until the bottom of the depression, and its recovery thereafter was not spectacular:

[1] Francisco Javier Gaxiola, Jr., *El Presidente Rodríguez*, pp. 375, 399.
[2] Vicente Fuentes Díaz, *El problema ferrocarrilero de México*, p. 121.

	Approximate Production (millions of barrels)[3]
1928	50
1929	45
1930	40
1931	33
1932	32.5
1933	34
1934	38

Feeling that the economic crisis would be better combatted by making payments which would have some likelihood of staying in the country, the Rodríguez Administration gave less comfort to the holders of the Mexican foreign debt than to holders of the internal public debt, and it devoted over 100 million pesos to amortizing the domestic obligations. Among the new authorized domestic debts was an issue of 40-year bonds (up to 100 million pesos) to be used in part to cover government obligations which had been accumulating for various years, and in part to liquidate finally the old banks of issue. The government also arranged to borrow 20 million pesos to be used in 1934 and 1935 to complete the work on the Laredo-Mexico City highway. This road-building loan was guaranteed by the Banco Nacional Hipotecario Urbano y de Obras Públicas, established in 1933, largely by government capital, to promote the building of pavements, market places, sewages, and water lines in small towns. Another financial institution established by the government of Abelardo Rodríguez, was Nacional Financiera, S.A., which, though not properly appreciated at the time, turned out, with the passage of years, to be the greatest lever for the industrial development of the country. Its function was the purchase and sale of securities.

In the September, 1934, presidential report to Congress, the nation learned that on May 21, 1934, the Mexican government had officially broken off relations with the International Bankers Committee. Not only did Mexico reject the idea of seeking to pay beyond her capacity by means of one refunding operation after another in a series of "capitalizations" which were believed to hide reality temporarily, but she also maintained that the International Bankers

[3] Secretaría de la Economía Nacional, *Anuario estadístico, 1938*, p. 203.

Committee acted illegally and was unfriendly to Mexico. Mexico referred to the Committee's "illegal and unjust" retention of about 7 million dollars which Mexico had paid under the Pani-Lamont Amendment of 1925 but which the Committee had not distributed to the bondholders.

Finance Minister Marte R. Gómez designated Eduardo Suárez to discuss in New York with Thomas Lamont the return to Mexico of the 7 million dollars "in gold." In the course of these talks Lamont first suggested that the Committee retain the funds as a basis of negotiation when Mexico was ready to work out a new debt agreement, but Mexico turned this suggestion down, making it clear that she did not recognize the Committee. Mexico likewise rejected Lamont's proposal of placing the disputed money in a bank or "neutral" institution pending an accomplished agreement. During the negotiations a third plan was proposed, that of distributing about 3 million dollars to the bondholders and of returning the remainder, less the distribution expenses, to the Mexican government. But subsequent messages from the Mexican Presidency to Marte Gómez, at the Waldorf Astoria in New York, made it clear that nothing should be done that might be interpreted as a renewal of relations with the Bankers Committee and that nothing less than the entire 7 million dollars should be accepted. President Rodríguez wished in no way to become involved in any compromises that might hamper the new administration which was about to take office.

When this matter went before the United States courts, the International Bankers Committee claimed to be acting as trustee for the bondholders, whereas Mexico, whose case was handled by Jerome Hess, argued that the Bankers Committee was acting as a paying agent and the United States courts should be considered ineligible to rule in the case. By this time the holders of Mexico's foreign bonds came to be represented by a new organization, the Foreign Bondholders Protective Committee.

Of the four or five formal Cabinet meetings which occurred during the presidential administration of General Rodríguez, two were called to deal with the controversy between the United States and Mexico in connection with defining the border.

The most serious border complication, that of El Chamizal in El Paso, had been festering for years, and the American Embassy seemed anxious that some definite resolution be reached prior to the

March, 1933, change of administration in Washington. El Chamizal is a section of the city of El Paso which had originally been south of the Río Grande (Río Bravo) and therefore originally Mexican. Natural forces caused the river to move gradually southward in 1853 and 1854. The Mexican government claimed that the more pronounced southward movement of the river in 1864 was an "abrupt and sudden change of the current" (not an erosive change) and therefore she should not lose her territory on account of that change. The problem became the subject of international arbitration, and in 1911 a Canadian arbiter, La Fleur, ruled that about one-third of El Chamizal belonged to the United States and about two-thirds belonged to Mexico. This gave Mexico about 160 hectares, but the United States government refused to accept the award, on the basis that it was "both impossible of performance and utterly void of law."[4] As El Chamizal became more and more an urbanized part of the city of El Paso, Mexican governments were unable to get the actual return of the land in accordance with the award, and therefore sought compensation. President Madero sought more Colorado River water for Mexico. Foreign Minister Aarón Sáenz on April 27, 1925, declared that "Mexico would not ask the material execution (of the Chamizal return), recognizing the great difficulty of it, but would take a just and fair compensation."[5]

By August, 1932, the United States ambassador (1930–1933), J. Reuben Clark, Jr., and Foreign Minister Manuel Téllez had worked out some ideas for a settlement of pending territorial problems. As part of the compensation for El Chamizal they looked to the matter of the Fondo Piadoso in California. The Hague Permanent Tribunal of Arbitration had in 1902 stipulated that Mexico should make certain annual interest payments on account of the Fondo Piadoso, or else a lump-sum payment of more than one million pesos, and by 1932 Mexico was behind on these annual payments by over 344,000 pesos.[6] The negotiators of 1932 furthermore

---

[4] Josephus Daniels, *Shirt-Sleeve Diplomat*, p. 117. See also Howard F. Cline, *The United States and Mexico*, p. 14, and Francisco Javier Gaxiola, Jr., *op. cit.*, p. 212.

[5] Francisco Javier Gaxiola, Jr., *op. cit.*, p. 213.

[6] When the Jesuits were expelled from Mexico in 1767 some assets (the Fondo Piadoso de California). which had been set up for their mission in Lower California, passed into the possession of the Spanish Viceroyalty. After Mexico's independence in 1821, the Mexican government put the Fondo at the disposition of the bishopric of the Californias. But in 1842 the Mexican government sold the assets, assuming the obligation of paying the bishopric 6 per cent yearly

proposed that the technical program of the International Boundary Commission be carried out so as to avoid future disputes like that about El Chamizal, and that of these engineering costs the United States pay 92 per cent and Mexico 8 per cent. The Mexican island of Córdoba, being north of the course of the Rio Grande, would go to the United States; and the United States island of San Elisario, south of the Rio Grande's course, would go to Mexico.

At the Cabinet meeting of October 23, 1932, Foreign Minister Téllez presented the projected settlement. It was attacked by Ing. Pani on the basis of a memorandum which he had earlier requested of Lic. Fernando González Roa, and it was also attacked by Lic. Bassols. Bassols pointed out that "territorial compensation should not be based on land area, but on the value of the land in El Chamizal." Ing. Pani brought up the question of possible claims against the Mexican government if she renounced rights of her nationals, and he also cited the Constitutional prohibition against parting with any of the national territory. He said that the Téllez-Clark proposals might be construed as meaning that Mexico was parting with El Chamizal for money. President Rodríguez expressed his opposition to the plan which Téllez had presented, and the Cabinet members, except for Téllez, voted against it.

President Rodríguez then called on Téllez and Bassols and Attorney General Portes Gil to submit a report by the next meeting, to be held on November 21, 1932. That meeting, however, did not take place, because in the meantime Dr. Puig Casauranc had taken over the Foreign Ministry. The next meeting was held at President Rodríguez' Cuernavaca home on January 7, 1933. Both Calles and Pani suggested the advisability of a settlement prior to the change of administration in Washington, Pani adding that the settlement should, of course, take into consideration his various objections and should recognize the La Fleur award. Puig recommended a pact stating that the considerable difference in the payments assumed by the two countries for rectifying the Río Grande boundary was due to the difference in the "economic returns of its waters to the two

---

interest on the value. The situation became complicated when the United States took over California, with Mexico insisting that the United States was replacing Mexico with respect to rights from and obligations to California. But in the case of the Fondo the Hague Tribunal ruled in 1902 that Mexico should cover back payments and should pay 45,051 pesos annually. At least until 1913 Mexico was up to date on making these payments. See José Bravo Ugarte, *Historia de México, tomo tercero, México II, Relaciones internacionales, territorio, sociedad y cultura,* p. 397.

nations." He proposed that not even one inch of Mexican territory be lost, and that he be authorized "to carry on publicity and propaganda to enlighten national opinion."

President Rodríguez authorized, at least for the time being, an agreement between Mexico and the United States for only the engineering works connected with the course of the Río Grande. He instructed his Foreign Minister to continue to negotiate about El Chamizal on the basis of "strict and exact compensation," but these negotiations were not at this time concluded, in spite of Dr. Puig's desire "not to leave such delicate problems to future governments, possibly weaker and less well supported by the masses."[7]

Another controversy which Puig was unable to resolve with Josephus Daniels, who succeeded Ambassador Clark, was that of apportioning the waters of the Río Grande and the Colorado River. The Colorado is made up of waters which originate in the United States, while the reverse is largely true of the Río Grande. "The American Commissions," says Daniels, referring to the Joint Commission on the Colorado, "had recommended that no more water be allotted to Mexico, after the construction of Boulder Dam was completed, than it had been receiving before; while the Mexican Commission had demanded a much larger amount." The Ambassador found the logic of the United States position on the Colorado was not helpful to the United States when applied to the Río Grande.[8]

The work of the United States-Mexican Claims Commissions, set up as a result of the Bucareli Conferences of 1923, was progressing very slowly and in a manner both costly and irritating. Both President Rodríguez and Foreign Minister Puig were concerned about the matter, and Ambassador González Roa pointed out the urgency of reaching some definite conclusion. Even before Ambassador Daniels presented his credentials, Foreign Minister Puig handed him a memorandum about the functioning of international commissions.

Commissions studying the smaller claims of other nations, such as France, Germany, Great Britain, Italy, and Spain, had concluded their work. Both President Rodríguez and Ambassador Daniels liked the idea of a lump-sum settlement to take care of the United States claims. Puig at the time was presenting additional lengthy memoranda to Daniels, one of them quoting from the Am-

[7] J. M. Puig Casauranc quoted in Francisco Javier Gaxiola, *op. cit.*, p. 223.
[8] Josephus Daniels, *op. cit.*, p. 116.

bassador's book about Woodrow Wilson and another presenting a claim based on the American occupation of Veracruz in 1914 when Daniels was Secretary of the Navy. He suggested an amount to take care of the United States claims, but Daniels, aided by Colonel A. Moreno of the American Embassy, found it to be insufficient.

At length Ambassador González Roa proposed that the United States accept as compensation for the claims a certain percentage of the total claims: the same percentage as that awarded on the same class of claims to the governments of Belgium, France, Germany, Great Britain, Italy, and Spain. Such a suggestion ran into objections from both sides. Mexicans pointed out that great duplication existed in United States claims, "over 1000" identical claims having been presented both to the Special and to the General Claims Commissions.

After Daniels had discussed the matter in Washington and had pointed out that until it was settled it would constitute "a running sore," the two agreements of April 24, 1934, were signed. One of these revised the procedure of the United States-Mexican General Claims Commission in order to simplify and speed up the work. Each government was to choose one commissioner, and each commissioner was to appraise claims individually. Then the commissioners were to get together and try to settle the differences. There was then to be a joint report to the two governments.

The other agreement of April 24, 1934, took care of the United States' special claims (for damages resulting from the Revolution). The amount was to bear the same proportion to total claims as the European awards bore to their total similar claims. But in making this computation, deductions from the total United States claims were to be made—deductions in the amounts corresponding to claims that had already been decided, and corresponding to duplications which inflated the claims figures. It was agreed that Mexico would pay half a million dollars yearly starting on January 1, 1935. The total to be paid was calculated to be seven million dollars, or 2.65 per cent of the special claims less the above-mentioned deductions.[9] In this way, more than ten years after the ratification of treaties worked out at the Bucareli Conferences, new agreements finally settled the complicated matter of United States claims arising out of damages caused by the Mexican Revolution.

[9] A. H. Feller, *The Mexican Claims Commissions, 1923–1934*, p. 62.

67.

Rodríguez Handles Agrarian and Labor Matters

In the agrarian and labor realms President Rodríguez went ahead with the program of the Revolution. As has been seen he pushed for, and achieved, the establishment of minimum wages. After the Six-Year Plan was adopted by the P.N.R. at the Querétaro convention in December, 1933, President Rodríguez used this Plan as the program of the last year of his own administration, and he issued a circular telling his collaborators to be guided by it.

As has been mentioned the Plan called for the renewal of land division under a more simplified system of greater federal (rather than state) administration. Under the old Local Agrarian Commissions and National Agrarian Commission not much land of late had been redistributed. Official statistics show merely 196,000 hectares for 1933, the lowest point since 1922 and a small fraction of the average year following 1922. An important reason for this slowdown had been the refusal of the central government to confirm the "provisional" redistributions which state governments had been continuing to make.

The President acted quickly to open up the floodgates of agrarian reform. He approved the new text of Constitutional Article 27, which had been formulated by Congress while Ortiz Rubio was President and which removed from the agrarian question the legal recourse to the court stop-order (*amparo*). By his creation in January, 1934, of an autonomous Agrarian Department he took the agrarian question away from the Agriculture Ministry, which of late had shown little sympathy or interest. Then he saw to it that all the "provisional possessions," which had been held up in recent years, were automatically confirmed wherever the local resolutions had not been the subject of specific actions taken in opposition. The Cuerpo Consultivo Agrario of the new Agrarian Department met at least twice weekly to act quickly on all these accumulated applications, with the result that land distribution went ahead at a rate which even exceeded that of the heyday of Portes Gil. The President's report of September 1, 1934, advised that between February 20, 1934, and August 31, 1934, 1,218,000 hectares had gone to 97,000 heads of families.[1]

President Rodríguez pushed for the possession of lands by individuals within the *ejidos*, rather than communal possession.[2] He also sought to provide the Banco Nacional de Crédito Agrario (National Bank of Agricultural Credit) with enough money to enable the many who were receiving parcels of land to get them into production. In a letter to Ing. Bartolomé Vargas Lugo, the Bank's manager, President Rodríguez said that unfortunately the economic crisis did not make available as much money as he would desire. He hoped to furnish the Bank with 30 million pesos, and was able to furnish it with 20 million.

As a result of the issuance of the Federal Labor Law of 1931 and the principles of the Six-Year Plan which affected labor, there was as

[1] Marte R. Gómez, letter, December 2, 1955; also Departamento Agrario, *Memoria, 1934–1935*.

[2] Francisco Javier Gaxiola, Jr., *El Presidente Rodríguez*, p. 467.

much activity in this field as in the agrarian realm. As one of President Ortiz Rubio's Ministers of Industry, Commerce, and Labor, General Rodríguez had been interested in plans to reorganize that Ministry, and as President he acted quickly, splitting the Ministry into two sections. The new autonomous Labor Department, which now reported directly to the President, could devote itself to the accumulating and increasing number of cases which, with the new labor legislation, were coming before the Boards of Conciliation and Arbitration. And the new Ministry of National Economy could devote its attentions to the ideas of state intervention called for by the philosophy of the Six-Year Plan.

The federal government took steps to see to it that contracts between labor and companies included clauses which made the unions exclusive bargaining agents with rights to say whom the companies should employ and should fire. This was a privilege of the unions which the President wanted to be used in a manner which would not allow the labor leaders to make reprisals harmful to the workers themselves, and he sought means of limiting it to cases where there were legal reasons why a worker should be removed.

With the new strength given to labor organizations considerable bickering appeared among their leaders. The preponderant C.R.O.M. was torn by internal strife, and Lic. Vicente Lombardo Toledano, long associated with Morones, formed his own federation of labor unions, the General Confederation of Workers and Peasants (C.G.O.C.). Still active was the Confederación General de Trabajadores (C.G.T.), which operated principally in the textile field; the Union of Railroad Workers of the Republic and the Union of the Mining and Metallurgical Industry were strong independents. On account of rivalries among labor leaders the newly created National Chamber of Labor failed to bring about any labor unification, and Gaxiola became moved to write that the directors of the laboring masses lost their character as leaders and became irresponsible agitators.

The President himself intervened to lay down the bases of settlement in a number of important labor disputes, and his award of December 10, 1933, settling a bus strike, was the first award to place in a labor contract the clause making it obligatory for the company to use exclusively workers belonging to the union.[3] When he intervened in a dispute between the National Railways of Mexico

[3] Departamento del Trabajo, *La obra social del Presidente Rodríguez*, p. 386.

and the Union of Railroad Workers of the Mexican Republic he not only helped this union obtain the recognition of the Railways, but ordered that the contracts include the union's exclusive rights in the case of hiring and firing.

The strike of the Union of Oil Workers of Southern Veracruz against Mexico's largest oil company, El Aguila Mexican Petroleum Company, and its subsidiary, Ingenieros y Constructores Martín, S.A., started on May 9, 1934. It had not been settled when the Head of the Labor Department, Ing. Juan de Dios Bojórquez, returned in June from a trip which he had made to New York "for reasons of health." It was at first announced that the El Aguila company and its workers had agreed to submit their differences to Bojórquez, but on the next day (June 6) it was learned that, at the suggestion of Bojórquez, President Rodríguez himself had been named arbiter.

The El Aguila strike ended soon afterward, although it was not until early in July that the details of Rodríguez' award became known. The presidential decision established "regional commissions to consider grievances and make awards. Each commission consisted of three members—a federal labor inspector, a representative of the interested labor organization and a representative of the company concerned."[4] The President's decision also established the union's exclusive rights in the determination of company employees; it reduced the work week to 46½ hours, called for obligatory payments on the weekly rest day, established numerous worker benefits, increased the number of holidays with pay, revised the vacation and retirement policy, and increased the workers' wages. Furthermore it established the methods to be used in granting promotions, based on years of service and competence.[5]

A result was that the workers' union of the Huasteca Petroleum Company asked for contract changes in accord with the principles established for the El Aguila workers. A strike notice was issued, but the conflicting parties agreed to submit the case to presidential arbitration, and on October 10, 1934, General Rodríguez issued his decision benefitting the workers of the Huasteca Petroleum Company. The Huasteca was associated with the Standard Oil of New Jersey group, whereas El Aguila, which worked the Poza Rica oil district, was affiliated with British interests (Lord Cowdray).

The President, recognizing that the near future would see important labor problems in the field of public services, due in part to

[4] Harlow S. Person, *Mexican Oil*, p. 48.
[5] Francisco Javier Gaxiola, Jr., *op. cit.*, p. 507.

"professional agitators," was personally inclined to favor the idea of obligatory arbitration. This matter he discussed at a meeting with Primo Villa Michel, Emilio Portes Gil, Aarón Sáenz, Juan de Dios Bojórquez, F. J. Gaxiola, the presidents of the Boards of Arbitration and Conciliation, and a consulting labor lawyer. Aarón Sáenz read a memorandum showing the constitutional possibility of obligatory arbitration in collective labor conflicts, and it apparently satisfied his listeners; it was unanimously agreed that obligatory arbitration was constitutional. It was felt that obligatory arbitration would not limit the constitutional right to strike but would follow the strike declaration.

On November 30, 1934, the police, recalling the unfortunate day of Ing. Ortiz Rubio's inauguration, took great precautions in connection with the ceremonies at which General Rodríguez turned over the presidency to General Cárdenas.

At about noon the Congress and a crowd estimated at between 30,000 and 35,000 persons installed themselves in the National Stadium. After the playing of the national hymn, followed by the bugles of the Army and the discharge of artillery, there was the customary March of Honor whereby the official committee came to the central platform amidst great applause. Besides Generals Rodríguez and Cárdenas, there was Cárdenas' Chief of Staff, Colonel Ramón Rodríguez Familiar. The Senate Commission included the president of the P.N.R., Senator Carlos Riva Palacio. The president of Congress, Lic. Enrique González Flores, sat between Generals Rodríguez and Cárdenas (the latter being at his left).

Cárdenas promised "to guard and have guarded the political Constitution of the United States of Mexico and the laws emanating therefrom." Then, following recent custom, the new Mexican President gave a brief address.

He said that the journeys of his political campaign had convinced him of the inequalities and injustices prevailing in Mexican social and economic life, especially among the indigenous groups. The government, he said, would seek to create new opportunities for labor in its material works, but as these could not be sufficient for all the needs, there would be better organization of the exploitation of the country's natural resources, in accordance with the Six-Year Plan. Mining, he said, constituted a private exploitation for the benefit of a few, and would be reorganized by the state with the creation of new opportunities for work.

In the course of his discussion of agrarian matters, Cárdenas said that the enemies of the Revolution were saying that the peasant was unable to increase agricultural production. To these enemies of the Revolution he replied that what the peasant had for hundreds of years been doing as a serf, he would in the future do much better as a free man. The new President announced that pending *ejido* resolutions would be activated, and that new lands would be given to those groups whose present *ejidos* were insufficiently large for their needs.

He spoke of his plans for unifying the laboring class, which, he said, was presently struggling on two fronts: (1) against the company owners, and (2) against other worker groups.

Cárdenas announced that he would give frank stimulus to socialistic education, so that the students might be identified with the aspirations of the proletariat and might also learn to work closely with labor unions, with co-operatives, and with agrarian committees; so that students might combat the forces which oppose the free march of laborers.

He made it known that the Constitution would be reformed so as to create a civil service, which would be formed for employees between the ages of twenty and sixty, once there had been a "purification" based on competency and on the employees' identification with the ideology of the regime.

He also advised his listeners that, in order to keep in contact with the people, he would dedicate one hour daily to hearing, by means of radio or direct phone wires, the people's complaints or suggestions about improving the government.[6]

After the applause which followed General Cárdenas' speech, General Rodríguez took off the presidential sash and placed it in the hands of his successor, thus concluding the ceremonies at 1:00 P.M. It had been arranged that the new Cabinet ministers would officially assume their functions in the course of a meeting at the Palacio Nacional on the following day, December 1.

Among the dignitaries who attended the inauguration ceremonies at the National Stadium were governors of the states, such as Matías Ramos of Zacatecas, Tomás Garrido Canabal of Tabasco, Rodolfo Elías Calles of Sonora, and Benigno Serratos of Michoacán. General Serratos, who in the recent past had had his differences with Cár-

[6] Lázaro Cárdenas' inauguration address as reported in *Universal Gráfica*, November 30, 1934.

denas, flew to Mexico City for the occasion, but was killed when his plane crashed in the course of the return trip to Michoacán on December 3.

The new President went to the airport on December 12 to say farewell to his predecessor, a man who in his short term at the helm had proved himself an able and active administrator. The departing general was accompanied by a man who had aided him excellently, Lic. Francisco Javier Gaxiola, Jr.

68.

December, 1934

At 11:00 A.M. on December 1, 1934, at the Palacio Nacional, President Cárdenas received the pledges of office of his Cabinet members and other associates in the following order (This list is incomplete.):

Minister of Gobernación
    Ing. Juan de Dios Bojórquez
Minister of Foreign Relations
    Lic. Emilio Portes Gil
Minister of Finance and Public Credit
    Lic. Narciso Bassols
Minister of War and Navy
    General Pablo Quiroga

Minister of Education
    Lic. Ignacio García Téllez
Minister of Agriculture
    Lic. Tomás Garrido Canabal
Minister of Communications and Public Works
    Sr. Rodolfo Elías Calles
Minister of National Economy
    General Francisco J. Múgica
Head of Labor Department
    Lic. Silvano Barba González
Head of Agrarian Department
    Lic. Gabino Vázquez
Head of Department of Federal District
    Lic. Aarón Sáenz
Attorney General of the Republic
    Lic. Silvestre Guerrero
Private Secretary of the President
    Lic. Luis I. Rodríguez
Chief Clerk of the Presidency
    Lic. José Hernández Delgado
Chief of Staff
    Colonel José Manuel Núñez
Head of Department of Fine Arts
    Lic. José Muñoz Cota
Manager of Petro-Mex
    Lic. Primo Villa Michel

Among the other officials named were Fernando Torreblanca as Undersecretary of Foreign Relations, Manuel Avila Camacho as Undersecretary of War and Navy, Efraín Buenrostro as Undersecretary of Finance, and Jesús Silva Herzog as Oficial Mayor of the Finance Ministry. General Vicente González, who in 1923 and 1924 had battled Delahuertismo in Tabasco, was appointed to replace General José Juan Méndez as Chief Police Inspector. General Manuel Medinaveytia, who had once been Pancho Villa's Chief of Staff, succeeded General Pedro Almada as Head of the City Garrison.

One of the many early acts of President Cárdenas was to bring to an end the law which, six years earlier, had provided that federal judges could not be removed by the Chief Executive. Cárdenas took this step against the advice of Portes Gil, who now, in spite of his preference for the Attorney Generalship, was Foreign Minister. Dissatisfied with the judges who had been appointed by President Portes Gil, the new President succeeded in obtaining their resignations. Then, after a careful study of the recommendations submitted by numerous organizations, he sent to Congress his lists of selected judges, including members of the Supreme Court of Justice and of the Superior Tribunal of Justice.[1] These lists were approved by Congress, there being no opposition in the Senate, and in the Chamber of Deputies only a few observations to the effect that some of the new appointees were not titled *licenciados*. Among those appointed to serve on the Superior Tribunal of Justice were Lics. Luis G. Corona and Miguel Alemán. The former was sponsored by the Union of Lawyers of the Federal District, and the latter, son of the late General Miguel Alemán, was recommended by a large number of labor and peasant groups, particularly those of his native state, Veracruz.

Other early acts of President Cárdenas included the shutting down of the fancy barroom at the Palacio de Bellas Artes (inaugurated on September 29), and the closing of gambling casinos, such as the Casino de la Selva and the Foreign Club, which in the immediate past had been very active. On December 8, 1934, the new President announced that between noon and 1:00 P.M. each day the people could send to the presidency free of charge telegrams relative to their problems and complaints. The President refused to follow the tradition of living in the great Castle of Chapultepec; he turned it into a museum.

Colonel Carlos Riva Palacio made two announcements with reference to the official party, which he headed. Advising that the Party treasury showed a balance of 427,000 pesos, he let it be known that these funds would be used for the construction of a P.N.R. building in front of the now almost completed Monument to the Revolution. The Colonel also announced his own resignation as Party president, an action which started rumors about his successor. Although Lic. Romeo Ortega, who had been director of the Comité Pro-Calles of 1924, as well as Calles' Attorney General and Undersecretary in

---

[1] The complete name of the Superior Tribunal of Justice is the *Tribunal Superior de Justicia del Distrito y Territorios Federales*. Important functions include the naming of judges of the Federal District and of the federal territories; also the naming of justices of the peace. The Supreme Tribunal of Justice is considered a part of the executive branch of the government (along with other tribunals, such as the boards of arbitration), whereas the Supreme Court of Justice is the highest authority in the judicial branch of the government.

Charge of Gobernación, figured in these rumors, the post went instead to General Matías Ramos, who had combatted the De la Huerta and Escobar rebellions.

Plutarco Elías Calles advised the nation that he was leaving Mexico City because his poor health required that he put in a period at some spot where he could relax. He said that he was departing full of confidence in the nation's future, a confidence inspired by the existence of a strong government and the Six-Year Plan. He said that the great pledges made to the nation would be fulfilled. However, Calles added a warning note: the job ahead required the strictest collaboration of all sincere Revolutionaries, and, now that the political struggle was over, everyone should co-operate and bring an end to unnecessary agitation. He went to "El Tambor" in Sinaloa in a special train, but after arriving there he found it necessary to go on north, to a sanitarium in Los Angeles, California.

The year 1934 ended with certain discords which were to be felt more acutely in 1935, and the brewing of which had stirred Calles to issue his warning. On the labor front the climate continued stormy. The Workers of the National Railways of Mexico issued a manifesto against the railroad management, and in a clash with the police a number of them were wounded. When the nation found itself with a general strike in the sugar industry, resulting from difficulties at Los Mochis, Sinaloa, the Congress of Workers and Peasants, which was assembled at the Palacio de Bellas Artes, decided to give its first attention to the Los Mochis conflict. The winds which had been blowing against the foreign oil companies gathered force as the workers demanded more and more. In spite of the recent settlement made by President Rodríguez, a new strike was announced for the El Aguila oil company; the talks between company and union representatives had arrived nowhere. The Huasteca Petroleum Company was having similar troubles. A general strike in Tampico left the port without transportation or light.

Congress ended its ordinary sessions for 1934 sharply split into two factions. A group which called itself "the leftists" had hoped to win for Senator Ernesto Soto Reyes of Michoacán the presidency of the Permanent Commission. Events did not so turn out. After Senator Vicente L. Beneitez had been chosen president of the powerful Permanent Commission, in about the closest possible vote, the Party bloc in the Senate offered a banquet in honor of the blocs in both houses. The lunch was scheduled for noon of December 29 at the San Angel Inn. By 3:00 P.M. only thirty federal legislators had shown up because there was so much ill-feeling about the elections for officers of the Permanente. The banquet was called off.

But at the same time the leftists held their own banquet in honor of Ernesto Soto Reyes at El Sabino Restaurant. The diners heard a speech by former General Cándido Aguilar, the Carrancista who, after years of exile following his role in the Delahuerta rebellion, had now returned to the Mexican scene as federal senator from his native state, Veracruz.

After Aguilar's speech, Senator Soto Reyes addressed the gathering. He declared that the leftists had not been defeated, and he went on to make the following explanation: "As was our duty, we have rejected the agreement whereby the Cia. Petrolera El Aguila would have conserved a privileged situation in the country. We lost the election of the Permanente because we hurt interests of men like Diputado Campillo Seyde. This is the real reason why the leftist group of the Congress lost the election of the Permanent Commission." Surprise was expressed at the selection of Senator Beneitez, and at his acceptance of the post in spite of his promise to back the candidacy of Senator Soto Reyes.

On the last day of December Beneitez publicly replied to attacks made against him at the El Sabino banquet shortly after the election of officers of the Permanent Commission. He said that these attacks made him look like an instrument of reactionaries and a man who did not keep his word, and he denied that the recent Permanente election was a triumph of the Felicista reaction. (Diputado Arturo Campillo Seyde had in the past served as a general under Félix Díaz.) Beneitez revealed that he had voted for Soto Reyes, adding that of the fourteen senators on the Commission, thirteen had voted for Soto Reyes and one for Senator Labra, but all of the fifteen *diputados* had voted for Beneitez.

This almost successful effort of Soto Reyes, Antonio Mayés Navarro, Luis Mora Tovar, and others to win in December, 1934, the Permanent Commission from the group which they felt to be Callista, was the result of the formation of what was called the "Left Wing" of Congress. This Left Wing originally consisted of only the nine federal deputies from Michoacán and about eleven other deputies. It had grown considerably. It "lacked confidence in the congressional majority precisely because of that majority's deference to the Jefe Máximo, and it believed that such a majority was a constant threat to President Cárdenas."[2]

The factor of greatest disturbance in Mexico City during this month of December, 1934, was the conduct of the "Red Shirts" who were sponsored by the Minister of Agriculture, Tomás Garrido Canabal.

[2] Victoriano Anguiano Equihua, *Lázaro Cárdenas: Su feudo y la política nacional*, p. 189.

69.

Garrido Canabal and Tabasco, "Laboratory of the Revolution"

Prior to obtaining increased prominence in the national spotlight as Minister of Agriculture, Tomás Garrido Canabal, for about thirteen years, had been dictator of the state of Tabasco. Before making his new impact on the national political scene and on the national capital, he had engaged in earlier activities which moved Cárdenas to cast his own vote for him in the 1934 presidential elections and which created of Tabasco what Cárdenas and Calles called the "lighthouse" or the "laboratory" of the Mexican Revolution.

Tabasco, the small southern state on the Gulf of Mexico, gets its name from an Indian word meaning "damp earth." Here Hernán Cortés first set foot on Mexican soil, and, although his men may have been disappointed at the lack of gold afforded them, it is hard to believe that they were not impressed with the vegetation. Tabasco is so plentiful in rivers and streams that it is known as Mexico's best-watered state. Its fertile soil provides an abundance of bananas, cocoa beans, and coconuts, as well as a large assortment of other products such as sugar cane, corn, rice, beans, tobacco, rubber, pepper, tropical fruits, and mahogany, cedar, and other fine woods. A particularly important occupation has been cattle ranching. Thus Tabasco is not, like Yucatán, a state depending largely on one product.

In 1890, in the neighboring state of Chiapas, Tomás Garrido Canabal was born into a family which owned and operated in Tabasco and Chiapas large ranches of the pre-Revolutionary type. As the son of a wealthy *hacendado* he did some studying in Tabasco, Veracruz, and Campeche, and in 1915 he became associated in Yucatán with the local government of Salvador Alvarado. In 1916 he was back in Tabasco, where he worked with Francisco J. Múgica and where in 1919 he served in the administration of Carlos Greene. He turned out to be neither an intellectual nor a soldier nor a public speaker. But he had other attributes. Those upon whom his power depended were impressed both by his apparent usefulness and by the course which he chose to follow and to associate with the Revolution. The way his sails were set indicated precise conformity with the course established by Calles, and, indeed, Garrido frequently appeared to be sailing along in Tabasco more boldly and spectacularly than the Jefe Máximo de la Revolución. Garrido, furthermore, was a man who managed to instill great discipline among his subjects, organizing large sectors of them under Revolutionary slogans. In his methods he was certainly not deterred by religious teachings.

One reason for Garrido's election to the constitutional governorship of Tabasco in 1922 was the opposition of Gobernación Minister Calles to the Partido Liberal Constitucionalista, and such was the pressure from Mexico City that Garrido's two opponents, including his cousin J. D. Ramírez Garrido, had to withdraw from the race before election day. Soon after that, and in spite of all that was done by the new governor and Ausencio C. Cruz and others to organize

Lic. Tomás Garrido Canabal. *Enrique Díaz.*

614

Ligas de Resistencia á la Carrillo Puerto, Tabasco became one of the bastions of Delahuertismo. More fortunate in his escape than Carrillo Puerto, Garrido was back in the governor's chair with the eventual military triumphs of the Obregonistas in 1924.

This blue-eyed admirer both of Obregón and of himself gave the impression of being more at ease wearing a wide-brimmed hat on a cattle ranch than in any kind of chair. After serving as Tabasco's governor during the four-year period which ended on December 31, 1926, he was succeeded by Ausencio C. Cruz, who was governor for the next four years. Garrido, acting as federal senator and president of the Liga Central de Resistencia del Partido Socialista Radical while his man Cruz was governor, returned to the governorship on January 1, 1931, and remained there until he became Cárdenas' Minister of Agriculture on December 1, 1934. Manuel Lastra Ortiz, a relative of Garrido, became governor of Tabasco on January 1, 1935. During the dictatorship members of Garrido's family played important roles in the state. Brother Pío exercised much control at Puerto Alvaro Obregón (Frontera); brother Manuel Garrido Canabal acted as administrator of the Villahermosa electric plant and manager of Cia. de Transportes Fluviales, S.A.; cousin Pío Garrido Llaven and uncle Manuel Garrido Lacroix acted as congressmen, the former travelling around well armed with guns.[1] The dictatorship was not harmful to various businesses in which Garrido and his friends were interested, such as cattle ranching or the activities of the Cia. de Transportes Fluviales. This last-named business transported bananas down the rivers of Tabasco and was a subsidiary of the Standard Fruit and Steamship Company of Mexico, Inc., a concern which paid a commission to Garrido and which enjoyed a monopoly in the purchases of bananas in the state. The dictator did not, however, enrich himself tremendously, and what he did accumulate came through his business enterprises and not through looting of the state treasury. If there was anything about the state finances which was perhaps not entirely admirable it was the contributions therefrom which served as retainers or gifts for important Callistas in Mexico City.

An outstanding feature of the dictatorship was the regimentation of persons and activities, and the strong-arm methods frequently used by Garrido and his subordinates to enforce discipline. Those

[1] Manuel González Calzada, *Tomás Garrido*, pp. 173–174; also Rodulfo Brito Foucher manuscript containing fourteen articles published in *El Día*, January 28, 1936–February 22, 1936, Article XI, p. 3.

who thought of their well-being co-operated as was necessary. Impressive indeed are the tales of killings, humiliations, punishments, acts of barbarism, and tortures with which the regimentation was brought about and maintained. Tabasco became, as Francisco J. Santamaría has made clear, no place for a free press.[2] It became a place where not even the slightest organized opposition to the regime was possible. Some vocal opponents existed outside of the state, but even away from Tabasco they were not always safe.

Laborers, of course, were organized into the Ligas de Resistencia, and if they were to continue laboring it was fairly advisable that they join up. So well were the Ligas dominated by Garridista politicians that strikes did not occur in all of Tabasco during the dictatorship. It might also be added that as the result of Garrido's decisions and the productivity of the state, wages were not low in Tabasco.

Producers and consumers were described as being organized into two or three hundred *cooperativas*, the control of which gave Garrido the opportunity to establish all sorts of rules on marketing. But for the most part the *cooperativas* which were listed lacked importance. An exception was the Co-operative of Cocoa Producers, by means of which Garrido set the prices to be received by the growers of this product.

Garrido maintained that the Revolutionary state should control all sorts of personal habits of the citizens. The assurance of the health and sleep of children was a responsibility of the state and therefore strict enforcement was given to the ruling that all children under eight be in bed before 8:00 P.M. As the policemen pocketed 50 per cent of the fines collected for violation of this rule, they were diligent in checking.

In 1932 was organized the Bloque de Jóvenes Revolucionarios, or "Red Shirts," a group which originated when students at Villahermosa's Instituto Juárez decided to combat Salvador Camelo Soler, a political enemy of Garrido. Other youths, particularly those employed by the Tabasco state and municipal governments, joined up, and soon Alfonso Bates Caparroso, cousin of Garrido's adviser Amado Caparroso, was placed in command. The Red Shirts got off to an active start when they shot two young supporters of Camelo Soler. It soon became compulsory for all men between the ages of fifteen and thirty to belong to the organization, to learn by

[2] See Francisco J. Santamaría, *El periodismo en Tabasco.*

heart the "Hymn of Youth" written by Napoleón Pedrero Fócil, Secretary General of the Bloque de Jóvenes Revolucionarios of Villahermosa, and to wear black pants, red shirt, and the black-and-red military cap. All of Tabasco's organized groups went in for much marching, but this activity was practiced particularly by the Red Shirts, who came to be a tool useful to the dictatorship when it wished to deal with those who might have aroused the official ire.

The social life of the people became the concern of Garrido's government, which forbade girls and women who were teachers or public employees from using color on their faces or wearing short hair. The Red Shirts organized the dances, and not only was it a serious mistake for anyone not to accept invitations, but it frequently became necessary to dance with the person indicated by the dance's leader. A section of the Bloque de Jóvenes Revolucionarios was formed for young women, so that they also could wear red shirts, parade, and stand at attention in various formations, the right arm typically in a horizontal position across the chest.

Lázaro Cárdenas remarked: "How much would we give that in other states of the Republic existed organizations of women, young people, workers, peasants, and all the components of our economy, similar to those that exist in Tabasco."

What was done with all of this dictatorial power, the like of which, according to one of Garrido's admirers, was never exceeded?

One thing was certain. Visiting dignitaries, particularly Presidents and official candidates campaigning for the presidency, were treated in Tabasco to a particularly warm and impressive reception featured by banners, bands, and parades made up of the various organized and uniformed groups. Uniforms for members of the Liga de Resistencia differed little from those of the Red Shirts except for the hat. "From the most distant places in Tabasco caravans of humble workers and peasants left on foot for Villahermosa, bearing on their backs a package of clean clothing and their only pair of shoes, which they had been obliged to buy especially for exhibition in those receptions."[3] Thirty thousand men and women between the ages of fifteen and fifty paraded before Garrido, Calles, and Cárdenas in 1934 when Cárdenas was campaigning for the presidency. The necessary financial contributions were obtained with little difficulty from people and businesses, according to their

[3] Rodulfo Brito Foucher, *op. cit.*, Article XIV, p. 10.

abilities, and it could be expected that notices of required attendance would not be ignored.

In the field of education Tabasco saw a great deal of activity, although this state, as the whole nation, at this time lacked adequate school facilities to handle all of the children of school age. "Rationalistic schools" began to make their appearance in Tabasco between 1925 and 1926, somewhat later than this development occurred in Yucatán, but considerably before the P.N.R. proclaimed the "socialistic" school as something for the nation as a whole. Tabasco's daily schoolteaching under the Garrido dictatorship was apt to begin and end with "optimistic and festive" dances and songs.[4] In the mornings theories were explained and in the afternoons the students were given practice at useful pursuits. Each school had a parcel of land for student cultivation. If a child had to be punished "his punishment consisted in depriving him of the pleasure of working."[5] In teaching, "the *cooperativista* thesis was sustained 'as the economic organization and the defensive recourse against capitalism.' "[6] Co-operatives of student groups were formed.

The state not only provided free education but also in some cases supplied students with food and transportation at no cost. Education was coeducational and compulsory, and parents who did not co-operate were fined. Many of the schools were "open air," and many others, such as the Lázaro Cárdenas rationalistic school, were housed in former church buildings.

Under the dictatorship was passed a divorce law whereby marriages could be terminated at the request of one of the two parties, with the result that on many an occasion a girl went to bed married and woke up in the morning divorced without even knowing it at the time.[7] Garrido himself did not make use of this law, but on the other hand he displayed a remarkably unrestrained interest in young women and devoted so much attention to satisfying his amorous desires that he became well known as quite a man in this realm of activity.

The dictator also showed much interest in typically Tabascan music and poetry. Once when a writer failed to produce a poem as ordered by the dictator he was thrown in jail, where in the next twenty-four hours he turned out what was to become one of the

---

[4] Roberto Hinojosa, *El Tabasco que yo he visto*, p. 10.
[5] Baltasar Dromundo. *Tomás Garrido*, p. 137.
[6] *Ibid.*, p. 132.
[7] Manuel González Calzada, *op. cit.*, p. 162.

more popular of Tabascan songs. It was made public at a great fiesta where Garrido presented a prize to the author.[8] Many were the literary products which were turned out to praise Garrido, and it is hardly necessary to add that in educational circles students were reminded, in songs and otherwise, of the virtues of Calles and Garrido Canabal. Local newspapers did not appear in Tabasco during the Garrido dictatorship, but people were not without reading matter: they had to subscribe to the official publication, *Redemption*.[9]

In such a well-disciplined state fiestas, fairs, expositions, and "congresses" were frequent. These fairs made much of local products and became famous throughout the Republic. There were cattle fairs, pineapple fairs, sugar-cane fairs, corn fairs, coconut fairs, etc., with prizes awarded to the exhibitors of remarkable Tabascan products. Garrido did much to identify himself with scientific progress in agricultural and livestock production, and he arranged for foreign importation of seeds and animals in order to improve upon the local varieties.

In July, 1934, the First Congress of Socialistic Students of the Republic assembled at Puerto Obregón (Frontera). It was attended by 235 delegates and 40 "honorary" and "worker" delegates from all over the country. Many of the delegates arrived from Veracruz on the steamer *Morazán* and at the opening session burst into revolutionary songs, cadences from "The International," and cries in favor of Marx and the leaders of the Mexican movement. Tomás Garrido Canabal never made speeches but the family was represented by the wife of one of Garrido's relatives: after speeches by Arnulfo Pérez H. and Lombardo Toledano, the flaming words of Sra. de Ramírez Garrido gave evidence that emancipated womanhood, "free of the dismal tutelage of the church,"[10] could orate in as strongly communistic a manner as the men.

Resolutions adopted at the Congress included a proposal for the suppression of religion in all of the nation, all church buildings to be turned into libraries, schools, cultural centers, etc. The students also called for the suppression of textbooks which were not clearly identified with socialistic educational tendencies. Since the Labor Arbitration Boards were considered to be protecting the interests of capitalists their suppression also was demanded. Plants and shops

[8] Baltasar Dromundo, *op. cit.*, p. 89.
[9] Rodulfo Brito Foucher, *op. cit.*, Article XIII, p. 10.
[10] Roberto Hinojosa, *op. cit.*, p. 61.

which would not increase salaries and reduce hours of work, said the students, should be expropriated and placed in the possession of the workers.[11]

Under the circumstances the Mexican socialistic students had strong words against alcoholic beverages. They stated that alcoholism was one of the weapons of the bourgeois in its fight against the emancipation of the proletariat, and was as dangerous as many of the religious dogmas. In taking a position against intoxicating drinks they subscribed to a point of view expressed by worker congresses in Yucatán and by Calles and Portes Gil. It was a point of view which was energetically and loudly pushed by Garrido in the state he completely dominated.

Garrido's earlier antialcoholic activities consisted of a series of regulations which irritated bartenders, one such regulation being that all bars should be a certain distance from work centers and schools, and should furthermore be of a determined height, a height which was very impractical, especially for short men.[12] Tabasco's first "dry law" was issued on May 31, 1928, and on April 30, 1931, Garrido made six years instead of one year the prison term for the handling of alcoholic beverages. It is perhaps well to mention that such laws frequently served merely as a basis for punishments differing from those stipulated. Compared with treatment sometimes administered by Garrido's henchmen to unfortunates who were known to have imbibed, the six-year jail sentence was merciful. When the author of the "Hymn of Youth" had to be punished for drinking he was forced to labor at the destruction of a church building.[13]

Garrido's best-known campaign was that which he directed against the Catholic Church and any belief in God. It is not extraordinary that Garrido, during the age of Calles, should have given trouble to the clergy; what was noteworthy was the thoroughness of his campaign against God. He did as complete a job as his absolute dictatorship would allow.

When Pascual Díaz became Bishop of Tabasco in 1922 he did not find that the people of the state were ardently Catholic. Rather, much indifference existed, and so the Bishop set out to remedy this, encountering at the time no official opposition. Three years later he

---

[11] *Ibid.*, pp. 65–70.

[12] Manuel González Calzada, *op. cit.*, p. 122; Baltasar Dromundo, *op. cit.*, pp. 156–157.

[13] Manuel González Calzada, *op. cit.*, p. 125.

found himself outside the state, which had decreed that priests must be married, observing in Tabasco the most savage attacks against God.

All churches in the state were closed and despoiled of any valuables they might have contained. These buildings were either destroyed or used for official purposes, meetings, and fiestas, at some of which God was denounced from the pulpits. The people were forced to participate in the destruction of church buildings and altars. All religious images, whether from churches, homes, or people's necks, were taken over by Garrido's men; some of them were exhibited in an obscene manner in official buildings and others were made the object of public ridicule. Eventually large piles of religious images were burned before multitudes singing atheistic songs.

Not only were crosses removed from graveyards and the use of flowers there prohibited, but all religious customs were outlawed. On days of religious fasting the eating of meat became obligatory. Christmas was not to be celebrated in any way and fines were imposed on any who suspended work on account of religious holidays. The word *adios* was suppressed.

At an exhibition of livestock a fine bull on exhibit would be called "God," a donkey named "Christ," a cow named "The Virgin of Guadalupe," an ox named "The Pope," a hog named "The Archbishop," etc.[14] Such animals often came from "La Florida," experimental stables belonging to the dictator.[15]

Among the children of the dictator was a son named Lenin and a daughter named Zoila Libertad (I am liberty), a name which at one time provoked the saying that the only liberty existing in Tabasco was the daughter of Garrido. Garrido was sometimes accompanied by a nephew named Luzbel (Lucifer).

Had Garrido been asked why more was not done in Tabasco to redistribute lands in accordance with the Federal Agrarian Code, or to grant to laborers certain rights provided in the Federal Labor Law, he would probably have replied that in these realms there were no problems in the unique state of Tabasco. Mexican law of the period notwithstanding, Garrido gave women the illusory right to vote in Tabasco; and so they went through with this formality in the local elections. Neither did Garrido countenance federal inter-

[14] Rodulfo Brito Foucher, *op. cit.*, Article XIII, p. 7.
[15] Mariano Tovar, *El dictador de Tabasco*, pp. 67–73.

ference, nor (although his position was due to federal favor) did he ever call for federal financial help even when such assistance might have been forthcoming as relief to a flood-damaged state.

Collaborators of this Red Shirt dictator, who always wrote with red ink, included Ausencio C. Cruz, Francisco Trujillo Gurria, Homero Margalli, Arnulfo Pérez H., Amado Caparroso, Alfonso Bates Caparroso, César A. Rojas, Napoleón Pedrero Fócil, as well as various relatives. Harmony was not always present in the ranks, and Trujillo Gurria found himself obliged to leave the state. Brother Pío Garrido Canabal was highly critical of the Caparrosos, of Red Shirt fame, and Pérez H. considered himself an enemy of the Red Shirts.

To take over the federal Ministry of Agriculture, Garrido Canabal arrived in Mexico City in his red-and-black plane, the *Guacamayo*. A few days earlier he had arranged a great event in Villahermosa to mark the close of an era: thousands of women participated in a great "burning of saints" on the ground which was formerly the site of the cathedral.

On November 29, 1934, the "vanguard" of the Red Shirts, about 200 youths highly practiced in marching and military music, reached Mexico City. This group paraded in honor of Cárdenas, Calles, and Garrido, and sang three hymns, one in honor of each of these leaders. When they were not parading or calling on Calles and other dignitaries, these young men were not always the city's most considerate guests.

Approximately 100 of these Tabasco Red Shirts remained in Mexico City, many of them to obtain posts in the Ministry of Agriculture and all of them to help promote the expansion of the Bloque de Jóvenes Revolucionarios del Distrito Federal, which came to number over 1000 including various Tabascans who were already in the capital as students. Following Cárdenas' election-campaign visit to Tabasco in 1934 Red Shirt organizations had been founded in the states of Puebla and Sonora, and now Garrido gave special attention to the establishment of these groups in Mazatlán, Guadalajara, Tampico, Morelia, Jiquilpan, Toluca, and elsewhere. In the nation's capital the Red Shirts received a building for their headquarters, and in public meetings they burned religious objects and proclaimed the greatness of Marx.[16]

[16] Eduardo J. Correa, *El balance del Cardenismo*, p. 22.

The new Minister of Agriculture organized meetings at the Hidalgo Theatre and at the Palacio de Bellas Artes and a program of three meetings weekly soon developed: "Agricultural Tuesdays," "Livestock Thursdays," and "Red Saturdays." At the Red Saturday sessions the clergy were ridiculed and shots were occasionally taken at a painting of Christ. It was advisable for employees of the Ministry of Agriculture to attend just as it was for them to subscribe to weekly publications which were inspired by Garrido: *Cristo Rey*, which attacked the Catholic Church, and *Juventud Roja*, the official journal of the Red Shirts.

In the patio of the Agriculture Ministry or in the Minister's waiting rooms might be heard singing to the accompaniment of the Red and Black orchestra. Red Shirts would salute the Minister in a martial form and then he would ask them "Does God exist?" and hear their drilled reply, "He has never existed."[17] The Ministry's offices were also full of girls, who would either take part in singing the praises of Cárdenas, Calles, and Garrido or form an audience for the music, and who at other times would distribute Garridista propaganda.[18]

The calling card of collaborator Arnulfo Pérez H., who had now become the Ministry's Chief Clerk, read as follows: "ARNULFO PEREZ H., CHIEF CLERK OF THE MINISTRY OF AGRICULTURE AND DEVELOPMENT. DEPUTY TO THE FEDERAL CONGRESS. MEMBER OF THE PARTIDO NACIONAL REVOLUCIONARIO. PERSONAL ENEMY OF GOD." It was Professor Arnulfo Pérez H. who, in a speech at the Open Air Theatre of the Education Ministry, proclaimed: "God, You do not exist; I apostrophize You and challenge You that if You really exist You strike down this building on my head." After a pause in the roofless open-air theatre the speaker went on to address his audience saying: "You see, gentlemen, the building has not fallen and so God does not exist."[19]

Following Garrido's instructions the Red Shirts undertook a series of anti-religious Sunday meetings, each meeting to take place in a different section of the Federal District. On the second Sunday of the series about seventy uniformed Red Shirts, some of them armed, gathered at about 10:00 A.M. on December 30, 1934, in the garden in front of the well-known church at Coyoacán on the outskirts of

[17] Rodulfo Brito Foucher, *op. cit.*, Article XIV, p. 23.
[18] Manuel González Calzada, *op. cit.*, p. 182.
[19] Rodulfo Brito Foucher, *op. cit.*, Article XIII, p. 13.

Mexico City. This was while the devout were attending Mass. On a large stone cross in the garden the Red Shirts placed a red-and-black flag and also a big picture of Homero Margalli. After two youths had made speeches and attracted a considerable crowd of unsympathetic listeners, it became the turn of Julio Díaz Quiroz to orate, and he let forth a particularly bitter diatribe against the Catholic Church and its followers. His sister, who happened to be passing, made some strong remarks condemning this activity of her brother, remarks which were soon supported verbally by the growing crowd. The noise had become considerable when at about 10:20 those who had attended Mass started leaving the church. The speaker was called upon to desist, and the Red Shirts, outnumbered by unfriendly residents of Coyoacán, were hissed.

The Red Shirts prepared to withdraw to a government office building on the square, but they did not leave before they had fired on the crowd and the worshippers, killing five and wounding many more. The outraged residents were furious and in the midst of the angry blows which followed one of the Red Shirts was killed. This was Ernesto Malda, who arrived late and walked into a tempest, becoming, on account of his death, a hero of subsequent Red Shirt protests against the injustice of his "lynching." The irate crowd might have done more against the Red Shirt murderers had it not been for the refuge which the latter, under protection of their pistols, found in some local government offices, together with the arrival of the police.

Things were not quite the same for Red Shirts in the capital as they had been for members of this organization in Tabasco. The police arrested sixty-five of those who had been involved in the Coyoacán murders and placed them in the penitentiary of the Federal District. Some residents of Coyoacán went to the home of President Cárdenas, at San Angel, to seek justice. They found the President out of town, but the President's secretary, Lic. Luis I. Rodríguez, stated that those responsible would be punished. General José Juan Méndez, who had apparently not yet quite given up his position of Police Chief, said that the affair was an armed aggression against the people by the Red Shirts.

Tomás Garrido Canabal, like Cárdenas, was out of town. He was turning over the Tabasco governorship to his successor, Manuel Lastra Ortiz, when he learned of the events at Coyoacán. At once he flew to Mexico City in his red-and-black *El Guacamayo* and took steps on behalf of his imprisoned followers. The police authorities, after studying the recent occurrences, freed twenty-five of the young men and left forty of them in jail, but these forty attained their liberty two days later (five days after the shootings) when Garrido put up bail amounting to about 200,000 pesos. The few days which the Red Shirts spent in prison were made more bearable than they otherwise would have been because of the girls whom Garrido sent with flowers and encouraging messages from the Ministry of Agriculture, and because of singers sent over during the nights. The antireligious songs may have proved more agreeable to the jailed Red Shirts than to some of the other prisoners who were in the same penitentiary, particularly Trejo Morales and Father Jiménez, who were in jail on charges of having been involved in activities of Castro Balda or Toral.[20]

Mexico City students issued a statement to the effect that the Red Shirts were not students and did not represent the views of students. The newspapers, which had never found much to admire about the Red Shirts, renewed their attacks, and many civic organizations expressed their disgust at the Coyoacán affair.

[20] Manuel González Calzada, *op. cit.*, pp. 89–91.

70·

Agitation and Strikes
in Early 1935

The nation's indefatigable new President went se-
renely ahead with what he felt to be the advancement of the
Revolution, the dictates of the Six-Year Plan, and his campaign
pledges to the people. But for many the first half of 1935 was a time
of strain. There was unrest among the Catholics and among the
students. The unrest was so great on the labor front that it was
reported that by June, 1935, about 1,200 strikes "had burst forth in
the Republic."[1] "Gold Shirts" (a new "shirt" group) now fought the
Red Shirts. And there were political differences.

[1] Archivo Casasola, *Historia gráfica de la Revolución*, p. 2115.

Late in January, 1935, Archbishop Pascual Díaz, who was still in Mexico in spite of Calles, stated that the "persecution" was worse than it had been in 1926 and in 1929. Catholic churches were closed in almost half of the states, and of the 375 churches still open in other states of the Republic 63 were in the state of San Luis Potosí, where General Saturnino Cedillo was opposing anticlerical laws and secular education.[2] In February President Cárdenas signed a law forbidding any religious material to go through the mails.

Early in March Archbishop Díaz and some of his companions were captured and jailed for a short while on the charges of having officiated in religious services when not authorized to do so (thus violating the state of Mexico law of May 24, 1932, regarding worship), for having worn religious garb outside of a church (thus violating the federal law of June 14, 1926), and for having received money contributions in a church (thus violating the federal law of January 4, 1926). The Archbishop said the charges were unfounded. Shortly after his release he wrote a letter to President Cárdenas pointing out that hundreds of Catholics had lost their government jobs because they were Catholics, and calling attention to rude attacks made by Education Minister García Téllez against religion. Priests, said the Archbishop, deprived of all means of livelihood, had to spend fifteen days in jail whenever caught celebrating Mass because they lacked ability to pay the 500-peso fine. In reply to the President's statement that the government was simply enforcing the laws, Díaz said that the laws had been issued precisely to hurt the Church, which, he added, had no interest in mixing in politics and only intervened in government affairs when it became necessary to defend itself. After making a reference to the achievements of the Catholic Church in Mexico in centuries past, the Archbishop pointed out that many important buildings now used by the government had been confiscated from the Church and from Catholic educational and charitable institutions. "Almost all of the secondary schools in this city have been established in buildings dedicated, up to a short time ago, to the functions of shelters and seminaries."

Education Minister García Téllez, who declared that he would employ all efforts to destroy the Catholic Church, inaugurated the First

[2] Nathaniel and Sylvia Weyl, *The Reconquest of Mexico*, p. 163.

Congress of the Proletarian Child, and decreed that in government educational establishments the word "Adios" be replaced by "Salud, camarada."[3] The greatest storm of controversy which arose in his field came when, with the help of the President, he took steps to make socialistic education the only education obtainable. Socialistic education was to be coeducational, "progressive," and "scientific"; it was to free the people from all forms of idolatry and superstition; it was to be useful, "co-operativistic," and Mexican. In the primary grades such education was to be obligatory for all those of school age, and it was to be free.

The Education Minister called on teachers to make every attempt to increase school attendance, which had been falling, and many of the parents who refused to have their children obtain the benefits of socialistic education were told to do so or be fined fifty pesos for disobeying the law. Even without the opposition of those who were dead set against socialist education, the federal teachers in the government's rural education program did not have an easy time of it, and they ran into a considerable amount of such opposition. Particularly in parts of Jalisco, such as in the Los Altos Plateau, they were given a rough time, and on occasion some lost their lives.

President Cárdenas ruled that private schools should either impart socialistic education or else close their doors, and a little later he declared that only the state could provide primary, secondary, and normal school teaching, because it was necessary to create in youth "an ideology guided toward the realization of social justice, feasible only in generations free of anachronous prejudices." The Education Ministry prohibited the offering of any secondary education without Ministry authorization, for such education had to be in accord with the official programs. Particularly strong protests arose in Guadalajara, where eighty private schools were closed,[4] and where students made a sizable manifestation against socialistic education. This demonstration was followed by rioting in which three persons were killed and many more seriously injured, so that the new governor, Everardo Topete, was forced to proclaim a state of practical siege and to forbid groups to gather in the streets. Governor Topete turned down a student request that the University of Guadalajara, like the National University and that of San Luis Potosí, be given full autonomy. He said that experience had shown no benefits to result from the granting of autonomy to universities.

[3] Eduardo J. Correa, *El balance del Cardenismo*, p. 62.
[4] *Ibid.*, p. 62.

When the Education Minister declared that the secondary school would not in the future serve as a preparation for the liberal professions, the autonomous National University in Mexico City reorganized its course of study in its more advanced Preparatory School, extending it so as to cover five years and at the same time making completion of all of their secondary schooling unnecessary for secondary school students desiring admission to the University's Preparatory School. García Téllez retaliated by announcing that the secondary studies had to be completed in order for the superior (Preparatory) studies to count for certificates. Then the University went to the courts to get an *amparo* (stop order) against a presidential decree which would prevent the University from extending its Preparatory course to five years, and the rector, Dr. Fernando Ocaranza, tried to explain the problem on behalf of the "autonomous" University.

After the President had called on the University youths not to be forgetful of the city workers and peasants, the Supreme Court denied the *amparo* sought by the University.

Students at the National University called for the resignation of Garrido Canabal, but they were not the only ones to clamor against the Red Shirts, one of whom was almost lynched when he went around the streets of Mexico City threatening, without any apparent reason, to kill individuals.

Mexico saw a new shirt organization. This was the fascist-like Acción Revolucionaria Mexicana (A.R.M.), more widely known as the "Gold Shirts," whose Jefe Máximo was the former Pancho Villa general, Nicolás Rodríguez. Early in March members of this new organization attacked the offices of the Communist Party, burning things and throwing out pictures of Lenin and Trotsky. After Gold Shirt leaders Nicolás Rodríguez, Ovidio Pedrero Valenzuela, and Andrés Morán had been jailed, they said that the Communists also should have been placed in jail. When they were freed on March 12 they were at once threatened by their enemies.

Later in March the Gold Shirts got into another well-publicized squabble and were apparently routed, leaving behind, as trophies for the victors, some of their clubs, hats, and shirts. This incident took place at the location where the Pasamanería Francesa was strike-bound, its place of business guarded by the representatives of the Felipe Carrillo Puerto Union of Workers. It was reported that the Gold Shirts wanted to tear down the red-and-black banners of the strikers. But General Nicolás Rodríguez declared that such a rumor was anti-A.R.M. propaganda. He said: "The idea of the A.R.M. is not to attack strikers, much less before the Labor Department has ruled whether or not they are right. If we have been involved with the Communists it is because their goal is to replace the present regime in Mexico by a soviet system which goes against our Constitution and customs." A few days later the Union of Gold Shirts explained that it was not a "rival of the laborer."

What the workers started late in December, 1934, against the El Aguila Petroleum Company turned into a series of strikes and demands. The El Aguila strike which took place on January 7 touched off other strikes, such as that of the Veracruz electricians, who cut off the port's electricity; when it was settled El Aguila's workers thanked their companions. But on February 4 the workers started another strike against El Aguila, and at the same time demanded payments from both the Huasteca and El Aguila oil companies in compensation for conditions in the past. For example, El Aguila was asked to pay half a million pesos for overtime from the years 1906 to 1933. Meanwhile gasoline became scarce.

In February the city of Puebla found itself subject to a general strike. On February 12 the taxi drivers of Mexico City went on a strike, which was settled favorably for them. Many of the chauffeurs appear to have been striking soon again and dividing themselves into two conflicting groups. Some of them, annoyed at the president of a conciliation and arbitration board, threatened him, and in addition destroyed the furniture in the board's office.

In March Veracruz had a general strike. In this particularly agitated state war was declared between the Cromistas and the Lombardistas. Relations between the senator from Veracruz, General Cándido Aguilar, and the Veracruz governor, Lic. Gonzalo Vázquez Vela, were not at all good, with the Senator accusing the Governor of making improper deals with the Huasteca Petroleum Company. The press went so far as to report a possible duel between these two individuals.

The railroad workers, who went on strike on March 7, were backed by the Mexico City streetcar workers in a strike of their own. On March 21 President Cárdenas agreed to act as arbiter in the case of the railroad strike, which was finally ended when it was three weeks old.

Presidential declarations backed up, and helped build up, the new strength of the labor groups. On March 22 General Cárdenas said: "It is urgent that opportunity be given to the laboring classes to incorporate themselves into civilization, for they have always suffered injustices, disregard, and privations."

When, on April 12, Senator Ezequiel Padilla mentioned to President Cárdenas that the first months of his administration had been "marked by an incessant agitation in labor organizations and by an extremist propaganda, the consequence of which has been the greatest anxiety in all investment circles," the President referred to the opportunity for the exaltation of Mexico in this "exceptional period." Lic. Padilla mentioned that capital might deserve some government stimulus, to which thought General Cárdenas replied by pointing out that "we must combat the capitalism, the liberal capitalistic school, that ignores the human dignity of the workers and the rights of the collectivity." He asserted his belief that the workers could be expected to conduct themselves so as to promote social solidarity and intelligent and patriotic co-operation, thus insuring the general prosperity of the Republic. "We must not forget that we are the continuers of a policy, initiated with the start of the Revolution, of stepped-up replevin, always limited by the facts of reality."

The Mexico City streetcar strike continued after the end of the railroad strike. The company said that it was losing 26,000 pesos daily, and not only rejected the workers' demands but refused to talk about paying salaries lost during the strike. However, with the end of the streetcar strike on May 6, the company was ordered to pay over half a million pesos in salaries lost during the strike; the company's property was attached to assure this payment.

In April, 1935, a general strike in Puebla, this time throughout the state, was occasioned by one labor group's opposing another. The Tampico electricians backed up the Huasteca Petroleum Company workers by paralyzing most of Tampico's activity. Then in turn the Tampico strikers were supported by strikes by the power plant workers of Celaya, Uruapan, León, Mérida, San Luis Potosí, and elsewhere, including parts of Jalisco. Conversations between the sugar workers and the sugar company owners broke off abruptly when representatives of the latter group became offended at remarks by the workers.

It was June, 1935. There were strikes by the telephone company employees, the bus drivers, the employees of the movie houses, and the workers at the paper factory, San Rafael y Progreso Industrial. The phone strike was brought to an end after several weeks, and the government stepped in to terminate the paper strike. As paper had become scarce and costly, the government, later in the year, invested half a million pesos in a new company which was to import paper and regulate its price.

According to the official statistics, those who proclaimed the occurrence of 1,200 strikes were exaggerating. It can be easily seen, however, that the effects of the Federal Labor Law and of the attitude of the Cárdenas Administration were considerable.

	Number of strikes	Strikers involved
1929	14	3,473
1930	15	3,718
1931	11	227
1932	56	3,574 (not a complete recording)
1933	13	1,084 (not a complete recording)
1934	202	14,685
1935	642	145,212

In April, 1935, the price of silver, which had fallen below 30 cents U.S. currency per troy ounce during the depression, made an advance above 72 cents. This meant that the silver coins, which in 1934 represented about 70 per cent of the money in circulation, were more valuable for their silver content than for their face value—at least as long as the dollar remained worth 3.60 pesos. (According to the law of October 27, 1919, the silver peso contained twelve grams of pure silver. The peso was 75 per cent silver.)

The Administration, in which Narciso Bassols was Finance Minister, decided against any shift in the rate of exchange between the dollar and the peso. Instead, by a law dated April 26, 1935, it decreed the withdrawal of silver coins from circulation, and ordered the holders of all such coins (peso or fraction thereof) to turn in their coins and receive paper pesos and new fractional currency.

On May 24 it was reported that long lines of people were exchanging their silver for new banknotes at the Bank of Mexico, but on the next day it was announced that the government had extended the one-month period in which the exchange was to be effected. The reason given was that a sufficient volume of the new money had not been issued. It is apparent, however, that not all of the public by any means turned in its silver coins. By the end of July over 157 million pesos in silver coins remained in circulation, more than 50 per cent of all the currency in circulation.[5] Needless to say there was complaint not so much against a provision of the new law which made it illegal to export or melt the silver coins which had been demonetized, but rather against the provision which obligated individuals and banks to exchange the coins for the new bills.[6] The law did, however, create a significant increase in the monetary reserve of the Bank of Mexico.

The Finance Ministry was aided by Supreme Court decisions refusing to recognize old concessions which had provided some tax exemptions for a number of companies. While the telephone companies, as the result of pressures, were improving the lot of their workers, at the same time they found themselves billed for back taxes which, on the basis of old concessions, they had not paid. The Compañía Mexicana de Petróleo El Aguila, S.A. made important payments to the government as a result of a similar ruling: Congress did not recognize advantageous tax concessions granted to S. Pierson & Son, Ltd. in 1906.

In all important realms tax collections between September 1, 1934, and July 31, 1935, exceeded estimates. The tax receipts from the exploitation of natural resources, mainly oil and metals, had been estimated at 16 million pesos for this period, but they actually came to over 31 million.[7]

Holders of the domestic forty-year bond issue which had been authorized during the administration of President Rodríguez were told that coupon No. 1, bearing a date of December 31, 1933, could be used for the payment of taxes. The government expressed its intent to do all possible to redeem some of the expired coupons on the domestic Banking Debt, on which service had been in suspense since 1933. Modifications were made to the contracts covering loans which, late in 1932, had been made to the government by the Pierce Oil Company, Huasteca Petroleum Company, and El Aguila Petroleum Company, and arrangements were made to liquidate these loans over a period ending in December, 1940.

Holders of Mexican foreign bonds were told that a solution to the problem would have to be tied strictly to Mexico's capacity to pay. It was pointed out that while the world was going through a

---

[5] Secretaría de Hacienda y Crédito Público, *La hacienda pública de México a través de los informes presidenciales,* p. 596.

[6] Alfonso Septien, *La última reforma monetaria.*

[7] Secretaría de Hacienda y Crédito Público, *ibid.,* p. 603.

difficult financial situation, which affected Mexico, it would be imprudent to enter into any arrangement.

Bassols found in Puig Casauranc a hearty admirer of his administration of the Finance Ministry. Puig observed that the Bank of Mexico had not always been conducted so as to fulfill its original intentions, one of which he felt to be assistance in the achievement of Mexico's economic independence and the elimination of the "dangerous actions of some foreign banks." Besides emphasizing that the Bank efficiently realized its original objectives while Bassols was Finance Minister, Puig came to feel that not until the regime of Cárdenas was the matter of agricultural credits for the *ejidos* handled in a really excellent manner.

71·

The Declarations
of General Calles

Early in May, 1935, General Plutarco Elías Calles, after medical treatments in Los Angeles, California, and his rest at "El Tambor," Sinaloa, arrived by plane in Mexico City. At the airport he was greeted by a large crowd which included President Cárdenas, Lic. Luis I. Rodríguez, Ing. Juan de Dios Bojórquez, Lic. Garrido Canabal, General Joaquín Amaro, and Ing. Rodolfo Elías Calles. General Calles made a public statement praising the work of the President, who was among those who accompanied him to his home. The two men had matters to discuss.

The federal Congress was breaking more sharply in a schism

between Cardenistas and Callistas, and the P.N.R., headed by General Matías Ramos, was having problems about gubernatorial elections, such as those in Nuevo León and Guanajuato.

In Guanajuato the Party backed Jesús Yáñez Maya, who was expected to continue the policies of the strongly Callista governor, Melchor Ortega. One of Sr. Yáñez Maya's opponents was Senator Federico Medrano, who at one time had headed Ortiz Rubio's Whites in the Chamber of Deputies. He now broke with the P.N.R., and was expelled by it. But he was supported by his fellow senators, and so this meant that the federal Senate was at odds with the official Party. Then the federal Chamber of Deputies backed the P.N.R.[1] Two observations might be made about this case of Senate support for a politician who had been thrown out of the official Party. For one thing, differences between Party officials and certain senators, particularly senators associated with the Left Wing, were not confined to the contest between Medrano and Yáñez Maya. For another thing, while there were differences between Medrano and Yáñez Maya, some felt that each of these men had at one time or another been identified with Melchor Ortega, so that to look for a candidate with a record more completely in opposition to Ortega they preferred to turn to Sr. Enrique Fernández Martínez, friend of Guanajuato's former Governor (1927–1931) Agustín Arroyo Ch.[2]

In Nuevo León the Party was backing Diputado Plutarco Elías Calles, Jr., against the popular General Fortunato Zuazua. The General was supported by a very strong anti-Government feeling and it would seem that he was the victor in the plebiscites, but on May 10 the Party announced the victory of the son of General Calles. After receiving this news, General Zuazua made a strong declaration in which he attacked President Cárdenas for not having respected the popular vote. In retaliation P.N.R. President Matías Ramos condemned any election that might be backed by religious women and vestrymen.

Mention has already been made of the situation in Veracruz, whose Senator Cándido Aguilar carried on against the governor and against the leadership of the congressional Permanent Commission. When P.N.R. Party members in Veracruz were attacked by gunmen and wounded, a report was circulated that supporters of Aguilar were responsible for the assault. Although Beneitez'

[1] Eduardo J. Correa, *El balance del Cardenismo*, p. 51.
[2] Agustín Arroyo Ch., interview, August 16, 1956.

election to the presidency of the Permanent Commission was brought about by the votes of *diputados* who were Party members, and although the *diputados* backed the P.N.R. in its differences with the Senate, it should not be supposed that all of the *diputados* supported the Party. Those from Cárdenas' home state of Michoacán shifted from the P.N.R.'s position.

By early June various declarations made it seem for a while that some kind of peace might be possible. It was pointed out to President Cárdenas that in spite of some differences between the majority of the deputies and the so-called "leftists," in reality all would cooperate with the Party. Then the senators declared themselves to be supporters of both Cárdenas and Calles, which is something that would have been easier had there not been profound differences in the philosophies of these two generals.

At this time a number of senators, representing Left Wingers who were having differences with P.N.R. President Matías Ramos, visited the senator from Guerrero, Ezequiel Padilla. It was arranged that a group would call on Calles at his home. Calles would give them guidance.

Accordingly, on June 11, 1935, about seven senators were received by Calles. The guidance they received was pretty strong stuff and included Calles' severe criticisms of recent strikes and of labor leaders Lombardo Toledano and Alfredo Navarrete. As the senators were about to depart, Padilla asked the General for his approval of issuing the declarations to the press, and Calles said he had no objection, as there was nothing secret about the matter.

Upon his return to Mexico City Padilla therefore made himself incommunicado in order to prepare a text for Calles' approval before giving it to the newspapers. Thus it was that Matías Ramos and Foreign Minister Portes Gil were unsuccessful in their efforts to reach him. It being known that Padilla was preparing a statement on the Calles interview for publication, a publication which the President thought would be unwise, Cárdenas had asked Portes Gil to persuade Padilla to visit the President. But Portes Gil's assistants could not reach Padilla.

On the day following the interview Padilla went alone to see Calles at Cuernavaca. The General furnished some excellent brandy and Padilla read the text which was to go to the press. Calles pronounced it perfect.

In it Calles said that he was speaking with his customary frankness; that what was most upsetting in Congress was that "personalistic divisions" were being pushed by persons who did not estimate the consequences:

What is happening now is exactly what happened during the period of President Ortiz Rubio. One group called itself Ortizrubista and another Callista. At that time, as soon as I found out what was going on, I tried, personally and through my friends, to stop it; but the perverse elements were stronger and carried on to the end, with what results you know. At this very moment this same personalistic movement is being carried on frankly and openly in the Chamber of Deputies and I could tell you the names of those who are promoting it. All those men who are trying to divide us are engaged in perfidious work. The recent history of our politics has taught us, with plenty of examples, that personalistic divisions lead only to final disaster. Therefore in the legislative chambers, the unjustified categories of Cardenistas and Callistas should be suppressed. When the division into groups based on persons begins, first the deputies, then the senators, governors, Cabinet ministers, and, finally, the Army, take sides.

"We come now," the statement continued, "to the matter of forming 'left wings,' which means that there will be 'right wings.' In this no one will wish to be left behind, and thus there begins 'the marathon of radicalism,' and with it the start of excesses that can lead to no good."

The words which Padilla read to Calles in Cuernavaca, and was about to have published, revealed the General's views about the labor situation:

For six months the nation has been shaken by constant strikes, many of them entirely unjustified, the labor organizations in many cases showing themselves to be ungrateful for what they have already received. These strikes hurt capital much less than they hurt the government, because they close the sources of prosperity. Thus the good intentions and untiring work of the President are constantly obstructed, and far from taking advantage of the present moments, so favorable for Mexico, we are going backwards, always retrogressing; it is unfair for the workers to cause this harm to a government headed by an honest citizen and a sincere friend of the workers like General Cárdenas. They have no right to create difficulties for him and obstruct his progress. I know the history of all the organizations, from their birth; I know their leaders, the old leaders and the new leaders. I know that they are not in agreement among themselves and that they go dragged in parallel lines by Navarrete and Lombardo Toledano, who are directing the disorder among them. I know what they are capable of, and I can affirm that in these agitations there are vigilant appetites, very dangerous to unprepared people and organizations. They are provoking, and playing with, the economic life of the nation, without respect for the generosity and frankly pro-labor position of the President . . . In a nation where the government protects them, helps them, and surrounds them with guarantees, to disturb the march of economic construction is not only ingratitude, but is treason. These organizations represent no force but themselves. I know them. In the hour of crisis, of danger, you will not see a one of them coming to the rescue, and it is we, the soldiers of the Revolution, who have to defend the cause. And we cannot stand tranquilly by while they, in order to defend bastard interests, are compromising Mexico's opportunities. They don't even know enough to select cases that are appropriate for their strikes. They declare a strike on the Streetcar Company [Compañía de Tranvías] which is in bankruptcy, which is losing money.

General Calles' remarks included mention of other prominent strikes, such as the one against the Telephone Company, which, according to Calles, had already conceded to labor all that could with justification be asked of it. In the case of Mata Redonda Calles pointed out that President Rodríguez, also a friend of the workers, had in the last months of his administration served as arbiter and given labor a favorable decision. "Then, when President Cárdenas has hardly started his government, new insatiable appetites mock the presidential award and start a new strike. In the San Rafael Paper Company the labor organizations declared a strike, their futile motive a dispute over the supremacy of worker groups, which could have been settled by a simple counting." Calles pointed to the serious harm done to the community by the strikes. He referred to León's 100,000 inhabitants without light, sanitation facilities, or water because of strikes carried out to support other strikers. "Nothing," he said, "checks the egoism of the organizations and their leaders. They have no morals, nor the most elemental respect for the rights of the collectivity."

After reading these words to his friend and host, Padilla suggested that it would perhaps be better for the General to handle the matter privately with President Cárdenas instead of by such a release to the press. Calles replied that on numerous occasions he had endeavored without success to convince the President of his views;

that being the case, Calles favored the publication of the interview statement.[3]

The newspapers on June 12, 1935, carried the "Patriotic Declarations of General Plutarco Elías Calles." They were sensational. Particular notice was given not only to the remarks about labor but also to the reference to ex-President Ortiz Rubio. This reference, in the opinion of Luis Montes de Oca, was not intended at all to be a threat to Lázaro Cárdenas but was included because Calles had seen the disaster that had resulted from Ortizrubistas clashing with Callistas, and early in the Cárdenas regime wanted to prevent a similar performance.[4]

[3] Ezequiel Padilla, conversation, 1956.
[4] Luis Montes de Oca, conversation, September 30, 1955.

72.

The Break between
Cárdenas and Calles

Telegrams congratulating General Calles poured into Cuernavaca by the thousands, and a great many prominent persons drove to Cuernavaca to express in person their agreement with the declarations.

The newspaper editorials were generally favorable to Calles, and news items showed that he was strongly supported in political circles. There were, on June 12, statements of praise by Senator Vicente L. Beneitez, president of the Permanent Commission, and by J. Jesús Vidales, president of the P.N.R. bloc in the Chamber of Deputies. It was reported that the Permanent Commission had held a session and agreed officially to send effusive congratulations to Calles for the statement's words which "came to mark firm plans of conduct for the country at moments when germs of confusion and error were in evidence in different economic and political sectors." The P.N.R. blocs of both Chambers, it was reported, were about to hold urgent sessions in order to congratulate the author of the declarations.

But one newspaper did not carry the words which Lic. Padilla had prepared on Calles' interview with the senators. This was *El Nacional*, the P.N.R. publication, at that time directed by Froylán C. Manjarrez, the former Puebla governor, who had spent five years in exile in Cuba after supporting the De la Huerta rebellion. Manjarrez' return to Mexico had been arranged through his friendship with Portes Gil, and now Portes Gil communicated with him, with the result that *El Nacional* omitted publication of the Calles statement.

Lic. Vicente Lombardo Toledano was quick to declare: "Once again, I have the honor of being considered, by those ignorant of the real causes of these conflicts, responsible for the strike movements which have occurred recently in the country."

The papers on June 13 reported that the members of the Permanent Commission had gone to Cuernavaca to present their congratulations. They also reported that in the Senate 8 members of the Left Wing were displeased with Calles, whereas now 50 senators did not wish to join this Left Wing. Reports pictured the Chamber of Deputies as having 45 Left Wingers, in opposition to whom majority leader Vidales claimed the support of 99 deputies and, in addition, 30 who indicated their adherence by telegram. To sum up these reports, figures were issued as of June 13 showing the following line-up: Callismo: 99 deputies and 45 senators; Cardenismo: 44 deputies and 9 senators.[1]

Rumors were afloat that Rodolfo Elías Calles, Fernando Torreblanca, and Aarón Sáenz were resigning their positions in the Cárdenas Administration. It was obvious that the government had a serious crisis on its hands.

As was to be expected, labor organizations made statements attacking Calles. Prominent among these were the pronouncements by the Railroad Workers Union and the National Labor Chamber, the latter declaring that "the declarations of Sr. General Calles

[1] Eduardo J. Correa, *El balance del Cardenismo* p. 55.

constitute an unjust charge against the working classes of Mexico."
Colonel Adalberto Tejeda asked that Calles be thrown out of the
country.

The President acted with speed and decision, both of which were
necessary in view of the uncertainty in the legislature. Almost at
once state governors and commanders of military districts received
visitors who represented the President personally and who had been
sent to determine the positions of those they visited.

At Los Pinos, where he was now living, Cárdenas showed Foreign
Minister Portes Gil the statement which he had decided to issue. In
it he said that he had never advised divisions. He referred to the
calmness which as President he had always recommended to his
friends and supporters in spite of those who, no doubt annoyed at
not receiving appointments which they wanted, openly and "with
full rage" had opposed the Administration and in so doing had
spread alarming gossip and even "reprehensible procedures of disloyalty and treason." Then the statement discussed the labor problems of recent months which had turned into strike movements. It
pointed out that even if these movements momentarily hurt the
nation's economy, they would, if resolved reasonably and in a spirit
of fairness and social justice, contribute in the course of time to a
stronger economic situation. This stronger economic situation would
be the result of a better condition of the workers, "obtained in
accord with the economic possibilities of the capitalistic sector."

Cárdenas' statement announced that the Federal Executive was
determined to work for the fulfillment of the program of the Revolution, the "laws that regulate the equilibrium of production."
and the P.N.R.'s Six-Year Plan, regardless of "the alarm of the
representatives of the capitalistic sector." At the same time the
President felt it his duty to advise workers and capitalists alike that
they would have all the protections guaranteed by the law, and
that the Chief Executive would not permit excesses, "unsatisfactory
agitations or acts implying transgressions of the law." Cárdenas,
in his statement, declared his full confidence in the country's labor
and peasant organizations, and he expressed himself as certain that
"they are competent of acting with the prudence and patriotism
required by the legitimate interests which they represent."

The document's concluding words were to the effect that the
President would know how to fulfill his responsibility and felt he
had the right to the nation's full confidence. "If I have committed

errors, they might have been from other causes but never have they sprung from perversity or bad faith."

Portes Gil found the President completely calm. He congratulated him on the message he was about to deliver and told him that it would raise the presidential prestige "already fallen in the six months that you have governed the nation." Enthusiastic about Cárdenas' dignified attitude, Portes Gil forecast that he would receive, as had Calles, thousands of congratulatory messages. "You will be surprised to find in many cases yours signed by those who signed messages to General Calles."

Cárdenas remarked to Portes Gil: "Tomorrow I think I shall call a Cabinet meeting to ask the resignations of all, so as to be free to name new collaborators. I want you to take over the presidency of the Party."[2]

With the issuance of the President's message to the nation and with the other steps he was taking, the Left Wing of Congress showed signs of strengthening. The Senate was now reported to have 23 Left Wingers. What is rather remarkable is that on the previous day only nine were reported as allied to Cardenismo in the Senate, where in the days before the crisis there had been so much Left Wing strength and opposition to P.N.R. management by Matías Ramos.

The President held his Cabinet meeting, as he had planned, on June 14, and all the ministers attended except for Communications Minister Rodolfo Elías Calles, who was out of town. Cárdenas reviewed the events of the last two days. "I regret very much that, in view of these events, the Government has experienced a crisis, from which it is absolutely certain to come out on top . . . I believe that we can expect the support of the immense majority of Mexicans and especially the labor and peasant groups."[3]

The President requested and received the resignations of all his ministers. Ing. Juan de Dios Bojórquez felt that if all those who had resigned would pay a call on General Calles at Cuernavaca, it would have a calming effect, and all but Lic. Portes Gil and General Múgica did this at once.

Following the news of the Cabinet resignations and the change

[2] Emilio Portes Gil, *Quince años de política mexicana*, p. 504.
[3] *Ibid.*, pp. 505–506.

644

in the presidency of the P.N.R., the Congressional Left Wing attained a majority.

Calles then announced that on June 18 he would depart for Sinaloa. His withdrawal, he said, was in order to bring an end to a situation which might be wrongly interpreted. He pointed out that when the senators had sought his opinion, he had given it "with full frankness and clarity." His statement, he said, had been made without any personal interest, its sole objective being "to orient the action of my party." He added that unfortunately his statement had been misinterpreted as meaning that he sought to intervene in government affairs.

When Portes Gil called on Calles, he found him ready to depart on the next day. Calles again expressed regret that his declarations "which have the seal of the best faith, for the good of the nation and the government, have been given a twisted interpretation." He added: "There is nothing to do about this now, unfortunately; and I have resolved to leave the Republic, retiring forever from all political activity. To my friends I recommend that they help the President and try to serve the country with full loyalty." Portes Gil observed to Calles that "the President could act in no other way than he did. The tone of your declarations was aggressive, and if he had remained silent, his authority would have been completely broken."

On the morning of June 19 a special plane, the *Electra*, was placed at the orders of General Calles. Among those who saw him off at the airport were Portes Gil (now head of the P.N.R.), Juan de Dios Bojórquez, Narciso Bassols, Sebastián Allende (ex-Governor of Jalisco), Senators Carlos and Manuel Riva Palacio and Fernando Torreblanca, and Generals Pablo Quiroga, Joaquín Amaro, and Pedro J. Almada (in charge of Veracruz Military Operations). All that reporters could get out of the departing celebrity was: "I have nothing to say." By 11:30 A.M. the plane had reached Mazatlán, Sinaloa.

In Washington, the Mexican ambassador to the United States, Dr. and General Francisco Castillo Nájera, announced that "the retirement of General Calles is complete."

As Portes Gil had foreseen, President Cárdenas received vast demonstrations of support, including almost 8000 messages. At the turn in events there was a good deal of rejoicing as well as admiration for the President's performance.

The composition of the new Cabinet was made known on the day of Calles' departure, and its most striking feature was the appointment of General Saturnino Cedillo to succeed Lic. Garrido Canabal as the Agriculture Minister. Cedillo, who opposed steps which were making life difficult for the Catholic Church, had been one of the earliest pushers of the Cárdenas presidential bandwagon. Not only were the religious in this way given the hope of less extensive Red Shirt activities, but some of the harshest anti-Church regulations were reversed. The President brought to an end the recent ruling against sending religious literature through the mails.

The new Cabinet:

Minister of Gobernación
　　Lic. Silvano Barba González
Minister of Foreign Relations
　　Lic. Fernando González Roa
Minister of Finance and Public Credit
　　Lic. Eduardo Suárez
Minister of War and Navy
　　General Andrés Figueroa
Minister of Education
　　Lic. Gonzalo Vázquez Vela
Minister of Agriculture
　　General Saturnino Cedillo
Minister of Communications and Public Works
　　General Francisco J. Múgica
Minister of National Economy
　　General Rafael Sánchez Tapia
Head of Labor Department
　　Lic. Genaro V. Vázquez
Head of Central Department
　　Sr. Cosme Hinojosa
Attorney General
　　Lic. Silvestre Guerrero

The Oficial Mayor of Cosme Hinojosa's Central Department, that handling Federal District matters, was Adolfo Ruiz Cortines, who had earlier been with the Department of National Statistics. Due to illness Fernando González Roa failed to accept the Foreign Ministry post, which was directed by Undersecretary José Angel Ceniceros until on November 30, 1935, Eduardo Hay was named Foreign Minister. Pascual Ortiz Rubio, who had returned to Mexico around Christmas time in 1934 after spending two years in San Diego, California, on June 16, 1935, was named Manager of Petromex (Petróleos Nacionales de México), the oil company operated by the government. On January 1, 1936, Luis Montes de Oca became the Director of the Bank of Mexico.

Party President Portes Gil recognized that General Zuazua had won a popular triumph over Plutarco Elías Calles, Jr., in Nuevo León. But he advised President Cárdenas that neither candidate was worthy of the governorship. He considered that young Calles had been defeated and was, besides, not friendly to the federal government. As for Zuazua, Portes Gil pointed out that he had "thrown himself into the arms of the reaction of Monterrey, which—in manifestations and noisy meetings—lost no opportunity to attack the federal government." So President Cárdenas agreed with the idea of declaring the recent voting in Nuevo León to be null and void. General Anacleto Guerrero became governor of Nuevo León. This selection may have been pleasing to Portes Gil, but apparently it was not entirely pleasing to General Múgica and others from Michoacán who became more and more unfriendly to the Party president and who were among those who resented the political strength he appeared to be building up.

The Chamber of Deputies became more strongly Cardenista following a battle therein on September 11, 1935, in which two of the nation's lawmakers were killed and various others were wounded. Luis Mora Tovar blamed the Callistas, and seventeen *diputados* were banished from the lower Chamber. Shortly after this happened General Cándido Aguilar was elected to the presidency of the Senate.

Although as the year progressed Garrido Canabal's Red Shirts dropped out of the picture, the Gold Shirts once again were involved in a spectacular and apparently useless fight. From the balcony of the Palacio Nacional on November 20, 1935, Luis I. Rodríguez addressed the various groups which had come to the Plaza de la Constitución to pay their respects to the President on the twenty-fifth anniversary of the Revolution.

During the applause which followed Lic. Rodríguez's words, the Gold Shirts, led by General Nicolás Rodríguez, arrived at the Plaza

"Leftists," in automobiles, fighting "Gold Shirts," on horseback, at the Plaza de la Constitución in front of the Palacio Nacional, November 20, 1935. Photo by "Chato" Montes de Oca. Casasola.

on horseback. When members of some labor groups arranged to have automobiles block the path of the horsemen, the gold-shirted riders prepared to advance on their adversaries, whirling cowboy ropes. Worker leaders, such as David Alfaro Siqueiros, Lorenzo Gómez, and Carlos Sánchez Cárdenas, called on their followers to resist the "fascists." In the struggle that followed, automobiles zigzagged around the Plaza with the object of running into the horsemen, and the great square became a battle field. When the police arrived half an hour later and brought an end to the hostilities, there were three dead and forty-six wounded. Nicolás Rodríguez was twice wounded with a knife.

The President was busy with more momentous matters. He was pushing the Revolutionary agrarian program at an unprecedented rate. In commenting on what had gone before, General Cárdenas pointed out that much of the land that had been redistributed had not been particularly satisfactory land. At the Agrarian Convention of September 7, 1935, the President admitted that in many cases the parcels which had theretofore gone to peasants had been too small to allow them to resolve their economic problems. He was particularly insistent on the need for unity among those who worked the soil, instead of division among all sorts of local and so-called national peasant groups, often under the domination of various political leaders. With unity, said Cárdenas, the peasant class could go ahead in a disciplined and rewarding manner.

While the 2,670,000 hectares of land which were redistributed in 1935 presented a smaller figure than those which were to follow, this was a terrific pace compared with anything that had gone before. The parcels redistributed, besides being more numerous than in the past, were individually larger. Government statistics revealed that about 70 per cent of the nation's laborers worked on the land. In April, 1935, about 25 per cent of all persons engaged in agriculture were *ejidatarios*. These 920,000 individuals produced about 27 per cent of the value of the nation's agricultural production, according to the official figures.[4]

Like his predecessor, General Rodríguez, President Cárdenas was particularly interested in providing funds so that the many *ejidatarios* could properly work their lands. During 1935 the National Bank of Agricultural Credit (Banco Nacional de Crédito Agrícola)

---

[4] Secretaría de la Economía Nacional, *La reforma agraria en México.*

loaned out over 15 million pesos, and during that same year a new entity was created: the National Bank of Ejidal Credit (Banco Nacional de Crédito Ejidal). This new institution was authorized to loan 20 million pesos to *ejidatarios* during 1936. The Banco Nacional de Crédito Agrícola was to continue to function, but was to make agricultural loans other than those needed by the *ejidos*.

73.

The Expedition to Tabasco

On June 21, 1935, Lic. Tomás Garrido Canabal was appointed General Director of Public Education of the state of Tabasco, to which he returned from Mexico City with many of his Red Shirts. Two days after this appointment, Mexico City University students gave a great demonstration in favor of the new Minister of Agriculture, General Cedillo, Garrido's successor in the Cárdenas Cabinet. Calmness was not now a feature of University circles and shortly after the demonstration of June 23 many of these same students were struggling against supporters of Lic. Vicente Lombardo Toledano.

At the time of the break between Cárdenas and Calles, Garrido Canabal, like many others, had a serious decision to make. Since the assassination of Obregón, Garrido had co-operated with Calles more fully than with anyone, co-operating at the same time with those whom Calles favored. Opponents of Garrido's Tabasco machine had from 1924 to date seen their hopes dashed by the support which Calles gave to Garrido. During the presidency of General Abelardo L. Rodríguez, when there seemed to be some possibility of changing things in Tabasco, Calles intervened in favor of the Tabasco dictator following a trip which Lic. Trujillo Gurría made on Garrido's behalf to "El Tambor," Sinaloa, where Calles happened to be at the moment.

The first reaction of Garrido to the differences between Cárdenas and Calles was to maintain the thesis that these two leaders should effect a reconciliation "for the good of the Revolutionary unity." When Garrido, who appears to have given more backing to Calles than to Cárdenas, subsequently lost his position in the Cárdenas Cabinet, and when Calles made his departure from the political scene, enemies of Garrido's Tabascan dictatorship had the idea that there might be some hope.

They focused that hope on a rather immediate objective. The Tabasco electoral law called for an election on August 18, 1935, to fill the state's single legislative chamber. By July 18, for this local election, nine *diputados* and nine substitute *diputados* representing the state's nine electoral districts would have to be registered in Tabasco.

We turn now to Rodulfo Brito Foucher, who headed up the idea of an anti-Garridista participation in this approaching state election. Lic. Brito Foucher, who like Garrido came from a background of Tabascan hacienda owners, had long been opposed to the Garrido dictatorship, considering it to be a tyranny without parallel in the history of Mexico and one of the most outstanding cases of perversity, degradation, and evil ever seen in the history of the world. After participating as a youth in the De la Huerta uprising, during which period he was Undersecretary and later Minister of Gobernación and Foreign Relations in the rebel government, Lic. Brito had spent two years in the United States. Subsequently he had been dean of the Law School of the National University of Mexico City and had served as a professor. In Mexico City he had plenty of experience with the regime in his home state, doing what he could legally for unfortunates who had incurred the displeasure of the dictator. He was now thirty-five years of age.

This avowed enemy of Garrido's machine was at this time determined to lead into the state a group who would participate in the local elections in an effort to have "Tabasco return to the institutional life." He spoke about the matter with two, and only two, important officials of the federal government. One of them was the President's Secretary, Lic. Luis I. Rodríguez, who was most cordial and did not hide his hostility towards Garrido. The other was General Francisco J. Múgica, who had been in 1915–1916 "pre-constitutional" governor of Tabasco and was now Minister of Communications and Public Works and particularly close to President Cárdenas. Múgica had in the past been friendly with Garrido Canabal, and had once announced the need of "Tabascanizing" all of the Mexican nation, but now he spoke against the dictator, saying to Brito and his followers: "You can go calm and confident that General Cárdenas is a man of honor who will not permit you to be assassinated."

But time was short and the raising of the necessary funds was disheartening. Of the 5,500 pesos put up for the adventure, only 1,500 represented contributions from outside of Brito's family (and only ten pesos from Catholics of Tabasco). With 500 pesos set aside as cash to be used for necessities in Villahermosa, the remainder was divided almost equally between the commissioning of two ten-passenger planes of Cia. Mexicana de Aviación to take men to Villahermosa and the purchase of an assortment of pistols and ammunition. This shortage of funds limited to twenty the number of one-way passages that could be purchased to Villahermosa, although many others were anxious to participate. Of the twenty who thus took off from Mexico City's airport on Sunday morning July 14, 1935, about one half were students. One student brought the number of *expedicionarios* up to twenty-one by taking earlier that same morning the regular scheduled airline flight and awaiting the others at the Villahermosa airport. Newspapermen of Mexico City declined invitations to go along and thus continued their long-drawn-out custom of not setting foot on Tabascan soil.

After a flight of about three hours the two chartered planes from Mexico City landed at Villahermosa's airport at approximately noon and promptly departed, leaving the members of the Expedition to Tabasco under a burning sun. Federal soldiers had, at the request of the airline, been placed at the airport in order to protect the planes in case of a possible conflict. The twenty-one members of the Expedition found themselves greeted at the airport by twenty-one unarmed residents of Tabasco and these helped the arrivals with their baggage on the march of about one and one-half kilometers, made on foot from the airport to Villahermosa. Not only had all of the city's automobile drivers been forbidden to transport the newcomers, but instructions had been given that cars should disturb the march by foot. Thus it was that automobiles went back and forth on the route sounding their horns derisively and whipping up clouds of dust. When the line of marchers reached a fork in the road, Brito decided that they would take the road which led past Garrido's well-guarded home, a happy choice since Garrido was seeking to avoid personal responsibility for a clash and since the alternate road, which passed through some woods, contained Garridistas lying in ambush.

Not far within the city limits the members of the Expedition and four or five others settled down in the humble dwelling of a Tabascan worker, one reason for this selection being that Villahermosa's hotels would not receive the new group. Here, in their unpretentious "headquarters," which consisted of a few simple rooms, Lic. Brito at once set to work to draw up a slate of eighteen names of persons who would participate in the August election of local *diputados* and substitute *diputados*, the slate which had to be filed by July 18. From the very start commissions of peasants from all over the state paid calls on the leaders of the Expedition and he lost no time in inquiring of these about their secret leaders, studying carefully the attributes of all in order to form a suitable list in opposition to the dictatorship. The candidates must be residents of Tabasco.

While this work was going on and while the newcomers ventured but little into a city which gave the impression of being almost deserted, a mass of anonymous letters from sympathizers forecasting all sorts of dire occurrences arrived for Brito and his men. One of these messages, a typical one, stated: "We advise you that tonight the city lights are going out, which is a custom of the government when it plans to assassinate anyone. Take care when the lights go out."

The city lights, whose power was supplied by a government-managed plant, did go out as the evening wore on. Members of the Expedition acted as guards both at the back and front of the abode they were occupying. One of the captains from the local contingent of the federal forces acted rather on his own when with a small escort that night he prevented the efforts of Garridista gunmen to throw bombs on the dwelling which housed Brito and his companions.

By early the next morning, Monday, July 15, having determined that, under the circumstances, it was necessary to move the headquarters to a more secure structure, Brito began some negotiations which would in one way or another provide either one or the other of two suitable homes on the opposite side of Villahermosa. In front of the lodging where Brito and his men had spent a troubled night, now rode a menacing array of about fifty Garridista horsemen with pistols and lassos.

After a decision to make the movement in two stages, the first contingent set forth to cross the city at about 10:00 A.M. This was a group which included fourteen of those who had come from Mexico City and ten others, local workers and peasants who had subsequently joined up. It included Brito's brother, Manuel, and all the students from Mexico City, as well as the other more youthful participants. Brito and some of the others who were thought to be the most hated by the Garridistas formed a group of seven which was to make a second crossing.

As the first group of twenty-four proceeded it ran into trouble, finding itself, before long, harried and followed by about three hundred Red Shirts headed by two members of the local legislature, Salatiel Córdoba and Onésimo Cortés. The Red Shirts hurled not only insults but also old fruit and other objects, and they even pushed some of those who made up the rear of the Britista group. In this manner they approached the corner of Juárez and Lerdo streets, in the central part of the city, where was another force of armed Garridistas, directed by federal Senator Ausencio C. Cruz, who handled a machine gun behind the barred window of one of the buildings. With the Britistas thus hemmed in from in front and behind, Cruz and his men opened fire. Britistas shot at the Red Shirts who had been pursuing them, but were easy game for the group directed by Cruz, particularly for the latter's machine gun. Manuel Brito Foucher, twenty-four–year–old brother of the Expedition's leader, fell dead with thirteen shots of the machine gun, and a good number of similar shots brought an end to the life of César Pedrero Gutiérrez. Other Britistas who lost their lives were Juárez Merino, Pedro Priego, and Jovito Pérez. The deaths of the last two mentioned, residents of Tabasco who joined the Expedition, occurred somewhat later and as the result of injuries received during the clash. Bernardo Calzada, Alfonso Pedrero, and Ricardo Castro, all three arrivals from Mexico City, were very seriously wounded.

Although Senator Ausencio C. Cruz and those who were with him suffered in no way, the large group of Red Shirts who from the start of this affair had pursued the Britistas did not come out of the encounter entirely unharmed. Five Red Shirts were killed, including the local *diputados* who were involved, Salatiel Córdoba and Onésimo Cortés. Various Red Shirts were wounded.

Thanks to an Army official's wife who became aware of the shooting, word of the combat reached the headquarters of the federal troops very quickly, with the result that a small contingent of federals arrived at the scene of the fighting and the last of the Garridistas hurried away. The news which reached Brito, who was interviewing more peasant groups in the house where he had spent the night, came from alarmed and humble women. One of them, a fruit vender, mentioned two hundred deaths, and a second spoke of a battle in which seventy-five had been killed.

Leading the six armed companions who had remained with him, Brito set forth. On passing the office of the Jefatura de Operaciones Militares he requested an escort of federal soldiers, but this request was denied on the basis that such protection was a matter for the local police. Brito was shown a telegram from the War Ministry in Mexico City which was addressed to the local Military Operations, headed by General Pilar R. Sánchez. It read as follows:

YOUR CODED WIRE OF THE TWELFTH. YOUR ACTION IN THE MATTER SHOULD BE LIMITED TO PROVIDING GUARANTEES NOT PERMITTING THE ALTERATION OF ORDER, BUT WITHOUT THE FORCE INVOLVING ITSELF IN MATTERS FOREIGN TO ITS MISSION . . . ANDRES FIGUEROA.[1]

As the group of seven was nevertheless determined to fire on any who obstructed its way, it was fortunate that the various assemblages of Red Shirts and uniformed students of the Juárez Institute which were encountered chose to flee rather than get involved in battle.

Brito and his companions, marching in formation, were thus able to reach the scene of disaster, a scene revealing a few bodies of dead and wounded strewn in the street, other bodies having by now been removed to the rooms of houses which faced the street. Brito kissed the face of his fallen brother and set to work to get medical attention for the wounded and sheets to cover the bodies of Manuel and of

---

[1] Rodulfo Brito Foucher, memorandum, September 17, 1958.

César Pedrero Gutiérrez. After hearing the details of the recent conflict he went to the telegraph office and sent to Mexico City a message that shocked the nation. Senator Ausencio Cruz and his armed followers reached the office shortly after Brito left it. President Cárdenas, who was at this time in Guadalajara, soon received telegrams from Governor Lastra, the local Tabascan Congress, Senator Cruz, and Senator Alcides Caparroso, who placed all the blame on Brito. Cruz used the *Guacamayo* to fly to Guadalajara with a direct report for the President.

Following receipt of this news, great demonstrations took place in Mexico City against the regime in Tabasco. From Guadalajara President Cárdenas on July 16 sent to the rector of the National University, Dr. Fernando Ocaranza, a telegram stating that an immediate investigation would be made. Students in Mexico City were quick to place on Governor Lastra and Colonel Cruz the responsibility for the tragedy.

Also on the sixteenth, as a result of the events of the fifteenth, two planes from Mexico City arrived at the Villahermosa airport, bearing sixteen youths who made up a second expeditionary group. Some of the new *expedicionarios* were practically children.

On the seventeenth a plane conveyed to Mexico City the bodies of the three who had reached Villahermosa on the fourteenth and had been killed on the fifteenth: Manuel Brito Foucher, César Pedrero Gutiérrez, and Juárez Merino. On the same plane went the wounded members of the Expedition (Ricardo Castro, Alfonso Pedrero, and Bernardo Calzada). On the following day stores and factories in the national capital closed for three hours of mourning. The University organized a parade, led by its rector and by professors. The thousands of students, many of them Americans attending summer school, marching under great banners calling for the removal of the "assassin Garrido," were joined by others who wished to participate. Catholics cried, "Viva Cárdenas!" and "Death to Calles and Garrido!" After passing through the principal streets of Mexico City the parade went to the cemetery. The newspapers of Mexico City, never supporters of Garrido, let loose indignant blasts against the dictator, and so strong were the pronouncements penned by Félix F. Palavicini that Garrido retaliated with a telegram in which he abused the newspaperman's forefathers and called him a profiteer in public opinion and in the Revolution.

From Villahermosa Brito on the seventeenth had sent a wire to an exiled Tabascan, José Suárez Naváez, who replied at once by putting at the disposal of the Expedition his unoccupied houses in Villahermosa. It might seem that the two floors of an entire block which were thus made available would have been ample for Brito's headquarters, but it happened that this was not at all the case. First of all twenty-five of the peasants who had been brought into town on July 21 to participate in the internal elections of the official political party slipped away from the fold and became Britistas. A little later an "army" of six hundred peasants, wielding knives and hiding pistols under their white jackets, paraded in front of the State Government Building crying, "Death to Garrido Canabal!" and "Viva Brito Foucher!" Tabascans who were working in the oil fields of southeast Veracruz formed expeditions and entered the state. Expeditions arrived from Campeche and Chiapas. When about two hundred Mexico City students sought to embark from the port of Veracruz they were prevented from doing so by orders of the federal government. Garrido ordered the suspension of Villahermosa's commercial activities, but the members of the Expedition nevertheless found themselves able to obtain provisions and services from sympathizers who co-operated day and night. The movement against Garrido Canabal was both local and national.

President Cárdenas withdrew General Pilar R. Sánchez as head of Tabasco's Military Operations, naming in his place General Miguel Henríquez Guzmán (who had participated in the fighting against Delahuertistas in Villahermosa in 1923 and 1924). General Henríquez Guzmán transmitted the following message to Garrido from the President:

The Permanent Commission of the Congress of the Union is now in session and within a few moments will have declared the termination of the powers of the state of Tabasco. In the face of this situation General Cárdenas offers you two choices, asking you to select the one you want: the open right hand, which is the hand of a friend, or the closed left hand, which is the fist of an enemy. On the selection which you make will depend the attitude of General Cárdenas toward you and your friends.

Garrido replied: "Tell General Cárdenas that I select his hand of friendship."[2]

On July 23 the Permanent Commission of Congress declared

[2] Rodulfo Brito Foucher, memorandum, July 11, 1958; also his memorandum

that the governmental powers of Tabasco had come to an end and named General Aureo L. Calles to take over from Governor Lastra Ortiz. There was much celebrating in Tabasco, especially in Villahermosa, where Red Shirts were quick to turn in their uniforms at the Brito headquarters.

On August 9 it was announced that Lic. Garrido Canabal would leave for Cuba to make an agricultural study. But on August 11 the *Guacamayo* took him to Costa Rica. He went there as a representative of the Mexican Diplomatic Service to carry out studies in the fields of agriculture and livestock. But he did not leave the state of Tabasco before Dr. Rodulfo Brito Foucher, at the insistence of the federal government, made an earlier departure. Toward the end of August the federal Minister of Gobernación declared to be unconstitutional most of the Tabasco decrees issued during the long dictatorship of Tomás Garrido Canabal.

---

of September 17, 1958. Most of this chapter is based on the earlier of these two memoranda.

74.

General Calles
Returns to Mexico

At 4:30 P.M. on Friday December 13, 1935, at Mexico City's Balbuena Airport, arrived a bi-motor plane XA-BEP, the *Electra*, coming from Los Angeles, California. It brought to Mexico City General Plutarco Elías Calles and Sr. Luis N. Morones. The XA-BEP had stopped at Hermosillo, Mazatlán, and Guadalajara, but at none of these points had Calles left the plane. His arrival in Mexico City was quite a surprise to the public, and this time he was not greeted at the airport, as he had been in May, by President Cárdenas and Lic. Luis I. Rodríguez. Those who turned out to welcome him, as he followed Morones out of the plane, included Senator Manuel Riva Palacio, Senator Bernardo Bandala, Senator Francisco Terminel, Ing. Rodolfo Elías Calles, Ing. Juan de Dios Bojórquez, Ing. Bartolomé Vargas Lugo, Ricardo Treviño, José López Cortés, General Manuel Medinaveytia (military commander of the México Garrison) and General Alejandro Mange.

This was at a time when President Cárdenas was ill with undulant fever. It was also a time when a terrific battle was going on at

Plutarco Elías Calles *and* Luis N. Morones *return to Mexico on December 13, 1935, the former announcing that he has arrived to defend the Callista regime from the slanders of which it has been the victim for six months. Casasola.*

the National University, where leftist students were taking over university buildings as a protest against anti-Marxist professors like Dr. Antonio Caso.

The car which took Calles, Morones, Alejandro Mange, and Fernando Torreblanca to the General's Anzures residence sought to avoid the most frequented streets. At Anzures Calles was greeted by old friends, among whom were General José María Tapia and General Joaquín Amaro (the director of Military Education).

Calles at first had nothing to say beyond the fact that he had come to reside definitely from now on in his own country, but later on that same evening he issued a press statement in which he made it clear that he had come to defend the Callista regime from the slanders of which it had been the victim for the past six months.

A storm of protest arose immediately against the fifty-eight–year–old former Jefe Máximo de la Revolución. Labor groups set up a howl. There was considerable speculation about the possible intentions of Calles and his intimates, and prompt steps were taken to weaken what position he might have and to prevent any serious internal conflict.

On the day following the arrival of Calles and Morones, five senators were expelled from the Senate, to be tried for having been engaged in seditious and subversive activities. These were Senators Manuel Riva Palacio (México), Francisco L. Terminel (Sonora), Bernardo Bandala (Puebla), Elías Pérez Gómez (Morelos), and Cristóbal Bon Bustamante (Sinaloa). In the halls of the Senate students agitated against Calles' presence in the country.

Only one of the expelled senators was present at the session when the expulsion resolution was adopted. This was Bandala, who said: "If, as I see it, the only motive for my removal is that I went to the airport to greet General Calles, who is my friend and who did not come to carry on seditious work, I accept the resolution and will leave the Senate, but I do not accept classification as a rebel." In reply to this statement, Senator David Ayala remarked that "in order to be a senator of the Republic it is necessary to have a political conscience; General Calles is no longer the leader of the nation, and it is logical to suppose that we must consider his political and personal friends to be conspirators." The expelled senators found that Mexico City newspapers would not publish their declarations.[1]

On Monday, December 16, following a session of Senate Left Wing elements, the senators took still further steps, this time against state governors who were considered to be pro-Calles. The senators officially declared that state powers had come to an end in Guanajuato, Durango, Sinaloa, and Sonora; the governors of these states (Jesús Yáñez Maya, Carlos Real, Manuel Páez, and Ramón Ramos) were thrown out of their offices and were accused of crimes. As Undersecretary of Gobernación, Agustín Arroyo Ch. participated in decisions which affected state governorships. Yáñez Maya, as-

---

[1] Luis L. León (pseud. "Ignotos"), *El regreso del Gral. Calles*, p. 14.

sociated with Melchor Ortega, was replaced as chief executive of Guanajuato by Enrique Fernández Martínez, friend of Arroyo Ch. and of Luis I. Rodríguez.

During the Senate session which ousted the four governors, Ernesto Soto Reyes made a bitter attack against Melchor Ortega. Yáñez Maya was called the "product of an imposition" and was accused, by Guanajuato's Senator David Ayala, of being an enemy of the peasants. Sinaloa's Governer Páez was charged with having lost a large sum of money in one night of gambling at the extinct Foreign Club over a year earlier. Insults were hurled at Torreblanca. Governor Ramos of Sonora was pictured as being the "spiritual son of Rodolfo Elías Calles."[2]

The Chamber of Deputies was hardly able to equal the splash made by the Senate, both because the latter had jurisdiction as to the legality of states' powers and also because the Deputies had already cleaned house about six months earlier when they expelled seventeen Callistas. Nevertheless, the *diputados* held a lively session on December 17, wherein one speaker after another made unflattering remarks about the former "Strong Man of Mexico."

Military leaders who had greeted Calles on his arrival were not overlooked. Generals Amaro, Medinaveytia, and Tapia received news that was calculated to be unwelcome. By a presidential resolution dated December 15 Joaquín Amaro was removed as director of Military Education, and at the same time Manuel Medinaveytia was replaced by Rafael Navarro as commander of the First Military Zone and the Mexico City Garrison. José María Tapia was accused of working for a military rebellion, and Colonel Pedro Amaro, who had been among those present at the airport on December 13, lost his command of a regiment.

It was at this time that General Pedro J. Almada, who had been at the airport on June 18 when Calles made his departure, was removed from his job of chief of Veracruz Military Operations. He had put down some disorder in this disturbed state, and was apparently not pleasing to organized agrarian groups, which in the newspapers called for his removal and classified him as a Callista. Almada received word of his discharge during a telephone conversation with War Minister Figueroa on December 14.[3]

In the Senate J. Guadalupe Pineda said that Calles should be tried

[2] *Ibid.*, pp. 17–19.
[3] Pedro J. Almada, *Con mi cobija al hombro*, pp. 375–376, 384.

for his crimes and expelled from the Army because he was unworthy of belonging in it.

While worker and peasant organizations asked Cárdenas to throw Calles out of the country, P.N.R. President Portes Gil spoke: "I consider that the greatest error committed by General Plutarco Elías Calles in his life is his having returned, and, especially . . . accompanied by Sr. Luis N. Morones!"

The unsuccessful presidential opposition candidate, General Antonio I. Villarreal, and his supporters, Professor Aurelio Manrique, Jr., and Lic. Antonio Díaz Soto y Gama (all long-time haters of Calles), raised their voices in alarm. Newspaper stories carried such quotes as: "The rebellion that knocks at our doors is, without any argument, the most unjustified of the many that have taken place in the course of our history," and "Danger threatens the public liberties, the reforms, and the hopes for collective betterment."

Under the direction of Ing. Bartolomé Vargas Lugo a small daily publication entitled *El Instante* was started; in it Calles put forth his views. In the regular press the General did not get what seemed to him a satisfactory opportunity to defend his regime. The leading newspapers of the capital were careful not to print the declarations which he made from time to time, as they were careful not to print the statements of the senators who had in these days become ex-senators. Callistas came to feel that, in order to get paper, the newspapers had become dependent on Pipsa, the government-controlled organization which, with the help of favorable import tariffs, had been created to combat the monopolistic position once held by the San Rafael Paper Company.[4]

Only *El Instante* printed the statement which Calles drew up on the evening of December 16, following the removal of his friends from the Senate, governorships, and Army posts. In this statement Calles expressed his surprise that, on account of presidential orders, all other Mexico City newspapers failed to publish his remarks, thus nullifying his efforts to defend himself and his regime from "the torrent of insults, untruths, and slanders which for six months have been let loose against my person and the Callista regime." He pointed out that his actions had always been in accordance with the institutions of Mexico, and that it was necessary for the nation to know that he was not a conspirator and had not come to Mexico to

[4] Luis L. León, *op. cit.*, p. 37.

cause any agitation. What agitation existed, he said, was caused by such astonishing acts as the dismissal of legislators and governors whose sole crime was to be considered friends of his. He felt it would be both cowardly and improper for him to be seeking to defend his regime from outside his own country. He criticized officials of the Administration for not acting calmly.

Calles' words, published in *El Instante* on December 17, also made reference to a new political party being formed by friends of his. On that day various individuals separated themselves from the P.N.R., handing in resignations dated December 14. Among these individuals were: Bartolomé Vargas Lugo, Melchor Ortega, José María Tapia, Luis L. León, and Francisco L. Terminel. In their statement to the P.N.R.'s president they criticized recent "illegal" actions on the part of the Party. Also on December 17 *El Instante* published the declarations of the Organizing Committee of the new political party, the P.C.R. (Partido Constitucionalista Revolucionario). For the most part those who signed these declarations were the same as those who had resigned from the P.N.R.

On the next day Mexico learned that the P.N.R. had expelled a number of its members and formers leaders: Plutarco Elías Calles, Fernando Torreblanca, Manuel Riva Palacio, Agustín Riva Palacio, Bartolomé Vargas Lugo, Melchor Ortega, José María Tapia, and Luis L. León. A statement was made by P.N.R. President Emilio Portes Gil and P.N.R. Secretary-General Ignacio García Téllez: "The formation of an opposition political group made up of citizens expelled from the bosom of the P.N.R. in these moments, when all are identified with the President, is a beneficial result of the process of Revolutionary purification, and instead of weakening, is strengthening. A financial oligarchy has divided the ranks of the Revolution."

In the Senate there were further demands that Calles be thrown out of the Army. The Confederación Campesina accused him of being "a traitor, a disloyal person, a conspirator, an imposter, a concealer," etc., etc.

On December 18 the brief life of *El Instante* came to an involuntary end when a large group of workers invaded the building and prevented the printing of the issue which was then going to press. Nor could any future issues be printed, because of the troubles which resulted from this episode.

Calles therefore had to turn to representatives of the foreign press in order to express himself. This he did on the eighteenth. He said that he had found it impossible to remain quiet or away from Mexico while his opponents went to such extremes to slander him. One such example, he said, was the bringing of Madre Conchita to Mexico City in order to have her imply that Calles had been among those responsible for Obregón's death. Now, he said, the Government was doing everything possible to cause agitation and to make him appear as a conspirator.

Calles proceeded to tell the representatives of the United Press and of Universal Service that his only force was moral force. He admitted that he was not in agreement with the Government's procedures or tactics. "The most serious error they are committing is to take this country to Communism. I feel that that philosophical school of thought and economic-social system has not yet proved its excellence, and besides, neither our geographic conditions nor our ethnological conditions, nor the culture of our people, nor their psychology make us prepared for that social transformation; nor is there a directive group well prepared to implant it and bring it to fruition. The Communist sector, which has no ties with me, is always ready to carry out any act of disorder, since on this it lives, and this is its tactics, but the other worker sectors are being artificially agitated."

For Sunday, December 22, a great public demonstration of protest against the return of Calles to Mexico was planned. Labor leaders in particular urged their followers to participate and to listen to the speeches to be given. In the Senate Vicente L. Beneitez, who on June 12 had praised the "Patriotic Declarations of General Calles," referred to a problem which would be created:

Calles, with his ambitions to take over power, has been stirring up the restlessness which exists among the workers, as will be seen at the demonstration being prepared for next Sunday, and this will place the Cárdenas Government in a serious dilemma, because if a group of five thousand demonstrators seeks to attack General Calles at his home, the Government will have to choose between protecting General Calles, thus acting against the workers, or else letting the demonstrators give free rein to their hostility against him.

In the Chamber of Deputies, one of the nation's lawmakers said that "Calles should die like Robespierre."[5]

[5] *Ibid.*, p. 29.

But the public demonstration was quite orderly. Some of the eight labor leaders who spoke attacked Calles in no kind terms and prided themselves on their leftism. One speaker said that the nation should clearly understand that labor was now in full command, and another went so far as to say if Cárdenas should fail in his duty to labor, he, too, would receive the same treatment as was being applied to Calles. Lic. Lombardo Toledano spoke in a restrained manner. The final speech was that made by President Cárdenas who, among other things, pointed to various accomplishments of his regime. "In the first place we got rid of the centers of exploitation and vice; and who were those who were close to these centers of vice?" He referred to the Administration's definite and concrete steps in the field of agrarianism, and he spoke of the restitution of lands and forests which were earlier exploited by members of the previous regime. In conclusion he advised his hearers that "General Calles and his friends are no problem for the Government or for the working classes; let the working classes agree to allow the delinquents and turncoats of the Revolution to remain in Mexico, where they should stay so that they may feel the shame and the weight of their historic responsibility."

When the foreign correspondents asked Calles for his comments on the President's speech, he replied in these terms: the speech, which might have been made by any of the well-known Communists and which stirred up political passion and personal hate, was below the dignity of the presidency; Calles added that it was a speech which only created confusion and was unworthy of any head of any state.

The Mexican Ambassador to Argentina, Dr. Puig Casauranc, was following the latest developments. He sent a cable of advice to his old friend:

. . . NO POLITICAL OR SOCIAL GOOD CAN RESULT FROM YOUR ACTION IN A NEW POLITICAL PARTY. EVEN WITH THE BEST POLITICAL SUCCESS, WHICH IS IMPOSSIBLE, BECAUSE NOTHING CAN PREVENT IT FROM CONVERTING ITSELF INTO A PARTY OF EX-BUREAUCRATS AND SPITEFUL MEN AND COUNTER-REVOLUTIONARIES LYING IN AMBUSH, IT WILL ONLY INCREASE THE GREAT CONFUSION, WHICH IS THE TRUE AND ALMOST ONLY PRESENT DANGER AND IS THE RESULT—WE MUST CONFESS IT—OF A CHRONIC POLITICAL CRISIS WHICH WE OURSELVES PRODUCED AND DID NOT KNOW HOW TO CURE. YOU IRREDEEMABLY REPRESENT TEN YEARS OF ACTIVITY OF WHICH ONLY FIVE WERE BRILLIANT . . .

In this lengthy cable Puig said further to Calles that his [Calles'] only alternatives were to work within the camp of the President, strengthening his action, or else to remove himself ("an historical character whose hour passes"). Since the first alternative was impossible, Puig told Calles that if he would close himself up with his conscience he would end up by going like a good soldier to see the President and to ask his permission to leave for foreign places. He reminded Calles that in 1932 they had analyzed possible future situations similar to the existing one, and Calles had then agreed that all of his preaching of loyalty to the institutions, and all of his exaltation of military duties and virtues, obligated him to "turn the other cheek" before endangering the institutional life:

ALTHOUGH THE FIELD REMAINS PERFECT FOR LEGITIMATE PARTY ACTION, THE ONLY ONE INCAPACITATED—BECAUSE OF THE FETTER OF HONOR WHICH YOUR PROMISES OF ABSTENTION CONSTITUTE—IS YOURSELF. AFFECTIONATE-LY, PUIG.

The writer of all of this sent one copy to Cárdenas, at the same time submitting his resignation as ambassador. The press got hold of the cable and soon the Mexico City papers were publishing, for all to read, Puig's telegraphic lecture to Calles. By some it was considered to be the effort of one seeking to stand well with the new President. Hurt by its publication, Calles replied as follows:

YOUR MESSAGE. YOUR JUDGMENTS ARE ANSWERABLE TO INFORMATION OF OFFICIAL CHARACTER, FIRST, AND THE DESIRE OF FINDING A PLACE AFTER-WARDS. AS FOR THE PAST, YOU HAVE NO RIGHT TO JUDGE MY PERSONALITY AS YOU DID BECAUSE IT IS FIRM IN THE REVOLUTIONARY IDEOLOGY AND I RESPECT THE INSTITUTIONS OF THE NATION AND NO ONE BETTER THAN YOU KNOWS THAT I HAVE NO AMBITIONS OF ANY SORT. BEFORE SIX MONTHS OF UNJUSTIFIED INJURIES TO ME AND THE CALLISTA REGIME, WHICH AMONG OTHERS YOU WERE OBLIGATED TO DEFEND, BECAUSE INJURIES TO THIS RE-GIME ARE PRINCIPALLY INJURIES TO YOU, I CAME HERE TO MAKE CLARIFI-CATIONS. ANY OTHER WAY WOULD HAVE BEEN COWARDICE AND UNWORTHI-NESS TO YOU WHO FORMED THAT REGIME, ALWAYS WITH PRAISES AND WITH-OUT ONE ACT OF PROTEST. THE AGITATION PRODUCED IS THE WORK OF OF-FICIAL ACTS AND NOT MINE AND I AM NOT FORMING THE POLITICAL PARTY TO WHICH YOU REFER, ALTHOUGH PERSONS OF MY FRIENDSHIP FIGURE IN IT, AND NEITHER CAN I NOR SHOULD I AVOID IT. I UNDERSTAND THE OBJEC-TIVE AND END WHICH YOU SEEK WITH YOUR MESSAGE. THANKS FOR YOUR ADVICE. GENERAL CALLES.

In case the Mexico City press should print it, Calles added this note: "The fact that the message sent to me by Dr. José Manuel Puig Casauranc, ambassador of Mexico to Argentina, has been published in all the organs of the press in the capital, confirms to me that that message was not dictated with the intention of giving me advice, but seeking another end, and this obligates me, much to my dislike, to ask the press of the capital to publish my reply."[6]

Puig received two more cables:

RECEIVED YOUR PATRIOTIC MESSAGE TO GENERAL CALLES. I REPEAT MY CONFIDENCE IN YOU. PRESIDENT CÁRDENAS

and

I EMBRACE YOU CORDIALLY. SECRETARY RODRÍGUEZ

After the publication of Dr. Puig's cable of advice on December 20, 1935, the public was treated to another sensation. The police discovered numerous machine guns, rifles, and ammunition in the homes of Luis Morones in Tacubaya and in the Portales Colony. Morones was accordingly brought before the authorities, where, in answer to questions, he asserted that he had never had the idea of rebelling against the Government of Cárdenas. The arms, he said, had been held by him precisely to defend and guarantee the life of Mexican institutions. He produced evidence to show that the Obregón Government had given him permission to acquire arms and make them available to groups for fighting against those who might disturb the public order. The old permit was signed by Calles as a Cabinet official.

The Left Wing of Congress approved a suggestion by an organization of Tabasco workers to the effect that Calles be placed on trial. Brothers of the late General Serrano presented to the Senate a petition asking punishment of those responsible for the killings at Huitzilac in 1927. Others asked for investigations having to do with the personal wealth of Calles and with his involvement in the deaths of Lucio Blanco (1922) and of Alvaro Obregón (1928).

On January 9, 1936, the former Jefe Máximo de la Revolución appeared in court to answer charges of having committed a less serious crime: that of having smuggled arms into Mexico at Nogales, Sonora, far back in the past. In this court appearance Calles was accompanied by Luis León, Bartolomé Vargas Lugo, Juan Platt, and Francisco Javier Gaxiola, Jr.

[6] J. M. Puig Casauranc, *Galatea rebelde a varios pigmaliones*, pp. 563–568.

Following his return to Mexico with Luis N. Morones in December, 1935, unflattering caricatures of General Calles appeared in the streets. This picture was taken in front of the Chamber of Deputies. Enrique Díaz.

On the streets one could see gatherings of the populace carrying not only anti-Calles signs, but unflattering caricatures of the once "Strong Man"; also coffins marked with his name; a mule bearing a grim resemblance to his face and marked "This Mule for Sale"; a face of Calles with horns attached.

Under these circumstances the greying General answered the judge's questions:

QUESTION: To what activities did you devote yourself in 1915?

GENERAL CALLES: In 1915 I was governor and military commander of Sonora and I had complete authority in the field of warfare, given to me by the First Chief of the Constitutionalist Army, Citizen Venustiano Carranza.

QUESTION: In what work were you engaged?

GENERAL CALLES: At that time I organized the Fourth Division of the Northwest Branch of the Army, which came to have 5000 men. The units making up the division were then headed by many youths who since have occupied high posts in the National Army, and among those who were under my direct orders I recall the present President of the Republic, General Lázaro Cárdenas. Due to assignments made by me, those soldiers handled the command of the garrison of Agua Prieta, where the general barracks were established.

QUESTION: Did you distribute any arms?

GENERAL CALLES: In accordance with the authority given to me, I distributed, through the officers of the garrison, not one, but thousands of weapons . . .

While General Calles was testifying, a photographer of the Mexican Revolution, Miguel Casasola, appeared outside a window, having climbed along the balconies to record the event. Said Calles: "Mr. Judge, I have no objection to the photographer's coming in."

The questioning became specific. Because of the passage of years, Calles could not recall whether he had distributed a weapon to a certain Nemesio García Treviño, but he admitted that it was quite possible. A government agent took over the questioning:

QUESTION: Did you give arms only to youths loyal to Constitucionalismo?

GENERAL CALLES: Not only to youths loyal to Constitucionalismo, but also to my friends, as I can do today.

QUESTION: Was it your habit to make a present of weapons after a battle?

GENERAL CALLES: No serious military leader had the custom of author-

Plutarco Elías Calles *answering questions in court regarding the charge of having smuggled weapons into Mexico. January 9, 1936. Casasola.*

672

izing that kind of reward to those who were simply doing their duty; there are other compensations of a moral character that are authorized and that are of positive worth.[7]

General Calles left the court, surrounded by police agents furnished by the government to protect him from the curious and the hostile.

A group of women tried to take possession of his "Santa Bárbara" home. Rumors of a Callista plot against the government persisted.

A judgment as to who were responsible for General Calles' situation is rendered in a letter from ex-President Abelardo Rodríguez, written late in March, 1936, to his close and long-standing friend, Ing. Juan de Dios Bojórquez, whose resignation as Gobernación Minister had been accepted by Cárdenas the previous June. In this letter, which was not made public until 1939, General Rodríguez said in part:[8]

. . . I tried to explain to him [Calles] how the idea was spreading in public opinion that he wanted to make himself a dictator and that in the end some deplorable consequences would result if the right steps were not taken in time. I suggested to him that it was the opportune moment for him to retire completely . . . , disregarding the adulation of servile politicians and human parasites, who would abandon him the moment they found better accommodation. General Calles then thought that I was exaggerating things . . . [He] pointed out to me that he intervened only in those matters where he was consulted, which was perfectly true. Never when I was at the head of the government did he make any hint that I could interpret as the slightest indication that such and such a thing be done. It was the politicians and one or another of my collaborators who grovellingly requested his orders and are responsible for the present situation of the General . . .

Of my collaborators, you, León, Puig, and Bassols were perhaps those who most distinguished themselves with their eagerness to make General Calles appear as a dictator. You and León did so, I believe, through the affection you had for the General, but Puig and Bassols did so with complete falseness and iniquity, because thus it suited their personal interests, never failing to be always ready to drive the dagger into his back in his adversity and when the propitious moment should present itself. They will do the same thing to General Cárdenas should he give them the opportunity. To León, General Calles owes the title of

[7] Archivo Casasola, *Historia gráfica de la Revolución*, pp. 2152–2153.
[8] Armando de María y Campos, *Múgica*, pp. 257–258.

"Máximo" . . . In my opinion it is León who has indisputably hurt the public character of Calles the most. Leaving aside politics, you were a good collaborator for me . . . I personally exonerate you of any blame in the present political conflict, for in you there is not evil or bad faith. Furthermore a fondness that has been growing up between us, since our youth and comradeship within the same activities, cannot be so easily ended . . . Abelardo L. Rodríguez.

75.

The Curtain Falls
for General Calles

In April, 1936, the state of Veracruz was agitated on two accounts. For one thing, in progress was a gubernatorial election campaign in which early prominent candidates were Colonel Eduardo Hernández Cházaro, the former secretary of President Ortiz Rubio, and Diputado Manlio Fabio Altamirano, a former manager of the P.N.R.'s *El Nacional*. This campaign was to see the assassination of Altamirano in June and, in August, the election of Lic. Miguel Alemán, who became a strong candidate late in the campaign, after the assassination, and who had the support of General Cándido Aguilar.

Veracruz in April was also the scene of conflicts between Luis Morones' C.R.O.M. and Lombardo Toledano's recently founded C.T.M. (Confederación de Trabajadores Mexicanos). At Orizaba, Veracruz, the C.R.O.M. called a strike, which President Cárdenas, in a public statement, declared to be unjustified.

Mexico City was horrified when it received word from Orizaba and Córdoba that on April 7, at the nearby station of Paso Grande, the train of the Mexican Railway Company, Ltd. had been dynamited on its way from Veracruz to Mexico City. Thirteen persons were killed and eighteen were wounded. Gubernatorial aspirant Eduardo Hernández Cházaro, one of the train's passengers who escaped unharmed, told reporters that he was going to speak with President Cárdenas about the event. It will be recalled that during the Ortiz Rubio administration Colonel Hernández Cházaro had had difficulties with Callistas and had complained that Calles would not let the President govern in peace.

The federal Executive energetically condemned the assault. The C.T.M. came out with a strong protest, accusing various individuals of seeking to bring about anxieties and discords:

The reactionary elements, the most intransigent captains of the bourgeois, politicians already liquidated before history, and a group of dishonest labor leaders have in recent weeks increased their counter-revolutionary work and have sought to cause various sorts of upsets to the normal progress of the country . . . This treacherous work has as its ultimate objective the pressuring of the Government so that it will change its conduct . . . It goes so far as to seek allies abroad in order to present its own Government, headed by General Lázaro Cárdenas, as a demagogic administration, without any cohesion, dangerous to the public interests and even to the interests of international order.

On April 9, 1936, the Left Wing of the Senate issued an accusation in connection with the Paso Grande dynamiting: "It concerns a diabolic maneuver by a political sector recently displaced from the Administration."

On the same day on which the Senate's Left Wing made this accusation, Police Chief Vicente González, complying with orders from the top, instructed the acting head of the Safety Commission, Lorenzo Díaz González, to take the necessary steps to place Calles, Morones, Luis L. León, and Melchor Ortega under guard. They were to be thrown out of the country.

Díaz González gave instructions to his men, with some of whom, between 4:00 and 5:00 P.M., he looked over Calles' "Santa Bárbara" farm outside Mexico City on the road to Puebla. Calles, because of an attack of the grippe had moved, a few days before, to "Santa Bárbara" from his Anzures residence in town. Sr. Díaz González was in touch with General Rafael Navarro Cortina, who had replaced General Medinaveytia as commander of the Military Forces of the Federal District and who was in charge of handling the expulsion of General Calles.

Shortly after 10:00 P.M. on April 9 Calles was in bed, wearing blue and white pajamas and reading Adolf Hitler's *Mein Kampf.* General Navarro Cortina, accompanied by Othón León Lobato and Colonel Adolfo Echegaray, paid a call on the ex-President at "Santa Bárbara."

Calles learned from Navarro Cortina that he would be forced to abandon Mexican territory on the following morning. This was, said Navarro Cortina, a ruling of the President of the Republic. A plane would be ready at the Balbuena Airport.

"What is the reason for my expulsion?" asked the former President and strong man.

His visitor pointed out that he was not familiar with the reasons. "I am a soldier and I comply with an order." Then Navarro Cortina added that the order was related to the public welfare.

Calles replied: "If it were a matter of my own choice I would not leave the country, but if it is an order of the President I have nothing to do but to obey. I'll prepare for my trip."

Calles also said that what they were trying to do to him was an "outrage." He made some telephone calls.

Soon after General Navarro Cortina had left General Calles, another visitor reached "Santa Bárbara." This was Sr. Lorenzo Díaz González, acting head of the Safety Commission, who had been checking up on the arrests of Morones, León, and Ortega. He announced himself to one of Calles' three aides and was taken to the General's bedroom.

Díaz González notified him that he had orders to establish a special guard until the morning, when Calles would be driven to the airport.

"Very well," replied Calles in a somewhat irritated fashion.

"Also, I hope you won't be surprised at the number of agents whom I must station, because perhaps it would seem to you—"

"Nothing surprises me. Aren't there enough with the federal forces which are stationed here?"

"I have nothing to do with those federal forces, as I am a commander of agents of the police, a civilian institution."

"Do your duty and leave all the agents you want."

"Very well, then. Good night."

"Hasta luego, boy."

Late in the night, General Navarro Cortina advised President Cárdenas of what had been accomplished.

The others were also taken into custody without difficulty.

Sr. Morones was accosted at 2:00 P.M. on April 9 when he was on his way to his home.

"Excuse me, Sr. Morones, but General Vicente González wants to speak with you."

"Good. I'll go to see him at once."

"No, you must come in my car."

Morones turned a bit pale but he obeyed, turning his small "Star" pistol over to the detective. From the Police Headquarters he was taken, energetically protesting his arrest, to a cell of the Sixth Commissariat. He sought to find out what was to be his fate and the names of others who were arrested. He got little or no sleep.

Sr. Melchor Ortega was arrested at Tehuacán, Puebla.

"We have instructions to take you to México. We belong to the police."

"But why are you arresting me? Do you have written orders?"

In México, Ortega spoke with Díaz González, who agreed to his request to be allowed to retain some money which he had with him. He too was placed in a cell of the Sixth Commissariat.

Ing. Luis L. León had destroyed many papers, including all the copies that he had of his publication *El regreso del General Calles* (*The Return of General Calles*), a booklet whose rareness had already been increased through its destruction by anti-Callistas. He was not arrested until 6:00 P.M., when he was on his way to Anzures accompanied by two armed men. Like Morones and Ortega, Luis L. León spent the night at the Sixth Commissariat. He appeared nervous and got but little sleep that night.

At 6:30 on the morning of April 10, General Rafael Navarro Cortina returned to "Santa Bárbara," where General Calles had been breakfasting with some of his family, among them Alfredo Elías Calles and Sra. Ernestina Calles de Pasquel, and others of the household, which included his secretary, Sra. Soledad González de Ayala González, his doctor, Abraham Ayala González, and his aide, Captain Manuel Fuentes.

Said Calles to the officials: "I am at your orders."

On the porch they awaited as several cars drew up. General Calles

Forced departures from Mexico, April 10, 1936: Ing. Luis L. León (*with blanket*), Sr. Melchor Ortega (*with light-shaded coat*), Sr. Luis N. Morones (*with bow tie*). *Enrique Díaz.*

rode in the first car. The fallen leader was accompanied to the airport by Navarro Cortina, León Lobato, and Colonel Echegaray, as well as by those who had breakfasted with him.

At Balbuena Airport they found Luis N. Morones, Luis L. León, and Melchor Ortega, who had been conveyed from their cells at 6:00 A.M. They also found the Police Chief, revolutionary warrior Vicente González. Calles was rather uncommunicative and he concentrated on his reading of *Mein Kampf,* but before entering the plane he said goodbye to those around him with the exception of General Navarro Cortina.

The plane, carrying the four exiles, went to Brownsville, Texas, where Calles told reporters that he would never return to his homeland. He went on to Los Angeles, California, by way of San Antonio and Dallas. At Los Angeles he said that he was not responsible for the Veracruz train wreck and added that he had not been a traitor to his country. He was received at Los Angeles by his son-in-law, Fernando Torreblanca, who took him to a hotel pending the finding of a permanent residence.

Melchor Ortega went to San Diego, California. Luis Morones spent a short time in California and then he went to New York.

In Mexico City P.N.R. President Portes Gil referred to conspiracies against the national institutions. "This is the time when General Plutarco Elías Calles is declaring to American reporters that Mexico lives in complete anarchy." Twenty-five laborers tried to take over the Anzures residence, but the police prevented them from breaking in.

The leader of the Senate Left Wing, Ernesto Soto Reyes, asked the War Department to throw Calles out of the Army.

Lázaro Cárdenas made a statement to the nation in which he said that the executive power, under his leadership, had been observing carefully the incessant maneuvers of some political groups who wished to provoke "a permanent state of alarm and of social restlessness." He had, he said, deferred any intervention by the public authorities until there could be no mistaking the work of the agitators. But, he went on to explain, the situation had reached an extreme condition, with these political elements carrying on "a criminal work" which not only tended to obstruct the development of Mexican institutions and the most noble ends of the state, but opposed the feeling of Mexico's social struggle. The government was finally forced to abandon the watchful attitude and to take emergency measures "so as to prevent greater upheavals coming to the nation which, if not averted, would threaten to crush the very organization of the collectivity, and might, in addition, place in danger the conquests which have been made, at the cost of so many sacrifices, in our replevying movements."

In conclusion the Cárdenas statement said:

. . . Conscious of its responsibilities and anxious not to follow the lamentable precedents existing in the history of our cruel political struggles, in which the principle of respect for human life has frequently been underrated, the Government over which I preside judged that circumstances demanded, on behalf of public safety, the immediate

680

departure from the national territory of Señores General Plutarco Elías Calles, Luis N. Morones, Luis L. León, and Melchor Ortega.

April 12 was a Sunday, and on that day occurred a large manifestation of support for President Cárdenas at the Plaza de la Constitución.

In May, 1936, the President appointed Adolfo de la Huerta to be Visitor of the Consulates of the Mexican Republic, thus ending Don Adolfo's years of exile, largely spent in giving lessons in voice in California. De la Huerta received a warm reception when he re-

General Plutarco Elías Calles *is forced to leave Mexico on April 10, 1936. This photograph (taken at the airport by Julio León a few minutes before the departure) shows* Rafael Navarro Cortina, *the uniformed general standing closest to Calles. Calles is flanked by two of his sons,* Rodolfo *and* Alfredo *(extreme right). Enrique Díaz.*

turned to a land in which now could be seen the faces of many whose quarrels with past regimes had kept them abroad.

Cárdenas opened the doors to all political exiles. Back came Porfirio Díaz, Jr., after an absence of twenty-three years; also José María Maytorena, ex-governor of Sonora, who had been responsible for Obregón's receiving his first army commission and who had been opposed by Calles at the time of the break between Venustiano Carranza and Pancho Villa.

Mexico now saw such prominent participants in the 1923 rebellion as Rafael Zubaran Capmany and Enrique Estrada, the general whose treatment of Cárdenas in 1924 had been considerate and whose exile had been spent in great poverty. Such, however, had been the bloody conclusion of that disaster that many of the great military participants were to appear no more, a remark less applicable to the 1929 rebellion, whose José Gonzalo Escobar, Fausto Topete, Francisco Manzo, and Marcelo Caraveo returned from exile with the fall of the curtain for the nation's former "Strong Man."

Two civilians who had played notable parts in past years resumed at this time their residence in Mexico. These were José Vasconcelos, who had been ordered by the Mexican government of December, 1929, to stay out of the country, and Gilberto Valenzuela, whose Plan of Agua Prieta had ushered in the once-powerful "trio from Sonora": De la Huerta, Obregón, and Calles.

It is clear that the fall of General Calles as a political factor was quite complete by the middle of June, 1935. But it was not until April 10, 1936, that he joined the other members of the "Triangle from Sonora" in being forcibly eliminated. As of that date this had happened in different ways and at different times to each of the triad. It had happened to Adolfo de la Huerta in 1924 and to Alvaro Obregón in 1928. And now, after his long career on the Mexican political scene, it had happened to Plutarco Elías Calles.

APPENDIXES

Appendix A[1]

Presidents of Mexico, December 1, 1884, to November 30, 1940

General Porfirio Díaz[2]	December 1, 1884—May 25, 1911
Lic. Francisco León de la Barra	May 25, 1911 —November 5, 1911
Francisco I. Madero	November 6, 1911—February 19, 1913
Lic. Pedro Lascuráin	February 19, 1913—February 19, 1913
General Victoriano Huerta	February 19, 1913—July 15, 1914
Lic. Francisco Carbajal	July 15, 1914 —August 13, 1914
General Eulalio Gutiérrez	November 6, 1914—January 16, 1915
General Roque González Garza	January 16, 1915 —June 10, 1915
Lic. Francisco Lagos Cházaro	June 10, 1915 —July 9, 1915
Venustiano Carranza[3]	May 1, 1917 —May 21, 1920
Adolfo de la Huerta	June 1, 1920 —November 30, 1920
General Alvaro Obregón	December 1, 1920—November 30, 1924
General Plutarco Elías Calles	December 1, 1924—November 30, 1928
Lic. Emilio Portes Gil	December 1, 1928—February 4, 1930
General e Ing. Pascual Ortiz Rubio	February 5, 1930 —September 4, 1932
General Abelardo L. Rodríguez	September 5, 1932—November 30, 1934
General Lázaro Cárdenas	December 1, 1934—November 30, 1940

[1] Data furnished for the most part by Eduardo Terrones Langone.

[2] General Porfirio Díaz had been President of Mexico from 1876 to 1880. He became President for a second time when on December 1, 1884, he succeeded General Manuel González, who had been President from 1880 to 1884.

[3] Venustiano Carranza became Constitutional President of Mexico on May 1, 1917. For some time prior to that date he directed the affairs of Mexico, using the title of First Chief of the Constitutionalist Army. He established his administration in the city of Veracruz on November 6, 1914, and therefore the "Pre-Constitutional Regime" is considered as running from then until May 1, 1917. On October 19, 1915, Carranza was recognized as First Chief of the Revolution by the government of the United States. Carranza in February, 1917, called for the popular election of the Constitutional President and of federal senators and congressmen, in accordance with the Constitution of 1917. In the elections which took place on March 11, 1917, Carranza was chosen President.

Appendix B[1]

Presidents of the Partido Nacional Revolucionario, March, 1929, to August, 1936

March 4, 1929	—February 5, 1930	General Manuel Pérez Treviño
February 5, 1930	—April 28, 1930	Professor Basilio Vadillo
April 28, 1930	—October 15, 1930	Lic. Emilio Portes Gil
October 15, 1930	—August 30, 1931	General Lázaro Cárdenas
September 1, 1931	—May 12, 1933	General Manuel Pérez Treviño
May 12, 1933	—June 7, 1933	Sr. Melchor Ortega
June 7, 1933	—August 25, 1933	General Manuel Pérez Treviño
August 25, 1933	—December 14, 1934	Colonel Carlos Riva Palacio
December 14, 1934	—June 18, 1935	General Matías Ramos Santos
June 18, 1935	—August 24, 1936	Lic. Emilio Portes Gil

[1] Data furnished by Eduardo Terrones Langone.

NOTES ON SOURCES OF MATERIAL

Notes on Sources of Material

To a larger extent than has been indicated in the notes below, information received during conversations and from newspaper items was utilized in this study. To get at significant issues of newspapers of the period we were fortunate in having at our disposal the library of General Rafael Aguirre Manjarrez in Mexico City.

Casasola's *Historia gráfica de la Revolución* (Vols. III, IV, and V) was referred to so frequently that we have (with one exception) omitted mentioning it in the following notes in order to avoid tedious repetition.

Two helpful books which cover events in the manner of a diary are the Antigua Librería de Murguía's *Colección de las efemérides* and Alfonso Taracena's *Mi vida en el vértigo de la Revolución.*

Reference books which were useful are Miguel A. Peral's *Diccionario biográfico mexicano* and Francisco Naranjo's *Diccionario biográfico revolucionario.* Also the Fondo de Cultura Económica's *Planes políticos y otros documentos* (edited by Manuel González Ramírez).

Those interested in a bibliography may wish to consult Roberto Ramos' *Bibliografía de la Revolución Mexicana, Tomo III.*

1. General Alvaro Obregón and the Constitutionalist Revolution

The "Constitucionalista" Revolution is described in detail in two lengthy volumes by Juan Barragán Rodríguez, *Historia del ejército y de la Revolución Constitucionalista;* also in Alvaro Obregón's *Ocho mil kilómetros en campaña.* J. A. Tamayo, in *El Gral. Obregón y la guerra* has something to say of Obregón's activities. Interesting interpretive comments may be found in parts of Ramón Puente's *Hombres de la Revolución: Calles.* An excellent new book in English describing events in 1914 and 1915 is Robert E. Quirk's *The Mexican Revolution 1914–1915.*

The second volume of Roberto Blanco Moheno's *Crónica de la Revolución Mexicana* has recently appeared; this, and the earlier Volume I, add to the array of accounts of Revolutionary times. Two relatively short studies which cover events from the last days of Porfirio Díaz up to the 1950's are José Mancisidor's *La Revolución Mexicana* and Gabriel Ferrer de Mendiolea's *Historia de la Revolución Mexicana.* Both these books include good bibliographies. A lengthy and interesting book covering the same period is *La Revolución Mexicana; Orígenes y resultados* by Jorge Vera Estañol, an expert in education who served in Cabinets of Porfirio Díaz and Victoriano Huerta and who was in exile from 1914 to 1931. Villa's story is given in Martín Luis Guzmán's *Memorias de Pancho Villa.* See also Rafael Muñoz' *Pancho Villa.*

J. M. Maytorena defends his own position and attacks Obregón in his *Algunas verdades sobre el General Alvaro Obregón.* Reports from Calles to Obregón in 1915 are recorded in *Partes oficiales de la Campaña de Sonora rendidos por el Gral. P. Elias Calles al C. Gral. Alvaro Obregón.*

Obregón's career and qualities are described, for the most part favorably, by Miguel Alessio Robles (*Obregón como militar*), Carlos Barrera (*Obregón: Estampas de un caudillo*), E. J. Dillon (*President Obregón: A World Reformer*), Juan de Dios Bojórquez (*Obregón: Apuntes biográficos*) and Roberto Quirós Martínez (*Alvaro Obregón: Su vida y su obra*). Pro-Obregón propaganda issued in 1924 includes Gutiérrez Cruz's *El brazo de Obregón* and Juan B. Cervantes' *Obregón ante la historia.*

Not quite so well impressed was Vicente Blasco Ibáñez, whose *El militarismo mejicano* is more witty than complimentary to Mexico's leaders of the period.

2. The Presidential Campaign of 1919–1920; 3. The Plan of Agua Prieta

The presidential campaign and also the military phase of the struggle are covered in the documents and items published in the five-volume *Campaña política del C. Alvaro Obregón, candidato de la presidencia de la República, 1920–1924*. There is also a large collection of material and photographs on the same subject in *Sonora y Carranza* by Amado Chaverri Matamoros and Clodoveo Valenzuela. The movement in Michoacán is recorded in Rodrigo López Pérez' *El movimiento obregonista en Michoacán*. Hermila Galindo supports the candidacy and record of Pablo González in a campaign biography, *Un presidenciable, el General D. Pablo González*.

Most of the books about Obregón mentioned in connection with Chapter 1 cover this effort to reach the presidency. Other books which were found useful are Miguel Alessio Robles' *A medio camino* (pp. 25–56), Vicente Fuente Díaz's *Los partidos políticos en México* (II, 15–16), Amado Aguirre's *Mis memorias de campaña* (pp. 305–323), Andrés Osuna's *Por la escuela y por la patria*, and Francisco G. Luque's *La causa Obregón–Cejudo*. Use was made of typewritten information furnished by Pascual Ortiz Rubio, Luis N. Morones, and S. J. Romero.

Adolfo de la Huerta's *Memorias* (pp. 143–149) have comments on this campaign. Their publication in 1957 was followed by debates in the Mexico City newspapers, which brought forth additional material.

Manuel González Ramírez has edited *Planes políticos y otros documentos*, giving the text of the "Plan de Agua Prieta" and other "Plans" and pronouncements issued "yesterday" in Mexico.

4. Tlaxcalantongo; 5. From Tlaxcalantongo to Mexico City

Francisco L. Urquizo's *México-Tlaxcalantongo* and his *Carranza* are both good reading. Another Carrancista who was at Tlaxcalantongo and who recorded his experience is Gerzayn Ugarte (*Por qué volví a Tlaxcalantongo*). Carrancistas have their say in *La verdad sobre la muerte de Carranza*, in which publication appears a short account by Luis Cabrera.

A rather complete story, including the background and succeeding events, is *El verdadero Tlaxcalantongo* by Miguel B. Márquez, who served under Rodolfo Herrero.

Magazines and newspapers often come out with articles about the Tlaxcalantongo tragedy and usually they are rather sensational. Among the more reliable newspaper stories is the series of five articles by Gustavo de la Torre in *El Universal*, May 24–29, 1956. Roberto Blanco Moheno interviewed Rodolfo Herrero for *Impacto* (July 16, 1958).

Later (August 13, 1958) that magazine gave Ignacio Suárez' observations and followed this by more stories in September and October, 1958. Marciano González has at times attacked in the press the story given by Herrero.

6. The Selection of an Interim President

Information about De la Huerta's attainment of the provisional presidency can be found in greatest detail in *Campaña política del C. Alvaro Obregón*. Other books, which also have been mentioned earlier and which cover this event, are the *Memorias* of Amado Aguirre and of Adolfo de la Huerta. Pascual Ortiz Rubio's manuscript, "Medio siglo," throws light on the subject.

Alberto J. Pani was a prolific writer and various of his books deal with the news that reached him in Paris. Particularly helpful is his *Apuntes autobiográficos* (pp. 241–251).

7. Adolfo de la Huerta and Pancho Villa

Interviews with De la Huerta helped provide details and impressions of how he ran the provisional presidency.

Several books by Miguel Alessio Robles, including *A medio camino* and *Historia política de la Revolución*, shed light on the provisional presidency and also on the story of the "surrender" of Pancho Villa. So does De la Huerta's *Memorias* (pp. 153–162). There is an account of the "surrender" in Rafael F. Muñoz' *Pancho Villa*.

8. The Interim Regime and Other Restless Generals

The story of what transpired in Monterrey, leading to the trial of Pablo González, was obtained principally from interviews. The trial itself is the subject of a chapter in José P. Saldaña's *Episodios de ayer* (pp. 164–188). Miguel Alessio Robles writes about the matter in his *Historia política de la Revolución* (pp. 245–246).

Ramón Rodríguez F. describes the pacification of Lower California in *Excelsior* (February 13, 1958), giving an account which differs somewhat from that in De la Huerta's *Memorias* (pp. 168–174). Other data were obtained from Alfonso Salazar Rovirosa's *Cronología de Baja California*.

The action of the federal government regarding various states is mentioned in De la Huerta's message of September 1, 1920, to the Congress. De la Huerta's *Memorias* (pp. 149–174) has much to say about the pacification of the country. Among the publications telling of conditions in Tabasco is Joaquín Ruiz's *La Revolución en Tabasco*.

9. The Election of General Obregón

E. W. Kemmerer (*Inflation and Revolution: Mexico's Experience of 1912-1917*) tells of paper money issues. Some brief views about Alvarado and Calles, attributed to Obregón, may be found in Miguel Alessio Robles' *A medio camino* (pp. 45, 65–66). See also *Impacto* magazine of September 24, 1958. Alvarado presents some of his ideas about Mexican problems in *El problema de México*.

De la Huerta speaks of the financial achievements of the provisional presidency in a magazine article "Crisis y Cresos: Nuestra economía." They are also mentioned in his *Memorias* (pp. 174–176).

Some of Alfredo Robles Domínguez' accomplishments are revealed in Stanley R. Ross's *Francisco I. Madero: Apostle of Mexican Democracy*, and his role in 1914 is described by Barragán and Obregón in their histories of the "Constitucionalista" Revolution. Robles Domínguez receives harsh treatment from E. J. Dillon, whose *President Obregón* covers Obregón's political campaign against Robles Domínguez. De la Huerta (pp. 180–182) and Amado Aguirre (pp. 326–327) discuss the election in their *Memorias*.

10. International Relations during the Interim Regime

Félix F. Palavicini's diplomatic mission to Europe is recorded in his *Mi vida revolucionaria* (pp. 439–481).

Material covering relations between the United States and Mexico is described in connection with Chapter 18. But mention should be made here of Edgar Turlington's *Mexico and Her Foreign Creditors*, which is useful at this stage as well as later. The position taken by De la Huerta is described in his *Memorias* and in Miguel Alessio Robles' *Historia política de la Revolución* (p. 275).

11. General Obregón and the Agrarian Problem

"Short-hand notes of the impressions exchanged between the President-elect and a numerous group of Congressmen (October 1920)" are given in *The Agrarian Problem* published by the Mexican Foreign Relations Ministry in 1924. Alberto J. Pani, in his missives to United States diplomats, defends agrarian principles adopted by Obregón (*Las Conferencias de Bucareli* by Pani and *La cuestión internacional mexicano-americano durante el gobierno del Gral. Don Alvaro Obregón* issued by Relaciones Exteriores). Amado Aguirre discusses the "Caja de préstamos . . ." in his *Memorias* (pp. 327–329).

Books which cover the agrarian matter are mentioned in the second paragraph of the notes on Chapter 33. Figures about land redistribution, and other matters, are given in Economía's *Anuario estadístico, 1938*.

12. Obregón's Administration Gets under Way during a Depression

The story of Ortiz Rubio's resignation from Obregón's Cabinet was furnished orally, mostly by Faustino Roel.

Some idea of the effects of the Post World War I Depression is given in Obregón's *Informes rendidos ante el H. Congreso de la Union* and in Economía's *Anuario estadístico, 1938*. A letter from Manuel Gómez Morín and Turlington's *Mexico and Her Foreign Creditors* speak of De la Huerta's negotiations with the oil companies. Pani's *Memoria de la Secretaría de Hacienda y Crédito Público correspondiente a los años fiscales de 1923, 1924, 1925* tells of federal tax collections in 1922.

13. Combatting Francisco Murguía and His Associates

The troubles of Rodolfo Herrero early in the Obregón administration are fully covered in Miguel B. Márquez' *El verdadero Tlaxcalantongo*. The banquet which preceded Hill's death is described by Miguel Alessio Robles in *La cena de las burlas* (pp. 16–32) and *A medio camino* (pp. 83–85).

The most complete story of the efforts of Murguía and other Carrancistas to overthrow Obregón is that contained in the bitterly anti-Obregón two-volume work of Adolfo Manero Suárez and José Paniagua Arredondo, *Los Tratados de Bucareli: Traicion y sangre sobre Mexico!* Luis I. Rodríguez has discussed Murguía's sense of loyalty in a speech which has been published under the title of *Francisco Murguía: Paradigma de lealtad*.

14. Combatting Ignorance

The work of José Vasconcelos as Minister of Education is described in Vasconcelos' *El desastre*.

15. The Death of the Partido Liberal Constitucionalista

Minor references in a large number of books served to tell of the fall of the P.L.C. The more important discussions can be found in Volume II of Vicente Fuentes Díaz's *Los partidos políticos en México* (pp. 13–23) and in Miguel Alessio Robles' *La cena de las burlas* (pp. 13–32). Some incidents described by Vasconcelos (*El desastre*) and Taracena (*Mi vida en el vértigo de la Revolución*) add to the picture.

El último caudillo (Chap. III), by Luis Monroy Durán and Gonzalo Bautista, describes the Cooperatista Party's victory over the P.L.C.

16. Carrillo Puerto and the Ligas de Resistencia de Yucatán

A description of Yucatán in the early 1920's can be found in an edition of *Terry's Guide to Mexico* published about that time.

The story of Carrillo Puerto, the Ligas de Resistencia, and their efforts up to 1922 is reported fully and sympathetically in Juan Rico's two volumes, *Yucatán, la huelga de junio*. Unsympathetic observations may be found in Adolfo Ferrer's *El archivo de Felipe Carrillo—El Callismo: La corrupción del régimen Obregonista*. In *El desastre* (pp. 98–125) Vasconcelos describes a visit to the peninsula made during Obregón's administration.

There is an "official edition" of Carrillo Puerto's *Informe rendido por el gobernador constitucional de Yucatán ante la H. XXVII legislatura del estado, el 1° de enero de 1923*.

We were able to locate only Volume I of Alvaro Gamboa Ricalde's *Yucatán desde mil novecientos diez*. This covers 1910–1914. Volumes II and III should be of assistance to students of Alvarado and Carrillo Puerto.

17. De la Huerta Makes a Trip to New York

Both A. J. Pani (*Apuntes autobiográficos*, pp. 266–267, and other writings) and Edgar Turlington (*Mexico and Her Foreign Creditors*) provide information about De la Huerta's visit with Mexico's creditors in New York; Turlington covers the New York negotiations.

In 1924 Obregón published a small book recording messages exchanged between himself and De la Huerta when the latter was in New York, *Documentos oficiales relativos al Convenio De la Huerta-Lamont*. De la Huerta's *Memorias* (pp. 184–216) relates something about the New York negotiations and about De la Huerta's visits with Harding and Hughes in Washington. De la Huerta, in conversation, included some points not to be found in printed form.

A text of the De la Huerta-Lamont Agreement is included in *La deuda externa de México* issued by Hacienda in 1926. Additional information may be found in *Documentos y comentarios relativos a los arreglos financieros llevados a cabo entre el gobierno mexicano y el Comité Internacional de Banqueros* (Cia. Editora de *El Heraldo*, S.A., 1922).

18. The Bucareli Conferences

United States-Mexican relations have been covered in J. Fred Rippy's *The United States and Mexico*, James M. Callahan's *American Foreign Policy in Mexican Relations*, and, more recently, in Howard F. Cline's *The United States and Mexico*. In 1926 the Secretaría de Relaciones Exteriores published documents (1921–1923) about the controversy between the two countries: *La cuestión internacional mexicano-americana durante el gobierno del Gral. Don Alvaro Obregón*.

Guy Stevens gives the point of view of United States oil companies in his *Current Controversies with Mexico* and in *American Policies*

Abroad: Mexico, to which he is a contributor. See also *Mexican Oil* by
Harlow S. Person, *Two Strikes and Out,* edited by William E. Mc-
Mahon, and *Expropriation in Mexico* by Roscoe B. Gaither. In 1923 the
Mexican Cámara de Senadores issued a comprehensive study, *El
petróleo: La más grande riqueza nacional.* Further information about
the Mexican oil controversy may be found in *The Oil Conflict in
Mexico,* issued in 1937 and 1938 by the Universidad Obrera de México.

Attacks on the Bucareli Conferences and what the Obregón Government did are made by Antonio Gómez Robledo (*The Bucareli Agreements and International Law*), Manero Suárez and Paniagua Arredondo (*Los Tratados de Bucareli*), Vito Alessio Robles (*Los Tratados de
Bucareli*), De la Huerta (*Memorias,* pp. 216–240), and Vasconcelos
(*El Desastre,* pp. 288–292, and *Breve historia de méxico*). The first
two mentioned, like Pani (see below), give information about what
transpired at the meetings. Aarón Sáenz defends the Obregón Government in his long introduction to Carlos Barrera's *Obregón*; he does the
same in his thirty-two articles in *Excelsior* (early in 1958). Another
who defends the conferences is Manuel González Ramírez (*Los
llamados Tratados de Bucareli*).

Alberto J. Pani has devoted a book to the subject: *Las Conferencias
de Bucareli.* Miguel Alessio Robles, in his chapters about this matter
(in *Historia política de la Revolución*), does not appear to be critical,
even though one of these chapters is called "Los Tratados de Bucareli,"
terminology not accepted by Mexicans who defend the conferences.

Secretary of State Charles Evans Hughes' letter of January 15, 1924
to Senator Henry Cabot Lodge about the conferences is worth reading.
It can be found in the Congressional Record for January 23, 1924.

Mexico City newspapers have not been without letters and articles,
pro and con.

19. The Presidential Succession; 21. The Break between the Partido Cooperatista Nacional and Obregón; 22. Adolfo de la Huerta Breaks with Obregón; 24. The Struggle Becomes Intense

El último caudillo, by Monroy Durán, assisted by Gonzalo Bautista,
and *La rebelión sin cabeza,* by Alonso Capetillo, tell of the De la Huerta
rebellion, and both these books have much to say about the events
leading up to the rebellion. A text of the Torregrosa Pact may be found
in the Appendix of the first-mentioned. An article resented by Pani is
Portes Gil's "Pani, el villano del drama" published in *Hoy* magazine
in 1955. On the anti-Calles side we have observations by Vasconcelos,
Miguel Alessio Robles, and Vito Alessio Robles in their writings.

De la Huerta's *Memorias* (pp. 216–252) gives his version of the events
preceding the armed revolt. Some of the articles and letters published
in newspapers, following the publication of De la Huerta's *Memorias,*

are worth consulting. Among these are Sáenz' thirty-two articles, and also revelations given to the press by Martín Luis Guzmán, Jorge Prieto Laurens, and Jorge Carregha. In reply to Martín Luiz Guzmán, Roberto Guzmán Esparza on February 11, 1958, reproduced in *Excelsior* an interesting letter from De la Huerta to Froylán Manjarrez written in 1937.

For Chapter 24 the amount of information which comes from interviews is perhaps above average. Amado Aguirre's *Mis memorias de campaña* (pp. 335–337) gives a close-up of Obregón at the time of the outbreak of the rebellion. In *Múgica, crónica biográfica* (pp. 201–205) Armando de María y Campos tells of the situation of one who was out of Obregón's favor.

20. The Assassination of Pancho Villa

The assassination of Villa is best described in Elías L. Torres' *Como murió Pancho Villa*. It is mentioned in Roberto F. Muñoz' *Pancho Villa*. Vasconcelos has some words on the subject in *El desastre* (pp. 238–241).

23. The Pani-De la Huerta Controversy

See *La controversia Pani-De la Huerta*, published by Hacienda in 1924. To a lesser extent Pani's *Memoria de la Secretaría de Hacienda y Crédito Público correspondiente a los años fiscales de 1923, 1924, 1925.*

25. The First Stage of the De la Huerta Rebellion

The two books which best cover the De la Huerta rebellion are heavy with anti-De la Huerta propaganda. *El último caudillo* by Monroy Durán and Gonzalo Bautista contains a vast number of detailed messages from federal generals and reports from all over the country. Capetillo's *La rebelión sin cabeza* is quite a readable account. Roberto Guzmán Esparza, who edited De la Huerta's *Memorias*, has this to say about the author of *La rebelión sin cabeza:*

> Individuals without morals, like that Capetillo, an Obregonista spy, wrote filthily false versions and concocted slanders against the man whose pureness has been fully recognized.
>
> In passing one should note that that Alonso Capetillo, who was in Veracruz in 1923 as an agent of Obregón, carried out similar work around Serrano and Gómez when they were shot . . . On that occasion Capetillo. according to the narrative of a witness who was present, shouted explanations of his true mission, but he was not believed. He supplicated and groaned, imploring that the soldiers phone Calles to clear up the point, but Obregón's men did not believe him, and he fell pierced by the unmerciful bullets that ended his cries of terror and his lamentations. Thus justice came to Capetillo.[1]

[1] Roberto Guzmán Esparza in *Memorias de don Adolfo de la Huerta*, p. 204.

De la Huerta's *Memorias* includes informal recollections about incidents which took place during the rebellion and sheds some light on Don Adolfo's character.

Manero Suárez and Paniagua's *Los Tratados de Bucareli: Traición y sangre sobre México!* is more likely to please Carrancistas than Obregonistas or Delahuertistas. In these pages can be seen the influence of Capetillo. Also, like Capetillo (pp. 294–307), they provide (pp. 339–344) the comments of Rafael Zubaran Capmany on the rebellion. Zubaran, who played a most important part in the rebellion's government, had broken with De la Huerta by the time he wrote these comments and they reveal the seriousness of the break.

The events in Puebla are described in *El último caudillo* and *La rebelión sin cabeza*, but it was only after we incorporated material given in Juan Andreu Almazán's *Memorias* that our description of these events was considered by a former Delahuertista soldier to be satisfactory.

26. The Last Days of Carrillo Puerto

Carrillo Puerto's end is described in two books which devote themselves largely to this matter: Edmundo Bolio Ontiveros' *De la cuno al paredón*, and "Chato" Duarte's *Fatalismo . . . ?* Both were published in Mérida, Yucatán. After Carrillo Puerto's death, the federal government was not slow in putting out a brochure containing the indignant comments of various writers: *El asesinato de Carrillo Puerto*.

27. The Assassination of Field Jurado

Cándido Aguilar's comments on the De la Huerta rebellion may be found in Manero Suárez and Paniagua, *Los Tratados de Bucareli* (pp. 326–327).

The best description of the assassination of Field Jurado is that by Vito Alessio Robles in *Desfile sangriento* (pp. 31–140). Vito's brother, Miguel, has a short chapter on the matter in his *Historia política* (pp. 294–301), and Vasconcelos writes of the assassination in *El desastre* (pp. 261–268). In July and August, 1956, the columns of *El Universal* contained exchanges between Alfonso Romandía Ferreira, Luis N. Morones, and others; the Field Jurado assassination was among the subjects discussed.

28. Military Events; The Battle of Esperanza

Early aspects of the Enrique Estrada revolt in the west may be found in *Así Fué* (pp. 99–105) written by his chief of staff, J. D. Ramírez Garrido. Memoranda submitted by S. J. Romero confirm what was written by Ramírez Garrido and give information which has not been printed, such as incidents at Morelia.

Baltasar Dromundo's *Tomás Garrido* tells something of the De la Huerta rebellion in Tabasco. Sources cited in connection with Chapter 25 describe events in Tabasco, Pueblo, Veracruz, and Tamaulipas.

29. The Last Bloody Phases of the Rebellion

Information about the battle of Ocotlán was obtained from *El último caudillo* (pp. 159–172) and from a conversation with Roberto Cruz. The best account of the action at Palo Verde is that of J. D. Ramírez Garrido in *El combate de Palo Verde*. What happened to Estrada after the battle was told by Jorge Prieto Laurens over the lunch table.

Events in Oaxaca are described by Jorge Fernando Iturribarría (*Oaxaca en la historia*) and by Almazán, and it is Almazán's well-documented *Memorias* that tells most vividly of Maycotte's last days.

De la Huerta's manifesto of February 20, 1924, from Frontera, Tabasco, is dealt with in Manero Suárez, and Paniagua's book; these authors also tell of the differences which developed between rebel leaders when they reached the United States. The final phase of the military conflict in Mexico (that in Yucatán, Chiapas, Campeche, and Tabasco) makes interesting reading as presented by Capetillo. It is well also to get De la Huerta's point of view (as presented in his *Memorias*) (pp. 266–284) about events connected with his departure for the United States, and about his activities there. Our conversations with De la Huerta added something to the material on his departure.

Vasconcelos' story (pp. 273–274) about the shooting of Lic. Treviño was checked in Monterrey, with the result that we changed Treviño's name from that given in *El desastre*.

30. Obregón Finishes His Term

Rosalie Evans was a gifted letter writer as well as a spirited defender of what was dear to her. The "British White Paper" at the end of *The Rosalie Evans Letters from Mexico* throws light on the difficulties between Mexico and Great Britain.

Others who signed a spirited letter were Carranza's children; their letter to Obregón is reproduced by Manero Suárez and Paniagua (pp. 186–187).

A note about the Calles inauguration may be found in Pani's *Apuntes autobiográficos* (p. 296). Books which deal exclusively with Calles and his career appear to be less numerous than those about Obregón. Ramón Puente's *Hombres de la Revolución: Calles* is excellent reading. Other works about Calles are Juan de Dios Bojórquez' *Calles*, Luciano Kubli's *Calles y su gobierno* and Amado Chaverri Matamoros' *El verdadero Calles*. Calles' *Mexico before the World* contains a short sketch of his life and some notes about his manner of living and working. A recently published brief defense of Calles is Luis Encinas' *Calles y su obra ante las nuevas generaciones.*

31. Luis N. Morones and Organized Labor

A note about the end of Francisco J. Múgica's hiding is taken from Armando de María y Campos' *Múgica* (p. 207).

A very complete story of the Mexican labor movement, 1907–1922, is given in *Las pugnas de la gleba* by Rosendo Salazar and José G. Escobedo. It is a useful contribution to history. Another book on the subject is Rafael Ramos Pedrueza's *La lucha de clases a través de la historia.* It, too, is a large book; and it has comments on many of the episodes in Mexican history, including those between 1919 and 1936. Published more recently is Alfonso López Aparicio's *El movimiento obrero en México.* The story of railway labor is given in Marcelo N. Rodea's *Historia del movimiento obrero ferrocarrilero (1890–1943).*

The C.R.O.M. has described its work during a part of the Calles administration in *Memoria de los trabajos llevados a cabo por el Comité Central de la C.R.O.M. durante el ejercicio del 23 de noviembre de 1924, al 1° de marzo de 1926.* English books which glorify Morones are J. H. Retinger's *Morones of Mexico* and J. W. Brown's *Modern Mexico and Its Problems.* They were published when Morones was at the height of his power.

32. Government Finances during the Golden Days of President Calles

Tristán Marof, in *México de frente y de perfil,* is specific about names in his criticism of active generals owning large properties.

Thanks to Alberto J. Pani there is no lack of published data about government finances when he was Finance Minister. A particularly useful and complete study issued in 1926 is his *La política hacendaria y la Revolución.* Some of his other works, such as *El problema supremo de México, Mi contribución al nuevo régimen,* and *Apuntes auto-biográficos* add to the picture. So does Hacienda's recent study, *Compilación de leyes del impuesto sobre la renta (1921–1953).* Information about the Pani-Lamont Amendment may be found in Hacienda's *La deuda exterior de México* (1926) and in Turlington's *Mexico and Her Foreign Creditors,* as well as in Pani's writings.

33. Efforts of the Calles Administration To Develop the Nation

A good source of information on the Calles program of 1924–1928 is given in one of the sections of J. M. Puig Casauranc's *El sentido social del proceso histórico de México* (pp. 175–199). Julio Cuadros Caldas also deals with the subject in *México-Soviet.* Both these books include a discussion of efforts made prior to the Calles Administration.

Pani's *Apuntes autobiográficos* provides a little information which was used in this chapter, including his story about his resignation from the Cabinet. G. Butler Sherwell, in *Mexico's Capacity To Pay*, analyzes the effect of the Calles program on Mexico's ability to meet payments due on its foreign debt.

Books dealing with the agrarian program include J. H. Retinger's *Tierra mexicana*, Frank Tannenbaum's careful study, *The Mexican Agrarian Revolution*, and Eyler N. Simpson's very complete and more recent (1937) *The Ejido: Mexico's Way Out*. Books published in Mexico include Enrique González Aparicio's *El problema agrario y el crédito rural*, Alberto Terrones Benítez' *Informe del Sindicato de Campesinos Agraristas del estado de Durango* (January 1, 1925) and some official publications such as the Cámara de Diputados' *Reglamentación del Artículo 27 Constitucional: Fraccionamiento de latifundios (1925)*. A fine compilation of legislation affecting lands is the Comisión Nacional Agraria's *Recopilación agraria de las leyes y disposiciones referentes a restituciones y dotaciones de tierras para ejidos*. The second edition of this book (1924) gives the legislation put out in this realm from 1573 through 1923.

34. Struggle with the Catholic Clergy

Books which tend to support the point of view of the Calles Government are: Luis C. Balderrama's two-volume *El clero y el gobierno de México*, Arturo M. Elías' *The Mexican People and the Church* (also published in Spanish), Francisco Riveros' *El decreto del 2 de julio y la pastoral colectiva*, Alfonso Toro's *La iglesia y el estado en México* and Emilio Portes Gil's *La lucha entre el poder civil y el clero*.

Books which tend to support the point of view of the Catholic clergy are: *La persecución religiosa en Méjico desde el punto de vista jurídico* (introduction by Félix Navarrete and comments by Eduardo Pallares), María Elena Sodi de Pallares' *Los Cristeros y José de León Toral*, and Félix Navarrete's *Sí hay persecución religiosa en México*; also books published in the United States such as Charles S. MacFarland's *Chaos in Mexico*, Francis McCullagh's *Red Mexico*, and Wilfrid Parsons' *Mexican Martyrdom*.

The verbal debate between Luis L. León and Manuel Herrera Lasso was published in *Controversia: El movimiento revolucionario y el clericalismo mexicano*.

Many other works which are not limited to the state-church struggle deal with the subject. Among those consulted were Ernest Greuning's *Mexico and Its Heritage* (pp. 211–286), Puig Casauranc's *El sentido social* (pp. 194–199), Obregón's *Ocho mil kilómetros*, and Nathaniel and Sylvia Weyl's *The Reconquest of Mexico*. Statements by Elías Calles on "The Church Question" can be found in his *Mexico before the*

704

World (pp. 103–141). The point of view in Joseph H. L. Schlarman's *Mexico: A Land of Volcanoes* is anti-Calles.

35. The Cristero Rebellion and the Case of Padre Pro

Some of the information about the attack made against Obregón and his companions was received orally from Arturo H. Orcí.

The case of Padre Pro and his associates is given attention by such anti-Calles writers as Wilfrid Parsons, Francis McCullagh, and M. Elena Sodi de Pallares. It is given the fullest coverage in Fanchón Royer's biography *Padre Pro: Modern Apostle and Martyr*.

36. The Revolutionary Program and United States Relations; 37. The Arrival of Ambassador Morrow

J. M. Callahan's *American Foreign Policy in Mexican Relations* and H. F. Cline's *The United States and Mexico*, both mentioned before, tell of the strains between the two countries during the Calles administration. Calles' reply to Secretary Kellogg is reproduced in Capetillo's *La rebelión sin cabeza* (pp. 217–221).

The full story of the Claims Commissions is given in A. H. Feller's *The Mexican Claims Commissions, 1923–1934*. The findings of the General Claims Commissioners, February 4, 1926–July 23, 1927, were published in the Claims Commission's volume, *Opinions of Commissioners*. A study of the "Calvo Clause" has been made by Donald R. Shea in his *The Calvo Clause*.

American Policies Abroad: Mexico, with contributions by J. Fred Rippy, José Vasconcelos, and Guy Stevens, is helpful in understanding the controversy between Mexico and the United States. Stevens, who has also presented the position of the American oil companies in his *Current Controversies with Mexico*, would be likely to disagree with some of the viewpoints expressed by Amy Blanche Greene in her *The Present Crisis in Our Relations with Mexico*. The 1925 Petroleum Law and the 1926 "Reglamento" were published by the Secretaría de Industria, Comercio y Trabajo: *Ley del petróleo y su reglamento*.

An account of Morrow's activities as ambassador may be found in Harold Nicolson's *Dwight Morrow*. Turlington's splendid book, *Mexico and Her Foreign Creditors*, does not end before it covers some of the problems which faced Montes de Oca.

38. The Presidential Campaign of Generals, 1927–1928

On pages 218–220 of *Quince años de política mexicana* Emilio Portes Gil discusses with clarity the presidential candidates of 1927. Something can be found about them in *La sucesión presidencial de 1928*, written by Antonio Islas Bravo in 1927. Fernando López Portillo has an interesting letter in *El Universal* of November 11, 1956. At times in that newspaper Higinio Alvarez García has told of amending the constitution regarding re-election, and one of his accounts has been reproduced in Pani's *La historia, agredida* (pp. 47–51).

References to the election campaign can be found in the writings of Vito Alessio Robles, Alfonso Taracena, Ramón Puente, Vasconcelos, and in the two-volume *Discursos del General Alvaro Obregón* (published in 1932). The campaign is covered in the first section (*La última campaña política del General Obregón*) of Felipe Islas and Manuel Múzquiz Blanco's very informative *De la pasión sectaria a la noción de las instituciones*. Palavicini, in *Mi vida revolucionaria* (pp. 485–499), describes the failure of the supporters of Serrano and Gómez to agree on a single opposition candidate.

39. Bloody Climax of the 1927–1928 Presidential Campaign

A personal account of events in Cuernavaca preceding the killing of Serrano and his companions is given by Francisco J. Santamaría in *La tragedia de Cuernavaca en 1927 y mi escapatoria célebre*. In his letters to *El Universal* early in October, 1956, Higinio Alvarez García gives a picture of the group at Chapultepec Castle, and he seldom fails to reveal his dislike of Calles. The tale of Serrano's last moments is completed in a section of Vito Alessio Robles' *Desfile sangriento* (pp. 231–244), which includes Claudio Fox's description of the shootings. In telling of what happened at this time Don Vito does not limit himself to the story of Serrano's death. Palavicini (*Mi vida revolucionaria*, pp. 500–509) has something to say of the events of this period.

A fully documented report on steps taken to put down the military uprising is given in the second section (*La infidencia militar*) of Islas' and Múzquiz Blanco's *De la pasión sectaria*.

40. The Re-election of General Obregón

Morones' speech which upset Obregón was recorded in the press. So also were Obregón's speeches; but they are easier to get at in *Discursos del General Alvaro Obregón* (published in 1932). In *La historia, agredida*, Pani has reproduced (pp. 69–75) Luis L. León's *El Universal* article ("Las conjeturas del Ing. Pani") describing Obregón's plans for the future.

Orcí and Sáenz, in conversations, have spoken of Obregón's interest in bringing the Cristero conflict to an end. Orcí has also told of efforts to warn Obregón of dangers in Mexico City.

41. The Assassination of General Obregón

The words of Toral, Madre Conchita, and her friends about their activities before Obregón's death are to be found in the two-volume stenographic text of the murder trial, *El jurado de Toral y la Madre*

Conchita (listed under Toral in our "Sources of Material"). For more information about Toral and Madre Conchita see M. Elena Sodi de Pallares' *Los Cristeros y José de León Toral.*

The text of the trial gives Toral's description of the shooting and it includes the testimony of R. Topete and Orcí. A small book on the "Bombilla" tragedy is *Quiénes mataron al General Obregón* published by Editorial Popular, S. en C. A particularly complete story of what happened at La Bombilla is given in the fourth section (*Toral en el crimen, el cautiverio y la ejecución*) of Islas and Múzquiz Blanco's *De la pasión sectaria.* Orcí, in a conversation, mentioned the scheme devised to have Obregón not show up at the banquet.

42. An Investigation and Some Accusations

Investigation of the crime has been described in *El jurado de Toral,* in Hernán Robleto's *Obregón, Toral y la Madre Conchita,* and in Islas and Múzquiz Blanco's *De la pasión sectaria.* In *Quince años de política mexicana* (pp. 14–16) Portes Gil tells of the call of Obregonistas on Calles. Conversations with Orcí covered both the detective work and the call on Calles.

During the latter half of 1956 the columns of *El Universal* published letters from Romandía Ferreira, Pablo Meneses V., Higinio Alvarez García, Arturo H. Orcí, and Luis N. Morones about Obregón's assassination and related matters.

43. A Memorable Presidential Address; 44. The Selection of a Provisional President

In his *Historia política de la Revolución* (pp. 331–334) Miguel Alessio Robles describes the setting in which Calles made his September 1, 1928, address to Congress.

Political events preceding and following that address are described in Volume I of Froylán C. Manjarrez' *La jornada institucional* and in Portes Gil's *Quince años de política mexicana.*

45. The Murder Trial

See Ma. C. Acevedo y de la Llata (Madre Conchita) *Obregón: Memorias inéditas de la Madre Conchita* and Hernán Robledo *Obregón, Toral y La Madre Conchita.* Also *El jurado de Toral y la Madre Conchita* (text of the trial). María Elena Sodi de Pallares, daughter of Toral's defense lawyer, makes her observations in *Los Cristeros y José de León Toral.*

46. President Portes Gil and the C.R.O.M.

See Portes Gil *Quince años de la política mexicana* and Puig

Casauranc *Galatea rebelde a varios pigmaliones.* Ezequiel Padilla discusses, in *Los nuevos ideales en Tamaulipas,* the work which Portes Gil had done in Tamaulipas.

The P.N.R.'s organizing committee published in January, 1929, its *Proyecto de programa de principios y estatutos* for presentation at the Querétaro Convention.

The story of railroad labor during the Portes Gil administration, and part of that of Ortiz Rubio, is told in *Tres años de lucha sindical* by Gudelio Morales.

47. Background for the Querétaro Convention; 48. The Querétaro Convention of the Partido Nacional Revolucionario

As far as the convention itself is concerned, the contemporary newspapers, and also the discussions with eight who were familiar with the convention, supplemented the information given in Portes Gil (*Quince años*), Puig Casauranc (*Galatea rebelde*), Francisco Díaz Babio (*Un drama nacional*), and Mauricio Magdaleno (*Las palabras perdidas*).

Data on the background for the convention can be found not only in the four above-mentioned books but also in Vasconcelos' *El proconsulado* and Volume I of Manjarrez' *La jornada institucional.* See also Manuel González Ramírez *Planes políticos* and F. J. Gaxiola *El Presidente Rodríguez* (pp. 82–85) for material about Fausto Topete's letter to Rodríguez. Roberto Cruz's comments on his relations with Portes Gil are expressed in his article in *El Universal* of August 19, 1949, "Las falsedades del Licenciado Portes Gil."

49. The Outbreak of the Escobar Rebellion; 50. The Campaign East and North; The Battle of Jiménez; 51. The Campaign in the West

Accounts of the military events have been recorded not infrequently, but invariably by supporters of the federal government: *La rebelión militar contra el gobierno legítimo del Sr. Presidente Lic. D. Emilio Portes Gil* by an anonymous "Observer"; *La jornada institucional* (Vol. II) by Manjarrez; Emilio N. Acosta's *Historia de la campaña de la Columna Expedicionaria del Norte, marzo 4–mayo 17, 1929;* Alfonso León de Garay's *El palpitar de las casta: Compaña del Norte hasta la toma de Torreón;* and the accounts given in Juan Andreu Almazán's lengthy *Memorias.*

Additional information was obtained from Portes Gil's *Quince años,* Vasconcelos' *El proconsulado,* and M. Magdaleno's *Las palabras perdidas;* also from interviews with some of the generals who participated (on both sides).

708

52. The Resumption of Catholic Services

For the story of the Church matter see Portes Gil's *Quince años* (pp. 283–318); also Schlarman's *Mexico: A Land of Volcanoes* and Nicolson's *Dwight Morrow*.

53. Autonomy for the National University

Portes Gil's *Quince años* (pp. 319–338) covers the University matter very adequately. Additional comments were secured from Puig Casauranc's *Galatea rebelde* (p. 338) and M. Magdaleno's *Las palabras perdidas* (pp. 91–92) and from conversations.

Ezequiel Padilla discusses education in *La educación del Pueblo*.

54. The Vasconcelista Campaign of 1929

The Vasconcelista campaign is fully covered in three books: Magdaleno's *Las palabras perdidas*, Vasconcelos' *El proconsulado*, and (with less enthusiasm for Vasconcelos) Vito Alessio Robles' *Mis andanzas con nuestro Ulises*.

José E. Villalobos Ruiz submitted a memorandum (March 11, 1957) to Ezequiel Padilla: "Breves datos biográficos-políticos de Don Nazario S. Ortiz Garza." For an account of the campaign in Coahuila, see Vito Alessio Robles' *Desfile sangriento* (pp. 165–222).

55. A Bad Inauguration Day for President Ortiz Rubio; 56. Rough Times for the Convalescent

Political aspects of the Ortiz Rubio administration are covered from different points of view in Puig Casauranc's *Galatea rebelde*, Francisco Díaz Babio's *Un drama nacional*, and Portes Gil's *Quince años*. Pani's *Apuntes autobiográficos* contains a few observations. Both Portes Gil and Simpson (*The Ejido: Mexico's Way Out*) deal with the agrarian program at this time.

A book with sensational revelations about the fate of Vasconcelistas, and the Topilejo massacre, is Alfonso Taracena's *Los Vasconcelistas sacrificados en Topilejo*. Magdaleno's *Las palabras perdidas* (pp. 207–211) deals with the matter, although less extensively and with fewer data.

The series of books by Luis G. Franco, including his *Glosa del período del gobierno del C. Gral. e Ing. Pascual Ortiz Rubio, 1930–1932: Ramo de Gobernación*, cover the Ortiz Rubio Administration in a manner sympathetic to Don Pascual. Observations about the "Estrada Doctrine" may be found in Franco's *Relaciones exteriores en una actuación histórica* and in *La opinión universal sobre la Doctrina Estrada* published by the Instituto Americano de Derecho y Legislación Comparada.

Information about Pascual Ortiz Rubio's earlier career may be obtained from some of his own works, such as *Memorias de un penitente* and "Medio siglo: Memorias"; also from Francisco Díaz Babio's *Actividades de Pascual Ortiz Rubio* and José Ugalde's *Quién es Ortíz Rubio*.

57. The Great Depression Sets In

Government finances of this period (and all periods from Mexico's independence until 1950) are described in Hacienda's monumental work, *La Hacienda pública de México a través de los informes presidenciales*. Gustavo Velazco was helpful in conversations. Almazán's *Memorias* have references to the Plan Calles. See *El Universal*, December 13–21, 1958.

The foreign debt and the Montes de Oca-Lamont Agreement are covered in Hacienda's "Convenio Montes de Oca-Lamont" (typewritten manuscript) and in Turlington's *Mexico and Her Foreign Creditors*. Salvador Mendoza (*Las objeciones al Convenio Montes de Oca-Lamont*) and Francisco Vázquez del Mercado (*La deuda exterior de México*) published their objections to the Montes de Oca-Lamont Agreement.

58. Pani Returns to the Finance Ministry; 59. Some Cabinets of President Ortiz Rubio

Financial matters of this period are discussed in two of Hacienda's publications: *La crisis económica en México y la nueva legislación sobre la moneda y crédito* and *La Hacienda Pública de México a través de los informes presidenciales*. The first-mentioned deals exclusively with this period. Pani writes of the matter in *Mi contribución, Apuntes autobiográficos*, and *El problema supremo de México*.

The Labor Law of 1931 is discussed in Tannenbaum's *Peace by Revolution* and briefly in Person's *Mexican Oil* (pp. 30–31). A Mexican labor lawyer reviewed and improved our paragraphs. The fate of the National Railways during the depression is brought out in Vicente Fuentes Díaz's *El problema ferrocarrilero de México*.

Commentators on the political "crises" include Puig Casauranc (*Galatea rebelde*), Díaz Babio (*Un drama nacional*), Almazán (*Memorias*), and Portes Gil (*Quince años*).

60. Acute Religious and Political Problems; 61. The Resignation of President Ortiz Rubio

In Antigua Librería de Murguía's *Colección de efemérides* there are some references to religious matters in Veracruz and elsewhere. A book having to do with the attempt to assassinate Governor Tejeda, and about the reaction to that attempt, was written by José C. Escasan and published by the Veracruz state government: *La ley de los trece, el atentado y las represalias*. The assault on Leonides Andreu Almazán and conditions in Puebla are discussed in Almazán's *Memorias* (in *El Universal* January 24–26, 1959) and in the anti-Almazán brochure (*Puebla bajo el terror Almazanista*) edited by Daniel Blumenkron and Luis Campomanes. Limits on the number of priests who could practice in the various states are given in a number of books; one of the best compilations is that in M. Elena Sodi de Pallares' *Los Cristeros y José de León Toral* (pp. 151–155).

Political developments at the time when Ortiz Rubio resigned, and just before, are covered in Puig Casauranc's *Galatea rebelde*, Pedro J. Almada's *Con mi cobija al hombro*, F. J. Gaxiola, Jr.'s *El Presidente Rodríguez*, Almazán's *Memorias*, Pani's *Apuntes autobiográficos*, and Díaz Babio's *Un drama nacional*. An official account of the selection of a successor to Ortiz Rubio is given in *La jornada institucional del día cuatro de septiembre de 1932* (perhaps published by the P.N.R. or the government).

Soon after Rodríguez took office appeared Guillermo Durante de Cabarga's *Abelardo L. Rodríguez: El hombre de la hora*, telling of the new President's background. This was followed by Emilio Uribe Romo's *Abelardo L. Rodríguez*.

The Rodríguez Administration is best described in Gaxiola's book and in the Departamento del Trabajo's *La obra social del Presidente Rodríguez*. More recent activities of Rodríguez are given attention in Enriqueta de Parodi's *Abelardo L. Rodríguez: Estadista y benefactor* and in Francisco Sánchez González' *Obra económica y Social del Gral. Abelardo L. Rodríguez*.

62. Pani's Departure from President Rodríguez' Cabinet; 63. Narciso Bassols and the Catholic Clergy

See Gaxiola's *El Presidente Rodríguez*, the Departamento del Trabajo's *La obra social del Presidente Rodríguez*, Josephus Daniels' *Shirt-Sleeve Diplomat*, and Pani's *Los origenes de la política crediticia, Mi contribución al nuevo régimen, La historia, agredida* and *Apuntes autobiográficos*. One source of information concerning the abolishment of the Comptroller Generalship is that given in Hacienda's *Informe sobre la revisión de la contabilidad del gobierno federal* (1958). Portes Gil's *Quince años* (pp. 481–493) adds to what Gaxiola has to say about the conflict with some members of the Catholic clergy. See also Portes Gil's *La lucha entre el poder civil y el clero*.

Something on socialistic education is given in J. Jesús de la Rosa P.'s *La escuela socialista mexicana*.

E. David Cronon's *Josephus Daniels in Mexico* (University of Wisconsin Press) came out so recently that we were unable to make use of it.

64. The Official Party Selects a Presidential Candidate; 65. Efforts by the Opposition in 1933 and 1934

The election and pre-election activities in 1933 and 1934, besides being fully described in newspapers, are dealt with in Gaxiola's *El Presidente Rodríguez*, Nathaniel and Sylvia Weyl's *The Reconquest of Mexico*, Portes Gil's *Quince años*, and De María y Campos' *Múgica* (pp. 249–250). Numerous persons were interviewed in order to learn how the selection of Cárdenas came about. The Six-Year Plan was published in *Plan Sexenal del P.N.R.*

Opposition efforts are discussed in Luis Cabrera's *Veinte años después* (pp. 133–198). Also see the Partido Nacional Antirreeleccionista's *Discursos pronunciados por Juan Ramón Solís, José R. Saucedo, Antonio Díaz Soto y Gama, Diego Arenas Guzmán y Antonio I. Villarreal.*

66. Negotiations with the United States under President Rodríguez; 67. Rodríguez Handles Agrarian and Labor Matters

Economic and financial matters during the Rodríguez administration are discussed in Gaxiola's fine book. Some additional information can be found in the writings of Pani and in the presidential messages to Congress. Fuentes Díaz tells about the railways (*El problema ferrocarrilero*).

To supplement Gaxiola's discussions of negotiations with the U.S. government one can read Josephus Daniel's *Shirt-Sleeve Diplomat* and refer to Feller's *The Mexican Claims Commissions*. Also useful is Cline's *The United States and Mexico*. Puig Casauranc has a few words about his term as Foreign Minister in *Galatea rebelde* (pp. 472–476).

The Rodríguez agrarian program is described by Gaxiola, by Eyler N. Simpson (*The Ejido: Mexico's Way Out*), and in *Memoria, 1934–5*, published by the Departamento Agrario. See also Alberto Terrones Benítez' *El Departamento Autónomo Agrario y el problema de la distribución de tierras*. A letter from Marte R. Gómez, which included a discussion of this matter, proved very helpful.

In the Departamento del Trabajo's *La obra social del Presidente Rodríguez* there is something about the agrarian matter, but this book is devoted mostly to an account of the Administration's work to improve the lot of laborers. Gaxiola has interesting comments on labor matters.

68. December, 1934

Numerous books have been written about Cárdenas and his administration, which is not the main theme of this study. Some of these books are Victoriano Anguiano Equihua's *Lázaro Cárdenas: Su feudo y la política nacional*; Juan de Dios Bojórquez, *Lázaro Cárdenas: Líneas biográficas*; J. Manuel Carro Viña's *Cárdenas frente a Calles*; Eduardo J.

Correa's *El balance del Cardenismo;* the Departamento Autónomo de Prensa y Publicidad's *México en acción;* Paul Nathan's "México en la época de Cárdenas"; the book sponsored by Nayarit's Governor Parra, *Síntesis biográfica del Divisionario Michoacano, Lázaro Cárdenas;* the P.R.M.'s *Cárdenas habla* (speeches by Cárdenas 1935–1940); William Cameron Townsend's *Lázaro Cárdenas; Mexican Democrat;* and Nathaniel and Sylvia Weyl's *The Reconquest of Mexico.* Portes Gil's *Rectificaciones a un libro* contains his comments about Townsend's book.

Our Chapter 68 is for the most part derived from newspaper items.

69. Garrido Canabal and Tabasco, "Laboratory of the Revolution"

See Salvador Camelo Solver's *Tomás Garrido Canabal: El Sátrapa;* Baltasar Dromundo's *Tomás Garrido; Su vida y su leyenda;* Tomás Garrido Canabal's *Informe ante la legislatura local, el 16 de septiembre, 1934;* Graham Greene's *El poder y la gloria* (which originally appeared in English as *The Power and the Glory*); Manuel González Calzada's *Tomás Garrido (al derecho y al revés);* Roberto Hinojosa's *El Tabasco que yo he visto;* Manuel R. Mora's *Ensayo sociológico de Tabasco;* Joaquín Ruiz's *La Revolución en Tabasco;* Francisco J. Santamaría's *El periodismo en Tabasco;* the book of political propaganda called *Tabasco Revolucionario;* and Rosendo Taracena's *Historia de Tabasco.* Of these, Dromundo's book, sympathetic to Garrido, is the most formal biography.

Brito Foucher contributed a 138-page manuscript containing 14 articles by him about Tabasco, published in *El Día* January 28 through February 22, 1936.

70. Agitation and Strikes in Early 1935

To supplement newspaper items reference was made to Eduardo J. Correa's *El balance del Cardenismo* (pp. 21–52) and Cándido Aguilar's *Por qué voté contra el dictámen de la Comisión Permanente del Congreso de la Unión en el caso de "Cerro Azul."*

Information about financial matters was provided by Hacienda's *La hacienda pública de México a través de los informes presidenciales* and by Alfonso Septien's *La última reforma monetaria.* Puig, in *El sentido social* (p. 180) comments favorably on Bassols' work.

71. The Declarations of General Calles

Here again our information comes largely from newspaper items and interviews, but with an assist from Correa's *El balance* (p. 53) and Portes Gil's *Quince años* (pp. 497–499). Ezequiel Padilla was particularly helpful. Correa (pp. 596–606) reproduces the *Patrioticas declaraciones del General Plutarco Elías Calles* as given in *Excelsior* on June 12, 1935.

72. The Break between Cárdenas and Calles

Books which describe events following Calles' declarations are Portes Gil's *Quince años* (pp. 499–509) and Correa's *El balance* (pp. 53–58), particularly the former.

Something about agrarian matters can be found in Economía Nacional's *La reforma agraria en México* (1937).

73. The Expedition to Tabasco

The expedition to Tabasco is described most fully in Rodulfo Brito Foucher's twenty-five page memorandum of July 11, 1958, with some slight changes which are given in his shorter memorandum of September 17, 1958. It is also given attention in the writings of González Calzada (pp. 189–200) and Dromundo (see notes on Chapter 66) and in Correa (pp. 61–70).

74. General Calles Returns to Mexico

In addition to turning to the press, it is interesting to consult *El regreso del Gral. Calles* by "Ignotos" (Luis L. León). Additional information is furnished by Pedro J. Almada's *Con mi cobija al hombro*, Puig Casauranc's *Galatea rebelde*, De María y Campos' *Múgica*, and Casasola's *Historia gráfica de la Revolución*.

75. The Curtain Falls for General Calles

This chapter contains little that was not obtained from newspaper items.

SOURCES OF MATERIAL

Sources of Material

Acevedo y de la Llata, María Concepción. *Obregón: Memorias inéditas de la Madre Conchita*. Libro-Mex, Mexico City, 1957.

———. (SEE Toral, José de León.)

Acosta, Emilio N. *Historia de la Campaña de la Columna Expedicionaria del Norte, marzo 4–mayo 17, 1929*. Impresa Azteca, Mexico City, 1930.

Agrario, Departamento. *Memoria, 1934–1935*.

Agricultura y Fomento, Secretaría de. *Decreto refundiendo, adicionando y modificando las prevenciones de los distintos ordenamientos vigentes relacionados con el uso y aprovechamiento de aguas de propiedad nacional*. Imprenta de la Dirección de Estudios Geográficos y Climatologicos, Tacubaya, D.F., 1927.

Aguilar, Cándido. *Por qué voté contra el dictámen de la Comisión*

Permanente del Congreso de la Unión en el caso de "Cerro Azul." Mexico City, 1935.

Aguirre, Amado. *Mis memorias de campaña: Apuntes para la historia.* 1953.

Aguirre Manjarrez, Rafael. "Discurso ante la tumba del Gral. Joaquín Amaro en el IV aniversario de su deceso." *El Legionario,* April 15, 1956, pp. 60–62.

―――. Conversation, June 11, 1956.

Alessio de Guemes, Carmen. Interview, September 20, 1957 (comments on manuscript).

Alessio Robles, Miguel. *Antología selecta.* Editorial Patria, Mexico City, 1946.

―――. *La cena de las burlas.* Ediciones Botas, Mexico City, 1939.

―――. *Contemplando el pasado.* Editorial Stylo, Mexico City, 1950.

―――. *Historia política de la Revolucion.* Tercera edición. Ediciones Botas, Mexico City, 1946.

―――. *A medio camino.* Editorial Stylo, Mexico City, 1949.

―――. *Obregón como militar.* Editorial cultura, Mexico City, 1935.

Alessio Robles, Vito. *Desfile sangriento.* A. del Bosque, Mexico City, 1936.

―――. *Los Tratados de Bucareli.* Mexico City, 1937.

―――. *Mis andanzas con nuestro Ulises.* Botas, Mexico City, 1938.

―――. Interview, January 31, 1957.

Almada, Pedro J. *Con mi cobija al hombro.* Editorial Alrededor de América, Sección de México, 1936.

Almazán, Juan Andreu. "Memorias," appearing in *El Universal,* 1957, 1958, 1959.

Alvarado, Salvador. *El problema de México.* 1920.

Alvarez García, Higinio. Articles in *El Universal,* October 5 and 6, 1949, reproduced in part on pp. 47–51 of A. J. Pani's *La historia, agredida.*

―――. Letters in *El Universal,* October 4, 5, 6, and 8, 1956.

Andrade, Manuel (ed.). *Constitución política mexicana, con reformas y adiciones* [and other laws] *anotadas y concordadas.* Editorial información Aduanera de México, Mexico City (n.d.).

Anguiano Equihua, Victoriano. *Lázaro Cárdenas: Su feudo y la política nacional.* Editorial Eréndira, Mexico City, 1951.

Arroyo Ch., Agustín. *Obregón: Discurso pronunciado en el XX aniversario de su muerte.* Mexico City, July 17, 1948.

―――. Interview, August 16, 1956.

Asesinato de Carrillo Puerto, El. Contemporary comments by legislatures, organizations, Lic. Castillo Torre, Dr. Siurob, Sr. Morones, General Calles, D. H. Dubrowsky, Hernán Robleto, etc. Mexico City, 1924.

Balderrama, Luis C. *El clero y el gobierno de México: Apuntes para la historia de la crisis en 1926.* Editorial Cuauhtemoc, 1927.

Barragán Rodríguez, Juan. "El héroe de León es el General Murguía." Articles in *El Universal,* August 19 and 20, 1958.

―――. *Historia del ejército y de la Revolución Constitucionalista.* 2 vols. Antigua Librería Robredo, Talleres de la Editorial Stylo, Mexico City, 1946.

Barrera, Carlos. *Obregón: Estampas de un caudillo.* Mexico City, 1957.

Bautista, Gonzalo. SEE Monroy Durán, Luis.

Beals, Carleton. *Mexico: An Interpretation.* B. W. Huebsch, Inc., New York, 1923.

Bienes Nacionales e Inspección Administrativa, Secretaría de, Dirección Técnica de Organización. *Directorio del gobierno federal, poderes legislativo, ejecutivo y judicial, 1956.* (No publication data.)

Blair, Albert E. Conversation, July 11, 1958 (also comments on second half of manuscript).

Blanco Moheno, Roberto. *Crónica de la Revolución Mexicana* (Tomo II, Querétaro-Tlaxcalantongo-La Bombilla). Libro-Mex, Editores, 1959.

―――. "La muerte de la política tropical." *Impacto,* July 4, 1956.

―――. "Habla Rodolfo Herrero," an interview with Rodolfo Herrero, presented as Chap. XXVII, Vol. II, of *Crónica de la Revolución Mexicana. Impacto,* July 16, 1958; "La muerte de Murguía" (Vol. II, Chap. XXXI, *Crónica*), *Impacto,* August 13, 1958.

Blasco Ibáñez, Vicente. *El militarismo mejicano (1921).* In *Obras completas de Vicente Blasco Ibáñez.* Aguilar, S.A. de Ediciones, Madrid, 1949.

Blumenkron, Daniel, and Luis Campomanes (eds.). *Puebla bajo el terror Almazanista: El libro rojo de un mal gobierno.* Puebla, 1933.

Bojórquez, Juan de Dios (pseud. Djed Bórquez). *Calles.* Segunda Edición. 1925.

―――. *Obregón: Apuntes biográficos.* Ediciones Patria Nueva, 1929.

―――. *Lázaro Cárdenas: Líneas biográficas.* Mexico City, 1933.

Bolio Ontiveros, Edmundo. *De la cuna al paredón: Anecdotario de la vida, muerte y gloria de Felipe Carrillo Puerto.* Mérida, Yucatán (n. d.).

Bonillas, Ignacio, Jr. Interview, March, 1956.

Braddy, Haldeen. *Cock of the Walk.* University of New Mexico Press, Albuquerque, 1955.

Brandenberg, Frank. Conversation, November 25, 1957.

Bravo Ugarte, José. *Historia de México, tomo tercero, México, II, Relaciones internacionales, territorio, sociedad y cultura.* Editorial Jus, Mexico City, 1959.

Brenner, Anita. *The Wind That Swept Mexico.* Harper & Brothers, 1943.

British Embassy in Mexico, Information Section. Conversation, December, 1956.

Brito Foucher, Rodulfo. A 138-page manuscript containing 14 articles about Tabasco published in *El Día*, January 28, 1936, through February 22, 1936.

————. A 25-page memorandum about the expedition to Tabasco of July 14, 1935. Dated July 11, 1958. Also Brito's memorandum of September 17, 1958.

————. Various conversations, including those of September 21, 1957, December 19, 1957, and June 27, 1958; also correspondence and comments on manuscript.

Brown, J. W. *Modern Mexico and Its Problems*. The Labour Publishing Company, Ltd., London, 1927.

Cabrera, Luis. *El balance de la Revolución* (Conferencia sustentada en la Biblioteca Nacional de México, la noche del día 30 de Enero de 1931). Mexico City, 1931.

————. *La herencia de Carranza*. Imprenta Nacional, S.A., Mexico City, 1920.

————. (pseud. Blas Urrea). Statement in *La verdad sobre la muerte de Carranza*, pp. 26–27. SEE Quiroga, Librería.

————. *Veinte años después* (3a. Edición). Botas, Mexico City, 1938.

Cacho Galván, Joaquín. "Persecución de Maycotte" (in Almazán's "Memorias"). *El Universal*, July 25, 26, and 27, 1958.

Caldas, Julio Cuadros. *México-Soviet*. Santiago Loyo, Puebla, 1926.

Callahan, James Morton. *American Foreign Policy in Mexican Relations*. Macmillan, New York, 1932.

Calles. SEE Elías Calles.

Cámara de Senadores, Sección de Estadística y Anales de Jurisprudencia. *El petróleo: Las más grande riqueza nacional*. Mexico City, 1923.

Camelo Solver, Salvador. *Tomás Garrido Canabal: El sátrapa*, Mexico City, 1933.

Campomanes, Luis. SEE Blumenkron, Daniel.

Capetillo, Alonso. *La rebelión sin cabeza*. Botas, Mexico City, 1925.

Cárdenas, Lázaro. *Cárdenas habla*. Partido de la Revolución Mexicana, La Impresora, S. Turanzas del Valle, Mexico City, 1940.

————. "Informes Presidenciales del 1° de Sept. de 1935 y del 1° de Sept. de 1936" (from *Diario de los debates de las Cámara de Diputados*).

————. Presidential inauguration address as reported in *Universal Gráfica*, November 30, 1934.

————. Speech at Durango, June 30, 1934, published in *El Universal*, July 1, 1934.

Cárdenas, Lázaro (Administration). *Seis años de gobierno al servicio de México, 1939–1940.* Talleres tipográficas La Nacional Impresora, S.A., November 28, 1940.

Carranza, Julia. Statement in *La verdad sobre la muerte de Carranza,* pp. 61–63. SEE Quiroga, Librería.

Carrasco Puente, Rafael. *Iconografía de Educación, 1905–1946.* Mexico City, 1946.

———. *Iconografía de Hacienda: Secretarios y Encargados del Ramo, desde que se inició la Revolución Mexicana de 1910 hasta la fecha.* Mexico City, 1948.

Carregha, Jorge. "La memoria de don Adolfo." *Excelsior,* January 24, 1958.

Carrillo Puerto, Felipe. *Informe rendido ante la H. XXVII legislatura del estado, el 1° de enero de 1923.* Mérida, 1923.

Casas Alatriste, Enrique. Conversations.

———. Memoranda with comments on manuscript, January and February, 1959.

Casas Alatriste, Roberto. Conversations.

Casasola (Archivo Casasola). *Historia gráfica de la Revolución.* Vols. III, IV, and V.

Cervantes, Juan B. *Obregón ante la historia.* Mexico City, 1924.

Chaverri Matamoros, Amado. *El verdadero Calles.* Editorial Patria, S.A., 1933.

Chaverri Matamoros, Amado, and Clodoveo Valenzuela. *Sonora y Carranza.* Casa Editorial "Renacimiento" de G. Sisniega y Hno., Mexico City, 1921.

Claims Commission, United States and Mexico. "Opinions of Commissioners under the Convention concluded September 8, 1923, between the United States and Mexico; February 4, 1926, to July 23, 1927." U.S. Government Printing Office, Washington, 1927.

Cline, Howard F. *The United States and Mexico.* Harvard, 1953.

Comisión Nacional Agraria. *Recopilación agraria. Segunda edición oficial de las leyes y disposiciones referentes a restituciones y dotaciones de tierras para ejidos.* Imprenta de la Dirección de Estudios Geográficos y Climatológicos, Tacubaya, D.F., 1924.

Comité Militar de Historia. SEE Peral, Miguel A.

Confederación Regional Obrera Mexicana (C.R.O.M.), Comité Central Saliente. *Memoria.* 1926.

Contreras Torres, Miguel. Series of four articles about Ing. Alberto J. Pani, under the heading *Los civiles en la Revolución. El Universal,* starting on April 19, 1958.

———. *Los civiles en la Revolución.* "Gloria y ocaso de Carranza: La nefasta imposición de un sucesor." *El Universal,* May 26, 1958.

————. *Los civiles en la Revolución*. "De la Huerta y el crimen de Tlaxcalantongo." *El Universal*, September 30, 1958.

Correa, Eduardo J. *El balance del Cardenismo*. Talleres Linotipográficos "Acción," Mexico City, 1941.

Corro Viña, J. Manuel. *Cárdenas frente a Calles* (n.d., n.pub.).

Creel, Enrique C. *Exportación e importación: Saldo de cuentas internacionales*. Mexico City, 1931.

Cruz, Roberto. "Las falsedades del Licenciado Portes Gil." *El Universal*, August 19, 1949.

————. Conversation, May, 1956.

Daniels, Josephus. *Shirt-Sleeve Diplomat*. University of North Carolina Press, Chapel Hill, 1947.

De la Huerta, Adolfo. *Memorias de don Adolfo de la Huerta, segun su proprio dictado: Transcripción y comentarios del Lic. Roberto Guzmán Esparza*. Ediciones Guzmán, Mexico City, 1957.

————. Letter of June 23, 1937, to Froylán Manjarrez. Published in "Contestación a Martín Luis Guzmán" (Part II) by Roberto Guzmán Esparza. *Excelsior*, February 11, 1958.

————. Interviews, March 22, 1954, and June 6, 1955.

———— (pseud. "Alex Hamilton"). "Crisis y Cresos: Nuestra economía," *Nuevos Horizontes*, July 15, 1954.

————. "Informe del C. Presidente de la República don Adolfo de la Huerta, 1° de Septiembre de 1920" (copiado del diario *Excelsior* y del *Diario de los debates*).

De la Rosa P., J. Jesús. *La escuela socialista mexicana*. Mexico City, 1935.

De la Torre, Gustavo. Five articles about the Tlaxcalantongo tragedy in *El Universal*, May 24–29, 1956.

Delgado, Ricardo (ed.). *Directorio General del Estado de Jalisco* (1940): *Una verdadera enciclopedia comercial e histórica*. Guadalajara, Jalisco. Tomo I.

De María y Campos, Armando. *Múgica: Crónica biográfica*. Editorial Populares, Mexico City, 1939.

De Parodi, Enriqueta. *Abelardo L. Rodríguez: Estadista y benefactor*. Gráfica Panamericana, S. de R.L., Mexico City, 1957.

Departamento Agrario. SEE Agrario, Departamento.

Departamento Autónomo de Prensa y Publicidad (D.A.P.P.). SEE Prensa y Publicidad, Departamento Autónomo de.

Departamento del Trabajo. SEE Trabajo, Departamento del.

Díaz Babio, Francisco. *Actividades de Pascual Ortiz Rubio*. Imprenta Aguilar, Mexico City, 1929.

————. *Un drama nacional*. M. León Sánchez, Mexico City, 1939.

Díaz Soto y Gama, Antonio. *Discurso en la Gran Convención del Partido*

Nacional Agrarista *(November 12, 1923)*. Imprenta Altamirando, 1923.

———. Interviews, October 3, 1955, and June 10, 1958.

Dillon, E. J. *Mexico on the Verge*. G. H. Doran, New York, 1921.

———. *President Obregón: A World Reformer*. Small, Maynard, and Company, Boston, 1923.

Distrito Federal, Departamento del. "Acta de defunción de la Señora Natalia Chacón de Calles" (copy of typescript in official files; copy dated December 7, 1956).

Dromundo, Baltasar. *Tomás Garrido: Su vida y su leyenda*. Editorial Guarania, Mexico City, 1953.

Duarte, "Chato." *Fatalismo . . . ? Obra histórica que contiene: El movimiento de la Huertista en Yucatán; Salida del Gobernador Carrillo Puerto y compañeros; Captura de Estos; Consejo sumarísimo, sentencia y ejecuciones*. Mérida, March, 1924.

Durante de Cabarga, Guillermo. *Abelardo L. Rodríguez: El hombre de la hora*. Ediciones Botas, Mexico City, 1933.

Economía Nacional, Secretaría de la (Dirección General de Estadísticas). *Anuario estadístico, 1938*. Departamento Autónomo de Publicidad y Propaganda, Mexico City, March, 1939.

———. *La reforma agraria en México*. Departamento Autónomo de Publicidad y Propaganda, Mexico City, 1937.

———. *Programa de los fundadores de Petróleos de México, S.A. ("Petromex," S.A.)*. Talleres Gráficos de la Nación, Mexico City, 1934.

Elías, Arturo M. *The Mexican People and the Church*. A. M. Elías, New York, 1927.

Elías Calles, Plutarco. "Informe presidencial del 1° de septiembre, 1928." *Excelsior*, September 2, 1928.

———. *Informes rendidos ante el H. Congreso de la Unión los días 1° de septiembre de 1925 y 1926*. Talleres Gráficos de la Nación, Diario Oficial, Mexico City.

———. *Mexico before the World: Public Documents and Addresses of Plutarco Elías Calles*. The Academy Press, New York, 1927.

———. *Partes Oficiales de la Campaña de Sonora, rendidos por el Gral. P. Elías Calles, Gobernador y Comandante Militar del Estado de Sonora, al C. Gral. Alvaro Obregón, Jefe del Cuerpo del Ejército del Noroeste*. Talleres Gráficos de la Nación, Mexico City, 1932.

Elías Calles, Jr., Plutarco. Interview, January 19, 1959.

Encinas, Luis. *Calles y su obra, ante las nuevas generaciones (discurso)*. Publicación del Bloque de Obreros Intelectuales de Sonora, Mexico City, 1955.

Escasan, José B. *La ley de los Trece: El atentado y las represalias*.

Talleres Linotipográficos del Gobierno del Estado, Jalapa-Enríquez, 1932.

Escobedo, José G. see Salazar, Rosendo.

Estrada, Roque. Interview, December 13, 1957.

Evans, Rosalie and Daisy Caden Pettus. *The Rosalie Evans Letters from Mexico*. Bobbs-Merrill, Indianapolis, 1926.

Fabela, Isidro. Interview ("Punto final de Fabela a la polémica acerca de los Tratados de Bucareli"). *Excelsior*, May 8, 1958.

Fabila, Gilberto and Francisco A. Ursua. *Reglamento del Artículo 27 Constitucional, fraccionamiento de latifundos, bases para la ley federal sobre esta materia*. Imprenta de la Cámara de Diputados, Mexico City, 1925.

Feller, A. H. *The Mexican Claims Commissions, 1923–1934*. Macmillan, New York, 1935.

Fernández del Castillo, Rafael. Conversations.

Fernández MacGregor, Genaro. "Las reclamaciones internacionales y don Adolfo de la Huerta." *El Universal*, February 11, February 17, 1958.

Ferrer, Adolfo. *El archivo de Felipe Carrillo—el Callismo: La corrupción del Régimen Obregonista*. Carlos López Press, 108 Fulton St., New York City, June, 1924.

Ferrer de Mendiolea, Gabriel. *Historia de la Revolución Mexicana*. Ediciones el Nacional, Mexico City, 1956.

Fondo de Cultura Económica. see González Ramírez, Manuel.

Fort, Daniel P. Conversations, including those of August, 1956, and January 14, 1958; also comments on first half of manuscript.

Franco, Luis G. *Glosa del período del gobierno del C. Gral. e Ing. Pascual Ortiz Rubio, 1930–1932: Departamento del Distrito Federal.* "Gobernar a la ciudad es servirla." Mexico City, April, 1948.

———. *Glosa del período de gobierno del C. General e Ingeniero Pascual Ortiz Rubio, 1930–1932: Ramo de Educación.* Mexico City, 1944.

———. *Glosa del período del gobierno del C. Gral. e Ing. Pascual Ortiz Rubio, 1930–1932: Ramo de Gobernación; Narraciones históricas; el Partido de Ingenieros, Arquitectos y sus Colaboradores (PIAC).* Mexico City, 1947.

———. *Relaciones exteriores en una actuación histórica.* El Partido de Ingenieros, Arquitectos y sus Colaboradores (PIAC), Mexico City, 1947.

———. *Tres años de historia del Ejército de México.* Mexico City, 1946.

Fuentes Díaz, Vicente. *Los partidos políticos en México* (Tomo II, *De Carranza a Ruiz Cortines*). Mexico City, 1950.

————. *El problema ferrocarrilero de México*. Edición del autor, Mexico City, 1951.

Gaither, Roscoe B. *Expropriation in Mexico*. William Morrow and Company, New York, 1940.

Gamboa Ricalde, Alvaro. *Yucatán desde mil novecientos diez* (Vol. I, 1910–1914). Imprenta Standard, Veracruz, 1943.

García, Francisco E. Conversation in Zacatecas, Zacatecas, December 5, 1957.

García, José A. Conversations.

García Naranjo, Nemesio. "Aarón Sáenz y las memorias de don Adolfo; Antes que historiador, hay que ser caballero." *Novedades*, March 26, 1958.

García, Severo. *El Indio Gabriel* (Prologue by Luis Islas García). Editorial Jus, S.A., Mexico City, 1957.

Garrido Canabal, Tomás. *Informe ante la legislatura local el 16 de septiembre, 1934.* (n.d.)

Gaxiola, Francisco Javier, Jr. *El Presidente Rodríguez*. Cultura, 1938.

————. Interview, January 14, 1959.

Gómez, Arnulfo R. *Estudios militares*. Mexico City, 1926.

Gómez, Marte R. Conversations, 1955; interview, January 11, 1957; letters, December 2, 1955, and February 4, 1957.

Gómez Morín, Manuel. Interview, September, 1956; letters, September 29, 1956, October 3, 1956, November 24, 1956, and February 4, 1957.

Gómez Robledo, Antonio. *The Bucareli Agreements and International Law* (trans. Salomón de la Selva). The National University of Mexico Press, Mexico City, 1940.

González Aparicio, Enrique. *El problema agrario y el crédito rural*. Imprenta Mundial, Mexico City, 1937.

González Calzada, Manuel. *Tomás Garrido (al derecho y al revés)*. Mexico City, November, 1940.

González, Marciano. "Vuelvo a la carga sobre la mentira del asesinato del Presidente Don Venustiano Carranza." *El Universal*, p. 3, May 22, 1958.

————. "Rodolfo Herrero continúa mintiendo." The Monterrey *El Porvenir*, August 28, 1958.

————. Interview, June 26, 1958.

González Ramírez, Manuel. "Glosa al pastor: La ligereza de las memorias." *Novedades*, February 13, 1958, and February 27, 1958.

————. Letter of December 2, 1957, with memorandum attached containing 8 pages of "Observaciones" on manuscript; letter of March 29, 1958, and attached comments on manuscript.

————. *Los llamados Tratados de Bucareli: México y los Estados Unidos en las Convenciones Internacionales de 1923*. Mexico City, 1939.

González Ramírez, Manuel (ed.). *Planes políticos y otros documentos.* Fondo de Cultura Económica, Mexico City, 1954.

Gorena, Abelardo. Conversations.

Greene, Amy Blanche. *The Present Crisis in Our Relations with Mexico.* George H. Doran Company, New York, 1927.

Greene, Graham. *El poder y la gloria.* Imprenta Pérez, Mexico City, 1954.

Greuning, Ernest. *Mexico and Its Heritage.* D. Appleton-Century, 1942 (copyright, 1928).

Gutiérrez Cruz, C. *El brazo de Obregón: Ideario de la Revolución Mexicana.* Ediciones de la Liga de Escritores Revolucionarios, Mexico City, 1924.

Guzmán Esparza, Roberto E. "Contestación a Martín Luis Guzmán." *Excelsior,* February 10, 1958, and February 11, 1958.

————. "La verdad no siempre es bien recibida." *Excelsior,* January 30, 1958, and January 31, 1958.

————. "Prieto Laurens contra don Adolfo de la Huerta." *Excelsior,* January 20, 1958.

————. SEE De la Huerta, *Memorias de don Adolfo.*

Guzmán, Martín Luis. "Cartas vistas." *Excelsior,* February 21, 1958.

————. "Causas de la renuncia de don Adolfo de la Huerta." *Excelsior,* January 27, 1958.

————. *La sombra del Caudillo* (Novela). Tercera edición. Ediciones Botas, Mexico City, 1938.

————. *Memorias de Pancho Villa.* Cia. General de Ediciones, S.A. Second edition, 1954.

Hacienda y Crédito Público, Secretaría de. *La controversia Pani-De la Huerta.* Mexico City, 1924.

————. "Convenio Montes de Oca-Lamont." Typescript, Finance Ministry, Mexico City.

————. *La crisis económica en México y la nueva legislación sobre la moneda y crédito.* Editorial Cultura, Mexico City, 1933.

————. *La deuda exterior de México.* Editorial Cultura, Mexico City, 1926.

————. *La hacienda pública de México a través de los informes presidenciales.* Talleres Gráficos de la Nación, 1951.

————. (Comisión de Revisión Contable). *Informe sobre la revisión de la contabilidad del gobierno federal.* Mexico City, October, 1958.

————. *Compilación de leyes del impuesto sobre la renta (1921–1953).* Dirección General del Impuesto sobre la Renta, Mexico City, 1957.

Hardy, J. K. Conversations.

Heraldo, El, Cia. Editora de, S.A. *Documentos y comentarios relativos a los arreglos financieros llevados a cabo entre el gobierno mexicano y el Comité Internacional de Banqueros.* Mexico City, 1922.

Herrera Lasso, Manuel and Luis L. León. *Controversia: El movimiento revolucionario y el clericalismo mexicano.* Tacubaya, D.F., 1926.

Herrero, Rodolfo. "Habla Rodolfo Herrero," an interview with Roberto Blanco Moheno. *Impacto*, July 16, 1958.

Herring, Hubert and Herbert Weinstock (eds.). *Renascent Mexico.* Covici Friede, New York, 1935.

Hidalgo, Cutberto. Documents used as basis of articles about Tlaxcalantongo tragedy. *Impacto*, September and October, 1958.

Hinojosa, Cosme. Conversation, January 14, 1958.

Hinojosa, Roberto. *El Tabasco que yo he visto.* Mexico City, 1935.

———. *El tren olivo en marcha.* Impreso en los Talleres Gráficos de la Nación, Mexico City, 1937.

Hughes, Charles E. Letter of January 15, 1924, to Senator Henry Cabot Lodge about the "Bucareli" conferences. In the Congressional Record of January 23, 1924, pp. 1325–1327.

Hurley, H. F. Conversations.

Impacto. "Estampas de la Revolución: Quién Mató a Carranza—una entrevista del Doctor Cutberto Hidalgo con Rodolfo Herrero," September 10, 1958; "La culpa de Mariel," September 24, 1958; "El plan de Hermilo," October 1, 1958.

Industria, Comercio y Trabajo. *Ley del petróleo y su reglamento.* Talleres Gráficos de la Nación, Mexico City, 1926.

Instituto Americano de Derecho y Legislación Comparada. *La opinión universal sobre la Doctrina Estrada, expuesta por el gobierno de México, bajo la presidencia de don Pascual Ortiz Rubio.* Mexico City, 1931.

Islas Bravo, Antonio. *La sucesión presidencial de 1928.* Imp. Manuel León Sánche, Mexico City, 1927.

Islas, Felipe and Manuel Múzquiz Blanco. *De la pasión sectaria a la noción de las instituciones.* Mexico City, 1932.

Iturribarría, Jorge Fernando. *Oaxaca en la historia: De la época precolombina a los tiempos actuales.* Publicaciones de la Universidad Benito Juárez de Oaxaca, Editorial Stylo, Mexico City, 1955.

Jiménez Rueda, Alberto. Memorandum of observations about manuscript. December, 1956.

La jornada institucional del día cuatro de septiembre de 1932. Juan José Ríos, P. Ortiz Rubio, A. L. Rodríguez, L. L. León, A. Sáenz. Mexico City, 1932.

Kemmerer, Edwin Walter. *Inflation and Revolution: Mexico's Experience of 1912–1917*. Princeton University Press, Princeton, 1940.

Kubli, Luciano. *Calles y su gobierno*. Leopoldo J. Miranda, 1931.

——. *Sureste Proletario*. Mexico City, April, 1935.

León de Garay, Alfonso. *Catorce rojo: Crónicas de Puebla*. Imprenta Nacional, S.A., Mexico City, 1922.

——. *El palpitar de la casta: Crónicas militares sobre la campaña del Norte contra los pronunciados de Durango, Nuevo León y Coahuila, hasta la toma de Torreón*. Linotipografía Guadalupana, José M. Aguirre, Puebla, 1929.

León, Luis L. "Las conjeturas del Ing. Pani." Reproduced on pp. 69–75 of A. J. Pani's *La historia, agredida* (appeared originally in *El Universal*, 1949).

——. Conversations, including those of June 6, 1955, December 11, 1957, and June 9, 1958.

——. *La doctrina, la táctica y la política agraria de la Revolución: Discurso pronunciado en la convención de la Liga Nacional de Campesinos*. Publicación del "Bloque de Obreros Intelectuales," Talleres Linotipográficos de "El Nacional Revolucionario," Mexico City, 1930.

—— (pseud. "Ignotos"). *El regreso del Gral. Calles: La tragedia del oportunismo mexicano*. Imp. Constitución, Mexico City, December 31, 1935.

——. SEE Herrera Lasso, Manuel.

López Aparicio, Alfonso. *El movimiento obrero en México: Antecedentes, desarrollo y tendencias*. Editorial Jus, Mexico City, 1952.

López Pérez, Rodrigo. *El movimiento obregonista en Michoacán*. Mexico City, 1920.

López Portillo, Fernando. "Algunas aclaraciones: Las memorias de D. Adolfo de la Huerta." *El Universal*, February 4, 1958, and February 11, 1958.

——. Letter in *El Universal*, November 1, 1956.

Luna Morales, Ricardo. *Mi vida revolucionaria*. 1942.

Luque, Francisco G. *La causa Obregón-Cejudo o el tirano hacia el abismo*. Mexico City, 1920.

MacFarland, Charles S. *Chaos in Mexico*. Harper, 1935.

Madero, Raúl. Conversations, 1955 and 1956.

Magdaleno, Mauricio. *Las palabras perdidas*. Fondo de Cultura Económica, Mexico City, 1956.

Magner, James A. *Men of Mexico*. The Bruce Publishing Company, Milwaukee, Second Edition, 1943.

SOURCES OF MATERIAL

Mancisidor, José. *La Revolución Mexicana.* Ediciones de Gusano de Luz, February, 1958.

Manero Suárez, Adolfo and José Paniagua Arredondo. *Los Tratados de Bucareli: Traición y sangre sobre México!* 2 vols. Mexico City, 1958.

Manjarrez, Froylán C. *La jornada institucional.* 2 vols. Talleres Gráficos Editorial y Diario Oficial, Mexico City, 1930.

Marof, Tristán. *México de frente y de perfil.* Colección Claridad, Crítica Social, Buenos Aires, 1934.

Márquez, Miguel B. *El verdadero Tlaxcalantongo.* A. P. Márquez, Mexico City, 1941.

Martínez del Sobral, Enrique. Conversation. November, 1958.

Martínez, Roberto Quirós. *Alvaro Obregón: Su vida y su obra.* 1928.

Maytorena, J. M. *Algunas verdades sobre el General Alvaro Obregón.* Imprenta de El Heraldo de México, Los Angeles, California, 1919.

McCullagh, Francis. *Red Mexico.* Louis Carrier, 1928.

McMahon, William E. (ed.). *Two Strikes and Out.* Country Life Press, Garden City, N.Y., 1939.

Mena Brito, Bernardino. *Felipe Angeles, Federal.* Ediciones Herrerías, Mexico City, 1936.

Mendoza, Salvador. *Las objeciones al Convenio Montes de Oca-Lamont* (privately printed).

Menéndez, Gabriel Antonio. "Peláez no fué guardia blanca." *Impacto,* July 16, 1958.

Meneses V., Pablo. Letters in *El Universal,* November 3, 5, and 6, 1956.

Mexican Light & Power Company. Annual Report for 1955.

Monroy Durán, Luis (also Gonzalo Bautista). *El último caudillo.* José S. Rodríguez, Mexico City, 1924.

Montes de Oca, Luis. Conversation, September 30, 1955.

———. Seven handwritten sheets of notes *re* manuscript, written shortly before his death in 1958.

Mora, Manuel R. *Ensayo sociológico de Tabasco.* Mexico City, 1947.

Morales, Gudelio. *Tres años de lucha sindical (1928–1931).* 1931.

Morones, Luis N. "Discurso en El Teatro Hidalgo, April 30, 1928." *El Universal* of May 2, 1928.

———. Letter in *El Universal,* August 12, 1956.

———. Interview, January 30, 1957; letter, February 16, 1957.

Muñoz, Rafael F. *Pancho Villa: Rayo y azote.* Populibros La Prensa, División de Editora y Periódicos, S.C.L., Mexico City, 1955.

Murguía, S.A., Antigua Librería. *Colección de las efemérides publicadas en el calendario del más antiguo Galván, desde su fundación hasta el 30 de junio de 1950.* Vol. 2; Antigua Librería de Murguía, S.A.; Mexico City, 1950.

Múzquiz Blanco, Manuel. SEE Islas, Felipe.

Naranjo, Francisco. *Diccionario biográfico revolucionario.* Imprenta Editorial Cosmos, Mexico City, 1935.

Nathan, Paul. "México en la época de Cárdenas," No. 3, Vol. VII, *Problemas agrícolas e industriales de México* (with comments by various writers). Mexico City, 1955.

Navarrete, Félix. *Sí hay persecución religiosa en México.* California Printing Co., San Francisco, 1935.

Navarrete, Félix, Eduardo Pallares, and others. *La persecución religiosa en México desde el punto de vista jurídico (Leyes y Decretos).* Mexico City (n.d.).

Nicolson, Harold. *Dwight Morrow.* Harcourt Brace and Company, New York. Fourth Printing, December, 1935.

Nosotros (magazine). "Un informe presidencial memorable." September 8, 1956.

Obregón, Alvaro. *The Agrarian Problem.* Secretaría de Relaciones Exteriores, 1924.

————. *Campaña política del C. Alvaro Obregón, candidato de la presidencia de la República, 1920–1924.* 5 vols. Mexico City, 1923.

————. *Discursos del General Alvaro Obregón.* 2 vols. Biblioteca de la Dir. General de Educación Militar, Mexico City, 1932.

————. *Documentos oficiales relativos al Convenio De la Huerta-Lamont.* (Exchange of documents between Obregón and De la Huerta; also Introduction and Conclusion by Obregón.) Mexico City, 1924.

————. *Informes rendidos ante el H. Congreso de la Unión durante el período de 1921 a 1924, y contestaciones de los CC. Presidentes del Citado Congreso en el mismo período.* Talleres Linotipográficos del *Diario Oficial,* Mexico City, 1924.

————. *Ocho mil kilómetros en campaña.* Librería de la Vda. de Ch. Bouret, Paris, France, and Mexico City, 1917.

Obregón: Aspectos de su vida. Rubén Romero, Juan de Dios Robledo, Dr. Atl, Alfonso Romandía Ferreira, Carlos Trejo y Lerdo de Tejada, Juan de Dios Bojórquez, Ezquiel Padilla, and Aarón Sáenz. Editorial Cultura, Mexico City, 1935.

Obregón M., Vicente. Narrations about De la Huerta rebellion (quoted in Almazán's "Memorias"), *El Universal,* July 13 and July 21, 1958.

Observador, Un. *La rebelión militar contra el gobierno legítimo del Sr. Presidente de la República Lic. D. Emilio Portes Gil.* San Antonio, Texas.

Orcí, Arturo H. Interviews, August, 1956, and December 6 and 31, 1956; letter of September 14, 1957.

————. Letter dated August 31, 1956, and published in *El Universal,* September 3, 1956.

Ortega, Melchor. Conversation, September 13, 1956.

Ortiz Rubio, Pascual. *De mis memorias.* Quoted pp. 227–228 in Luis G. Franco's *Glosa del período del gobierno del C. Gral. e Ing. Pascual Ortiz Rubio, 1930–1932, Ramo de Gobernación.* Mexico City, August, 1947.

———. Interviews, including that of February 2, 1956; letter, February 8, 1956.

———. "Medio siglo: Memorias para la Sociedad de Geografía y Estadística." Typewritten manuscript, January 27, 1954.

———. *Memorias de un penitente.* Imprenta Francisca, Mexico City, 1916.

———. *La Revolución de 1910: Apuntes históricos.* 2a Edición, Botas, Mexico City, 1936.

Padilla, Ezequiel. Conversations; letters; comments on manuscript.

———. *La educación del Pueblo.* Editorial Herrero Hnos., Sucs., 1929.

———. *Los nuevos ideales en Tamaulipas.* Mexico City, 1929.

Palavicini, Félix F. *Como y quienes hicieron la revolución social en México.* Editorial Cultura, Mexico City, 1931.

———. *Mi vida revolucionaria.* Ediciones Botas, Mexico City, 1937.

Palleres, Eduardo. SEE Navarrete, Félix.

Pani, Alberto J. *Apuntes autobiográficos.* One-volume edition by Editorial Stylo, Mexico City, 1945; two-volume edition by Porrua, 1951.

———. *El cambio de regimenes en México y las asonadas militares* (síntesis histórica). Paris, 1929.

———. *Las Conferencias de Bucareli.* Editorial Jus, Mexico City, 1953.

———. *Cuestiones diversas.* Imprenta Nacional, S.A., Mexico City, 1922.

———. *La historia, agredida.* Editorial Polis, Mexico City, 1950.

———. Interview in *El Universal,* August 6, 1949, p. 1.

———. Interview, June 1, 1955.

———. *Memoria de la Secretaría de Hacienda y Crédito Público correspondiente a los años fiscales de 1923, 1924, 1925.* Talleres de la Editorial Cultura, Mexico City, 1926.

———. *Mi contribución al nuevo régimen, 1910–1933.* Cultura, Mexico City, 1936.

———. *Obsesiones y recuerdos.* Mexico City, 1953.

———. *Los orígenes de la política creditica.* Editorial Atlante, S.A., Mexico City, 1951.

———. *La política hacendaria y la Revolución.* Editorial Cultura, Mexico City, 1926.

———. *El problema supremo de México.* Copyright by Inversiones, A.R.P.A., S.A., Mexico City, 1955.

Paniagua Arredondo, José. SEE Manero Suárez, Adolfo.

Parkes, Henry Bamford. *A History of Mexico.* Houghton-Mifflin, 1938.

Parra, Francisco (Governador Constitucional del Estado de Nayarit). (Book published under his auspices). *Síntesis biográfica del Divisionario Michoacano, Lázaro Cárdenas.* Talleres Gráficos del Estado, Tepic, Nayarit, 1934.

Parsons, Wilfrid. *Mexican Martyrdom.* Macmillan, New York, 1936.

Partido Nacional Antirreeleccionista. *Discursos pronunciados por Juan Ramón Solís, José R. Saucedo, Antonio Díaz Soto y Gama, Diego Arénas Guzmán y Antonio I. Villarreal.* Speeches at November 19, 1933 meeting.

Partido Nacional Revolucionario. *Plan sexenal del P.N.R.* Mexico City, 1934.

———. *Primer informe anual que rinde el Comité Ejecutivo Nacional del P.N.R.* June, 1936.

———. *Proyecto de programa de principios y de estatutos que el Comité Organizador del Partido Nacional Revolucionario somete a la consideración de las agrupaciones que concurrirán a la Gran Convención de Querétaro.* Mexico City, January, 1929.

Peral, Miguel A. Comité Militar de Historia. *Diccionario biográfico mexicano.* Comité Militar de Historia, 1956.

Person, Harlow S. *Mexican Oil.* Harper & Brothers, 1942.

Pettus, Daisy Caden. SEE Evans, Rosalie.

Phillips, Henry Albert. *New Designs for Old Mexico.* National Travel Club, New York, 1939.

Ponce, Bernardo. *Adolfo Ruiz Cortines.* Biografías Gandesa, Mexico City, 1952.

Popular, Editorial, S. en C. *Quiénes mataron al General Obregón? Relato histórico de la tragedia de la Bombilla.* Mexico City (n.d.).

Portes Gil, Emilio. Conversation, January 15, 1959; letter, July 20, 1957.

———. *La lucha entre el poder civil y el clero.* Mexico City, 1934.

———. "Pani, el villano del drama." *Hoy* (magazine), 1955.

———. *Quince años de política mexicana.* 2a Edición. Botas, Mexico City, 1941.

———. *Rectificaciones a un libro (de Wm. G. Townsend que contiene la biografía del Sr. General Cárdenas).* Mexico City, 1955.

Prensa, La (Mexico City newspaper). News items, courtesy of library of General de División Rafael Aguirre Manjarrez.

Prensa y Publicidad, Departamento Autónomo de. *México en acción.* Mexico City, 1938.

Prewett, Virginia. *Reportage on Mexico.* E. P. Dutton & Co., Inc., New York, 1941.

Prieto Laurens, Jorge. Articles in *El Universal,* January 12, 13, 14, and 15, 1958, pointing out errors in *Memorias de don Adolfo de la Huerta.*

————. *Balance moral y político de la XXX Legislatura: Documentos para la historia.* Imprenta Franco Elizondo Hnos., Mexico City, 1935.
————. Conversation, November 9, 1955; letter, October 15, 1956.
————. "Habla el Señor Jorge Prieto Laurens," letters on pp. 263–273 of Bernardino Mena Brito's *Felipe Angeles, Federal.*
————. "La memoria del Lic. Sáenz y el caso de San Luis Potosí." In *El Universal,* March 15, 1958.
————. "La República Cooperativa" and "El Banco Nacional Cooperativo Rural" in No. I of *Cooperación: Revista publicada por la Academia de Estudios Sociales y Políticos del Partido Cooperatista Nacional.* Mexico City, December, 1922.
————. *Texto completo del discurso pronunciado por el C. Jorge Prieto Laurens, Presidente del Congreso de la Unión (XXX Legislatura Federal), el día 1° de septiembre de 1923, en respuesta al mensaje presidencial del C. Gral. de Div. Alvaro Obregón.* Mexico City, August 30, 1956.
Puente, Ramón. *La dictadura: La Revolución y sus hombres.* Mexico City, 1938.
————. *Hombres de la Revolución: Calles.* Los Angeles, California, 1933.
Puig Casauranc, J. M. *Galatea rebelde a varios pigmaliones.* Impresores Unidos, Mexico City, 1938.
————. *Mirando la vida.* Mexico City, 1933.
————. *El sentido social del proceso histórico de México.* Ediciones Botas, Mexico City, 1936.

Quevedo M., Rodrigo. Conversation, May, 1956.
Quirk, Robert E. *The Mexican Revolution, 1914–1915; The Convention of Aguascalientes.* Indiana University Press, Bloomington, 1960.
Quiroga, Librería. *La verdad sobre la muerte de Carranza.* San Antonio, Texas (n.d.).
Quiros Martínez, Roberto. *Leonor Llorente de Elías Calles.* Talleres Gráficos de la Nación, Mexico City, 1933.

Ramírez Garrido, J. D. *Así fué.* Mexico City, 1943.
————. *El combate de Palo Verde, reseña y crítica.* 1925.
Ramos Pedrueza, Rafael. *La lucha de clases a través de la historia de México: Revolución democraticoburguesa.* Mexico City, 1941.
Ramos, Roberto. *Bibliografía de la Revolución Mexicana.* Tomo III. Secretaría de Educación Pública, Mexico City, 1940.
Rébora, Roberto E. Conversations.
Relaciones Exteriores, Secretaría de. *La cuestión internacional mexicano-americana durante el gobierno del Gral. Don Alvaro Obregón.* Secretaría de Relaciones Exteriores, Mexico City, 1926.

Retinger, J. H. *Morones of Mexico*. The Labour Publishing Company, Ltd., London, 1926.

———. *Tierra mexicana: The History of Land and Agriculture in Ancient and Modern Mexico*. Noel Douglas, London, 1928.

Rico, Juan. *Yucatán, la huelga de junio*. 2 vols. Mérida, 1922.

Rippy, J. Fred. *The United States and Mexico*. Knopf, 1926.

Rippy, J. Fred, *et al. American Policies Abroad: Mexico*. The University of Chicago Press, 1928.

Riva Palacio, Manuel. Conversation, January 22, 1959.

Rivero del Val, Luis. *Entre las patas de los caballos: Diario de un Cristero*. Segunda Edición. Editorial Jus, Mexico City, 1954.

Riveros, Francisco. *El decreto del 2 de julio y la pastoral colectiva*. Talleres Gráficos de la Nación, Mexico City, 1927.

Robleto, Hernán. *Obregón, Toral y la Madre Conchita*. Ediciones Botas, Mexico City, 1935.

Rodea, Marcelo N. *Historia del movimiento obrero ferrocarrilero en México (1890–1943)*. Mexico City, 1944.

Rodríguez, Abelardo L. "Informe presidencial del 1° de septiembre de 1934" (from *Diario de los debates de las Cámara de Diputados*).

———. Interviews.

Rodríguez F., Ramón. "La pacificación de Baja California." *Excelsior*, February 13, 1958.

Rodríguez, Luis I. *Francisco Murguía, Paradigma de Lealtad*. Ediciones Humanismo, Mexico City, November 1, 1955.

Roel, Faustino. Conversations, letters, and memoranda containing historical data.

Romandía Ferreira, Alfonso. Letters in *El Universal*, July 4 and 6, 1956, and August 7, 1956.

Romero, J. Rubén. *Alvaro Obregón: Discurso pronunciado el día 17 de julio de 1938* ... Mexico City, 1938.

Romero, Salvador J. Memoranda of December 13, December 18, and December 20, 1956; also letters of December 13 and December 21, 1956; comments on manuscript.

Romero Flores, Jesús. *México: Historia de una gran ciudad*. Juan Pablos, 1956.

Ross, Stanley R. "Dwight W. Morrow, embajador de México." A series of articles in *El Universal*, of which Parts IV and V appeared on April 8 and 9, 1958.

———. *Francisco I. Madero: Apostle of Mexican Democracy*. Columbia University Press, New York, 1955.

Royer, Fanchón. *Padre Pro*. P. J. Kennedy & Sons, 1954.

Ruiz, Joaquín. *La Revolución en Tabasco*. Mexico City, 1934.

Sáenz, Aarón. Interviews, including that of February 2, 1956.

————. "Las 'Memorias' de De la Huerta y la política internacional de Obregón." Series of 32 articles. *Excelsior*, February 17, 1958, through March 30, 1958.

————. A 37-page "Prologo" for Carlos Barrera's *Obregón: Estampas de un caudillo*. Mexico City, 1957.

————. "El Vencedor de León fué el Gral. Alvaro Obregón." Articles in *El Universal*, August 14 and 15, 1958.

Salazar, Rosendo. *México en pensamiento y en acción*. Editorial Avante, Mexico City, 1926.

Salazar, Rosendo and José G. Escobedo. *Las pugnas de la gleba*. Editorial Avante, Mexico City, 1923.

Salazar Rovirosa, Alfonso. *Cronología de Baja California: Del territorio y del estado, de 1500 a 1956: Cuadernos Bajacalifornianos*. 10 books. Impreso en "Litografía Artística," S.A., Mexico City, January–October, 1957.

Saldaña, José P. *Episodios de ayer*. Sistemas y Servicios Técnicos, S.A., Monterrey, Nuevo León, 1959.

Salido Orcillo, Rubén. "Las memorias de don Adolfo de la Huerta." *Excelsior*, May 20, 1958.

Salinas, León. Interview, January 16, 1956; letter of January 30, 1956, *re* notes on the interview. Also conversation of February 16, 1956.

Santamaría, Francisco J. *El periodismo en Tabasco*. Ediciones Botas, Mexico City, 1936.

————. *La tragedia de Cuernavaca en 1927 y mi escapatoria célebre*. Mexico City, 1939.

Schlarman, Joseph H. L. *Mexico: A Land of Volcanoes*. Bruce Publishing Co., 1950.

Secretaría de Bienes Nacionales e Inspección Administrativa. SEE Bienes Nacionales e Inspección Administrativa, Secretaría de.

Secretaría de Hacienda y Crédito Público. SEE Hacienda y Crédito Público, Secretaría de.

Secretaría de Industria, Comercio y Trabajo. SEE Industria, Comercio y Trabajo, Secretaría de.

Secretaría de la Economía Nacional. SEE Economía Nacional, Secretaría de.

Secretaría de Relaciones Exteriores. SEE Relaciones Exteriores, Secretaría de.

Septien, Alfonso. *La última reforma monetaria*. Publicaciones de la Academia Mexicana de Jurisprudencia y Legislación Correspondiente de la España, Mexico City, 1936.

Serrano, Francisco R. *Manifiesto a la nación del Ciudadano General de División Francisco R. Serrano, candidato antirreeleccionista a la presidencia de la República*. Mexico City, July 23, 1927.

Shea, Donald R. *The Calvo Clause.* University of Minnesota Press, Minneapolis, 1955.

Sherwell, G. Butler. *Mexico's Capacity To Pay: A General Analysis of the Present International Economic Position of Mexico.* Washington, 1929.

Simpson, Eyler N. *The Ejido: Mexico's Way Out.* University of North Carolina, Chapel Hill, 1937.

Simpson, Lesley Byrd. *Many Mexicos.* G. P. Putnam's Sons, New York, 1941, 1946.

Sodi de Pallares, María Elena. *Los Cristeros y José de León Toral.* Editorial Cultura, Mexico City, 1936.

Stevens, Guy. *Current Controversies with Mexico: Addresses and Writings (1926–1928)* (no publication facts available).

Stevens, Guy, *et al. American Policies Abroad: Mexico.* The University of Chicago Press, 1928.

Strode, Hudson. *Timeless Mexico.* Harcourt, Brace and Company, New York, 1944.

Suárez, Eduardo. Interviews, including that of June 23, 1955.

Suárez, Ignacio. Account of events at Tlaxcalantongo, May 20–21, 1920. In *Impacto,* August 13, 1958.

Tabasco Revolucionario (1929? P.N.R.?) (No date, publisher, or author shown. Tabasco and the Ortiz Rubio presidential campaign.)

Tamayo, J. A. *El Gral. Obregón y la guerra.* Talleres Linotipográficos de El Mundo, Tampico, Tamaulipas.

Tannenbaum, Frank. Conversation, June 19, 1955.

————. *The Mexican Agrarian Revolution.* The Macmillan Company, New York, 1929.

————. *Peace by Revolution: An Interpretation of Mexico.* Columbia University Press, New York, 1933.

Taracena, Alfonso. *Mi vida en el vértigo de la Revolución.* Botas, Mexico City, 1936.

————. *Los Vasconcelistas sacrificados en Topilejo.* Colección Resplandor, Clásica Selecta. Editora Librera, Mexico City, 1958.

Taracena, Rosendo. *Historia de Tabasco.* Ediciones Botas, Mexico City, 1937.

Terrazas, Alfredo. Conversation, June 14, 1957.

Terrones Benítez, Alberto. Conversations.

————. *El Departamento Autónomo Agrario y el problema de la distribución de tierras.* Décima Convención Nacional de Ingenieros, Mazatlán, Sinaloa. Imprenta Reveles, Mexico City, 1934.

————. *Sindicato de Campesinos Agraristas del Estado de Durango, Informe que el Lic. Alberto Terrones Benítez, Presidente del Consejo Ejecutivo, rinde ante el Quinto Congreso Agrarista del Estado reunido en la C. de Durango el 1° de enero de 1925.* (no publication facts)

Terrones Langone, Eduardo. Historical data.

Terry, T. Philip. *Terry's Guide to Mexico.* Houghton-Mifflin, 1925.

Thompson, Wallace. *The Mexican Mind.* Little, Brown and Company, Boston, 1922.

Topete, Ricardo. Conversations.

Toral, José de León, and others. *El jurado de Toral y la Madre Conchita.* Stenographic text, 2 vols. Mexico City (n.d.).

Toro, Alfonso. *La iglesia y el estado en México.* Secretaría de Gobernación. Talleres Gráficos de la Nación, Mexico City, 1927.

Torreblanca, Fernando. Interview, 1955.

Torres, Elías L. *Como murió Pancho Villa.* El Libro Español, Mexico City, 1955.

Tovar, Mariano. *El dictador de Tabasco: Reivindicación y justicia.* Villahermosa, March, 1936.

Townsend, William Cameron. *Lázaro Cárdenas: Mexican Democrat.* Wahr, 1952.

Trabajo, Departamento del. *La obra social del Presidente Rodríguez.* Talleres Gráficos de la Nación, Mexico City, 1934.

Trejo, Francisco. *El Banco Unico de Emisión y las demás instituciones de crédito en México.* Mexico City, 1921.

Trejo Lerdo de Tejada, Carlos. *Norte contra sur: Obregón, Calles, Ortiz Rubio.* Talleres Gráficos de la Nación, Mexico City, 1931.

Treviño, Jacinto B. Conversations, October 17, 1955, and August 8, 1956.

Trujillo, Rafael. "El Gral. Calles y los Tratados de Bucareli." *Excelsior,* April 10, 1958.

Turlington, Edgar. *Mexico and Her Foreign Creditors.* Columbia University Press, New York City, 1930.

Ugalde, José. *Quién es Ortíz Rubio.* Talleres Linotipográficos, Papelería Nacional, 1929.

Ugarte, Gerzayn. *Por qué volví a Tlaxcalantongo.* Mexico City, 1954.

United States Department of the Interior, Bureau of Mines. *Four Hundred Years of Mining History in Mexico, 1521 to 1937.* Mineral Trade Notes, Special Supplement No. 13 to Vol. 24, No. 4. Washington, D.C., April 21, 1947.

Universal, El. "Que es apócrifo el recado de Cárdenas a Herrero, ordenando la muerte de Carranza." August 21, 1958.

————. News items.

Universal Gráfica (Mexico City newspaper). News items, courtesy of library of General de División Rafael Aguirre Manjarrez.

Urquizo, Francisco L. *Carranza.* 6a Edición. Mexico City, 1954.

————. *Mexico-Tlaxcalantongo—Mayo de 1920.* Segunda Edición. Editorial Cultura, Mexico City, 1943.

738

Uribe Romo, Emilio. *Abelardo L. Rodríguez; De San José de Guaymas al Castillo de Chapultepec; Del Plan de Guadalupe al Plan Sexenal.* Talleres Gráficos de la Nación, Mexico City, 1934.
Ursua, Francisco A. SEE Fabila, Gilberto.

Valenzuela, Clodoveo. SEE Chaverri Matamoros, Amado.
Valenzuela, Gilberto. Conversation, May 30, 1956.
Vasconcelos, José. *Breve historia de México.* Sexta Edición. Botas, Mexico City, 1950.
———. *El desastre.* Ediciones Botas, Mexico City, 1951.
———. "La Flama." Articles in magazine *Hoy,* September, 1958.
———. *El proconsulado.* Tercera Edición. Botas, Mexico City, 1946.
Vasconcelos, José, *et al. American Policies Abroad: Mexico.* The University of Chicago Press, 1928.
Vázquez del Mercado, Francisco. *La deuda exterior de México.* Mexico City, 1931.
Velasco, Gustavo R. Conversations, August, 1956, and January 15, 1959. Notes and observations on manuscript, May 27, 1958.
Vera Estanol, Jorge. *La Revolución Mexicana: Orígenes y resultados.* Editorial Porrua, S.A., Mexico City, 1957.
Villa, Eduardo W. *Compendio de historia del estado de Sonora.* Editorial Patria Nueva, Mexico City, 1937.
Villalobos Ruiz, José E. "Breves datos biográfico-políticos de Don Nazario S. Ortiz Garza." Memorandum for Señor Licenciado Ezequiel Padilla, Mexico City, March 11, 1957.

Weinstock, Herbert. SEE Herring, Hubert.
Weyl, Nathaniel and Sylvia Weyl. *The Reconquest of Mexico.* Oxford University Press, 1939.

Zambrano, Santiago M. Conversations; comments on manuscript.
Zubaran Capmany, Rafael. Letter of September 27, 1924, to Adolfo de la Huerta, reproduced in Capetillo's *La Rebelión sin cabeza,* pp. 294–307 and in Manero Suárez and Paniagua Arredondo's *Los Tratados de Bucareli: Traición y sangre sobre México!,* pp. 339–344.

INDEX

Index

746

748

750

Calles, Plutarco Elías—*continued*
  Portes Gil, 404; in Portes Gil Cabinet, 441; and Portes Gil's candidacy in Tamaulipas, 519–520; confers with Portes Gil, 520; enthusiasm of, for Portes Gil's Catholic study, 564–565
  —power of: increasing influence of, 132; "tyranny" of, 396; and rebuke of Cabinet officers, 509; and seeming rebuke of Cabinet members, 509; as "Jefe Maximo," 521–522; functions of, defined by Puig Casauranc, 525; as "Iron Man" of Mexico, 557–558; as "strong man of Mexico," 559; dynasty of, 582; as dictator, 672–673
  —as public official: as police commissioner of Agua Prieta, 5; as governor of Sonora, 14; as Minister of Industry and Commerce, 20; named head of Sonora military operations, 23; and internal state conflicts, 103; declines to intervene in state election, 182; inauguration of, 268–269; as executive, 269–270; new Cabinet of, 273; Cabinet of, in debate, 306; annual message of, to Congress, 306–308, 383–386; pardons prisoners, 311; in Cabinet, 526; suggests Cabinet changes, 527; as War Minister, 532; as Finance Minister, 555
  —and public works: 281; road building, 290; and irrigation, 291
  —in religious problem: and work at Cubilate, 299; supports schismatic Mexican church, 300; makes decree on La Soledad, 300; orders compliance with religious rulings, 301; takes legal action against Mora y del Río, 302; and punishment of rebellious acts, 303; insures penal laws on religion, 303; government of, boycotted, 303–304; suggests solutions for Catholics, 306; and Pro brothers, 315; and Roberto Pro, 315; and religious problem, 329–330; on spiritual functions of the Church, 460; and religious question, 463; and expulsion of Catholic bishops, 564; reviled by Catholics, 656
  —return of, to Mexico: 659; statement of, on return, 660–661; protested, 661, 665–666; intentions of, 661; steps to weaken position of, 661–663; mistake of, in, 663; as center of rebellion, 663; views of, in *El Instante*, 663; and statement on anti-Callista actions, 663–664; uses foreign press, 664–665; "Patriotic Declarations of . . . ," 665; replies to Puig's telegram, 667–668; defends himself, 667; makes final statement, 679; fall of the curtain for, 681
  —trial of: 668; charges against, in, 668–669; tried for smuggling arms, 668–670; testimony of, in, 670–672; under guard after, 675; sentenced to expulsion, 676–679
  —as soldier: as expert in fortifications, 14; orders Guajardo against Villa, 73; against Villa, 177; in military function, 222; recruits forces, 223; at Irapuato, 250; in charge of campaign against rebels, 444; in Escobar rebellion, 442; on northern campaign, 446–448; weakens Aguirre's position, 444–445; at Aguascalientes, 446; at Bermejillo, Durango, 449; and construction of railroad, 449; air force of, 449; headquarters of, moved, 452; reports to Portes Gil, 452; and treatment of prisoners, 455; confers with Almazán, 455
  —support of: 306; political, 174; by Manrique, 181; and advisers of, 264; and orders of, to followers, 538
Calles, Plutarco Elías, Jr.: as brother-in-law of Sáenz, 434; pro-Cárdenas sentiment of, 572; and Nuevo León, 582; backed by P.N.R., 635; as gubernatorial candidate, 646; mentioned, 662
Calles, Rodolfo Elías: and constitutional amendment, 509; and re-election, 509; and Rodríguez, 571; work of, for Cárdenas, 572; influence of, for Cárdenas, 573; as political leader, 579; as "Prince" of Sonora, 582; at inauguration, 603; in Cabinet, 606; meets Plutarco Elías Calles, 634; resignation of, rumored, 641; welcomes Calles, 659–660
Calles Dam: 292, 404
Calles de Pasquel, Ernestina, Sra.: at "Santa Barbara," 678
Calles Doctrine: Ortiz Rubio's loyalty to, 538
Callismo: and Obregonismo, 395; "Death to —," 581; attacked, 581–582; and looting, 585; membership of, 641
Callistas: led by De la Huerta, 175; attack De la Huerta, 204; and Ortizrubistas, 490; not to form opposition to Ortiz Rubio, 537; retained by Garrido Canabal, 614; schism between, and Cardenistas, 634–635; and fight in Chamber, 646; expelled from Senate, 661; expelled from governorships, 661–662; plot of feared, 661, 662, 663, 664, 668, 672;

766

Gil Farías, Pedro: as Carrancista, 42; as prisoner of Herrero, 49; and "suicide" document, 50; mentioned, 45, 52, 109
gold: confiscation of, 65. SEE ALSO currency
Gold Shirts (Acción Revolucionaria Mexicana): fighting Red Shirts, 625; as new organization, 628; and striking laborers, 628–629; in battle, 646–648
Gómez, Abundio: 34, 67, 389
Gómez, Arnulfo R.: assistance of, to Calles, 11; and candidacy of Obregón, 24; deserts Carranza, 34; supports Plan of Agua Prieta, 53; as ally of Calles, 53; fights Hernández, 116; harasses Delahuertistas, 223; at Calles' inauguration, 269; on trip for military studies, 332; as presidential candidate, 333, 335; campaign of, 336–337, 338; health of, 342; leaves Mexico City, 342; solicitude of, for supporters, 342–343; troops of, routed, 353; in hiding, 353; trial and execution of, 353; burial of, 353; and conflict with Obregón, 353–354; and Vasconcelos, 418; mentioned, 73, 110, 210, 215, 216, 234–235, 271, 333, 334, 335, 337, 338, 340, 343, 346, 351, 352, 396, 420, 422, 445, 472, 581
Gómez, Filiberto: as presiding officer, 268; in P.N.R., 433; mentioned, 432, 575
Gómez, José F. (Che Gómez): executed, 255
Gómez, Lorenzo: fights Gold Shirts, 648
Gómez, Marte R.: and agrarian legislation, 291; comments on Serrano and Arnulfo Gómez, 353; advises Calles, 380; and Morones, 381; leads anti-Topete group, 391; in Cabinet, 407; cancels contracts, 407–408; and land expropriation, 479; and shooting of Ortiz Rubio, 485; suspected, 487; at London Economic Conference, 550; on wages commission, 553; befriends Pani's brothers, 556; as Finance Minister, 556; and Cárdenas candidacy, 571; and debt agreement with U.S., 593; mentioned, 393, 395, 555
Gómez, Rodrigo: accompanies Obregón, 86; and Sáenz, 355
Gómez Arias, Alejandro: and Vasconcelos, 419, 473–474
Gómez Morín, Manuel: as one of "Seven Wise Men of Greece," 81; and Bank of Mexico, 283–284; aids

Vasconcelos, 472; advises against rebellion, 476; and permanent opposition party, 478; and monetary law, 505; and silver coinage, 516; mentioned, 477
Gómez Robledo, Antonio: Bucareli Conferences interpreted by, 169
Gómez Vizcarra, Francisco: with Arnulfo Gómez, 353
Gompers, Samuel: at Calles' inauguration, 268–269; and Pan-American Federation of Labor, 274, 276
Góngora, Victorio: and P.N.A., 419; on election results, 476; requests investigation of Topilejo, 488
González, Bernabé: 454
González, Cholita: on Morones, 372
González, Eulogio: in poison plot, 363; at Toral trial, 399; treatment of, by General Police, 401
González, Gonzalo: 278
González, Lucas: in Yaqui rebellion, 312; pursues rebels, 452; mentioned, 245
González, Marciano: as Carrancista, 42; freed by De la Huerta, 66; mentioned, 45, 50, 58, 113
González, Otilio: 348, 581
González, Pablo: traits of, as general, 6; and Obregón, 9, 25, 39, 58; campaign of, against Zapatistas, 13; refusal of, to back Bonillas, 20; announces candidacy, 20; as opposition candidate, 24, 35; military force of, 35; endangers Carranza, 35–36; enters Mexico City, 36; as head of Liberal Revolutionary Army, 38; and Plan of Agua Prieta, 38; manifesto of, 39; congratulations for, 39; and Interim President, 56; requests Pani's support, 60; as problem for De la Huerta, 71; revolt of, 73; disloyalty of, 73–74; trial of, 74; withdraws as presidential candidate, 84; mentioned, 11, 38, 52, 56, 57, 59, 61, 72, 78
González, Porfirio: 73
González, Vicente: withdraws to Villahermosa, 243; declares for De la Huerta, 244; at Esperanza, 244; on mission to New Orleans, 245; advances on Diéguez and Vigil, 255; gets revenge in Tabasco, 261, 262; in danger, 347; at Balbuena Airport, 678; mentioned, 230, 606, 675, 677
González Aparicio, Enrique: and Vasconcelos, 419
González de Ayala González, Soledad, Sra.: at "Santa Barbara," 678
González Flores, Enrique: at inauguration, 602

770

lem, 551; and religion, 359; schools
for, 559–560; and Six-Year Plan,
567–568; and Cárdenas, 588; agitation of, 608; unrest in, 625. SEE ALSO
Morones, Luis R.; Partido Laborista
Mexicano; Partido Socialista del
Sureste
—disputes: dockworkers in, 141; railway workers in, 141–144; power-
company workers in, 143; utility
workers in, 273; negotiation of, 513,
514; bases for settlement of, 600;
and national economy, 638, 642;
mentioned, 200. SEE ALSO strikes
—leaders of: and Madre Conchita,
377–378; honesty in, 469; and workers, 600; bickering among, 600; as
agitators, 600; criticized by Calles,
637–638
—legislation: 94, 156, 493; criticized
by Murguía, 116; code of, promised
by Obregón, 357; federal, 411, 413,
513; state, 413; and Article 123,
513, 514; minimum wages in, 554
—organization of: in Yucatán, 137;
and Morones, 273; and confedera
tion of labor unions, 274; as world
movement, 423; and unification,
603; in Tabasco, 615; mentioned,
274, 275, 278. SEE ALSO labor, unions
—problems of: and working and living
conditions, 98, 287, 293, 514, 553,
601; and remedial benefits, 213, 514,
551, 553; and social security benefits, 276–277; and low-cost housing,
287; and relief of conditions, 296;
activity for, 599–600; welfare of,
and Cárdenas, 642; wages of, 513,
553, 554, 598, 601, 615
—unions: membership of, 292–293;
support Calles, 306; and Obregón,
380–381; as means of oppression,
567; as bargaining agents, 600;
privileges of, 600; added strength of,
600; most important of, 600; rights
of, 601; strengthened by Cárdenas,
629–630; Cárdenas' confidence in,
642; ask expulsion of Calles, 663;
protest return of Calles, 665–666
Labor Department: creation of, 546,
600
Labor, Ministry of: reorganization of,
600
Laboristas. SEE Partido Laborista
Mexicano
Labor Party. SEE Partido Laborista
Mexicano
Laborde, Hernán: as Communist presidential candidate, 586
Labougle, Emilio: 315

Labra, Senator: and Permanent Com-
mission, 609
La Cruz, Sinaloa: 499
La Fleur (Canadian arbiter): in El
Chamizal dispute, 594; award of, to
Mexico, 595
"La Florida": 620
Laguna del Carmen, Campeche: 142,
143, 247
"La Hormiga": 416
Lake Chapala: 191, 192, 215, 250, 251
Lamont, Thomas W.: heads Interna-
tional Committee of Bankers, 148;
visits Mexico, 148; in Pani-De la
Huerta dispute, 201; discussed by
De la Huerta, 202; and U.S. debt
agreement, 593. SEE ALSO De la
Huerta-Lamont Agreement; Pani-
Lamont Amendment; Montes de
Oca-Lamont Agreement
land problem. SEE agrarian problem
Lane, Arthur Bliss: greets Ortiz Rubio,
478
La Piedad, Michoacán: 251, 253, 561
Lara, J. Félix: protects Villa, 178–179;
in Yaqui rebellion, 312
Laredo, Texas: 22, 115, 310, 352, 418
Lasso de la Vega, Arturo: 352
Lastra, Agapito: executed, 349
Lastra Ortiz, Manuel: as governor of
Tabasco, 614; installed as governor,
623; blames Brito, 656; blamed by
students, 656; removed, 658
Las Vargas, Chihuahua: 454
"Las Viejas": leak military plans, 253
Las Vigas, Veracruz: 225
La Unión, Puebla: 50
Law of *Ejido* Patrimony: enacted, 291
Law School (of National University):
284; examinations in, 464; student
strikes in, 464–465; and violence in,
465; petition of students of, to Portes
Gil, 465; students of, request resig-
nations, 465
League of Nations: approved by labor,
276; Julio Pani at, 556
Leagues of Agrarian Communities:
support Cárdenas, 571
League To Defend Religious Liberty.
SEE Liga Defensora de la Libertad
Religiosa
Lechuga, César: 43, 52
"leftists": in Congress, 608–610. SEE
ALSO Left Wing
Left Wing
—of Congress: supports Cárdenas,
609–610; formation of, 610;
strengthened, 643; attains majority,
643–644; approves trial of Calles,
668

784

788

YESTERDAY IN MEXICO

petroleum problem—*continued*
—legislation for: proposed by Carranza, 160; regulation of, 163; and Petroleum Law of 1925, 319, 320, 328; U.S. complaints against, 321
—production in: taxes against, 198; collapse in, 294; and Russian schemes, 480; recovery in, 591–592
—and petroleum district: in rebellion of De la Huerta, 225; and De la Huerta rebel government, 229; Delahuertistas in, 246; U.S. occupation of, 247; mentioned, 34
Phoenix, Arizona: 263
Piedras Negras, Coahuila: 448
Piedritas, Durango: 116
Pierce Oil Company: loans from, 632
Pineda, J. Guadalupe: and trial of Calles, 662–663
Pineda O., Alberto: deserts Carranza, 34; rebellious attitude of, 75; spy of, 75; revolts against Obregón, 243; mentioned, 244, 254
Pino Suárez, José María: assassination of, 91–92
Pipsa: and newspapers, 663
Plan Calles: and relation between gold and silver, 506; deflationary effects of, 508; as cause of Montes de Oca's fall, 510; mentioned, 505, 506, 515
planes. SEE airplanes
Plan of Agua Prieta: formulation of, 33; signers of, 33; writers of, 33, 52; declarations of, 33–34; and Treviño, 35; and Hernández, 43; and Herrero, 50; Valenzuela's role in, 52; supporters of, in Tampico, 53; triumph of, 60; and state constitutional powers, 76; and Plan of Veracruz, 219; mentioned, 38, 39, 55, 64, 102, 192, 416, 439. SEE ALSO Agua Prieta movement
Plan of Guadalupe: starts revolution against Victoriano Huerta, 34
Plan of Guaymas: drawn up by Vasconcelos, 475; and rebellion, 476; publication of, 477; and death of Bouquet, 478
Plan of Hermosillo: as basis of Plan of Agua Prieta, 33; against "imposition," 438; as call of people to revolt, 438; written by Valenzuela, 438; as recital of Calles' crimes, 438; and Portes Gil, 438; mentioned, 448
Plan of Liberators: 397
Plan of Saltillo: by Murguía, 113
Plan of Veracruz: and De la Huerta, 218, 218–219; and Plan of Agua Prieta, 219; charges in, 219; mentioned, 222
Plan of Xilitla: revealed, 218

Plan of Zaragoza: issued by Murguía, 116
Plan Revolucionario de Oaxaca. SEE Oaxaca Plan
"Plans": defined, 33
Platt, Juan: at Calles trial, 668
Plaza de la Constitución: as scene of Gold Shirt battle, 646; mentioned, 129, 306, 680
Plaza de la República: Pani's plans for, 548–550
P.L.C. SEE Partido Liberal Constitucionalista
P.L.D. SEE Partido Liberal Democrático
P.L.M. SEE Partido Laborista Mexicano
P.N.R. SEE Partido Nacional Revolucionario
Policía Constitucionalista. SEE Constitutionalist Police Force
Politeama Theatre: 581
political parties: and power, 335–336; improvised, 357; and democracy, 358, 457–458; large number of, 409–410; consolidations of, 409–410; of permanency, 410; advisability of two rival, 410; financial systems of, 435; in stable government, 542; used for personal ends, 579
political party, Revolutionary: propitious time for, 409
Pope Pius XI: demands of, 462; and Mexican clerical legislation, 562; mentioned, 304, 461
"populace": in presidential election, 340–341
Portales Colony: 668
Portes Gil, Emilio: supervises relief work, 107; as president of P.C.N., 134; opposes Prieto Laurens, 186; and No Re-election, 333; and Cruz, 372, 423; in Cabinet, 381, 482, 546, 605; opponents of, 392, 646; supporters of, 392; and program of the Revolution, 393, 406, 679; as leader, 402; and free election, 404; and federal debt, 406, 501; and differences with Montes de Oca, 407; and fraud in office, 408; and freedom of speech, 411; and Vasconcelos, 420; and Toral case, 425; on Sáenz, 429; belief of, in Tejeda, 437; high regard for, 467–468; and Germán de Campo, 474–475; danger to, from Russia, 480; and Daniel Flores, 486–487; replaces Vadillo, 496; and Morrow, 502; as minister to France, 519; and Tamaulipas governorship, 520; in El Chamizal dispute, 595; and Froylán C. Manjárrez, 641; on P.C.R., 664;

790

Progreso de Zaragoza, Veracruz: 52
Pro Juárez, Ana María: 312
Pro Juárez, Humberto: and Liga Defensora, 312; executed, 315; as friend of José de León Toral, 364; mentioned, 313
Pro Juárez, Miguel: undercover activities of, 312, 313; and police force, 312; executed, 315; and Toral, 364; mentioned, 327
Pro Juárez, Roberto: and Liga Defensora, 312; exiled, 315; mentioned, 398
Pro Juárez brothers: arrested, 313–315; and Madre Conchita, 362–363
property rights, foreign. SEE agrarian problem; Bucareli Conferences; Claims Commissions; Mixed Claims Commission; General Claims Commision; petroleum problem; Special Claims Commission
public works: funds for, 91, 286; encouraged by Calles, 281; promoted, 287; and irrigation, 291–292; interest in, of Ortiz Rubio, 494; program of, 592; and Rodríguez, 592; mentioned, 282
Puebla: and Carranza's final march, 42; provisional governor for, 77; troubles in, 103; troops from, 209; defended by Almazán, 221; strategic importance of, 223, 225; Vasconcelistas in, 474; government of, 529; Red Shirts in, 621; general strike in, 629, 630; mentioned, 20, 38, 43, 51, 53, 57, 110, 116, 128, 133, 185, 189, 207, 224, 225, 237, 245, 256, 266, 383, 444, 529, 568, 641, 661
Puebla, Puebla: 220, 224, 225, 256
Puente, Ambrosio: and message from Calles, 346; captives of, 349; mentioned, 347
Puerto Alvaro Obregón (Frontera), Tabasco: 614, 618
Puerto Angel, Oaxaca: 256, 258
Puerto Escondido, Oaxaca: 258
Puig Casauranc, Carlos: 184
Puig Casauranc, J. M.: opposes Prieto Laurens, 186; in Cabinet, 269, 382, 407, 482, 524–525, 546; and roads, 290; and farm credit, 291; and schools, 292; in debate on church-state, 306; at Chapultepec, 349; fears of, for Manrique, 386–387; and Portes Gil, 392, 467–468; and P.N.R., 408–409, 410; as ghost writer, 412, 457; and Sáenz candidacy, 415; and student strikes, 465; and autonomy of National University, 466–467; oath of office of, 485; questions Flores, 486; resignation

of, 497; on Montes de Oca in politics, 508–509; named ambassador to U.S., 522; and resignation of Pani's brothers, 556; and lunch for Daniels, 558; in El Chamizal dispute, 595, 596; writes memorandum on international commissions, 596; on Bank of Mexico, 633; mentioned, 270, 351, 410, 434, 485, 509, 519, 530, 536
—and Calles: works for Calles, 184; directs Calles campaign, 194; clears Calles, 239; advises Calles, 264, 666–667; with Calles, 265; for longer Calles term, 383; and Calles' address, 384; on Calles, 490–492; on Calles' sons in politics, 509; defines functions of Calles, 525; with Calles in Boston, 532; and Calles as dictator, 672
—and Ortiz Rubio: with Ortiz Rubio, 478; and Ortiz Rubio Cabinet, 479; and Ortiz Rubio's candidacy, 429–430; as joint-author of Ortiz Rubio statement, 525–526; refuses Ortiz Rubio appointment, 534
Púlpito Canyon (Púlpito Pass): as invasion route, 5; mentioned, 357, 448, 454
Putla, Oaxaca: 256

Querétaro: provisional governor for, 77; limits Catholic Church, 531; mentioned, 34, 213, 340
Querétaro, Querétaro: as scene of P.N.R. convention, 427, 470, 567; mentioned, 428
Querétaro Congress: 83
Querétaro Constitutional Assembly: 213, 427
Querétaro Convention: 427–433; influence of generals in, 429, 430; rebellion as factor in, 429; and Six-Year Plan, 598; mentioned, 417, 436, 439. SEE ALSO Partido Nacional Revolucionario
Quevedo Moreno, Rodrigo: at Esperanza, 244; against Catholics, 310–311; at Jiménez, 449; with Almazán, 454; mentioned, 226, 245, 449
"Quinta Chilla": 4
Quintana, Valente: sent to protect Vasconcelos and students, 123; in Padre Pro case, 313; and Toral case, 374, 399; dismissal of, requested, 465; injured, 475; confusion over tenure of, 485; mentioned, 425
Quintana Roo: 139, 231
Quintero, Rafael: and labor in politics, 276

Villarreal, Antonio J.—*continued*
presidential aspirant, 418; agreement of, with Vasconcelos, 418;
campaign of, 422; at Monterrey,
422; lost eligibility of, 471; as candidate for nomination, 579; as opposition candidate, 580; and presidential candidacy, 583; nominated
for president, 584
—in Serrano rebellion: 343; in Serrano
"Cabinet," 344; in Cuernavaca, 345;
warning of, 346
Villarreal, Irineo: revolt of, against
De la Huerta, 73
Villarreal, Julián: at Red Cross Hospital, 485
Villarreal, Rafael: defeats Portes Gil,
521
Villarrealistas: violence of, 589
Villistas: in opposition to Obregón, 3;
and De la Huerta, 78; fought by
Calles, 177; and Special Claims Commission, 318; mentioned, 11, 13, 42,
69
Virgin of Guadalupe: altar of, violated,
298; 400th anniversary of, 529, 530
Vizcana, Rubén: 210

wages: discussed by Obregón, 96; real,
553, 554; minimum, 553; commission on, 553–554; and minimum
wage commission, 553–554
Waldorf Astoria: 593
Wall Street: 328, 338
Walsh, Edmund: 461
Ward Line: shuns Yucatán, 235
Warren, Charles Beecher: represents
U.S. at Bucareli Conferences, 163;
treatment of, in Mexico, 164; replies to welcome, 164; and "Panama" crisis, 165; and Vasconcelos,
169; statement of, on Bucareli Conferences, 169, 170; received by Obregón, 265; and Mrs. Evans, 266, 267;
mentioned, 166, 202
Washington, the: surrenders to federals, 453
Washington, D.C.: 65, 202, 228, 229,
259, 262, 318, 328, 443, 477, 478,
498, 550, 594, 595, 644
water-apportionment dispute: 596; and
Boulder Dam, 595
White House: visited by De la Huerta,
155–156; mentioned, 265
Whites: 481–482; defeated by Calles,
496; mentioned, 495
Wiechers, Luciano: and monetary law,
505
Wilson, Woodrow: and support of De
la Huerta, 75; Administration of,

159; Fourteen Points of, 498; mentioned, 597
"wolves of Wall Street"; 155
Wood, U.S. Consul: 229
Worker Congress of Izamal: 139; condemns tobacco, 139; mentioned, 138,
139, 143
Worker Congress of Motul: 138–139;
and liquor, 138; and marihuana,
138; mentioned, 138
World Monetary and Economic Conference in London: Pani at, 550;
silver agreement of, 590; helpfulness of, 591; mentioned, 550
World War I: henequen sales during,
81; alignment of Mexicans in, 89
World War II: effect of, on people,
371

Xaltepuxtla River: 51

Yáñez, Miguel E.: replaces Topete in
Obregonista bloc, 391
Yáñez Maya, Jesús: as Callista Candidate, 635; backed by P.N.R., 635;
replaced and accused, 661–662;
charges against, 662
Yaqui Indians: as cause of political
conflict, 23; as prison guard, 27;
support Obregón, 27; at inauguration of De la Huerta, 64; esteem
De la Huerta, 65; in battle, 226; in
Veracruz, 246; at Ocotlán, 251; and
train holdup, 311–312; rebellion of,
311–312; surrender of, 312; pleased
with railway, 312; at Perote, 437;
mentioned, 424
Yaqui River: land allotment on, 97
"Year of Hunger": 14
Yocupicio, Román: 454
Yucatán: provisional governor for, 77;
troubled government of, 77; visited
by Vasconcelos, 121; and Carrillo
Puerto, 128; failure of P.L.C. in,
136; and henequen, 137; and control
of railroads, 141–142; sensation in,
over Carrillo Puerto killings, 234;
increasing restlessness in, 235; rebel
control of, 259; under Aguilar, 261;
limits number of clergy, 302; labor
law in, 413; as one-product state,
612; mentioned, 72, 81, 110, 128,
132, 142, 152, 230, 234, 245, 262,
356, 383, 432, 575
Yúdico, Samuel: and C.D.O., 21; and
Morones, 273; and Communism,
274–275; credentials of, 275; supports Calles, 306; and Madre Conchita, 377; mentioned, 142–143